A FINE AND PRIVATE PLACE: THE ARCHAEOLOGY OF DEATH AND BURIAL IN POST-MEDIEVAL BRITAIN AND IRELAND

Annia Cherryson

Zoë Crossland

Sarah Tarlow

Leicester Archaeology Monograph No. 22

© Individual authors

ISBN 978-0-9560179-8-7

Typeset and printed by 4word Ltd, Bristol

Printed in 11/13pt Baskerville. Named after John Baskerville, printer and typographer (d.1775) buried in the garden of his house 'Easy Hill'; later moved to the crypt of Christ Church, Birmingham and finally to the catacombs of Warstone Lane Cemetery.

Contents

	Preface	iv
	List of Figures	v
	List of Tables	vii
	Summaries	viii
1	Introduction: the context of death in post-medieval Britain and Ireland	1
2	The preparation and presentation of the post-medieval corpse	22
3	Enclosing the corpse	45
4	The burial landscape of post-medieval Britain and Ireland	81
5	By choice, circumstance or compulsion: unusual burials in post-medieval Britain and Ireland	105
6	The medical body: the archaeological evidence for the use of the corpse for medical research and teaching	133
7	Conclusions	156
	Appendix 1: Burial Legislation, c.1500–1902	162
	Gazetteer	164
	References	196
	Index	265

Preface

This volume has been several years in the making, during which time Zoë Crossland, the first research assistant on the project, moved to an academic position at Columbia University and was replaced by Annia Cherryson. Annia and Sarah built on Zoë's sturdy foundations to bring the book to completion. We have been heavily dependent on the goodwill and patience of others who have given us access to their unpublished site reports, and drawn our attention to sites, sources or connections we had missed. In particular we thank our funders the Leverhulme Trust, and our colleagues on the 'Changing Beliefs of the Human Body' project: John Robb, Dušan Borić, Preston Miracle, Marie Louise Sørensen, Katharina Rebay-Salisbury, Robin Osborne, Jessica Hughes, Maryon McDonald and Oliver Harris.

For their kind assistance in making material available to us we are most grateful to Oxford Archaeology especially Lousie Loe and Ceri Boston, University of Leicester Archaeological Services especially Harriet Jacklin, Museum of London Archaeological Services especially Natasha Powers, Nigel Jeffries and Andy Chopping, Jo Adams of the Birmingham University Field Archaeology Unit, Kath Mahoney, Steve Tucker and Francis Grew of the London Archaeological Archive and Research Centre, Declan Moore of Moore Archaeological and Environmental Services Ltd, Keith Wade of Suffolk County Council, Sue Anderson of CFA, Steve Driscoll of Glasgow University Archaeological Research Division, Robin Turner of the National Trust for Scotland, Victor Buckley and his colleagues at the National Monuments Service in Dublin, Nick Pearson and On-Site Archaeology, Warwick Rodwell for Barton-upon-Humber, Bruce Williams and Annsofie Witkin, Bristol and Region Archaeological Services, Jo Buckberry of Bradford University, Andrew Chamberlain, Richard O'Neill and Christie Cox of the University of Sheffield, Mike Smith of Southampton City Archaeology Unit, Duncan Sayer of the University of Lancaster, Tom Addyman at Addyman Associates, Sue Anderson at CFA Archaeology, Alison Cameron at Aberdeen City Council Archaeological Unit, Susan Fox at the Roman Baths Museum & Pump Room, Bath, Steve Preston at Thames Valley Archaeological Services, Brett Thorn at Bucks County Museum, Colm Donnelly for the Centre for Archaeological Fieldwork, Queens University Belfast, Bill White at the Museum of London, Melissa Melikian and AOC Archaeology, Nigel Neil of Neil Archaeological Services, Rachel Sloane of ACS Ltd., John Smith and Carl Thorpe at Cornwall County Council and Liz Popescu of Cambridgeshire Archaeology. Our Leicester colleagues have been offered both moral and practical support and we thank them all, but particularly for help with maps we are most grateful to Mark Gillings, and for editorial and production advice we would like to thank David Edwards.

All maps have been prepared for this volume by Annia Cherryson; the following figures were drawn for publication by Debbie Miles-Williams of the School of Archaeology and Ancient History, to whom we are most grateful: 3.3, 3.6, 3.7, 3.12, 3.13, 3.15, 3.16, 3.17, 3.18, 3.20, 4.1, 4.3, 4.8, 4.9, 4.10, 5.1, 5.3, 5.6, 5.7, 5.9, 5.11.

For the other figures we would like to thank the Pepys library for 2.1; Mark Ynys-Mon for 2.3; the British Library for 2.4; the Natural History Museum for 2.5, 2.6; MoLA for 2.7, 3.8, 3.14, 3.19, 3.21, 6.8; Warwick Rodwell for 2.8, 3.22, 6.3; ULAS for 2.9, 3.11; Oxford Archaeology for 2.10, 5.2, 5.12, 6.4; Graham Norrie, Institute of Archaeology and Antiquity at Birmingham for 2.11; the Mary Rose Trust for 2.12; Archaeology South-East for 2.14, 3.9; the London Archaeological Archive and Resource Centre for 3.1, 4.5, 5.5; John Cooke for 3.4; Birmingham Archaeology for 3.5, 3.10; On-site Archaeology for 5.4; Ruthann O'Connor for 5.10; Wilkinson's Auctioneers of Doncaster for 5.15; Wellcome Institute for 6.1; Annsofie Witkin for 6.2 and 6.7; John Dalrymple for 6.5; Laureen Buckley for 6.6; the Hunterian Collection for 6.9. Remaining pictures are © the authors.

List of Figures

Figure 1.1	Geographical distribution of the sites	3
Figure 1.2	Site distribution by country and county	4
Figure 1.3	Chronological distribution of sites	4
Figure 1.4	Geographical distribution of English, Welsh and Scottish sites in use during the sixteenth century	5
Figure 1.5	The distribution of sixteenth-century sites compared with the whole dataset	6
Figure 1.6	Bar chart of distribution of site type	7
Figure 1.7	Number of burials per site	7
Figure 2.1	Image of a shouded burial from the 'Ballad of the Inhumane Butcher of the Leaden-Hall Market'	23
Figure 2.2	Shroud pins from the New Churchyard, London	24
Figure 2.3	Affidavit in accordance with the Act for Burial in Woollen Onely	25
Figure 2.4	London's charity and the country's cruelty	25
Figure 2.5	Shroud from Christ Church, Spitalfields	27
Figure 2.6	Funeral cap from Spitalfields, London	28
Figure 2.7	Eighteenth-century livery button, St Marylebone, London	30
Figure 2.8	Corpses with leather truss, St Peter's Church, Barton-upon-Humber in	31
Figure 2.9	Coins over the eyes, Ebenezer Chapel in Leicester	32
Figure 2.10	Skull with a full set of dentures	33
Figure 2.11	Large, gold mourning ring, St Martin's-in-the-Bull Ring, Birmingham	36
Figure 2.12	Rosary from the Mary Rose	37
Figure 2.13	Oliver Cromwell's head	40
Figure 2.14	Glass viewing panel from Kingston upon Thames	42
Figure 3.1	Uncoffined burial from the New Churchyard, London	46
Figure 3.2	Catch on the Easingwold parish coffin	47
Figure 3.3	Common post-medieval coffin shapes	48
Figure 3.4	Anthropomorphic lead coffins, Farleigh Hungerford Castle, Somerset	48
Figure 3.5	Fish tailed coffins, St Martin's-in-the-Bull Ring, Birmingham	49
Figure 3.6	Exploded drawing of a coffin with multiple shells	51
Figure 3.7	Re-used wood in a coffin from the burial ground of Newcastle Infirmary	57
Figure 3.8	Coffin plate of Robert Wilson, 1660	58
Figure 3.9	Initials and a date (1696) in nails on the coffin lid, Quaker Burial Ground at Kingston-upon-Thames	59
Figure 3.10	Copper alloy letters forming the initials, age and date of death	60
Figure 3.11	Large coffin-plate from Leicester	60
Figure 3.12	Inner and outer coffin plates from Kingston-upon-Thames Quaker burial ground	63
Figure 3.13	Some commonly used coffin plate shapes	63
Figure 3.14	Highly decorated coffin plate from St Marylebone	65
Figure 3.15	Burial from Hemingford Grey in Cambridgeshire	67
Figure 3.16	Examples of variation in grip handle form	68
Figure 3.17	Examples of variation in grip plate form	68
Figure 3.18	Examples of 19th-century lid motifs	68
Figure 3.19	Burial from St Marylebone Church, London with ornamental coffin fittings	70
Figure 3.20	Witch bottle from All Saints' Church, Milton Keynes	76
Figure 3.21	The death masks and hand interred at St George's Bloomsbury	77
Figure 3.22	Burial with his feet resting on a white ceramic plate, St Peter's Church, Barton-upon-Humber	78

Figures

Figure 4.1	Early modern burials in front of altar at St Oswald's Priory Gloucester	83
Figure 4.2	Bolton Priory showing continued use of nave as a parish church	83
Figure 4.3	Putative recusant burials, Eynsham Abbey	84
Figure 4.4	Post-Reformation Catholic cemetery of St James Winchester	84
Figure 4.5	Burials at the New Churchyard, London	87
Figure 4.6	Bunhill cemetery, London	88
Figure 4.7	Non-conformist gravestone Bunhill cemetery, London	90
Figure 4.8	Plan of the Quaker Burial Ground at Kingston-upon-Thames	92
Figure 4.9	Disturbed burial from the Baptist Burial ground at West Butts Street, Poole	93
Figure 4.10.	Expansion of burial capacity at St Martin's-in-the-Bull Ring, Birmingham	95
Figure 4.11	West Hill Cemetery Winchester	98
Figure 4.12	Undercliffe Cemetery, Bradford	99
Figure 4.13	Area of Quaker burials at Undercliffe Cemetery, Bradford	100
Figure 4.14	Re-landscaped churchyard of St George in the East, London	101
Figure 4.15	Plaque recording the location of the Quaker part of the cemetery at Bunhill Fields	101
Figure 5.1	Grave of John Rawls, Glastonbury Tor	106
Figure 5.2.	Civil War cemetery at Abingdon Vineyard	109
Figure 5.3.	Plan of 17th-century cemetery, Edinburgh Castle	110
Figure 5.4	Mass grave from York Barbican	111
Figure 5.5	Collective burial, New Churchyard, London	114
Figure 5.6	Burial of drowned bodies at Braigh, Aignish on the Isle of Lewis	116
Figure 5.7	Isolated burial of an adult male from Alresford in Hampshire	118
Figure 5.8	The body of murderer/suicide of John Williams	121
Figure 5.9	Woman and neonate from the Carver Street Methodist Chapel, Sheffield	122
Figure 5.10	Maamtrasna cillín, County Mayo	123
Figure 5.11	Special cemetery at Tintagel in Cornwall	124
Figure 5.12	Early modern burials from the filled-in moat of Oxford castle	126
Figure 5.13	Sixteenth-century image showing the display of severed heads at Dublin Castle	127
Figure 5.14	Thomas More's head	128
Figure 5.15	Anthropodermic bibliopegy	129
Figure 6.1	The day of judgement at William Hunter's anatomy school	135
Figure 6.2	Skulls recovered from the burial ground at the Newcastle Infirmary	140
Figure 6.3	Skeleton 219, St Mary's, Barton-upon-Humber	146
Figure 6.4	Burial from Oxford Castle moat	147
Figure 6.5	Mortsafe from St Mary's, Holystone	150
Figure 6.6	Cranium of a skull found at Cotton Court, Hill Street, Belfast	151
Figure 6.7	Tibia from the burial ground of Newcastle Infirmary with saw marks	151
Figure 6.8	Assemblage of cut bones from grave at the Royal London Hospital	152
Figure 6.9	Skeleton of "Mr. Jeffs"	154

List of Tables

Table 2.1.	Examples of buttons and dress fittings found associated with seventeenth- to nineteenth-century burials	29
Table 2.2.	Examples of jewellery found in association with eighteenth- and nineteenth-century burials	35
Table 2.3.	Interval between death and burial at the Quaker burial ground at Kingston-upon-Thames	38
Table 3.1.	Comparative incidence of wood, lead and other metal coffins	52
Table 3.2.	Distribution of coffin type by burial location at St. Luke's Islington, London	52
Table 3.3	Incidence of lead coffins	52
Table 3.4	Example of zinc and iron coffins	55
Table 3.5.	Distribution of types of wood by site	55
Table 3.6.	Distribution of coffin wood by burial location at St. Martin's-in-the-Bull Ring, Birmingham	56
Table 3.7.	Examples of information provided on the depositum plates from St. George Bloomsbury, London	62
Table 3.8.	Metals used for breastplates	64
Table 3.9.	Metals used for the grips, grip plates, lid motifs and escutcheons from St. George's Church Bloomsbury and St. Luke's Islington in London	64
Table 3.10.	Examples of variation of coffin cover colour	71
Table 3.11.	Examples of coins found in post-medieval burials	74
Table 3.12.	Examples of items found with post-medieval burials	75
Table 4.1.	Examples of excavated hospital and workhouse burial grounds	96
Table 6.1.	Archaeological examples of autopsy	138
Table 6.2.	Burial contexts of autopsied individuals from churchyards and community burial grounds	140
Table 6.3.	Summary of demographic composition of examples of autopsy and dissection from different types of sites in Table 6.1	143
Table 6.4.	Individuals subject to autopsy exhibiting paleopathological lesions	144
Table 6.5.	Non-funerary assemblages of human bone with evidence for medical intervention	148

Summary

Only a few decades ago the post-medieval burial grounds of Britain and Ireland were routinely destroyed or damaged in the course of development without any archaeological recording having taken place. However, during the 1990s influential site reports such as the crypt clearance at Christ Church, Spitalfields in London demonstrated that the detailed archaeological study of such sites can tell us a great deal of historical information, help us to refine our own methods and capture the imagination of the wider public. Since then numerous archaeological recordings, investigations, excavations and watching briefs have taken place in burial grounds, although it is still the case that only a relatively small number of these are published and readily accessible. Despite the publication of a number of very good site reports in recent years, there is almost no archaeological literature which brings together the primary archaeological evidence from several sites, and nothing approaching the size or scope of this book, the first interpretative and synthetic discussion of the below-ground archaeology of death and burial in post-medieval Britain and Ireland.

The book itself is in two parts. There is a gazetteer of over 500 sites of archaeologically excavated post-medieval human burial, with references, site summaries and other details; and preceding that is a an extensive synthetic discussion of the evidence in its historical context. After an introduction setting out the context of death in post-medieval Britain and Ireland, chapters review the evidence for the preparation of the corpse; the coffin and other things that accompanied the corpse to the grave; the burial landscape including the different kinds of cemeteries and burial places used in the period; unusual burials (criminals, suicides, excommunicants, victims of war or shipwreck and others); and evidence of the development of scientific knowledge of the body through anatomical dissection, embalming and display. There is an appendix covering historical legislation. The volume brings together not only the empirical evidence relating to mortuary practices, but also provides some preliminary interpretation of the significance of religious change and difference (such as between Catholics and Protestants, or the Established Church and nonconformist groups), of political and legislative change and of changing beliefs about the nature of the dead body.

It ends with a number of recommendations for research and practice, and a hope that this book marks the beginning of a valuable dialogue in this comparatively neglected area of archaeological study.

Résumé

Un lieu privé et excellent: l'archéologie de la mort et des pratiques funéraires dans la Grande-Bretagne et l'Irlande post-médiévales: résumé

Annia Cherryson
Zoë Crossland
Sarah Tarlow

Il y a de cela quelques décennies seulement, les lieux funéraires post-médiévaux de Grande-Bretagne et d'Irlande étaient fréquemment détruits ou endommagés dans le cadre de travaux d'aménagement sans que le moindre enregistrement archéologique n'ait eu lieu. Néanmoins, dans le courant des années 1990, d'influents rapports de fouilles, tels que les travaux à Christ Church, Spitafields à Londres, ont démontré que l'étude archéologique détaillée de ces sites pouvaient nous fournir une quantité importante d'information, nous aider à raffiner nos propres méthodes, et capturer l'imagination du grand public. Depuis de nombreux recherches, fouilles et suivis de travaux archéologiques ont eu lieu sur des lieux funéraires, bien que peu de ces travaux aient été publiés et rendus accessibles. En dépit de la publication de quantité d'excellents rapports de fouilles ces dernières années, il n'y a presque aucune littérature archéologique qui rassemble les données archéologiques primaires de plusieurs sites, et rien qui ne se rapproche de l'étendue de cet ouvrage, la première discussion interprétative et synthétique de l'archéologie de la mort et des pratiques funéraires dans la Grande-Bretagne et l'Irlande post-médiévales.

Le livre est organisé en deux parties: d'une part, un inventaire comprenant plus de 500 sites avec restes humains post-médiévaux fouillés, incluant références bibliographiques, résumés des sites et autres détails; d'autre part, une large discussion synthétique des données dans leur contexte historique. Après une introduction présentant le contexte de la mort en Grande-Bretagne et Irlande post-médiévales, les chapitres passent en revue les données liées à la préparation du corps; au cercueil et autres éléments qui accompagnent le corps dans la tombe; au paysage funéraire, y compris les différents types de cimetières et de lieux funéraires utilisés à cette période; aux tombes inhabituelles (criminels, suicides, personnes excommuniciées, victimes de guerre ou de naufrage,...); aux informations relatives au développement de la connaissance scientifique du corps grâce aux dissections anatomiques et aux pratiques d'embaumement et de présentation du corps. Est également comprise une annexe couvrant la législation historique. Ce volume combine non seulement les données empiriques relatives aux pratiques funéraires, mais fournit également de premiers éléments d'interprétation de la signification des changements et différences religieux (par exemple entre Catholiques et Protestants, ou entre Eglise Etablie et groupes non-conformistes), des changements politiques et légaux, et des changements de croyance concernant la nature du cadavre.

Ce volume se termine par un certain nombre de recommandations pour la recherche et la pratique, et l'espoir que ce livre marquera le début d'un dialogue productif dans ce domaine relativement négligé de la recherche archéologique.

Zusammenfassung

„Ein guter, ruhiger Platz." Die Archäologie von Tod und Bestattung im neuzeitlichen England und Irland

Annia Cherryson
Zoë Crossland
Sarah Tarlow

Noch vor ein paar Jahrzehnten wurden die neuzeitlichen Gräberfelder von Großbritannien und Irland routinemäßig bei Baumaßnahmen zerstört oder beschädigt, ohne archäologisch dokumentiert worden zu sein. Doch in den 1990er Jahren zeigten einflussreiche Grabungsberichte, wie etwa anlässlich der Räumung der Krypta der *Christ Church*, Spitalfields in London, dass die detaillierte archäologische Untersuchung solcher Fundorte zahlreiche historische Informationen liefert, uns hilft, unsere eigenen Methoden zu verfeinern und die Fantasie der breiten Öffentlichkeit anregt. Seitdem haben zahlreiche archäologische Aufnahmen, Untersuchungen, Ausgrabungen und Baubeobachtungen von Begräbnisstätten stattgefunden, obwohl immer noch nur eine relativ kleine Anzahl veröffentlicht wurde und leicht zugänglich ist. Trotz der Publikation einer Reihe sehr guter Grabungsberichte in den letzten Jahren gibt es fast keine archäologische Literatur, die Daten mehrerer Fundstellen zusammenführt, und nichts, was auch nur annähernd an den Umfang dieser Monographie heranreicht. Es handelt sich um die erste interpretative und zusammenfassende Diskussion der Archäologie von Tod und Bestattung unter der Erdoberfläche im neuzeitlichen England und Irland.

Das Buch selbst hat zwei Teile. Es ist ein Verzeichnis von über 500 archäologisch erfassten neuzeitlichen Menschenbestattungen, mit Literaturangaben, Zusammenfassungen von Grabungsberichten und anderen Details, davor befindet sich eine umfangreiche Erörterung der Daten in ihrem historischen Kontext. Nach einer Einführung, die den Kontext von Tod und Bestattung im neuzeitlichen England und Irland herstellt, behandeln die einzelnen Kapiteln Hinweise für die Präparation des Leichnams, den Sarg und andere Dinge, die den Leichnam ins Grab begleiteten, die Bestattungslandschaft inklusive der verschiedenen Arten von Gräberfeldern und Bestattungsplätzen, die in dieser Periode in Gebrauch waren, ungewöhnliche Bestattungen (Verbrecher, Selbstmörder, Exkommunizierte, Gefallene, Schiffbrüchige und andere), Hinweise auf die Entwicklung wissenschaftlicher Erkenntnisse über den Körper anhand von anatomischer Obduktion, Einbalsamierung und Ausstellung. Im Anhang wird die historische Gesetzgebung abgedeckt. Das Buch sammelt nicht nur die empirische Evidenz in Bezug auf die Bestattungspraxis, sondern bietet auch einige vorläufige Interpretation der Bedeutung des religiösen Wandels und religiöser Unterschiede (wie zwischen Katholiken und Protestanten oder der Staatskirche und nonkonformistischen Gruppen), der politischen und rechtlichen Änderungen und der wechselnden Ansichten über die Natur des toten menschlichen Körpers.

Das Buch endet mit einer Reihe von Empfehlungen für Forschung und Praxis und der Hoffnung, dass es den Beginn eines wertvollen Dialogs in diesem vergleichsweise vernachlässigten Bereich der archäologischen Forschung markiert.

1 The context of death in post-medieval Britain and Ireland

In their survey of the archaeology of health and disease in Britain from prehistory to the modern age, Roberts and Cox were frustrated that "only a handful" of mortuary contexts dating from the post-medieval period in Britain had been archaeologically excavated (2003: 289), and of these, only a small proportion had been subject to systematic osteoarchaeological analysis. Their demographic and palaeopathological observations were therefore based upon a fairly small number of sites. Many archaeologists attempting to work on this period have faced similar problems. Although there are a few good text-based histories of death and burial in post-medieval England (e.g. Gittings 1984; Litten 1991; Harding 2002), there is no synthetic overview of the archaeological evidence, and indeed only a few individual sites are widely known and easily accessible. Certainly there has been no attempt to consider the whole of Britain and Ireland together. The paucity of published excavations of post-medieval burial, at the time Roberts and Cox published their article, stood in contrast to the archaeological study of commemoration, which had been the subject of several published articles and books in recent years (e.g. Tarlow 1999; Finch 2000; Mytum 2000, 2004). Observations from excavation had not been subject to the same degree of analysis and explanation as standing monuments. In the past few years, however, a good number of post-medieval cemetery excavations have been published as monographs or lengthy articles – especially though not exclusively in London (e.g. Brickley et al. 2006; Bashford and Sibun 2007; Adams and Colls 2007; Miles and White 2008; Miles et al. 2008; Boston et al. 2009). This has gone some way towards redressing the balance, although publications of post-medieval cemeteries still tend to be less interpretive than those of comparable sites belonging to medieval or earlier periods. There are a few reasons for this: the great size of many post-medieval cemeteries, especially urban cemeteries in use during the eighteenth and nineteenth centuries, makes it necessary to use some kind of sampling strategy; in many cases archaeological involvement may be limited to a watching brief while the cemetery is cleared by a commercial company with no archaeological expertise. In some parts of Britain and Ireland, the archaeological value of such sites is not recognised by law and any archaeological investigation is carried out only as a result of personal commitment to the archaeology of later historical periods by individuals who have decision-making powers. Also where the excavation is on Church land, there may not be much money to fund the kind of detailed excavation that a commercial developer might be able to underwrite. Even the deeper pockets of developers might not be equal to the financial demands of cemetery sites with hundreds or thousands of graves, as were common in the nineteenth century.

Unlike the mortuary archaeology of earlier periods, where excavations are still carried out as long-term, research-driven projects, all archaeological excavation of post-medieval human remains is carried out by professional archaeological units in response to immediate threat. The expeditious reburial of human remains is usually a condition of excavation, and often includes the reburial of all material associated with interments, such as coffin fittings and any personal items. Because of the way British archaeology is presently managed and funded, the excavators of post-medieval burial sites rarely have the time, money or access to materials to undertake a detailed contextual review of the literature. On the other hand, academic archaeologists who are in a better position institutionally to undertake slow, detailed excavation and carry out wide-ranging background research are not practically able to work on post-medieval burial grounds, for legal, ethical and logistical reasons. They have therefore often preferred to undertake the recording and analysis of surviving above-ground memorial monuments from this period, for which no formal permission is usually required, and which provides excellent material for student projects, for all the reasons set out in Mytum (2004). Nevertheless, the study of post-medieval burials is still in its infancy in Britain and Ireland, and a clear research agenda is yet to emerge.

The aims of this book

This volume provides a brief descriptive overview of archaeological evidence relating to the treatment of dead bodies from the sixteenth century to approximately the end of the nineteenth. Our period runs from the time of the Reformations, which marked

1 The context of death in post medieval Britain and Ireland

changes both in the relationship between the living and the dead, and in the social and economic organisation of Britain and Ireland, to around the end of the nineteenth century. The end date is not chosen for academic reasons, but because burials from after this period in Britain and Ireland are not usually excavated archaeologically (archaeology of twentieth-century mortuary practices mostly relates to the hasty or secret burials of victims of war and massacre (e.g. Haglund et al. 2001; Crossland 2002; Saunders 2007; Robertshaw and Kenyon 2008) which did not occur in Britain). The first and, as it turned out, the greatest task in compiling this book, was to find out where post-medieval burial sites had been archaeologically excavated, and to track down reports. Most of the written material we were able to study was in the form of unpublished grey literature reports. Because this is the first time an attempt to draw this material together has been made – we have not even found regional syntheses to help us here – we were not at all sure to start with how many sites we were likely to find. Roberts and Cox (2003) believed that there were only "a handful", and it is certainly true that only a small number of sites are well-known and fully published. However, the gazetteer we have compiled now contains over 500 sites. Neither the gazetteer nor the database on which it is based is exhaustive, but we have tried to make them as complete as possible in the time available to us. New sites are being published all the time now, and chances are that a few more will be published between the time this volume goes to press and by the time it is available for purchase, so it cannot be regarded as definitive. Our intention is to maintain and periodically update the gazetteer (see Chapter 7 for more information). We have been ambitious in our coverage, and included Ireland as well as England, Scotland and Wales. There are advantage and disadvantages to this approach. We strongly believe that only by considering evidence from across Britain and Ireland will a good understanding of trends emerge. It also enables us to note, for example, the relative significance of local tradition, religion and politics on burial (surprisingly, perhaps, the history of post-medieval burial in Catholic Ireland is not very different to staunchly Protestant England – class and legislation appear to be much more significant influences on practice). On the other hand, in order to outline these larger trends it is possible – in fact likely – that we have missed significant regional variation. One unfortunate result of the geographical imbalance in our coverage is that England, and big cities, especially London, are over-represented (figure 1.1 and figure 1.2). This is a shame because whatever London might be, it is certainly not typical of the rest of Britain, let alone Ireland. Our hope is that as the field of post-medieval archaeology develops, the archaeology of rural and provincial areas will become better known. In the mean time it seemed to us that, rather than writing a book limited to London, or to urban England, the better option was to include archaeological evidence from rural areas and from the other countries of the British Isles where we have been able to find it.

The gazetteer is biased towards London and other major urban centres because archaeology follows development. Thus, burial grounds in cities subject to major redevelopments in recent years are more likely to have been investigated than quieter rural settlements where development can take place in greenfield sites. There is also a chronological imbalance, in that the cemeteries of known eighteenth and nineteenth-century date are both more numerous and larger than early modern (sixteenth- to mid eighteenth-century) ones (figure 1.3). This is in many ways a product of historical circumstance: we are more likely to know secure foundation dates for later burial grounds than for early ones, and they are more likely to contain diagnostic datable material because the use of coffins provides fittings which are typologically distinct. By contrast, in early modernity, most burials were in parish churchyards and where there is no coffin they are indistinguishable from late medieval ones. Thus a much larger proportion of the sites in the survey that were in use the sixteenth century contain atypical burials in marginal locations when compared with the overall distribution of site types within the study (figure 1.4 and 1.5).[1] This is why the burials of criminals and shipwrecked sailors, the hurried disposal of victims of war or disease, the furtive or unorthodox burial of unbaptised babies and excommunicates – are actually better represented in the archaeological record than the conventional mortuary practices of respectable parishioners during the sixteenth century. Although not as marked, a similar trend can be seen among the sites in use during the seventeenth century. Normative burial throughout the period was in a parish churchyard (figure 1.6). These landscapes are rarely redeveloped – especially outside the cities – and are often still in use as burial grounds. Archaeological investigation tends to be limited to narrow strips of land which are opened in order to install new cables or lay a path – often yielding only fragments of disarticulated bone which do not lend themselves to extensive interpretation. Many sites consist only of one or two burials found during small-scale developments in the churchyard (figure 1.7). In making the final selection for inclusion in the gazetteer, sites which comprise only disarticulated bone of uncertain date have been omitted.

This chapter is a brief introduction to the social and religious history of the period between the Reformation and the end of the nineteenth century. It

The aims of this book

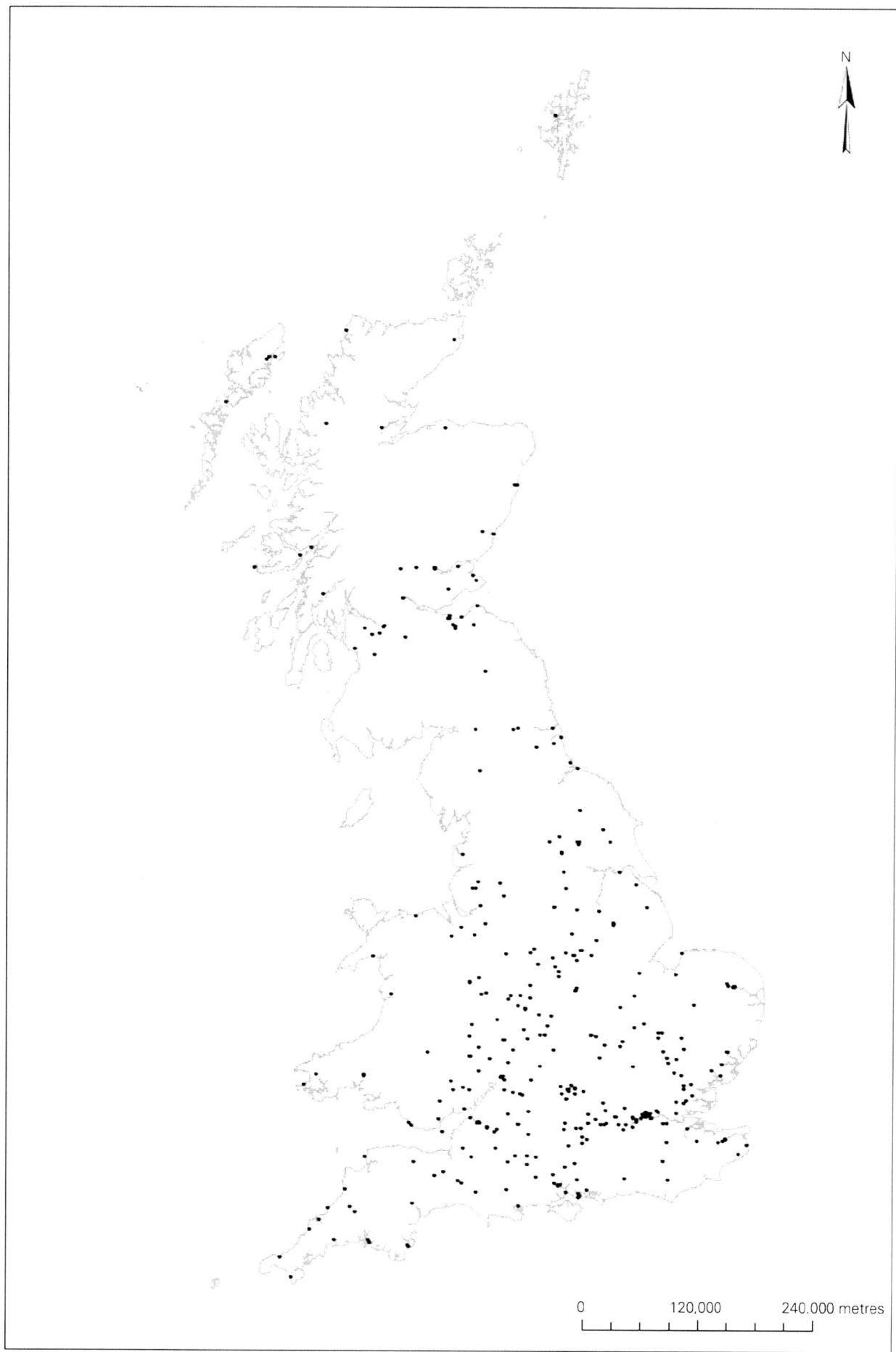

Figure 1.1 Geographical distribution of the sites in survey in England, Wales and Scotland. Sites in Ireland cannot be included on this map for copyright reasons.

1 The context of death in post medieval Britain and Ireland

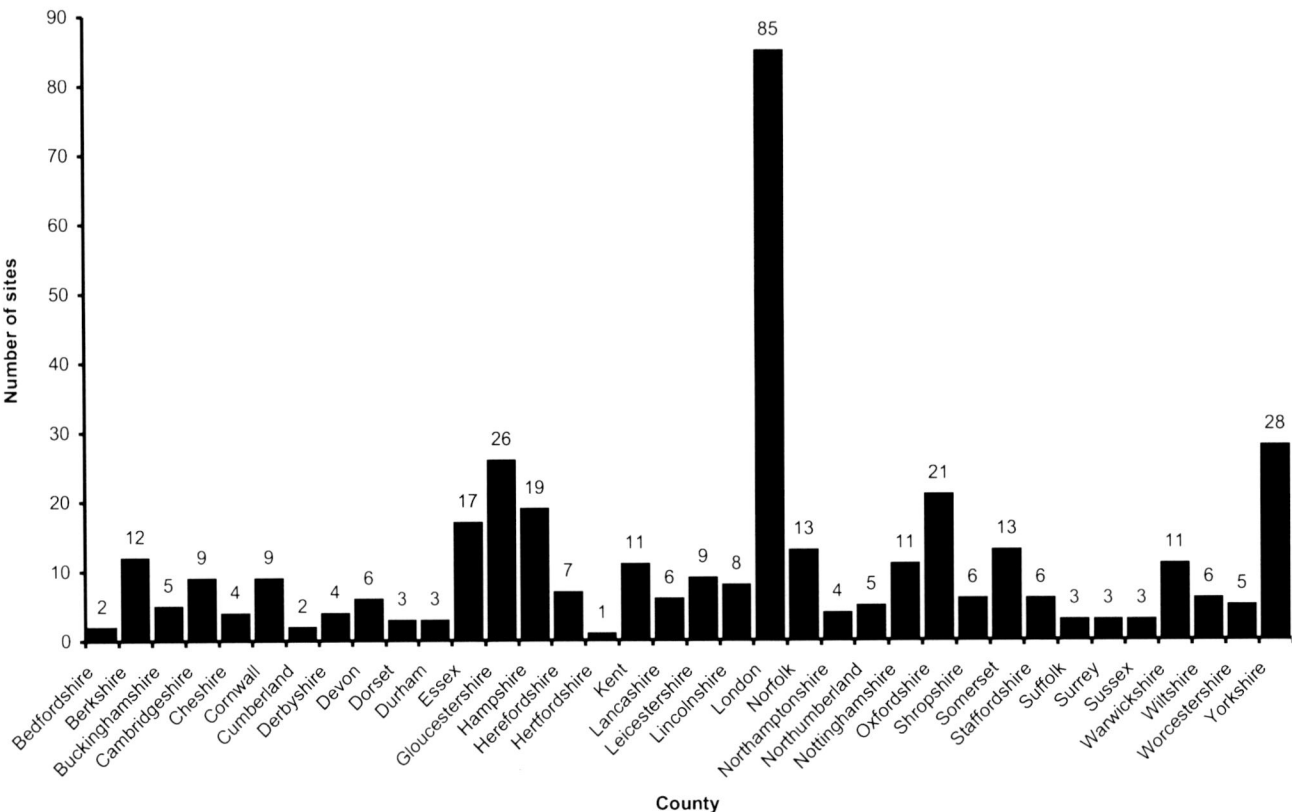

Figure 1.2 Site distribution by country a) and by county for b) England; c) Wales; d) Scotland and e) Ireland.

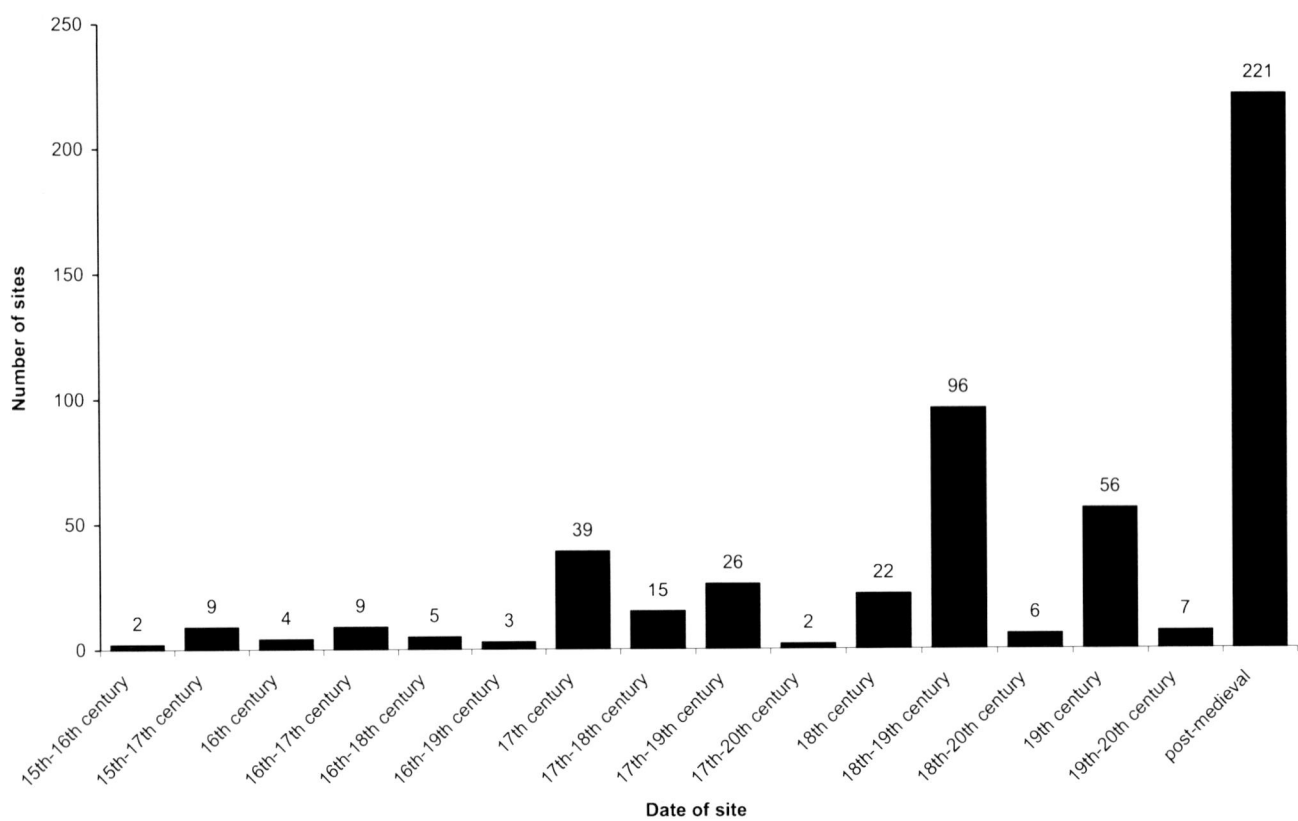

Figure 1.3 Chronological distribution of sites.

The aims of this book

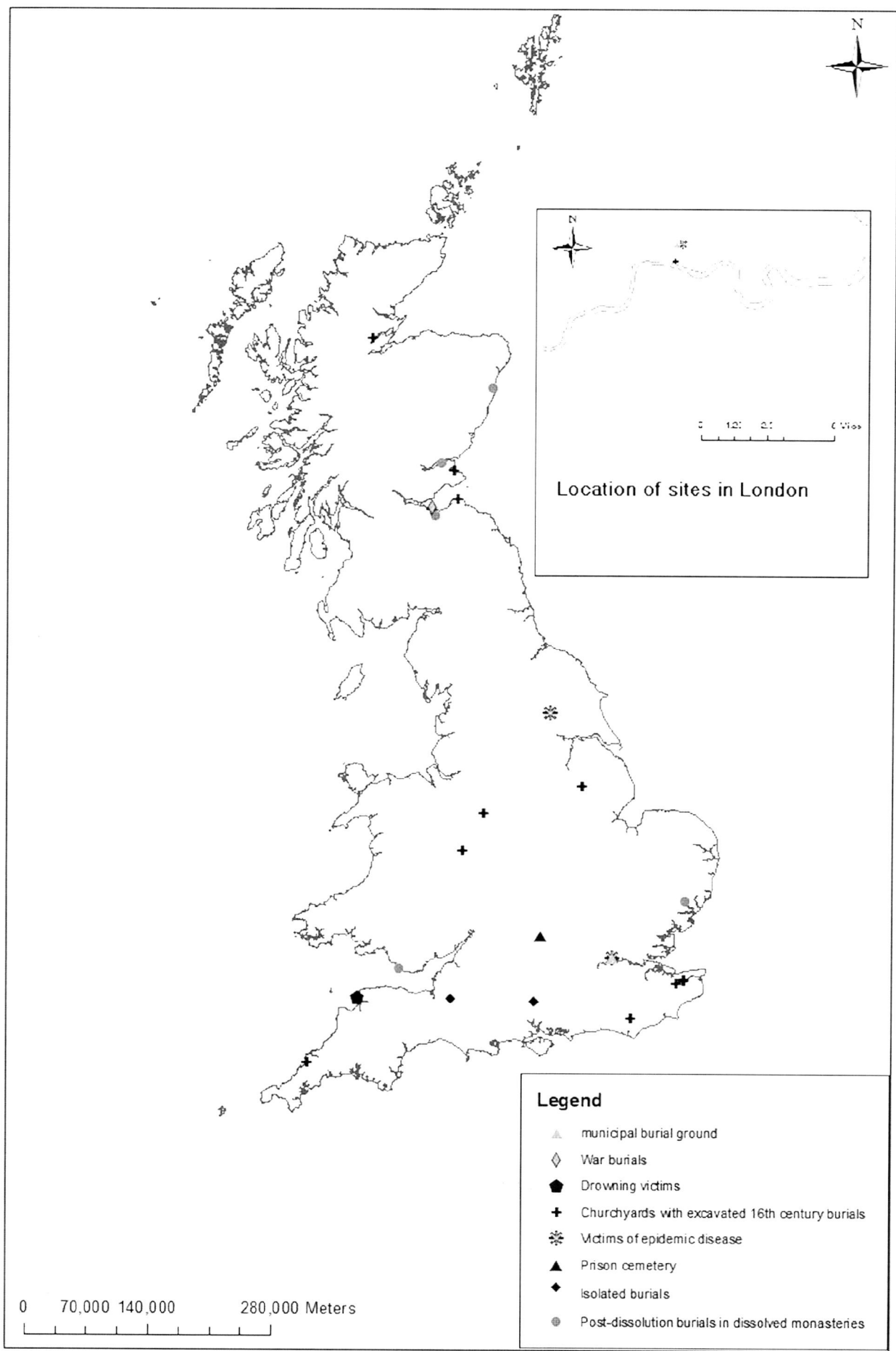

Figure 1.4 Geographical distribution of English, Welsh and Scottish sites in use during the sixteenth century. Sites in Ireland cannot be included on this map for copyright reasons.

1 The context of death in post medieval Britain and Ireland

(a) Sites in use during the sixteenth century by type (first digit is number of sites; second is percentage of total number)

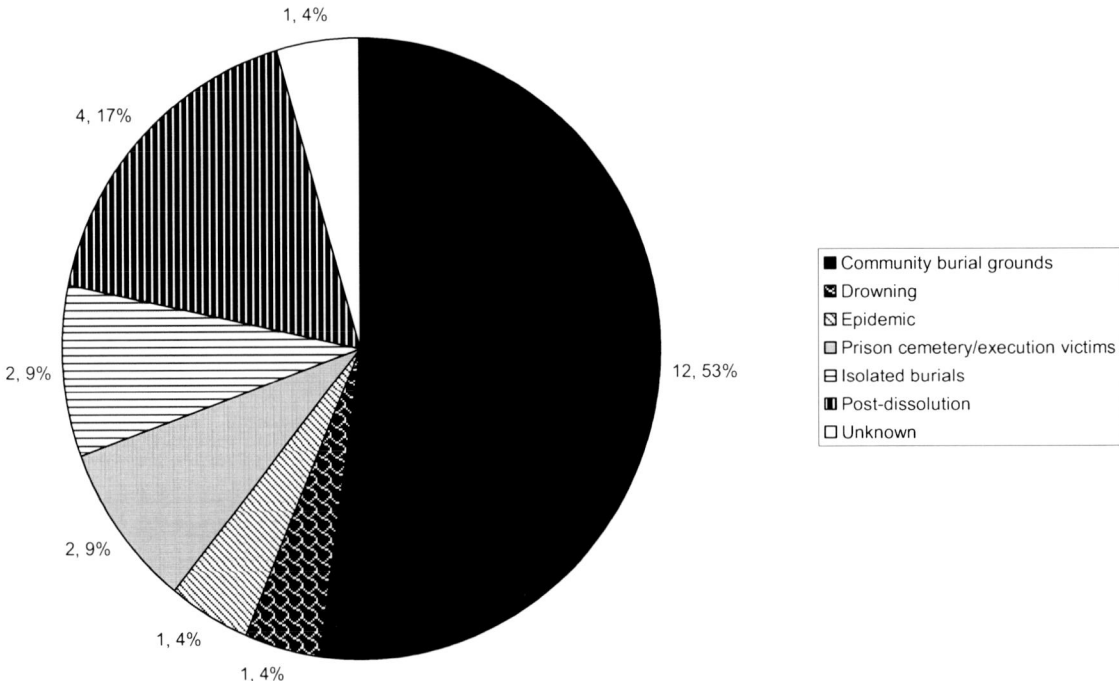

(b) All sites including within the study by type

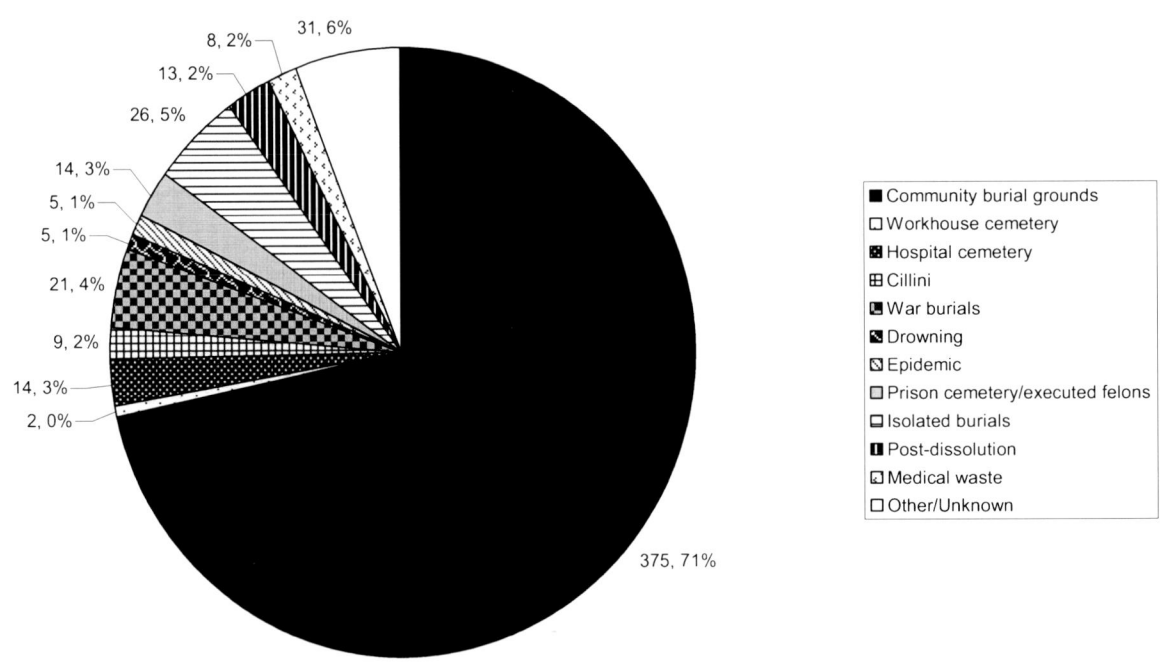

Figure 1.5 The distribution of site type for sites in use during the sixteenth century compared with distribution within the whole dataset.

The aims of this book

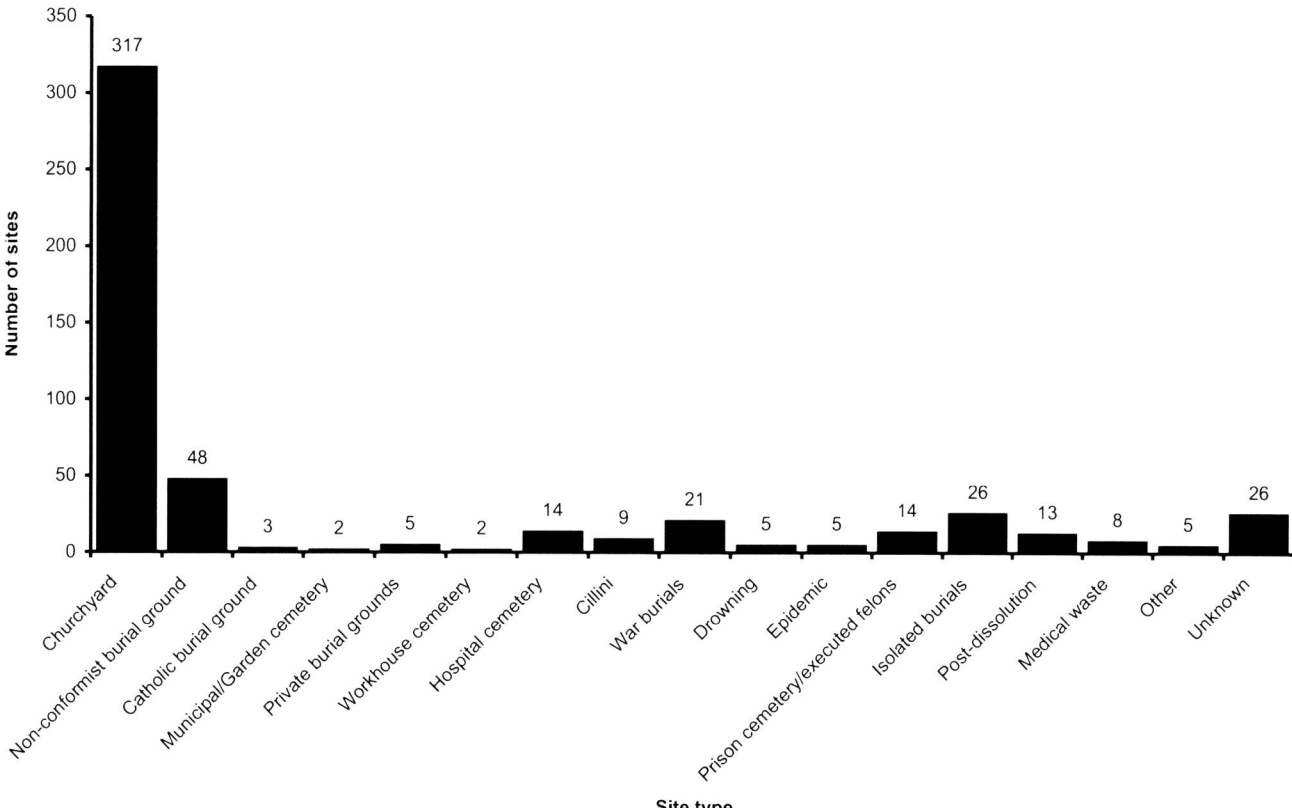

Figure 1.6 Bar chart of distribution of site type within the survey.

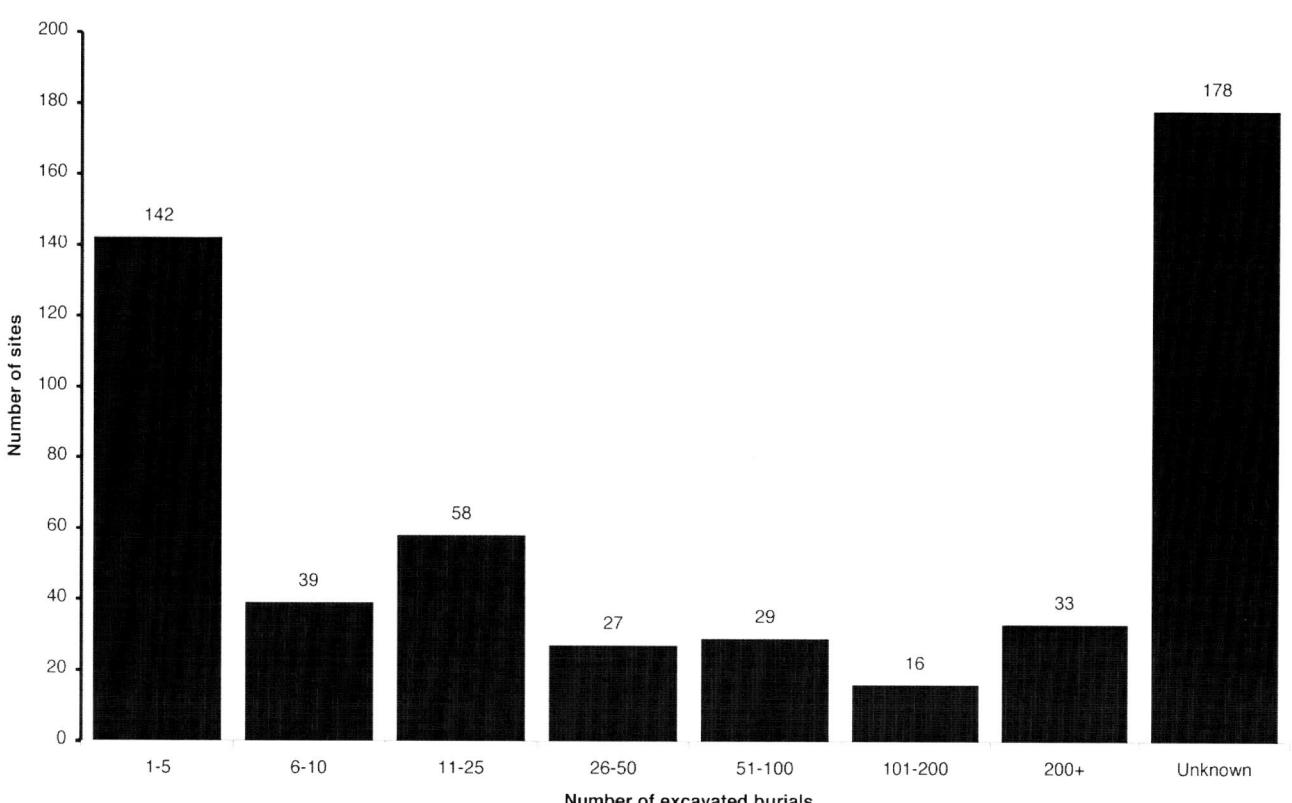

Figure 1.7 Number of burials per site.

focuses on the aspects of social and cultural history that had greatest bearing on mortuary practices and concludes with a short list of the factors which were most significant in the treatment of the body after death.

The Religious Context

The events of the Protestant Reformation are the single biggest factor in tracing attitudes to mortality and relationships with the dead during this period. The Reformation was part of a series of changes in the distribution of political power and adherence to religious doctrine across Europe particularly focused in a series of schisms and ruptures in the second quarter of the sixteenth century, but whose effects continued to shape the political and religious landscape of Europe for over a century afterwards. During the late medieval and early modern centuries, the operation of power changed at all levels, from the decline of feudal relations, to the rise of nation states; from the development of common (as opposed to canon) law, to the possibility of relatively unrestricted flows of information and knowledge offered by the development of the printing press. These changes precipitated new relationships to Papal power and new interpretations of, or outright rejection of, Catholic doctrine. In much of continental Europe the Reformation affected the local administration of the Church, but left Catholicism itself fundamentally unchallenged, continuing to recognise Papal authority. In England, Scotland and Wales, however, like some other parts of northern Europe, traditional Catholic beliefs were rejected alongside respect for existing Church hierarchy.

There is no agreement between historians about how best to tell the story of the English Reformation. While some have emphasised the high-level international politics, others have looked at local and popular belief, as evident in material practices (Gaimster and Gilchrist 2003). Conclusions can be contradictory: depending on the exact period studied, the location of the study and the kind of evidence examined it has been possible to argue either for a mood of popular Protestantism, or for generally conservative adherence to Catholicism) (e.g. Haigh 1987; Duffy 1992; Todd 1995; Doran and Durstan 2003). Equally, for some the Reformation was experienced and described as a series of political shifts and ruptures, but it was also a set of theological and doctrinal beliefs that were profoundly held and earnestly promoted by others, and for which many people sacrificed their liberties or lives.

From the late fifteenth century critics of the Catholic church and certain Catholic teachings had acquired followers in Europe. Their disagreements with Catholicism were often entwined with local and European power politics and, particularly in northern Europe, involved a rejection of the nepotic and centralised power of the Italian papacy. However, there were also theological grounds for critique. Reforming preachers took issue with some or all of a number of aspects of Catholicism which principally included:

1. the literal transubstantiation of the host (Protestants did not believe that the bread and wine transformed into the actual flesh and blood of Christ at communion and saw communion as a symbolic socio-religious act rather than a mystery)
2. the role of saints' images and relics (Protestants accused Catholics of idolatrous image worship and tended to trust words rather than images)
3. the role of the clergy (Protestants advocated a less mediated relationship between ordinary people and God, to which end they promoted the translation of the Bible into the vernacular and the power of private prayer. The job of the priest was to promote private piety rather than to act as an intermediary between parishioners and God)
4. the existence of Purgatory and the utility of prayers for the dead (of which more in a moment)
5. the kind of double-entry tallying encouraged by Catholicism whereby sins on one hand could be compensated by acts of penitence on the other (mostly the repetition of particular prayers, either personally, or one's behalf by others)
6. the value of religious orders

In England, the precipitating circumstance of the Reformation was the Pope's refusal to grant Henry VIII an annulment of his marriage, but in fact the political power struggles between Rome and England, as between Rome and the other nascent national states of Europe, were deep-seated and complex. When he seized and redistributed the power and property that had formerly been held by the Catholic church, Henry also opened up a space to challenge and reform aspects of church teaching that had already focused the minds of church critics.

One doctrine had particular importance for the relationship between the living and the dead. Late medieval Catholicism taught that at the moment of death, when the soul left the body, the soul of a baptised Christian could go to one of three places: either straight to Heaven, in the case of the saints; straight to Hell, in the case of those irredeemably damned; or, for everyone else, to Purgatory (Marshall 2002). Purgatory was a kind of antechamber to judgement, where minor sins might be expiated. It was an unpleasant place where the dead person would be purged by fire and with pain. Depending on the extent of your sins, you might be required to spend a very long time there. However, a sentence in Purgatory could be reduced by prayers said on behalf of the dead by the living, or by the intercession of saints asking for clemency. It was thus open to the bereaved to take active steps to ameliorate conditions for their departed kin and friends. It also meant that those who had the necessary financial or human resources available to them could make plans before death to ensure that as much as possible would be done to shorten their time in Purgatory. The wealthiest were able to endow chantry priests for the main purpose of repeating masses and prayers for their souls and those of their kin. For the less well-off their name might be included in the Bede-roll, a register of names and dates of death, which the bedesman would consult so that the appropriate prayers and masses could be said on the occasions of the 'month's mind' and 'year's mind' – anniversaries of the death. All sorts of other bequests to orders, guilds or parishes might be accompanied by conditions specifying the dates, types and numbers of prayers that had to be said for the soul of the deceased, and provisions of dole for the funeral were also often conditional on the paupers' willingness to pray for the benefactor's soul. Obviously this led to some social asymmetry in the afterlife, with the wealthy more able to buy out their time in Purgatory. This undermined the doctrine of equality at death and seemed to go against the scriptural valorisation of material poverty.

Reformers, starting with Luther, held instead that divine grace could only be secured by faith, and was of an individual nature. This undermined the elaborate system of masses for the dead that structured the main calendar and responsibilities of the Catholic clergy. It also challenged the efficacy of pious works, which had mostly been interpreted as material benefactions and underwrote church finances. Standing alone before God, the Protestant's relationship with the divine was highly personal, enabled by the availability of printed Bibles in English and Welsh. Protestants attributed much importance to the word – to scriptural authority – and were suspicious of such aspects of traditional Catholic worship as images, the mediatory role of the priesthood, and collective mysteries.

This section has so far dealt with the Reformation in England and Wales. The path of reform was different in Scotland, and very different in Ireland. In Scotland the Protestantism founded upon the Calvinism of John Knox drew the country closer to England and further from France – indeed Scottish Protestantism was of an altogether purer and more consistent kind than in England. In Ireland the reformed Anglo-Irish elite never managed to convert the majority of the people to Protestantism, and throughout the early modern and modern period Ireland remained an overwhelmingly Catholic country, as it is today. Heal (2003) is one of a small number of authors who have attempted to examine the effects and courses of Reformation across the islands of Britain and Ireland, with all its contradictions. Ireland is fascinating because there the will of the people apparently prevailed against governmental and official attempts and the Catholic Counter-Reformation was ultimately the dominant force.

Dissenters

Although there was an established, state-approved church in all countries of Britain after the Reformation, there were also many people who belonged to dissenting churches. There were always large numbers of Catholics, although they were prevented from participating in the public life of the nation in a number of ways and, particularly in the sixteenth and seventeenth centuries, subject to institutional and popular persecution. There were also numerous fundamentalist Protestant churches who found the established church conservative. In the sixteenth and seventeenth centuries Puritan denominations, particularly the Quakers and Baptists, had influence in some parts of the country, and were indeed dominant for a short period during the interregnum, under Cromwell's Protectorate. However, the greatest number of dissenting churches were founded in the eighteenth century, and most prominent among them were the Methodists. Methodism had its greatest following among the working and lower-middle orders in the north and the south-west of England and in Wales.

Puritans and dissenters sought to distance themselves from what they saw as the crypto-Catholicism of the high Anglican church – bells and smells, elaborate robes, ritualistic ceremonies and so on. In various ways the Dissenters and Puritans embraced what they saw as the values of the early Christians – fellowship, simplicity, a high regard for scripture and a distrust of ostentation, luxury and image in religious devotion.

All of these 'dissenting' churches, like recusant Catholics, endured some degree of social disadvantage until at least the nineteenth century, with the repeal of the Test Acts[2] that had specified Anglicanism as a prerequisite for rights or offices, and the liberalisation of the universities. In the history of death and burial the dissenting churches were sometimes rendered less visible because, unless there was a local dissenters' burial ground, final control of mortuary rites and the disposal of the dead lay with the established parish priest. Usually the Anglican minister would allow burial in parish ground to all residents of a parish, including dissenters, but they were within their rights to deny burial to non-communicants or to insist that it be carried out according to Anglican rites, and this was sometimes a source of tension and resentment (Laqueur 1983; Rugg 1998). The most common kind of non-Anglican burial grounds were Quaker grounds, especially in the seventeenth and eighteenth century, together with a limited number of Methodist grounds. A few Catholic cemeteries and a very small number of Jewish cemeteries also existed over this period.

Rugg (1998) has argued that the dissatisfaction of dissenters was a major factor in the cemetery reforms of the 1830s and 1840s. In any case, the foundation of large, non-denominational, suburban cemeteries in the nineteenth century secured unconditional access to burial space for all city residents, including dissenters, and indeed these cemeteries also sometimes served neighbouring villages and small towns. After the establishment of cemeteries the importance of dissenters' ground declined, but many remained in use into the twentieth century and some are still used today.

Theological Orthodoxy and Folk Belief

Although clergymen and theologians debated the finer points of eschatology, becoming very exercised over such questions as the fate of unbaptised infants, the mechanics of bodily resurrection or the geography of the afterlife, these questions did not always interest ordinary people, and the orthodox answers to them did not necessarily define what people actually did. Many popular religious and spiritual beliefs over this period had no biblical foundation, nor any solid basis in the pronouncements of learned men.

One example of this is the treatment of the dead body. For early modern theologians, as for late medieval ones, discussion of the body is usually conjoined with discussion of the soul, its complement and foil. The soul is eternal, glorious, divine and the part that animates and ennobles the body. In the metaphorical alignment of the body and the state which pervades the discourse of the period, the soul was analogous to the king or ruler; it was the origin of power and meaning. In much religious discourse, both Catholic and Protestant, the body, by contrast, was transitory and mortal, a thing of dust. The body was only important because the soul inhabited it; when the soul left it lost significance. Although the soul could and would survive without the body, a body without a soul was nothing. The body was thus referred to as a prison or a gaol. In the poet Andrew Marvell's 'Dialogue between the soul and the body', the soul complains of being "hung up, as 'twere, in chains/ Of nerves, and arteries, and veins". Alternatively, the profane corporeality of the body was emphasised by using words that carried connotations of decay, like 'carcase' and 'carrion', or of waste, like one seventeenth-century writer who described the body as a 'jakes' [toilet] (Sherlock 1690). Once the soul had left the body, the body was of no account. Money spent on disposal of the corpse was money wasted:

> "Oh the folies of mens hearts, who vainelie and needleslie waste upon their dead vanities that which might builde houses for the poore ... God will never inquire of a mans Soule where was thy body buried? But how hast thou lived into that bodie?"

wrote Zacharie Boyd (1629: 1045–6). For Boyd, and zealous Protestants like him, monuments and expensive funerals would not improve one's chances of salvation, and crowds of paid mourners only signalled vanity and pride (in contrast to the Catholic position where masses said by people who were being paid to say them could still help reduce the period of Purgatory and provide solace to the pains of those who suffered there). For Protestants, even the resurrection of the body, which was a matter of faith to most early modern reformed theologians, did not require the preservation of the corpse. Citing St Augustine, learned writers asserted that even if bodies were reduced to ashes or consumed by wild beasts, they could still be recomposed for the resurrection, such was the power of God.

These writings provide no theological grounds for disposing of the body with any ceremony whatsoever. There was no religious imperative behind the use of special sanctified ground for burial, and certainly none for embalming the body, burying it in the same place as ancestors or kin, or keeping wakes. Nevertheless, all these practices were normal in Britain throughout most of the period under examination here. Although religious change undoubtedly did have a major influence on burial practice, it would be a mistake to think that responses to death and the dead were wholly shaped by doctrine. Neither were they wholly shaped by the emergence of scientific knowledge of the body, or in some process of negotiation between 'science' and 'religion'. The most enduring aspects of post-medieval mortuary practice owed little to religious or scientific orthodoxy, but a great deal to unsystematic folk beliefs about death and the dead, many of which were incompatible with religious and scientific teaching. These include a deep-rooted anxiety about revenants and ghosts (evident in the care taken to pin down the bodies of those likely to 'walk' or cause mischief, such as suicides or witches). Associated beliefs involved an anxiety about causing pain or discomfort to the dead body, expressed most clearly in the near-universal horror of being 'anatomised' but also in the care taken to bury the deceased with kin and the appropriation of the criminal corpse by the criminal justice system. This last practice enacted social vengeance upon the dead body, by quartering, gibbeting, dissection or partition. All of these attribute to the newly dead body a degree of awareness, suggesting that the body could still feel and sense, and that it could retain a personal and social identity equivalent to the living self it had formerly been. Katharine Park (1995) has argued that in the late medieval period, Northern Europeans understood death as a process rather than a single event and therefore attributed more significance to the treatment of the new corpse, its place of burial, its need for protection and so on. This was in contrast, claims Park, to the Italian view of death as an abrupt separation of body and soul, leaving the body an empty husk which had meaning only as a mnemonic for the dead person. She points out that the German judicial system recognised 'bier-right' (or cruentation), the phenomenon that a murdered body would bleed in the presence of its murderer, until the seventeenth century. This practice was also part of legal practice in Scotland and England, and remained a popular belief through the nineteenth century (Brittain 1965).

The Social Context

The Reformation had major consequences for the ordering of civic and secular society, as well as in religious belief. Pre-Reformation social power was closely bound up with the structures of the Church and the religious world. In the towns, civic life was controlled by guilds, orders and fraternities, and much of the nation's wealth was expended on the construction of devotional buildings and endowments to maintain clerics. Much of rural Britain was owned and administered by the major religious houses. Bendix (1980) estimates that about 25% of the agricultural land of England and Wales was in the hands of religious houses on the eve of Reformation. Universities, schools, hospitals and other institutions were founded by pious benefactions and controlled by men in holy orders. Moreover, the endowments upon which many of these religious institutions were built were made specifically to ensure that prayers and masses for the soul of the benefactor and his or her family continued to be made regularly and indefinitely. The Reformation removed this funding structure from institutions of power. At the same time the monastic estates were taken from the religious orders and re-allocated by the monarch in a series of individual land and title grants. In towns the old hierarchies of clergy were toppled. Those whose jobs had been primarily concerned with intercessions on behalf of the dead, such as chantry priests and bedesmen had no place in the new order. The fate of parish clergymen depended on a variety of factors: the extent to which they were prepared to support the new elite; their reformatory zeal; local politics and personalities, particularly the match between the religious and political affinities of the local landowner and those of the parish priest; personal connections; and so on. Because the Reformation was a process rather than a single event, and was carried out under three monarchs (Henry VIII, Edward VI and Elizabeth I) who had differing priorities and degrees of enthusiasm for Protestantism, with a Catholic counter-Reformation (under Mary) in between, the second two thirds of the sixteenth century was a very unstable time in Britain. The best chance of survival for most lay in moderate compliance and careful avoidance of any practice that showed ostentatious adherence to any position or faction. Practices in death and burial, and especially in commemoration around this time show a rise in the number of people making the cautious choice of a secular or non-denominational memorial. There were, however, people who were willing to risk their wealth, social positions and even their lives for deeply held religious convictions. Adherence to Catholicism is evident archaeologically in the continuing surreptitious use of monastic burial grounds after they had been closed down (see Chapter 5) and in the adaptation and concealment of Catholic symbols and relics within the fabric of reformed ecclesiastical buildings (Tarlow 2003).

While the Reformation unseated, or at least agitated the old social hierarchy, it also created a new ruling class. After the Reformation the Church was no longer such a significant career pathway for an ambitious young commoner. Alongside clerical education there were many new routes to power through the secular structures of civic office and political preferment. In order to rise through these structures it was necessary to possess sufficient wealth to establish oneself as a private gentleman. Politically the franchise depended on property ownership, and social influence was cemented through the ability to entertain one's peers and demonstrate one's stability and influence in material ways. These ways included architecture, estate and urban landscapes, clothing, art, material culture, ceremony and commemoration.

A link between the possession of wealth and the exercise of social and political power is, of course, not unique to post-Reformation Britain. However, the reduction in the power of the Church, and the investment of powers formerly in the hands of the Roman church into the Head of State changed the way that wealth operated. In comparison to medieval times, society was more fluid and social structures more responsive to change in the distribution of wealth. This meant that there was always a large number of arriviste property owners, insecure in their status and in constant need of the support and approval of their peers at local and national level. It also opened up the upper levels of society to members of the mercantile class to a greater extent than the late medieval period, although many merchant families had attained social prominence even before the Reformation. Status based on wealth was more precarious than status based on blood. It also created an environment where status gains were always under threat from other aspirational nouveaux riches entrepreneurs.

Much recent critique has challenged the received wisdom that the Reformation marked a decisive break between a backwards-looking, traditional, medieval society, dominated by the church, and a progressive, rational, fluid modernity. Many of the processes associated with the Reformation were in fact underway for decades, or even centuries, before the big changes of the mid sixteenth century. Historians, notably Eamonn Duffy (1992) and Christopher Haigh (1987), have argued that the majority of the English population remained loyally Catholic right up to the very eve of Reformation. Popular Protestantism was not widespread, and in many parts of the country there is little evidence of discontent or any reduction in such Catholic practices as endowing chantries or celebrating mysteries and saints' days before they were banned by the legislative changes of the Reformation. Nevertheless, once the Reformation did take place, it took hold with relative quiet and peace in comparison with other parts of Europe. Its effects were profound and enabled new structures of power to be formulated more quickly and more fully than might have been the case had England continued to be a Catholic country. While the religious changes of the Reformation profoundly altered the relationship between the living and the dead, the accompanying social changes had a fundamental impact on social relations between the living. Both of these kinds of change underlie practices of burial and commemoration in Britain not only during the sixteenth century but right up to the present day.

The Self and the Body

Since the nineteenth century cultural historians have theorised that from the Renaissance/ Reformation, Europe saw the formation of a new kind of self: the individual. Individuals, as characterised by Jakob Burckhardt (1878) and those who followed him, are autonomous, self-created beings, with an inner, authentic 'core' self, and an outer social surface that could be cultivated in terms of improving its skills, shaping its behaviour through codes of etiquette, and developing its appearance by careful use of clothing, cosmetics and so on.

Burckhardt's individual has been thoroughly deconstructed on numerous grounds, with criticism turning around three key issues. The first is that his account ignores much evidence of medieval selves as individuals, claiming instead that pre-modern selves were aware of themselves only as members of groups. Second, the writings of a small group of Italian men was taken to stand for all society. Third, at all periods there have been numerous and contradictory understandings of the self (Porter R. 1997); the changing relationship between body and self is not easily or cleanly divisible into chronological chapters. Most cultural historians of the early modern period have concentrated their analyses on the dualistic relationship between self and body, and inner and outer worlds. However, most of the early modern literature that is explicitly dualistic is theological in orientation – it is concerned with the relationship between body and soul. Other dualisms, such as the Cartesian distinction between mind and body, or between nature and culture may be viewed as later reworkings of older dualistic theological traditions around the self. However, it should be noted that although this dualistic conception of body and soul had ancient roots, there were other non-binary views of the self prevalent in medieval Christianity (as Caroline Bynum has shown 1995a, 1995b). Equally, non-dualistic concepts of the self also permeated early modern beliefs about the body, as attested to by apotropaic devices associated with witchcraft (Crossland 2010: 395–401).

If there is one firm thing we can say about the early modern self and the early modern body, in life as in death, it is that beliefs were multiple, contradictory and contextual. So in some contexts, such as theological discourse, it was appropriate to consider the body as a corruptible carcase, to compare it to meat or to clay, or to emphasise its ephemerality because it was a foil for the eternal and incorruptible soul. In other contexts, such as early scientific and anatomical writings, the human body was seen as a glorious thing to be marvelled at as the most wonderful and perfect of all God's creations – think of Leonardo da Vinci's depiction of the human body as mathematical ideal. In still other contexts, the dead human body, according to the results of archaeological observation, was treated as the locus of the social self – it was elaborated and beautified so the relationships between the living and the dead, as individualised persons, could be created and recreated through the medium of the corpse. These different concepts all existed before the Reformation and continued to be found in discourses and material practices long afterwards. For this reason, cultural histories of the body that arrange different ideas sequentially are necessarily simplifications of what were complex and contextually specific ideas.

Nevertheless it is true that some ideas or representations of the body are more prevalent and frequently refered to at particular times. For example, ideas about the body as a scientifically known and anatomised material object occur very often in poetry, literature or as artistic depictions during the seventeenth to nineteenth centuries, and at the same time there is a concentration of evidence from archaeological contexts of bodies having been cut up before burial. The dominant 'self' that emerged over the last 500 years in the Atlantic world was individualistic with a comparatively high degree of introspection, self-determination and autonomy. This kind of self was more easily realised by men and by the wealthy than by children, women or the poor, but it was significant in shaping personal relations, which in turn affected the social response to death, dying and remembering.

Emotional Codes and Family Life

Given all the caveats and the complexity discussed above, what we can say about the self in the early modern and especially the modern period, is that it is frequently discussed as an autonomous, individual and unique person. A person's experience of the world was positioned as coming from an inner subjectivity and a particular personality. This meant that everyone's experiences, thoughts, relationships and knowledge were personal and individual. This is not to suggest that other forms of self-fashioning were inadmissible or nonexistent, just that an individualised kind of self was widely presupposed in the literature, the values and the practices of early modernity, particularly at an elite level. Protestantism worked to elaborate beliefs around this kind of self because Protestant doctrine prioritised a personal relationship with God. This was enacted through individual meditation and prayer, rather than the collective worship mediated by a priest that characterised Catholic practice. Many of the progressive and 'improving' values of the period required an autonomous self capable of actively affecting the world (Tarlow 2007). What is (now) less controversial in discussions of the modern self is that in written discourse that self was, implicitly or explicitly, gendered – and the privileged gender was male. Through all the dualistic thought of the period, women and the feminine were associated with nature, with passivity and with disorder. This is visible in the pervasively negative valuation of women, women's experiences and women's bodies, in texts of the period. In addition to the low esteem in which women's ability to contribute to social life was generally held, women's experiences were simply uninteresting to most of the writing, painting, philosophising men whose productions form the majority of orthodox historical sources. The self was assumed to be male and to have all the privileges of agency and autonomy that goes with it. Many women were denied the possibilities of being the protagonists of their own individualised lives; and their opportunities were more narrowly circumscribed. And yet women did, of course, experience new forms of 'modern' subjectivity, making different choices in other spheres of action that are less visible to historians than men's. There is, of course, real potential here for archaeological studies to open up to our analysis some of the material experiences and values of women's lives in the past.

Over this period developing gender ideologies, combined with new ideas about the constitution of the self, promoted particular codes of feeling and a new emotional self that valorised relationships of love. The most important relationships of love were family relationships between close kin (such as parents and children or between siblings) and romantic love. In the transformation of the early modern world into modernity, Philippe Ariès (1981) has suggested that one of the key changes in the understanding of death was the switch in emphasis from the death of the self (apprehension of one's own mortality) to the death of the other (grief occasioned by bereavement). Looking at Orcadian commemorative practices for example, that change seems to occur in the late eighteenth century (Tarlow 1999a). Other aspects of mortuary practice, such as the beautification and attempted preservation of the dead body, suggest that in England it might have occurred rather earlier.

The new codes of sensibility and of affective individualism attributed high value to a person's emotional sensitivity, their proclivity to form emotional bonds with others and to be moved by aesthetic and humane stimuli (the beauty of a mountain view would be an example of the first; an abandoned child or maltreated animal could be (and often was) an example of the latter (see too Laqueur 1989a). In cultural history these values informed the Romantic movement of the end of the eighteenth and much of the nineteenth century; and its overwrought progeny of melodrama, sentimentalism and schmaltz. In private life the same positive values placed on feelings promoted marriage for love and an ideal of strong bonds of affection between parents and children. By the nineteenth century most Britons, at least most middle class Britons, would hope to feel love for their spouse and would understand that the most desirable filial attachments should also be those of love (Campbell 1987). The objects and subjects of love were understood as highly individualised people, unique in their selfhood, which was located in their individual body. At the moment of death, therefore, grief at separation was often profound for the bereaved (Stone 1977). The removal and decay of the body posed a problem for emotional selves of the modern period. The body itself became the focus of attempts to express and mediate the very personal relationship between the dead and the bereaved as the beautiful corpse was made to do much of the emotional 'work' of the dead person.

Over the same time an increasingly tender attitude towards children and childhood accompanied a recognition of childhood as a separate state, and children as vulnerable innocents requiring adult protection. Parental involvement in child rearing, by fathers as well as mothers became acceptable and even praiseworthy among the well-to-do (the poor had never had much choice in the matter of raising their own children). At a national level new laws were passed to protect child workers from excessive exploitation (admittedly the conditions of child employment set up by the industrialising nation were probably worse than most pre-industrial child workers had endured).

Roberts and Cox (2003: 303–4) have examined the bills of mortality for London between 1728 to the 1840s. The population of London was probably more affected by infectious disease than most other parts of Britain and Ireland, except for other large industrial towns, but their analysis shows a particularly high rate of child mortality in the capital. In the eighteenth century over 30 per cent of all recorded deaths were of infants under two years old, a proportion that fell to around 25 per cent by the middle of the nineteenth century. The next age category, children between 2 and 6, accounted for a steady 10 per cent of all deaths, and overall throughout the period about half the population died before reaching the age of 20. Child mortality only saw a substantial drop in the later part of the nineteenth century with the hygienic reforms of the water and waste infrastructure, and medical advances in preventing infection. However, there is no indication that high mortality rates discouraged emotional investment in babies and children, as is sometimes claimed. In fact, numerous diaries, letters and accounts left by bereaved parents testify to the anguish they experienced at the death of a child (Stone 1977), although these expressions of grief also varied by social class and by region (Strange 2005).

Industrialisation, urbanisation, mortality

Over the 500 years or so covered by this book the social geography and economy of Britain and Ireland changed in most areas to something that would have been unrecognisable to its sixteenth-century inhabitants. The early modern period was a time of growth for the market towns and regional centres that were important in the economic integration of town and country (Johnson 1996). Towns in the late middle ages had been walled strongholds which acted as commercial, judicial and administrative centres (Aston and Bond 1976). Often they were also centres of church power, exercised through abbeys and monasteries, colleges, guilds, churches and hospitals. In the late middle ages there had been a decline in population (due to the Black Death and its aftermath). Few new towns were established, nor did many established ones expand (Dyer 1989).

Only London attained the sort of size that really marked it out as what later Britons would recognise as a city. By the sixteenth century it was more than ten times the size of Norwich, its nearest rival. Outside London it was not until the later seventeenth century that many towns began their rapid growth. This growth accompanied a change in function, or rather changes in the importance of many of the existing functions of towns, especially trade and exchange, as the economy became more mercantile and then capitalist. Towns had an increasingly important role in the manufacture and production of goods, although it was not until the early nineteenth century that we see the widespread establishment of factories (Palmer and Neaverson 1998). The market town of Frome in Somerset was a typical example (Leech 1981). Frome experienced considerable urban growth in the seventeenth and eighteenth centuries due to the success of local cloth industry. Frome became an important market and an affluent centre for the emerging middle classes.

Town growth in early modern Britain and Ireland took the form of both infilling of empty space and expansion of the area of the town. Re-use of urban monastic sites also contributed to the formation of the modern town. By the sixteenth century the town's defensive role was largely irrelevant, and redundant walls were often pulled down, permitting urban expansion, although at the time of the Civil War in the mid seventeenth century, some old defences were refurbished or non-defensive structures were pressed into military service.

It was during the eighteenth and nineteenth centuries, however, that the greatest changes and most rapid growth of towns took place. London continued to grow at a spectacular rate, unequalled in Europe. In 1801 only seven cities in Britain had populations of over 50,000; London had over a million. Until the late eighteenth century, the urban economy was still largely based on trade; in the nineteenth century, manufacture played an increasingly important role, as changes in the sources of industrial power enabled factories to be located close to the workforce, rather than limited by convenient access to water for power and transport. Manufacture shifted from the largely home-based, small-scale production of goods for local or regional markets to factory-based bulk production of specialist goods for a global market. Towns such as Birmingham and Newcastle grew rapidly into motors of colonial and imperial expansion through the development of manufacturing and export industries. Other cities such as Bristol, Glasgow and Liverpool developed as a manufacturing hinterland to the big ports of the Atlantic trade. In places like Belfast and London, shipbuilding was itself a major industry. These huge towns had large populations, swelled by immigration from rural areas.

There was, however, a dark side to this urban expansion most evident in the slums and bills of mortality. Poor hygiene and overcrowding made some parts of towns very hazardous to health. High mortality among the urban poor was a source of concern to nineteenth-century civic improvers and played a significant role in the reform of burial practices. Heavy extractive industries such as coal mining, steel production and stone quarrying expanded and came to dominate some regions, including north Wales (slate) and the north-east of England (coal). Concurrent developments in transport and communication enabled goods and materials to be moved quickly to markets and ports for distribution around the world. Merchants, traders and shippers grew rich, and port cities such as Bristol and Liverpool thrived. However, the spread of wealth was uneven, both geographically and socially. Much of Scotland, Ireland and Wales, as well as parts of England were less well connected by transport links, less endowed with valued natural resources and, for a variety of other reasons, less willing or able to adopt capitalist forms of commodity production. Neither were more rural communities often willing to embrace the ethics of personal and community enrichment that underwrote capitalist development. In Highland Scotland, for example, the lack of exploitable resources, the shortage of roads, ports and seaways able to handle heavy traffic, and the persistence of traditional, clan-based systems of community subsistence farming combined to frustrate full integration into an industrialised, capitalist global economy.

Large-scale factory production encouraged the development of towns and cities as the rural population migrated to supply the factories' needs for waged labour. While the growing urban centres attracted the young and mobile, the same people were also being pushed out of the rural villages of their ancestors. Great increases in agricultural productivity were accomplished by changes to the organisation and management of farms (Dalglish 2003; Tarlow 2007; Forsythe 2007). Small tenant farmers were bought out by enclosing and improving landlords, and the only options left for many of the rural poor were the insecurity of casual agricultural labour or immigration to a centre that offered the possibility of paid work. The process of enclosure also deprived the very poorest of their traditional subsistence strategies. When lands that had been previously exploited as common were consolidated in private hands, those who had no strict legal claims on the land, but whose presence had been tolerated in the past, were turned out without any compensation. At the same time a series of new laws criminalised practices like foraging, gleaning and low level seasonal exploitation of 'wild' resources, which were reclassified as trespass, poaching, and theft.

These economic changes altered the geography of Britain. Even taking Dyer's (2003) unusually high estimate that 20% of the population of Britain lived in towns during the fourteenth to early eighteenth centuries (most estimates are considerably lower), the rise to 50% by the time of the 1851 census is remarkable. To some extent the developed capitalism of the nineteenth century opened up possibilities for individuals to improve their social position and grow rich, the traditional legitimatory ideology of liberal capitalism. However, the possibilities of autonomous Improvement were nevertheless constrained. As already noted, women's life choices were restricted by the legal and cultural limits imposed on their capacity for independent action. Those without the social or personal resources to seek out education and opportunity were almost certain to "waste their sweetness on the desert air". Thus, along with the upwardly mobile entrepreneurs and auto-didacts there was also a large population of very poor and destitute people. Unsurprisingly, levels of mortality among the very poor were high, especially in urban areas (Lunn 1991; Harris 2004). Even the middle classes suffered from endemic and epidemic disease, especially in towns; and some evidence suggests that adult mortality among the elite was actually as high as among the very poor, due to lifestyle factors (Razzell and Spence 2006). A number of factors contributed to high levels of urban mortality: the new city population was living in very crowded conditions, especially in the slums and shanties that mushroomed to accommodate new immigrants from rural areas and, in the nineteenth century, refugees from the rural famines of Ireland and northern Scotland and the wars and persecutions of continental Europe. Devastating epidemics of infectious disease ravaged the population from time to time. Diseases like cholera and typhus thrived in the polluted and crowded cities. In the absence of proper sewers, people used rivers, soakaways and simple dumps, which meant that drinking water, whether obtained from rivers or wells, became more polluted and regularly bore cholera. Although modern theories of infection did not take hold until the mid nineteenth century, concerns about the effects of miasmas (bad air emitted from decaying things) and effluvias (flowing or seeping liquid pollution) on human health drove a number of reforms from the late eighteenth century. Reformers condemned, among other unhygienic practices, the overcrowded city graveyards, from which the smell of rotting bodies disturbed the neighbours and congregations of city churches. In the middle third of the nineteenth century most inner city parish burial grounds were closed to new interments, and large new non-denominational cemeteries were established in the suburbs (see Chapter 4).

Archaeological excavation of urban churchyards shows the degree of overcrowding present by the end of the eighteenth century, with the same plots used for sometimes scores of successive burials, and earlier grave cuts obliterated by numerous later cuts and recuts for new shafts. Burial densities of 3 bodies per square metre or higher were normal in London parish burial grounds (Miles et al. 2008: 35). This frequent re-use of burial plots was hard to reconcile with a prevalent cultural rhetoric of death that emphasised rest, peace and the possession of an undisturbed grave in perpetuity.

Hospitals, prisons and workhouses

The rapidly increasing population, combined with the particular social and political context of Britain in the eighteenth and nineteenth centuries produced a large social underclass of paupers, criminals and indigents. The new legal and cultural context promoted a view that these groups were a problem demanding a social solution. In the case of criminals, for example, traditional practices were redefined as crimes in order to protect increasingly individualised property rights. At the same time the break-down of traditional family and community based networks and systems of support made people more likely to turn to crime to supply basic needs. Medieval and early modern regimes of judicial punishment tended to be direct, retributive, physical and often carried out in (and by) the community (for example, stocks, 'rough music', beatings, brandings, and execution or transportation for more serious crimes). In contrast, eighteenth- and nineteenth-century sensibilities demanded that punishment be aimed also at reform, be more coolly and impartially carried out, and that the community be protected by containment of the criminal threat in some place removed from other people (Ignatieff 1978). These changing 'disciplinary' practices around the body, may also be seen in developments in institutional architecture (Markus 1994; Brodie et al. 1999; Spencer-Wood et al. 2001) as well as changing attitudes towards the disposal of the bodies of the poor and criminals (see Chapter 6). However, while there was certainly an important shift in attitudes towards legal punishment after the early modern period, Thomas Laqueur (1989b) has noted the continued carnivaleque elements of public executions until their cessation in 1868, and suggests that these tend to be downplayed by historians (e.g. Foucault 1977; Hay et al. 1988).

Similarly, the numbers of people living in extreme poverty also increased over this period. Changes to the organisation of agricultural labour to a situation where much rural employment was casual and short-term removed the expectation that farmers would care for labourers and their families as part of the extended farm household, as had been the practice in Britain and Ireland in the late medieval and early modern periods (Snell 1985; Mingay 1994). In industrial areas too, more alienated forms of labour came to dominate many parts of Britain, as the anonymity of the factory, paying wages for time, or the large-scale 'putter out', paying money for piece work, replaced smaller workshops (Palmer and Neaverson 1998). Work was not always easy to find, and in times of unemployment people's final recourse was generally to apply for parish poor relief. But short-term contracts and a mobile population made it easier for parishes to refuse to support those who were not settled there. The number of beggars, tramps and people living rough rose, unsurprisingly. At the same time, civic pride and a spirit of Improvement made the established middle classes less tolerant of the sight of paupers on the streets and less happy to accept the destitute, unemployed or 'profligate and over-fertile' as worthy recipients of charitable maintenance. Lack of paid work, disorderliness and dirt were widely believed to be the result of personal failures of will, morality and discipline: there was no concept of unemployment as an economic phenomenon with human victims – and reminders of the continued existence of paupers alongside respectable society was experienced as a social evil.

By the eighteenth century, both criminals and paupers had become 'problems' that needed to be removed, or at least contained. In response to this perceived need a range of new institutions were established with the aim of deterring or reforming social deviants, and protecting the rest of society from their disruptive and contaminating presence (Morrison 1997). For the poor, the workhouse was transformed from a kind of refuge for those with nowhere else to go, to a place for the ordering and moral improvement of those who could not be persuaded to conform by other means. Parishes grouped together to provide 'union' workhouses which had to be 'less eligible', that is, less desirable, than the conditions of the poor outside (Fraser 1976). Given the levels of disease, malnutrition and material deprivation among the non-institutional poor, this was a pretty tall order. Because it would have been inhumane to starve or freeze workhouse inmates, the poor were discouraged from applying for help by instituting a psychologically and emotoinally miserable regime of segregation by sex and age, as well as the splitting up of families. These disincentives were coupled with long and arduous work programmes and the de-individualising practices of a stigmatising uniform and a dull and monotonous diet. After the 1832 Anatomy Act a further deterrent was added by the ruling that 'unclaimed' bodies of paupers who died in the workhouse be made available for anatomical dissection.

Until the later eighteenth century, custodial sentences were not commonly passed on criminals. those who were not fined, corporally punished or executed were removed from British society by the simple expedient of shipping them en masse to the new world, mainly the plantations of Virginia, Maryland and Barbados, until American independence. After 1775, although many convicts were transported to Australia, some after being held on disease-ridden 'floating hulks' for some time, many more custodial sentences were imposed (Ignatieff 1978). Old gaols were totally inadequate for these new demands, since they had only been intended as temporary holding places. New prisons were established, designed to enable surveillance and the removal of prisoners from both a vulnerable public and the moral contagion of one another.

Numerous other institutions were founded in the later post-medieval period, from the late eighteenth to the late nineteenth century, prominently including schools, colleges and other institutes of education, orphanages and young people's reformatories. Given the scope of this volume, however, the most significant institutions in tracing a history of death and burial are those in which people most commonly died, and which made provision for the disposal of their bodies. As well as workhouses and prisons, the institutions that most commonly owned their own burial grounds were hospitals.

Hospital patients were not regarded as wicked or feckless deviants in the same way that the inmates of prisons and workhouses were, but they were nevertheless subject to some of the principles of social control adopted by those coercive institutions. There was an imbalance of power between patients and the medical and administrative staff of the hospital, with the body of the sick person functioning as the place where inequalities were created and played out. Even after death the body of a hospital patient could be subjected to the intrusive attentions of doctors, as we shall see in Chapter 6.

Medical Science

We have seen already how mortality rates were affected by urbanisation, hygiene and other factors, including the introduction or evolution of new strains of pathogens. Medical knowledge was transformed over this period. Galenic theories of disease, which informed medieval medical practice, held that illnesses were the result of imbalances in the 'humours' or elements of which the body was composed and which also determined personal character. Gilchrist and Sloane suggest that these beliefs may have influenced the differential treatment of burials of women and the young in plague cemeteries of the period (Gilchrist and Sloane 2005). These beliefs gave way to a more modern conception of pathology which understood disease as a result of infection or malfunction, with consequent shifts in the forms of medical intervention that are visible in burial contexts. What this meant, among other things, was that death went from being an event whose timing and course was known only to God, to a consequence of bodily failure. Death became an anomalous departure from a systemic equilibrium and therefore required explanation and investigation.

The treatment of disease was carried out by physicians, pharmacists and surgeons and was closely linked to research and the development of medical sciences like biology and, especially, anatomy. There was no separation between medical research and clinical practice; the same people carried out both, although medical education was a more specialised field. Traditional medical knowledge in Europe was passed in two distinct lines: folkloric knowledge mixed traditional herbal treatments with ritual practices and religious elements, so that folk rituals, charms, prayers, botanical preparations or a combination of all four could be used to treat ailments. Such medical knowledge was often in the possession of women, was transmitted mostly orally and was available at low cost. Scientific medicine, by contrast, was based on the writings of classical authors and their continental interpreters. It was a masculine, pedantic tradition. From the seventeenth century, both traditions were challenged and eventually marginalised by a new kind of medical science, based on empirical observation and practical experiment. This privileged practice and experience above the authority of ancient authors and received wisdom. The need for ongoing observational research to benefit human health was often advanced as an argument for facilitating access to cadavers for anatomists, surgeons and medical students. On the whole, however, until the mid nineteenth century, medical science contributed very few major benefits to human health (Roberts and Cox 2003: 358), with a small number of exceptions such as successful and widespread vaccination against smallpox. Whether or not they were convinced of the potential benefits of scientific medicine, most of the population of Britain and Ireland remained hostile to the practice of anatomical dissection. Some authors, both in the nineteenth century and today, attribute public reluctance to support anatomical study through the dissection of dead human bodies to a literal belief in the resurrection of the dead (e.g. Roberts and Cox 2003: 289). However, the history of the relationship between religious and scientific belief over this period is complicated and contradictory, especially as far as concerns the dead body. There is little historically documented evidence to suggest that people believed that dissection (or indeed any other non-normative treatment of the corpse) would compromise a Christian resurrection. This supposition was primarily cited by educated supporters of dissection in order to support their case and ridicule the opposition (Richardson 1987: 273). There were certainly a range of beliefs around post-mortem intervention and whether or not it was viewed negatively depended to a large extent on how the intervention was positioned politically and socially (Crossland 2009a; Park 1994; Weiss-Krejci 2005). Equally, no straightforward opposition can be demonstrated between scientific and religious beliefs around post-mortem surgery. Most of the early modern texts on anatomy state that the ultimate aim of anatomy is greater knowledge of the self – "cognoscere te ipse" – and thus a more perfect understanding of God. Religious devotion, in these early texts, is given far greater emphasis than any more tangible benefit in terms of human health. It is certainly not the case that religious belief was squeezed out or replaced by the rise of empirical science, as progressivist histories of the modern period might suggest. Scientific and religious convictions not only co-existed throughout this period, but continued to inform each other, even in cases where the beliefs appear incompatible (Tarlow 2011).

In the latter part of the nineteenth century mortality rates among vulnerable groups such as infants, children, parturitive women and workers in dangerous industries began to fall. Mean life expectancy at all ages began to rise. Improvements in sanitation, nutrition, and better legal specification of minimum working and living conditions were probably more significant than medical knowledge in improving human health, but a better scientific understanding of the causes of disease underlay beneficial legal and social developments.

'The Afterlife'

Despite the post-modern critique which valorizes open-ended and fluid forms of writing, the discursive formations of the post-Enlightenment academic world tend to privilege narratives about past styles of thinking that present coherent and relatively closed accounts. This can translate into an expectation that any beliefs under study will relate their 'true facts' to each other in an internally consistent manner that coheres without obvious incompatibilities or contradictions. Beliefs about death and the dead, reveal the inadequacy of these expectations. People's ideas about what happens after death were complex, contradictory and often incoherent. This is still true today as attested to by the persistence of vague beliefs in ghosts, spiritual presences, Heaven, angels and so on. People may accept the teachings of biological science and offer their organs for transplant after death, but many are still disturbed by the retention of body parts for research (see too Bynum 1998).

For these reasons it is not possible to provide a neat history of 'belief' as it relates to death, with new theological or cultural ideas succeeding one another in a linear narrative, each set of beliefs expressed through a coherent set of material practices. Throughout this period – and before and afterwards too – several incompatible discourses of belief existed in parallel. These beliefs were drawn upon contextually. To give an example, at an academic conference, one might work from the assumption that after death the self ceases to exist, and the body simply rots, insensibly, in the ground. And yet archaeologists frequently feel the spectral presence of those they exhume (Boyle 1999; Kirk and Start 1999), and it is common to endow the dead body with some agency and to talk about how it 'speaks' or 'testifies' (Crossland 2009b). Walking past a graveyard late at night, or engaging in the shared emotional experience of watching a horror film, one might feel that some aspect of personhood survives death, and that dead bodies might be sensible and animate. Particularly in culturally and emotionally difficult times such as bereavement, the same person might participate in discourses about Heaven, angels and souls, grasp at the promise of future reunion or a continuing personal bond with somebody who is 'watching over' you. It is hard to pin down what exactly we 'believe' about the afterlife even today. The point is that while we should not expect a closed and coherent system of human belief, we can recognise that in certain contexts many members of a group can agree to talk about about belief in the same terms, both linguistically and in material practice. This book does not, therefore, try to identify a clear set of beliefs in the afterlife, but does draw upon ways of 'talking' about the dead – with words and with actions – that gained prominence in particular historical contexts.

What factors affected the treatment of the body after death?

Religion

While religious belief alone did not determine postmortem treatment, it was nevertheless an important factor. The established church controlled most places of burial and specified the outline of funerals. Until the nineteenth century even non-conformist burials were usually subject to Anglican control. Religious beliefs about the existence of Purgatory, the efficacy of prayers for the dead and the bodily nature of resurrection were also clearly important in structuring the relationship between the dead and the living and thus affected the treatment of the corpse both directly and indirectly. Religious affiliations were often as much about identification with a particular social group as adherence to specific dogma. Here, the maintenance of particular burial grounds provided a locus for the reproduction of community identity. In the aftermath of the Reformation, either strength of faith or tenacious fidelity to a shared Catholic identity moved some people to risk the wrath of the law and the new church by continuing to use monastic burial grounds, for example.

Status and wealth

Traditionally, mortuary archaeologists have often chosen to interpret the archaeology of death and burial in terms of the demonstration or negotiation of status. This approach risks ignoring or minimising the significance of the other factors listed here, which all affect disposal (Tarlow 1999), although undoubtedly the possession or lack of wealth and high standing in society affected the kind of treatment a body received. Aspiration could be as significant as actual wealth; people might choose to spend disproportionately on a funeral as a social investment (as described by Parker Pearson 1981, for example). The funeral was an opportunity to generate social capital and esteem by publicly demonstrating not only wealth, but also appropriate emotions, tastes, political and religious sympathies and cultural attitudes, all of which could enhance the social position of a family. Wealth was perhaps most usefully deployed in the ceremony of the funeral and the erection of lasting monuments to the deceased. However, the ability to access an exclusive or expensive place of burial, an elaborate coffin (or indeed, in early periods, any coffin at all), or fine grave clothes was a way of showing wealth. Additionally the corpse's style of hair and clothes, and the use of good dentures or other prosthetics usually suggest possession of material wealth in life.

The absence of wealth and status could also have a great effect on the treatment of the body. The scientific development of anatomical knowledge was acquired through the exploitation of the dead bodies of the poor and marginal in ways that enacted and reproduced inequalities of power. Even if left unexamined, the bodies of the poor, the socially deviant, and those of ethnic or religious 'others' could be stigmatised in the form or location of burial.

Emotional relationships between the living and the dead

Death and bereavement were often accompanied by feelings of love and grief and the body of the deceased could mediate those emotional relationships in various ways. The place of burial sometimes became the locus of a continuing relationship between the living and the dead, especially after Protestant reformers had denied the value of prayers for the souls of others. For most Britons, especially in the eighteenth and nineteenth centuries, the decay of the body was a horrifying prospect, especially the body of a beloved individual whose selfhood was very closely linked to his or her unique body. Accordingly, measures were taken among the wealthy to delay or prevent the onset of decay, through embalming or preservation in wax cloths or lead-lined coffins. Where this was not possible, the dead body was often subject to attempts at beautification through the use of cosmetics, false hair and teeth, special clothes, flowers and foliage, opulent textiles, ruffles and frills (Tarlow 1999b). In the early modern period the dead body seems to have been viewed as less horrifying, and body parts were even used by the living as symbols of a dead person with whom an emotional relationship was still active. This is attested to, for example, by the curation of Sir Thomas More's head by his daughter and its eventual deposition in his son-in-law's family vault (Tatton-Brown 1980).

Emotions towards the dead include fear and revulsion as well as love and grief. On a personal level emotions of guilt and fear, especially fear of one's own inescapable death, were also significant factors in trying to represent death or the relationship between the dead person and their survivors in particular ways. As Alan Swedlund (2009) observed, "Bereavement and commemoration were intertwined in complex ways as personal emotions and social conventions came together."

Beliefs about the dead body

As we have noted already, beliefs do not always conform to religious teaching or indeed to any apparently coherent position. Other significant kinds of beliefs include the attribution of sentience to the dead body, care for its 'comfort', and whether the corpse is a source of dread and fear or is lovingly curated. There are also metaphorical or figurative beliefs about the body such as whether the dead person is seen as embarking on comparisons of death to a journey, or is compared to a planted seed, or a person falling asleep. All these metaphors can inform the material treatment of the corpse.

Practical and economic constraints

Death rituals are not, however, free expressions of belief and cultural value. There are material limits to the resources available for burial that impact and limit cultural ideals. Because bodies decay quickly, and death can happen suddenly, there is often little time to prepare the body exactly as either the deceased or the bereaved would wish. Living in a particular place or being a member of a particular group could constrain the options available for disposal – outside London, there were limited numbers of dissenters' burial grounds, for example. What we encounter archaeologically is often the result of a compromise between the ideals promoted by religious, political or social interests; the personal, economic resources available and the constraints of law and convention.

In particular the rise of the undertaking profession over the period considered in this volume saw the removal of the preparation of the corpse and the management of the funerary rites from the family home to the death professional (Litten 1991: 5–31). Material accoutrements of death – the coffin and its fittings, grave clothes and so on – were more frequently chosen from nationally distributed ranges. Professionalisation of disposal resulted, predictably, in a smaller degree of regional and local variation. Paradoxically it often resulted in a greater degree of choice for the bereaved, but a choice that was largely constrained to a set of pre-defined options.

The law

The disposal of the dead had to meet certain legal strictures. Appendix 1 lists the most significant legislation affecting burial. The law could stipulate what methods of disposal were acceptable (not cremation, for example, until 1880), where the dead could be buried (most urban churchyards, for example, were closed in the mid nineteenth century) and even what the dead could wear (English wool, to support the woollen industry and prevent valuable linen from going out of circulation when it was in great demand by the paper industry). The law could also insist that an autopsy take place as part of a coroner's inquiry where there was any suspicion about the cause of death.

Tradition

Of course, not all decisions about funerary practice were reached after a careful consideration of social, cultural, religious and philosophical factors. Most of the time mortuary practices simply followed the traditions and conventions of the period and place. The slowness and conservatism of death ritual has been noted by a number of archaeologists and anthropologists (e.g. Goldstein 2004: 251). In the context of post-medieval Britain, Harold Mytum (2007) has shown how the coffin and below-ground material culture was more resistant to change and less inflected by fashion than the commemorative monuments erected in graveyards. This was partly to do with the greater opportunities for ostentation provided by the erection of an enduring and public monument compared to the coffin itself which would only be briefly on open display, but it also relates to the willingness of the bereaved to conform to local expectation and to be guided by the undertaker in times of emotional and psychological stress. Two of the remarkable features of the mortuary archaeology of the period covered by this book are, first, the lack of major rupture with the preceding medieval period, and second, the similarity and continuity in the burials of the vast majority of people throughout the period. Although we have perhaps paid more attention to the unusual, deviant or unique examples, most people continued to be buried in graveyards, in simple shrouds and single-shell coffins, with no durable grave goods. In this respect the modally average nineteenth-century burial was very similar to that of the sixteenth century, or indeed that of the fourteenth, except for the increasing use of coffins.

Politics

Political sympathies and statements were sometimes significant in determining funerary practice or burial location. In the case of the wealthy aristocratic and political elite, ostentatious funerals could be used to demonstrate the locus of political power. Burial – and especially commemoration – in prestigious locations inside churches and cathedrals was often accompanied by state or church-sponsored solemnities, and the pronouncement of funeral sermons, usually published afterwards, which used the occasion to make political propaganda. However, even the means of disposal could sometimes be seen as a political statement. In the nineteenth century, for example, the campaign for the legalisation of cremation was regarded as a radical cause, supported by the same people who believed in other 'eccentric' causes, such as vegetarianism or votes for women (Jupp 2006).

Manner of death

Finally the way in which somebody died could affect or even determine the treatment of their corpse. Victims of judicial executions were sometimes legally required to be buried at their places of execution, to be displayed in gibbets, or to have their bodies handed over to anatomy schools (Richardson 1987: 32–37). Those who died at times of plague or major epidemics were sometimes buried in mass pits with minimal ceremony, as frequently also happened to those killed in battle. Health and public decency required bodies to be quickly interred in such times of crisis. Those who died as victims of crime, or in some kinds of accidents like falling into bogs or being drowned at sea might receive no formal burial: some individuals have entered our gazetteer as isolated bodies that might have been deliberately concealed or whose place and manner of death was not discovered at the time.

About this book

The book falls into two major sections: a gazetteer of the archaeologically-investigated post-medieval sites of human burial in England, Scotland, Wales and Ireland, preceded by a descriptive account of the archaeological evidence in its historical and cultural context. The gazetteer lists sites, rather than individual burials, and aims to give an indication of the kind of evidence that was recovered from each of the locations, together with references, so that people interested in post-medieval burial practice can identify sites of possible relevance. We have drawn on summaries published in *Post-Medieval Archaeology*, the *British and Irish Archaeological Bibliography*, together with published articles, online reports, and grey literature publications obtained from archaeological units across Britain and Ireland.

The first seven chapters outline and describe the archaeological evidence for post-medieval human burial in Britain and Ireland, drawing out (we hope) major themes and offering some preliminary analysis of the data. The first chapter outlines the historical context of the material – including major religious and political changes affecting mortuary practices, and something of the social, cultural and economic background. This is necessarily a brief and selective history and obviously cannot stand as a general introduction to the period. There is, unfortunately, no single introductory work of history that covers the whole period considered here across all the countries of the British Isles, nor even good histories of its constituent nations over the whole of the last 500 years, but introductions limited by period and place are easy to locate.

The chapters that follow address different aspects of the material and archaeological characteristics of burial over this period. We have tried to construct a synthesis which we hope will be useful, drawing on examples from across Britain and Ireland, as well as to draw attention to local differences which we are not able to cover comprehensively.

Notes

1. In figure 1.4, the term community burial ground include churchyards, garden cemeteries, private burial grounds, municipal cemeteries and non-conformist burial grounds.
2. The Corporation Act of 1661, the Test Act of 1673 and the Test Act of 1678.

2 The preparation and presentation of the post-medieval corpse

At the centre of any funerary rite lies the body of the deceased, for it is the loss of life which sets all funerary rituals in process and it is the disposal of the mortal remains of the deceased that forms the focus of virtually all mortuary practices. As such the body provides the most pertinent subject with which to start a survey of the archaeological evidence for post-medieval burial practices. This chapter focuses on the preparation and presentation of the corpse prior to burial from the beginning of the sixteenth century to the end of the nineteenth century. The cleaning, adornment and display of the corpse has formed a constant component of funerary rites throughout the historic period in Britain and Ireland. The body of the Anglo-Saxon Saint Cuthbert, was washed and re-dressed prior to burial in the seventh century as were the bodies of the dead during the reign of Victoria over a millennium later (Colgrave 1940: 131; Webb 1965b: 97; Richardson 1987: 17). During this period attitudes to the body and its role in the afterlife moved from emphasising the resurrection of the body during the early medieval period to the early modern trope of death marking the soul's release from a putrefying prison of flesh (Bynum 1995: 10; Tarlow 1999). What is remarkable about the treatment of the dead body over this period of some 1400 years is the degree of continuity at the core of normative burial practice. The west-east interment of a supine, washed and prepared body in an ecclesiastical burial ground was as normal for most of the rural population of Britain and Ireland in nineteenth century as it had been for their ancestors more than a thousand years earlier. While some unusual treatments of the dead are historically particular – anatomical dissection for example did not occur before the period considered in this book – the ways of distinguishing transgressive or exceptional individuals, such as prone burial, or burial in marginal locations – are notable for their great antiquity (Reynolds 2009).

Washing the dead

Throughout the last 1400 years regardless of contemporary eschatological beliefs a degree of care towards the corpse persisted, ensuring the corpse was washed, garbed, and usually displayed prior to interment. This in part may be explained by the fact the corpse resembled the body of a known and often beloved individual, and as such was due the care befitting that individual (Richardson 1987: 16; Cressy 1997: 387). This reverential treatment of the deceased was particularly important as according to some post-medieval folk beliefs, the soul was thought to linger around the body after death, at least for a short time, and a sentient corpse would be well aware of its treatment (Richardson 1987: 7, 17; Porter 2003: 217). Yet while the need to prepare and display the body prior to interment remained a constant throughout the historic period, the form these practices took did change over time. This was particularly true of the way the corpse was dressed for the grave, which during the post-medieval period was influenced by contemporary eschatological views, the rise of the undertaking profession and even state legislation.

During the medieval period, following death the body was washed, laid out and dressed in appropriate funerary attire, usually a winding sheet or shroud (Gilchrist and Sloane 2005: 23). This practice continued during the post-medieval period. A French visitor, writing in the early eighteenth century, described the English custom of washing the body, shaving it if male, and then clothing it (Misson 1719: 89). Death is a messy process: the body is often soiled with blood, pus and sweat while the release of the anal sphincter after death results in the soiling of clothes and bedding (Janaway 1993: 104; Cressy 1997: 425). To send the body on its final journey so defiled was considered inappropriate by most people. Yet the antiquity of the tradition of washing and laying out the corpse suggests that the emphasis on washing the bodies of the dead has more than a practical function attributed to concerns about hygiene, particularly when most of the living post-medieval population bathed infrequently (Cox M. 1998: 114). The cleansing of the body may also have a more symbolic role perhaps linked to the preparation and purification of the body for its final journey. Once washed, precautions were taken to prevent the release of the products of decomposition from soiling the body by plugging the orifices with fabric (Cox M. 1998: 114). Only a few examples of such textiles have been recovered archaeologically and this is probably a result of problems in the preservation and recognition these fabrics. A pad of fabric found bound between the legs of one of the bodies from Christ Church Spitalfields may have been used to absorb the products of decomposition and accidentally left in place (Cox M. 1998: 114; Janaway 1993: 104). Alternatively, the pad may have been used to treat a pressure sore or incontinence in life and retained in death (Cox M. 1998: 114). A porcelain plug recovered from the pelvic region of an individual buried at Goswell Road in London was also probably used to seal the body's orifices (Deeves 2002: 26).

Those responsible for the preparation of the body varied during the post-medieval period both with the passage of time and the social standing of the deceased. Francis Tate writing in the early sixteenth century said of the preparation of the body that "by whom it is done, I think at this day is little regarded amongst us" (1600: 217). Not necessarily a pleasant task, the washing and laying out the body was often performed by members of the family, although these duties were frequently designated to others by those of means, such as servants, the poor or neighbours (Litten 1991: 72; Cressy 1997: 428–9). Probate accounts from the sixteenth and first half of the seventeenth century often mention that women were involved in laying out the body, but give few other details (Gittings 1984: 112). From the seventeenth century laying out the bodies of the well-to-do was increasingly performed by individuals supplied by the coffin maker or, later, the undertaker (Litten 1991: 72). This delegation of duties could lead to complaints. In an address on premature death and interment in 1780 William Hawes complained that the bodies of those thought to be dead were "committed to the management of an ignorant and unfeeling serf, whose care extends no further than laying the limbs straight" (1780: 30). Indeed despite the increasing use of undertakers, in many middle- and upper-class Victorian households laying out remained the duty of a family servant or the nurse who had attended the deceased during their final illness (Jalland 1999b: 211).

Dressing the dead

While the washing of the dead appears to have been a constant element of the funerary process during the post-medieval period, there were significant changes in the way the body was clad for interment. Most burials during the late medieval period were simply wrapped in a shroud or winding cloth prior to burial (Gilchrist and Sloane 2005: 106). This practice appears to have continued up to the end of the sixteenth century when Francis Tate described how "as the funeral approaches, the body is wrapt up with flowers and herbs in a faire sheet" (Tate 1600: 217). Unfortunately, textiles rarely survive in funerary contexts from the sixteenth and seventeenth centuries and much of the information on how the corpse was dressed for interment during this period is derived from artistic representations of the deceased. Images on funerary monuments of the sixteenth century suggest that the widespread use of shrouds appears to have continued beyond the Reformation (Litten 1991: 61–70). Although caution should be exercised when using artistic representations, images, such as a shrouded corpse on the 1592 Foljambe family monument at Chesterfield in Derbyshire (1991: 64), are suggestive of the persistence of shrouded burial and provide some indication of the form of the sixteenth-century shroud. In contrast to the images of the tightly swaddled enshrouded corpse from the late medieval period, the sixteenth-century shroud appears to have been a voluminous sheet some three times the width of the body and twelve inches longer to allow it to be tied above the head and below the feet (figure 2.1) (Litten 1991: 57, 60). From the 1630s a cap or bonnet was often added to the ensemble, and an undershirt or smock was more frequently placed on the body before it was wrapped in a shroud (Litten 1991: 76; Gittings 1984: 112). In 1638, Reginald Shrawley, a member of the community of the hospital of St John, Canterbury, was interred wearing a sheet (shroud), shirt and cap (Gittings 1984: 112).

While textiles rarely survive for long in the grave, shroud pins have been found accompanying sixteenth- and seventeenth-century burials. Fifty-seven of the burials interred in the seventeenth-century burial ground at Abingdon vineyard in Oxfordshire were interred accompanied by wound wire-headed shroud pins of sixteenth- to seventeenth-century type (Allen 2006). Copper alloy shroud pins were found with seven of the sixteen burials in the late seventeen- and early eighteenth-century Quaker burial ground at

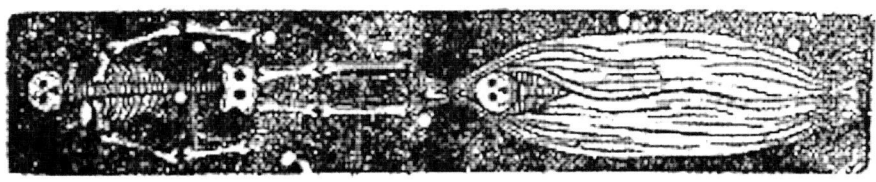

Figure 2.1 Image of a shrouded burial from the 'Ballad of the Inhumane Butcher of the Leaden-Hall Market'. The corpse appears to be loosely wrapped in a large piece of cloth which is then tied above the head and below the feet (Picture courtesy of the Pepys Library).

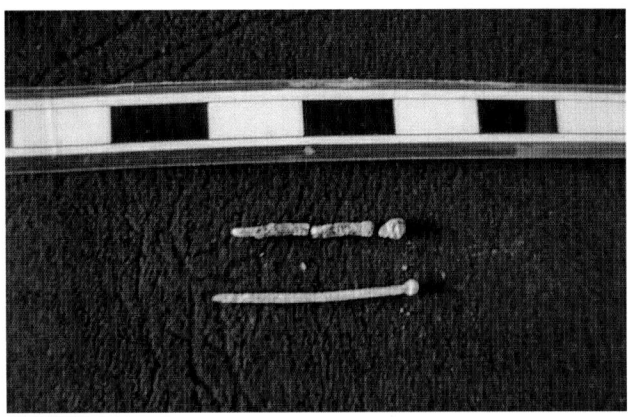

Figure 2.2 Shroud pins from the New Churchyard, London (Photograph by Annia Cherryson).

Hemingford Grey, Cambridgeshire (McNicol *et al.* 2007: 5), and pins of a similar age were recovered from London's New Churchyard (figure 2.2). Shroud pins are not found with all burials and when present, their numbers are relatively low. This suggests that pins were not the primary means of securing shrouds (Gilchrist and Sloane 2005: 110). Some may have been dress accessories but many are likely to have been used for pinning shroud material. Individuals were known to be sewn into shrouds at the time of the Reformation. In 1516 Alice Bumpstead bequeathed 2d in her will to the two women responsible for sewing her into her winding sheet (Dinn 1995: 154). As such the pins might, at least in some cases, have simply served to secure fabric during this process and subsequently been accidentally interred with the body (Gilchrist and Sloane 2005: 110).

During the early modern period, shrouds were often sheets belonging to the family, although there are examples of the purchase of fabrics especially for shrouds (Gittings 1984: 111–112; Litten 1991: 71; Cressy 1997: 430). During the late medieval period, linen was the fabric most often used for winding clothes and shrouds (Cox M. 1998: 115) and its use continued into the early modern period although the use of fabrics such as calico, crepe and worsted for shrouds also appears in the accounts of the period (Cressy 1997: 429). This changed in 1660 with the passing of the first Act for Burying in Woollen Only. This legislation, requiring the corpse to be interred in woollen cloth, was designed to support indigenous wool industry (Gittings 1984: 56). Initially, adherence was far from universal, requiring the legislation to be reinforced by an additional act in 1678 imposing a fine on those failing to obey the regulations (1678 30. Cha 2 c.3; Litten 1991: 74). An affidavit was required confirming only woollen fabrics had been used to garb the dead, although it was possible to purchase an exemption from the act for £5 (1680 32 Cha 2 c.1; Gittings 1984: 113, figure 2.3). It had been possible to procure ready-made shrouds from the mid-seventeenth century and the burial in woollen legislation enhanced this trade by allowing under-takers to stock large numbers of woollen shrouds in many sizes (Litten 1991: 72, 74).

While most of those interred during the early modern period were simply enclosed within a shroud, there is a little evidence suggesting a small proportion of individuals were interred in clothes. Bishop Mayo, who died in 1516 and was interred in Hereford Cathedral, was buried in his episcopal robes accompanied with a crosier and gold ring (*Anon* 1844: 47). Remnants of a brocade band, presumably from ornate vestments were found in St Augustine's Abbey in Canterbury, Kent with the body of Abbot John Dygon, who died in 1510 (Thorn 1981: 74, 81). The abbot also had a lead mitre on his head, decorated and painted to mimic a real preciosa mitre (Thorn 1981: 76). Interment in clothing does not appear to have been just confined to the ecclesiastical elite. Four burials dated to c.1450–1525 from the priory of St Mary Sandwell, Staffordshire were found with the remains of footwear (Thomas 1991: 102, 110) and a buckle of probable late fifteenth- to early sixteenth-century date was found with a burial at the Austin Friars in Leicester (Clay 1981: 133). Fragments of a leather belt with three buckles and fragments of metal, possibly from the belt, were found in a grave in Stradbally North, Castleconnell in County Limerick (Coyne 2003: 24, 46). A pipe found with the burial suggests a seventeenth century date and it is possible that the buckles were part of a military uniform (Coyne and Lynch 2003a: 15). Five hook-and-eye fasteners, presumably from clothing, were found with a skeleton interred in a small seventeenth-century cemetery in Abingdon West (Norton *et al.* 2005: 14). Three burials from the Civil War cemetery of Abingdon vineyard contained lace chapes, which are the metal tags found at the ends of clothing ties (Allen 2006). The Abingdon evidence suggests that the practice of occasional clothed interment persisted into the seventeenth century, although both cemeteries have been linked to the Civil War and circumstances during periods of conflict may have prevented adherence to the usual funerary conventions. The rarity of such finds does suggest that the vast majority of interments were in shrouds only. Indeed a seventeenth-century pamphlet contrasting London's charity with the "crueltie" of the countryside in the matter of plague burials shows the mass pit burial of clothed bodies as an indication of improper and uncharitable treatment of the dead (figure 2.4) (Anon 1641).

Funerary representations suggest that the use of loose shrouds fastened at head and foot declined during the last quarter of the seventeenth century as

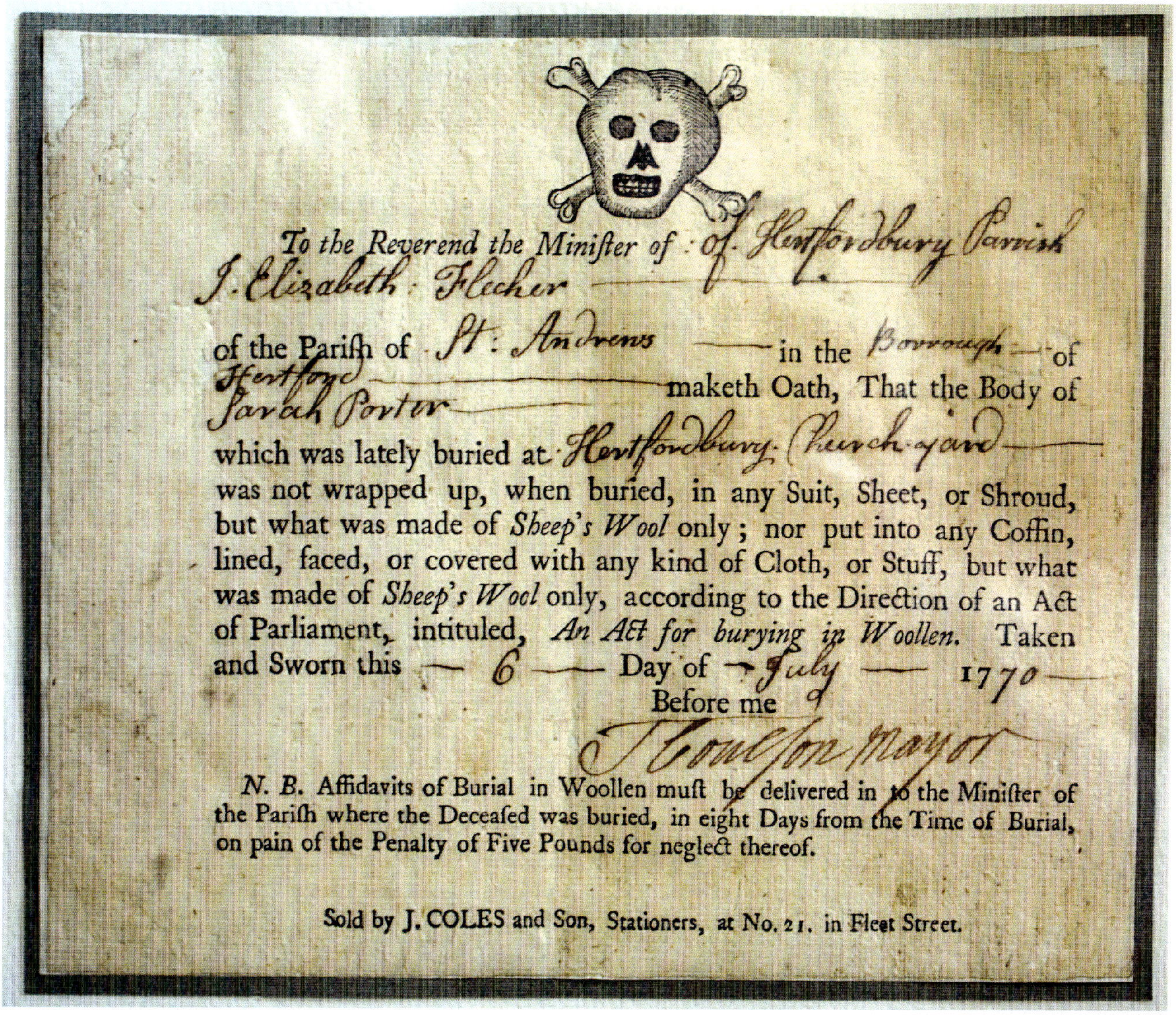

To the Reverend the Minifter of : of Hertfordbury Parish
J. Elizabeth : Fletcher

of the Parifh of St : Andrews —— in the Borrough —— of Hertford —— maketh Oath, That the Body of Sarah Porter ——
which was lately buried at Hertfordbury : Church-yard ——
was not wrapped up, when buried, in any Suit, Sheet, or Shroud, but what was made of *Sheep's Wool* only; nor put into any Coffin, lined, faced, or covered with any kind of Cloth, or Stuff, but what was made of *Sheep's Wool* only, according to the Direction of an Act of Parliament, intituled, *An Act for burying in Woollen.* Taken and Sworn this — 6 — Day of — July — 1770 —
Before me
J. Coulson Mayor

N. B. Affidavits of Burial in Woollen muft be delivered in to the Minifter of the Parifh where the Deceafed was buried, in eight Days from the Time of Burial, on pain of the Penalty of Five Pounds for neglect thereof.

Sold by J. COLES and Son, Stationers, at No. 21. in Fleet Street.

Figure 2.3 Affidavit confirming that the body of Sarah Porter, buried in 1770, was buried in only woollen clothing, in accordance with the Act for Burial in Woollen Onely (Photograph courtesy of Mark Ynys-Mon).

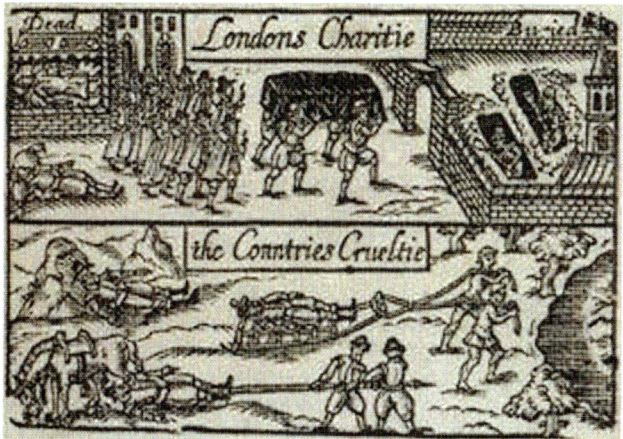

Figure 2.4 A pamphlet of 1641 contrasts London's charity with the country's cruelty. The decent treatment of the plague dead in the city includes burial in single graves, in draped coffins carried by bearers and followed by mourners carrying sprigs of rosemary. The (grossly unfair) caricature of rural plague burial shows the dead dragged (by a rope around the ankles in one case) to mass burial pits still clad in their everyday clothes. None of the ceremony of normal, decent burial attends them and they are unaccompanied by any mourner (London's Lamentation (1641). Picture courtesy of the British Library).

they were replaced by open backed shifts with drawstrings at the wrist and neck (Litten 1991: 76). A French visitor, writing in the early eighteenth century, describes how the body was first dressed in a garment akin to a long flannel shirt, decorated with lace or embroidery at the wrist or neck (Misson 1719: 89). The shirt was of sufficient length to allow fabric to be folded over the feet and tied with woollen thread. The ensemble was completed with gloves, a cravat around the neck and a cap with a broad chin strap. The chin strap would presumably have functioned in part to secure the jaw in place. The embalmed body of the Duke of Lauderdale who died in 1682 had been wrapped in a fine linen shroud before being swaddled in lanolin-impregnated linen (Caldwell 1976: 27). Unfortunately, it was unclear from the archaeological evidence whether the shroud took the form of one of the new shift-like shrouds or

the older, looser form, although the fact the body appeared to be wrapped perhaps suggests it was the earlier, more voluminous kind.

In principle, changes from a tightly shrouded form, to one which is loosely wrapped ought to be visible archaeologically, according to techniques developed by Henri Duday (Duday 2009; also Nilsson Stutz 2003). This form of fieldwork recording and analysis, known as '*anthropologie de terrain*', pays close attention to the disposition of bones and grave furniture, and takes careful account of the way that the body decomposes in the grave. Tightly wrapped and shrouded burials would tend to be characterized, for example, by patellae that remain in place, rather than falling to the side as the body decomposes and the femurs rotate outwards in the hip joint. Tightly wrapped burials can also be characterised by clavicles that are angled sharply downwards reflecting the compressed shoulders. Unfortunately, much skeletal recording has by necessity to be undertaken rapidly by the marking of presence and absence of bones on standardized forms; only careful recording of the disposition of the body *in situ* will preserve this information.

The changing nature of the shroud may in part be linked to a shift in attitudes towards the dead and alterations in the funerary behaviour. Coffins were rarely used during the medieval period but this gradually changed during the early modern period so that by the end of the seventeenth century interment without a coffin was uncommon.[1] The increased use of coffins changed the role of the shroud. No longer was it used to encase and contain the corpse during the funeral and protect it in the grave. This function was now served by the coffin, which provided the body with a much higher level of protection than was possible with a shroud. Freed from this more functional role, the form of shroud began to be shaped by contemporary perceptions of death and the corpse. The early modern perception of death was of something to be feared – an enemy whose arrival had to be prepared for by acts of faith, penitence and fortitude (Porter 2003: 212, 222). The Enlightenment saw the repopularisation of old metaphors of death, which served to soften its impact. Death became the transition between two states, often seen as a final sleep, something not to be feared and for those reaching the end of long and painful illnesses a more than welcome visitor (Porter 1989: 85–6).[2] The analogy between death and sleep was reflected in the shift-like form of shrouds which often mimicked contemporary nightwear (Rogers 2006: 163), while the rise of the undertaking profession imposed a degree of standardisation of form.

The impact of these influences can be clearly seen in the textiles recovered from the late eighteenth- and nineteenth-century burials from Christ Church Spitalfields in London (Janaway 1993). The long sleeved shrouds, designed to cover the body from head to foot, were backless, presumably to make dressing the corpse simpler (figure 2.5) (Janaway 1998: 26). Shrouds were usually of woven wool in accordance with the Burial in Woollen Act; cotton was not used until after the repeal of the Act in 1814 (Janaway 1998: 24–5). The shrouds were embellished with gathered strips of cloth in the form of frills or ruffles on the chest, and the garments often had pinked or scalloped edges (Janaway 1998: 26). The garments were often roughly sewn with long tacking stitches. Hems and edges were often cut with pinking shears and there was no oversewing of any of the punched decoration on these garments, since they would not need to withstand the stresses placed on clothing by the living (Janaway 1993: 106; 1998: 26, 29). Their backless form and poor finishing suggests that the majority of shrouds were made for the single purpose of dressing the dead, as they only had to look good for a short period before being consigned to the grave. The burial ensemble for both males and females was finished off with burial cap or bonnet, often of the same fabric as the shroud, and in some cases a pair of stockings, examples of which, made from wool, silk and cotton, were found at Spitalfields (Janaway 1993: 106, 108). Not all of the shrouded burials at Spitalfields had burial caps and it may be that their use was not universal although differential preservation may also have been a factor. While the textiles recovered from Spitalfields represent the largest known assemblage of eighteenth- and nineteenth-century funerary clothing, examples of shrouds are known from other sites. The bodies of Sarah Latimer and Sarah Brook, interred in New Bunhill Fields London in 1844 and 1839 respectively, were found dressed in shrouds, the former also wearing stockings (Miles 1997: 46). At St George's Bloomsbury, a linen shroud with raglan sleeves adorned with punched lace was found in the coffin of Catherine Morris, who died in 1825 (Boston 2009: 170). Two child burials from the Cross Bones cemetery in London were found with the remains of shrouds, one also having a pair of knitted booties (Brickley and Miles 1999a: 27). Fragmentary remains of a shroud were found on the body of Catherine Harrison, who was interred at St Phillip's Cathedral in Birmingham in 1870: it was gathered at the waist using a band of cloth tied with a bow, and there was a drawstring at the neck (Patrick 2001: 28). A shroud with a frill on the front and a ribbon at the neck was found on the body of General Sir Alexander Mackenzie, who was interred at St Nicholas's Church, Bathampton in 1853 (Cox and Stock 1995: 140), while a woollen stocking was found with a male burial from St Martin's-in-the-Bull Ring in Birmingham (Rogers 2006: 172).

Figure 2.5 Shroud from Christ Church, Spitalfields. Made specially for the grave, the shroud was open at the back (Photograph courtesy of the Natural History Museum).

The textiles recovered from the burials at Spitalfields have significantly enhanced the understanding of shrouds of the eighteenth and nineteenth centuries, as have the smaller assemblages from other sites. Yet it is important to recognise the limitations of the evidence. Due to the vagaries of preservation the majority of the surviving textile evidence for burial clothing comes from within triple-shelled wood and lead coffins, often from vaults or brick-lined graves (Janaway 1998: 18). For example the majority of the textiles from the burial vault in Spitalfields were from 72 lead and 30 wooden coffins (Janaway 1993: 100). Triple-shelled coffins, with a middle-shell of lead, were not cheap, and nor was interment in a vault or brick-lined grave. As such, the surviving textiles provide an insight into the burial dress of those of the middling and upper classes, while probably telling us very little about the funerary clothing of the poor. A second consideration is to what extent the findings at Spitalfields can be assumed to be typical of burial dress of this period. The church at Spitalfields served a very distinctive community – an urban one of some affluence and containing many individuals of French Huguenot descent (Molleson and Cox 1993: 94). Can the burial clothes of this distinctive Protestant community be assumed to be similar to those of non-conformist groups or Catholics or those living outside the metropolis? Similarities in the general form of the shrouds found at Bathampton and New Bunhill Fields do suggest a degree of standardisation, probably due in part to the professionalisation of undertaking, although with only a small sample from fairly affluent contexts we are not yet in a position to say how extensively these forms were used.

The shroud was far from ubiquitous in burials of the eighteenth and nineteenth centuries. As in earlier centuries, a small but significant number of individuals were interred in everyday clothing (Janaway 1998: 19). In many cases, the individual was attired as for bed, in their own night clothes. One nineteenth-century burial from St Nicholas Sevenoaks, Kent was interred in a cotton nightshirt that bore evidence of darning (Janaway 1998: 29), while some of the sixteen individuals buried at Spitalfields in their own clothing wore linen shirts with buttons, shifts or chemises, all of which could conceivably be worn to bed (Janaway 1993: 111). Others interred at Spitalfields however definitely wore day clothes, including a jacket, a lace dress, and a silk waistcoat (Janaway 1993: 109; 1998: 18). All the evidence from Spitalfields was for clothing from the upper body; presumably the lower body was covered by coffin sheets. In contrast, David Dallas, who was interred in 1829 at St Nicholas' Church, Bathampton Somerset wore a suit with a jacket and trousers made of felt fabric (Cox and Stock 1995: 140). The trousers had plain metal buttons down the outside seams, possibly suggesting some form of livery or uniform. Dress accessories have also been found in number of burials. Two pairs of silk gloves and a pair of mittens made from the same fabric as the shroud were found on the hands of three individuals interred at Christ Church Spitalfields (Janaway 1998: 31) and a pair of knitted gloves found on the hands of a female skeleton from the burial ground associated with the Catholic mission of St Mary and St Michael in London. Other examples of accessories include a length of green and cream silk, thought to be a cravat, found around the neck of a male burial from St Luke's Church, Islington (Boyle *et al* 2005: 100). Although caps and bonnets were often made especially for the funeral, often from the same fabric as the shroud with similar decoration, there are also many examples of use of existing headwear in a funerary context (figure 2.6) (Janaway 1993: 27). Of the fifteen caps in the Spitalfields assemblage, only ten were part of specially constructed sets of funerary attire. The remaining items, including a knitted night cap, were items of normal dress. The remnants of leather caps were found with two skeletons at the Quaker burial ground in Kingston-on-Thames (Bashford and Sibun 2007: 121) and a female burial from All Saint's Church, Pavement in York was found wearing a wire-framed indoor cap of the early to mid-nineteenth century (MAP Archaeological Consultancy Ltd 1998: 94). Fragments of leather, thought to be from a belt and pouch, were found in a burial from St Mark's Church in Lincoln (Mann 1986: 41). It is also worth noting that being buried in clothes did not necessarily preclude the use of a shroud and there are a number of burials from Spitalfields interred in clothes with a shroud on top (Janaway 1993: 108). Why some individuals were interred in clothes as opposed to shrouds is not clear. Choices made by the individual prior to death or by the family are likely to be the explanation in many cases, especially when the body was interred in garments that had a personal significance to the deceased or the bereaved. Although not actually worn by the individual, this was clearly the case when Everilda Chesney was interred with her husband Francis's military uniform in 1840 at St Barnabas's Church, West Kensington, London (Black and Scheuer unpublished referenced in Janaway 1998: 18, 20). In other instances, circumstance may have dictated that burial in clothes was necessary perhaps due to infection or advanced decomposition.

Figure 2.6 Funeral cap from Spitalfields, London. By the eighteenth century it was common for people to be buried wearing garments specially made for the grave, but this bonnet was drawn from the everyday wardrobe of the deceased (Photograph courtesy of the Natural History Museum).

Even when textiles do not survive, the presence of clothes as opposed to shrouds in some burials can sometimes be inferred from the presence of fasteners such as buttons and hooks (table 3.1). While it is possible that buttons found at the wrists and necks my have originated from shrouds, the textile evidence recovered from Spitalfields suggests buttons were rarely used on shrouds, the garments instead being fastened by woollen or cotton ties or ribbons. Yet not all shrouds were commercially produced. Some were home made, and even if the shrouds were supplied by the undertaker, chronological and geographical uniformity cannot be assumed during the eighteenth and nineteenth centuries. So while small glass, bone, shell or even mother of pearl buttons often found at the wrist and necks are probably from shifts, shirts, chemises or nightgowns (Cowie, Bekvalac and Tausmally 2008: 38), it is possible that a few may be from shrouds. More elaborate buttons made from metal or cartwheel buttons are unlikely to be found on shrouds. The five plain copper alloy buttons found within the grave of Richard Gideon Hand, who died in 1839 and was interred at 2–4 Church Street in Chelsea in London, are thought to have come from a

Table 2.1. Examples of buttons and dress fittings found associated with seventeenth- to nineteenth-century burials.

Site	Date	Dress fittings	Reference
Abingdon Vineyard, Oxfordshire	17th century	3 lace chapes	Allen 2006
Abingdon West, Oxfordshire	17th century	5 hook and eye fasteners from one burial	Norton et al. 2005: 14
Hemingford Grey, Cambridgeshire	1680s–1720s	2 copper alloy aglets	McNichol et al. 2007: 28
St Benet Sherehog Burial Ground, London	17th–19th century	7 copper alloy buttons with 1 burial	Egan 2008:68
2–4 Church Street, Chelsea, London	Late 17th–mid-19th century	5 plain copper alloy buttons from single grave; shell buttons	Cowie et al. 2008: 38
City Bunhill Burial Ground, Golden Lane, London	1833–1853	Buttons	Connell and Miles 2010: 10
Quaker Burial Ground, Kingston on Thames	1664–1814	Leather ties in area of sternum of one burial. Cuff-links found with another	Bashford and Sibun 2007: 121
Launceston Castle (Prison burial ground)	18th century	Buttons of copper alloy and iron; copper alloy lace tags	Saunders 2006: 161, 164
Baptist Burial Ground, Kings Lynn	1773–1841	1 cartwheel button	Boston 2005: 146
Catholic Mission of St Mary and St Michael, London	1843–1854	Glass and shell buttons, wire hooked fasteners	Miles and Powers 2006: 34
St Marylebone Church, London	18th to 19th century	Copper alloy buttons, livery button	Miles, Powers and Wroe-Brown 2008: 53
St Paul's Church, Hammersmith, London	1828–1853	Shell buttons, possible cartwheel buttons	Oxford Archaeology 2009
Bow Baptist Church Burial Ground, London	c.1810–1837	Copper alloy, bone, shell and glass buttons; copper alloy rings, probably eyelets	Miles and Powers 2007: 29
St Nicholas' Church, Forest Hill, Oxfordshire	Post-medieval	Buttons of copper alloy, mother of pearl, enamel and wire circles from cloth or cartwheel buttons	Boston 2004
Carver Street, Sheffield	1805–1855	Buttons, often of bone	McIntyre and Willmott 2003
Ebenezer Chapel, Leicester	19th century	Buttons	Jacklin 2006a: 5
Bond Street Congregational Chapel, Leicester	1824–1892	Buttons	Jacklin 2006b: 3
Sheffield Cathedral	18th–mid-19th century	Buttons of bone, shell and copper alloy	Symonds and Sayer 2001: 4, 6
St Martin's-in-the-Bull Ring, Birmingham	18th–19th century	Buttons of bone and copper alloy	Rogers 2006: 183
Southwark Cathedral, London	18th century	Copper alloy and ivory buttons and a copper alloy hook and eye	Divers 2001: 108–9
York Prison	19th century	Bone and copper alloy buttons	York Archaeological Trust 1998: 13–14
Newcastle Infirmary	19th century	Buttons of bone, pewter and shell	Nolan 1998: 58
Kinoull graveyard	18th–19th century	small button, probably of glass, found with child burial; fragment of mother of pearl button found with adult burial; fragment of safety pin	Cox, A. 1998: 292
Leslie	18th–19th century	18th century cuff-links	Cox, A. 1998: 292

jacket (Cowie, Bekvalac and Tausmally 2008: 38) The single livery button found inside the eighteenth to nineteenth-century coffin of an adult male burials at St. Marylebone may also have been from clothing, although it has been suggested that it may have may have been a token from a former employer (Egan 2008b: 65) (figure 2.7). The seven copper alloy buttons from a burial at St Benet Sherehog burial ground are also likely to have originated from clothing (Egan 2008a: 69) as are the row of 5 wire circles, likely to be remains of cartwheel buttons, found overlaying the ribcage of a young woman interred at St Nicholas' Forest Hill in Oxfordshire (Boston 2004: 21).

Leather, particularly in comparatively recent interments, is more likely to survive than textiles yet leather footwear is rarely found in post-medieval burials. There are a few examples such as the boots discovered with a burial in the eighteenth- and nineteenth-century Cross Bones burial ground in London (Brickley and Miles 1999a: 27) and a pair of leather shoes found in the mid-nineteenth-century burial ground associated with the Catholic mission of St Mary and St Michael also in London (Miles and Powers 2006: 39).³ In addition, a shoe buckle was found with a male burial from the burial ground associated with St Marylebone Church (Egan 2008b: 65) and a pair of child's shoes were found in a burial from St Mark's Lincoln (Mann 1986: 41). The scarcity of such finds suggests that shoes and boots were not considered necessary or appropriate attire for burial. Indeed, it has been suggested that the shoes from the Catholic mission burial ground remained on the corpse because it was impossible to remove them (Miles and Powers 2006: 39). The burial from Cross Bones was also dressed in the remains of trousers and a shirt (Brickley and Miles 1999a: 27). It is possible that this individual died from an infectious condition and that the relatives or undertaker were unwilling or unable to strip, wash and re-dress the body prior to burial. Illness may also explain the pair of slippers and woollen socks found on the body of a sixty year old male buried in Christ Church, Spitalfields in 1798 (Janaway 1993: 112). The slippers were of different sizes and the legs had possibly been bandaged under the woollen socks, suggesting that this individual suffered from an affliction affecting the lower limbs, possibly gout (Janaway 1993: 117). The retention of medical dressings may also explain the two corpses interred wearing leather trusses at St Peter's Church, Barton-upon-Humber in Lincolnshire (figure 2.8) (Rodwell and Rodwell 1982: 306). Trusses of varying constructions were used in the treatment of hernias to secure the viscera in place after surgery (Buchan 1789: 662; Andrew 1847: 603).⁴ Given the build-up of gases within the abdominal cavity as the body begins to decompose perhaps the trusses were left in place to prevent the extrusion of the viscera prior to burial, thus maintaining a pleasant appearance.

Unlike the winding sheets and tightly bound shrouds of the early modern period, the looser funerary attire of the eighteenth and nineteenth centuries allowed the body to move around (Janaway 1993: 95). From the eighteenth century onwards, ties were used to hold the body in position during viewing and also to prevent the distress caused by the limbs knocking against the coffin during the funeral (Janaway 1993: 104). Textiles, often commercially-produced ribbons but sometimes torn strips of fabric, were found securing the legs of a number of burials, either by binding the ankles or by tying the big toes together, at Christchurch Spitalfields, London (Janaway 1998: 24). Although less frequent, fabric securing the arms to the torso were also encountered. The presentation of the face was also important, especially during the nineteenth century with the increased emphasis on the beautiful corpse, sometimes recorded in drawings and photographs, for commemorative purposes (Jalland 1999b: 288; Tarlow 1999b: 194). The jaw was secured to prevent the mouth gaping open. Ties attached to the bonnets or caps, which were a common element of funerary attire during this period, would in many cases have been sufficient to prevent the jaw dropping. Other options included securing the jaw with silk ribbons or the use of a jaw cloth which was pinned to a cap or bonnet. The use of the latter may explain the green patination observed on some skulls, possibly from contact with copper alloy pins. Surviving jaw clothes include examples from

Figure 2.7 Eighteenth-century livery button found with a male burial at St Marylebone, London, suggesting that this individual was buried in normal day clothes (Photograph courtesy of MOLA).

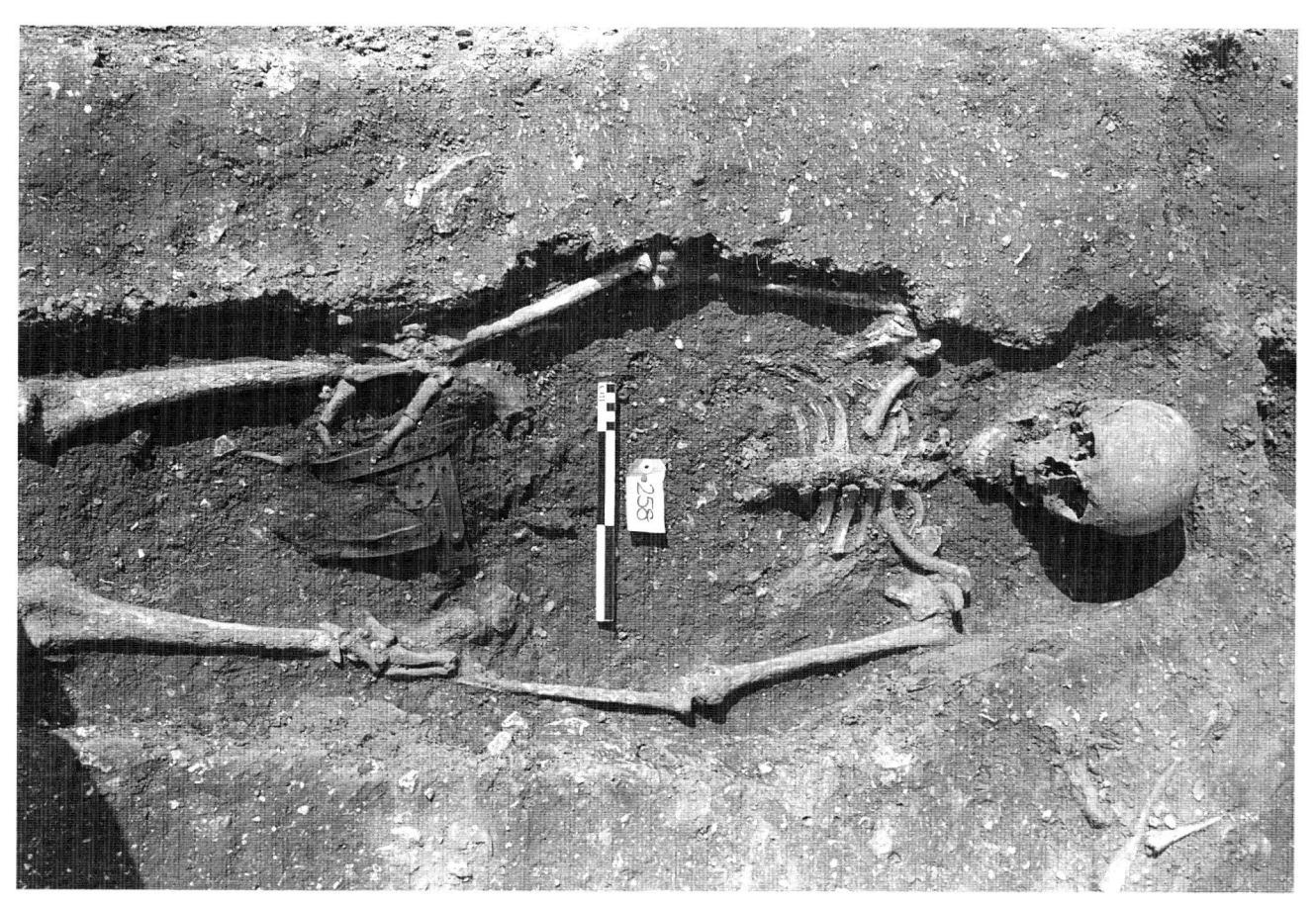

Figure 2.8 A need to keep the corpse looking presentable might have led to the interment of two corpses still wearing leather trusses at St Peter's Church, Barton-upon-Humber in Lincolnshire (Photograph courtesy of Warwick Rodwell).

Spitalfields where triangular pieces of fabric were wrapped twice around the head and jaw and then tied under the chin and covered by caps and bonnets, while Colonel John Hume, who was interred in a brick-lined grave at Bathampton Somerset in 1815, had his jaw strapped up (Cox and Stock 1995: 140).

Coins were sometimes used to hold the eyes closed, if *rigor mortis* had set in, to improve the appearance of the corpse (Richardson 1987: 19). Coins have been found in association with a number of burials (table 3.11) and some were found covering the eyes suggesting that they were not always removed prior to interment (figure 2.9).[5] The number of examples is small but geographically and chronologically diverse. An early example comes from Fowlis Wester Church in Perthshire where two "Turners" (Scottish two pence coins) dating to the reign of Charles I (1642–50) were found (Rees and Strachan 1998: 68). Later examples include two from London, both children. At Spitalfields, a two year old infant, who died in 1826 was found with pennies over the eyes (Cox 1996: 115) while two George III half pennies dating to 1799 and 1806–7 had been placed over the eyes of a child of about three years buried at St Marylebone (Miles, Powers and Wroe-Brown 2008: 50). Of a similar date were the two coins covering the eyes of an adult male skeleton from the nineteenth-century non-conformist burial ground at Ebenezer Chapel in Leicester (Jacklin 2006b: 5). The two coins found stacked to the right of the skull of the burial at the eighteenth- to nineteenth-century Baptist burial ground in Kings Lynn, Norfolk may have originally been placed over the eyes but then removed prior to interment and placed next to the head (Boston 2005a: 146). Similarly, a George III penny dating to 1806 was found to the right of the skull in a coffin at St Phillip's Cathedral in Birmingham (Patrick 2001: 20).

The display of the body prior to burial required not only the appropriate attire but also that the hair be suitably dressed. The simple combs found accompanying four eighteenth- and nineteenth-century burials of both sexes from St Martin's-in-the-Bull Ring in Birmingham are thought to have been used to comb the hair prior to burial, and are different from the tortoiseshell combs which seem to have been used to dress the hair of adult women (Bevan 2006: 180; Brickley and Buteux 2006: appendix 5). The inclusion of the combs within the coffin may be due to a reticence to retain items used intimately in the preparation of the corpse for the grave. Combs were also found with burials from St Peter's, Barton-upon-Humber (Waldron 2007: 159–160). Women's hairstyles, particularly among the middling and upper classes, were often quite elaborate during the

Figure 2.9 Coins have been found in association with a number of burials and some were found covering the eyes suggesting that they were not always removed prior to interment. This nineteenth-century burial is from the non-conformist Ebenezer Chapel in Leicester (Photograph courtesy of University of Leicester Archaeological Services).

eighteenth and nineteenth centuries, but whether these were always recreated while preparing the corpse is unclear (Bevan 2006: 181). Indeed, the popularity of funerary bonnets would by their very nature have negated the need to recreate elaborate coiffures. Moreover the analogies between death and sleep reflected in funerary attire were likely to have extended to the way the hair was dressed. Just as elaborate coiffures were not appropriate when retiring for the night, similarly simple styles might have been favoured for those going to their final rest. Yet there is a little evidence to suggest that at least a few women went to the grave with elaborate hairstyles.

The keratin in hair can lead to its survival in the archaeological record, particularly in recent burials. Occasionally the level of preservation is sufficient to determine the nature of the hairstyle as with the bun of hair held together with hair grips from the nineteenth-century burial of a thirteen to eighteen year old female from the burial ground associated with the Catholic Mission of St Mary and St Michael in London (Miles and Powers 2006: 22). Large tortoiseshell combs used to support elaborate hairstyles were found with two female burials from St Martin's-in-the-Bull Ring in Birmingham (Bevan 2006: 180). A small hair comb and a fragment of a tortoiseshell comb were found with a third female burial. A poorly preserved decorative bone comb was found with one of the male burials. This burial also contained a second simple bone comb. A large comb of horn or tortoiseshell was found by the head of a female burial from St. Paul's Church, Hammersmith in London and a fragment from an ivory comb were found with a burial from the City Bunhill Burial Ground in London (Oxford Archaeology 2009: 9; Connell and Miles 2010: 10). St Martin's also produced a possible hairpin from a burial from 1866 (Bevan 2006: 181), while a decorated ball-headed pin and fragments of copper alloy found with a large amount of hair at the Catholic Mission of St Mary and St Michael in London are though to be the remains of a hair pin used to secure a funerary cap (Miles and Powers 2006: 34–5). An account of the clearance of the Quaker burial ground at O'Meara Street in London in 1860 describes the opening of a coffin where among the hair found with the skeleton were a tortoiseshell comb and the remains of a pad used to support and add volume when the hair was worn up (Brickley and Miles 1999b: 51). Wigs and hairpieces were often worn during the eighteenth and nineteenth centuries and hair pieces, wigs, a wig base and a queue were recovered from among the eighteenth- and nineteenth-century burials from Christ Church Spitalfields, London (Janaway 1993: 109). One elderly lady was buried in a wig of long dark hair at Spitalfields. Similarly, the blonde hair recovered from the coffin of Anna Barnard who was interred in the Quaker Burial Ground at Kingston-upon-Thames was probably a wig (Bashford and Pollard 1998: 162). Adorning the corpse with the wigs and hairpieces that the individual had worn in life, particularly when combined with the other evidence for the use of hair combs and elaborate hairstyles, does suggest that in some cases a good coiffure was an important element of the presentation of the corpse.

Changes in diet have led to increasing levels of dental decay since the Roman period (Whitaker 1993: 49). By the eighteenth and nineteenth century, high levels of refined sugars and carbohydrates combined with a more processed diet and poor levels of oral hygiene to produce high levels of dental decay (Whitaker 1993: 53; Brickley 2006: 145). Poor dental health can also result in tooth loss due to periodontal disease, caries and deliberate extraction. (Brickley 2006: 139). An early post-medieval example of a dental prosthesis used to replace lost teeth was found at Christ Church Spitalfields, London where silk ligatures were used to tie two carved replacement teeth to the real teeth of Deborah Peck, who died in 1739

(Whitaker 1993: 56). The body of the prosthesis appears to have been made of ivory with polished ivory or enamel from the animal's dentition used to create the teeth. Eight other individuals interred in the vault at Spitalfields between 1729 and 1857 were also buried wearing dentures or bridges, including three individuals with both upper and lower dentures (Whitaker 1993: 54). One of the complete sets of dentures consisted of porcelain teeth mounted on a gold alloy base, while the other two contained real teeth mounted on ivory or metal (Whitaker 1993: 55, 57–9). Real teeth or "Waterloo" teeth were harvested from cadavers on the battlefield or bodies exhumed from earth graves or crypts.[6] A mixture of Waterloo and ceramic teeth were used in the dentures that accompanied Mary Hume, who died in 1843, to her grave at St Nicholas's Church in Bathampton, Somerset (Cox and Stock 1995: 141). According to *Cassell's Household Guide*, ceramic or porcelain teeth were more hygienic than using organic materials such as ivory or real teeth and less prone to discolouration (1870: 130). French émigré Archbishop Dillon, who died in 1806, was interred at St Pancras Old Church with a full set of porcelain dentures with springs linking the upper and lower sets (Powers 2006: 460–1). Ann Maria Browett was interred in 1891, wearing a set of vulcanite and porcelain dentures, with coiled springs linking the upper and lower jaws, in a family vault at St Martin's-in-the-Bull Ring in Birmingham, and a similar set was found in association with a male burial in an earth-cut grave in the churchyard (Buteux and Cherrington 2006: 54; Brickley 2006: 140). Six examples of dentures or bridges were recovered from coffins in the crypt of St Andrew, Holborn in London (Miles 2006: 33), but these cannot be securely dated since the site was in use from the late seventeenth century.

Eighteenth- and nineteenth-century dentures were custom-made and expensive, something which is reflected in the high status funerary contexts in which most of the archaeological examples were recovered. Some were particularly finely made, and the rich may have owned more than one set. A man was interred in the vault of St George's Church in Bloomsbury, London wearing a set of dentures, consisting of porcelain teeth riveted onto gold plate with springs joining the upper and lower jaws (figure 2.10) (Boston *et al* 2009:136). A second pair of dentures of identical construction was also placed in the coffin. A lead coffin, from St Nicholas's Church in Sevenoaks in Kent, also contained two set of dentures, although it was not possible to determine whether either pair actually belonged to the coffin's occupant Maria West who died in 1785 (Boyle and Keevil 1998: 92).

Enhancing the appearance of the corpse may offer an explanation for those individuals interred wearing

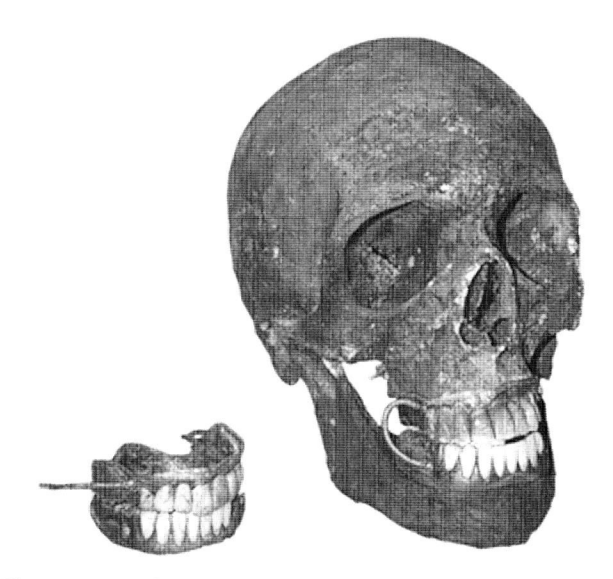

Figure 2.10 The skull of male skeleton 3044, from the vaults of St George's church, Bloomsbury, London, who had been interred wearing a full set of dentures. A second pair, also pictured, was found within the coffin (Photograph courtesy of Oxford Archaeology).

a full set of dentures as this would have masked the hollowing out of the lower face, which can occur in edentulous individuals. Whether the comparative rarity of dentures in burial contexts is representative of the level of use is unclear, as in some cases they may have been removed prior to burial (Molleson and Cox 1993: 54). Also inserting the dentures could be problematic. An account of the laying out of the Dowager Duchess of Atholl in 1897 described the difficulties encountered by those preparing the body in putting in her false teeth (Jalland 1999b: 211). As the presence of *in situ* dentures enhances the appearance, and given the nineteenth-century focus on the beautification of the corpse (Tarlow 1999b: 194), it seems likely that the dentures may have been placed in the mouth whenever possible. However, attempts to improve the appearance of the corpse cannot explain the wearing of all dental prostheses, nor the cases where additional sets were placed in the grave. Perhaps dental prostheses were too intimate, personal and idiosyncratic to be useful to anyone else after the death of their owner. Being worn daily, and seeming to be almost a part of the body, dentures may also have come to take on some of the personhood of the dead and been viewed as a part of the corpse in ways that that differed from other personal effects such as eyeglasses and jewellery.

The eighteenth- and nineteenth-century preoccupation with the "sleeping" corpse extended beyond the body itself. The corpse was often displayed on the bed before being placed in a coffin (Jalland 1999b: 214) and once in the coffin, the textiles around the body were arranged to mimic bedding (Litten 1991: 79). The all-encompassing winding sheets of the early modern period were all but replaced by the 1770s by coffin sheets which were wrapped around the corpse in a manner similar to sheet on a bed to suggest that the dead were simply sleeping (Litten 1991: 214; Janaway 1998: 25). These could take two forms: either the fabric was attached to the base of the coffin, or to the sides of the coffin, usually to the wooden beading used to support the coffin lid, and held in place by iron tacks and tacking stitches (Janaway 1993: 102–3). Examples of side sheets from the burials at Christ Church Spitalfields were made of plain woven wool or cotton with pinked or scalloped edges and punched decoration. In some instances the face of the deceased was covered by a 'face cloth' (Janaway 1993: 109). Five of these rectangular pieces of cloth, often with punched decoration and scalloped edges, were found at Spitalfields while evidence for the use of face cloths was also observed at St Nicholas' Church Sevenoaks (Janaway 1998: 26; Cox and Stock 1995: 140). The death as sleep theme is continued in some burials with the use of pillows, often decorated with ribbons and bows, to support the head (Rogers 2006: 163). Pillows, stuffed with a variety of materials including wool, feathers and hay, were recovered from Spitalfields (Janaway 1993: 103), while imprints of pillows were seen among the burials from the Quaker burial ground at Kingston-upon-Thames (Bashford and Pollard 1998: 159). Pillows stuffed with animal hair and straw were observed during the excavation of the privately owned eighteenth- and nineteenth-century Backchurch Lane burial ground in London (Watson 1993: 17). Pillows, stuffed with horsehair and kapok, were found with burials at St Luke's Islington in London (Boston and Boyle 2005: 87) while wood shavings and textiles found beneath the skull of a burial from the nineteenth-century Bond Street Congregational chapel burial ground in Leicester are thought to represent the remains of a pillow (Jacklin 2006a: 3).

During the eighteenth and nineteenth centuries, the base of the coffin was often covered with a thin layer of bran or sawdust, usually covered with fabric (Litten 1991: 92). Misson describes how "some would put a layer of Bran, about four inches thick, at the bottom of the coffin" (1719: 89). This lining not only served to absorb the liquids from the corpse, but also ensured "that the corpse may lie softer" (Misson 1719: 89). Rosemary or balm was often added to the bran to obscure the odours produced by decomposition (Litten 1991: 92). Sawdust and bran were observed in coffins from St George's Bloomsbury and St Luke's Islington (Boston *et al* 2009: 150; Boyle, Boston. and Witkin 2005: 103), and one of the coffins from St Nicholas's church in Bathampton, Somerset (that of Mary Lucy Lewis, who died in 1857), contained sawdust (Cox and Stock 1995: 139). Sawdust was also found in a zinc coffin from a late eighteenth- and early nineteenth-century Quaker burial ground in Kings Lynn (Mahoney 2005: 100) and in late eighteenth- and early nineteenth-century coffins from the graveyard of St Paul's Church in Sheffield (Belford and Witkin 2000). In some instances more substantial provision was made for the comfort of the deceased by fitting mattresses into the base of coffins. The mattresses were usually shaped to fit the coffin and served to further emphasise the analogy between death and sleep (Janaway 1998: 22). Six mattresses, stuffed with horsehair or kapok, were discovered in coffins at St Luke's Islington, including one covered with silk and decorated with tassels (Boyle, Boston and Witkin 2005: 87). Mattresses stuffed with hair, wool and straw were found during the excavations at Spitalfields (Janaway 1998: 22) and mattresses were also observed in some of the burials from St Nicholas's Church in Bathampton, Somerset (Cox and Stock 1995: 139).

Adorning the dead

While the presentation of the corpse had become increasingly important by the eighteenth and nineteenth centuries, personal adornment in the form of jewellery is a rare inclusion in burials of this period, suggesting it was not generally considered an appropriate addition when preparing the body for burial. Jewellery was often an emotionally and financially important part of a person's estate, commonly inherited by friends or family. Indeed, early modern and modern wills often made explicit provision for the inheritance of jewellery. Jewellery has been found *in situ* in a small number of post-medieval graves (table 2.2). Finger rings are the most common form of personal adornment encountered and can be divided into three categories; wedding rings, mourning rings and decorative rings. Three gold wedding rings were found at Christchurch, Spitalfields in London, one with a date mark 1800 and another of 1784 (Reeve and Adams 1993: 89). Three gold bands also thought to be women's wedding rings were recovered during excavations at St Martin's-in-the-Bull Ring, Birmingham (Bevan 2006: 179). One manufactured in 1835–6 was found with the body of Ann Maria Browett who died in 1894, while another with a hallmark suggesting manufacture in 1842–3 was found on the left hand of Eliza Haines who was 60 years old when she died in 1904. The latter ring was older than the individual it was interred with, suggesting that it may have been some form of family heirloom. The final ring, which came from the grave of a probable male, was very thin and worn and may represent a memento. The body of Margaret Swallow who died

Table 2.2. Examples of jewellery found in association with eighteenth- and nineteenth-century burials

Site	Date of site	Number of burials	Jewellery	Reference
Christ Church, Spitalfield, London	1729–1867	968	3 gold wedding rings 1 mourning ring 1 pair of earrings	Reeve and Adams 1993
St Luke's, Islington, London	18th–19th century	896	1 gold earring	Boyle, Boston and Witkin 2005
Burial ground associated with Catholic mission of St Mary and St Michael, London	1843–1854	747	1 gold ring 1 copper alloy ring Religious pendants and rosaries	Miles and Powers 2006
Portchester Castle, Hampshire	18th century	4	1 rosary	Cunliffe and Garratt 1994
St Peter's Church, Wolverhampton			3 copper alloy rings 1 gold earring	Bevan 2007
St Nicholas' Church, Bathampton, Somerset	19th century	6	2 gold rings	Cox and Stock 1994
St Martin's-in-the-Bull Ring, Birmingham	18th–19th century	505	3 gold wedding rings 1 mourning ring 1 copper alloy ring 2 necklaces of glass beads	Bevan 2006
Sheffield Cathedral	18th–19th century	—	2 bracelets of glass beads	Ponsford 2006
St Peter's Church, Barton-upon-Humber	1700–1855[1]	427	1 bronze finger ring 1 gold wedding ring 1 lead pendant	Rodwell 2007
Glasgow Cathedral	Post-medieval	—	1 gold earring	Driscoll 2002
St Peter's Church, Waterford	Post-medieval	—	1 gold ring 1 copper alloy ring bone cross 1 lead medallion	Hurley and McCutcheon 1997
Workhouse Burial Ground at Manorhamilton	19th century	73	3 rosaries	Moore Group Archaeological and Environmental Services 2001; 2002
St Ann's Graveyard, Shandon	Post-medieval	—	1 rosary	McCarthy 2001

1 Only phase A – post-medieval burials included

in 1845 was interred with a wedding ring at St Peter's Church, Barton-upon-Humber, Lincolnshire (Rodwell 2007: 28). Wedding rings were in common use by the early modern period although Puritans tried to abolish them in the seventeenth century, deeming them symbols of Popery (Oman 1974: 35). However, the practice of continuously wearing a wedding ring only became general practice in the eighteenth century (Bury 1984: 15). The scarcity of wedding rings found in burial contexts suggests that wedding bands were retained by family of the deceased as mementoes or heirlooms rather than being routinely consigned to the grave with the corpse. The few occasions where a wedding ring is present represent a conscious decision to inter the ring with the body or perhaps, in a few instances, the inability to remove the ring.

The bequeathing of rings as mementoes in remembrance of the deceased is a longstanding tradition (Oman 1974: 71). During the early modern period money was left in wills for specially commissioned rings. These rings took a variety of forms; some were inscribed with appropriate inscriptions or featured an enamelled skull, while others bore little evidence of their function. Mourning rings became very popular in late eighteenth and nineteenth century as the advent of mass production in the latter part of the eighteenth century allowed them to be commissioned in batches (Bury 1984: 47). The rings were given out at funerals and worn to commemorate the deceased during and after the period of formal mourning (Jalland 1999b: 298). The rings were often inscribed on the outside and two examples have been found in

2 The preparation and presentation of the post-medieval corpse

Figure 2.11 A large, gold mourning ring, dedicated to the memory of "Mr Thos Martin died 13 Sept 1808 aged 53" found with the burial of a middle-aged male at St Martin's-in-the-Bull Ring in Birmingham (Photograph courtesy of Graham Norrie, Institute of Archaeology and Antiquity).

funerary contexts. A large mourning ring, dedicated to the memory of "Mr Thos Martin died 13 Sept 1808 aged 53" was found with the burial of a middle aged male at St Martin's-in-the-Bull Ring in Birmingham (figure 2.11) (Bevan 2006: 179). Another mourning ring commemorating "Judith Mesman obit 15th May 1763 AET 29" with blue enamel surrounding the lettering was found with a burial at Christ Church, Spitalfields in London (Reeve and Adams 1993: 89).

Apart from wedding and mourning rings, a number of other rings made from gold and copper alloy have been found in funerary contexts. Examples of gold rings include two found on one finger of the left hand of Mary Hume who was buried at St Nicholas' Church, Bathampton Somerset in 1843 (Cox and Stock 1995: 141), and a gold finger ring with gem or imitation gem intaglio found on the right hand of an individual from the burial ground associated with the Mission of St Mary and St Michael in London (Miles and Powers 2006: 35). A gold ring was also found with a burial at St Peter's Waterford (Hurley and McCutcheon 1997: 227). Examples of copper alloy rings include the three found at St Peter's, Wolverhampton. Two of the rings were associated with a female burial, the wider of the two rings appears to have been plain, while the other had a broken bezel originally inlaid with five stones, two of which remained *in situ* (Bevan 2007: 35). The third ring was also found with a female burial. Single examples of copper alloy rings were found at a number of sites including the burial ground associated with the mission of St Mary and St Michael in London (Miles and Powers 2006: 35), St Peter's Waterford (Hurley and McCutcheon 1997: 227) and St Martin's-in-the-Bull Ring in Birmingham (Bevan 2006: 179).

Other forms of personal adornment are rare. Examples of a single burial with of a pair of gold earrings have been found at a number of sites including Glasgow Cathedral (Driscoll 2002: 64), Christ Church Spitalfields (Reeve and Adams 1993: 89) and St Peter's Church, Wolverhampton (Bevan 2007: 35). Single earrings or fragments of gold or bronze earrings have also been recovered from several sites including St Luke's Church, Islington (Boyle, Boston and Witkin 2005: 100), the burial ground associated with the Catholic Mission of St Mary and St Michael London (Miles and Powers 2006: 35) and St Peter's Church, Wolverhampton (Bevan 2007: 35). Even more unusual were the two necklaces found at St Martin's-in-the-Bull Ring, Birmingham (Bevan 2006: 180). One was an almost complete necklace of over 300 loose pink opaque glass beads from a child's grave. The associated copper alloy fastener had four beads attached suggesting the beads were from a four strand necklace. Part of a second necklace consisting a number of coloured beads with associated fragments of thread were found with a fragment of textile fused to a piece of coffin wood from a second grave. A lead pendant was found with an adult female interred at St Peter's Church, Barton-upon-Humber in Lincolnshire (Waldron 2007: 153) and a lead medallion in a burial from St Peter's Waterford (Hurley and McCutcheon 1997: 227). Two bracelets of glass beads were found during the excavations at Sheffield Cathedral (Ponsford 2006: 376). As with the rings discussed above, the rarity of other forms of jewellery implies that this form of adornment was not considered appropriate or necessary to the presentation of the corpse. Jewellery belonged to the living and not the dead. Pieces that had belonged to the deceased frequently became heirlooms and mementoes, passed on to the living and sometimes used to commemorate the dead. As such, when jewellery is found in a funerary context, it can be assumed in the majority of cases that its inclusion was the result of wishes of the deceased or the bereaved and that the item had a personal significance, although accidental oversight or difficulties in removal may account for a few of the examples.

Jewellery of a more devotional nature was found in several Catholic graves. A bone cross was found with a burial from St Peter's Waterford and pendants depicting religious figures were found with four burials in the burial ground of St Mary and St Michael Mission in London (Hurley and McCutcheon 1997: 227; Miles and Powers 2006: 34). Several graves in the latter burial ground contained rosaries, some with wooden beads with copper alloy attachments, and others possibly made from glass beads (Miles and Powers 2006: 35). A number of copper alloy crosses were also recovered from burials at the Mission, some simply worn on a chain and others associated with rosaries (2006: 34). At Portchester Castle, one of the bodies in an eighteenth-century multiple burial of French prisoners-of-war has a rosary of bone beads with a copper alloy crucifix placed over his chest (Cunliffe and Garratt 1994: 119). The ritual repetition of set numbers of certain prayers counted using a string of beads, a rosary or pater noster, was an important element of late medieval devotional practice (Dillon 2003: 451), although the incorporation of rosaries and prayer beads into medieval funerary contexts is rare (Gilchrist and Sloane 2005: 93). Late medieval examples include an elaborate amber and jet rosary with a silver gilt crucifix found in a late fourteenth- or fifteenth-century grave at the Benedictine nunnery of St Mary Rusper in Sussex (Way 1857: 304) and another consisting of forty-two bone beads in a fourteenth- to sixteenth-century grave at the Dominican friary in Cork (Hurley and Sheehan 1995: 114–5). Partly because of its association with the Virgin Mary, the rosary came under attack after the Reformation when the Royal Injunction of 1538 rejected Marian devotions as diverting honour due to Christ alone (Dillon 2003: 452); nevertheless more than one rosary was recovered from the wreck of Henry VIII's flag ship the *Mary Rose* (figure 2.12). When the Act of Uniformity in 1559 made Protestantism the only legal religion in England and Wales, Catholicism was outlawed and the next century saw the loss of many elements of the Catholic liturgy. Yet against this background of the loss of Catholic places of worship, priests, rituals and objects, the rosary survived as a portable and easily concealed symbol for followers of the old faith. In Ireland where the numbers following the Catholic faith remained high rosaries are a more common finding. Three burials from a nineteenth-century workhouse burial ground in Manorhamilton, County Leitrim each had a set of rosary beads (Moore Group Archaeological and Environmental Services 2001; 2002: 23). In one of the burials the beads lay around the neck, on the left shoulder of another and in the third burial the rosary lay below the skull. This later burial also contained a heart-shaped religious medal and a medallion by the neck. About one third of the burials at the Jesuit cemetery at Manresa House, London, which was in use between 1867 to 1962, included a rosary or crucifix, usually around the neck, in the hands, or placed on the torso (Melikian 2004a: 12). These burials were all either ordained priests (including a bishop and an archbishop), monks or priests in training. A wooden and cord set of rosary beads was found wrapped around the end of the radius of a burial from St Ann's graveyard in Shandon, Co. Cork (McCarthy 2001). An account of a wake held by an Irish Catholic family in Cumberland in the early years of the twentieth century which described the corpse lying in the coffin with his rosary beads in his hands

Figure 2.12 Sixteenth-century rosary recovered from the wreck of the Mary Rose (Photograph courtesy of Mary Rose Trust)

gives an indication of how such items might be incorporated into a burial context (Roberts 1989: 197). As with more secular jewellery, rosaries, crucifixes and religious pendants are found infrequently which suggests their inclusion was not routine but the result of choice or circumstance

Preservation of the body

The time between death and interment appears to have been highly variable throughout the post-medieval period and based on individual circumstances. Francis Tate writing in 1600 said that "among us there is no set or determined time how long a corpse should be kept, but as seems best to friends of the deceased (Tate 1600: 217). In the second half of the seventeenth century, 70% of those dying in the London parish of St Mary Woolnoth were interred within three days of dying and nearly 90% had been interred by the fourth day (Porter 1982: 76–80) while the interval between death and burial ascertained for 366 individuals interred between 1792 and 1852 in the vaults below Christ Church Spitalfields, London ranged between 1 and 21 days (Molleson and Cox 1993: 186). A comparison of the interval between death and burial at the Quaker burial ground at Kingston-upon-Thames showed a marked increase in the period prior to interment during the eighteenth century (table 2.3). A number of factors influenced the interval between death and interment including allowing viewing of the body, the complexity of the funeral arrangements, fears of premature interment and rate of decomposition.

The Reformation may have removed the concept of Purgatory but could not expunge its influence from traditional customs (Porter 2003: 217). Some folk beliefs suggest that the soul was thought to linger around the body after death, at least for a short time, while other traditions held that the actions of friends and family could influence the soul's final destination, behaviour unlikely to be sanctioned by Protestant theology (Richardson 1987: 7,17; Porter 2003: 217). Such beliefs may in part explain why the body was retained at home prior to burial and the custom of visiting the dead, holding wakes and keeping vigil over the corpse. Tate writing in 1600 noted that the body was "continually attended or watched" (1600: 216). The amount spent on some early modern wakes suggests the numbers attending could be quite high (Gittings 1984: 106). Wakes, with their origins in Catholic eschatology, were unpopular with the post-Reformation ecclesiastical authorities and although the practice persisted well into the seventeenth century, the opposition of the clergy combined with political and social changes, such as the turmoil of the Civil War, saw its rapid decline in the south and east of England during the later part of the seventeenth century; it persisted only a little longer in the north of the country (Gittings 1984: 107; Cressy 1997: 427). In contrast, wakes survived into the early twentieth century if not later in Irish, Welsh and Scottish communities (Porter 2003: 217). Even with the disappearance of wakes, the body was still kept at home and viewed by friends and family in England, providing both proof of death and an important part of the mourning process. Misson, writing in the early eighteenth century described how "Before funeral the body is lain on coffin on two stools for viewing, then they take off the top of the coffin and the facecloth is removed from the face" (Misson 1719: 90). In contrast, the Victorians preferred to view the dead shortly after death, ideally before rigor had stiffened the features, so the face had a more relaxed appearance (Jalland 1999b: 213). Moreover, the loss of the wake did not mean the body was left unguarded prior to interment, but a more solitary vigil held by the immediate family took the place of the more communal wake (Gittings 1984: 109). Time was also needed to arrange the funeral, particularly for more elaborate affairs. Misson described how the body lay in the coffin for three to four days prior to interment while the funeral was arranged (1719: 90). Children's funerals were generally simpler affairs not requiring as much planning or organisation. The time between death and burial of those children interred in Christ Church Spitalfields London does overall appear to be shorter than for many of the adults (Molleson and Cox 1993: 186).

Table 2.3. Interval between death and burial at the Quaker burial ground at Kingston-upon-Thames (based on data from Basford and Sibun 2007)

Date	Number of burials	% interred within 1 day of death	% interred within 2 days of death	% interred after 2 days	Maximum time between death and burial
1664–74	36	41.6	77.7	22.2	9 days
1675–82	54	39.1	81.5	18.5	4 days
1683–90	40	20	82.5	17.5	4 days
1691–1731	16	6.3	43.7	56.3	5 days
1732–1814	92	2.2	9.8	90.2	14 days

Accidental interment of the living was always a subject of concern to any society, particularly when there was limited medical knowledge. Revival of the dead was not unknown during the post-medieval period. In the late sixteenth century, Matthew Wall of Braying Hertfordshire revived when his coffin, which was being carried to his grave, was dropped by one of the bearers (Jones-Baker 1977: 164). Indeed Misson described how the corpse lay in the coffin for a few days "to give the dead person an opportunity of coming to life" (1719: 90). Watchers were paid to watch the bodies of those dying in suspicious circumstances or as the result of accidents prior to examination by the coroner (Gittings 1984: 108). While their primary purpose was to prevent any tampering with the corpse, they were also on hand should anyone revive. Concerns about premature interment were further exacerbated by advances in medical knowledge during the eighteenth century. The publication of papers and articles on such topics as on the uncertainty of determining whether a person was dead, circumstances where a premature diagnosis of death might occur and methods of reviving the apparently dead all served to fan fears of interment alive as did accounts of premature burial (Hawes 1780; Finch 1788; *Times* 6th May 1874: 11). Since putrefaction was the only reliable indicator of death, delaying the interment for a time to ensure life was truly extinguished is understandable. How great the grounds for such fears were is unclear. However, a rather gruesome nineteenth-century burial from the graveyard of the Holy Trinity Church in Coventry suggests that burial alive was a real possibility (Soden 2000). This supine burial had unusually flexed arms, as if in an attempt to push up the lid of the coffin.

The time between death and burial was also determined by the rate of decomposition. Rapid putrefaction could curtail the length of time the body was displayed in the coffin and lead to an early interment (Jalland 1999b: 213). Bills for wakes often include perfume, which was presumably used to mask the odours of bodily decay (Gittings 1984: 106). For example, 10d was spend on perfume for the wake of a Cambridge student who died in 1618 (Porter 1969: 34). It is noticeable among the burials at Christ Church, Spitalfields London that the interval between death and burial was usually shorter in the warmer months of the years, and most of the longest intervals occurred in the colder winter months (Molleson and Cox 1993: 186). While this may in part be a result of difficulties in travel during winter, it seems likely that the deleterious effect of warm weather on the recently dead was a major factor. Unpleasant by-products of rapid decomposition included noxious odours which in some cases were masked by coffin bearers smoking tobacco, body liquor escaping from the coffin as it was transported and occasionally, and horrifically, the build up of the gaseous products of putrefaction resulting in the explosion of lead coffins prior to interment (Chadwick 1843: 13,15).

In some circumstances rapid interment of the corpse was not an option. This was the case for those dying away from home but destined for a final resting place in the family mausoleum or those of high social status requiring an elaborate funeral. In these circumstances, it was often necessary to retard the process of putrefaction, usually by embalming. This could allow the corpse to be returned home or provide time to plan the funeral and allow the display of the body some time after death. Misson described how "among persons of quality it is customary to embalme the body and expose it for a fortnight or so on a bed of state" (Misson 1719: 93). The need to delay putrefaction was nothing new and while never routine, bodies were occasionally embalmed during the medieval period, usually to facilitate the repatriation of remains from overseas or retain the integrity of the body allowing identification and public display, which was particularly important for those in possession of high position (White 1978: 25). Antiquarian discoveries of the preserved bodies of Humphrey, Duke of Gloucester, brother of Henry V, and Thomas Beaufort, Duke of Exeter, uncle to Henry V, both of whom died in the fifteenth century and had been soaked "in pickle" (Litten 1991: 38) suggests that embalming was a practice used at least occasionally by those of high status. In cases of individuals dying abroad, one method used, *mos teutonicus*, involved dismembering the body, followed by boiling to separate soft tissues. The soft tissues were then buried at the place of death and the skeletal remains returned home (Litten 1991: 37). A modified version of this method was employed after the death in Normandy of Henry V in 1422, when the king's soft tissues and bones were sealed in a lead case for eventual interment in Westminster Abbey some two months after his death (White 1978: 27; Litten 1991: 37).

The practice of embalming appears to have continued into the sixteenth and seventeenth centuries, again mostly for the bodies of those of high status, particularly royalty. The body of Henry VIII was eviscerated and embalmed prior to his burial in 1547 (Gittings 1984: 216). Similarly, the body of Charles I, with head sewn back in place, was embalmed following his execution in 1649, then encased in an anthropoid lead coffin (Litten 1991: 157), while the corpse of his nemesis Cromwell was subject to both autopsy and embalming in 1658 (figure 2.13) (Pearson and Morant 1935: 7). Embalming was not always successful. Sometimes, as in the case of the corpse of Ludovic Stuart, Duke of Richmond and Lennox, failure of the embalming process required rapid, often nocturnal,

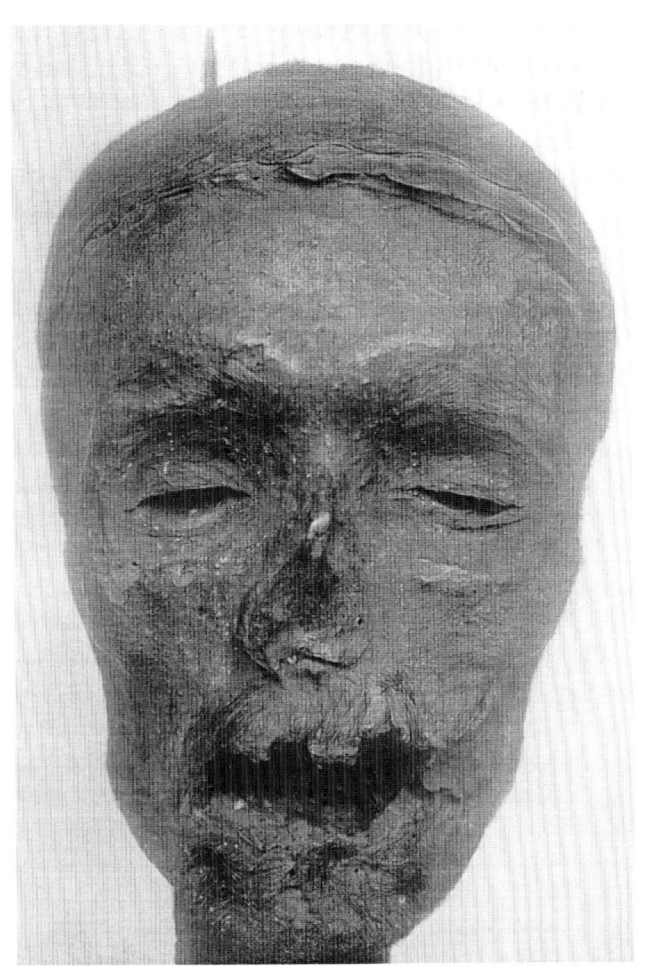

2 The preparation and presentation of the post-medieval corpse

Figure 2.13 Oliver Cromwell's head. His body had been embalmed and subject to autopsy. After craniotomy his skull had been repaired and the scalp stitched back into place. The stitches are visible on the top left of this picture. Notice also the protruding spike from the post-mortem display of his head (Photograph reproduced from Pearson and Morant 1935).

disposal of the putrefying remains (Gittings 1984: 167). Such was the political and social importance of the funeral during this period that the Duke was given a sumptuous funeral some two months later with an effigy in place of the body (Gittings 1984: 168). In fact the burial of an effigial body in place of a carnal one was a strategy frequently adopted at early modern elite funerals (Llewellyn 1991; Tarlow 2008).

The bacteria contained in the intestines, which are released after death, are an important element of the process of bodily decomposition and removal of the viscera or "emboweling", virtually an universal element of medieval and early modern embalming, would have retarded the onset of putrefaction (Read 1696: 710). The embalmed body of Duke of Lauderdale, who was interred in the burial aisle of St Mary's Church, Haddington, East Lothian in 1682, had been eviscerated, and the abdominal cavity packed with sawdust (Caldwell 1976: 27). Embalming also usually involved opening the cranium to remove the brain (Guibert 1639: 144; Read 1696: 710). The Wilkinson head, thought by many to be that of Oliver Cromwell exhibits clear evidence of a craniotomy cut, with needle holes in the skin demonstrating that the skull cap had been reattached (Pearson and Morant 1935: 6) (figure 2.13). Once the internal organs had been removed, the next stage in the embalming process is to make cuts in the body to remove the blood (Guibert 1639: 144–5; Read 1696: 710). The body was then treated with a variety of spices and solutions thought to have preservative characteristics, such as turpentine and vinegar, and wrapped in cerecloth, a waxed fabric, or a material imbued with similar properties (Guibert 1639: 145–6). The embalmed body of Duke of Lauderdale was found to have been dressed in a shroud and wrapped in several layers of linen heavily impregnated with lanolin with the fabric being tightly bound around the body using linen ties, and the coffin sealed with a combination of lanolin and possibly gum ammoniacal (Caldwell 1976: 27).

Treatment of the body parts removed during the embalming process varied. In some cases they were simply discarded, but more usually they were also interred, often in close proximity to the body, either within the coffin or in separate containers. For example, when the coffin of Charles Lethieullier, who died in 1737, was interred in a vault attached to St Mary's Church, Little Ilford, it was accompanied by a viscera chest that on opening in 1984 was found to contain the internal organs including the heart packing in aromatic bran (Litten 1991: 54). The coffin of the Duke of Lauderdale was accompanied by a lead box containing a canopic jar and bearing an inscription (Caldwell 1976: 28). The coffin would be placed adjacent to the viscera on the completion of the requisite formalities which, depending on the nature of the ceremonies, could take some time. It was nineteen days before the coffin of Henry VIII was reunited with his internal organs in St George's Chapel, Windsor in 1547. The Duke of Lauderdale died away from home at Tunbridge Wells and the body had to be transported some distance back to Haddington making embalming the corpse essential (Caldwell 1976: 34). Given the distance involved it is also probable that the viscera had been embalmed before being placed in the canopic jar (Guibert 1639: 144). The need to return the dead home has been suggested to explain the two unlabelled lead drums found in the Cavendish Vault in Derby Cathedral, Derbyshire. These might contain the entrails of family members who died some distance away and required embalming (Butler and Morris 1994: 26). The drums are thought to contain the viscera of Mary and Henry Cavendish who died in London in 1698 and Parma in 1821 respectively, although other possible origins include Colonel Charles Cavendish and the second Earl of Northumberland, both Civil War fatalities.

The late sixteenth and early seventeenth century saw a decline in embalming and the procedure appears to have been performed infrequently by the early eighteenth century (Gittings 1984: 105). This may in part be a result of the distaste expressed by some members of the nobility for having their corpses manhandled by so many people and concerns, particularly of women, about having their body intruded upon (Gittings 1984: 190). Also the decline in elaborate heraldic funerals during the seventeenth century reduced the need to keep bodies in a state to be ceremonially displayed for many days or even weeks after their death (Litten 1991: 193). Embalming would still have been necessary for those dying away from home but who wished to be buried close to their ancestors.

The latter half of the eighteenth century saw changes in the nature of embalming and a new reason to embalm bodies: scientific enquiry. By this time, anatomy had become an important means of understanding the normal functions of the body and of determining the aetiology and treatment of pathological conditions. Dissection was also an essential element of the education of any aspiring medical student.[7] Preserved specimens of body parts had become a vital tool for both teaching and research and this resulted in considerable advances in the preservation of soft tissue.[8] It was only a matter of time before these advances were harnessed to preserve the bodies of the dead for cultural reasons (Baillie 1812: 12). The results of integrating the latest advances into the embalming process are well illustrated by the methodology described by William Hunter in a lecture in 1776. The initial stage involved injecting large quantities of an antiseptic solution, such as oil of turpentine, into the blood vessels and then allowing time for this to permeate through the body (Hunter 1776: 534–5). The thoracic and abdominal cavities were then opened to allow removal of internal organs as with earlier methods (Hunter 1776: 536). More antiseptic solution was then injected into the disembowelled corpse and also into excised organs (Hunter 1776: 537–8). The internal organs were replaced in the body with nitre, resin and camphor packed around them before the body was sewn closed (Hunter 1776: 540–1). Unlike in early modern methods, the brain was not removed (Hunter 1776: 539).

The application of science to the art of embalming changed not only the methods used to preserve the dead but also the reasons behind such treatment. While bodies continued to be embalmed, often by undertakers, to allow their transport over great distances, in the hands of the anatomist preservation of corpses became an arena for experimentation and display. William Hunter is known to have embalmed two bodies to illustrate the practical applications of his endeavour to improve methods of preservation (Litten 1991: 35). The identity of the first body is unknown but the second was probably the most famous embalmed body of the era, Maria Van Butchell (Litten 1991: 46). Embalmed in 1775 at the request of her husband Martin – a former student of Hunter's brother John, the preserved corpse was not buried but instead kept in his house even after his remarriage (*The Times*, Aug 25th 1787; Dobson 1953: 436; Litten 1991: 46, 49). Several decades earlier, the surgeon Charles White had embalmed the body of septuagenarian Hannah Beswick and displayed the embalmed corpse as the centrepiece of his collection of anatomical specimens at his home in Manchester (Litten 1991: 44–45; Dobson 1953: 433). White was not alone in having a freshly embalmed corpse as part of his private museum; the surgeon John Sheldon also embalmed the body of one of his patients and kept it in his home (Dobson 1953: 437).

There is little archaeological evidence for embalmed corpses from the eighteenth and nineteenth centuries. Some of the nineteenth-century burials from Ashton-under-Lyme in Lancashire appear to have been embalmed by injecting formalin into the body (Duff and Johnson 1974: 564). Liquid mercury was found at the base of one of the coffins from the vault under St Luke's Islington, London, and in the abdominal region of a burial from St Peter's Church Wolverhampton (Adams and Colls 2007: 87). Mercury was used in the treatment of syphilis in the eighteenth and nineteenth century (Waldron 1993: 85) and this may explain its presence in the grave, although neither of the skeletal remains exhibited any of skeletal changes characteristic of the disease (Boyle *et al.* 2005: 87).[9] Alternatively a common homeopathic remedy Mercurius vivus was used to treat a variety of ailments including fevers, skin disorders and toothache (Adams and Colls 2007: 87–8). Mercury is also toxic to many bacteria and may have been used to retard putrefaction and thus preserve the corpse. A small open topped wooden box full of sawdust was found above the feet in a coffin from the vault at Christ Church, Spitalfields (Reeve and Adams 1993: 82). It is possible that it held viscera.[10] There are also a small number of coffins in various vaults which have never been opened but which documentary evidence suggests contain embalmed bodies. Elizabeth Cavendish, wife of the 5th Duke of Devonshire, died in Rome in 1824 and her body was embalmed before being returned to England in a lead coffin with a glass window (Butler and Morris 1994: 26). Her coffin now lies in the Cavendish Vault in Derby Cathedral, and while its external appearance has been recorded, it has never been opened. A late nineteenth-century edition of Cassell's Household Guide describes the use of glass panels in coffins of those dying some distance from home to allow friends and family a final opportunity to look on the face of the deceased. However, the presence of glass panels may not necessarily indicate that the body within had been embalmed, as in some instances attempts to retard decay could be confined to placing pitch between lid and shell of coffin (*Cassell's Household Guide* n.d. 344). Glass panels were also found with two late seventeenth-century burials from the Kingston-upon-Thames Quaker burial ground and it has been suggested they may have been used to contain infection as an alternative to an open coffin (figure 2.14) (Bashford and Sibun 2007: 121).

The absence of archaeological evidence for embalming during the eighteenth and nineteenth centuries may reflect the comparative rarity of the practice, something perhaps suggested by the notoriety of some of the examples discussed earlier. Indeed Matthew Baillie writing in 1812 stated that embalming occurred so rarely that many surgeons would not be sure how to embalm a body (1812: 7). Another point to consider is how identifiable embalmed remains are within an archaeological context. If the preservation process was unsuccessful, there would be little to distinguish the embalmed body from one buried in its natural state. Craniotomies allowing the removal of the brain would be the most obvious evidence for embalming on skeletal remains from the early modern period, but by the eighteenth century many of the methods for preserving the body did not require the opening of the cranium (Hunter 1776: 539). Moreover, the increasing numbers of post-mortems performed during the eighteenth and nineteenth centuries meant than evidence of post-mortem cutting of the bones is more likely to be the result of determining the cause of death than preserving the corpse.[11] Even if the embalming had been successful, the situation is little better as current health and safety regulations often require the immediate reburial or cremation of bodies with surviving soft tissue without investigation or recording (Kneller 1998: 186; Boyle 1999: 190). Finally it is worth noting that many of the more infamous embalmed bodies of the eighteenth and nineteenth centuries were not interred, but were instead displayed as scientific curiosities above ground (Dobson 1953: 433, 440).[12]

Cremation

Inhumation is not the only means of disposing of the bodies of the dead and cremation has been practiced by many societies in many periods. By the beginning

Figure 2.14   Burial 1085 from the Quaker burial at Kingston-upon-Thames showing the glass viewing panel from Kingston upon Thames (Photograph courtesy of Archaeology South-East).

of the early modern period, inhumation had been the standard means of disposal in Britain and Ireland for some 700 years and it continued to be so throughout the period examined by this book. The destruction of the body by flames was practiced during the early modern period, when women guilty of certain crimes, notably treason, were normally burned at the stake (Gatrell 1994: 315–6).[13] Yet, the flames in this instance were the cause of death and not the means of disposing of the dead (although sometimes the woman was hanged or strangled before being burned, in which case the consumption of the body by fire was a part of the post-mortem punishment). Perceptions of cremation changed in the nineteenth century when the process began to emerge as a viable alternative to inhumation (Jupp 1990: 1). During the nineteenth century the potentially deleterious effects of the decomposing dead on the living had been a subject of increasing concern (Walker 1839: III-IV). The unprecedented population growth experienced by many industrial centres during the first half of the nineteenth-century had overwhelmed existing burial provision (Rugg 1998: 44). As the population of urban centres soared, conditions within the burial grounds and churchyards deteriorated.[14] The gases or 'miasmas' produced by the decomposition of the corpses in these over-crowded burial grounds were thought to be responsible for a number of diseases (Walker 1839: 109). These concerns over the risk to public health led to the burial legislation of the 1850s and the shift of the control of the disposal of the dead from the Church to the State. The same concerns also in part lay behind the Cremationist movement (Tarlow 1992: 129; Curl 1993: 303).

The Cremation Society was founded in 1874 and campaigned for the legalisation of cremation. By 1879 the society had built a crematorium at Woking, to the great ire of the local vicar (Jupp 1990: 15; Curl 1993: 309–10; White 2002: 179). The use of cremation to dispose of the dead was seen as abhorrent by many, tainted by both criminal and pagan connotations. In addition, both the Anglican and Catholic churches were opposed to the process, which was seen in some quarters as irreligious (Jupp 1990: 15; Tarlow 1992: 132). Perhaps more important than society's perceptions in the eyes of the Cremation Society was the uncertain legal status of the process in the absence of any specific legislation either prohibiting cremation or requiring that the bodies of the dead be buried (White 2002: 173). Protests to the Home Secretary over the Woking Crematorium led to a ban on cremation there on the grounds it might destroy vital forensic evidence in instances of suspicious death (Jupp 1990: 15). This did not stop some individuals seeking to be cremated after their death and the Cremation Society provided assistance by arranging transportation to Milan, where the first facility to cremate human remains had been established in 1876 (Curl 1993: 305; White 2002: 173). Henry Crookenden died aged 57 on 21st of December 1875 and was interred in Brompton cemetery (White 2002: 172). On the 14th of March 1878, his body was exhumed by his sister-in-law and taken to Milan for cremation and then buried in Manafon churchyard in August of that year (White 2002: 174–5).

Others were less willing to go abroad. In 1882, Major Hanham of Sturminster Newton in Dorset sought permission to use the Cremation Society's crematorium to cremate the bodies of his wife and mother who had died in 1876 and 1877 respectively (Jupp 1990: 16; White 2002: 177). Permission was not forthcoming so Hanham built his own crematorium and burnt the bodies himself (White 2002: 179). He died a year later and was also cremated. A more controversial cremation was that of Jesu Grist Price, cremated in a cask of oil by his father in 1884. The father was charged with cremating rather than burying his son. The charges were dismissed, the judge ruling that cremation was not unlawful as it was not expressly prohibited provided there was no nuisance caused (Jupp 1990: 16; Curl 1993: 310; White 2002: 185). A year later the first individual was cremated at the Cremation Society's Woking facility (White 2002: 1840). A total of three individuals were cremated that year, ten the following year and 104 in 1892 (Jupp 1990: 16). Furthermore, a number of authorities, such as Manchester (1892), Glasgow (1895) and Liverpool (1896), acquired statutory powers to build crematoria in the decades prior to the 1902 Cremation Act (Curl 1993: 310). Cremation was very much a minority rite at the end of the nineteenth century, but that was to change significantly during the course of the twentieth century (Jupp 1990).

Conclusion

During the post-medieval period attitudes towards the corpse change significantly from the decaying flesh of the post-Reformation period to aesthetic sleeping corpse of the later eighteenth and nineteenth centuries (Tarlow 1999b; 2002; 2011). This is reflected to some extent in the preparation of the body. During the early modern period the corpse was swaddled in voluminous shrouds, obscuring all recognisable features of the individual, and then encased within a coffin – treatment appropriate for a rotting corpse. Representations of the dead and decaying body were normal. Yet before being obscured from view the body was washed, prepared for the grave, and viewed during a wake – elaborate treatment for decaying flesh. The contradictions in the perception and treatment of the corpse during the early modern period are not surprising, as they were governed not only by contemporary religious and scientific orthodoxy but by traditional beliefs and practices (Tarlow 2011). The decaying flesh about which the theologians sermonised was once a living person, and to friends and family still retained the identity of a loved one after death and was thus deserving of care. Washing the dead is mentioned in some of the earliest British documentary sources, and the practice probably dates back much earlier (Webb 1965a: 97; Webb 1965b: 181). Such long-held ideas on the appropriate treatment of the corpse are deep-seated and may not be greatly affected by changing fashions and religious doctrines concerning the treatment of the dead.

By the eighteenth century, the archaeological evidence shows how attitudes to death and the corpse had changed. Historical accounts demonstrate how the social process of separation at death was rationalised and understood by a range of metaphors including those of a journey, the diurnal cycle and sleep. The evidence of the presentation of the corpse suggests that in the burial context, sleep emerged as the dominant metaphor. The shroud was no longer voluminous, obscuring the body, instead it resembled night clothes with the coffin often made up like a bed (Tarlow 2002: 87). Care was taken in the presentation of the corpse to create a whole and beautiful body – the hair was combed and styled, wigs and false teeth put in place, and shrouds and pillows were decorated with bows and ribbons. The attention to these aspects illustrates the importance of the body as a focus of mourning and remembrance. The impression of the body when viewed by loved ones for the final time was increasingly important. By the second half of the nineteenth century photographs were commonly taken of the corpse, sometimes in its coffin, to commemorate the dead, as Jay Ruby has explored for the US (1995).

Finally, it could be argued that the development of the less substantial shrouds of the eighteenth and nineteenth century was only made possible by the virtually universal use of coffins by the end of the seventeenth century. With increased coffin use, the shroud was no longer the corpse's sole protection from the earth of the grave and the loss of this role allowed a greater flexibility in design. The post-medieval period also saw increasing state, as opposed to ecclesiastical, regulation of burial and some of the earliest legislation, the Burial in Woollen Acts of the seventeenth century, had a direct impact on funerary attire. This legislation also proved advantageous to the fledgling undertaking profession allowing bulk purchases of woollen shrouds in a variety of sizes and removing the requirement to provide funerary attire in a range of fabrics.

Notes

1. See chapter 3 for a more detailed discussion of changes in coffin use.
2. However, this shift in perceptions did not entirely displace the brutal Death. Some religious groups, such as Scottish Calvinists, continued to see Death as the final enemy (Porter 1989:86).
3. Part of a worn shoe was found in a coffin in the Newcastle Infirmary burial ground (Nolan 1998: 68). It is unclear why only one shoe was included with the burial.
4. A belt formed from a continuous metal sheet thought to be a hernia truss was found over the pelvis of a fourteenth- to sixteenth-century burial from the Augustinian Church of St. Mary Merton in Surrey (Miller and Saxby 2007: 101–2).
5. See chapter 3 for a more detailed discussion of coins found elsewhere in the grave.
6. See chapter 6 for archaeological evidence for the removal of teeth from corpses.
7. See chapter 6 for more information.
8. See discussion in chapter 6 and Knox 1836 for an idea of methods employed.
9. Changes to the skeleton only occur in 10–12% of individuals affected with venereal syphilis (Roberts and Manchester 1999:153).
10. Although an account of the burial of Elvira Horsley in 1852 describes how a pine box containing letters was added to the coffin (Jalland 1999b: 214).
11. See chapter 6 for a more detailed discussion of the archaeological evidence for autopsy.
12. The eighteenth century "Manchester Mummy" – Miss Hannah Beswick – was kept in the Manchester Natural History Museum until it closed in 1836 when it was buried in Harpurhey Cemetery (Dobson 1953: 433), while the embalmed body prepared by John Sheldon and that of Mrs Van Butchell were housed by the late nineteenth century in the Museum of the Royal College of Surgeons where they remained until their destruction in 1941 during the Blitz (1953: 440).
13. See chapter 5 for a further discussion of this subject.
14. See chapter 4 for further discussion of this subject.

3 Enclosing the corpse

Having considered the treatment of the body, our focus now shifts to the grave and this chapter will consider the use, form and adornment of coffins during the post-medieval period. Coffins can serve a multiplicity of functions, concealing, protecting and containing the corpse, as well as providing a means of conveying the body to the grave and making claims about the individual inside. The post-medieval period saw important changes in the frequency of coffin use, as well as the standardisation of coffin form. There were also significant changes in decoration of coffin and how status was signalled. This chapter will also consider the items placed within and on the coffin and the flowers and floral tributes that accompanied the corpse to the grave.

Coffin use and construction

The most common container for the corpse during the early medieval, medieval and post-medieval period is the wooden coffin, yet like many organic materials, wood is often poorly preserved, and survival is dependent on particular environmental conditions. Its survival thus varies significantly both between and within sites. Nonetheless it is possible to make some generalised inferences about coffins using archaeological evidence (Gilchrist and Sloane 2005: 114). It is clear that during the medieval period coffin use was far from universal. The majority of individuals were still carried to their grave in a communal or parish coffin (Gilchrist and Sloane 2005: 111). The body was then removed from the coffin and placed into the grave in just a shroud. Evidence for coffin use varies between sites during the medieval period, but it was a minority practice. Evidence from eight medieval monastic cemeteries shows that coffins were used for between 3.7–34.1% of all burials (Gilchrist and Sloane 2005: 114), yet by the end of the seventeenth century coffins were virtually universal. Determining the exact timing of this change is problematic because of variations in the preservation of wooden coffins, and the difficulties in identifying burials that can be securely dated to the sixteenth and early seventeenth centuries (Gilchrist 2003: 402–3). Moreover many of the coffins that can be identified tend to be the expensive lead coffins of those who lie interred in burial vaults, rather than more perishable, and more common, wooden coffins. The wealthy elements of society preferred their own coffin in the early modern period and would not have been seen dead in the common parish box that was used to transport bodies to the church for burial (Cressy 1997: 433). Significant change in coffin use appears to post-date the Reformation. Harding has noted that there are few documentary references for burial in coffins in London prior to the mid-sixteenth century and has suggested that the majority of intramural burials (those beneath the floor of the church itself) were not placed in coffins until the mid-sixteenth century and that most of extramural (graveyard) burials remained uncoffined for a further half century (2002: 59).

The archaeological evidence for this period also seems to suggest that the major shift to universal coffin burial occurred during the seventeenth century. The rather fragmentary burial evidence from the sixteenth century appears to indicate that the majority of the population continued to be interred wrapped in shrouds. For example only 13% of the pre-1600 single burials from the New Churchyard were in coffins (figure 3.1) (Gilchrist and Sloane 2005: 241). The New Churchyard is admittedly atypical as it was one of the earliest municipal cemeteries, designed to serve as an overflow cemetery during outbreaks of epidemic disease. The cemetery was not particularly popular as its peripheral location raised logistical problems in the transportation of corpses for interment. Moreover, many parishioners were reticent to abandon traditional burial grounds with the result that the New Churchyard soon contained a disproportionate number of immigrants lacking local parochial ties (Hunting 1991: 33). However, a similar pattern of funerary provision can be seen at St Oswald's Priory in Gloucester where only three of the ten intramural burials dating to c.1550–1650 were interred in coffins (Heighway and Bryant 1999: 219). These individuals had been interred in front of the altar, a prestigious location, and the low level of coffin use even here suggests that shroud burial was still the standard practice. In comparison the level of coffin use among a group of seventeen-century intramural burials interred at St Benet Sherehog in London prior to the Great Fire of 1666 is 83% (Miles and White 2008: 59) and the incidence of coffin use at the New Churchyard

3 Enclosing the corpse

Figure 3.1 This burial from the New Churchyard, London, did not have a coffin, judging by the position of the body and the absence of any evidence that the body had a solid container. It was probably wrapped in a winding sheet. Only 13% of the pre-1600AD single burials from the New Churchyard werue in coffins. (Photograph courtesy of the London archaeological archive and resource centre)

after c.1600 is 52% (Gilchrist and Sloane 2005: 116). All the burials from the Quaker burial ground at Kingston-upon-Thames which was founded in 1664 were in coffins (Bashford and Sibun 2007: 112) as were those from the Quaker burial ground at Hemingford Grey, which was in use during the late seventeenth and early eighteenth century (Clough 2007a: 31). The parish coffin was rendered largely obsolete during the seventeenth century as coffin burial became universal (Litten 1991: 86). Yet the surviving examples of two Yorkshire parish coffins, from Easingwold and Howden Minster, date to c.1645 and 1664 respectively which implies that, at least in rural Yorkshire, some individuals were still being interred in shrouds without coffins in the second half of the seventeenth century (figure 3.2) (Litten 1991: 86, 97–8). This also raises the issue of regional variation. Much of the evidence for early modern burial comes from only a few sites and many of these are in London. It is possible that the universal use of coffins occurred earlier in London than elsewhere. Nor can it be assumed that the increased use of coffins occurred at the same time throughout the British Isles and Ireland. It is possible that shrouded burial persisted longer in some parts, particularly in rural areas, and these late parish coffins are an example of that phenomenon.

So why did the coffin become an essential element of funerary provision during the seventeenth century? Coffins had been used during the early medieval and medieval period but were very much a minority rite. There is no simple single explanation as to why this changed during the seventeenth century, but a number of factors seem likely to have contributed. The early modern period saw a greater emphasis placed on bodily privacy, particularly among the middle and upper classes (Tarlow 2011). This may have been extended to the corpse by concealing the body within the coffin following a period of display immediately after death, so concealing any loss of proprietary engendered by the decay of the body. Indeed some have suggested that the unseemly sight of cartloads of corpses during the Great Plague of London hastened the adoption of coffins (Litten 1991: 100). Moreover, the enclosing of the body has parallels elsewhere in early modern society with the enclosure of bounded and private spaces within buildings (Johnson 1996). In addition the increasing use of coffins also occurs at a time when the corpse was acquiring a greater significance within mortuary practices in the aftermath of Reformation (Tarlow 2011). The 1547 Chantries Act denied the existence of Purgatory, stripped the chantries from within churches and ended the practice of praying for the

Figure 3.2 Catch on the Easingwold parish coffin, dating to about 1645. Because this parish coffin was made for repeated use, it was not hammered shut, but closed with a simple catch so that the body could be removed for burial. The coffin is in Easingwold parish church, North Yorkshire (Photograph by Sarah Tarlow).

dead, in effect removing many traditional methods of structuring a relationship between the living and the dead. In this void the body of the deceased acquired a greater importance providing one of the few remaining foci for mortuary rituals and for the commemoration of the dead (Houlbrooke 1989: 38). The enhanced personal significance of the corpse thus resulted in the body of the deceased being afforded greater protection in the grave by enclosing it in the more robust coffin as opposed to a shroud. Finally, economic improvements during the Elizabethan period made coffins more affordable to a greater proportion of the community resulting in a gradual change to the perceptions of the coffin from a luxury item to an essential one (Litten 1991: 12).

Medieval coffins, when present, were usually of wood, using wooden dowels or iron nails for their construction, and were either rectangular or trapezoid in shape (see figure 3.3, types a and b) (Gilchrist and Sloane 2005: 112). Far less common were lead coffins and these are usually found in intramural contexts (Gilchrist and Sloane 2005: 117). The majority of medieval lead coffins were trapezoid in shape with anthropomorphic coffins making an appearance from the fourteenth century (figure 3.3, type c) (Gilchrist and Sloane 2005: 118). Medieval variations in coffin shape persisted into the early modern period and examples of rectangular, trapezoid and anthropoid forms have been identified in seventeenth-century contexts. A rectangular lead coffin thought to contain the body of Elizabeth, Countess of Shrewsbury who died in 1607 was identified in the Cavendish vault in Derby Cathedral (Butler and Morris 1994: 25). Three of the intramural burials dating to c.AD1550–1650 from the St Oswald's Priory were interred in rectangular wooden coffins (Heighway and Bryant 1999: 221). Three seventeenth-century trapezoid coffins were identified in the nave of Glasgow Cathedral (Driscoll 2002: 102) and two early modern trapezoid lead coffins were found in the nave of Canterbury Cathedral (Blockley, Sparks and Tatton-Brown 1997: 39). A third lead coffin of an anthropoid form was also encountered at Canterbury Cathedral. The number

3 Enclosing the corpse

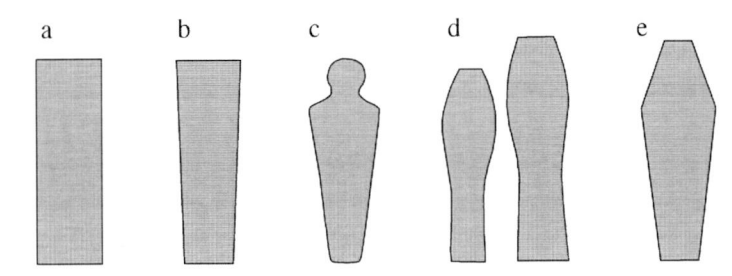

Figure 3.3   Most frequently encountered post-medieval coffin shapes. a: rectangular; b: trapezoidal; c: anthropomorphic; d: fishtailed; e: single-break. Most medieval coffins were rectangular or trapezoidal, with a small number of anthropomorphic coffins appearing in late medieval and post-medieval vaults. Fishtailed coffins were a local variation in the Birmingham area, but the majority of coffins from the whole period were of the single-break type (Drawn by Debbie Miles-Williams).

of anthropoid coffins declined in the 1660s and 1670s (Litten 1991: 92), but there is a splendid collection of anthropomorphic lead coffins in the vault of the chapel at Farleigh Hungerford castle in Somerset (Moffett and Hewlings 2009) (figure 3.4). Some of those coffins even have 'masks' over the facial area to emphasise the representation of the body. A late example post-dating the 1690 refurbishment of the crypt was recovered from St Andrews Holborn in London (Litten 1991: 92; Miles 2006: 23). Anthropoid coffins are almost invariably found in burial vaults, such as the Poulett family vault in Hinton St George in Somerset, and have been associated with the heraldic funerals of the early modern period (Litten, Dawson and Boore 1988: 259). The use of lead coffins was not confined to adults. The corpses of three infants were placed in anthropoid coffins in the Barnardiston vault in Keddington Church, Suffolk (W.H.B. 1918: 46). One coffin dated to 1671, another 1667 and the final was undated.

The early modern period also saw the emergence of a new coffin shape. The single-break coffin, widest at the shoulders and tapering towards both head and feet (figure 3.3, type e) appeared during the latter part of

Figure 3.4   Anthropomorphic lead coffins from the chapel vault at Farleigh Hungerford Castle, Somerset. Some of these sixteenth and seventeenth-century coffins have 'masks' over the faces (Photograph courtesy of John Cooke).

the sixteenth century (Litten 1991: 96). Single-break coffins thought to date to between 1570 and 1590 were found during excavations at the New Churchyard in London (Gilchrist and Sloane 2005: 241). Another early example of a lead single-break coffin was that of Lady Elizabeth Howard who died in 1591, while a wooden example with a gabled lid was found below the ledger stone of William Averie who was buried at St Peter's Church, Exton, Somerset in 1608 (Litten 1991: 90, 97). Gable-lidded coffins are often seen in artistic depictions of funerals between the fourteenth and seventeenth centuries but infrequently encountered archaeologically (Litten 1991: 96).

The seventeenth century saw the increasing standardisation of coffin form. As coffin use became virtually universal, variations in form disappeared so that rectangular, anthropoid, trapezoid forms were rarely used by the later part of the century, and in their place was the flat-lidded single-break coffin which appears to have become the dominant coffin form between c.1660–75 (Litten 1991: 99). For example, all of the coffins found at the Quaker burial ground at Kingston-upon-Thames, which was founded in 1664, were the single-break form with a flat lid (Bashford and Sibun 2007: 124). At Christ Church, Spitalfields only four of the eighteenth- and nineteenth-century coffins were not single-break (Reeve and Adams 1993: 78). All four were of wood and one was trapezoid, the other three rectangular. Yet although the single-break becomes the dominant coffin shape during the eighteenth and nineteenth centuries, occasional regional variations do occur. 80% of the 37 coffins from the vaults in the churchyard at St Martin's-in-the-Bull Ring in Birmingham whose shape could be determined were fishtailed in shape, in that they taper inwards around the legs but flare out again at the foot of the coffin (figure 3.3, type d, and 3.5) (Hancox 2006: 154). Fishtailed coffins were observed during excavations at St Phillip's Cathedral also in Birmingham (Patrick 2001: 16–18). This regional variation seems to disappear in the late 1860s/1870s at St Martin's when the incidence of fishtailed coffins declined to be replaced by the ubiquitous single-break form (Hancox 2006: 155). Why the single-break coffin becomes the dominant form by the end of the seventeenth century is not clear. The disappearance of the anthropoid coffin can be attributed to the decline in heraldic funerals, but why this period also saw the virtual disappearance of both rectangular and trapezoid forms is more problematic. The shift from gabled to flat lids can be explained in purely practical terms as it allowed coffins to be stacked above each other in vaults or graves if no shelving system was present. In 1615 St Mary Colechurch prohibited the use of "a ridged coffin" for burials within the church requiring the use of "square flat

Figure 3.5 Fish tailed coffins from vault 10 in the churchyard of St. Martin's-in-the-Bullring, Birmingham. The coffin on the left is that of Frances Home, who died in 1833, and to the right that of John Home, who died in 1828. (Photograph courtesy of Birmingham Archaeology).

coffins" to facilitate the interment of more than one body in a grave if necessary (Harding 1989: 117). Yet expediency alone cannot entirely explain growing dominance of the single-break coffin. The rectangular and trapezoid forms were as practical and much easier to construct than the single-break coffin, but both were rarely used after the end of the seventeenth century. Perhaps as coffin use became universal and with the beginning of a commercial funerary industry, it became important to have a distinctive container for the corpse. The single-break chest or box is not used outside funerary contexts and even in basic outline is easily recognisable.

The undertaking trade had its origins in the later part of the seventeenth century (Litten 1997: 52). Prior to this the majority of the population were interred comparatively simply by family and friends, who in some instances may have used the services of tradesmen such as carpenters and joiners. The funerals of the nobility during the sixteenth and early seventeenth century were organised by the College of Arms, a corporation of heralds and part of the Royal household (Litten 1991: 14). The College was also the arbiter and regulator of funerary etiquette – in particular dictating which aspects of funerary behaviour were the preserve of those of nobler birth. Yet although they managed the funerals the College often drew on the expertise of tradesmen such as upholsterers, coffin makers and tailors (Fritz 1994–5: 241). During the 1670s tradesmen such as William Boyce and William Russell set up undertaking businesses arranging funerals in London (Litten 1991: 17; 1997: 52–53; Fritz 1994–5: 242). The development of the undertaking industry should be seen as a reflection of social and economic changes during this period (Fritz 1994–5: 246). The second half of the seventeenth century saw a growth in trade and commerce and the development of London's middle class. The members of this group were keen to demonstrate their taste and acquaintance with fashion, and had the monetary means to do so, thus providing a market for the undertakers. The undertaking industry was initially based in London, spreading first to the larger cities in the provinces, and then during the course of the eighteenth century to smaller cities, market towns and villages.

During the later medieval period when the vast majority of individuals were interred in shrouds, a coffin was a usually a mark of status. However, coffin use appears to have been determined by a number of factors including attitudes towards the body. Age, sex and the cause of death were also influential (Gilchrist and Sloane 2005: 111, 114). Certainly, the use of more expensive materials such as lead was an indication of wealth and therefore status (Gilchrist and Sloane 2005: 119). The expense – and therefore prestige – of using large quantities of lead persisted into the early modern period (Cressy 1997: 434). As coffin use became universal and coffin form increasingly standardised, the coffin functioned to signal the status, real and aspired, of the deceased and their family (Litten 1991: 86; Adams *et al.* 2006: 223). During the sixteenth and early seventeenth century under the auspices of the College of Arms, all aspects of aristocratic mortuary practice, including the form and adornment of the coffin had been strictly regulated, and a precise form of funerary provision enforced for members of each rank in society (Fritz 1994–5: 247). With the growth of middle-class funerals during the latter part of the seventeenth century, funerary provision became as much an indicator of wealth as rank. Coffins became a vital medium for social display during the eighteenth and nineteenth century as the complexities of construction, the raw materials used and the form of the ornamentation were all used in the negotiation of social position.

The basic container during the eighteenth and nineteenth centuries was a wooden single-break coffin with a flat lid. Single-break coffins were constructed from a minimum of six pieces of wood; a base, lid, two sides and two ends. The joins were usually butt-ended rather than mitred or dove-tailed and secured with glue and/or iron screws and nails (Litten 1991: 90; Miles and White 2008: 59). All the single-break coffins from Spitalfields were constructed with butt joints (Reeve and Adams 1993: 78). The joints in the adult coffins were fixed using small nails or panel pins, having some instances been first glued. Variations from the usual construction methods have been found at a number of sites. At Chelsea Old Church in London, the majority of the coffins were nailed together but screws were found in some (Cowie, Bekvalac and Kausmally 2008: 31). A coffin from the Quaker burial ground in Kings Lynn had mitred joints secured with iron nails and resin or glue (Mahoney 2005: 99). Another coffin from the same site contained no nails but was secured with a combination of carpentry techniques and glue. Wooden coffins in the adjacent Baptist burial also used mitre and tenon joints in their construction (Boston 2005a: 145). Usually a series of saw-cuts or 'kerfs' were made on the internal surfaces of the side planks so the wood could be bent to form the distinctive shoulder of the single-break coffin, although the break in coffin sides from North Dalton Church were created not by kerfing, but by joining two pieces of wood together (Mytum 1988: 186). Carpenters' marks were observed on nineteen coffins from Spitalfields including one with the internal length and shoulder width, 5'6" and 19" respectively, marked in white chalk (Reeve and Adams 1993: 82). More elaborate containers involved the addition of an extra lid and /or multiple coffins, often termed shells, one placed within the other like Russian dolls (figure 3.6) (Litten 1991: 100). Four burials from the Quaker burial ground in Kings Lynn, Norfolk were in wooden double case coffins while another burial was in a wooden triple-shelled coffin (Mahoney 2005: 98). Double-shelled wooden coffins were also recovered from the burial ground associated with the workhouse in Manorhamilton, Co. Leitrim (Moore Archaeological and Environmental Services 2001). The presence of double-shelled coffins in a workhouse cemetery is a little surprising and may be linked to concerns over infection. Several single-shelled wooden coffins from the burial ground of the Church of St John of Wapping in London had double lids (Miles 1998: 18) while a damaged wooden coffin from the Davidson vault at St Benet Sherehog also appears to have a double lid (Miles and White 2008: 58). Double lids may just have been used for aesthetic reasons or as an indication of status but it is possible that the space between the lids was packed with charcoal to reduce the odour produced by decomposition (Litten 1991: 101). There is little evidence for the use

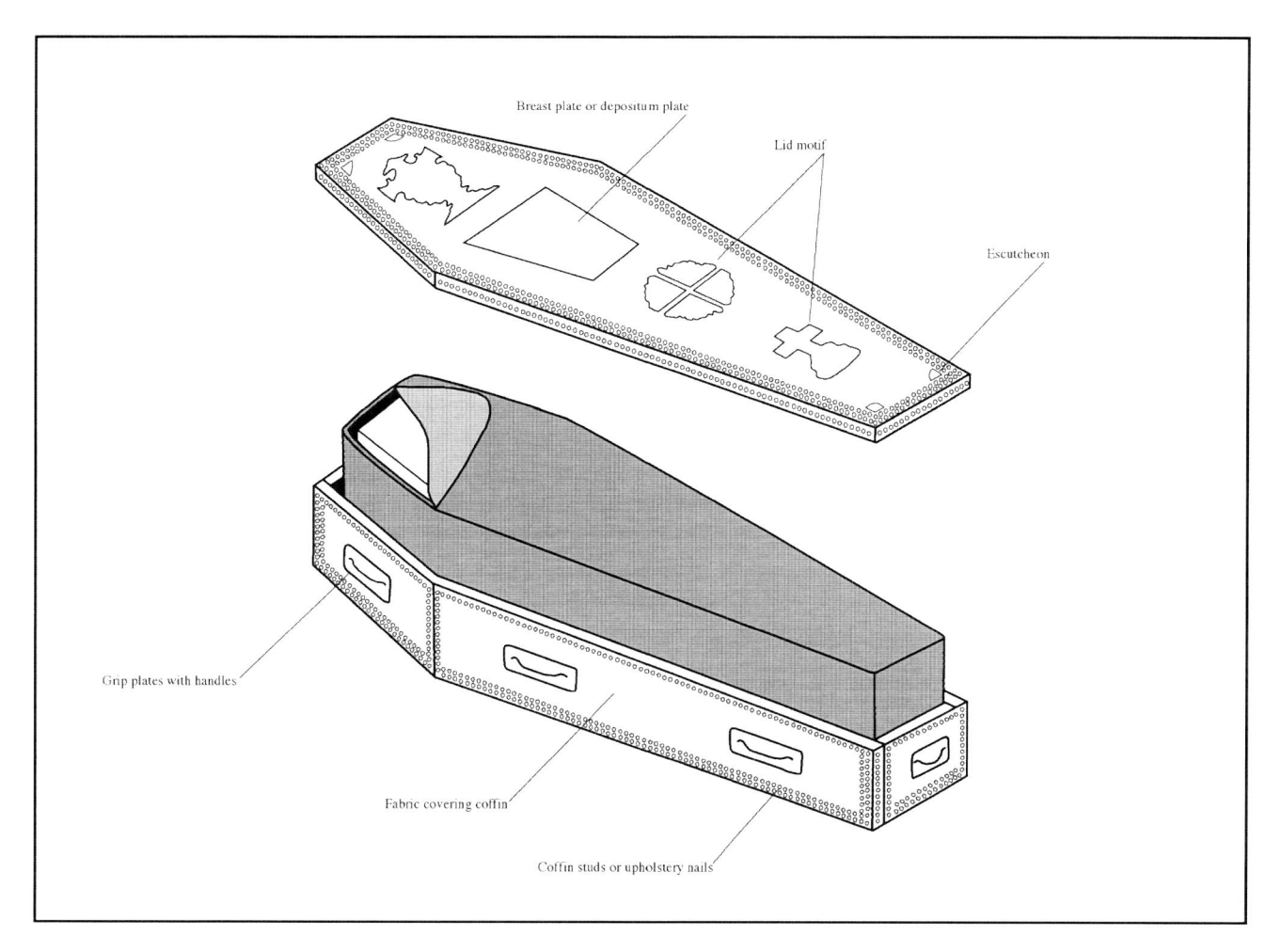

Figure 3.6 Exploded drawing of a coffin with multiple shells, showing the different parts. Triple-shelled coffins often consisted of outer and inner coffins of wood with a middle case of lead (Drawn by Debbie Miles-Williams).

of additional lids and multiple shells during the medieval period and these variations in coffin construction appear to have developed during the early modern period.

Wood was not the only material used in the construction of coffins during the post-medieval period. Lead was also used in more expensive containers for the corpse, either alone or more frequently in combination with timber (table 3.1). The shape of anthropomorphic coffins would appear to rule out the presence of an outer or inner wooden case, as does the presence of human features on some of the coffins, although it should be noted that a square shouldered lead coffin with a head recess from the Willoughby vault in St Catherine's Church, Cossall, Nottinghamshire did have evidence of an outer wooden shell (Litten 1991: 94; Elliott 2000a: 90, 92). During the seventeenth century when lead and wood were combined it was usually in a double-shelled coffin, with an inner wooden coffin surrounded by an outer one of lead. While there is always a possibility that the outer wooden coffin had decayed, the finishes of many of these coffins suggest this is unlikely. The two lead grips at the ends of a single-break lead coffin of 1685 from the Willoughby vault in St Catherine's Church, Cossall, Nottinghamshire suggest there was never an outer wooden shell (Elliot 2000a: 92), as does the lengthy inscription on a brass plate affixed to a lead coffin in the family burial aisle of St Mary's church in Haddington, East Lothian (Caldwell 1976: 27). This coffin contained an inner wooden shell and within this lay the embalmed body of the Duke of Lauderdale who died in 1682. In contrast during the eighteenth and nineteenth centuries, the vast majority of lead containers were part of triple-shell coffins, consisting of three coffins one inside the other, usually with the inner and outer coffins of wood sandwiching a middle coffin of lead (figure 3.6), although other variants continued in use in small numbers. Double-shell coffins with a inner wooden shell encased by an outer layer of lead have been found at a number of sites including St George Bloomsbury in London (Boston 2009: 151). The outer surface of lead coffins encased by outer wooden shells at a number of other sites, such as Christ Church Spitalfields (Reeve and Adams 1993: 82) and St Martin's-in-the-Bull Ring in Birmingham (Hancox 2006: 155), are simply

3 Enclosing the corpse

Table 3.1. Comparative incidence of wood, lead and other metal coffins

Site	Date	Location	Wood only		Containing Lead		Containing Zinc or Iron		Reference
			Number of coffins	% of all coffins	Number of coffins	% of all coffins	Number of coffins	% of all coffins	
Quaker Burial Ground, Kingston-upon-Thames	1664–1813	Earth-cut graves and churchyard vaults	334	95.4	16	4.6	-	-	Bashford and Sibun 2007
Baptist Burial Ground, West Butts, Poole	c.1735–1851	Earth-cut graves	83	100	0	0	-	-	McKinley 2008
St Andrew's Holborn, London	1690–1854	Crypt	739	41.19	895	-	1	-	Miles 2006
St Mary and St Michael Roman Catholic Church	1843–1854	Earth-cut graves	747	100	-	-	-	-	Miles and Powers 2006
Quaker Burial Ground, Kings Lynn	1780–1835	Earth-cut and brick lined graves	29	96.7	-	-	1	3.3	Mahoney 2005
Baptist Burial Ground, Kings Lynn	c.1773–1841	Earth-cut graves	17	94.4	-	-	1	-	Boston 2005

Table 3.2. Distribution of coffin type by burial location at St. Luke's Islington, London (data from Boston and Boyle 2005:99)

Burial location	Earth-cut graves in the churchyard	% of earth-cut graves	Vaults and shaft graves in churchyard	% of vaults and shaft graves	Church crypt	% of burials in church crypt	Total number of burials
No surviving coffin	330	52.1	5	8.0	-	-	335
Wooden coffin	236	37.3	17	27.4	1	0.3	254
Lead shell	63	9.9	40	80.6	351	99.4	454
Zinc	1	0.2	-	-	1	0.3	3
Iron	3	0.5	-	-	-	-	3
Total number of burials	633	-	62	-	353	-	1047[1]

1 Excludes one burial from unknown location

Table 3.3. Incidence of lead coffins

Site	Date	Earth-cut graves	Churchyard vaults and brick-lined graves	Church crypt	Reference
Quaker Burial Ground, Kingston-upon-Thames	1664–1813	7/227 (3.1%)	9/9 (100%)	-	Bashford and Sibun 2007
St Luke's Islington	c.1740–1853	63/303 (20.8%)	40/57 (70.2%)	351/353 (99.4%)	Boston and Boyle 2005
St Bartholomew's Church, Penn, Wolverhampton	18th–19th century	2/22[1] (9.1%)	20/22 (90.1%)	-	Boyle 2002
St Martin's-in-the-Bull Ring, Birmingham	18th–19th century	0/806 (0%)	57/122 (46.7%)	-	Hancox 2006

1 Based on figures in table 3.1

decorated with a wire-carded cross-hatch design. The large lead letters soldered to the lead case to form the inscription "Catherine relict of Robert Morris of Brunswick Square Died 6th August 1825 Aged 55 years" on a coffin from St George Bloomsbury in London were not designed to be covered up by an outer lead shell (Boston 2009: 151). Similar assumptions can be made about the lead coffin of Bridget Sale, who was interred in the Carrington vault at All Saints Church in High Wycombe in 1737, which had an ornate appliqué breast plate with appliqué lettering (Boyle 1998: 60) and the lead coffin found below the floor of nave of St Cyngar's Church in Hope, Flintshire with the initials WH, a date of 1746 and a skull and crossbones embossed on the lid (Jones, Silvester and Edwards 2001: 44). A more unusual variation in coffin construction was encountered at St George Bloomsbury in London. Here the body of David Edwards who died in 1831 was found within a coffin consisting of an inner wooden shell, a lead shell and two outer wooden cases (Boston 2009: 151; Boston, Boyle and Witkin 2006: appendix 3, p. 17). Both outer wooden coffins bore breast plates and it has been suggested that this individual may have originally been interred in a triple-shelled coffin which was then reboxed prior to being placed in the crypt. Lead coffins had to be specially made, often requiring the skills of a plumber (Litten 1991: 102). Construction methods do not appear to have been standardised during the eighteenth and nineteenth centuries: nine different methods of assembling lead coffins were observed among the lead coffins Christ Church, Spitalfields and additional variants observed at other sites (Reeve and Adams 1993: 82; Cowie, Bekvalac and Kausmally 2008: 31; Miles, Powers and Wroe-Brown 2008). The lead shell of the triple-shelled coffin could either be constructed around the occupied inner wooden coffin, or used to line the outer wooden coffin (Litten 1991: 102; Reeve and Adams 1993: 82). Evidence for the latter construction method was identified at Christ Church Spitalfields, where fragments of waste solder were found trapped in the kerfs of some of the outer wooden coffins. Other coffins had nails punched through the lead shells from the inside to attach the lead to the outer wooden case.

Triple-shelled coffins tend to be found in burial vaults and brick-lined graves (Litten 1991: 101). All the coffins from the earth-cut graves in the churchyard of St Martin's-in-the-Bull Ring in Birmingham were of wood, while 53.7% of the 122 coffins from vaults and brick-lined graves within the churchyard were of wood and 46.3% of lead (Hancox 2006: 153). Burial in lead coffins appears to become more prevalent among the later burials at St Martin's (Hancox 2006: 154). Lead coffins are not unknown in earth-cut graves but are less frequently found there than in mortuary structures within the churchyard or in church crypts (tables 3.2 and 3.3). For example of the 57 lead coffins found at St Marylebone church in London, only four (7%) came from the earth-cut graves in churchyard compared to 23 (40.4%) from within the church and 30 (52.6%) from vaults within the churchyard (Miles, Powers and Wroe-Brown 2008: 50). For those unable to afford a lead coffin a thin lead lining nailed to the inner surfaces of single-cased wooden coffins introduced early in the nineteenth century provided a cheaper alternative. Examples of such linings were found during excavations at St Phillip's Cathedral in Birmingham (Patrick 2001: 51). Lead was not the only metal used for coffins. Zinc and iron coffins are occasionally encountered both as part of triple- and single-shell coffins (table 3.4). These metals had the advantage of being lighter than lead, but in some instances could cost more to inter (Litten 1991: 86). For example, officials at St Peter-le-Poore in London charged an additional £50 to inter an iron coffin compared to only £20 for lead.

Whether made from wood, lead, or both, all coffins had to conceal the evidence of bodily decomposition, at least for a short while. Airtight lead coffins would have done much to eliminate the malodorous by-products of decay. Single-shelled wooden coffins would have been less effective in reducing odours, and coffin bearers were known to smoke tobacco to mask the stench of decay in instances of advanced decomposition, often having first fortified themselves with alcohol (Chadwick 1843: 13). Smell was not the only problem faced by those charged with conveying the deceased to the grave. Bodily fluids occasionally escaped from coffins and onto the clothing of the coffin bearers (Chadwick 1843: 13). The sawdust and bran packing observed within coffins at many sites including Chelsea Old Church, St George's Bloomsbury and St Luke's Islington would have absorbed some of the liquid products of decomposition (Cowie, Bekvalac and Kausmally 2008: 31; Boston, Boyle and Witkin 2006: 87; Boyle, Boston. and Witkin 2005: 103).[1] In addition, pitch or resin was used to coat all or part of the base and in some instances the sides of the coffin. This enhanced the waterproof qualities of single-shelled coffins and of the inner wood shell of triple-shelled coffins. Examples are known from many sites including Christ Church Spitalfields, St Luke's Islington, and Chelsea Old Church (Litten 1991: 102; Reeve and Adams 1993: 82; Boston and Boyle 2005: 86; Cowie, Bekvalac and Kausmally 2008: 31). For those coffins destined for vaults or crypts below the floor of the churches, the long-term containment of the by-products of decomposition was more important because it had to prevent unpleasant aromas seeping into the nave. For instance at the Enon Baptist Chapel in London, only a floor of wooden boards separated the living from the dead interred in the crypt below (Jupp 1997: 94). Contemporary witnesses spoke of the overpowering smell and the infestations of insects (Walker 1839: 155). Not only was the smell unpleasant, but there were growing concerns about the potential health risk from the vapours produced by decomposition (Walker 1839: 109). These vapours were often referred to as miasmas and were held to be responsible for a number of medical conditions.[2]

By the early decades of the nineteenth centuries, many churches insisted on a lead coffin for interment in the church crypt or below the floor. At St George's Bloomsbury, vestry minutes from 1810 state "that hereafter no corpse be permitted to be placed in the vaults except in leaden or metal coffins" (Boston 2006: 86), and similar restrictions were in place at Christ Church, Spitalfields from 1813 (Reeve and Adams 1993: 78). Two coffins found at Spitalfields consist of an outer lead shell encasing double-shelled wooden coffins. In both instances the middle wooden shells were decorated and had breast plates more in keeping with the appearance of an outer case. It has been suggested that these double-shelled wooden coffins were encased in lead to comply with the new regulations (Reeve and Adams 1993: 78). These new regulations were not often extended to vaults and brick-lined graves in the graveyard where the vapours were released directly to the open air, a process often aided by the ventilation vents incorporated into some structures (Hancox 2006: 153). That said, those who could afford the expense of constructing brick structures within the churchyard often interred their dead encased in lead. 46.3% of the coffins found in the vaults and brick lined graves in the churchyard of St Martin's-in-the-Bull Ring were of lead (Hancox 2006: 153). Interestingly, the incidence of lead coffins was markedly higher in the vaults (at 59.5%), whereas lead coffins were present in only six of the 24 brick-lined graves. The differences can be attributed to a combination of cost, chronology and practical considerations (Hancox 2006: 154). Brick-lined graves were generally used for a shorter period and perhaps the comparatively rapid decay of wooden coffins presented less of a problem. The act founding a general cemetery in Winchester in 1840 required all burials below the chapel to be enclosed in lead or in a double wooden coffin with a half inch layer of pitch between the two shells (3 and 4 Vict. c.8). Pitch was not the only material placed between shells. A coffin was also found with lime between the lead shell and outer wooden case of a triple-shelled coffin containing the body of a young woman interred at St George Bloomsbury in 1818 (Boston 2009: 151).

Elm is often considered the traditional wood for coffins. It is durable, easy to work and its cross grain makes it less prone to splitting, thus imbuing it with a degree of water resistance. Elm has been identified among coffins from a number of sites (table 3.5) (Chisham 2008: 48; Litten 1991: 90). Elm accounted for 85.4% of the 185 inner wooden coffins and 74.3% of 553 outer coffins at Spitalfields (Reeve and Adams 1993: 80), while the majority of coffins recovered from the chambered burial vault and the family vaults at St Martin's-in-the-Bull Ring were of elm, as were 67.8% of the coffins recovered from earth-cut graves (Gale 2006: 161). However, as illustrated in tables 3.5 and 3.6, elm was not the only wood used for the construction of coffins nor was elm present at all sites. Oak tended to be more expensive than elm (Litten 1991: 90) and appears to have been used less frequently accounting for 4.9% of outer and 1.1% of inner coffins from Christ Church, Spitalfields (Reeve and Adams 1993: 80), while at St Martin's-in-the-Bull Ring 18.5% of the coffins analysed contained oak compared with 76.5% of elm[3] (table 3.6) (Gale 2006). At Spitalfields, the majority of non-elm coffins are of soft woods such as pine, larch and spruce, which account for 20.8% of outer and 13.5% of inner coffins. These woods, generically known as deal, were cheaper than elm and oak. The lower cost made deal a popular option for the poorer members of society. Evidence given to the Commission investigating the nature of urban interment in 1843 stated that the cheapest coffin – described as an adult pauper – consisted of a deal coffin with shroud, but with no nails, cloth, nameplate or handles (Chadwick 1843: 108). Many of the coffins at Cross Bones, a burial ground for the poor of the parish of St Saviour's in London, were poorly preserved, but when wood type could be identified it was deal (Brickley and Miles 1999a: 6, 25). Cost was also a consideration for institutions such as hospitals, workhouses and prisons, which interred unclaimed bodies in coffins made from cheaper woods.[4] When the coffins from the nineteenth-century Newcastle Infirmary burial ground were analysed, all were found to be made of the cheaper deal woods: pine, larch or spruce (Nolan 1998: 72). Similarly, the fragments of wood from the coffins in the burial grounds associated with the Ballinasloe and District Lunatic Asylum in Co. Galway and with Manorhamilton Workhouse, County Leitrim were from thin, poor quality planks of spruce (Moore Archaeological and Environmental Services 2003: 56; Stuijts 2003). The fact that the indigent and marginal were buried in coffins at all, however, even in parts of Britain and Ireland that lay far from London, attests to how pervasive the custom of containing and hiding the bodies of the dead had become by the nineteenth century.

Coffin use and construction

Table 3.4. Examples of zinc and iron coffins

Site	Date of site	Type of metal	Coffin type	Reference
St Andrew's Church, Holborn, London	1690–1854	1 zinc	Unknown	Miles 2006
St Luke's, Islington	c.1740–1853	2 zinc 3 iron	All single shell except one triple shell with zinc	Boston and Boyle 2005
Mary-le-Port, Bristol	17th–19th century	1 possible zinc	Unknown	Watts and Rahtz 1985
Baptist Burial Ground, King's Lynn	c.1773–1841	1 iron	Triple shell	Boston 2005
Quaker Burial Ground, King's Lynn	1780–1835	1 zinc	Triple shell	Mahoney 2005
Christ Church Spitalfields, London	1729–1867	1 iron	Unknown	Reeve and Adams 1993
St John the Baptist, Cardiff	19th century	1 tin or metal plate	Unknown	Tavener 1998a

Table 3.5. Distribution of types of wood by site

Site	Date	Oak	Elm	Hazel	Ash	Pine	Walnut	Mahogany	Beech	Larch/Spruce	Other species	Evidence for composite coffins	Reference
Quaker Burial Ground, Kingston-upon-Thames	1664–1813	•	•				•						Bashford and Sibun 2007
Christ Church, Spitalfields, London	1729–1867	•	•			•[1]							Reeve and Adams 1993
Cross Bones Burial Ground, London	Post-medieval					•							Brickley and Miles 1999
St Peter's Church, Barton-on-Humber	Post-medieval	•	•			•							Waldron 2007
St Peter's Church, Wolverhampton	19th century	•				•		•				Yes	Gale 2007
St Martin's-in-the-Bull Ring, Birmingham	18th–19th century	•	•	•		•				•	Unidentified exotic wood	Yes	Gale 2006
West Butts Baptist Burial Ground, Poole	1735–1855	•	•								Yew	Yes	McKinley 2008
St Nicholas's Church, Bathampton, Somerset 1994	19th century		•			•							Cox and Stock
Carver Street Methodist Chapel, Sheffield	19th century	•	•									Yes	Bagwell and Tyers 2001
Newcastle Infirmary	1743–1845				•				•			Yes	Groves and Boswijk 1998
Llangar Church, Merionethshire	Post-medieval								•				Hood 1980
Glasgow Cathedral	17th–19th century	•				•						Yes	Bain and Ramsey 2002
Cille Bhrea Chapel, Lemlair	17th–19th century									•			Rees 2004
Ballinsloe and District Lunatic Asylum Burial Ground	19th century									•			Moore 2003

1 Conifer rather than pine

3 Enclosing the corpse

Table 3.6. Distribution of coffin wood by burial location at St. Martin's-in-the-Bull Ring, Birmingham (based on data from Gale 2006)

Location		Elm	Oak	Pine	Alder or Hazel	Composite coffins
Earth cut graves	Wood only coffins	19	6	2	1	No
Burial vaults	Wood only coffins	6	2	-	-	1 of oak/elm
						1 of pine/exotic wood
	Lead and wood coffins	25	5	-	-	1 of oak/elm
Brick lined graves	Wood only coffins	6	-	-	-	1 of elm/pine
	Lead and wood coffins	4	1	-	-	1 of elm/pine

It is temping to create a hierarchy of wood types with oak and mahogany at the top of the scale and deal at the bottom. However, this would be too simple: it is important to remember that pine was used for the construction of coffins from the high status vault below Christ Church, Spitalfields as well as the parish poor ground at Cross Bones. Moreover, any such scheme would fail to take into account factors such as local availability of timber and the use of composite coffins. For example, all bar one of the 34 samples of wood from Cille Bhrea, Lemlair were of Scots pine and the other was either larch or spruce (McCullagh 2004: 204). A similar pattern is observed at Glasgow Cathedral with only one occurrence of oak while all the rest were Scots pine (Richmond and Bain 2002: 102). Pine[5], like larch and spruce, is not native to England and although reintroduced during the early modern period many of the conifers used in the construction of coffins during this period may have been imported (Bagwell and Tyers 2001). The situation was slightly different in Scotland as the Scots pine was a native species. The use of pine has been noted at a number of Scottish sites and may represent the use of local timbers, in the same way that elm coffins predominate at many southern English sites (Richmond and Bain 2002: 102).

Pine and oak account for most of the wood recovered from eight nineteenth-century coffins from the Carver Street Methodist Chapel in Sheffield (Bagwell and Tyers 2001). These coffins were composites. The top and sides of the coffin were of oak, except in one instance where elm had been used, while the base boards of all containers were of Scots pine. Of a similar date, composite coffins of oak and pine were also found at Church of St Martin in Wharram Percy (Bell *et al.* 1987: 151), while a combination of oak and ash was observed in some of the coffins from Llangar Church, Merionethshire (Hood 1980: 94). Presumably the cost of the coffin was reduced by using cheaper and more easily obtainable wood for part of the structure and it is notable that at Carver Street the cheaper pine seems to be confined to the least visible part of the coffin: its base (Bagwell and Tyers 2001), although a more random approach was taken at Llangar. The coffin in grave seven had a base and lid of oak with sides of ash while that in grave nine was predominately oak with a lid of ash (Hood 1980: 94). The incorporation of additional wood species may also have been used as decoration. The small sample of coffin wood from the Baptist burial ground at West Butts in Poole was dominated by elm, but examples of yew were also recovered (Chisham 2008: 48). Yew is a hard wood and not easy to work and so tends to be used for decoration. At Poole, yew and elm were found in the samples from the burial of an adolescent female. The yew was associated with copper studs arranged to give the year of death of the deceased and may have been part of the decoration on the lid of the coffin.[6] A slightly more unusual form of wooden decoration was observed on a single-break wooden coffin found at the eastern end of Llangar Church in Merionethshire (Shoesmith 1980b: 91). The lid of the coffin appears to have been covered by bark, thought to have been stripped from the tree, probably ash, and fastened to the top of the coffin either by glue or by the copper studs used to spell out EH 1687 (Hood 1980: 94).

Cheaper coffins were often poorly constructed. This can be seen at the Cross Bones burial ground where only four or five internal saw cuts were normally used to bend the sides of the coffin (Brickley and Miles 1999a: 26). This may be contrasted to the more usual six or seven, as used in the construction of the coffin of Martha Butler, who died in 1739 and was interred in the family vault at Chelsea Old Church in London (Cowie, Bekvalac and Kausmally 2008: 31). Cost could be reduced by using several planks for the sides, base or lid of the coffin as opposed to more expensive single wide planks. The lids, and less frequently bases, of some of the coffins from the Cross Bones burial ground consisted of three planks laid side by side and nailed in position, with internal braces used to strengthen the coffin (Brickley and Miles 1999a: 26). A similar method was used to construct the some of the coffins from the burial ground associated with Newcastle Infirmary except only two planks were used (Nolan 1998: 70). The use of two or more planks rather than a single plank in coffin construction was not just confined to poorer burial grounds, as evidenced by examples found at Spitalfields and in other vault burials, but in these instances the quality of the construction of the coffin was better. There, planks had first been joined together using panel pins before being cut to form a lid or base, rather than being just nailed on to the sides of the coffin (Reeve and Adams 1993: 80). The thickness of the wood used in the construction of a coffin could significantly affect its cost. The thicker the wood, the more expensive the coffin (*Cassell's Household Guide* 1870: 291). The most frequent thickness of the wood used in the construction of the coffins from Spitalfields was 25mm, although planks of 70mm were used in the construction of some of the outer cases and 20mm for the inner cases (Reeve and Adams 1993: 80). Institutions such as workhouses often had contracts with undertakers to supply coffins, usually specifying the minimum thickness of the wood to be used in constructing the coffin. There were, however, complaints that these standards were sometimes ignored, and the coffins supplied were of such poor quality that they would break while en route to the grave (Chadwick 1843: 108; Crowther 1983: 241). The re-use of wood could reduce costs. Cut marks seen on the base of one of the coffins from the Newcastle Infirmary burial ground point to this having occurred in at least one instance (figure 3.7) (Nolan 1998: 70). The purchase of coffins by contract could also result in individuals being forced into coffins that were too small for them, as at Carver Street Methodist Chapel Sheffield (McIntyre and Willmott 2003: 12). Occasionally a post-medieval skeleton will be found with one or more coffin nails piercing the body. During the excavations of the St Benet Sherehog Burial Ground – nails had pierced the skeleton in 23 cases (8.7% of the sample) and the number of occasions on which a nail went into soft tissue must surely be much higher (Miles and White 2008: 67). While this burial ground had once been quite high status, there was a decline in the number of high status burials during the eighteenth century and the number of skeletons pierced by nails may be indicative of scrimping on wood resulting in some individuals being interred in coffins that were too small for them (Rowsome 2000: 70; Miles and White 2008: 53). The use of standardised containers by an institution is also suggested also at the Old Gaol in Portlaoise, where the feet of all of the burials appear to have been squashed into the coffins (Keeley 1988: 5).

Adorning coffins

As coffin use became virtually universal during the seventeenth century, the decoration of the outer surface of the corpse's container became increasingly important in conveying status. This does not mean

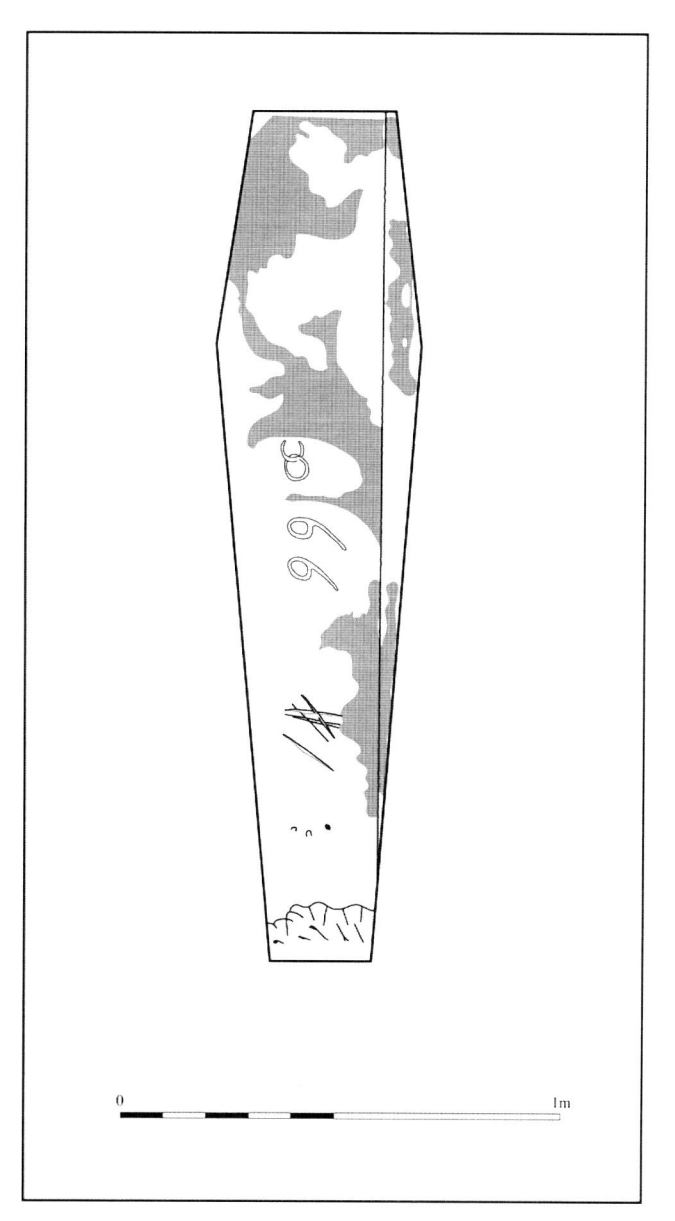

Figure 3.7 Re-used wood used as a base board in a coffin from the burial ground associated with Newcastle Infirmary (Drawn by Debbie Miles-Williams adapted from Nolan 1998).

that all medieval coffins were unadorned. Despite the poor preservation of medieval wooden coffins, examples of their decoration can be traced back to the seventh century. The inner wooden coffin of St Cuthbert, who died in AD 687, had the image of Jesus surrounded by symbols of the four Evangelists incised into the lid, with the twelve apostles, seven archangels and the virgin and child depicted on the sides (Campbell 1982: 80). Incised designs have also been found on mid-fourteenth-century coffins from the Augustinian Friary in Hull (Gilchrist and Sloane 2005: 119), while a coffin from Hereford Cathedral was covered in linen (Mereweather 1847: 61). Documentary sources have referred to painted wooden coffins and a late medieval lead coffin from the friary at Guildford had a green painted border and cross as well as the name Margareta Daubney incised into the lead (Poulton and Woods 1984: 52).

3 Enclosing the corpse

More elaborate means of identifying the deceased were encountered at St Augustine's Abbey in Canterbury in the form of lead plates giving biographical details from the graves of Abbot John Dunster and Abbot John Dygon, who died in AD 1497 and 1510 respectively (Potts 1920: 147; Thorn 1981; Gilchrist and Sloane 2005: 120). More practical metal fittings were occasionally used on medieval coffins, such as the coffin from Greyfriars Hartlepool with three iron bands on its base (Daniels 1986: 271). While unusual, a few medieval coffins have been found with handles and these tend to take the form of metal rings (Gilchrist and Sloane 2005: 112–3). What is unclear is how widespread the use of decoration was during the medieval period. Coffin use was a minority practice at this time, but poor preservation of many coffins makes it impossible to determine whether all or just a few were decorated, or what form that decoration took (Gilchrist and Sloane 2005: 120).

There is evidence for the growing importance of biographical information about the deceased on the coffin during the seventeenth century. Many coffins recovered from crypts and vaults bear inscribed coffin plates (figure 3.8). A lead coffin from the vault at Blandford Parish Church carries the inscription;

Figure 3.8 Coffin plate of Robert Wilson who died in 1660 and was buried at St Benet Sherehog in London. This is one of the earliest coffin plates in the study but the trend towards labelling the coffin with the name and date of death grows during the period (Photograph courtesy of MOLA).

"Here lieth the body of Rogersa daughter and coheir to mr Richard Rogers of Brianston by dame Ann his second wife daughter to Sr Thomas Cheeke she married S'r Henry Belasyse Knight of the most honourable of the Bath sonne and heire to the Right Ho^{bl} John Lord Belasye Baron of Worlaby in ye county of Lincolne she departed ye 22nd of Sep^{br} Anno Dni 1661. Aetatis suae octodecimo" (Goodall 1970: 154).

Other late seventeenth-century coffin plates include one found on the lead coffin of Judith Davidson, who was interred in the family vault at St Benet Sherehog in 1685 (Miles and White 2008: 58). The Duke of Lauderdale, who was interred in the family burial aisle at Haddington in 1682, had a brass plate with a fine italic inscription attached to his lead coffin (Caldwell 1976: 27). The majority of the population was unable to afford inscribed coffin plates and the use of dome shaped coffin studs of copper or brass to spell out the initials, age and date of death on the lid of the coffin provided a cheaper alternative (Litten 1991: 99). This practice appears to have developed during the second half of the seventeenth century, c.1660–75. A burial from the Quaker burial ground at Kingston-upon-Thames had the initials F H and part of the date [1]696 spelt out on the lid (Bashford and Sibun 2007: 113) (figure 3.9), while at the Church of St Botolph in London a date interpreted as 1665 was marked on the lid of a coffin using dome-headed nails (Schofield et al. 1999: 47). Two seventeenth-century coffins from Llangar Church, Merionethshire, bore biographical details, one the initials E H and the date 1687 and the other the initials I O and the date 1688 (Shoesmith 1980b: 91).

Coffin studs were usually made of brass or iron, with the iron often enamelled or painted black. Initially the use of coffin studs appears to have been primarily functional to secure fabric to the external surfaces of the coffin. In the late seventeenth- and early eighteenth-century Quaker cemetery at Hemingford Grey, the comparatively small numbers of coffin studs associated with the burials suggest a purely functional role (Clough 2007: 29). By the second half of the seventeenth century, however, they were also used provide biographical information by forming the initials of the deceased and the date of death. Coffin studs were found on 38 of the coffins recovered from the seventeenth- to nineteenth-century Quaker burial ground at Kingston-upon-Thames. In nineteen they were used only to provide biographical information, while in the remaining nineteen they were used for both biographical information and decoration or solely for decoration (Bashford and Sibun 2007: 128). One coffin at Kingston-upon-Thames bore the initials A.G. the date 1706 and the outline of a heart (Bashford and Sibun 2007: 113, 120, 129). The heart decoration is reminiscent of the so-called 'sankofa' symbol made out of tacks on the lid of a coffin recovered from New York's African Burial Ground which has widely been interpreted as a West African symbol expressing an element of African identity in the cultural practices of those African-Americans buried there. However, the occurrence of similar symbols in Anglo-American burial contexts, and here at the Quaker burial ground, add weight to Seeman's (2010) argument that the so-called 'sankofa' could equally well be a reworked element of European mortuary practices.

The growing emphasis on attaching labels to the bodies of the dead during the early modern period is likely to have been the result of several factors. From a purely practical perspective, the increasing use of coffins provided a more permanent and stable surface on which to place labels than a shrouded body. Yet coffins had been in use throughout the medieval period, albeit by a comparatively small proportion of the population, and while examples are known, putting personal information on coffins does not

Figure 3.9 Burial from the Quaker Burial Ground at Kingston-upon-Thames, showing how intitials and a date (1696) were marked out in nails on the coffin lid (Photograph courtesy of Archaeology South-East).

appear to have been commonplace (although see the three late medieval examples cited above). It is possible that labelling may have occurred using more ephemeral materials such as paint, or that the details were carved into the wood of the coffins. However, such practices are not known to us. In contrast, the metal plates and coffin studs used to convey biographical information during the post-medieval period survive reasonably well within the archaeological record. Thus it is possible that the perceived increase in the use of labels during the post-medieval period may in part be linked to a change in the materials used. However, the early modern period saw two fundamental changes that are likely to have influenced these developments; on the one hand an increasing familiarity with the written word through the medium of printed texts, and on the other a shift in the relationship between the living and the dead. The abolition of Purgatory and the end of the practice of praying for the dead meant other ways were required to remember the deceased. The body of the deceased increasingly became the focus for commemoration. Within this context, the labelling of the dead makes sense particularly given the shift from images to lettering and increasing levels of literacy (Houlbrooke 1989: 39). In addition, it has been argued that the labelling of coffins was part of the post-medieval continuation of strong personal identities beyond death (Gittings 1984: 164).

A variation on the use of coffin studs was seen on two coffins from a Baptist burial ground in use from 1735 to 1855 at West Butts, Poole. Here, letters cut from sheet iron were used instead of upholstery studs (McKinley 2008: 25). Something similar was also seen on a coffin from St Martin's-in-the-Bull Ring, which was decorated with large copper-alloy letters attached to the lid, giving the initials of the deceased, date of death and age at death of 85 (figure 3.10) (Hancox 2006: 153). The eighteenth century saw the increasing use of coffin plates which became more affordable following the introduction of stamped iron coffin fittings, and were able to provide more detailed biographical information (Litten 1991: 106; Mepham and Avery 2008: 47). The use of coffin studs as a means of conveying information gradually dwindled, although the practice persisted late into the eighteenth century despite the increasing availability of stamped iron coffin fittings from 1730s (Litten 1991: 106). Late examples include a burial from the Quaker burial ground at Kingston-upon-Thames dating to 1796 (Bashford and Sibun 2007: 113, 128) and two from the Baptist burial ground in Poole dating to the 1770s (Mepham and Avery 2008: 45).

The use of coffin plates was widespread by the beginning of the nineteenth century. Simple, single-shell wooden coffins tended to have only a single breast plate on the outer surface. On more elaborate coffins this was sometimes augmented with endplates, a headplate and a footplate, and side plates all placed on the outer case, as well as an additional inner breast plate on the middle lead shell of a triple-shelled coffin (figure 3.6, 3.9 and 3.11). The end and side plates appear to have been used to aid the identification of coffins in those situations when the breast plates might be obscured, such as when coffins were stacked in parochial crypts, allowing the coffins of relatives to be

Figure 3.10 Copper alloy letters from St Martin's-in-the-Bull Ring, Birmingham, forming the inititals, age and date of death of the deceased (Photograph courtesy of Birmingham Archaeology).

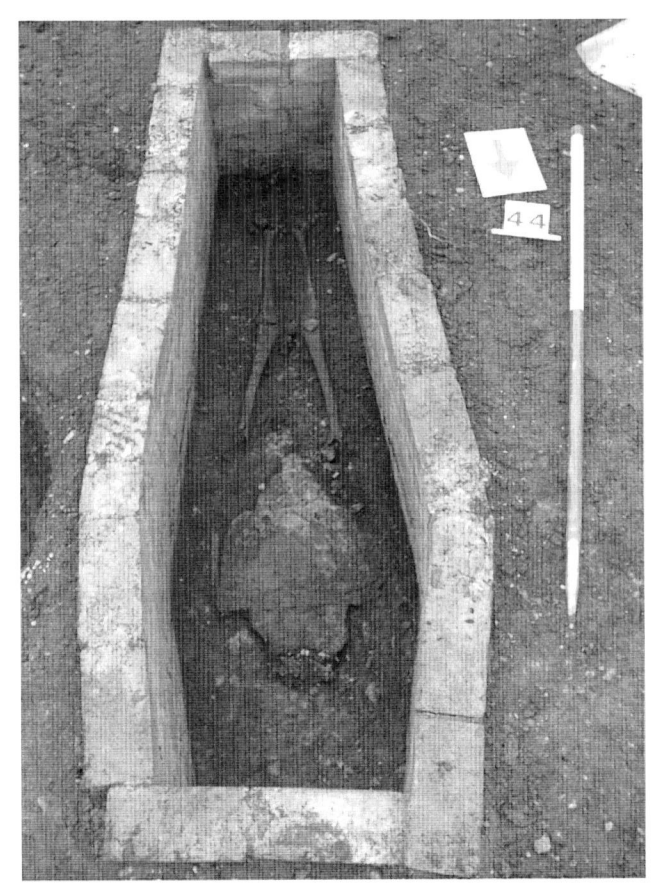

Figure 3.11 Large coffin-plate from a brick-lined grave, Leicester (Photograph courtesy of University of Leicester Archaeological Services).

placed in close proximity (Reeve and Adams 1993: 88). The parochial crypt at Christ Church Spitalfields contained the coffins of two members of the same family both with sideplates who lay adjacent to each other, despite a gap of 21 years between their deaths. The information provided on these departum or depositum plates was usually confined to name, date of death and age at death. The outer breast plate tended to provide the most information with the inner breast plate either duplicating this information or slightly truncating it (table 3.7). Details on the endplates were usually limited to name and year of death. Additional biographical information was occasionally included on depositum plates. Most frequent was profession in the instance of males and for women and children the name and in some instances profession of husbands or parents. Plates for both sexes sometimes include the address of the deceased or their family and where they had originally come from (table 3.7) (Boston 2009: 164). Sometimes the need for an inner breast plate was negated, as in a number of burials from St George Bloomsbury in London, by etching the biographical details directly onto the inner lead coffin (Boston, Boyle and Witkin 2006: appendix 3). A small proportion of coffins exhibit discrepancies in the information on the headplates, footplates, and outer and inner breast plates. These include differences in the year of death, different age at death, and variations in the spelling of names (see examples in table 3.7 and figure 3.12) (Bashford and Sibun 2007: 127; Boyle, Boston and Witkin 2006: appendix 3). The occasional reuse of coffin plates is suggested by the coffin plate of Samuel Dawson who was interred at Christ Church Spitalfields in 1815 (Cox 1996: 105). The reverse of this coffin plate bears the inscription 'Miss Maria Serle died 1st August 1815, aged 3 yrs'. While there are occasional exceptions such as the breast plate of Gilbert Gollan in table 3.7, religion and religious concepts are notably absent from depositum plates, as is information about an individual's achievements in life. Professions are occasionally mentioned but the information on depositum plates by and large is very utilitarian; it labelled the body – rarely anything more.

There are significant variations in the shape, the materials used and the methods of construction of depositum plates. While side and endplates tended to be rectangular, there was much greater variation in the shape of breast plates, which could be oval, diamond, rectangular, quadrilateral or shield-shaped (figure 3.13). The outer and inner breast plates were often but not always the same shape (Boston 2009: 165). Some of the shapes used may have had their origins in heraldic practices: for example a lozenge shape for a girl or spinster, a shield for a boy or young man (Litten 1991: 109). It is unclear how long these meanings remained commonly understood, as the use of heraldic convention appears to have declined from the early eighteenth century. Indeed there are seven nineteenth-century female burials among the dated interments from the vaults and brick-lined graves at St Martin's-in-the-Bull Ring, Birmingham with shield-shaped breast plates suggesting that the specific meanings of heraldic symbolism were not a significant factor in the selection of breast plate shape by the nineteenth century (Hancox 2006: 157–8). The shield was the most popular shape among the dated burials from the vaults and brick-lined graves at St Martin's and was used for men, women and children. In contrast at Christ Church Spitalfields rectangular breast plates were the most commonly encountered among the crypt burials, with trapezoid or diamond-shaped accounting for most of the others (Reeve and Adams 1993: 86).

A number of metals, including lead, iron and brass, were used in the manufacture of breast plates and table 3.8 gives the incidence of the materials used at several sites in London. At the majority of the sites lead appears to be the most frequently used metal. The exception is at New Bunhill Field where 95.7% of depositum plates were of iron. This is a reflection of the context of the burials. The majority of those interred at New Bunhill Fields were interred in earth-cut graves – a less prestigious and cheaper burial location than family vaults, brick-lined graves or the parochial crypt. Iron breast plates were generally less expensive than those of brass and lead and thus might be expected to be found in higher levels in less expensive burial contexts. A similar pattern can be seen at St Martin's-in-the-Bull Ring in Birmingham where all but one of the depositum plates found in the earth-cut graves were made of stamped iron, painted black, with the information about the deceased painted on in white rather than engraved (Hancox 2006: 153). In contrast the breast plates from the brick-lined graves and vaults were a mixture of brass, lead and iron (Hancox 2006: 157–8).

When more than one depositum plate is present on a coffin, they are not necessarily made from the same metal. 99.3% of the inner breast plates from St George's Church Bloomsbury are made of lead while only 61.6% of outer breast plates were of lead and 31.7% were of brass (table 3.8). The coffin of William Phelps, interred at St George's in 1831, had a rectangular lead inner breast plate and a copper alloy tapered outer breast plate (Boston, Boyle and Witkin 2006: appendix 3). Not only were several different metals used, but the contemporary trade catalogues for coffin furniture list a variety of finishes, including bronze, brass, silver and white (tin dipped iron, sometimes with silver leaf added), black (tin dipped iron paint with black paint) and coloured (tin dipped iron

3 Enclosing the corpse

Table 3.7. Examples of information provided on the depositum plates from St. George Bloomsbury, London (from Boston, Boyle and Witkin 2006: appendix 3)

Coffin number	Outer breastplate	Inner breastplate	Headplate	Footplate
1093		Amy Rangemont, Born 19th Aug, 1842, Died 29th Feb, 1844	Amy Rangemont, 1844	Amy Rangemount, 1844
1107	Mrs Sarah Dove, Died 20th May, 1837, Aged 46 Years	Mrs Sarah Dove, Died 20th May, 1837, Aged 46 Years		Sarah Dove 1837
1144	Adam Lymburne, Esq, Died 10th Jany, 1836 in the 90th Year of his Age	Adam Lymburne, Esq, Died 10th Jany, 1836 in his 96th Year		
1504		MARY, Widow of, John Williams, many years Vestry Clerk of St. Dunstan in the West, Whose remains were interred at , Fryern Barnet, Died 9th March 1835, Aged 74 Years		
1528		Joseph Planta, Esquire, T.P.S. (?), Principal Librarian of , The British Museum, Born 21st February 1744, Died 9th December, 1827		
1545	Phoebe Eliza, the Infant Daughter of Thos & Eliza Stooks, Died 11th of May 1830, Aged 13 Mons	Phoebe Eliza, the Infant Daughter of Thos & Eliza Stooks, Died 11th of May 1830, Aged 13 Mons		
1574	Thomas Atkinson, Esqr, of Lincoln's Inn Fields, and of Bedford Place, Died 4th August, 1836, Aged 80Years	Thomas Atkinson, Esqr, of Lincoln's Inn fields, and of Bedford Place, Died 4th August, 1836, Aged 80 Years	Thos Atkinson, Esqr, 1836	
3025	Mrs Mary Ann Watts, Died 11th Jan, 1804, aged 33 Years	Mrs Mary Ann Watts, Died 14th Jan, 1804, aged 33 Years		
3033	Mary Isabella Youngest daughter of Samuel Heywood Sergeant at Law and Susanna his wife daughter of John Cornwall, Esq. Died on the 16 day of October 1822 Aged 27 Years	Mary Isabella Heywood Died October 1822 Aged 27 Years		
5007	Henry Whitfield Cresswell Esqr Died 17th Feby 1828 in the 36th Year of his Life	Henry Whitfield Cresswell Esqr Died 17th Feby 1828 in his 36th Year		Henry Whitfield Cresswell Esqre 1828
6001	Lieut. Colonel Joseph Gasgoyne Honble East India Company's Service Died 21st March 1830 Aged 71 Years	Lieut. Colonel Joseph Gasgoyne Honble East India Company's Service Died 21st March 1830 Aged 71 Years	Lieut Colonel Joseph Gasgoyne H.E.I.C.S. 1830	
7043	Here are deposited the remains of Gilbert Gollan late of the Island of St. Vincent Esquire after a most painful and …ious illness which he bore with Christian fortitude and resignation …….. Life on the 26th Jany 1809 …. 62 Years	Gilbert Gollan Esqr late of the Island of St. Vincent Died Jany 26th 18..6.. Aged 62 Years		
7065	Millicent Waters Died 14th Decr 1818 Aged 14 Years	Millicent Waters Died 14th Decr 1818 Aged 14 Years	Millicent Waters Died Decr 1818	Millicent Waters 1818

painted white, and some details highlighted with water-gilding) (Litten 1991: 107). Traces of black paint were found on iron breast plates from the vaults and brick lined graves at St Martin's-in-the-Bull Ring, while gold paint was found on another iron breast plate (Hancox 2006: 157, 159). Enamelling or black paint was observed a small number of lead breast plates from St George's Bloomsbury (Boston 2006: 109). A more expensive finish in the form of ormolu coffin fittings, which involved gilding bronze with a thin layer of gold, was found on four coffins from the Quaker burial ground at King's Lynn (Mahoney 2005: 102).

Depositum plates were usually embellished with decorative borders and an array of motifs drawing on classical and Christian imagery (figure 3.14). Common motifs included angels, bibles, sunbursts, crowns, flames and cherubs (Boston 2006: 106). Floral images, especially lilies, roses and chrysanthemums, were also popular images (Boston 2006: 107). The use of classical imagery, such as urns, inverted torches and cherubs, was criticised by some as un-Christian (Pugin 1844) but was popular nevertheless. The inner breast plates and end and side plates usually exhibit less decorative embellishment (Boston 2006: 109). Available designs were largely subject to the control of those supplying coffin fittings, and it was in their interests to promote sales, even of outdated and unpopular designs, achieving this by selling such fittings cheaply or in sets (Reeve and Adams 1993: 77). The eighteenth century saw marked changes in the manufacture of depositum plates, and other forms of coffin furniture. After c.1720–30 these were produced more efficiently using hand-operated die-stamping machines. The process was further mechanised by the introduction of power-assisted machines from 1769 and coffin fittings were manufactured this way until the 1950s when the method was replaced by moulding and casting (Litten 1991: 106; Richmond 1999: 150). Changing the complex designs on the die-stamps meant that alterations or redesigns cost both time and money and this may account of the longevity of many of the designs which appear on the coffin fittings of the eighteenth and nineteenth

Figure 3.12 Inner and outer coffin plates from the coffin of Elizabeth Barber from the Kingston-upon-Thames Quaker burial ground. Note the discrepancies in the date of death (D. Miles-Williams adapted from Bashford and Sibun 2007).

Depositum Plates

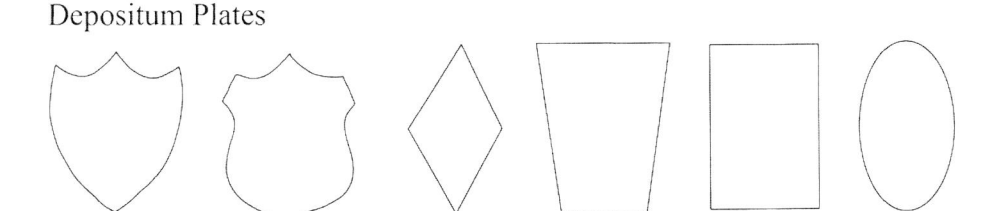

a b c d e f

Figure 3.13 Some commonly used coffin plate shapes: a and b: shield; c: diamond; d: trapezoid; e: rectangle; f: oval (D. Miles-Williams).

3 Enclosing the corpse

Table 3.8. Metals used for breastplates

Site	Date	Location	Type of depositum plate	Metal used					Reference
				Lead	Copper/Brass plate	Iron	Silvered tin		
St. Marylebone Church, London	1767–1857[1]	Crypt, churchyard, external vaults	Inner and outer breastplates	71 (84.5%)	10 (11.9%)	3 (3.6%)	-		Miles, Powers and Wroe-Brown 2008
New Bunhill Fields, London	1818–1853	Churchyard	All departum plates	46 (3.1%)	17 (1.2%)	1405 (95.7%)	-		Miles 1997
St. George's Church Bloomsbury, London	1800–1856	Crypt	Outer breastplate	244 (61.9%)	125 (31.7%)	11 (2.79%)	-		Boston 2006; Boston et al. 2009
			Inner breastplate	424 (99.3%)	-	3 (0.7%)	-		
St. Luke's Islington, London	c.1740–1853	North and South churchyard, crypt	Endplate	173 (98.3%)	-	3 (1.7%)	-		Boston and Boyle 2005
			All departum plates	153 (75.4%)	15 (7.4%)	19 (9.4%)	16 (7.8%)		

1 Based on dates on coffin plates

Table 3.9. Metals used for the grips, grip plates, lid motifs and escutcheons from St. George's Church Bloomsbury and St. Luke's Islington in London

Site	Fitting type	Number	Iron	Brass	Lead	Silvered tin	Tin pewter	Ormolu[1]	Reference
St. George Bloomsbury[2] c.1800–1856	Grips	134	108 (80.6%)	25 (18.7%)	0	0	0	1 (0.7%)	Boston, Boyle and Witkin 2006
	Grip plates	67	21 (31.3%)	30 (44.8%)	3 (4.5%)	8 (11.9%)	5 (7.46%)	0	
	Lid motifs	49	19 (38.8%)	21 (42.9%)	4 (8.1%)	2 (4.1%)	3 (6.12%)	0	
	Escutcheons	53	16 (30.2%)	32 (60.4%)	4 (7.5%)	0	1 (1.9%)	0	
St. Luke's Islington c.1740–1853	Grips	243	241 (99.2%)	2 (0.8%)	0	0	0	0	Boyle, Boston and Witkin 2005
	Grip plates	142	122 (85.9%)	0	6 (4.23%)	2 (1.4%)	12 (8.45%)	0	
	Lid motifs	23	17 (73.9%)	0	2 (8.7%)	0	4 (17.4%)	0	
	Escutcheons	15	8 (53.3%)	2 (13.3%)	0	1 (6.67%)	4 (26.7%)	0	

1 Brass mercurially gilded with gold
2 Only includes those fitting where metal composition was recorded

Figure 3.14 Highly decorated coffin plate from St Marylebone, London, decorated with an array of motifs and foliate designs (Photograph courtesy of MOLA).

centuries (Richmond 1999: 150). Subtle variations seen in the central panel motifs and the border designs were observed among the breast plates from St George Bloomsbury. Inner and outer borders designs were found in different combinations and with a variety of central panels (Boston 2006: 108). This suggests that rather than use a single die in the manufacture of a breast plate, a combination of dies may have been used to create the image allowing a greater range of possible designs. Typologies for metal coffin fittings were established during the Spitalfields excavations and expanded using data from later excavations (Reeve and Adams 1993: 83; Boston and Boyle 2005: 88–9). While the importance of establishing a systematic basis for the identification of the styles of metal coffin fittings in use during the post-medieval period cannot be overemphasised, a detailed consideration of typology lies outside the remit of this particular work.

The depositum plates were not the only form of coffin ornamentation but part of a suite of metal embellishments. Handles, termed 'grips' by the burgeoning funerary trade, were standard on all but the most basic of coffins for much of the post-medieval period. Coffin handles are known from the medieval period but are rare (Gilchrist and Sloane 2005: 112–3). While the absence of securely dated interments from the early modern period makes it difficult to determine exactly when the use of handles on coffins became commonplace, the available evidence suggests that the practice may be linked to increased coffin use so that grips and grip plates had become pretty common by the end of the seventeenth century (Litten 1991: 99). None of the three late sixteenth- to early seventeenth-century coffined intramural burials from St Oswald's Priory in Gloucester had grips (Heighway and Bryant 1999: 219, 221). Six handles, two on each side and one at each end, had been soldered directly on to the outer lead coffin of Judith Davison, who had been interred in the family vault in the burial ground of St Benet Sherehog, London in 1685, and eight iron grips were attached to the wooden coffin of Dorothy Spenser, who was buried within St Paul's Cathedral in 1687 (Miles and White 2008: 57–8; Wroe-Brown 2001: 30). Seventeenth-century grips and grip plates were also recovered from the North family vault in All Saints' Church in Kirtling, Cambridgeshire (Ponsford and Jackson 1998: 145). Two coffins from within Llangar church, dating to 1688 and 1691, both had iron grips and grip plates (Shoesmith 1980b: 91–2). The use of grips was not confined to Anglican family vaults: square cut iron grips were found with some of the seventeenth-century burials at the Quaker burial ground at Kingston-upon-Thames (Bashford and Sibun 2007: 125, 127). Iron grips were also found with two of the 16 burials from the Quaker burial ground at Hemingford Grey in Cambridgeshire (figure 3.15) (Clough 2007: 28). The cemetery dates to between the 1680s to the 1720s and these coffins are thought to date to the later decades of its use (Clough 2007: 29). The evidence from the Quaker cemeteries suggests that although grips were increasingly used on coffins by the end of the seventeenth century they were by no means universal. The eighteenth century saw a wider use of grips as the increasing mechanisation of the manufacturing practices made them more affordable.

By the eighteenth century, the most common arrangement of grips was three on each side and one at each end for adult coffins and two on the side panels and one at the head and foot on the coffins of children (figure 3.6) (Reeve and Adams 1993: 83). While the grips could possibly have been used to lift a single-break wooden coffin, triple-shell coffins with a middle lead shell could weight up to quarter of a ton. Coffins were usually borne on the shoulder and lifted from the underside, suggesting grips were only required to stabilise the coffin during lifting and thus may have had a primarily decorative function (Bashford and Sibun 2007: 126–7). Grips were attached to grip plates, which in turn were fastened to the coffin. The robust nature of grips meant they were usually made from either iron or brass, with a greater diversity of metals used in the construction of grip plates (table 3.9) (Boston and Boyle 2005: 95). Analysis of the grips from the seventeenth- to nineteenth-century Quaker cemetery at Kingston-upon-Thames indicates that the incidence of the two metals changed over time with iron dominating during the seventeenth century while the incidence of brass increased during the eighteenth century (Bashford and Sibun 2007: 127). Further research is required to determine whether a similar pattern occurs elsewhere. While the grips and grip plates generally matched each other in both design and materials there were exceptions, and three coffins from St Nicholas' Church, Forest Hill in Oxfordshire had mixed sets of grip plates made from different metals while three coffins from the Baptist burial ground at West Butts Poole had coffin fittings of differing types (Boston 2004: 18; Mepham and Avery 2008: 44). At the latter site, two coffins combined grips of iron and tin and the other had iron and brass. The more functional origins of the grips appear to have limited variations in their form and opportunities for elaboration (figure 3.16). In contrast, the flat surfaces of the grip plates, which were relatively unadorned during the seventeenth century, had greater potential. Iron stamped grip plates decorated with winged cherub heads appeared towards the end of the seventeenth century and by the eighteenth and nineteenth centuries they were often embellished with elaborate designs using the same repertoire of motifs seen on

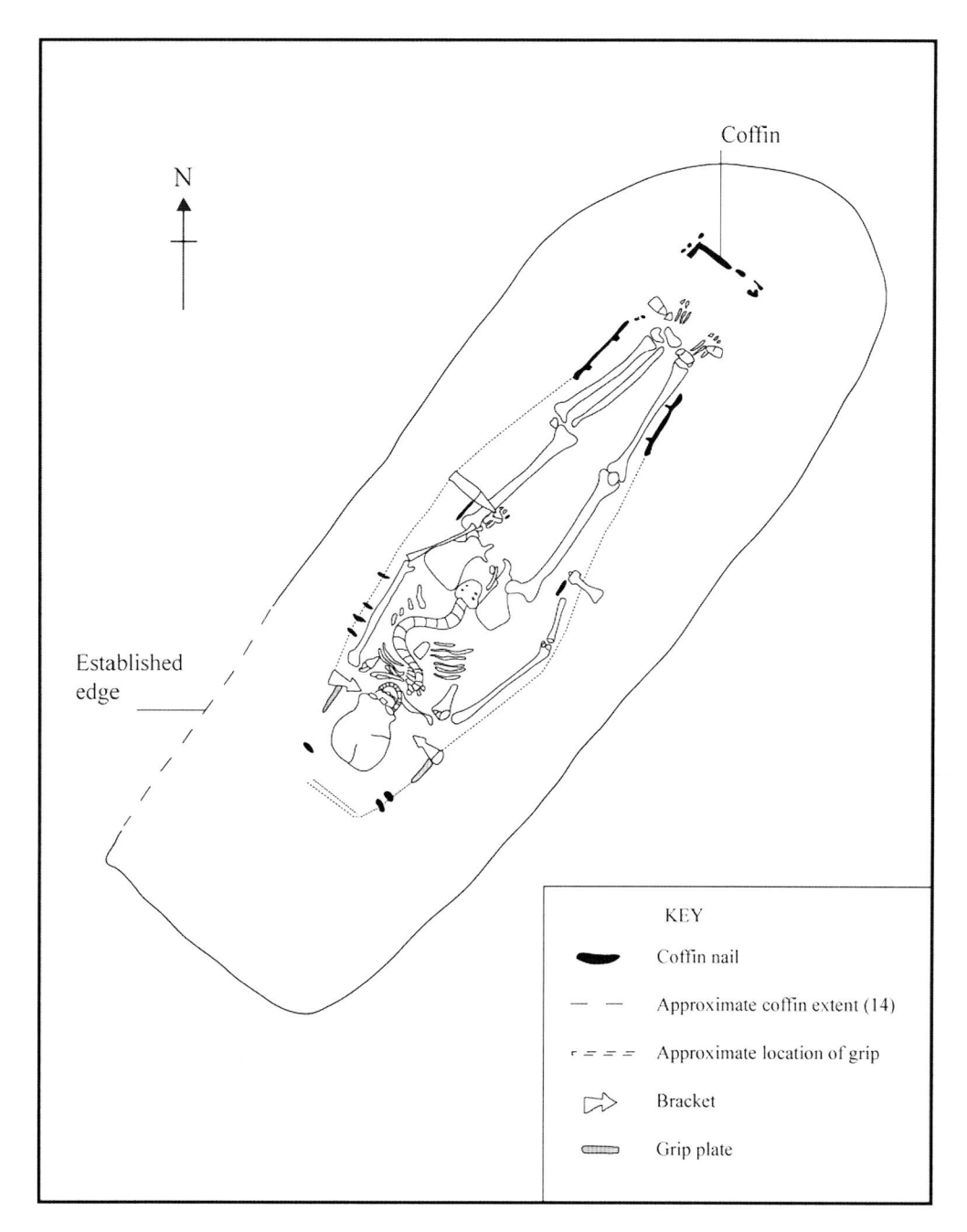

Figure 3.15 Burial from Hemingford Grey in Cambridgeshire, showing the positions from which iron coffin grips were recovered (D. Miles-Williams adapted from McNichol, Clough and Loe 2007).

contemporary breast plates (figure 3.17) (Litten 1991: 107).

In some instances, additional ornamentation on the most elaborately decorated coffins was provided by the addition of small pieces of embellished metal, often referred to as escutcheons or drops (figure 3.18) (Reeve and Adams 1993: 83). While these could occur all over the coffin, they were often placed in the corners, or incorporated into the designs created on the external surface of the coffin using coffin studs (Reeve and Adams 1993: 87). Larger pieces of decorative metal, referred to as lid motifs, were added to the lid, often above and/or below the breast plate. While lid motifs and escutcheons could be made from a variety of metals (table 3.9), iron appears to dominate. This may explain the relative rarity of these fittings in archaeological contexts (Boston and Boyle 2005: 96–97; Boston 2006: 110). Lid motifs and escutcheons by their very nature would have been largely confined to more expensive coffins, but these fittings were made from thin stamped sheets of metal and are more prone to corrosion than more substantial fittings such as grips and breast plates. Moreover, the majority were made of iron and may have simply rusted away. If this is the case then the comparatively low numbers of these fittings encountered even in crypt excavations may result from poor preservation and may not reflect their true incidence.

The practice of covering coffins with fabric is known from the medieval period, but appears to have

3 Enclosing the corpse

Figure 3.16 Examples of variation in grip handle form from 19th-century coffins from St. George's Bloomsbury in London (top and bottom) and Mary-le-Port, Bristol (centre) (D. Miles-Williams from Boston et al. 2006 and 2009; Watts and Rahtz 1985).

Figure 3.17 Examples of variation in grip plate form from 19th-century coffins from St. George's Bloomsbury in London (top and bottom) and the 17th- to 19th-century Quaker burial ground at Kingston-upon-Thames (centre) (D. Miles-Williams from Boston et al. 2006 and 2009; Bashford and Sibun 2007).

Figure 3.18 Examples of 19th-century lid motifs from St. George's Bloomsbury in London (D. Miles-Williams from Boston et al. 2006, 2009).

become increasingly common during the post-medieval period (Gilchrist and Sloane 2005: 119; Litten 1991: 102). The coffin of William Averie, who died in 1608 and was interred beneath St Peter's Church, Exton in Somerset, was covered with a pitched cambric or linen (Litten 1991: 97). Coffins were covered with wool baize or silk velvet and the choice of textile depended largely on the wealth of the individual. Wool baize is most common among the surviving coffin covers from St Luke's Islington in London, 28 of which were of baize, two of velvet and three of a loosely woven coarse fabric, possibly shoddy (Boston and Boyle 2005: 91). Shoddy was used as a backing for velvet and these coffins were probably originally covered in velvet (Boston and Boyle 2005: 92). A blue shiny fabric, thought to be raw silk, was used to cover some of the coffins containing infants at St George Bloomsbury in London (Boston 2009: 163). Coffin covers were usually dyed black and scarlet during the eighteenth century. Black, rather than scarlet, tended to be used on coffins destined for an earth-cut grave (Litten 1991: 112). Additional colours, such as midnight blue, holly green and turquoise appeared in the early nineteenth century and have been encountered at a number of sites (table 3.10). An early burial at little Ilford (1670) – "showed evidence of purple velvet" in its covering (Crowfoot 2001) and there is another purple example among the eighteenth- to nineteenth-century burials at St Martin-at-Palace, Norwich. Colours could also be combined to enhance the appearance of the coffin (Litten 1991: 112). For example, contrasting colours were used to the highlight the border between coffin nails. Despite the introduction of other colours the evidence from excavations suggests that black remained a popular shade. The remains of fabric covers from eight late eighteenth- and nineteenth-century coffins from the vaults in the churchyard of St Martin's-in-the-Bull Ring in Birmingham were analysed and all were of black wool baize (Walton Rogers 2006: 165, 173). Woollen baize dyed black or dark green was also used to cover the majority of the coffins from Spitalfields (Janaway 1998: 22). Most of the coffin covers from St Luke's were black with only two exceptions; one coffin was covered in green and another in yellow. Black was also the dominant colour at St George's Bloomsbury, although covers of mustard yellow, dark blue, dark green, red and brown were also present (Boston 2006: 107). Turquoise was often used for the very young and a number of the infant coffins found at St George Bloomsbury were upholstered in that shade (Boston 2006: 107). Uncovered pauper coffins were often painted black, perhaps in an attempt to mimic the effect of cloth covering (Fowler 2007: 180). Among the more affluent, woollen coverings could be teased to give the impression of napped velvet as at Wharram Percy (Crowfoot 2001:45). The inside of the coffin was also lined, usually with plain or waxed cambric and fragments or this internal lining have been encountered adhering to the inside of coffins from a number of sites including St Luke's Islington in London (Litten 1991: 102; Boston and Boyle 2005: 86). Coffins could also be covered with a loose cloth, called a mort cloth, for the funeral, and then removed before the interment. However, a find from the vaults of the White Kirk, Comrie, Perthshire, dating from some time after 1805 suggests that it might occasionally have been left over a coffin. In that case the existence of the cloth is indicated by the imprint of a finely woven textile in the corrosion products on the exterior surface of some coffin brackets. The excavators suggest that a mort cloth covered the coffin and decayed *in situ* (Cachart and Cox 2001).

The fabric was fixed to the outside of the coffin using dome-headed nails or tacks, often arranged in elaborate designs as discussed above (Reeve and Adams 1993: 83) (figure 3.19). While further research is required, the available evidence suggests that the last decades of the seventeenth century and early years of the eighteenth century saw the increasing use of coffin studs for decoration, although there may be significant geographical variation and the wealth of the deceased family may also be a factor. This shift in the use of coffin studs is perhaps best exemplified by the burial of the members of one family in St Paul's Cathedral in London (Wroe-Brown 2001). Dorothy Spenser died in 1687 and was interred beneath the floor of the cathedral in a coffin with a breast plate, eight iron grips with grip plates and several smaller decorative iron plates (Wroe-Brown 2001: 30). Her husband and son, both called Lawrence, died within five months of each other in 1719–20. Their coffins, placed one above the other in a single grave cut, each had a breast plate, six iron grips with grip plates and decorative lines of coffin studs.

By the mid-eighteenth century, coffin studs were arranged in rows around the edges of the sides of the coffin and often used to sub-divide the sides into a series of panels containing elaborate designs. In some instances, "coffin lace" was used to fix the fabric. These narrow strips of metal with a filigree designs, which often just had a decorative function, were available in two shades, white made from tinned-metal or black from lead (Litten 1991: 109; Reeve and Adams 1993: 83; Hancox 2006: 155; Adams *et al.* 2006: 224). Another variation seen at the Quaker burial ground at Kingston-upon-Thames was the use of studs in strips three or four abreast (Bashford and Sibun 2007: 128), while at Christ Church Spitalfields thin strips of metal resembling double rows of coffin studs were found on two coffins (Reeve and Adams 1993: 86). The use of

Figure 3.19 Burial from St. Marylebone Church, London illustrating ornamental coffin fittings (Photograph courtesy of MOLA).

cloth to cover coffins persisted into the second half of the nineteenth century. Examples dating to 1851, 1863 and 1864 were recorded at St Martin's-in-the-Bull Ring in Birmingham, although the practice was increasingly replaced by the use of waxed and French-polished woods (Litten 1991: 117; Walton Rogers 2006: 165). The De La Warr vault in Withyham contains a number of polished oak coffins dating to between the 1870s and 1890s (Litten 1991: 118). Finally there is some limited evidence for the decorative use of paint on coffins. One instance was found at Pershore Abbey, among burials dating from the seventeenth to early nineteenth centuries. Here, two interior lead shells showed rectangular patches of white paint that seemed to be decorative in nature (Blockley 1996, 2000a, 2000b).

While a vast array of coffin fittings was potentially available to adorn and embellish coffins during the eighteenth and nineteenth centuries, there were significant variations in both the quality and number of fittings found on coffins. Wealth was a major determining factor and in an era where material possessions and monetary wealth were indicators of success the funeral became the final stage to display an individual's achievements and reinforce a family's standing (Litten 1991: 165). At one end of the spectrum are the burials of the upper and middle classes from crypts, such as at Spitalfields (Reeve and Adams 1993), St Luke's Islington (Boyle, Boston and Witkin 2005) and St George's Bloomsbury (Boston, Boyle and Witkin 2006), which have provided ample evidence for the use of the more expensive triple-shelled coffins embellished with depositum plates, grips and grip plates, decorative coffins studs, and in many instances escutcheons and lid motifs. Extensive suites of coffin fittings would not have been cheap, particularly if made from more expensive metals and thus were beyond the resources of many. Most people during this period were interred in single-shell wooden coffins. Coffin fittings were still present, although made of less expensive metals, of poorer quality and in smaller numbers. Because these coffins were buried directly in the earth, they rarely survive well, and their fittings are most frequently recovered in a fragmentary and corroded condition. It is not always possible to relate such remains to individual interments. For the poor there were the lowest priced coffins, often described as an 'adult pauper'. According to evidence given to the Commission investigating the nature of urban interment in 1843 these consisted of a deal coffin without nails, nameplate or handles (Chadwick 1843: 108). This explains the paucity of coffin fittings in some burial grounds serving poor communities such as the Cross Bones burial ground in London. Only 23.4% of the coffins recovered were decorated, the decoration usually taking the form of just name plates or coffin studs (Brickley and Miles 1999a: 26). In cases of hospital and workhouse burials, which

Table 3.10. Examples of variations in coffin cover colour

Site	Date	Colour	Reference
St Martin's-in-the-Bull Ring, Birmingham	18th–19th century	Black	Walton Rogers 2006
St Luke's Islington, London	c.1740–1853	Black, yellow, green	Boston and Boyle 2005
St George's Bloomsbury, London	1803–1856	Black, mustard yellow, dark blue, dark green, red and brown, turquoise	Boston 2006
Wharram Percy, Yorkshire	Post-medieval	Dark red, dark blue	Bell *et al.* 1987
Carrington burial vault, All Saints, High Wycombe	Post-medieval	Dark blue, orange-brown-probably originally red	Boyle 1998
All Saints Church, Pavement, York	Post-medieval	Black	Walton Rogers 1998

were institutionally funded, coffin fittings are even rarer. None were found associated with any of the 210 burials from the burial ground associated with Newcastle Royal Infirmary (Nolan 1998: 70), nor were there any among the burials associated with Ballinasloe and District Lunatic Asylum in Co. Galway or the workhouse at Manorhamilton, Co. Leitrim (Moore Archaeological and Environmental Services Ltd. 2001 and 2002: 60). Only one of the six burials excavated at the Edinburgh Royal Infirmary had any surviving coffin fittings and this took the form a single coffin handle (Henderson, Collard and Johnston 1996: 935), while only one of the five eighteenth-century skeletons from Old Addenbrooke's Hospital had coffin fittings (Welch 1994: 4–5).

In the medieval period burial of the dead was a Christian act of mercy. This act of charity survived the Reformation and during the early modern period the dependent poor, foundlings and vagrants were interred by the parish (Harding 2002: 229). While not elaborate, burial by the parish usually constituted the minimum necessary for a decent funeral (Gittings 1984: 61). For example, when Thomas Laines was buried by the parish in 1653, costs covered not only the preparation of the grave but also the bell ringers' fees and the purchase of bread, beer and butter for the feast for the mourners, which formed an integral part of the early modern funerals. During the eighteenth century attitudes towards those on the margins of society changed (Gittings 1984: 64). Vagrants and the destitute were perceived to be the authors of their own misfortune (Tarlow 2007). Assistance given to the poor was increasingly thought to encourage indolence and vice (Crowther 1983). To remedy this, the assistance provided by poor relief became so unpleasant and degrading that it would only be sought by the most desperate (Rugg 1999: 224). In a similar vein, the increasingly punitive nature of poor relief removed many of what were deemed to be the more ritualistic elements of the parish funeral, such as bell ringing and the provision of food. The result was a stark demeaning burial, stripped down to just the bare essentials. For example J.H. Wick, an undertaker providing contract funerals for the London Poor Union at the beginning of the nineteenth century, charged £1 15s for a basic funeral consisting of plain pine coffin, four bearers and the hire of a baize pall (Litten 1991: 165). In a society where funerals could indicate upward aspiration or economic success, a pauper's burial was a visible sign of social failure, a stigma that would reflect badly on the bereaved family (Laqueur 1983: 109; Litten 1991: 165). A pauper's burial was therefore to be avoided at all costs. Poor families would deprive themselves of necessities and delay interment of the corpse until sufficient funds were raised, often with the body occupying the only bed in overcrowded slum housing (Chadwick 1843: 32; Litten 1991: 165). Some would go into debt rather than see a relative deposited in a pauper's grave. The desire to avoid such a fate lay behind the development of many burial societies in the first half of the nineteenth century – where participants saved to ensure a decent burial. Indeed death was often the only thing that the poorest classes saved for. Relatives who had allowed individuals to enter a workhouse would often reappear to claim the body for burial – thus avoiding the ignominy of a pauper burial (Crowther 1983: 242).

While the wealth of the deceased and the aspirations of their family were significant factors in determining the type of coffin fittings on a coffin, they were was not the only factors. Two largely contemporary family vaults in the churchyard of St Martin's-in-the-Bull Ring exhibit striking differences in the types of breast plate used (Hancox 2006: 159). In one vault five of the six coffin plates were of brass, while in the other four of the seven were of iron, painted black. The first vault was constructed by William Jenkins, a brass founder, the other by Joseph Warden, an iron merchant. Here the choice of coffin fittings appears to have been at least in part conditioned by the professional interests and is a reminder

3 Enclosing the corpse

that an individual's specific circumstances and choices may have a significant influence on the nature of funerary provision. Another factor is geographical variation. Much of our knowledge of the material culture of the burials of the eighteenth and nineteenth centuries is based on the analysis of a comparatively small number of sites, many in London and the majority in large urban centres. Yet the nature of burial practice is unlikely to have been uniform at a national level. Even in this sweeping survey of the data, regional variations are apparent, such as the fashion for fish-tailed coffins in Birmingham and variations in the types of wood used in coffin construction; this is clearly an area which requires further investigation. More research is also needed to establish the nature of differences between rural and urban communities in the funerary provision and their relative chronologies. A comparison between the coffin fittings from the Baptist burial ground at West Butts Street, Poole and those seen in many of the London cemeteries is interesting. The winged cherub motif, which was popular throughout the eighteenth and nineteenth century and is the most common design on the grip plates from Christ Church, Spitalfields (Reeves and Adams 1993: 87), was absent from the Baptist burial ground in Poole (Mepham and Every 2008: 47). The grip plates and grips are thought to be of local manufacture, the grip plates having similarities to latch fittings on cottage doors. The use of locally produced coffin fittings may indicate that commercially produced items were less readily available outside large urban centres, or simply that they were beyond the means of the members of the Poole Baptist community (Mepham and Every 2008: 47). However, another possibility in the latter case is that their Baptist faith informed the community's rejection of more expensive and elaborate coffin fittings.

As we've seen, religious beliefs significantly influenced the changing nature of funerary provision in the post Reformation period. One of the aspects most available to archaeological study is the rejection of ostentatious mortuary styles by a number of non-conformist groups. Here archaeology can allow us to study the gaps between what was professed and actual practice. The difficulty lies in distinguishing whether wealth or religious convictions are the major determining factor in the funerary provision accorded an individual. In many cases it may well be a combination of both. The Quakers are known to have advocated simplicity in their funerary practices (Stock 1998a: 133). Only 14 of the 32 coffin interred in the Quaker burial ground at King's Lynn had coffin fittings, and when present they were simple. For example, there was no decoration on the grip plates, unlike the more embellished contemporary fittings found at other sites (Mahoney 2005: 102). While it is possible this may be a straightforward reflection of the middling income of the individuals interred in the burial ground, the expensive materials used suggest otherwise. Some of the coffin grips had an ormolu finish (brass plated with gold), indicating that despite the simple designs, some of the families of the dead had sufficient means to afford elaborately decorated fittings but chose those more in keeping with the simple style of funeral expected of Quakers. Similarly, despite the presence of a few costly burials, the coffin fittings from the Quaker burial ground at Kingston-upon-Thames were characterised by a simplicity of form (Bashford and Sibun 2007: 141). Like the Quakers, Baptists disapproved of elaborate display and this may account for the simplicity seen in the iron coffin fittings from the Baptist burial ground in Kings Lynn (Boston 2005a: 146). However, many Baptist communities during this period were working class and the relative poverty of the community may also have influenced the nature of coffins and coffin fittings seen in the Kings Lynn burial ground.

The Quakers also rejected usual conventions regarding the orientation of the bodies. West-east orientation characterised most burials in contemporary churchyards, but Quaker doctrine rejected the traditions of the established church (Stock 1998b: 145). In the late seventeenth- and early eighteenth-century Quaker burial ground at Hemingford Grey in Cambridgeshire nine of the 16 burials were orientated north-east/south-west. Six of the nine had their heads to the north-east and three had their heads to the south-west (McNichol, Clough and Loe 2007: 5). The graves of the remaining seven inhumations were orientated north-west/south-east and of these five had their heads to the north-west and two to the south-east. Similar variation was also observed among the seventeenth-century graves from the Quaker burial ground at Kingston-upon-Thames with both north-south and east-west orientations observed, although there is a suggestion that the north-south orientation was preferred (figure 4.8). East-west orientation generally occurred only in the vicinity of boundaries or where the gravedigger had tried to squeeze additional burials in between the existing rows to maximise the limited space of interment (Bashford and Sibun 2007: 122). This preference for north-south graves was also observed at the Quaker burial ground in Bathford in Somerset founded in 1703 (Stock 1998b: 144). In contrast, all but one of the graves from the Quaker burial ground in Kings Lynn, which was in use between c.1780 and 1835, were interred west-east (Mahoney 2005: 76). The one exception was interred east-west (Mahoney 2005: 96). Thus it appears that some, but not necessarily all, Quaker communities may have selected a grave orientation as far away as possible from the usual conventions as a means of emphasising their separation from the established church. Variation from west-east orientation was also observed in the Baptist burial ground at West Butts Street Poole where 92.6% of the burials were orientated south-west/north-east, at right-angles to the alignment of West Butts Street (McKinley 2008: 21). The remaining four graves were south-east/north-west or north-west/south-east lying at right angles to the majority of the burials and parallel to the street. Uniformity in body orientation does not appear to have been an important consideration for those using the Baptist burial ground in Kings Lynn. All fifteen burials lay in west-east graves, but seven had their heads to the west and eight their heads to the east (Boston 2005a: 144). In contrast, all 348 burials from the Bow Baptist Church burial ground in London were orientated west-east with their heads to the west (Miles and Powers 2007: 12).

Grave goods

The deposition of items within the coffin does not appear to have formed part of normal funerary practices during the post-medieval period. Objects are rarely found in association with post-medieval burials and when present usually constitute items associated with the preparation of the corpse, such as clothing fasteners, hair combs, jewellery and false teeth, which have been discussed in the previous chapter. However, there are also a small number of items recovered from graves that cannot be linked to the preparation of corpse (tables 3.11 and 3.12). These include coins, which have been found with a number of burials but can be difficult to interpret (table 3.11). In some instances they may have been used to hold the eyelids in place. In this case the coins were usually removed prior to interment but, as illustrated by the examples discussed in the previous chapter, on some occasions the coins were overlooked and interred with the body. In other examples the connection is more tentative. Numerical discrepancies suggest that the presence of the four coins found by the head of a burial from the Methodist burial ground at Carver Street, Sheffield and the single 1806 George III penny found to the right of the skull of a burial at St Phillip's Cathedral, Birmingham may be the result of other factors (McIntyre and Willmott 2003: 10; Patrick 2001: 20). Another possible explanation for the presence of coins within burials is provided by John Aubrey. Writing in the seventeenth century he recalled an account he had heard in childhood of an old custom of placing a coin in the mouth of the deceased for St Peter (1881: 159). In Protestant eschatology St Peter has no special role, but the Catholic origins of the custom might not have mattered to those who continued to practice long-standing traditions.

Coins have been found not only in the vicinity of the head, but also on the chest, and arms (table 3.11), nor were the coins always placed above the body. For example, two seventeenth-century coins were found below the body, but within the coffin at the White Church, Comrie, Perthshire (Cachart and Cox 2001: 123–4) and a coin was placed below the skull of a burial from Drogheda Abbey, County Louth (Murphy and Stirland 2006: 9). Tokens could also be used in a similar way to coins: two seventeenth-century Cork City of Refuge tokens were found on the left and right shoulders of a skeleton from St Brendan's Cathedral, Ardfert, Co. Kerry (www.excavations.ie site no. 1991: 062). The purpose served by the inclusion of coins placed on or below the body is unclear. It is possible they had some form of votive or apotropaic role. The practice is not unique to the post-medieval period, and while far from common, coins have been found in medieval burials, often in similar locations on or below the body (Gilchrist and Sloane 2005:100; Gilchrist 2008: 135). For example, a coin was found below the skull of a late fifteenth-century burial from Kirkstall Abbey, another on the chest of a twelfth- or thirteenth-century burial from Gorefields Nunnery, Buckinghamshire, while several medieval burials have two coins placed in the vicinity of the shoulders (Gilchrist and Sloane 2005: 100). The antiquity of the practice may be indicative of the persistence of folk traditions.

A well-preserved burial from the East Kirk, St Nicholas's Church, Aberdeen had four coins, the latest dating to 1691, placed on the lid of the coffin where they remained corroded to the wood (Cameron 2006: 15). It is possible that these coins represent some form of grave-side offering and were thrown onto the top of the coffin. Finds of coins from grave fills are not uncommon and it is conceivable that some of these may once have lain on coffin lids. Coins have also been found with a number of atypical burials, including a drowning victim from Braigh, Aignish, Lewis (Holmes 1991: 81), putative murder victims from Gunnister in the Shetland Islands (Henshall and Maxwell 1952: 40) and Quintfall Hill, near Wick, Caithness (Orr 1921: 213), and an isolated burial from Old Alresford in Hampshire (Fitzpatrick and Laidlaw 2001: 222–3).[7] In these cases the inclusion seems to have been accidental or incidental to the circumstances of burial. Surviving textiles suggest the coins from Lewis, Gunnister and Wick were in purses or some form of fabric wrapping, while the position of the coins from Alresford point to the use of some form of container. All of these individuals appear to have to have been interred wearing the garments in which they died. The individuals from Lewis, Gunnister and

3 Enclosing the corpse

Table 3.11. Examples of coins found in post-medieval burials

Site	Date of coins	Position	Demographic information	Reference
St Peter's Church, Barton-on-Humber	Georgian and Victorian	Left humerus + 7 in graves either as accidental or deliberate inclusions	Older female (other seven unknown)	Rodwell 2007
St Marylebone, London	1799, 1806–7	Over eyes	3 years old	Miles, Powers and Wroe-Brown 2008
Christ Church, Spitalfields, London	1826[1]	Over eye sockets	2 years old	Cox 1996
Ebenezer Chapel, Leicester	19th century	Over eye sockets	Adult male	Jacklin 2006b
Kinnoull Church, Fife	c.1837–1860	On chest	Child	Cox A. 1998
Fowlis Wester Church, Perthshire	1642–50	Over eye sockets	None	Strachan 1997; Rees & Strachan 1998
White Church, Comrie, Perthshire	17th century	Below body within coffin	None	Cachart and Cox 2001
East Kirk, Aberdeen	16th–17th century	1 with body, 4 on lid of coffin with another burial	None	Cameron 2008
Drogheda Abbey, Co. Louth	16th–17th century	Below skull	None	Murphy and Stirland 2006
Killalee Church, Kilarney	1737–1738	2 coins	Adult, possibly female	Dennehy 2001
Braigh, Aignish, Lewis	1607–1681	17 coins between the legs	Male, aged 22–24	McCullagh and McCormick 1991
Gunnister, Shetland	1681–1690	3 coins in purse	Adult male	Henshall and Maxwell 1952
Quintfall Hill, near Wick, Caithness	Late 17th century	19 coins in a purse – right side of pelvis	Adult male	Orr 1921
Pinglestone Farm, Old Alresford, Hampshire	1553–1603	9 coins left side of pelvis	Adult male	Fitzpatrick and Laidlaw 2001

1 Date of burial

Table 3.12. Examples of items found with post-medieval burials

Site	Date	Object	Demographic information	Reference
Quaker Burial Ground, Kingston-upon-Thames	1664–1813	4 walnuts – 1 in mouth, 1 between knees, 1 between feet, 1 fallen out of decayed base of coffin	Adult male	Bashford and Sibun 2007; Bashford and Pollard 1998
Launceston Castle, Cornwall	18th century	Flint & stone strike-a-light	Male, 20–25 years	Saunders 2006
St George's Bloomsbury, London	1800–1856	Small round box, thought to be snuffbox	Older adult male	Boston, Boyle and Witkin 2006
St Peter's Church, Barton-on-Humber	19th century[1]	3 plaster effigies; two death masks & the cast of a right hand	7 year old Anna Stringfield (d.1835)	Rodwell 2007
		White china dinner plate	Older adult male	
		A blue-and-white china bowl below the base board of the coffin	Adult female	
		Small silver bell	Male, 50+	
		Fob watch	–	Rodwell and Rodwell 1982
St Peter's Church, Wolverhampton	mid-19th century	China cup	Adult	Adams and Colls 2007
Waterloo Road, Bristol	1793–1854	Spongeware cup	Infant	Lankstead 2005
General Baptist Chapel, Priory Yard, Norwich	1726–1854	Post- 1825 green transfer printed ware cup	Adolescent, c.17–18	Shelley 2004
St Mary's and St Michael's Mission, London	1843–1854	Wooden fragments from a grave, covered in three layers of paint. Possibly from furniture, small cart or wooden toy	Unknown	Powers and Miles 2006
Christ Church, Spitalfields, London	1729–1867	Turned box-wood barrel containing extracted third molars (not from burial)	Unknown	Cox M. 1998
St Marylebone, London	18th–19th century	Umbrella	Adult male	Miles, Powers and Wroe-Brown 2008
St Benet Sherehog	17th century	Hourglass	–	Miles and White 2008
New Bunhill Fields Burial Ground, London	1853[2]	Glass vial containing paper with details of burial	Infant	Miles 1997
St Phillip's Cathedral, Birmingham	1845	Water smooth pebble	Nine year old girl	Patrick 2001
Cloughvalley Upper, Co. Monaghan	18th or early 19th century	Metal object possibly a knife	Unknown	Excavations.ie site 2003:1485
Arnish Moor, Lewis	Early 18th century	Bag containing horn spoon, wooden comb, two quills, lengths of wool	Young adult male	Bennett 1975
Braigh, Aignish, Lewis	Late 17th–early 18th century	Iron whittle tang knife	Young adult male	McCullagh and McCormick 1991
Gunnister, Shetland	Late 17th century	Horn spoon, wooden staff, wooden tub, wooden knife handle, 2 tablets of wood, purse	Adult male	Henshall and Maxwell 1952
Quintfall Hill, near Wick, Caithness	Late 17th century	Purse	Adult male	Orr 1921

1   Date of burials, not necessarily the date range of the cemetery   2   Date of burial

3 Enclosing the corpse

Wick were also accompanied by a variety of other objects such as a spoon, quills, length of wool and a knife (table 3.12). All were items carried by these individuals at the moment of death which then accompanied them into the grave. Accidental inclusion probably also explains the flint and stone strike-a-light found with a male of 20–25 years buried at Launceston Castle, Cornwall (Saunders 2006: 161). The castle was used as a prison during the late seventeenth and eighteenth century and the four copper alloy buttons, probably from a jacket, indicate that this probable prisoner was interred in day clothes. While interment in clothes is not unknown in this period[8] and of itself is not indicative of a lack of care, the position of the strike-a-light suggests that it was concealed within a pocket and the fact it was interred with the body may point to a rapid interment after death without observation of normal funerary treatment.

Folk traditions and beliefs may explain the walnuts found in the mouth and between the knees and feet of an adult male burial from the Quaker burial ground at Kingston-upon-Thames (Bashford and Sibun 2007: 121). Walnuts were used in popular medicine to treat a variety of conditions such as worms, mental conditions including epilepsy and also as an antidote to some poisons, and the skeleton of this individual exhibited pathological changes. A steeple bottle of late seventeenth- or eighteenth-century date was found lying between the left humerus and upper chest of the burial of a young adult of indeterminate sex interred in the churchyard of All Saint's Church, Loughton in Buckinghamshire (figure 3.20) (Bonner 1994). It contained several copper pins along with liquid and the remnant of a cork stuck with pins was still in the neck of the bottle. The bottle is thought to have served as a counter-measure against the effects of witchcraft, often called a witch-bottle. On the basis of the contents of other examples, the bottle may originally have contained human urine. Witch-bottles were meant to be prepared by the victim and either concealed, to cause the slow and painful death of the witch, or heated until they exploded for a more rapid death (Merrifield 1955: 195). Why such an item would be placed in a grave is unclear. Perhaps the death of the occupant had been attributed to witchcraft? Certainly a grave or churchyard location is consistent with the other 'threshold' places where such devices are commonly found (Crossland 2010: 395–401). The presence of witch-bottle and walnuts perhaps point to the persistence of more distributed and permeable understandings of the body.

Stones were sometimes used as protective amulets (Gilchrist 2008: 145) and it is possible that the water smooth pebble found in the hand of nine year old Selina Harrison, who was interred at St Phillip's Cathedral in Birmingham in 1845, had some protec-

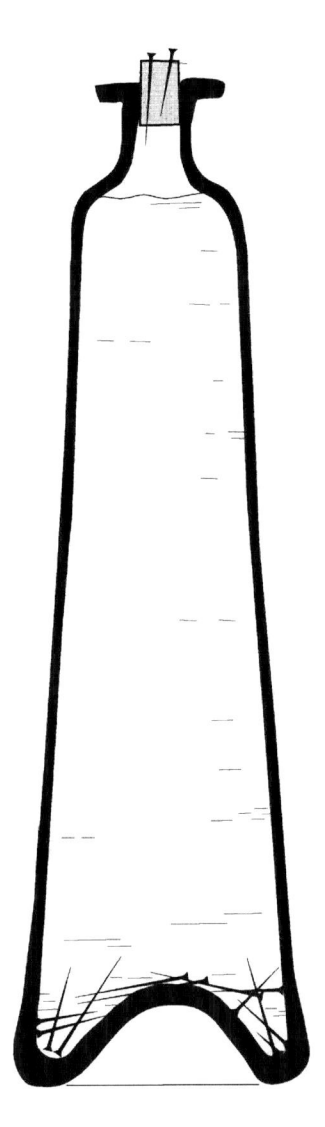

Figure 3.20 Witch bottle from All Saints' Church, Milton Keynes. Witch bottles were used curatively or apotropaically, but were normally smashed in order to make them work. A few witch bottles have been discovered buried or built into houses (Illustration drawn by Debbie Miles-Williams from Bonner 1994).

tive or curative role (Patrick 2001: 31). The practice of placing a stone in the hand, or mouth, is known from the early medieval and medieval periods; white quartz pebbles in particular are often found in Ireland, Scotland and the Isle of Man (Gilchrist 2008: 138). The use of quartz in a funerary context persisted into the post-medieval period in these regions. Small white pebbles, usually of quartz, were found scattered in several post-medieval graves from a churchyard of St Ronan's Church on Iona (O'Sullivan 1994: 334). Small quantities of quartz stones appear to have been added to the infant burials from a cillin at a monastic site at Inishcealtra, County Clare (de Paor 1974: 5, cited in Donnelly and Murphy 2008: 202), while several graves from the cillin at Reask in County Kerry were covered by layers of quartz and sea pebbles (Fanning 1981: 74). Small quartz pebbles were found in and around the graves of a group of child burials from Tintagel in Cornwall (Nowakowski and Thomas 1992: 28). It has been suggested that quartz may have possessed connotations of purity and salvation during the medieval period and it is possible that this association persisted into the post-medieval period (Gilchrist 2008: 139). The persistence of old practices may also explain the small clump of sheep's wool found at the bottom of a grave cut at the graveyard of Christ's Kirk on the Green, Leslie, Fife (Cox 1998: 292), and the small bell found with the body of an elderly male interred at St Peter's in Barton-upon-Humber (Waldron 2007: 160). Small bells have been found occasionally within medieval graves (Gilchrist and Sloane 2005: 177). Bells were rung as a deterrent against evil during the medieval period and it may be the practice persisted into the post-medieval period in some areas. Alternatively, during the nineteenth-century period of anxiety about premature interment, bells might have been included in the coffin for emergency use if the 'corpse' revived.

The inclusion of a wooden barrel containing wisdom teeth, not from the deceased, in a coffin from Christ Church, Spitalfields may be linked to folk beliefs (Cox 1998: 117), although they may also have had some personal significance to the deceased. The inclusion of items commemorating relatives of the deceased may provide a possible explanation for the two death masks and a cast of a right hand in the coffin of seven year old Anna Stringfield, who was interred in St George's Bloomsbury in 1835 (figure 3.21) (Boston 2009: 171). The death masks were both of the same elderly woman while the hand was small and very narrow, with wrinkled skin, again suggestive of an older female. There was a green patination on the palm of the hand suggesting that a copper alloy item, possibly a coin, had originally lain there and the coffin also contained a silk shawl. Why these items were placed in the coffin of this young girl is unclear, but it has been suggested the death masks and cast of the hand may be of the grandmother of the deceased. Her paternal grandmother is known to have predeceased her as did both her parents. Items placed within the grave not only commemorated deceased relatives but may have had personal significance to either the deceased or the bereaved, or both. According to Tate writing in 1600, "the body is put into a coffin of wood or stone or wrapped in lead, and sometimes there is put up with it something which he (the deceased) principally esteemed". This seems the most probable explanation for the small round box, thought to be a snuff box, found in the coffin of an older male interred at St George Bloomsbury (Boston 2009: 170) and the fob-watch found with one of the burials at St Peter's Church, Barton-upon-Humber (Rodwell and Rodwell 1982: 306). During excavations at Kinnoull parish churchyard, as well as a coin on the chest of a child, an oyster shell with a single roughly square perforation through the thicker end was also found in the grave cut of one of the deepest burials (Cox A. 1998). It is possible that the copper-alloy skeleton of an umbrella found in the grave of an adult male from the burial ground of St Marylebone Church in London may have been of personal significance but accidental inclusion is a more probable explanation (Egan 2008b: 65).

Ceramic vessels were found with five burials: two plates, one bowl and three cups (table 3.11). A male burial from the site of St Martin Vintry Church had an inverted delftware plate, dating to c. 1680, placed over the abdomen (Schofield 1998: 86), while the feet of an early nineteenth-century male burial from St Peter's Church, Barton-upon-Humber, Lincolnshire lay on a white china plate (figure 3.22) (Waldron 2007: 27). Another burial from St Peter's had a blue-and-white transfer printed bowl under the coffin below the skull (Waldron 2007: 28). A nineteenth-century green transfer printed cup was found on the left side of the chest, in the vicinity of the heart, of the body of an adolescent of seventeen to eighteen years interred in burial ground of the General Baptists, Priory Yard, Norwich (Shelley 2004: 38). A sponge-ware cup was carefully placed adjacent to the skull of an infant burial at Waterloo Road, Bristol (Lankstead 2005: 7), and a printed earthenware cup with missing handle was found with an adult burial from St Peter's Church in Wolverhampton (Adams and Colls 2007: 87). In France, it was customary to keep a ceramic stoup by the coffin before the funeral (Cox 1998: 117). These vessels were then thrown into the grave onto the coffin. It is not possible to draw parallels between funerary behaviour in Catholic France and largely Protestant post-medieval Britain given the rarity of ceramic finds in graves, but it is possible that the cups and bowl found in the burials in the table may have contained holy water and were then placed in the coffin before it was closed. Alternatively salt is known to have been placed on the body to ward off evil sprits

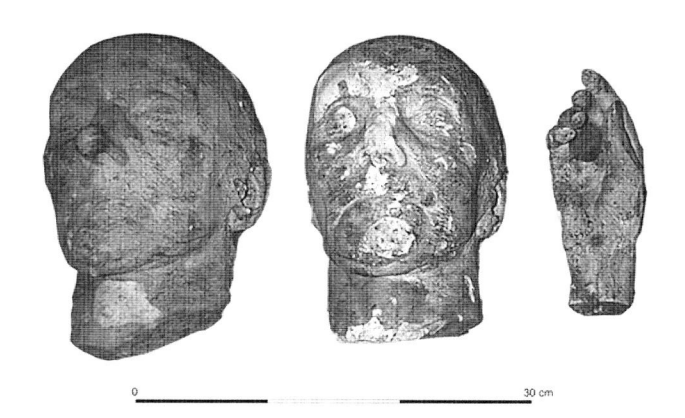

Figure 3.21 The death masks and hand found in the coffin of 6 year old Anna Stringfield interred at St. George's Bloomsbury (Photograph courtesy of Oxford Archaeology).

3 Enclosing the corpse

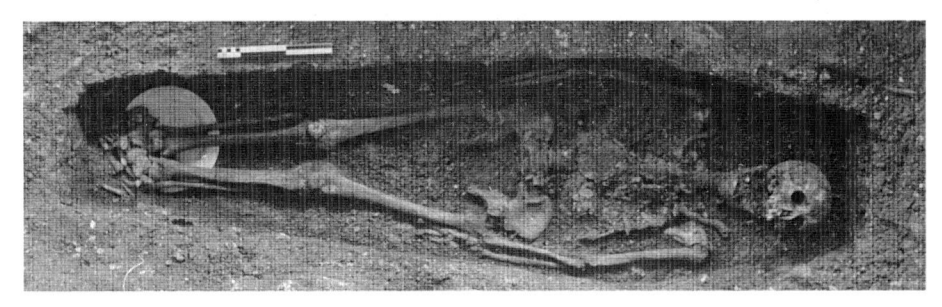

Figure 3.22 Adult male burial, dating to around the beginning of the nineteenth century, from St Peter's Church, Barton-upon-Humber. The man was buried with his feet resting on a white ceramic plate (Photograph courtesy of Warwick Rodwell).

and stop the body from swelling (Leather 1912: 120; Baddeley 1891: 93; Gittings 1984: 111). Traditionally the salt was placed on a pewter vessel, usually a plate, but it is possible that ceramic vessels may have been substituted in some instances.

The two halves of an hourglass were found in a pre-1666 seventeenth-century grave from St Benet Sherehog in London (Willmott 2008: 68). Given the strong association of hourglasses with *memento mori* at this date it seems likely to have been associated with the funerary context. While it is possible that it might have been accidentally incorporated within the grave, an account of a grave robbing incident in 1601 describe how the accused were charged with selling a lead coffin, an hourglass and a garland of flowers. Another grave was uncovered in the eighteenth century in Clerkenwell with an hourglass to the left of the skull. These incidents suggest that the hourglass had been purposefully included (W.P. 1746: 640; Harding 2002: 145). Hourglasses are known to have formed the centrepiece of some burial ('maiden's') garlands symbolising mortality (E.S. 1747: 265). These garlands, associated with the burial of virgins, were carried to the grave during the funeral and then displayed within the church. The custom fell out of favour during the seventeenth century when burial garlands were deemed inappropriate decoration for churches, at least in the London area. The practice persisted in a modified form, whereby the garland was carried to the grave and then placed on the coffin over the face of the deceased.

Finally, although not strictly a grave good, a brief mention should be made of the funerary coronet placed on top of some aristocratic coffins, such the one found on top of the velvet covered triple-shelled coffin of Robert, 1st Baron Carrington who was interred in the Carrington vault in All Saint's Church, High Wycombe in 1838 (Boyle 1998: 60). Funerary coronets occurred as both an embossed metal fitting on the coffin and as a three-dimensional object placed on the lid of the coffin (Litten 1991: 112). Their appearance in the first quarter of the eighteenth century has been linked to the revival of interest in heraldry during this period and it has been suggested that they may represent the final vestiges of the early modern funeral effigy.

Flowers and floral tributes found in mortuary contexts

The deposition of plants with the bodies of the dead is known from the medieval period both within the coffin or shroud and by casting plant material on the body within the grave. Samples of oak, bay laurel and willow have been recovered from within medieval coffins (Gilchrist and Sloane 2005: 145), while bunches of box and hyssop had been thrown onto the coffin in a well preserved late fourteenth-century grave from the Augustinian friary in Hull (Hall *et al.* 2000, cited in Gilchrist and Sloane 2005: 180). These practices persisted into the early modern period. Misson described how mourners carried sprigs of rosemary during the funerary procession, which were then thrown into the grave (Misson 1719: 91). Drury (1994) mentions early modern sources for the funerary use of bay, rosemary, yew and sage, as well as for various flowers. Plants were also deposited within the coffin: one early seventeenth-century commentator noted how the body was "wrapped up with flowers and herbes in a faire sheet" (Tate 1600: 217). Large quantities of leaves and twigs of bay and rosemary were found in a lead coffin containing body of young girl from the seventeenth-century vault in the Blandford Parish Church in Dorset (Goodall 1970: 155), while box was found above and behind the skull of one of the burials from Llangar Church, Merionethshire (Hood 1980: 95). Analysis of a sample from the stomach area of the burial from Llangar Church also contained evidence for viola species, possibly field pansy, which were was probably part of some floral offering (Hood 1980: 95). The incorporation of plants into the funerary process represented a combination of custom, symbolism and practicality. Evergreens, like box, bay laurel and rosemary, were used as symbols of the immortality of the soul and were used at both weddings and funerals during the early modern period (Dekker 1603; Coles 1656: 64; Gittings 1984: 110;

Drury 1994: 102). Plants such as bay, box and rosemary, also had the advantage of not wilting too rapidly after being cut (Coles 1656: 64). The scents produced by aromatic plants, such as rosemary, may also have aided in masking the odours of death (Litten 1991: 72; Cressy 1997: 454). These early modern practices appear to have persisted into the eighteenth and nineteenth centuries. Traces of flower petals were found in a number of wooden coffins from St Nicholas' Church in Sevenoaks, both below and above the human remains, and the coffin of Peter Nouaille, a Huguenot who died in 1845 aged 79, contained bunches of lavender and rosemary (Boyle and Keevill 1998: 94). Box leaves with traces of gold paint or gilding, probably from some form of floral arrangement, were found in the chest area of a burial in a wooden coffin at St Peter's Church, Carmarthen (Page 2001: 57). A branch of box was found in burial from the City Bunhill burial ground in London (Connell and Miles 2010: 10). Box, bay and possibly yew were recovered in burials from St. Pancras, London (Giorgi 2005 referenced in Connell and Miles 2010). At Dalton, woody vegetation was seen in the 1748 coffin of Ramsden Barnard close to the head (Mytum 1988: 186). Evidence for the placement of flowers within the coffin comes from six burials from St Martin's-in-the-Bull Ring in Birmingham (Ciaraldi 2006: 186). Fragments of box were found in three of the burials and another evergreen, privet, was found with the body of a young adult female in an earth-cut grave (2006: 185). A burial, thought to be that of Mary Elizabeth Warden who died in 1867 aged twenty or twenty-one, from one of the vaults contained cherry leaves. Another coffin that was placed in the same vault in 1871 contained the evergreen juniper. Juniper has medicinal properties and its presence may have been linked to the last illness of the deceased. Juniper also produces a strong aroma when burnt and twigs may have been burnt before the coffin was closed.

The increasing use of floral wreaths placed on the top of the coffin in the vault or in the grave may represent a nineteenth-century adaptation of the practice of throwing rosemary onto the coffin (Cox M. 1998: 116). The use of floral wreaths is thought to have been introduced in the 1860s (Litten 1991: 170). This tends to be borne out by the archaeological evidence, with examples from securely dated contexts coming mostly from the last decades of the nineteenth century. In one case five funeral wreaths were found associated with the coffin of Jane Emily Phillips, who died in 1897 aged 63, and was interred at St Bartholomew's Church in Penn (Boyle 2002: 15). Another example, that of an iron ring with some associated foliage from a wreath, had been laid on the coffin of Hannah Harrison, interred at St Phillip's cathedral in Birmingham in 1890 (Patrick 2001: 30).

The coffin also contained a short spiral of wire which appears to have been wrapped around something with a small diameter, perhaps a floral tribute. Wreaths were also recovered from a number of burials at St Nicholas' Church in Sevenoaks in Kent (Boyle and Keevill 1998: 94) and in the overspill graveyard of the Church of the Holy Trinity in Coventry (Soden 2000). In addition, it has been suggested that the metal ring found on the chest of one burial at St Peter's Church in Wolverhampton may have been remains of wreath placed on the coffin (Bevan 2007: 35). Unusual instances of wreaths dating to the first decades of the nineteenth century include the remains of one found on a coffin interred at St Bartholomew's Church in Penn, Wolverhampton in 1806 (Boyle 2002: 14), and a floral tribute on top of the coffin of a young woman from St Luke's Islington who died in 1830 (Boston and Boyle 2005: 91). While these may represent unusually early examples of the use of floral arrangements, the possibility that they were originally associated with another burial, or placed on the coffin at a later date cannot be excluded. Where burial location could be determined all wreaths were found in crypts and vaults rather than in earth-cut graves. Interment in such places was far from cheap, and during the nineteenth century wreaths were expensive. Only the well-off could easily afford these formal tributes, and this is reflected in the context in which they are encountered. However, plant remains tend not to survive in the environment of an earth-cut grave, so wreaths or other more informally composed floral arrangements are less likely to be found in these contexts (Adams and Colls 2007: 87). The increasing popularity of visible floral arrangements in the later nineteenth century may be placed in the broader context of changing metaphorical associations with the dead. Flower motifs became common on breastplates and grip plates in the eighteenth and nineteenth century, as found at St Luke's Islington (Boyle *et al.* 2005: 90–91). Excavations in pre-nineteenth-century contexts at Kilbarchan Old West Parish Church, Scotland found coffin lids decorated with strips of zinc impressed with floral motifs (Addyman *et al.* 2002; 98). Floral decoration was also present on the coffin furniture of the nobility from the end of the seventeenth century (Litten 1991: 106). Alongside softer imagery that related death to sleep, the nineteenth century saw the elaboration of the imagery of flowers, together with metaphors of planting, growth and harvest, both in graves and on gravestones (e.g. Tarlow 1995:112).

Conclusion

The early modern period saw significant changes in both the form and embellishment of the coffin, changes that continue to determine how the dead are encased. Central to these changes was the growth of coffin burial from a minority to majority rite during the seventeenth century. Several factors combined to contribute to this change but at its heart lay a changing attitude to the body, related to the redefinition of the relationship between the living and the dead. The adoption of the coffin resulted in other changes in funerary provision. As has been discussed in chapter 2, the shroud, once freed from its protective role, began to reflect contemporary attitudes to death and the afterlife. Similarly, the exterior sides of the coffin provided a medium during the eighteenth and nineteenth century for the display of wealth, taste and personal qualities to a society with a developing middle class and one where these attributes were important in determining status and religious affiliation. Interestingly, while there was diversity in the materials and decoration of coffins, this period also saw a standardisation in coffin form. The single-break coffin that first appeared during the early modern period rapidly became the standard coffin form due in part to the emergence of the undertaking industry. The combination of the undertaking trade and the mechanisation of the production of coffin fittings were to have significant influence over the form and cost of funerals during the eighteenth and nineteenth century. Changes in mortuary behaviour during the post-medieval period were not just confined to funerary provision. The period also saw significant changes in the geography of burial and this will be discussed in the next chapter.

Notes

1   The use of bran and sawdust to increase the comfort of the corpse's final rest is discussed in chapter 2.
2   The impact of these concerns on burial location during the nineteenth century is considered in more detail in chapter 4.
3   Numbers include composite coffins.
4   Some hospitals made those sponsoring patients liable for the cost of interment should the patient die.
5   Pine was present in England until the Bronze Age, but with a possible existence of a few isolated relict forests was not grown in the country until reintroduced during the early modern period (Groves and Bopswijk 1998: 85).
6   Yew may also have been associated with a second burial but the remains were too fragmentary to allow a full identification of the wood.
7   See chapter 5 for more information on atypical burial during this period.
8   See chapter 2.

4 The burial landscape of post-medieval Britain and Ireland

On the eve of the Reformation, the vast majority of the population were interred, as they had been for the last 700 to 800 years, within their parish in consecrated ground associated with a church or chapel. While the nature of the religious establishment varied and included parish churches, monasteries, friaries and hospitals, consecrated ground was the only socially acceptable burial location, making the Church's control over burial absolute. Religious change, population growth, non-conformism, the industrial revolution and concerns over health and sanitation would combine to reshape Britain's burial landscape between the Reformation and the death of Queen Victoria. The dissolution of the monasteries resulted in the loss of many long-standing burial grounds within a single generation. The rise of non-conformism meant the end of the monopoly over burial by the established Church, and the aftermath of the 1689 Act of Toleration (1 Gulielmi and Mariae c. 18), which granted freedom of worship to non-conformists, saw the foundation of many new burial grounds to serve the needs of new religious groups. The burgeoning populations of many British towns and cities after the industrial revolution created logistical problems as the growing numbers of dead overwhelmed existing burial provision. The resulting municipal and private cemeteries created to address this problem further eroded the Church's control and increasingly secularised burial. Concerns about the potential health risks posed by burials brought an end to the ancient tradition of interring the dead in the midst of the living. Instead, the dead were relocated to more marginal locations, often on the edge of towns. This chapter examines the major factors behind the changes in the burial landscape of post-medieval Britain and Ireland, with a particular emphasis on the impact of the Reformation and the origins and development of cemeteries.

The Reformation and the fate of monastic burial grounds

The dissolution of the monasteries had a profound impact on the burial landscape. While the primary function of monastic cemeteries was to provide a final resting place for members of the religious community, these cemeteries also provided an alternative to burial in a parish church or a cathedral for some elements of lay society (Gilchrist and Sloane 2005: 56). Patronage of monastic houses by the wealthy often earned them the right to burial within the monastery. Thus monastic churches or chapels could become the burial place or mausoleum for a particular family, as Earls of Lincoln (the de Lacy family), for example, used Barling's Abbey (Everson and Stocker 2003: 150). Within a generation all this was to change. The dissolution of the monastic houses started under Henry VIII and completed in Ireland by his daughter Elizabeth I resulted in the loss of many associated churchyards. Removed from ecclesiastical control, many monastic buildings and estates were sold by the Court of Augmentations and passed into lay ownership (Phillpotts 2003: 299–300). Rural monastic houses such as Netley Abbey were converted into great country mansions (Hare 1993: 216), while others in urban centres become high status town dwellings: a number of London's dissolved religious establishments were, for example, converted in the homes for prominent courtiers (Phillpotts 2003: 300). While the conversion of monastic houses to domestic dwellings could take many forms, the abbot's or prior's house which had already been used for domestic occupation often formed the core of these new houses. The church and other religious buildings, along with associated churchyards were commonly converted into open or landscaped areas.

A key element of the dissolution of many monastic houses was the stripping and destruction of the church to prevent any possibility of the religious community returning (Aston 1973: 239). In Coventry, the destruction of St Mary's Cathedral and Benedictine Priory, dissolved in 1539, commenced in or soon after 1545 when the corporation's attempt to save the Cathedral failed and the ruined nave of the church became a dumping ground for the city's butchers (Soden 2003: 281). The funerary monuments inside the monastic building were not exempt. Monumental tombs were dismantled and the brasses, ornamental slabs, stone and alabaster used in their construction were sold at auction (Lindley 2007: 12). Nor was the destruction just confined to above-ground monuments; examples of grave robbing in the aftermath of the dissolution have been identified at a number of sites. At Lewes

Priory, the backfill of two stone cist graves within the Priory Church contained destruction debris suggesting that they had been opened at the time of the dissolution[1] (Lyne 1997: 73,75). The disturbance of the east end of a third burial was also suggestive of post-dissolution looting. In addition, three floor tombs were plundered and largely destroyed (Lyne 1997: 78). At the Dominican Friary in Guildford, the fill of three graves contained demolition debris (Poulton and Woods 1984: 52). The disarticulated remains of the graves' occupants were found either within the grave fill or just outside the grave. Again, the looting of graves, perhaps for lead coffins, has been suggested. A fourth grave at Guildford was disturbed but in this case the body appears to have been completely removed, suggesting a purposeful exhumation probably for reburial elsewhere. The absence of demolition debris suggests this occurred either prior to the dissolution of the monastery or immediately after the suppression order. A number of "translations" are noted in Leland's itinerary of 1553–4; including the relocation of the tomb of the Countess of Westmorland from the White Friars in Doncaster to the parish church of St George and the removal of Geoffrey Barbour's remains from Abingdon Abbey to the parish church of St Helen's (Gilchrist 2003: 408). The fear of looting may be a factor behind the exhumation and relocation of these burials, although being interred in a church or churchyard where members of the family were likely to be buried in the future was probably a more important consideration.

Monastic graveyards were rarely the main burial location for the lay community. That function was served by the parish church. The monastic houses tended to provide an alternative to the parish church and with their loss burial reverted to the parish graveyard. However in a few cases, the loss of a monastic house could rob a community of the only consecrated ground in which to inter their dead. When the church at Monk Nash, Glamorgan was granted to Neath Abbey in the eleventh century all of its parochial rights including burial were lost and it became a chapel (Locock 1993). Following the dissolution of the abbey, the chapel became a church again but it was not until 1607 that a burial licence was granted and a graveyard was established adjacent to the church (Locock 1993: 24). A group of three interments dating to the sixteenth or seventeenth century have been excavated on the foreshore at Cwm Nash within Monk Nash parish (Locock 1993: 4). These burials lie close to the site of a holy well and it has been suggested that the site was used by parishioners during the period when there was no official burial ground in the parish (Locock 1993: 25).

The dissolution of the monasteries did not lead to the loss of all monastic graveyards for the wider population, particularly if there was a parish church associated with a religious community's church. In a survey of the fate of nineteen of London's monastic houses, six survived in some form as parish churches with associated cemeteries (Schofield and Lea 2005: 182). The northern side of the abbey church at Romsey, Hampshire, had served as the parish church of St Laurence (Caldicott 1989: 151). After the monastic house had been dissolved, the churchwardens and parishioners were allowed to buy the entire abbey church for one hundred pounds although most domestic buildings and cloisters were cleared (Scott 1996: 99). Lands around the church, including the community's burial ground, were included in the sale to provide a cemetery and processional way for the parish (Caldicott 1989: 151). In Gloucester, the north aisle of the ruinous church of St Oswald's Priory was modified by blocking the arcades and inserting windows and doors, so that the north transept formed the chancel of the new church (Heighway and Bryant 1999: 22). Ten post-Reformation burials have been excavated close to the new altar within the restructured church (figure 4.1) (Heighway and Bryant 1999: 219). A similar situation arose after the dissolution of Bolton Priory in West Yorkshire in 1540, where the nave of the priory church became the parish church while the rest of the monastic buildings were allowed to decay (figure 4.2) (Timbs and Gunn 2006). In Chester, the abbey church became the cathedral. Some shallow graves excavated within what was then an unpaved nave appear to date from the period of the Reformation (Ward 2003: 268, 275; 1998: 43). Even in Scotland, where the triumphant Calvinists demanded the suppression of all non-parochial religious buildings, some monastic houses, such as Melrose and Dunfermline abbeys, and the cathedrals of Aberdeen and Brechin survived by becoming parish churches (Spicer 2003: 31).

Religious buildings abandoned and destroyed during the Reformation retained their significance for some becoming the foci of covert devotion (Walsham 2011: 166). There is evidence that burial in limited numbers continued in some monastic graveyards after the destruction of the religious house and their churches. At Perth, fourteen burials were cut into the demolition layer of the Carmelite Friary (Hall 1989: 106), while at least six burials in the chancel at Holy Trinity Abbey, Lough Hey in County Roscommon postdate the canons' abandonment of the monastery in 1607–8 (Clyne 2005: 61). Ten uncoffined and intercutting post-dissolution burials were uncovered in the nave of the abbey church at Balmerino in Fife (Kenworthy 1980: 6). Burial also continued at the Carmelite Friary in Aberdeen after the dissolution although it is unclear for how long (Stone 1989: 42). At Linlithgow Friary a child of four to eight years

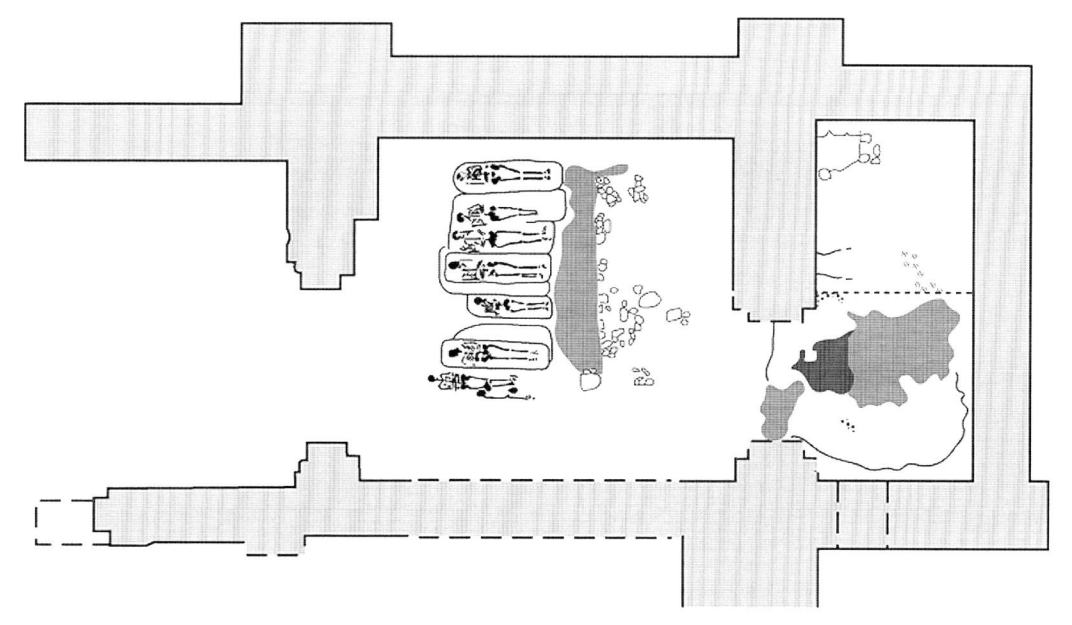

Figure 4.1 Plan of 16th-17th century burials interred in front of altar at St. Oswald's Priory Gloucester (Illustration drawn by Debbie Miles-Williams adapted from Heighway and Bryant 1999).

Figure 4.2 Bolton Priory showing continued use of nave as a parish church and the ruinous nature of the rest of the monastic church (Photograph by Annia Cherryson).

buried to the west of the church is thought to post-date the dissolution (Lindsay 1989: microfiche 1.D4). A number of post-medieval burials, some cut through the demolition rubble, were excavated at Carmarthen Greyfriars (Manning 1998b: 29). The burials at these sites may represent the continued use of monastic graveyards by former members and ancillary staff of the religious house, and perhaps the families of those already interred within the graveyard. Burial also appears to have persisted at Warrington Friary in Cheshire after the destruction of the church although here the friary church remained in use as a place of worship for some time after its dissolution and continued to receive burials in the area of the nave and north transept (Heawood 2002: 134, 151–3). It was only in the latter part of the seventeenth century that the church fell into disrepair and presumably disuse. By the beginning of the eighteenth century little remained standing. Yet at least ten graves dating to the late seventeenth and eighteenth centuries have been excavated, primarily from the area of the nave (Heawood 2002: 154–5, 182). There is documentary evidence for the interment of excommunicated Catholic recusants around Eynsham Abbey, Oxfordshire (Hardy, Dodd and Keevill 2003: 519). Three burials found cut through the demolition rubble over the west end of the refectory at Eynsham and thought to date to between the dissolution and the early seventeenth century may be recusants denied interment elsewhere (figure 4.3) (Hardy, Dodd and Keevill 2003: 152–3; 519). When Nicholas Tychbourne, imprisoned for recusancy, died in Winchester prison in 1589, he was denied interment in any church or cemetery within the city (Silverira 1836). He was eventually laid to rest on a hill a mile from the city by the ruins of a chapel dedicated to St James. This site, which became the Catholic cemetery of St James, continued to be used for interments throughout the seventeenth, eighteenth and nineteenth centuries (figure 4.4). The Catholic dead were brought there for interment from all over Hampshire (Bogan 1999: 26).

The Reformation appears to have had less of an impact on the geography of burial in Ireland where the pattern of monastic burial survived to a much greater extent (Tait 2002: 77). Many monastic graveyards continued in long-term use after the ecclesiastical buildings had been reduced to ruins. At Clonmacnoise in Co. Offaly, excavations identified both post-medieval and "modern" burials despite the monastic

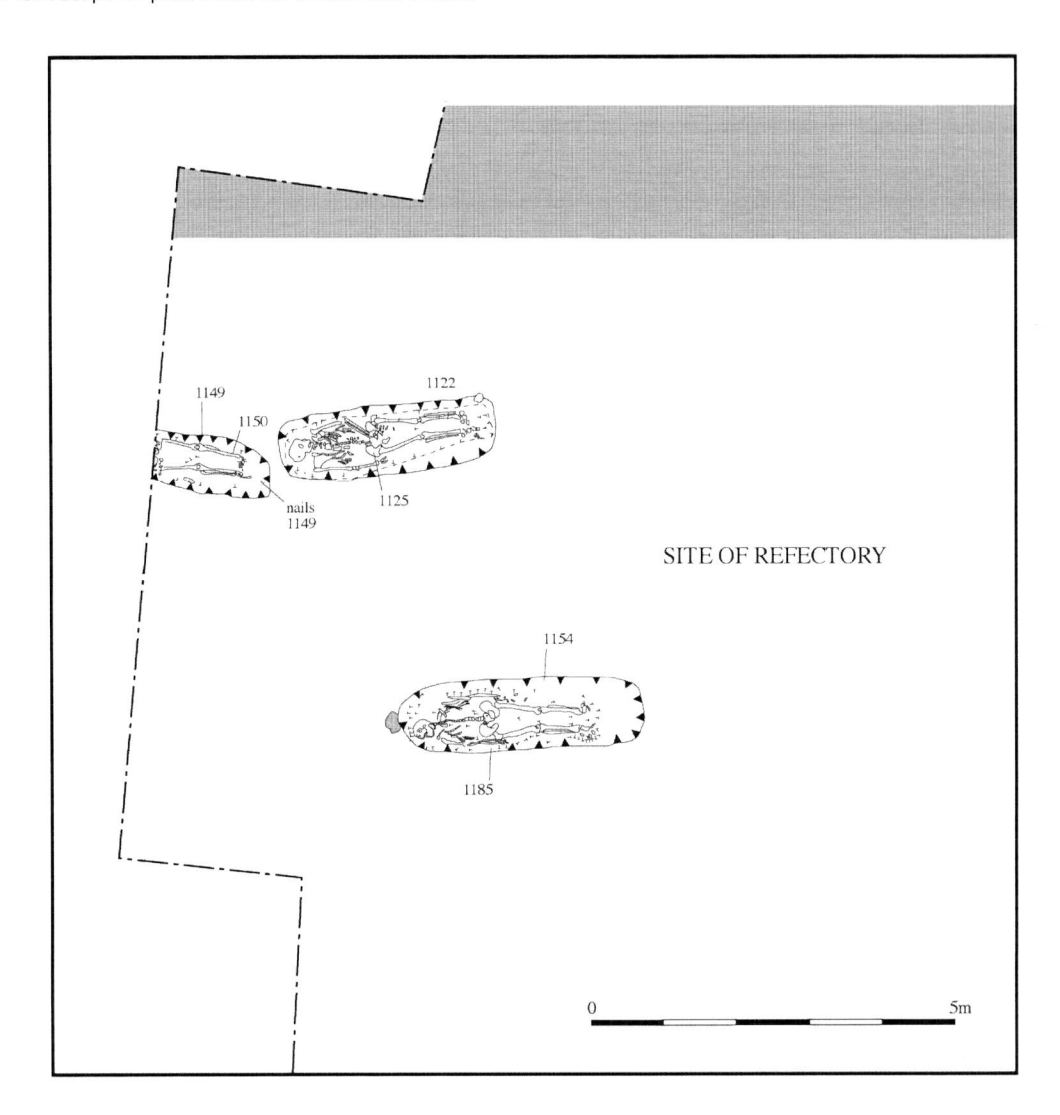

4 The burial landscape of post-medieval Britain and Ireland

Figure 4.3 Putative recusant burials, dug through the demolition layers of Eynsham Abbey in the early post-Reformation period (Plan drawn by Debbie Miles-Williams from Hardy, Dodd and Keevill 2003).

Figure 4.4 The post-Reformation Catholic cemetery of St James Winchester. Nicholas Tychbourne, who died a recusant Catholic in 1589, was buried by a ruined chapel outside the city. Over the next three centuries St James cemetery became the main Catholic burial place for Hampshire (Photograph by Annia Cherryson).

buildings being destroyed in 1552 (King 1993; 1994; 1995). Even if the ownership passed to others, the new owners rarely prevented the continued use of the monastic precincts for burial (Tait 2002: 77). When the lands of the Franciscan Friary of Creevelea in County Leitrim passed to a new English owner, the Friary was converted into a house and the church re-thatched. Catholic burial continued in the graveyard in exchange for a fee to the new owner (Tait 2002: 78). This latter phenomenon may explain the presence of burials found on the site of the Cistercian abbey in Newry, County Down, even though there is no associated church and the ruins of the abbey were used to build a private house. Nicholas Bagenal, marshal of the army in Ireland, was granted the recently dissolved abbey in the late 1540s and converted the ruins of the precinct into a tower house, Bagenal's Castle (Dawkes and Buckley 2006: 31). A cemetery, dating to between 1550 and 1650, has been excavated to the north of the tower house, lying over the stone foundations of the monastic buildings.

The sites of former religious houses could also provide a burial location with religious significance for those excluded from community burial grounds. There was a large proportion of children among the later burials at the Carmelite Friary in Aberdeen (Stone 1989: 43), while the graves of four infants were found cut through the demolition layer at the Augustinian Priory of Lanercost, Cumberland (Whitworth 1998: 135) Unbaptised children were often excluded from churchyards, and it is possible that the bereaved sought to inter their bodies in locations which had religious significance, such as former monastic graveyards. This may explain the clusters of post-dissolution infant and child burials seen at some of these sites.[2]

The Reformation also changed the spatial organisation of British and Irish church buildings. The long tradition of intercession by the living on behalf of the souls of the dead through prayer, masses and donations was rejected. The Chantries Act of 1547 abolished prayers for the dead and dissolved the chantries (1 Edw. VI, c.14; Roffey 2003: 341). The passage of the act led to the removal of fittings and furniture associated with the now outlawed practices, such as chantry chapels, rood screens and representations of saints (Graves 1997; Finch 2003: 444; Aston 2003: 9). Many chantries were completely destroyed while others were put to other, often more secular, uses such as vestries (Roffey 2007: 130). In many urban parish churches, chantries could have occupied up to half of the internal space (Roffey 2003: 344) and their absence significantly changed the internal geography of many churches. In some cases, chantries survived in a modified form becoming burial chapels or family mausolea (Roffey 2003: 349; 2007: 133). In Canterbury, Kent, the chantry built by the Roper family in 1402 continued in use after the Reformation as a burial chapel for the family (Tatton-Brown 1980: 227). In Scotland the survival of chantries as burial places provided a means of circumventing the kirk's prohibition on burial within churches (Spicer 2000: 150,156). For example, the chantry chapel built by the Lindsay family at Edzell Old Church in Angus was converted into a burial aisle (Bowler, Perry and Middleton 2000: 140). The exclusion of burials from the kirk interior met with opposition as it threatened the long-standing tradition of burial close to ancestors, and also in some cases impinged on the legal rights of lairds (Bowler, Perry and Middleton 2000: 151). Chantries were not the only means of ensuring continued burial within the church. Collegiate chapels established to pray for the souls of founders often became family burial places (Bowler, Perry and Middleton 2000: 156). The chapel established at Carnwath in Lanarkshire by the first Lord Somerville became the family's place of burial after the Reformation. Other churches constructed burial aisles in the form of annexes or projections (Bowler, Perry and Middleton 2000: 153). The burial aisle at St Mary's Parish Church in Haddington, East Lothian was created from an earlier vestry (Caldwell 1976: 25). Changes in liturgical practice meant that parts of the church such as the chancel were not used for worship, and these areas were in some cases used for burial (Bowler, Perry and Middleton 2000). In some cases, the chancels were blocked off from the rest of the building to create burial chapels. At Glasgow Cathedral burial continued within the former nave after an outer kirk was created by partition in 1647 (Driscoll 2002).

The impact of the Chantries Act on the geography of burial was not confined to intramural interment. During the medieval period, the Church played a central role as a mediator between the living and the dead as the prayers of the living congregation were believed to affect the fate of the soul of the deceased (Le Goff 1984: 11; Geary 1994: 90). In its rejection of Purgatory, the 1547 Chantries Act changed the relationship between the living and the dead (1 Edw. VI, c.14). No longer could the prayers and actions living affect the final destination of the soul after death (Daniell 1997: 198). Nor was there any longer a spiritual advantage in being interred close to altars or the shrines of saints (Houlbrooke 1998: 33; Harding 2002: 55). Indeed the influence of Swiss Reformed and Calvinist theology on the reformation in Britain and Ireland with its emphasis on the omnipresence of the divine meant many no longer believed that specific places could be sanctified (Walsham 2011: 82) This did not, however, lead to the abandonment of burial in consecrated ground adjacent to churches. Only the most radical of Protestants (such as the Quakers) rejected burial on consecrated ground as superstitious. A combination of demotic practice and familial ties meant that churches and churchyards continued to be perceived as the appropriate place to inter the deceased (Harding 1998: 54; Houlbrooke 1998: 334). Yet it could be argued that this change in the relationship between the living and the dead was the first step in a process of distanciation between the living and the dead that resulted in the major changes in the geography of burial seen during the post-medieval period.

The burial of Catholics after the Reformation

The imposition of the Protestant faith in the British mainland was not welcomed by all, and many continued to follow the old faith. In Ireland the situation was very different as the majority of the population remained Catholic although ownership of ecclesiastical buildings passed into Protestant hands (Tait 2002: 78). In mainland Britain, recusancy did not always result in excommunication. Many Catholics were still interred in consecrated ground, which they perceived to belong to God and not just to the established church (Cressy 2000: 119; Cressy 1997: 465). That anti-Catholic legislation of 1606 imposed a fine of £20 on any recusant who had not been excommunicated and was not interred within a churchyard might also have influenced the choice of burial location. Despite differences in religion, the majority of Catholics continued to be interred in family chapels and churchyards throughout the seventeenth and eighteenth centuries, and some Catholic communities had their own customary burial area in parish churchyards (Houlbrooke 1989: 336; Aveling 1976: 70).Yet this does not alter the fact that those choosing to be interred within a church or churchyard had to use the Church of England burial service administered by an Anglican priest (Aveling 1976: 70; Blackmore 1775: 392). In some instances, earth blessed by a priest was interred with the deceased as a means of 'offsetting' the Reformed service and minister (Houlbrooke 1989: 336). The more observant buried their dead illicitly, smuggling coffin and priest into churches and churchyards at night (Aveling 1976: 144). Some made little effort to disguise their religious affiliations and the stone coffin of the alleged recusant George Willoughby, who was interred in the family vault at St Catherine's Church at Cossall in Nottinghamshire in 1691, bears the distinctly Catholic inscription "on whose soul God be merciful" (Elliot 2000a: 93). There was often a close physical connection between the Catholic gentry and their local parish church, which in many instances lay closer to the manor house than the rest of the village and many known recusant gentry were interred within the local church close to their pre-Reformation ancestors (Aveling 1976: 144). Those of the gentry dwelling some distance from the local church often constructed manorial chapels close to their homes and in the aftermath of the Reformation some became private chapels and family mausoleums. One particularly unusual example is the Fitzalan Chapel at Arundel Castle. The eastern half of the chapel was sold by Henry VIII to the family of the founder, the Earl of Arundel and a brick wall was constructed to separate the two halves (Martin 2006: 29). The western half remained in use as a parish church while the eastern part became a private chapel and family mausoleum for the Catholic family (Martin 2006: 30).

Excommunication for adherence to the old faith was generally confined to the sixteenth and seventeenth centuries and even then usually restricted to those exhibiting contempt for the new Protestant faith or thought to be leaders of recusant groups. For excommunicated papists, burial location was often dependent on the attitudes of the local clergy but usually an accommodation was reached (Cressy 1997: 465). For example thirteen excommunicated Roman Catholics were interred in the churchyard at Hathersage in Derbyshire between 1629 and 1631, although the burials were all nocturnal (Gittings 1984: 77). Elsewhere, burial was only permitted if there was a faculty from the Bishop. When the body of Richard Lumbye, an excommunicated papist, was brought for burial at his local church in Leeds in 1604, it was stopped at the gate of the churchyard where it remained for seven days until a faculty allowing burial was obtained.

Others were less tolerant. In 1611, Catholics in Lancashire were denied burial in all churches, leading to their interment in fields, gardens and highways (Cressy 2000: 119). Some of those denied churchyard burial sought interment in locations with some religious significance, often using the sites of earlier ecclesiastical buildings, such as the monastic burial grounds described above, to provide them with the sanctity denied them by the established church.

The origins and growth of non-parochial burial grounds and cemeteries

The loss of the monastic churchyards had altered the specific geography of burial but the underlying rules remained the same. The only socially acceptable burial location for the majority of people was on consecrated ground either adjacent to or within a church, and the Church's control over who was accorded this rite was absolute. Over the next four centuries, however, increasing numbers of individuals were interred in burial grounds or cemeteries independent of the Church of England. The development of these alternatives to churchyard burial was a gradual process and the result of a combination of religious, demographic and social factors.

Pestilence and population growth: London's new cemeteries

The dissolution of the monasteries may have been a contributory factor in the establishment of the first non-parochial burial grounds in London. The loss of the monastic cemeteries was accommodated in most towns and in rural areas, in part due to the parishes obtaining land formerly owned by the dissolved monastic communities (Harding 2002: 50). This was not the case in the capital. London was easily the largest city in Britain and a major centre of immigration (Harding 2002: 14; Hunting 1991: 31). The century following the Reformation was one of exceptional demographic growth for the metropolis and this was accompanied by high mortality rates (Harding 2002: 14–16; 1998: 55). Moreover, due to poor sanitation and housing, the already high urban mortality rates rose even higher in epidemic years. Diseases, such as influenza, typhus and, particularly during the early modern period, plague resulted in large numbers of deaths concentrated over a comparatively short period of time (Harding 1993: 54; 2002: 21). The capacity of London's parochial churchyards, already stretched after the loss of the monastic cemeteries, particularly the large burial ground associated with St Mary Spital, could not cope (Harding 2002: 93; Hunting 1991: 33).

Six years after the plague outbreak of 1563 and fearing another outbreak would overwhelm the city's churchyards, the so-called "New Churchyard" was established in 1569 by mayoral proclamation (Hunting 1991: 33; Harding 2002: 93). The cemetery was established on land already owned by the city on the north-east fringe of the metropolis. The first of the early modern non-parochial burial grounds, the foundation of the New Churchyard marked the start of secular control over burial and began the erosion of the Church's monopoly (figure 4.5). The land, part of Old Moorfield, lying close to Bethlehem Hospital was prone to flooding so before it could be used for burial, the ground level was raised by dumping of earth from elsewhere in the city (Hunting 1991: 33; Harding 2002: 93). When the site was excavated in the 1980s, some of the earliest burials were sealed by earth of similar composition to that used to raise the ground level, suggesting that burial had began while the site was being prepared in 1569 (Hunting 1991: 33). The small number of early burials also implies that initially interment in the New Churchyard was not particularly popular. This was probably in part the result of a reticence to abandon traditional burial grounds and also a reflection of the initial logistical difficulties in arranging the transportation of corpses to the site from other parts of the city (Hunting 1991: 33). Hunting (1991: 33) suggests that many of the earliest burials in the cemetery may have been those of immigrants lacking parochial ties.

After the initial interments, there was a marked change in the nature of burial on the site. The earlier single inhumations were replaced by several large pits, each containing between four and sixteen individuals (Hunting 1991: 33). The cemetery had been designed

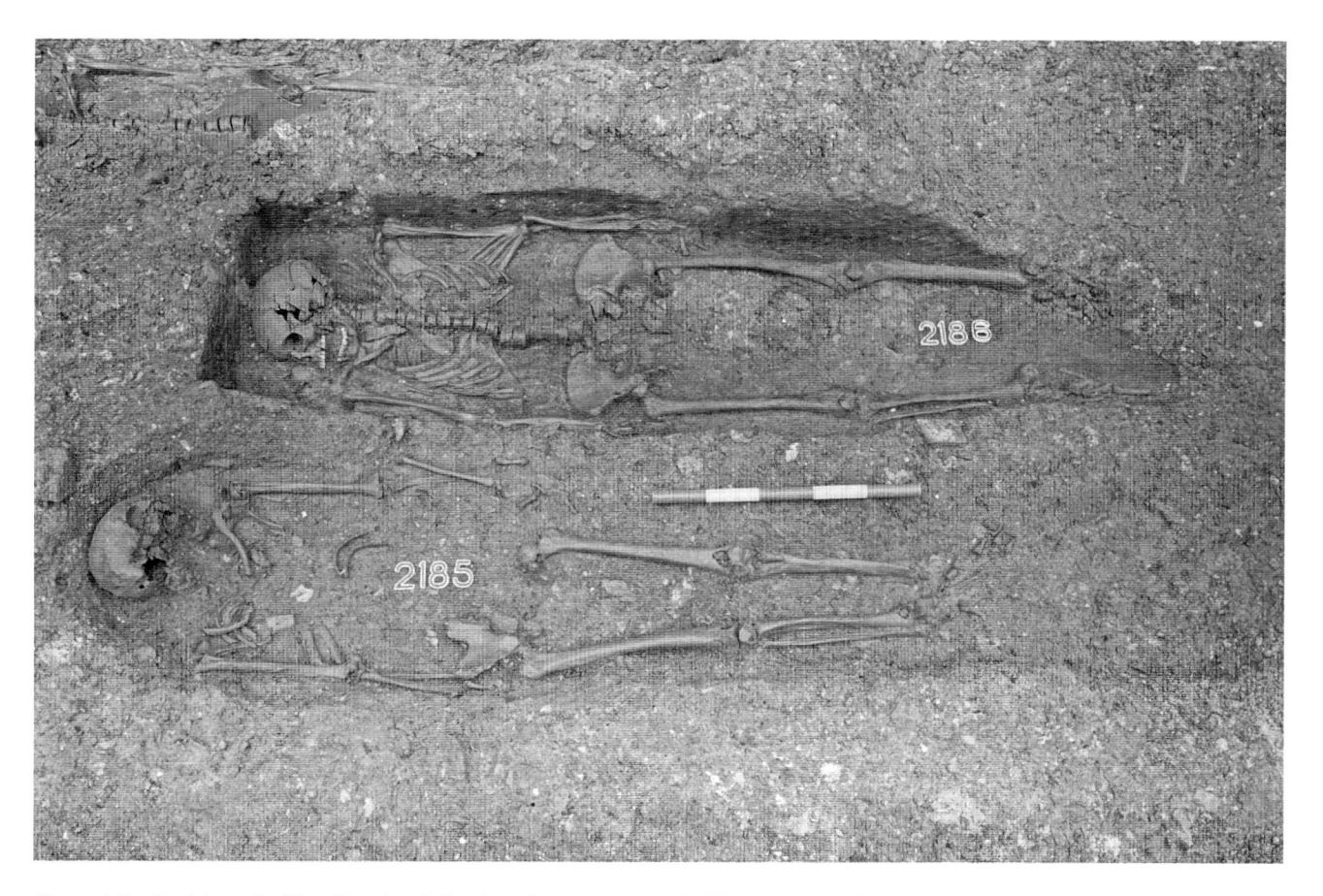

Figure 4.5 Burials at the New Churchyard, London, the first non-parochial burial ground of the early modern period, founded in 1569 (Photograph courtesy of London Archaeological Archive and Resource Centre)

to take the overflow from London's parish churchyards during epidemics, and these burial pits are thought to contain victims of the plague outbreaks of either 1593 or 1603. The possibility that these mass graves contain pauper burials cannot be completely excluded. However, over half of those interred in the burial pits were less than seventeen years old. This abnormal mortality curve is suggestive of plague as younger individuals would have lacked the immunity conferred by early visitations of the disease.

After the burial pits, interment along more conventional lines resumed: single inhumations arranged in rows or groups within the site (Hunting 1991: 33). The cemetery attracted an interesting cross-section of London society. On the one hand, the marginal location of the cemetery combined with its proximity to the hospital for the insane at Bethelehem, and the comparatively low cost of interment, meant that many on society's periphery were interred there. Those parishes with little space in their churchyards preferentially interred their poorer residents, especially servants, strangers, and foundlings, in the New Churchyard (Harding 2002: 96–7). The bodies of prisoners from Newgate and suicides were also buried in the New Churchyard (Harding 2002: 96). In contrast, the recovery of some highly decorated coffins from the site indicates that not all of those interred in the New Churchyard came from poorer parts of society (Hunting 1991: 35). Documentary sources indicate that individuals from more expensive parts of town and members of middle-income families were also buried in the New Churchyard (Harding 2002: 98).

In 1665, plague stretched the resources of the parochial churchyards again, and the over-use of the New Churchyard resulted in the mayor and aldermen obtaining and consecrating land at Bunhill Fields to the north of the city as London's second non-parochial burial ground to ease the burden on the city's parish churchyards (figure 4.6) (Harding 1993: 61; Hunting 1991: 36).

The second half of the seventeenth century also saw the appearance in London of another group of cemeteries lying outside the parochial system – the burial grounds of the city's growing Jewish population (e.g. Halliday and Susser 2002). The medieval Jewish population of England had been expelled in 1290 by Edward I. In the centuries that followed there is little evidence for a Jewish presence in the country. This changed following the expulsion of Jewish communities from Spain and Portugal in the late fifteenth century. Some of those exiled sought refuge in Britain and a small and secretive Jewish community was present by the first half of the seventeenth century (Katz 1994: 108). When Oliver Cromwell convened the Whitehall Conference in 1655 to consider the formal re-admission of Jews, it

Figure 4.6 Bunhill cemetery, London. London's second non-parochial burial ground, opened in response to the burial crisis of the 1665 plague (Photograph by Annia Cherryson).

turned an unwelcome spotlight on the existing Jewish community while doing little to resolve their status (Katz 1994: 108, 134). Resolution of the matter came indirectly as a result of the outbreak of war with Spain in 1656. This led to the confiscation of all Spanish property including that of Jews of Spanish birth living in the capital. One of them went to the courts claiming as a Jew he should not be seen as Spanish and thus not an enemy alien. The court agreed and in doing so indirectly authorised the re-admission of the Jews (Katz 1994: 135, 137). The new arrivals were mainly from Holland, Portugal, Spain, Germany and France, and a Jewish community was firmly established by the time of Cromwell's death in 1658 (Marks 2009: 182; Katz 1994: 104).

The growing community needed places to worship and inter their dead and the first Jewish cemetery was founded by the Sephardic community in 1657 when land was rented at Mile End, then a village about a mile outside London (Diamond 1955: 168). Ashkenazi Jews arriving in London after 1656 initially used the Sephardic cemetery but in 1696 they bought land contiguous to the existing cemetery for their own burial ground (Sussex 1997: 14). As the Jewish communities grew during the eighteenth century and the existing cemeteries filled up, additional cemeteries were established by both communities. In 1733 a new Sephardic cemetery was established and in 1761 a new cemetery was opened for the Ashkenazi in Brady Street (Marks 2009: 184–5). Not all of London's Jewish population were interred in Jewish burial grounds. The Christianised Jews, the Marranos, were usually interred in Christian burial grounds. Initially Jewish settlement was confined to London but the population gradually spread (Susser n.d.: 1). By 1725 small communities were present in a number of provincial towns (Susser n.d.: 1). Where no cemetery was present, the practice was usually to inter the dead in land belonging to members of the Jewish community. This practice was probably followed by London's Jewish community prior to the foundation of their own burial grounds. A similar practice occurred in Plymouth where land on Plymouth Hoe belonging to Sarah Sherranbeck was used to inter members of that city's Jewish community. Eventually ownership of the land was passed to the Jewish community and it became the city's first Jewish burial ground (Susser 1993).

Dissenter burial grounds

After centuries of Catholic monopoly in Western Europe, the sixteenth and seventeenth century saw the fragmentation of the Christian faith. It wasn't simply a case of Catholic and Protestant, but the development of non-conformist (dissenting) groups who disagreed with the established church on the interpretation of the Bible and the practice of Reformed Christianity. The turbulence of the Civil War and the tolerant climate of the interregnum allowed dissent to flourish and minority denominations, such as Baptists, Quakers and Independents, to enjoy a greater freedom of worship (Gittings 2007: 324). Indeed the 1644 Directory for the Publique Worship of God removed any religious connotations from the act of burial (Gittings 1984: 48). During the 1640s and 1650s, individuals enjoyed unprecedented freedom to inter the deceased where they wished and using whatever rites they felt appropriate (Cressy 1997: 417). This climate of religious tolerance was to be short-lived. The restored state church was hostile to dissent in the aftermath of Restoration. The primacy of the Anglican Church was enforced by a series of parliamentary measures known as the Clarendon Code. One of these measures, the 1662 Act for the Uniformity of Publick Prayers; and Administration of the Sacraments, and other Rites and Ceremonies: And for Establishing the Form of Making, Ordaining, and Consecrating Bishops, Priests and Deacons of the Church of England (13 and 14 Cha. II c.4), imposed a single form of worship based on the ceremonies and rituals set out in the Book of Common Prayer, outlawed other religious denominations and established criteria to be adhered to by the Anglican clergy (Spurr 1996: 236). Failure to inter the deceased in a churchyard or church using the prescribed Anglican rites could result in an appearance before the ecclesiastical authorities or excommunication (Cressy 1997: 418).

Given the intolerant climate, it is not surprising that many groups continued to use parish churchyards and were interred by the parish priest using Church of England burial services, despite otherwise distancing themselves from the observances of the Church of England (Cressy 1997: 418). In other instances an accommodation was reached with the local clergy allowing interment without the usual Anglican rites (Cressy 1997: 419). Yet this was not without its problems: the delayed baptism of Baptists or failure to acknowledge the Trinity during baptism by the Unitarians led to some members of these congregations being excluded from churchyards, or exiled to the burial ground on the north side of the church to be interred with the unbaptised and suicide victims, on the grounds of not being properly baptised (Jupp 1997: 93; Rugg 1998: 46). In some instances Quakers were refused burial by incumbent ministers who alleged that they were not Christian (Mullet 1991: 104). This exclusion of non-conformists could lead to illicit burials as friends and family sought to inter the deceased close to kith and kin in community burial grounds often raising the ire of the local clergy. For example, at Over in Cambridgeshire, Silvester Burrowes was buried in the churchyard in 1678 by his brethren without a minister. John Woolman, another dissenter, was surreptitiously interred in the same churchyard seven years later (Stevenson 1995: 364).

For others, burial in consecrated ground within or adjacent to the parish church was to be avoided as a matter of principle, some rejecting church land altogether in favour of burial on private ground (Cressy 1997: 418). In London, the New Churchyard's non-parochial status made it popular with non-conformists from its earliest days. A number of stauncher Puritans were interred there during the Elizabethan period (Harding 2002: 96; Houlbrooke 1998: 334). The seventeenth century saw the continued use of the site for non-conformist burials, including that of the Leveller activist Robert Lockyer in 1649 (Gentles 1996: 219). Yet until its closure in the early eighteenth century the New Churchyard remained, in the eyes of many, a burial place for those on society's margins even despite the presence of more affluent burials within its bounds.[3] The same could not be said about London's other non-parochial cemetery, Bunhill Fields. Although like the New Churchyard, it was established in 1665 to provide extra burial capacity when epidemic disease visited the metropolis (Hunting 1991: 36; Harding 1998: 61), Bunhill Fields appears never to have been used for plague victims. Instead it was leased by John Tyndall who converted it into a dissenter's burial ground that came to be the final resting place for many non-conformists including John Bunyan in 1688 and Thomas Rosewell in 1692 (figure 4.7) (Mullet 1996: 114). Bunhill Fields became a popular burial place for non-conformists until its closure in 1853, including those of the Baptist,

Figure 4.7 Non-conformist gravestone Bunhill cemetery, London. Non-parochial burial grounds offered greater freedom of burial for Catholics, non-conformists and other non-Anglicans. Thomas Rosewell, whose monument this is, was sentenced to death for treason in 1684 after criticising Charles II's 'popery', but later pardoned. Rosewell died in 1692; this stone is a nineteenth-century memorial (Photograph by Annia Cherryson).

Independent, and Presbyterian ministries, and was later associated with the Calvinist Methodist Islington Chapel (Hunting 1991: 36; Harding 1998: 61; Arnold 2006: 71; Houlbrooke 1998: 334).

Outside London, there was little choice of burial place for dissenters other than the parish churchyard. For some this was unendurable, particularly in the case of the Quakers, who viewed the consecration of ground for burial as superstitious idolatry (Stock 1998a: 129). In their view, all ground was God's ground and thus suitable for burial. Quakers therefore sought to inter their dead outside the usual burial place favouring instead gardens, fields and orchards (Bashford and Pollard 1998: 155; Cressy 1997: 418). At Over in Cambridgeshire, twelve Quakers were buried between 1667 and 1677 in the orchard belonging to another of their denomination, George Nash (Stevenson 1995: 364). The Quakers' beliefs also meant that they insisted from the outset upon having their own burial grounds when possible (Morris 1989: 396), and where there were sufficient numbers, the Friends would purchase or lease land for burial. Sixty-seven members of the Quaker community from Alton in Hampshire and the surrounding area donated amounts of between £40 and 6d for the purchase of a burial ground and the building of a meeting house in the town in 1672 (HRO 24M54/60). The Alton community were not unique: for example, ground within an orchard was leased and then purchased for use as a burial ground at Kingston-upon-Thames in 1663 using money raised by 37 subscribers (Bashford and Sibun 2007: 102). A more unusual location was used by the Quaker community of Felsted in Essex, who interred their dead in and around a mound of probable prehistoric origin. Excavation of the barrow in the 1940s uncovered nine inhumations of probable late seventeenth- or early eighteenth-century date some with fragments of wood and coffin handles suggesting the presence of coffins (Essex SMR record 1256). While the Quakers' rejection of consecrated ground meant that many of the earliest dissenter cemeteries tended to be owned by the Friends, early examples belonging to other dissenting groups are known such as the burial ground of the Baptist community of Amersham in Buckinghamshire established in 1676 (Morris 1989: 396). The importance of the rejection of established burial places and mortuary rituals by some dissenters cannot be over-emphasised. Not only were they making a conscious decision to reject tradition and the pull of ancestral burial places, but also embracing the normally stigmatised practice of burial outside the parochial churchyard.[4]

The late seventeenth century saw the increased toleration of Protestant dissent, notably with the passing of the 1689 Act that allowed non-conformists to worship in their own meeting-houses, provided these places were licensed. While this legislation did lead to an increase in the number of non-conformist burial grounds in London and elsewhere (Harding 2002: 100), most Presbyterians, Baptists and Congregationalists continued to be buried in churchyards long after 1700. As late as the 1740s, it was estimated that 0.19% of Protestant burials were in non-conformist burial grounds (Houlbrooke 1989: 336). The majority of non-conformists interred in churchyards were buried by the parish priest using Church of England burial services, but in some instances an accommodation was reached with the local clergy allowing interment without the usual Anglican rites (Cressy 1997: 418–9). For example, at Haddenham in Cambridgeshire, Quakers John Dobson and Nathaniel Purver were interred in the churchyard by the Society of Friends in January 1715/6 and June 1716 for a mortuary fee of 10s (Stevenson 1995: 364). The continued use of traditional burial locations by many non-conformists is likely to be the result of the interplay of a number of factors. Many dissenting groups had no doctrinal differences with the Church of England around the liturgy of death. Thus interment in parochial churchyards with Anglican rites was perfectly acceptable, although the attitude of the incumbent minister could affect the ease with which this was accomplished. Another consideration is tradition, and the appeal of interment with kin in often ancient burial grounds. Moreover, not all non-conformists severed all ties with the established church: many continued to attend their parish church as well as dissenting meetings, although this attendance might be sporadic and they might only stay for part of the service (Spurr 1996: 242).

Given the Quakers' rejection of interment on consecrated ground, it is perhaps not surprising that most of the excavated examples of early dissenter cemeteries belong to Quaker communities, including burial grounds at Kingston-upon-Thames (Bashford and Sibun 2007), O'Meara Street in London (Brickley and Miles 1999b), Calne in Wiltshire (Mumford 2006) and Hemingford Grey in Cambridgeshire (figure 4.8) (Clough 2007). The creation of new burial grounds was also dependent on the size of the dissenting community in any one area and its ability to raise sufficient funds to either lease or purchase land (Jupp 1997: 91). In 1668, there were only two Quakers in Bromyard, Herefordshire, and they attended meetings in a nearby village (Lewis and Pikes 2004: 21). In terms of burial options, it was either the local churchyard, their gardens or a Quaker burial ground in a neighbouring settlement. Indeed, some early Quaker cemeteries, such as that at Hemingford Grey in Cambridgeshire, would have served a number of surrounding communities (Clough 2007). As the Quaker community in Bromyard grew it was able to establish its own meeting house with associated burial ground in 1677 (Lewis and Pikes 2004: 22). A second Quaker meeting house was established in 1726, which acquired its own burial ground in 1744. Non-conformist numbers, and thus numbers of burial grounds, could also vary as a result of local factors. For example the 83 articulated skeletons from the Baptist Chapel and burial ground at West Butts in Poole were the remains of members of two different Baptist communities (McKinley 2008: 58). The burial ground was initially used by the members of the West Butts Street Baptist chapel which was founded in 1735. The congregation dwindled in the 1780s following the death of their pastor John Bird and the chapel was demolished. The burial ground was later used by congregation of the Hill Street Baptist Chapel which was founded in 1804. It is worth noting that for all the rejection by dissenting communities of the burial practices of the established church some aspects of traditional practices persisted. Many dissenter cemeteries were located adjacent to meeting houses, echoing the close geographical tie between the place of worship for the living and resting place of the dead seen in the established church.

Overall numbers of non-conformist burial grounds increased during the eighteenth and early nineteenth century. In Leeds, for example, only two dissenting chapels had their own burial grounds in 1730 compared with six in the 1810s (Morgan 1989: 95–6). The number and distribution of burial grounds was dependent on the fortunes of the varying dissenting communities. At a national level, the rise of new dissenter groups, especially Methodists, was to have a significant effect on the fortunes of the various dissenting congregations. The period saw the emergence of Wesleyan Methodism under the leadership of John Wesley and Calvinistic Methodism under George Whitfield. The Calvinistic Methodists often continued to inter their dead in Anglican cemeteries while the Wesleyan Methodists, like the Quakers, objected to the use of consecrated ground. Wesley himself described it as unauthorised by any law of God, leading to the foundation of chapels and burial grounds such as the nineteenth-century Methodist Chapel in Carver Street in Sheffield (McIntyre and Willmott 2003). The evangelical revival also affected the older dissenting communities, reinvigorating the Baptist and Congregational ministries and contributing to the decline of the Quakers and older Presbyterians.

While non-conformist burials grounds changed the burial landscape of post-medieval England, the vast majority of the population continued to be interred in Anglican churchyards. For example in Leeds, 96% of the town's dead were interred in Anglican churchyards in the 1730s and 93% between 1811 and 1820 (Morgan 1989: 95–6). Yet the non-conformist burial grounds provided an alternative burial location independent of the Church of England and demonstrated that it was possible to have an 'acceptable' burial outside of a churchyard.

The origins and development of cemeteries

Space has always been at a premium within churchyards. The practice of continually interring the dead within the same small area over a long period of time, often many centuries, means regardless of the size of the churchyard, its capacity will be exceeded (Cherryson 2007). The result is the high levels of inter-cutting and post-burial disturbance that characterise so many medieval and post-medieval churchyards (Gilchrist and Sloane 2005: 50, 194–5; Brickley and Buteux 2006:25).[5] During the post medieval period, ease of disposal seems generally to have determined the fate of human remains disturbed

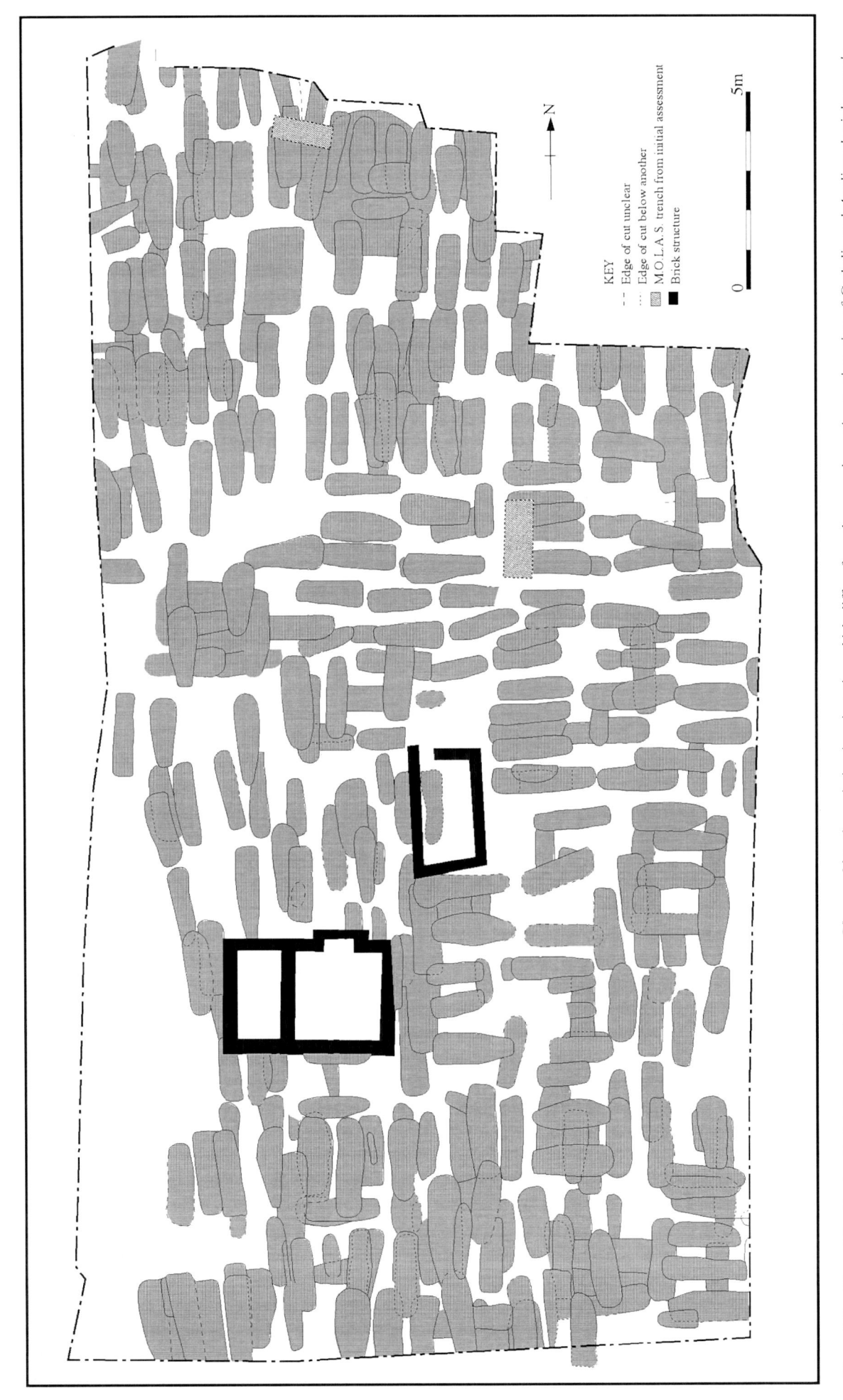

4 The burial landscape of post-medieval Britain and Ireland

Figure 4.8 Plan of the Quaker Burial Ground at Kingston-upon-Thames. Note the variation in orientation which differs from the normal west/east orientation of Catholic and Anglican burial grounds during this period (Plan drawn by Debbie Miles-Williams from Bashford and Sibun 2007).

by later graves. Often the bones were simply deposited back into the fresh grave along with the backfill with varying degrees of care. Disturbed remains were found in the base of several graves at St. Marylebone in London (Miles, Powers and Wroe-Brown 2008: 35). In this instance the bones appear to have been used to reinforce the base of the grave cut. The re-interring of disturbed bones in small charnel pits cut into the base of the intrusive grave was observed in seven graves in the Quaker burial ground at Kingston-upon-Thames in London (Bashford and Sibun 2007: 114). Similar behaviour was observed in four graves from the eighteenth-century Baptist cemetery at West Butts in Poole (figure 4.9) (McKinley 2008: 18, 29–30). Other modes of disposal involved the excavation of large pits specifically for the disturbed human remains. In 1616, workmen at St. Margaret's Church in Westminster were paid to dig a pit to inter the bones scattered across the churchyard (Gittings 1984: 139). Large quantities of disarticulated bone were recovered from charnel pits during the excavations at St Martin's-in-the-Bull Ring in Birmingham (Brickley and Buteux 2006: 25). More bone was discovered within archaeological layers as soil in the churchyard was continually churned by new burials. There is limited archaeological evidence for the use of charnel houses (buildings used to store human remains displaced by later activities) during the late medieval period (Gilchrist and Sloane 2005: 194). Charnel houses appear to have been largely the preserve of cathedrals and major churches in larger towns (Gilchrist and Sloane 2005: 42). While there is little evidence for the widespread use of charnel houses during the post-medieval period, documentary sources point to their sporadic use at least during the early modern period. For example, payment for the collection of bones and their deposition in a "bone house" is included the accounts of St Mary's Church in Warwick for 1653–4 (Gittings 1984: 139).

The post-medieval period saw the rapid growth of urban populations, initially in London but then elsewhere as the impact of the industrial revolution was felt (Rugg 1998: 44). Between 1801 and 1841, the population of Bradford increased by 444%, of Huddersfield by 247%, and of Leeds by 186% (Murray 1991: 3). Even in the non-industrial city of York, the population increased by 71% in the same period. When population growth was combined with poor sanitation and housing, the result was high levels of urban mortality, further exacerbated by endemic and epidemic disease (Rugg 1998: 44). This surfeit of bodies overwhelmed existing urban burial provision, leading to levels of overcrowding that would have been unimaginable in earlier centuries, and making traditional methods of churchyard management obsolete.

There were some attempts to expand burial capacity within urban centres, although these were not very systematic to begin with. In many towns and cities, there was a degree of ecclesiastical reorganisation as additional churches with associated burial grounds and vaults were built to minister to the growing population. The new church of St Paul's was built on the edge of Sheffield in the 1720s, although the town gradually expanded to surround it during the following decades (Belford and Witkin 2000: 3). Attempts were also made to expand the capacity of existing churchyards. In York, earth was brought in from outside town and deposited on the churchyards to increase the depth of soil for burial (Murray 1991: 3). Parishes looked to acquire additional land for burial, although within crowded urban centres this was rarely simple. The church of St Benet was destroyed in the Great Fire of London in 1666 and never rebuilt (Miles and White 2008: 4). Yet such was the pressure on burial space in the capital that burial continued

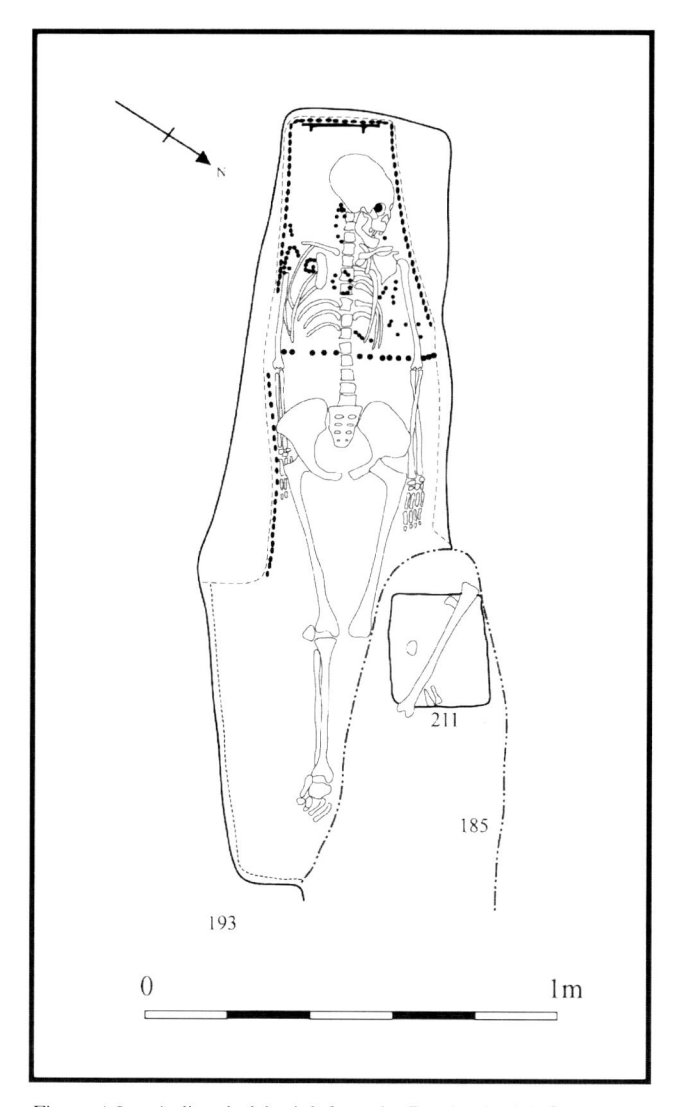

Figure 4.9 A disturbed burial from the Baptist Burial Ground at West Butts Street, Poole. The displaced bone has been placed in a pit cut into the base of the intrusive grave (Plan drawn by Debbie Miles-Williams from McKinley 2008).

on the site, which became a subsidiary burial ground for the new parish of St Stephen Walbrook. Similarly, excavations at Old Church Chelsea centred on a part of the churchyard which appears to have come into use at the end of the seventeenth century (Cowie, Bekvalac and Kausmally 2008: 27). By the eighteenth and nineteenth centuries the problems of a rapidly expanding population were not just confined to London, and parishes in other large cities sought to expand their churchyards. In Wolverhampton, the church of St Peter had acquired the gardens associated with the Deanery Hall for use as an overflow cemetery by 1819 (Adams and Colls 2007: 1,13). In Coventry, the nave and aisles of the ruined cathedral were re-consecrated for use as an overspill cemetery for the adjacent Holy Trinity Church in 1776 (Soden 2000). It was not always possible to obtain land adjacent to the current churchyard. The initial expansion of the churchyard of St Martin's Church, Birmingham in 1781 involved the purchase of land to the south of the churchyard following the clearance of the buildings surrounding the churchyard (Brickley and Buteux 2006: 16). However, when further space was required for burial in 1807 the only land available was a short distance from the church in Park Street (figure 4.10). In an era when proximity to the church remained an important mark of prestige, overflow burial grounds were often less popular than the original churchyards, particularly if detached, despite the reduced burial fees. Not surprisingly, the detached burial ground at Park Street was unpopular and was mostly used by the parish's poor. Extensions to churchyards were financed by the church levying a rate on property owners within the parish (Morgan 1989: 98). During the early nineteenth century, this means of raising revenue was increasingly challenged by non-conformists (Morgan 1989: 98) who objected to being charged for an extension to a churchyard they were unlikely to use.

The eighteenth century also saw the development of an increasing number of privately owned non-parochial burial grounds, predominately in London (Watson 1993: 5). There were fourteen such grounds in London by 1835, including Spa Fields Clerkenwell which started out as tearooms until converted to the more lucrative venture of human burial (Arnold 2006: 97). The Backchurch Lane burial ground in London was in existence by 1776 and was bought by a local undertaker in the 1830s. Private enterprise was not just confined to burial grounds. There were many private burial vaults, popular due to the widespread fear of body-snatching (Richardson 1989: 108). Many of the private burial grounds and vaults were owned by dissenting communities, with the latter often lying below non-conformist chapels. Many dissenter burial grounds were restricted to members of the community while others accepted the bodies of those outside their faith. 11.6% of the 241 registered burials in the Quaker burial ground at Bathford, Somerset did not belong to the Society of Friends (Stock 1998b: 139). The New Bunhill Fields burial ground in Islington Green, London, also known as the Jones burial ground and the Islington Chapel Ground, were owned by the non-conformist minister Reverend Jones and attached to the Islington Chapel (Miles 1997: 17). The fact that approximately 14,300 burials were removed during the commercial clearance of the burial ground provides an illustration of the size of this private venture (Miles 1997: 6). Construction of the Presbyterian Church in Regent Square, London in the 1820s was preceded by excavation of burial vaults which were sold and the revenue used to fund the construction of the church (Jupp 1997: 93). Other private cemeteries appear to have been founded and purchased as simple speculative ventures, in an attempt to capitalise on the chronic overcrowding of London's comparatively small parish churchyards (Holmes 1896: 191; Jupp 1997: 92). These private enterprises survived by undercutting the prices of local churchyards (Holmes 1896: 192; Miles 1997: 18). This made them particularly popular with the poor, offering some a means of avoiding the indignity of a pauper burial (Jupp 1997: 92–3).

Private burial grounds and vaults became a subject of increasing concern during the first half of the nineteenth century, especially in London (Holmes 1896: 191). While some were run with all customary propriety, other owners were less scrupulous. Much was probably dependent on the motivation of their owners. One particularly infamous case, and one that garnered much publicity in the mid-nineteenth century, was Enon Chapel in London (Holmes 1896: 193). The Baptist Chapel opened in 1822 (Jupp 1997: 91) and consisted of an upper storey used for worship and a lower one for burial with only a floor of wooden boards separating the living from the dead. Conditions were far from pleasant (Jupp 1997: 94). Contemporary witnesses spoke of an overpowering smell and infestations of insects (Walker 1839: 155). Some 12,000 individuals were thought to have been interred in a space of only 59 ft by 29 ft by 6ft (Walker 1839: 155; Jupp 1997: 94). Bodies were removed to make space for new interments and the coffins used for firewood (Jupp 1997: 98). The estimated number of burials was questioned at the time and later examination of the events has identified discrepancies (Jupp 1997: 98–99). It is possible that the events and conditions at Enon were exaggerated by those seeking burial reform. Yet, the discovery of large quantities of bone below the flagstones during building work when new occupants moved into the minster's house next door in the 1840s point to the

The origins and development of cemeteries

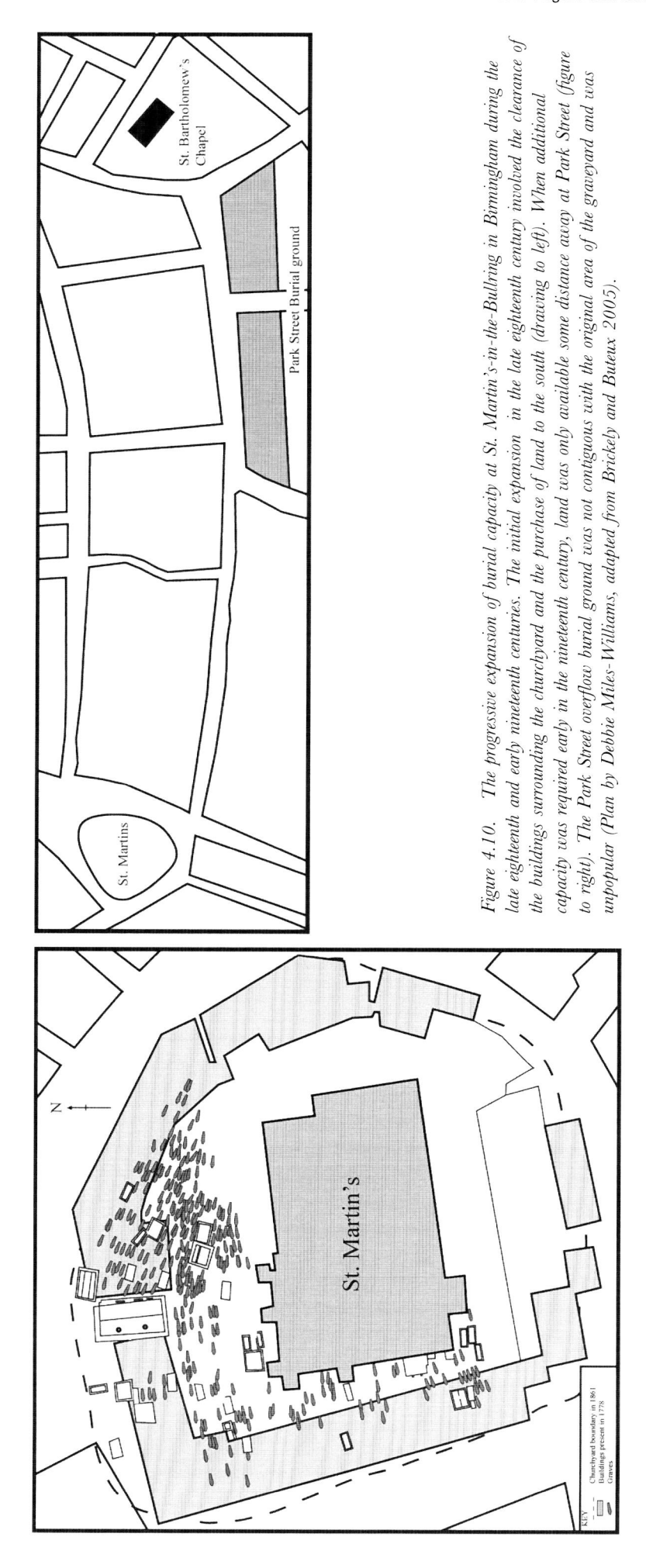

Figure 4.10. The progressive expansion of burial capacity at St. Martin's-in-the-Bullring in Birmingham during the late eighteenth and early nineteenth centuries. The initial expansion in the late eighteenth century involved the clearance of the buildings surrounding the churchyard and the purchase of land to the south (drawing to left). When additional capacity was required early in the nineteenth century, land was only available some distance away at Park Street (figure to right). The Park Street overflow burial ground was not contiguous with the original area of the graveyard and was unpopular (Plan by Debbie Miles-Williams, adapted from Brickely and Buteux 2005).

95

4 The burial landscape of post-medieval Britain and Ireland

inappropriate disposal of the dead at Enon and suggest that the claims made had some basis in fact (Jupp 1997: 100).

Along with the development of private grounds the eighteenth and nineteenth century saw the increasing development of institutional burials grounds for those dying in hospitals, workhouses and asylums. While the majority of the bodies of those dying in workhouses and in hospitals were claimed by family and taken away for burial, those that remained unclaimed were usually interred either in a local churchyard or burial ground (Morrison 1997: 99). Some institutions established their own burial grounds, some of which have been subject to archaeological investigation (table 5.1).[6] For example, Old Addenbrooke's Hospital in Cambridge, which was founded in 1766, initially interred its dead in the churchyard of St Benet's church at the expense of the hospital, but in 1771 the hospital acquired its own burial grounds in a piece of land consecrated by the Bishop of Ely (Welch 1994: 6). This only lasted until 1778 when subscribers sponsoring patients became liable for the cost of burial and the assumption is that this included removal of the body to a churchyard. Thus, the five graves excavated in the grounds of the hospital are thought to date to between 1771–8. Occasionally industrial complexes could have their own burial grounds. The settlement at North Fasagh, Loch Maree in the Scottish highlands is thought to have housed those working at the nearby ironworks in the seventeenth century (Lelong 1999: 81). A small graveyard of 24 graves lies some 620 meters from the ironworks at Fasagh and it has been suggested that the remains of those working at the plant may have been interred there (Duncan 1999: 97).

During the late eighteenth and nineteenth century the restrictions placed upon Catholics were eased by the introduction of the Catholic Relief Acts of 1778,[7] 1791[8] and 1829[9] (18 Geo. III c.60; 31 Geo. III c.32; 10 Geo. IV c.7). The 1791 legislation allowed Catholics to worship without fear of prosecution. The Anglican monopoly over burial, however, remained in place. Catholic priests, like non-conformist minsters, were forbidden to preside over burial in any churchyard (Ward 1909: 314). Often a priest would officiate at a service held at the home of the deceased before they were interred in a churchyard using Anglican rites. Only with the greater tolerance towards Catholics during the nineteenth century was there an increase in the number of Catholic burials grounds and chapels. A number of nineteenth-century Catholic burial grounds have been subjected to archaeological investigations, including the Masonic lodge in Bath which was used as a Catholic Chapel in

Table 4.1. Examples of excavated hospital and workhouse burial grounds

Site	Date	Number of burials	Evidence for dissection and autopsy	Reference
Old Addenbrookes Hospital, Cambridge	1771–1778	5	No	Welch 1994
Newcastle Infirmary	1753–1845	210	Yes	Nolan 1998; Boulter, Robertson and Start 1998
St Thomas's Hospital	17th century	239	Unknown	London Archaeologist 1992: 420; Knight 2002
Royal London Hospital	1820–1854	265[1]	Yes	Vuolteenaho et al. 2008
Haslar Naval Hospital, Hampshire	1753–1859	19	No	Boston 2005
Greenwich Royal Naval Hospital, London	1742–1857	55	Yes	Boston et al. 2008
Edinburgh Royal Infirmary	Second half of 18th century	5	Yes	Henderson, Collard and Johnston 1996
Connaught Asylum, Ballinasloe, Co. Galway	Mid-19th–20th century	12	No	Moore Archaeological and Environmental Services 2003
Fever Hospital in Clonmel, Co. Tipperary	1841–1870	12	No	Mary Henry Archaeological Services Ltd 2000
Whitechapel workhouse, London	18th–19th century	60	No	Greater London Archaeology Advisory Service Annual Review 2007
Manorhamilton workhouse, Co. Leitrim	19th century	71	No	Moore Ltd Archaeological and Environmental Services 2001, 2002

1 Articulated burials from area A.

early and mid-nineteenth century (Moller 2003: 4). The basement was used to inter coffins and excavations uncovered eleven tombs, each containing up to three coffins. A total of 742 burials were excavated from the burial ground of the Catholic mission of St Mary and St Michael in London that was only in use for eleven years between 1843 and 1854 (Miles and Powers 2006). A hundred and eight burials interred between 1867 and 1962 were recorded during the exhumation of a late Jesuit cemetery at Manresa House also in London (Melikian 2004a and b).

The limited additional capacity provided by new private burial grounds, dissenter burial grounds and Catholic cemeteries as well as extensions to existing churchyards proved insufficient. As the population of urban centres soared, conditions within the burial grounds and churchyards deteriorated. A single interment within a grave was becoming an increasing rarity in churchyards in the larger urban centres, except for the wealthy who were increasingly buried elsewhere (Mytum 1989: 288). At St Mary Magdalene churchyard in London, graves were cut in rows parallel to each other and bodies placed on top of each other up to five deep within each single grave (BNY98 archive – LARC). Stacked burials were found in 37 graves at St. Marylebone Churchyard in London, with a maximum stack size of ten coffins (Miles, Powers and Wroe-Brown 2008: 35). Nor was the overcrowding confined to Church of England cemeteries. Graves in the burial ground belonging to the Catholic mission of St Mary and St Michael contained stacks of up to eight burials (Miles and Powers 2006: 16). Evidence from the coffin plates suggests each grave represented all those interred in a single day rather than family plots. At the Crossbones burial ground, large pits, seven or eight coffins wide and three or four coffins high, were excavated (Brickley and Miles 1999: 25). These pits would have been left open and only sealed when there was no more space for more coffins. The lack of space and soil with which to cover the bodies often left corpses exposed and in the most crowded churchyards, the attempts of the gravedigger and sexton to find space for another body would have been a familiar sight (Rugg 1998: 45). This was often accomplished by the use of an iron borer which could lead to inadvertent breaching of sealed coffins and the escape of noxious gases (Chadwick 1843: 141; Mytum 1989: 291). The practice of continually forcing new burials into already over-crowded burial grounds resulted in high levels of post-burial disturbance and intercutting of graves. The result was the large quantities of disarticulated bone seen in many churchyards, such as at St Martin's-in-the-Bull Ring, Birmingham (Brickley and Buteux 2006: 91). Unfortunately, the long term use of many churchyards means that it is impossible to determine whether the disarticulated remains recovered during the excavations of predominately eighteenth- and nineteenth-century burials at St Martin's are from contemporary inhumations or earlier interments. The high proportion of bodies in relation to soil seen in many churchyards and burial grounds also inhibited the decomposition of the bodies as conditions were unsuitable for the bacteria necessary to break down soft tissue, further exacerbating the already atrocious conditions (Mytum 1989: 268). This was especially a problem with public graves where the bodies in the centre of the mass graves decompose more slowly (Haglund 2002: 247).

The deplorable condition of many urban churchyards appears to have been tolerated by the majority of the population (Rugg 1998: 45). This is not to say that that the condition of the cemeteries was never raised or that no complaint were made. For example in 1720 the churchyard of St Andrew's Holborn was closed because its overcrowded condition led to the frequent disturbance of partially decayed bodies and the conditions were offensive (Gittings 1984: 140). Yet it was not until the first half of the nineteenth century that any serious and systematic attempts were made to alleviate the overcrowding and poor conditions seen in many churchyards and burial grounds with the foundation of large cemeteries on the edge of towns. Ironically given the poor state and overcrowding of many urban burial places, it was religious dissent and not concerns about conditions that lay behind the foundation of many of the earliest cemeteries (Rugg 1997: 109).

By the early 1820s, the focus of many non-conformist groups had began to shift away from instituting their own small burial grounds towards the foundation of larger cemeteries on the edge of towns (Jupp 1997: 93). The earliest English cemetery was the Rosary in Norwich (Brooks 1989: 8). Founded by the non-conformist minister Reverend Thomas Drummond in 1819,[10] the cemetery occupied a five acre former market garden on the edge of the city and served Norwich's dissenting communities (Elliot 1982: 2). The Rosary is slightly unusual in that it was founded and financed by one individual. Most of the new extra-mural cemeteries were financed by cemetery companies through the sale of shares – a method often used to underwrite town improvements during this period (Rugg 1997: 105–6). Ten of the earliest thirteen cemetery companies were non-conformist, mostly in towns with large dissenting populations and where non-conformist burial provision was limited (Rugg 1997: 109, 111). Despite their non-conformist origins, most of the new cemeteries could be used by those of any religious persuasion including Anglicans (Rugg 1998: 46).[11] Many, such as York Cemetery, established in 1837, had an area for dissenter burial and a consecrated area for Anglican burial (Murray 1991: 10). The cemetery's chapel was placed astride the dividing line between the consecrated and dissenter sections so it could be used by all.

Although non-conformity was a key element in the formation of cemeteries between 1820 and 1834, another important factor was the fear of body-snatching that had permeated all elements of society (Richardson 1989: 108). Prior to the 1832 Anatomy Act, the increasingly voracious needs of the private anatomy schools were met by the illegal acquisition of relatively fresh corpses, usually from local churchyards and burial grounds (Richardson 1987: 58–61; 1989: 109). During the eighteenth and nineteenth centuries the prevalent emotional attitudes to death and dying were shaped by relationships between highly personalised and individuated selves. The valorisation of the individual was manifest in a funerary context by an increased desire to maintain the uniqueness of the body after death (Tarlow 1999b).[12] Preserving the integrity of the body was an important element of this process. The activities of eighteenth- and nineteenth-century grave-robbers, popularly known as 'resurrectionists', who removed newly buried corpses for sale to anatomy schools threatened the body's integrity and offended moral sensibilities by disrupting the usual conventions surrounding death and burial, while dissection had criminal connotations and might popularly have raised questions over the spiritual state of the anatomised (Richardson 1989: 109; Rugg 1998: 48).[13] Reflecting the concerns of the time, security seems to have been of concern for many of the early cemeteries (Rugg 1998: 48). This often took the form of high walls, as at Kensal Green in London,[14] while at the York Cemetery, there was a guard dog until 1870 (Brooks 1989: 13; Richardson 1989: 113; Murray 1991: 12). This made the new cemeteries a popular alternative to less secure parish churchyards and burial grounds Until the 1832 Anatomy Act removed the probability of being disinterred, the bodies of the poor were particularly susceptible to being stolen and traded (Richardson 1989: 116).[15] Thus, the cheaper cost of burial in a public grave in one of the new cemeteries was one way of safeguarding the remains of loved ones against the anatomist's knife.

A final significant motivation for cemetery establishment was monetary gain. Just as some of the earlier burial grounds were simply speculative undertakings, the same is true of a few of the early cemeteries (Rugg 1997: 106; 1998: 48). In part a response to the rising demand for investment opportunities during the 1820s to 1840s, the financially opportunist cemetery company was a departure from their non-conformist origins (Rugg 1998: 49). Few of the purely speculative cemeteries lasted long and those that did, such as Highgate in London, tended to offer a luxury funerary service. The less favourable economic environment of the late 1830s and early 1840s affected cemetery foundations, which declined in number and were less ambitious in nature (Brooks 1989: 26). Private foundations during this period were often relatively small undertakings often in the overcrowded smaller towns such as the West Hill Cemetery in Winchester, established in 1840 (figure 4.11). The 1840s also saw the foundation of a few cemeteries by local authorities, such as those in Leeds, established 1842, and Southampton, founded in 1846 (Brooks 1989: 38; Morgan 1989: 102).

By the 1840s another factor became central to the cemetery foundation process: public health. Cemetery prospectuses start to mention health and sanitary conditions in the 1840s (Rugg 1998: 52). Much of this could be traced to the 1839 publication of Dr. George Walker's book *Gatherings from Graveyards*. Walker was concerned that the close proximity of the living and the dead in many of the nation's cities was deleterious to health and morality, particularly given the deplorable conditions of many burial places, which he described in grim and revolting detail in his writings (Walker 1839: iii–iv). To give an example, the burial ground of Whitechapel church in London was

> "so densely crowded as to present one entire mass of human bones and putrefaction....... It appears almost impossible to dig a grave in this ground without coming into contact with some recent interment, and the grave digger's pick is often forced through the lid of a coffin when least expected, from which so dreadful an effluvium is emitted" (Walker 1839: 168).

The potential hazards of the city centre churchyards were not just confined to physical health. Dirt and

Figure 4.11 West Hill Cemetery Winchester. This cemetery was founded as a private concern in 1840 (Photograph by Annia Cherryson).

pollution were also considered to be deleterious to moral well-being (Tarlow 2007: 114). As such, the appalling condition of city centre churchyards not only presented a risk to health but also endangered the moral well-being of the population.

Walker was not the first to raise concerns about the health risks associated with churchyards. For example, in 1721 Thomas Lewis published a pamphlet on 'Seasonable considerations on the indecent and dangerous custom of burying in churches and churchyards' (Jenner 2005: 617). The greater impact made by Walker's work can be attributed to a number of factors. His ideas reached a large audience due to the widespread dissemination of his writings. Extracts from *Gatherings from Graveyards* were published in periodicals and local papers, and his work was discussed in the *Lancet* (Rugg 1997: 115; 1998: 53). Walker's book was also published in a more receptive climate. The 1832 cholera outbreak had briefly heightened the general awareness of the dangers of disease (Jupp 1997: 96), although it had little effect on public and social reform during the 1830s (Morris 1976: 198). However, the outbreak was to influence and shape the ideas of a number of individuals at the beginnings of their careers who by the 1840s were in a position to influence the course of social and health reform as it became an increasingly important issue (Morris 1976: 200). During the 1830s increasing concern over living conditions and their impact on public health in London had led to the 1838 Poor Law report (Brooks 1989: 33). Its findings were of sufficient concern for the Government to order an inquiry into the sanitary conditions of the working classes throughout Britain, which included a special inquiry into the practice of interment in towns chaired by W.A. McKinnon (Chadwick 1843). Yet although the resulting report received considerable attention, there was no legislative change (Brooks 1989: 37) and while the 1847 Cemeteries Clauses Act provided a framework for the establishment and management of cemeteries, including stipulating the consecration of at least part of the cemetery for Anglican burial (10 and 11 Vict. c.65), it did little to address health concerns.

Outbreaks of typhus and fears of another cholera outbreak, combined with disquiet about the conditions endured by the working class, made public health a matter of increasing concern during the late 1840s and led to the first Public Health Act in 1948 (11 and 12 Vict. c.63; Morris 1976: 205; Brooks 1989: 43). While burial was not the primary focus of the Act, the legislation did give the newly created local Board of Health the authority to report any burial place thought to present a risk to public health, which could result in the prohibition of any further burials. London was excluded from this legislation. For example burial temporarily ceased in a section of the New Bunhill Fields burial ground in London after a special order was issued by the General Board of Health in September 1849 (Miles 2010: 18).[16] In the same year as the capital's existing burial provision was overwhelmed by the bodies of cholera victims, London's first medical officer issued a damning report on burial within the city (Brooks 1989: 44). The proposals made by the General Board of Health in response to the report became the 1850 Metropolitan Interments Act (13 and 14 Vict. c.52). The Act gave the General Board of Health powers to found new cemeteries, take over control of existing joint stock cemeteries and the ability to recommend to the Privy Council the closure of existing burial grounds for health reasons. However, since the Treasury was unwilling to release sufficient funds, the act made little impact (Brooks 1989: 46). Two years later the act was repealed and replaced by the 1852 Burial of the Dead in the Metropolis Act (15 and 16 Vict. c.85). This act allowed the Privy Council to prohibit burial in any burial place in London if it was deemed necessary for health reasons and required each parish to establish a burial board responsible for ensuring adequate burial provision with the parish, establishing new cemeteries if necessary. The legislation was extended to cover the rest of England and Wales in 1853 (16 and 17 Vict. c.134) as well as to Scotland in 1855 (18 and 19 Vict. c.68) and Ireland in 1856 (19 and 20 Vict. c.98). The establishment of burial boards following the legislation appears to have been relatively rapid and many existing Victorian cemeteries, such as the City of London Cemetery, are the product of the burial boards (Brooks 1989: 51). In a few instances private cemeteries, such as the Undercliffe cemetery in Bradford, were founded to take advantage of the changes in burial location (figure 4.12 and 4.13) (Rawnsley and Reynolds 1977: 215–6). Yet, in many ways the importance of the burial legislation of the 1850s lies not so

Figure 4.12 Undercliffe Cemetery, Bradford, founded in 1854 by the Bradford Cemetery Company (Photograph by Annia Cherryson).

4 The burial landscape of post-medieval Britain and Ireland

Figure 4.13 Area of Quaker burials at Undercliffe Cemetery, Bradford. In contrast to the ostentatious and individualistic monuments in other parts of the cemetery (see figure 4.11), the Quaker memorials are modest, low-lying and of a standard design (Photograph by Annia Cherryson).

much in the foundation of new cemeteries – cemeteries already existed on the periphery of many cities and towns – but in the powers to close existing burial grounds. Over the 1850s and 1860s the Privy Council ordered the closure of many city centre burial grounds, burial vaults and churchyards, some of which had been in use for over a thousand years. Away from the large metropolitan centres, closures often occurred in two phases. Initially burial in locations thought to pose the greatest risk to public health was prevented, including within and below churches, chapels and meeting houses and in close proximity to other buildings, with the closure of other grounds delayed for a few years to ensure adequate alternative burial provision could be put in place. This approach is exemplified by the Order in Council on 31st March 1855 regarding the closure of the burial grounds in Ringwood, Hampshire that forbade further burial

> "forthwith in the parish church, Presbyterian Unitarian chapel, the Independent Chapel, the Wesleyan Chapel, in the churchyard within four yards of all houses, in the Friend's Burial-ground and in the Independent Chapelyard within four yards of the day school, and from and after the 1st of January one thousand eight hundred and fifty-eight in the churchyard, in the Presbyterian Unitarian Chapel Burial-ground, and in the Independent Chapel Burial-ground" (HRO 22M84/PB4)

Family vaults and graves were sometimes excluded when a churchyard was closed. Burial was discontinued at St Martin's-in-the-Bull Ring in Birmingham in 1873 but occasional interments continued to be made in family vaults and graves, as exemplified by the coffins of Campbell Lloyd Haines, who died in 1878, and Eliza Haines, who died in 1904, found in the Haines family vault during recent excavations (Adams 2006: 22; Buteux and Cherrington 2006: 56–7). The burial legislation of the 1850s not only had the effect of moving burial from the centre to the periphery of many cities and towns, but marked the point at which the Established Church's monopoly over burial, was effectively lost. As we have seen, this had been gradually eroded since the seventeenth century, largely by the activities of the non-conformist groups (Laqueur 1993: 184). The church was no longer responsible for the mechanics of burial and the maintenance of the burial grounds as the new cemeteries came under the jurisdiction of burial boards that operated in accordance to guidance from the Home Office and Treasury (Jupp 1990: 11). The urban churches still conducted the ceremonies associated with the interment of the deceased but in many ways the focus of their role had shifted towards the care of the bereaved not the deceased (Jupp 1990: 12). It is also important to remember that although this legislation significantly altered the geography of burial in many urban centres this was not the case in many smaller towns and villages where ancient churchyards continued in use, sometimes by extending their existing grounds.

The fate of the closed inner-city churchyards varied. Many were converted into open areas or parks (figure 4.14). An appendix in Mrs. Basil Brown's book on London burial grounds surveys the condition of the capital's burial places in 1895 some forty years after the closure of the inner city cemeteries. Many, such as St Marylebone's burial ground, are listed as being maintained as a public garden, although others appear to have been neglected (Holmes 1896: 280). The conversion of former burial places to public areas took a variety of forms. Gravestones and other commemorative monuments were left in situ at many sites, although at others they were removed or were used to build walls and pavements in the new grounds, as at St Pancras, Widecombe in the Moor in Devon or Leeds parish church (St Peter's) on Kirkgate, Leeds. Other measures included planting with flowers and shrubs, the provision of benches or play apparatus, as at the additional burial ground in Drury Lane (Holmes 1896: 280, 285). Others, particularly those in poor condition, were simply covered in asphalt for use as children's playgrounds or as recreational areas (Holmes 1896: 286). Some churchyards were entirely or partially lost to development. The conversion of churchyards into open areas meant there was no need to disturb any of the burials. This was not often possible when a site was redeveloped (figure 4.15). Part of St Giles in the Field burial ground was lost to the railway (Emery 2006). The workmen were given little instruction on dealing with the bodies and the resulting spoil heap of bones, broken coffins and coffin fittings was reported in *The*

Figure 4.14 The church of St. George in the East in London showing the re-landscaped churchyard following its closure. The memorial monuments have been replaced by flower beds and ornamental trees (Brown 1896).

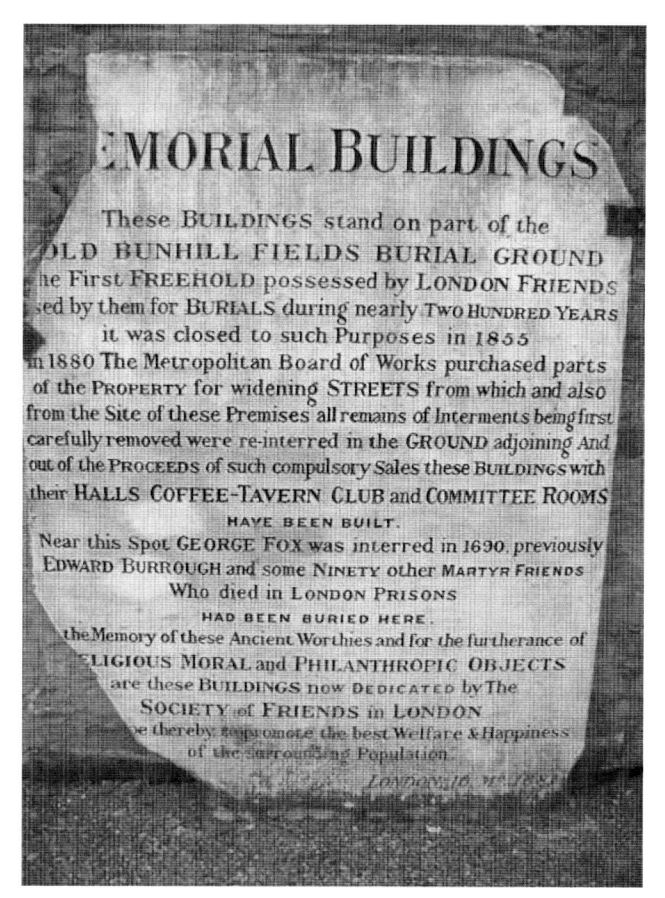

Figure 4.15 Nineteenth century plaque recording the location of the Quaker part of the cemetery at Bunhill Fields. Especially in urban areas, many small cemeteries have given way to expansion and redevelopment (Photograph by Annia Cherryson).

Times of 3rd July 1866. The ensuing controversy led to the suspension of work until the requisite licenses were granted and the remains were re-interred between the railway and burial ground. New Bunhill Fields in London was closed in 1853. Due to the pressure on space in London, the site was soon slated for re-development and the bodies removed (Miles 1997: 27). This led to a number of complaints and the subject was discussed in Parliament in 1854. In contrast, the Quaker cemetery at O'Meara Street closed long before the Burial Acts of 1850s but when the land was cleared for development in 1860, a Quaker was present every day and the remains were re-interred in the cemetery at Long Lane (Woolgar 1994: 32). Here some burials, perhaps interred at a greater depth, were encountered during excavations prior to construction in 1994 (Woolgar 1994: 35).

The 1850s legislation did not just close churchyards. A similar fate befell many inner-city burial vaults. Attempts appear to have been made to secure burial vaults prior to sealing them. At St George Bloomsbury in London, the coffins were covered with first with sand and then with a thick layer of charcoal (Boston, Boyle and Witkin 2006: 40; Boston *et al.*

2009: 29–30), while the coffins in the vault under St Bride's Church were covered with a layer of soil and above that charcoal (Milne 1997: 14). The sand or soil was used to stabilise the stacks of coffins, while the charcoal was to absorb the noxious products of decomposition. Deposits were also found covering the coffins in the vaults at Christ Church, Spitalfields, although in this case it consisted of 245 tonnes of a combination of soil, building materials, domestic waste and industrial refuse from a leather working shop (Reeve and Adams 1993: 89). The church at Spitalfields was undergoing renovation when the vaults were sealed in 1867. The vault proved an easy way of removing the spoil as well as meeting the requirement of an order of the Queen's Council to embed the coffins in soil prior to sealing the vault. Thin layers of sand and charcoal were then spread over the dumped material (Reeve and Adams 1993: 125).

In an era when being interred close to family was deemed to be important, the idea of leaving the remains of family members in the now defunct churchyards and burial vaults was upsetting to some. There is some evidence for the exhumation of remains to allow them to be re-interred close to family. A memorial within the church of St George Bloomsbury records the removal in 1853 of the body of "Mrs Sophia ….[indistinguishable]" to a family vault in Kensal Green (Boston, Boyle and Witkin 2006: 127). Nor was this just a London phenomenon. The bodies of two of the children of John Gowland, who was the first individual to be interred in the vaults beneath York Cemetery, were exhumed from their initial resting place so they could join him in death (Murray 1991: 13). Such was the changing nature of the geography of burial during the 1850s that considerable forethought was required to ensure a husband and wife could be reunited in death. A woman buried at Kensal Green left instructions that should the churchyard at Westminster be closed, her husband's remains were to be exhumed and re-interred next to her (Chadwick 1843: 104). Dorcas Ballingall applied for faculty for the removal of the body of her husband, Colonel David James Ballingall, from the churchyard of St James Foreton in Hampshire which was due to close on April 1st 1855, in the March of that year (HRO 21M65/166F/1). The body was to be reburied in the Portsea burial ground so that when she died her body could be interred next to it.

While religious dissent and health concerns were important factors in cemetery foundation, the popularity of the new foundations owed much to changing attitudes towards death and bereavement as well as towards property ownership (Tarlow 2000: 227, 232). The relationship between the living and the dead had become more personal during the eighteenth and nineteenth century and the body acted as both the focus of the grieving process and a visual symbol of remembrance (Jalland 1999b: 246; Tarlow 2000: 227). There is little evidence to suggest the living regularly visited the graves of the deceased until the late eighteenth century (Tarlow 1999a: 125). Indeed, few graves were marked before the eighteenth century making the identification of the location of the body impossible within a few years of burial. The growing use of gravestones from the late eighteenth century provided a long lasting indication of grave location and should in part be seen as a result of an increase in the custom of grave visiting. Ironically this focus on the grave coincided with unprecedented population growth in urban centres and a marked deterioration in the conditions of city centre burial grounds and churchyards. Visiting graves in many urban churchyards was not a pleasant experience and the new cemeteries offered much more attractive conditions (Tarlow 2000: 232). With the body becoming more central to the grieving process, post-burial disturbance of the dead also became less acceptable (Tarlow 2000: 227). The new cemeteries could offer the desired level of permanence – a final resting place in perpetuity. In the new cemeteries graves could be purchased freehold (Laqueur 1993: 184). In contrast, grave tenure within urban churchyards was invariably short-lived with bodies soon displaced to make room for new corpses.

The new cemeteries were increasingly designed not just as a place for the dead or even as a focus for the grieving process, but as a place for the improvement of the living (Loudon 1843: 1). The early cemeteries, such as the Rusholme Road and Evelyn Street cemeteries in Manchester founded in 1821 and 1824 respectively, were relatively modest affairs (Brooks 1989: 9). During the late 1820s and 1830s, however, cemeteries became increasingly elaborate, designed by leading architects and influenced by contemporary thinking on urban planning. For example, the St James cemetery in Liverpool, which opened in 1829, was landscaped and had architect-designed buildings. The rapid growth of many urban centres during the eighteenth and nineteenth centuries nurtured a nostalgia for a lost rural idyll: the countryside was imbued with all the moral virtues deemed absent from the crowded and polluted towns (Tarlow 2007: 99–100). The creation of open spaces in urban centres brought the moral benefits of the countryside to the town, with the enhanced light and ventilation counteracting the detrimental affects of pollution and overcrowding (Tarlow 2007: 101). The new cemeteries provided some of the earliest, and often only, open spaces in crowded industrial centres. They were places to partake of the 'fresh' air thought to be essential to good health. The vegetation that characterised the new cemeteries not only attempted to reproduce the countryside, but was thought to provide a purifying influence on the atmosphere counteracting the products of decomposition as well as creating a scene which was easy on the eye and soothing to the mind (Chadwick 1843: 132, 138). The perceived beneficial nature of the new cemeteries also extended to the moral and intellectual improvement enacted upon visitors by reading inscriptions on commemorative markers and the contemplation of the transient nature of life (Tarlow 2007: 114).

While the new cemeteries provided burial for all regardless of religious persuasion in the urban centres, non-conformists living in many smaller towns and villages remained disadvantaged. In these smaller communities, there had been no pressure on burial space and existing burial provision, the churchyard, had been sufficient (Morgan 1989: 102). Thus in those communities lacking non-conformist burial grounds, the non-conformists were left with no alternative but to use the local churchyard. Although, the existing rules could be circumvented by non-conformist ministers conducting services outside the church gate, this was an unsatisfactory state of affairs and entirely dependent on the discretion of the local minister (Stevens 2002: 342, 347). Righting this perceived wrong was in many ways the last of the major non-conformist campaigns pertaining to burial. It came to an end in 1880 with the passing of the Burial Laws Amendment Act allowing interment within a churchyard without a Church of England service (43 and 44 Vict. c. 41) and with this the last vestige of the Anglican monopoly over burial was lost.

Conclusion

The post-medieval period was witness to the most widespread change in the geography of death in Britain and Ireland since the introduction of churchyard burial. This transformation was the result of many factors but it can be argued that it had its origins in the Reformation. The Reformation prompted the closure of many monastic burial grounds, but more importantly rejected Purgatory. The masses and prayers for the dead were silenced, the chantries destroyed or converted and the role of the saints was diminished. The role of church buildings, for so long a focus in the commemoration of the dead passed to the body itself. This initially had little effect but would prove to be important in later centuries. The Reformation also heralded a period of religious turbulence and the development of a number of dissenting groups. While some of these were content to be buried in traditional churchyards, for others such a practice was unacceptable and they demanded their own burial grounds. Their wish was granted with the Act of Toleration of 1689 and a precedent set, albeit one that excluded Catholics. Burial grounds were established outside the auspices of the church and the Church's monopoly over the control of burial began to diminish, even though the vast majority of the population continued to be laid to rest in churchyards. The foundation of new non-conformist burial grounds provided new foci for burial away from the ecclesiastical buildings of the established church, although interestingly often associated with meeting places of the dissenting groups. No longer were the burying places of the established church the only acceptable location to inter the dead. The presence of alternative burial locations may in part have influenced the development of institutional and private burial grounds. It has also been suggested that the fragmentation of the Protestant faith in the aftermath of the Reformation meant that once the inheritance of Rome had been removed there was no consensus about death ritual and this may have contributed to the relatively early secularisation of death in England (Houlbrooke 1989: 41–2).

The increasing number of non-conformist, private and institutional burial grounds founded during the eighteenth and nineteenth centuries provided alternative burial locations to the churchyards, at least in the cities and larger towns. They also in many cases charged lower burial fees than the churchyards, allowing many poorer people to avoid the stigma of a pauper's grave. While the non-conformist burial grounds were usually associated with a meeting house or chapel, many of the institutional and private burial grounds had no such provision – in essence distancing these places of the dead from the foci of worship for the living. When the first of the new cemeteries appeared in the 1820s and 1830s, their chapels were used to conduct services for the dead, but not for the living – that remained the role of the parish church or the non-conformist meeting house. The dead were beginning to be physically separated from the religious foci of the living community. The separation of the dead from the living continued with the closure of many inner-city churchyards and burial grounds in the 1850s, 1860s and 1870s, pushing burial to periphery of many urban centres. Finally it is worth noting that in contrast to the profound changes seen in the urban centres, burial location in many smaller communities, such as hamlets, villages and some smaller towns remained largely unchanged with the local churchyard remaining the focus of burial. Even in the relatively quiet rural parishes, however, some individuals were not buried according to normal custom and tradition. These atypical burials are examined in the next chapter.

Notes

1. The disarticulated remains of another individual were found in one corner of another cist, but it unclear in this case whether this is another burial disturbed during the dissolution or whether this represents an earlier re-interment (Lyne 1997: 74).
2. The burial of the unbaptised is discussed in more detail in chapter 5.
3. Burial continued into the later part of the eighteenth century in the cemetery's vaults, with an inscription recording a burial in the Jenkes vault in 1774 (Hunting 1991: 36).
4. Burial outside community burial grounds is discussed in more detail in chapter 5.
5. Burials could also be disturbed by construction work and the bones found in a large pit in the churchyard of St. John the Baptist Church in Southover, Lewes may have been disturbed during the construction of the church tower in 1714–1738 (Grant 2009: 17, 24).
6. See chapter 5 for prison burial grounds.
7. An Act for relieving his majesty's subjects professing the Popish religion from certain penalties and

8   disabilities imposed on them by an Act made in the eleventh and twelfth years of the reign of King William the third entitled An Act for the further preventing the growth of popery.
8   An Act to relieve, upon conditions and under restrictions, the persons therein described from certain penalties and disabilities to which Papists or persons professing the popish religion, are by now subject.
9   An Act for the relief of his majesty's Roman Catholic subjects.
10   The land was purchased in 1819 but the first burial did not occur until 1821 (Elliott 1982: 2).
11   Abney Park cemetery founded by dissenters in London initially had no consecrated ground for the burial of Anglicans (Brooks 1989: 27).
12   See chapter 2 for more detail on the treatment of corpse.
13   Dissection and grave robbing are discussed in detail in chapter 6.
14   Kensal Green was founded after the Anatomy Act of 1832 removed the resurrectionist threat yet a display of security was still deemed to be important (Brooks 1989: 13).
15   In fact, their bodies were at greater risk of being dissected after 1832, only this time within the law, if they died 'unclaimed' in the workhouse.
16   This burial ground was also called City Bunhill Burial Ground and Golden Lane Burial Ground.

5 By choice, circumstance or compulsion: unusual burials in post-medieval Britain and Ireland

The vast majority of the population of post-medieval Britain and Ireland was interred in churchyards, burial grounds or cemeteries, according to a shared repertoire of contemporary burial mores. This chapter examines those post-medieval burials that differ from normative practice either in the nature of the interment or in the location of the burial. The previous three chapters have demonstrated that there is significant variation within post-medieval burial practices and that the dividing line between normal and unusual is at best blurred. While any burial practice that is statistically infrequent can be described as unusual, this chapter focuses particularly on those post-medieval burials that occur outside of community churchyards, burial grounds or cemeteries. Such burials, although they constitute a minority of interments during the post-medieval period, are nevertheless likely to be underrepresented in the archaeological record. Isolated and unaccompanied burials can be difficult to date without radiocarbon dating, and cost means that this is not always feasible. Classically atypical burials have been described as "deviant" in that they deviated from what was perceived to be normal for that period. The term deviant has somewhat sinister connotations and may not always be the most appropriate as the factors that may have led to an individual being given a distinctive burial are many and varied. It is not possible to elucidate all the factors that may have led to an interment that differed from the accepted norm, but many of the more likely possibilities can be grouped into three broad categories; choice, circumstance and compulsion.

Choice

Traditionally, interpretations of funerary behaviour have focused on the role of the community or society; individual choice is often subsumed into the collective whole. Yet the preferences of the deceased and the bereaved have a significant impact on the nature of funerary provision and selection of burial location. More often than not these choices are drawn from a contemporary repertoire of burial styles and locations. As has been discussed in the previous chapter, a combination of the Reformation and the rise of non-conformism changed perceptions of what constituted a suitable burial location. Rejection of the usual burial locations by some dissenting groups significantly altered the range of burial locations by demonstrating that it was possible to have an "acceptable" burial outside of a churchyard. As is demonstrated later in this chapter, the vast majority of those interred outside churchyards or dissenter burial grounds, during the post-medieval period were the victims of unavoidable circumstances or exclusion. However, there are a few examples of individuals or their families rejecting more conventional burial forms and locations in favour of a more individualist interment during the post-medieval period (Gittings 2007: 322). A study of twenty-six individuals accorded more individualistic interments, often away from conventional burial grounds, between 1689 and 1823 found they were predominately male, usually elderly and reasonably wealthy (Gittings 2007: 327). Wealth was an important factor as it gave these individuals a freedom of choice simply not available to those who struggled to raise funds for a normal burial. Given the religious component of funerary rites in this period, it is unsurprising that many of those rejecting a conventional burial location had been labelled as atheists during their lives although others were non-conformists or Anglicans (Gittings 2007: 326, 329). Their choice of burial location varied. Some, like Dr William Martyn, a physician from Plymouth who was buried on his estate in 1762, were interred in fields, while others, such as the Birmingham printer John Baskerville who died in 1775, were interred in their own gardens (Gittings 2007: 329–30).[1] Identifying individuals who chose to be interred outside community grounds in the archaeological record can be difficult. One possible candidate is John Rawls who had been interred on Glastonbury Tor in the earlier of the two ruined churches on the summit in an iron bound coffin in 1741 (figure 5.1) (Rahtz 1970: 42). The nature of the funeral provision and spectacular location of the burial suggests that his final resting place may have been the result of personal choice, rather than circumstance or compulsion.

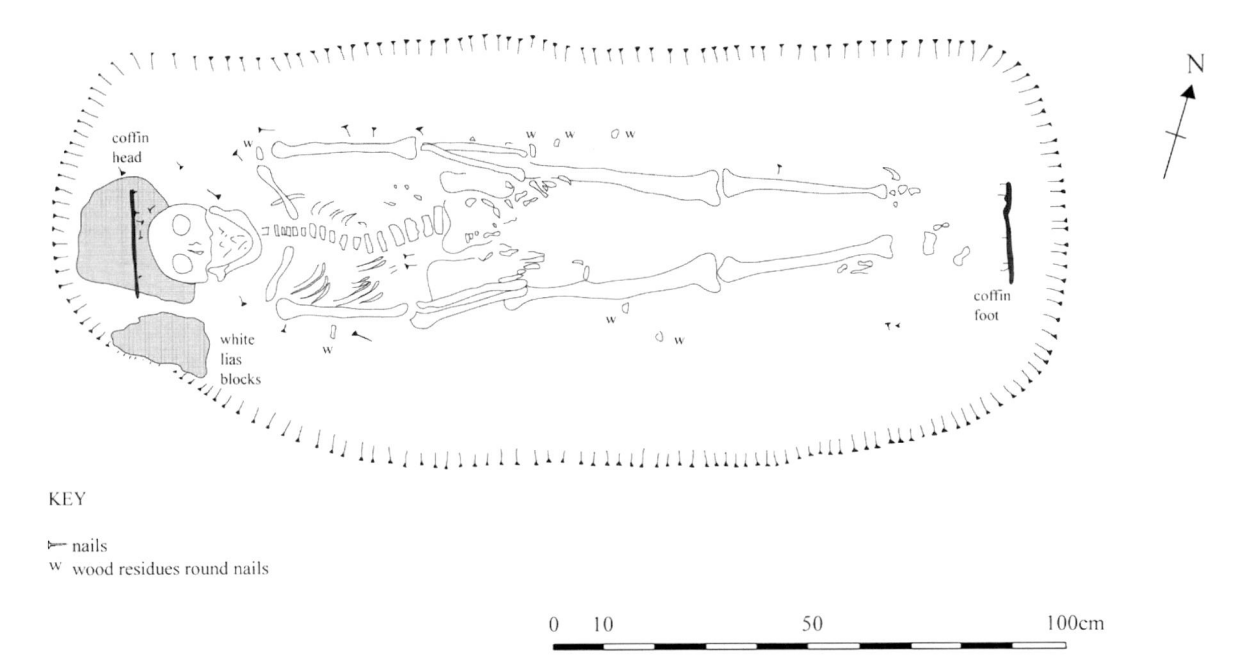

Figure 5.1 Grave of John Rawls, who was interred on Glastonbury Tor in 1741. The choice of such a spectacular location could suggest that Rawls's burial location was determined by his own wishes (Drawing by Debbie Miles-Williams, adapted from Rahtz and Watts 2003).

Circumstance

A "decent" burial was important throughout the post-medieval period and every effort was made to ensure the deceased were interred with respect. However, sometimes the circumstances of an individual's death could result in an atypical interment. Either the condition of the body, or the location or manner of an individual's death would prevent the usual burial practices being followed. Similarly, high levels of mortality or exigencies of war could overwhelm existing burial provision preventing, despite the best of intentions, adherence to the usual funerary customs.

The War Dead

A duty of care was owed to those who lost their lives on the field of conflict, yet in reality the degree of care given to each individual body decreased as the number of fatalities rose (Donagan 1998: 128,130). While attempts were normally made to provide a decent interment many of the war dead of the post-medieval period were denied a Christian burial. This was primarily a matter of logistics. Even allowing for exaggeration, the dead of many of the battles fought in Britain and Ireland during the post-medieval period numbered in the hundreds or even thousands. For example, contemporary accounts of the battle of Marston Moor in 1644 recorded that the occupants of the neighbouring villages buried 4150 bodies (Newman and Roberts 2003: 125). Accounts of the aftermath of battles during the Civil War, and in later conflicts such as the battles of Prestonpans (1745) and Culloden (1746), indicate that the majority of those killed in battle were interred not far from where they fell, usually in mass graves (Donagan 1998: 129). In 1642 following a battle in Herefordshire the Earl of Stamford "commanded pits to be made and their [the enemies'] bodies, with those of our men [Royalists] .... to be buried together" (Anon 1642: 6). Many of the mounds or tumuli located on the sites of known battles have traditionally been thought to mark the site of mass graves, such as the tumuli in Wilstrop Wood remembered as the final resting place of those killed in the battle of Marston Moor in 1644 (Fiorato et al. 2000: 3).

Despite the many battles fought on British soil during the post-medieval period, there are no carefully excavated examples of war graves comparable to the medieval mass burial containing casualties of the Battle of Towton in 1461 (Fiorato et al. 2000). Mass graves were discovered during the eighteenth, nineteenth and early twentieth centuries on the sites of the battle of Naseby (1645) in Northampton, Marston Moor (1644) in Yorkshire (Foarde 2001: 96) and Prestonpans, East Lothian (1745) (Pollard and Ferguson 2008:6). In 1842, Edward Fitzgerald discovered human bone when investigating one of several depressions in the ground at Naseby (Terhune and Terhune 1980: 342–3, 345; Foarde 1995: 356). Seven or eight skeletons were discovered when a trench was opened across this grave (Terhune and Terhune 1980: 345). The bodies were tightly packed laying alternating east and west, with one body jammed in across the others (Foarde 1995: 356). Estimates based on the size of the grave suggest it may have contained about 100 individuals (Terhune and Terhune 1980: 345). Burials were also found at Naseby during gravel digging on Mill Hill in 1792 and 1794 (Mastin 1818: 113; Foarde 1995: 356). At Marston Moor, many skeletons were discovered during drainage operations in 1858–9 and several more were discovered during the 1920s (Newman 1978: 30). At Prestonpans, the site of a key battle in the Jacobite rising, human remains were found during drainage works in the late eighteenth century. An 1883 account indicated that "the clothes covering the remains were so well preserved they could distinguish Royalist from rebel" (M'Neill 1883: 130, quoted in Pollard and Ferguson 2009: 6). Large quantities of human bone, including several irregularly orientated skeletons, were discovered near Aylesbury in the early nineteenth century (Anon 1820: 13–4). The skeletons appeared to have been hastily interred in pits and may be linked to the 1642 Battle of Aylesbury. Rows of burials were found during excavations adjacent to the fortified defences in the Newarke area of Leicester (Courtney and Courtney 1992: 69). It was thought that whole rows had been interred at one time and the discovery of seventeenth-century pottery found below one of the skeletons suggests that these burials may be linked to the Civil War. Documentary sources mention that the dead of the 1645 siege were buried in the Newarke, although other explanations such as plague pits cannot be excluded. A similar situation was encountered during excavations of the Taunton's medieval defences (Somerset Historic Record 57136). The ditch had been re-used during the Civil War and then used to inter the bodies of those killed during the conflict.

There are also examples of isolated human remains in the general vicinity of battlefields which may be linked to combatants fleeing the field of battle, possibly under pursuit, such as the two individuals wearing helmets found in 1817 in a gravel pit between Cold Ashby and Guilsborough, not far from Naseby (Terhune and Terhune 1980: 365; Foarde 1995: 357). The skeletons of four relatively young males found at Carlingford, County Louth, three roughly deposited in a single grave with the fourth interred in a single grave close by, probably died in combat (Buckley and McConway 2004: 40). The skeletons bore evidence of multiple injuries, particularly to the head. The osteological evidence suggests all were victims of a ferocious attack, one which did not cease once they were lying on the ground; neither does this appear to be their first experience of conflict, since two of them had healed head wounds. War was not just a series of large battles; skirmishes between smaller numbers of combatants made a significant contribution to war casualties. Of a sample of 126 Catholic nobility and gentry, who died for the Royalist cause, forty-five percent were killed in skirmishes (Carlton 1992: 206) and it is possible that those interred in Carlingford died in this type of incident. In 1823 workmen found several skeletons "huddled together" in the ditch on the outside of Newcastle upon Tyne's town wall, just outside the Carliol tower. One of them had a "cannon ball" lodged in the skull. Another 24lb ball was found embedded two and a half feet deep in the wall (*Archaeologia Aeliana* 1896: 17). Two adult males were found in north-south graves in the narrow strip of land between the star fort and boundary wall in the north-west corner of the artillery ground at Spitalfields market (Holder and Jeffries *forthcoming* 127). The backfill of the graves contained pottery dating to between 1580 and 1650 and the burials respect and probably post-date the star fort; thus suggesting a date of c. 1640–1650s. The graves are thought to contain members of one of the groups using the artillery ground, who were perhaps killed in a military accident or during the failed Presbyterian and City-backed counter revolution against Parliament in 1647.

Sadly, combatants are rarely the only victims of military action. Two mass graves, one containing nine individuals and the other six, were uncovered during the excavation of Carrickmines Castle, County Dublin, with a single inhumation lying between the two graves and an additional prone individual to the north-east (Fibiger 2004: 9, 14). Those within the mass graves were interred with little care (Fibiger 2004: 41). Ensuring as many individuals as possible were accommodated within the grave appears to have been the main concern. Bone preservation was poor and sex could only be determined for five individuals from the mass graves; all were probably female (Fibiger 2004: 20). The first mass grave also contained the remains of two children, one of approximately three years and the other of about four to five years. The skeletons of seven individuals from the site exhibited evidence of peri-mortem trauma, while the presence of a musket ball points to at least one victim of firearms (Fibiger 2004: 33). The area around Carrickmines saw much conflict between Catholic and Protestant forces during 1640s, which culminated with the many of the local Catholic population taking refuge in the Castle (O'Byrne 2003: 9–10). The castle was placed under siege by Protestant forces in March of 1642, and fell a few days later whereupon its civilian occupants were massacred to widespread condemnation from both sides (O'Byrne 2003: 10–11). It seems likely that the burials found in 2001 represent some of the victims (Fibiger 2004: 42).

The scarcity of British and Irish post-medieval mass war graves in the archaeological record is the result of a number of factors. There is a level of uncertainty regarding the precise location of some battlefields.

Even when the location of the battle is known the site may not have been subject to any excavations. Many post-medieval battlefields lie outside urban centres where much of modern developer-led excavation occurs. Moreover, the protection offered to many battlefields by the law further reduces the chances of these sites being excavated. In addition there are the usual issues of preservation. Documentary sources suggest many of those interred on the field of conflict lie in comparatively shallow graves, making them susceptible to disturbance by later activities, such as cultivation (Foarde 2001: 96). Levels of skeletal preservation may be a factor and it is worth noting that the bones found at Naseby in 1842 were described as being in poor condition (Terhune and Terhune 1980: 351). Whether any of these bones would now be visible some 160 years later is debatable. It should be noted that British war graves are also of course found at many sites outside of Britain, and that archaeologists are now investigating these contexts (e.g. Fraser and Brown 2008).

Burial without appropriate rites and away from recognised burial grounds was widely perceived as unfit for human dignity, and raised fears that improper interments condemned the spirits of the deceased to linger in torment (Cressy 2000: 119). Thus while the vast majority of those killed in battle were buried close to where they fell, efforts were made to recover the remains of some of the war dead and inter them in recognised burial grounds with the appropriate rites. Following the Battle of Cheriton in Hampshire in 1644, the royalists "fetched off cartloads of dead men, some they buried and some they carried with them" (Anon. 1644: 5). A couple of years earlier, following a skirmish near Southam in Warwickshire in 1642 the "enemy wheeled round, took their dead and fled" (Ellis 1853: 316). Many of the burials that appear in parish registers from York for the year of 1644 are of soldiers (Wenham 1970: 132–139). Some were casualties of the siege of the city between April and July of that year, but at least three individuals are known to have died at the battle of Marston Moor. Identifying combatants killed in battle but later interred in community burial grounds is difficult unless documentary or nameplate information is available. A lead coffin in the Cavendish Vault in Derby Cathedral has tentatively been identified as belonging to Colonel Charles Cavendish (Butler and Morris 1994: 19). The Colonel, who was killed at the battle of Gainsborough in 1643, was first buried at Newark and re-interred in the family vault in 1674 (Butler and Morris 1994: 16). Injuries are not only sustained on the battlefield, making the identification of military involvement tentative in some cases. Examples for such inter-personal violence include a seventeenth-century male burial from Glasgow Cathedral found with lead shot in his skull (Driscoll 2002: 42), or the three late sixteenth- or early seventeenth-century male burials from Bagenal's Castle, Co. Down with head trauma from sharp implements, probably a sword (Dawkes and Buckley 2006: 32),

The high levels of mortality associated with conflict could overwhelm existing cemeteries, as at Abingdon where the Parliamentarians used the site of a former orchard as an overflow burial ground (Allen 2006: 12). The cemetery was created after the Parliamentarians took Abingdon from the Royalists in 1644 and continued in use until c.1661.[2] While the cemetery contained the burials of close to 300 men, women and children, there was an imbalance towards men of military age (Allen 2006). The majority of those interred in the northern area of the cemetery were adult males making it likely that this area was designated for the burial of military casualties, whereas the lay population was buried to the south. The cemetery is near St Nicholas' Church but as the church remained staunchly Anglican throughout the Civil War with probable Royalist leanings, it is unlikely that the burials were associated with the church (Allen 2006).

The majority of burials at Abingdon were single interments but the cemetery also contained nineteen multiple interments, most of two or three individuals and one grave containing the bodies of nine males, including one individual with a musket ball in his chest (Allen 2006) (figure 5.2). Burial records from St Helen's Church, Abingdon from 1644–45 mention a payment made for the burial of nine men from the prison and this may correspond to the burials in the mass grave. It is not clear if these individuals were prisoners of war but the mass burial of prisoners of war is seen elsewhere. One of the two post-medieval graves found at Portchester Castle, Hampshire, contained the remains of three individuals and the arm of the fourth, the rest of the body having been removed by a nineteenth-century pit prior to excavation (Cunliffe and Garratt 1994: 27). These burials may have been part of a much longer row of burials. This mass burial, and that of the individual found in a single grave close by, date from the latter half of the eighteenth century when Portchester Castle was used to hold French prisoners of war (Cunliffe and Garratt 1994: 4, 27). Other examples of the possible interment of prisoners of war include the two burials found during excavations at Ely Place in Camden, London, which are thought to date to the Civil War period when the site was used as a prison and a hospital (Filer 1991b: 301). Remains of three individuals from a site off Sutton Road in Plymouth, Devon, are believed to be eighteenth-century French prisoners of war from when the area was a site of a prison (Cotswold Archaeological Trust 2001: 5, 13–4), and

Figure 5.2. Mass grave of nine men excavated in the Civil War cemetery at Abingdon Vineyard, 1989. The seventeenth-century graveyard population was dominated by adult men, especially in the northern part of the site, which suggests that the area acted as a graveyard for Parliamentarian casualties of the Civil War, as well as the civilian population (Copyright Oxford Archaeology).

human remains uncovered outside Perth Prison are thought to belong to French prisoners held there during the Napoleonic Wars (Ponsford 2001: 248).

Death on the field of conflict was not the only circumstance during time of war that could prevent an individual being interred in the usual burial grounds. The many sieges of castles during the English Civil War would have cut off the occupants from contact with the outside world, including access to burial grounds. At Sandal Castle in Yorkshire, the nine single male burials lying in the only part of the bailey relatively free of buildings are thought to be Royalist casualties of the siege of 1645 (Mayes and Butler 1983: 6–7, 80). Three of the graves contained irregular fragments of ferrous metal (Manchester 1983: 337). The metal may have come from one or more of the mortars known to have exploded within the castle during the siege and have been embedded in soft tissue of these individuals when they were interred. In addition, peri-mortem trauma to the skull and mandible was observed in three individuals, including one of those interred with fragments of ferrous metal (Manchester 1983: 338). The occupants of the three graves found along the curtain wall on the north side of the inner ward of Beeston Castle, Cheshire are thought to represent Royalist casualties of the siege of 1644 (Keen and Hough 1993: 120–1). The six graves found within Pontefract Castle in Yorkshire may be those of individuals interred when the Royalist garrison was completely surrounded and cut off from All Saint's Church in 1645 (Roberts 2002: 429). Sir Jarvis Cutler is known to have been interred in the chapel during the siege and then exhumed for reburial elsewhere in 1648 (Roberts 2002: 98). Two of the Pontefract Castle graves are empty and it is possible that the occupants of both were exhumed (Roberts 2002: 96). The upper half of a young adult of indeterminate sex found in a shallow grave on the Green at Nottingham Castle may also represent a Civil War fatality (Drage 1989: 78). Another possible siege victim, who does not appear to have been accorded a formal burial, is a young adult male whose skull and cervical vertebrae were found in a gully inside the Citadel Postern Gate during excavations at Basing House, Northamptonshire (Allen and Anderson 1999: 99). The remains probably date to the Civil War when Basing House was under siege. The top of the skull bears an unhealed cut, unlikely to have been the cause of death but possibly sufficient to stun this individual (Allen and Anderson 1999: 100–2). Two burials in shallow graves found within Clogh Oughter Castle in County Cavan may be

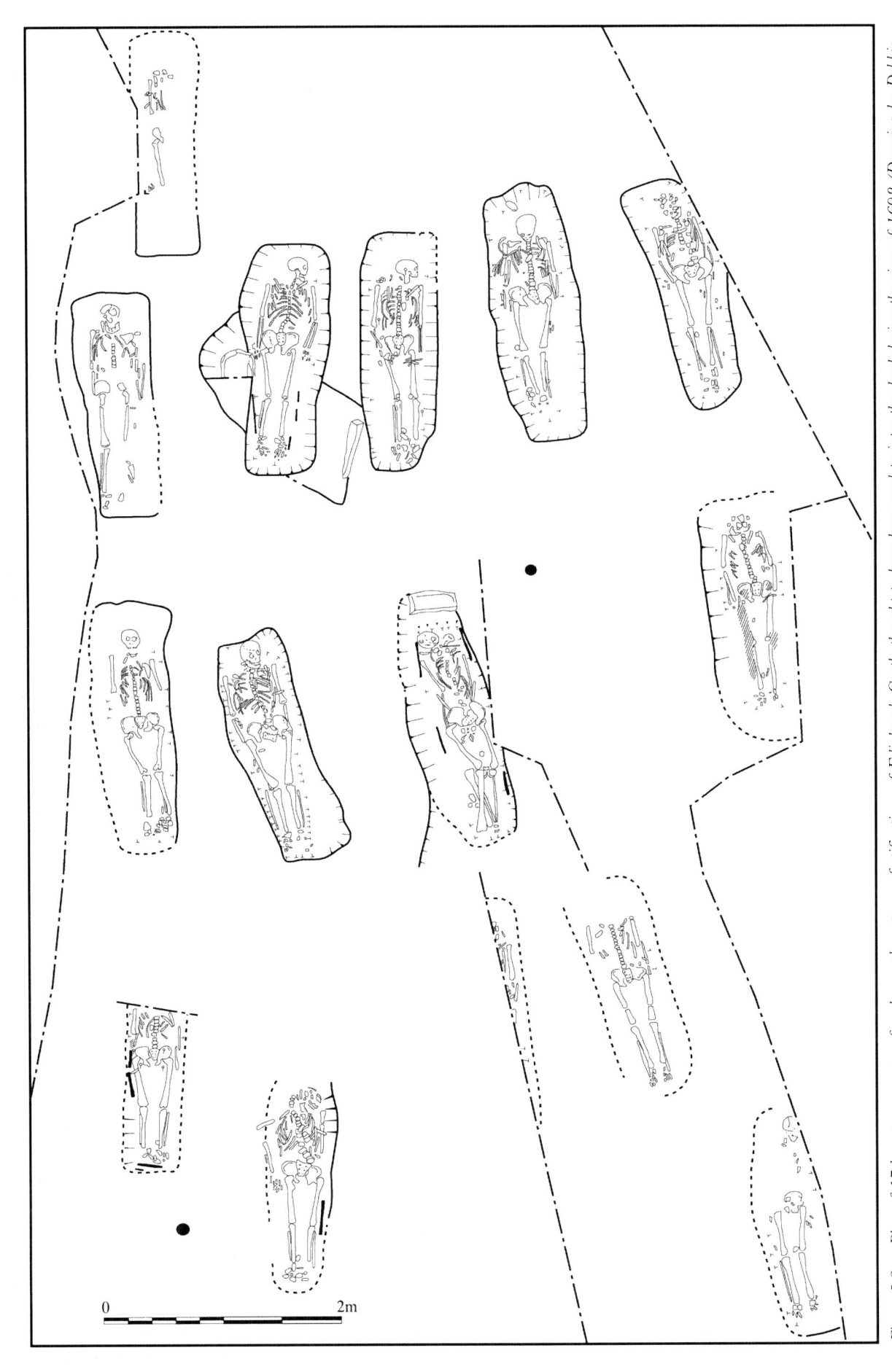

5 By choice, circumstance or compulsion: unusual burials in post-medieval Britain and Ireland

Figure 5.3. Plan of 17th-century cemetery found near the entrance fortifications of Edinburgh Castle thought to have been used to inter the dead during the siege of 1698 (Drawing by Debbie Miles-Williams, adapted from Driscoll and Yeoman 1997).

linked to the Cromwellian siege of 1653 (Egan 1988: 194–5).

Evidence of burials from siege warfare is not confined to the Civil War Period. A small burial ground of fifteen graves arranged in four rough rows has been excavated by the entrance fortifications of Edinburgh Castle (figure 5.3) (Driscoll and Yeoman 1997: 111). All the burials were men, the majority of whom were young adults. All had been wrapped in shrouds and interred in simple coffins lacking in coffin fittings. Two of the burials had been cut into demolition rubble which contained a forged coin dating to 1686 and it is likely that these individuals were interred during the siege of the castle in 1689 by William and Mary's forces. Supplies of food and water are known to have run low during the siege and outbreaks of disease were also reported. Epidemic disease could be a major cause of mortality during sieges as the conditions in besieged towns and fortifications provided ideal conditions for the spread of disease. Ten mass graves containing a total of 110 individuals, with between four and 18 individuals per grave, were discovered during the excavation of a medieval cemetery at the Barbican site in York (figure 5.4) (Chamberlain, Mcintyre and Pearson 2008; Bruce 2009). The graves date to the early modern period and the virtual absence of females and older males suggests a military cohort. Yet the absence of perimortem trauma makes it unlikely that these individuals died in conflict and it has been suggested that they were victims of epidemic disease, perhaps contracted during the siege of York in 1644.

Victims of epidemic disease and famine

As in times of war, the excess number of corpses produced by epidemic disease could stretch conventional modes of disposal beyond breaking point. Yet there appears to have been an attempt to adhere to usual funerary conventions for as long as possible, whether dealing with plague victims in the sixteenth and seventeenth centuries or cholera epidemics of the nineteenth century (Harding 2002: 65). During the initial stages of an epidemic, victims were interred within churches and churchyards according to the usual burial conventions, although health concerns and regulations could result in some modification of conventional burial practices (Morris 1976: 104).

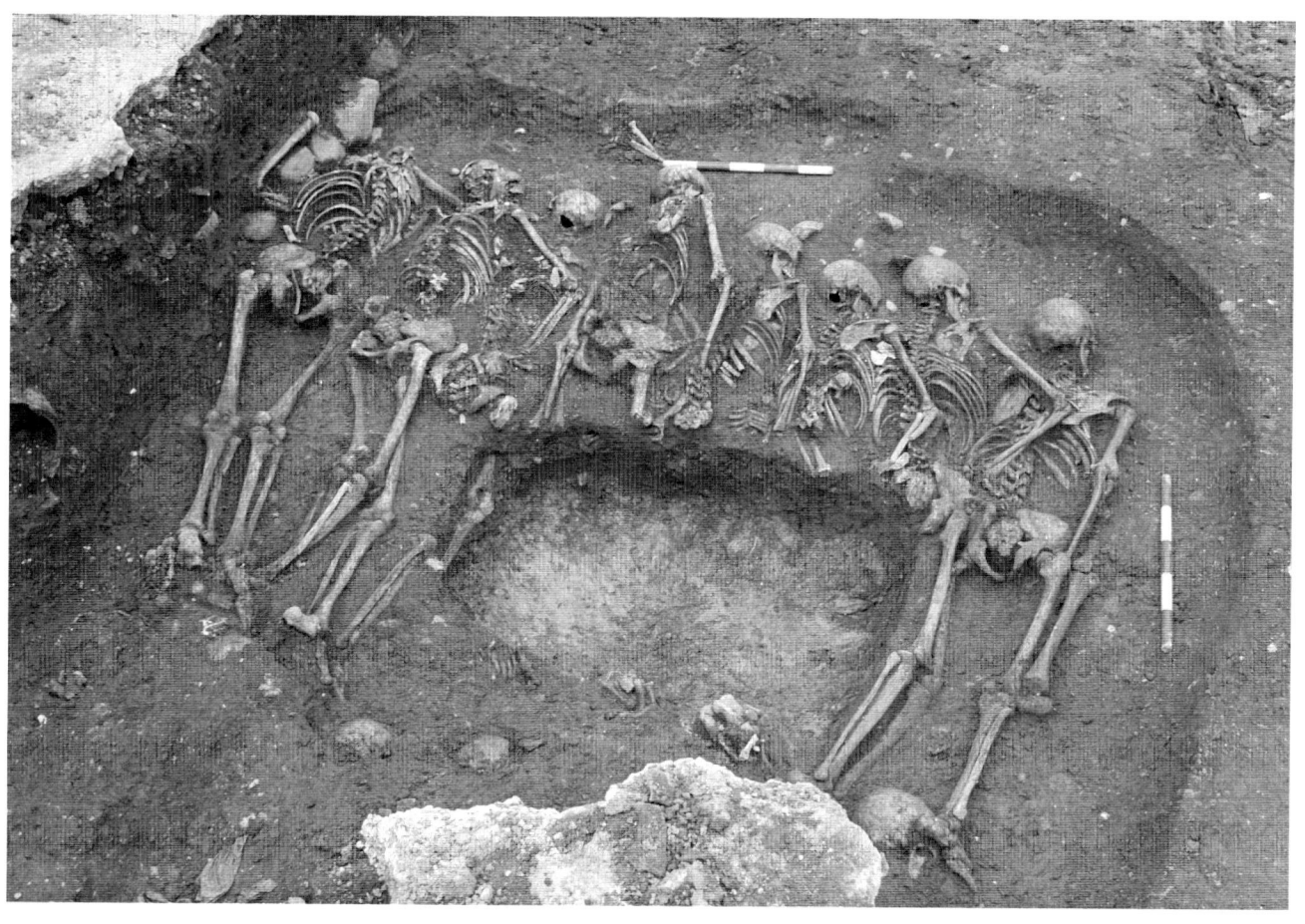

Figure 5.4 A mass grave from York Barbican. One of ten pits containing 110 individuals in total, this mid seventeenth-century burial probably dates to the siege of York during the English Civil War. All the bodies were young adult men, but they lack the perimortal trauma which one would expect to see if they died in battle. Andrew Chamberlain suggests that they might be the victims of epidemic disease, common in siege situations (Photograph courtesy of On-Site Archaeology).

During the 1665 plague outbreak, the church of St Bride Fleet Street, London instituted a ban on the burial of plague victims within the church, while burial in the upper churchyard was restricted to the well-known and wealthy (Harding 1993: 56). In York, cholera victims of the 1832 outbreak were not allowed within the church buildings; burial services were conducted in the churchyard (Barnet 1972: 29). During the same outbreak, the Central Board of Health required victims to be interred within 24 hours of death wrapped in cotton or linen cloth saturated in pitch or coal tar. Many of the regulations were unpopular as they curtailed the usual funerary rites such as wakes and viewing of the dead and increased fears of being buried alive (Morris 1976: 105–6, 112). The unpopularity of many health measures resulted in marked variation in the enforcement of many of the regulations.

Cholera victims were sometimes buried in quicklime (Morris 1976: 105). At St Anne's, Middlesex, early victims of the 1832 cholera outbreak were wrapped in blankets dipped in coal tar and buried in coffins full of lime (Morris 1976: 105). Burial with lime is not unknown in the archaeological record and in some instances the treatment of the body can be linked to epidemic disease. A body within a lead coffin in the Carrington burial vault in All Saint's Church, High Wycombe, Buckinghamshire was covered in a powder thought to be quicklime (Boyle 1998: 60). Elizabeth Carrington died of cholera in 1832 and it is possible that her body lies in this coffin. The Manse house in Mullingar, County Tyrone was used as a hospital during a nineteenth-century cholera epidemic and the three graves, some containing lime, excavated in its grounds are likely to be linked to the outbreak (excavations.ie 1999.187–1). It has been suggested that the lime packed between the lead shell and outer wooden coffin of a coffin from the vault of St. George's Church, Bloomsbury was designed to contain infection (Boston *et al.* 2009: 151). However, infectious disease was not the only reason for treating the body with lime. Lime can be used to break down organic matter. Honoretta Pratt, who died in 1769, left instructions that her corpse be treated with slaked lime to reduce it to ashes in an altruistic attempt to prevent the release of the gaseous by-products of decomposition, which she believed to have a deleterious affect on health of others (Gittings 2007: 335). Quicklime was added to coffins to make remains useless for dissection (Chadwick 1843: 95) and was also associated with the burial of felons. When dissection was removed as a punitive measure for those guilty of murder, it was replaced by burial within prison precincts in quicklime (Richardson 1987: 227). The bodies of those executed for treason in 1820 for their part in the Cato Street plot to kill the cabinet were interred in quicklime within the precincts of Newgate prison (Gatrell 1994: 308). The integrity of the corpse was greatly valued during this period and is discussed in more detail later in this chapter and in chapter 6. Judicial punishments often derived their potency from threatening this integrity. The destructive action of quicklime challenged the integrity of the body and the association between criminality and the use of quicklime upset many who were forced by health regulations to include the substance in the coffins of friends and family dying during the cholera outbreaks (Richardson 1987: 227). Thus the presence of lime within a burial should not be automatically linked to infectious disease in the absence of additional information. Thus the presence of lime in two late seventeenth-century burials from the Quaker burial ground at Kingston-upon-Thames, and several seventeenth-century burials in the nave of Glasgow cathedral (Driscoll 2002: 52) could be the result of a number of different factors (Bashford and Sibun 2007: 121). An alternative means of containing infectious disease may explain the thin layer of a yellow mortar-like substance covering the lid of a coffin from the Creswicke vault in St Mary's Church, Bitton in South Gloucestershire (Boore 1998: 79).

As mortality levels increased during epidemic outbreaks, the number of bodies eventually exceeded the capacity of the usual burial grounds and adherence to the usual burial conventions was gradually abandoned. The account of plague outbreak of 1665 in London described how at the height of the epidemic "they died by heaps, and were buried by heaps" with individual interments being replaced by mass graves (Defoe 1722: 337; Harding 1993: 56). In some cases, the pits were dug within existing churchyards. For example, the burial pits for the plague dead of the parish of St Bride Fleet Street were probably within the lower churchyard (Harding 1993: 57) while a great pit, about 40 feet in length and about fifteen or sixteen feet broad and up to 20 feet deep was dug in the parish churchyard at Aldgate (Defoe 1722). In 1665 the Earl of Craven bought a field to inter the plague dead (Chave 1969: 710). It has been suggested that bones uncovered during demolition work at the corner of Broadwick Street and Marshall Street in 1969 came from the Craven pest field. In 1832, a privy council order gave local Health Boards power to acquire special cholera burial grounds (Morris 1976: 73). This could involve the use of land adjoining existing cemeteries as when 196 cholera victims were interred in land adjacent to the overflow burial ground for Whitechapel, London in 1832 (Holmes 1896: 131). The remains of at least 80 individuals uncovered during construction work in Whitechapel in 1909 might have come from this burial ground (ILAU archive DAV 77).

The need to dispose of victims of the epidemic could also involve the urgent creation of new areas for burial, such as the new burial ground established for the burial of the York's cholera victims in 1832 (Barnet 1972). Seventeen years later, 147 of the 155 victims of the 1849 outbreak were interred in the new York Cemetery in thirty public graves with an average of five bodies per grave (Murray 1991: 15). The other eight victims were from better-off families and were interred within family graves or vaults. Clearly, relative wealth was an important consideration in the disposition of the bodies of those who had died in disease epidemics; those of means could avoid burial in communal pits. Concerns about burial in unconsecrated ground led to the subsequent consecration of the York burial ground containing the 1832 cholera victims by the archbishop (Murray 1991: 36). This was relatively unusual and many victims of epidemic disease were interred in unconsecrated ground. The disarticulated remains of three individuals were found buried in sand at York Place in Aberdeen (Ponsford and Jackson 1998: 214). The victims of the 1647 plague outbreak are known to have been buried in the sands along the coast; tradition suggests that York Place, close to the shore, was one of the main areas of burial. Interment of victims away from centres of habitation was not uncommon as such areas not only provided space for mass graves but also sequestered possible sources of infection away from the living. Three burial mounds south of St Catherine's Hill to the east of the city of Winchester mark the location of plague pits from the 1666 outbreak (Walker and Farwell 2000: 3). In later centuries, the development of fever hospitals meant that many of the victims of subsequent epidemics, such as the 1832 cholera outbreak, were interred within burial grounds attached to hospitals (Morris 1976: 105). It seems likely that some of the occupants of the twelve graves from the burial ground at the fever hospital in Clonmel, County Tipperary died in one of the many epidemics which swept across Ireland during the nineteenth century (Mary Henry Archaeological Services Ltd 2000: 5). Epidemic disease is also one of the possible explanations for a cluster of inhumations found in the burial ground of the Royal London Hospital, which comprised of several rows of stacked coffins that appear to have been placed on the contemporary ground surface and then covered in rubble (Vuolteenaho et al. 2008: 26).

Usually the problems caused by high levels of mortality were faced when they arose, but occasionally contingency plans were made. Recurrent outbreaks of plague combined with increasing pressure on burial space within the burgeoning metropolis resulted in the creation of London's New Churchyard in 1569 as the capital's administrators decided to prepare for the disease's next visitation, and create space for the overflow from the city's parish churchyards (Harding 2002: 93; Hunting 1991: 33).[3] Excavations of the cemetery have revealed a series of large pits, each containing between four and sixteen individuals (figure 5.5). These burial pits are thought to contain victims of the plague outbreaks of either 1593 or 1603.

Famine with its high mortality levels and disruption of social cohesion has, like epidemic disease, the potential to overwhelm existing burial provision. The famine in Ireland in the 1840s resulted in large scale depopulation of the Irish countryside due to a combination of starvation, epidemics such as typhus that had a devastating impact on the weakened survivors, and emigration. Excavations at McDonagh Station uncovered the burial ground of the Kilkenny workhouse which contained 64 3x3 metre burial pits containing the remains of approximately 900 individuals interred at the height of the great famine 1845–1850 (J. Geber *pers. comm.*). The excavated remains include approximately equal numbers of male and female adults but between 60 and 70% of the inhumations are children. The burials are properly laid out mostly in coffins, and a few accompanied with rosary beads. The pits appear to date to the famine period when people close to death chose to enter the workhouse to secure a decent burial. The pits are thoughts to have been used one at a time with each pit remaining open until filled. Such was the rate of mortality that the pits, each containing about fourteen bodies, would fill up at a rate of about one a week.

The Drowned

The sea is a treacherous place, and many lives have been lost in the waters surrounding Britain and Ireland over the centuries. For some the sea provided their final resting place. The disarticulated remains of at least 179 individuals from a crew of 415 were recovered during the excavation of the *Mary Rose*, which sank in Solent Waters in 1545 (Stirland 2005: 4, 76), while human remains have also been noted on a seventeenth-century wreck off Duart Point, Mull (Ponsford 1993: 223). Twelve wrecks in British waters are listed in the schedule of ships that are protected under the Protection of Military Remains Act (1986) because they are known or supposed to contain unrecovered bodies (Department for Transport, Receiver of Wreck 2011). All of these were lost during the twentieth century as a result of conflict, mostly the two world wars. Best known is probably the *Royal Oak*, sunk in Scapa Flow, Orkney in 1939 with the loss of 833 lives.

5 By choice, circumstance or compulsion: unusual burials in post-medieval Britain and Ireland

Figure 5.5   Collective burial, possibly a plague pit, from New Churchyard, London. This is one of a series of pits, each containing between 4 and 16 individuals, thought to be victims of the plague outbreaks in 1593 or 1603 (Photograph courtesy of the London Archaeological Archive and Research Centre).

The remains of others dying at sea were washed ashore in varying stages of decomposition. Prior to 1808 some, maybe most, drowning victims were interred outside consecrated ground, often on or close to the shore (Pollard 1999: 37). Evidence for this practice during the post-medieval period is provided by a group of eleven skeletons arranged in two pits in the sand dunes at Braigh, Aignish on the Isle of Lewis (figure 5.6) (McCullagh and McCormick 1991: 76). Nine of the eleven individuals were male; the sex of the other two was indeterminate, and all but two of them were in their late teens or twenties (Lorimer 1991: 77). Coins found with one of the burials suggest an early eighteenth century date for the interments. The demographic composition, predominately male, argues against these being victims of epidemic disease or famine and conflict seems an unlikely explanation (McCullagh and McCormick 1991: 86). Shipwrecks were common in this area and this offers the most probable explanation for these burials. Moreover, the coins, which included Dutch, Irish and Austrian denominations, suggest that those interred within the grave could have been foreigners or at least well-travelled (McCullagh and McCormick 1991: 87).

Another example of the interment of drowned individuals away from consecrated ground was the discovery of four burials interred on the southern edge of Croyde Bay in Devon (Gent 1998: 1, 3). The bodies, laid out slightly overlapping each other within a single grave, seem to have been washed ashore and then moved from the beach to the nearby headland for immediate burial (Gent 1998: 3). Sandy deposits found around the lower legs are probably beach sand, originally trapped in the men's now decomposed boots. Buttons found with the burials indicate a sixteenth-century date and a possible Dutch origin for some of the individuals (Gent 1998: 1). Other possible drowning victims are three mid-eighteenth to mid-nineteenth-century burials interred in a rubbish pit on the island of Flat Holm in the Bristol Channel (Coles 1986: 3). The bodies were partially disarticulated suggesting the remains were buried in a slightly decomposed condition. These bodies might have been washed ashore partially decomposed, or possibly to have been exhumed from elsewhere. Curiously, the lower left leg of the one of the burials had been sawn through, perhaps from an amputation, and then interred with the rest of the body (Coles 1986: 4). The rather disrespectful interment within a rubbish pit may be the result of having to rapidly dispose of bodies that were already decomposing (Coles 1986: 5). Isolated burials of adult males have been found among sand dunes between Hartlepool and Seaton Carew and also outside Portballintree, Co. Antrim (Waughman 1995; Ponsford 2000: 312). The presence of pipe facets in the teeth of the former burial suggests a post-medieval date while the latter has been radiocarbon dated to the late seventeenth or eighteenth century (Ponsford 2000: 312). The Portballintree burial was in a coffin, raising the possibility that other factors than drowning may have resulted in this individual being interred away from recognised burial grounds.

The practice of interring the drowned outside recognised burial grounds may reflect the urgent need to bury bodies that had decomposed due to prolonged periods of time in the water as appears to have been the case with the burials from Flat Holm (Pollard 1999: 39). However, it is also clear that some effort was made to arrange the bodies. At Braigh the dead were oriented with heads to north or south, against the usual pattern found in the nearby churchyard, but some care was taken to arrange the hands on top of the body, suggesting that the unusual orientation may have been a deliberate choice. The unusual place and nature of death of those lost at sea may have been a factor; perhaps they were perceived as being more dangerous. However, the exclusion of the drowned from the usual churchyards and burial grounds was not universal (Pollard 1999: 37). Unless the condition of the body necessitated rapid disposal, it was only the bodies of strangers that were buried along the shore while locals who drowned were interred in the parish churchyard. This is well illustrated at both Braigh and Croyde Bay where coins and buttons found with the bodies point may be indicative of the foreign origins of these individuals. In contrast, when those who died on board the *Royal George* in 1782 were washed ashore at Haslar their remains were interred in the cemetery belonging to the Naval Hospital, while those recovered from the shore at Portsmouth were buried within the town (Boston 2005b: 5).

This different treatment of outsiders drowned at sea may be linked to the territoriality of burial due to the parochial system. Those dwelling within a parish were automatically entitled to burial within its churchyard, unless excluded on grounds of excommunication, suicide or because they were not baptised (Harding 1998: 57).[4] Strangers dying within the parish had no such entitlement. In practice, many strangers were buried within community burial grounds, particularly if somebody paid for the privilege, although they were often interred in less favoured parts of the churchyard. Even unknown individuals with no money, such as the traveller found dead in the parish of Woodchurch in Kent in 1616, were often accorded at least the minimum acceptable funerary rites at the expense of the parish (Gittings 1984: 61). Others were less fortunate. Eight burials excavated in the garden of a riverside house at One Gun, Dartmouth, Devon had been interred well away from the local graveyard (Freeman 1985: 132). All but one of the burials had been

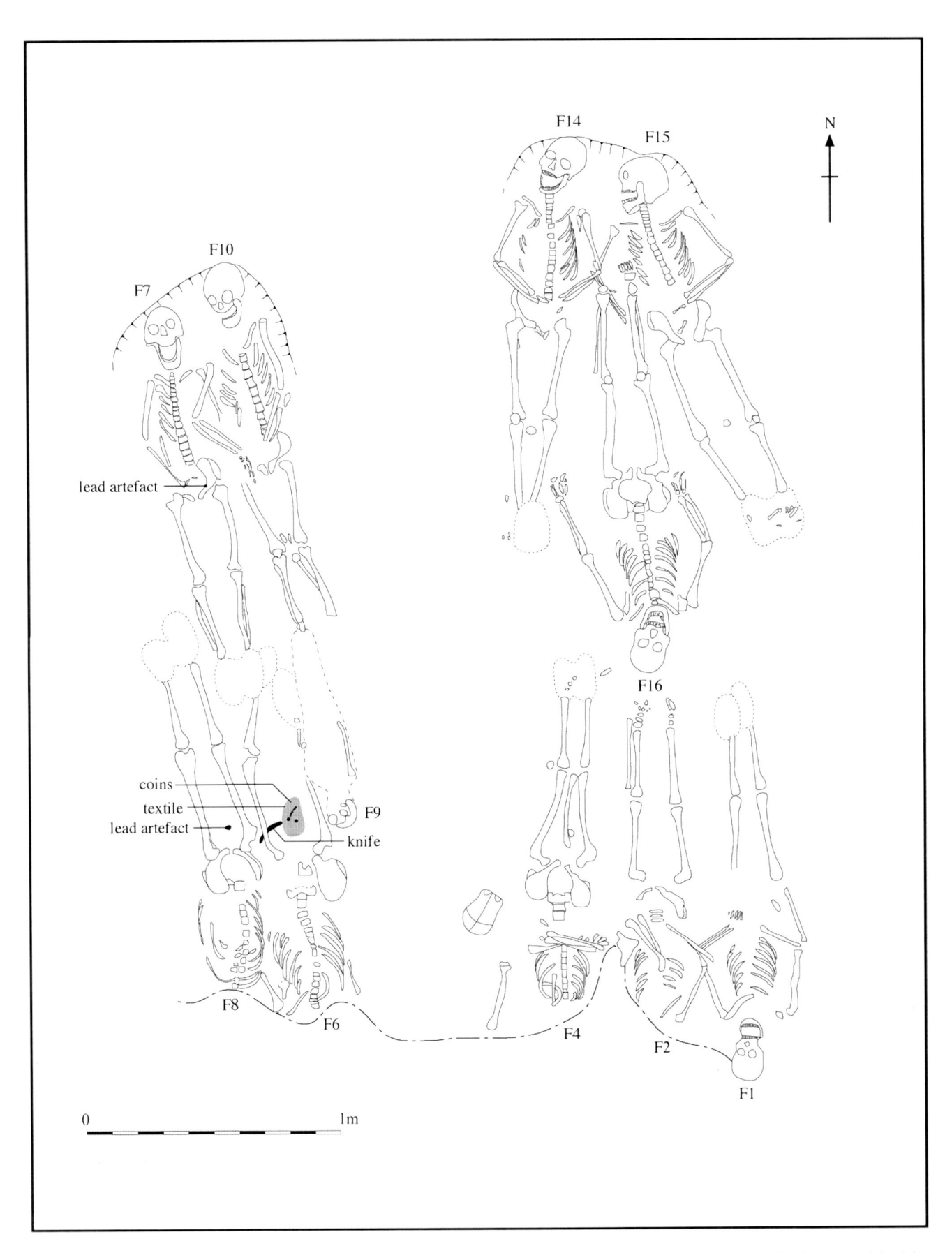

5 By choice, circumstance or compulsion: unusual burials in post-medieval Britain and Ireland

Figure 5.6 The burial of drowned bodies close to the shore at Braigh, Aignish on the Isle of Lewis. These burials differ from normal burials not only in their location, far outside the parish graveyard, but also in their lack of west-east orientation, in the deposition of two or three bodies in each grave and because the bodies were not prepared for burial in any way. They seem to have been wearing the clothes in which they died, including coins and other small objects in their pockets (Plan drawn by Debbie Miles-Williams from McCullagh and McCormick 1991).

interred in wooden coffins. The nature of the burials and artefacts from the grave fills suggest a post-medieval date (Freeman 1985: 133). The house where these burials were found was once called One Gun Cottage. Notes in the parish registers of the nearby St Petrox Church record two occasions when Frenchmen were buried at "One Gunn" during the seventeenth century: one from a ship from the West Indies and the other from a "banker"[5]. This suggests that One Gun was an area used for the burial of foreigners dying on the ships in the port; although it is possible drowning victims were also interred here. The intercutting of several of the graves suggests the occasional use of the site over a period of time. Interestingly, the use of coffins does seem to indicate some care was taken in interring these individuals, even though they were interred away from consecrated ground and mostly orientated with their heads to the south or south-west, as at Braigh. That unusual orientation suggests that that stranger burials were not just differently located but also seen as needing different treatment.

During the post-medieval period parochial ties were loosened. The foundation of non-parochial burial grounds and cemeteries offered alternative burial locations and increasing urbanisation broke down parish communities resulting in an erosion of the distinction between those belonging to the community and those deemed to be strangers (Harding 1998: 62). The sixteenth-century burials at Croyde Bay and the early eighteenth-century mass grave at Braigh date from a period when outsiders, whether drowned or nor, were more likely to be excluded from the parochial burial grounds. By the end of the eighteenth century these attitudes towards the burial of strangers had relaxed, with the majority of dead interred in some form of community burial ground. This not only reflected changing burial practices, but was in line with the shift towards the acknowledgement of 'humanitarian' common feeling (Laqueuer 1989a). Newspaper reports of the inquest into shipwrecks off the coast at Happisburgh in 1791 noted the coroner's determination to

"…enforce a Christian burial of those dead bodies that may unfortunately be washed on shore during storms on this coast, it having inhumanly been a common practice to bury them in holes near the beach without any ceremony being performed over them" (quoted in Halliday 1994:82).

This change in attitude was formalized in 1808, when all communities, rural and urban, in England were prohibited from excluding those dying at sea from the usual burial grounds by the Drowned Persons Act. The act required that those washed ashore, having died in the sea, should be given a Christian burial (48 Geo. 3 c. 75). The requirement was extended to bodies deposited on the shore from any navigable water in 1886 (19 and 20 Vic. c.20). The decomposed state of the bodies buried on the beach at Flat Holm in the eighteenth or nineteenth century suggests that their final resting place may have been determined as much by the condition of the bodies as their relationship to the local community. It is also possible that the differential burial of outsiders persisted to a much later date in smaller and more remote communities. In parts of rural Ireland the burial of strangers in cillíní alongside the unbaptised babies and suicides, was common in the nineteenth and even early twentieth centuries.

Illicit burial and accidental deaths

Some isolated burials may be the result of the illicit disposal of a body. Three Scottish post-medieval bog bodies, all adult males, are thought to be murder victims (Turner 1995: 117). The late seventeenth-century bodies from Quinfall Hill, Caithness and Arnish Moor, Lewis suffered blows to the head (Orr 1921: 213; Bennett 1975: 173; Turner 1995: 117), while the eighteenth- or early nineteenth-century body from Greenhead Moss, Lanarkshire had a cut through his cap that may have been caused by sword blow to the back of his head (Mann 1937: 47). Elsewhere, one possible interpretation of the prone north-south burial at Perth Carmelite Friary was that the individual had been murdered, thrown in a ditch and buried (Hall 1989: 106). A body, thought to date to the seventeenth century, thrown into the outer ring of a ringfort at Carrickmacross, County Monaghan could also be a murder victim, although the remains may be linked to the 1641–7 rising in Monaghan (Roycroft 2003: 5).

Other bodies may lie where they fell, having died as the result of accidents or environmental factors. The skeleton of one unfortunate individual was found below a fallen stone column in the chapter house at Rievaulx Abbey, Yorkshire (Coppack 2000: 129). After the dissolution, the buildings at Rievaulx were made unusable by pulling down the columns supporting vaults. The skeleton could have been one of those involved in this process. Sometimes an individual who met an accidental death was buried close to where he or she was found. A fully clothed late seventeenth-century male bog body from Gunnister, Shetland was found buried in a shallow grave (Henshall and Maxwell 1952: 30). This individual was interred with a number of items including a stick, two lengths of woollen cord, and a purse with a number of coins (Henshall and Maxwell 1952: 31): the sort of equipment carried by a traveller. The individual was dressed for cold weather with a long coat and a jacket as well as knitted gloves and two caps, one on his head and the other in his pocket (Henshall and Maxwell 1952: 30, 36). It has been suggested that this individual died of exposure in the winter and was later buried where he died (Henshall and Maxwell 1952: 41). A late sixteenth- or early seventeenth-century isolated burial from a Roman villa near Old Alresford in Hampshire might be the result of similar circumstances (Fitzpatrick and Laidlaw 2001). The adult male was interred in a small shallow grave orientated approximately south-west to north-east (figure 5.7) (Fitzpatrick and Laidlaw 2001: 222). The lace tags which accompanied the burial indicate that the body was at least partially clothed, which was not usual in a period of shrouded burials; neither was the presence of nine coins, presumably in a container at this individual's left hip (Fitzpatrick and Laidlaw 2001: 227). The location and nature of the grave is suggestive of rapid burial. The coins may rule out casual highway violence as the victim was not robbed. It is possible that this individual died close to where he was buried, perhaps from exposure, accident or disease and the condition of the body made rapid interment a necessity. Alternatively the body might have been deliberately concealed following a murder.

Unusual burial by compulsion

So far this chapter has focused on those accorded atypical mortuary rites due to choice or circumstance, but the denial of a "decent burial" was a powerful punitive measure in a society where the treatment of the dead body impacted the social standing of the bereaved and the regard in which the deceased was held. Inappropriate burial continued punishment beyond death for those guilty of transgressing certain ecclesiastical and secular laws.

Suicides

During much of the post-medieval period great emphasis was placed on a good death, one prepared for and faced with calmness and fortitude. A bad death was to be avoided at all costs and could lead to

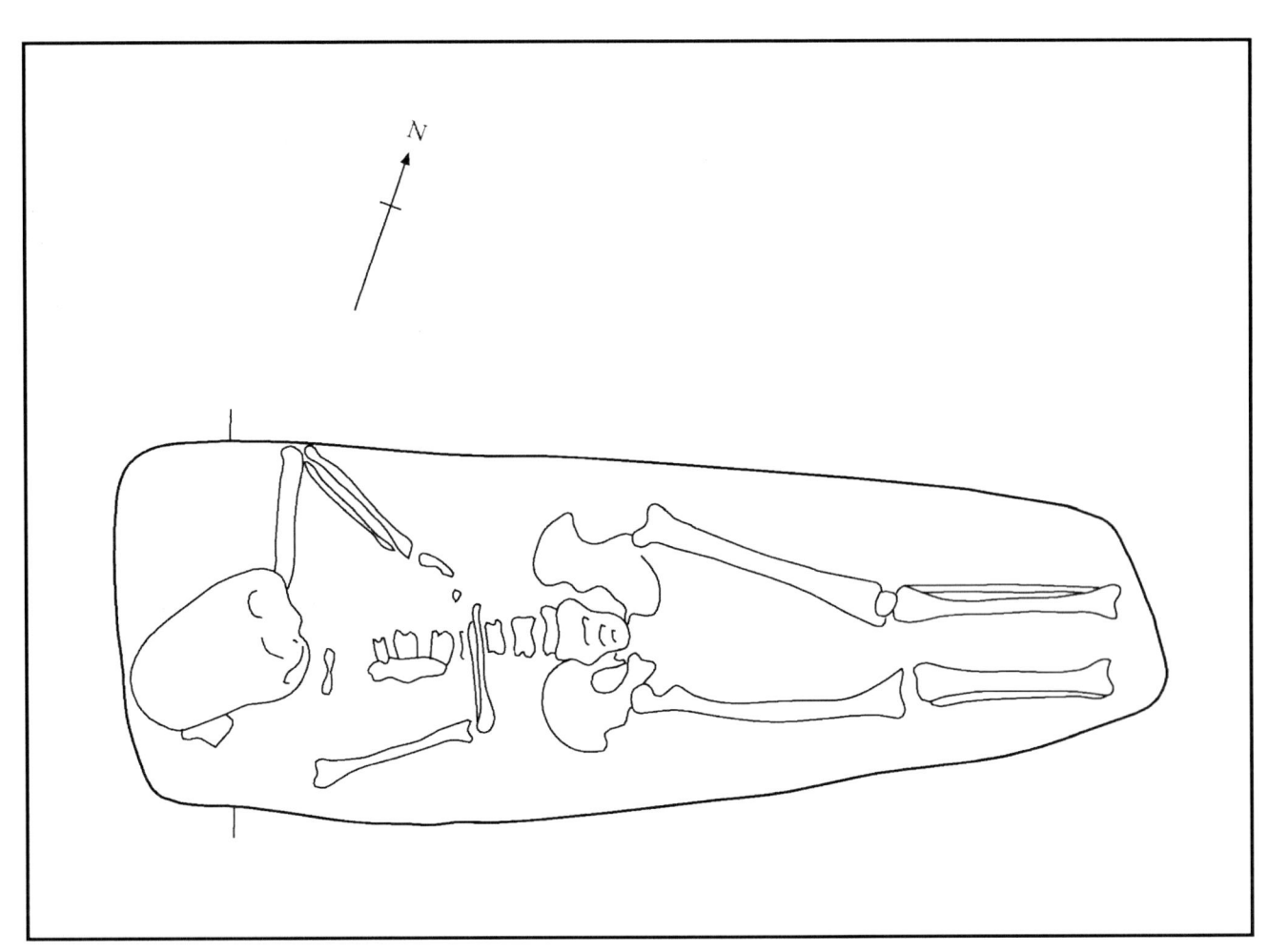

Figure 5.7 Plan of the isolated burial of an adult male from Alresford in Hampshire. Lace tags suggest that this man was buried in his normal clothes. That he was not robbed of the 9 coins in his pocket or purse makes it unlikely that he was the victim of casual highway crime. He might have died of exposure and been buried close to the place he was found (Plan drawn by Debbie Miles-Williams adapted from Fitzpatrick and Laidlaw 2001).

interment away from recognised burial grounds. Suicide was the very antithesis of a good death. It was considered a type of murder (*felo de se*)[6], a felony in the eyes of the state and an unforgivable sin in the eyes of the church (McDonald 1986: 53). Suicides were denied Christian burial rites. In their place, a profane parody of usual funerary practices was enacted, with the body interred in highways or at crossroads with a stake through the heart (McDonald and Murphy 1990: 15; Halliday 1997). The origins of the rituals governing the treatment of the corpse of suicides are obscure. Anglo-Saxon law codes prohibited the use of Christian rites when interring anyone who had taken their own life (Murray 2000: 264–5), and this is reiterated in a rubric inserted into the *Book of Common Prayer* in 1661 (Procter and Frere 1951: 636).[7] Yet, there is nothing in ecclesiastical legislation that specifies where or how the body should be interred (McDonald and Murphy 1990: 20). The rites for the desecration of the corpses of suicides seem to have developed during the medieval period from a combination of demotic customs and beliefs (McDonald and Murphy 1990: 18). Some elements of the treatment sometimes accorded to suicides, such as prone burial and north-south orientated graves, inverted the usual Christian burial practices (McDonald and Murphy 1990: 44). Other elements, including the distinctive practice of interring suicides in a grave on the highway or at a crossroads with a stake through the heart, may have their origins in folk beliefs. The spirits of suicides were considered to be restless and dangerous, coming back as ghosts and revenants (MacDonald 1986: 54; MacDonald and Murphy 1990: 46–7). The stake anchored the ghost within the grave preventing it from wandering. In addition, should the soul escape the confines of the grave, interment at a crossroads was thought to confuse the spirit and prevent it from finding its way home (Brown 1966: 123). The body of a suicide was also perceived to be a contaminant and interment in the highway or at a crossroad excluded the suicide from the community of the dead and prevented the corpse polluting recognised burial grounds (Gittings 1984: 73; MacDonald and Murphy 1990: 42, 47). The polluting effect of the body of a suicide may explain why the body of 20 year old Henry Apes, who hanged himself in 1665, was interred on the boundary of two parishes in Wiltshire impaled with two stakes, thus in essence removing the body from both parishes and echoing the liminal state of the suicide after death, so he belonged neither to the community of the living nor that of the dead (Rickard 1957: 8–9 in Reynolds 2009: 217).

Despite all the documentary evidence for the exclusion of the corpses of suicides from the usual burial grounds and their subsequent desecration, there is little evidence for this in the archaeological record for the post-medieval period. The lack of evidence may simply be the result of the bodies either not surviving or not being recognised. It has been suggested that the post-dissolution prone male burial aligned north-south in a ditch at Perth Carmelite Friary may have been a suicide (Gilchrist and Sloane 2005: 72; Hall 1989: 105–6). At least six post-medieval Irish bog bodies are known to be suicides (Ó Floinn 1995: 142). Water was considered to be an effective barrier to the dangerous undead during the medieval period (Caciola 1996: 30). It is possible this tradition persisted in the post-medieval period and watery places, like bogs, were used to contain the wandering spirits of those who took their own lives. Fear of wandering spirits may have determined the fate of an eighteenth-century woman poisoner from Aberystwyth who committed suicide (Halliday 1997: 6). The coroner had suggested burial at a crossroads with the requisite stake through the heart, yet such were the fears her spirit would join the ghosts tormenting a nearby village that burial on the beach was considered more appropriate. It is possible that a similar series of events lay behind the 100 to 200 year old burial of a woman of between 16 and 18 years found in a shallow grave in the intertidal zone on a beach at Fareham (Howard 1996).

It is unclear how frequently the bodies of suicides were given highway or crossroad burial or consigned to a watery grave. That it did happen is indisputable, but it was not inevitable. Suicides are known to have been simply interred in open fields (MacDonald and Murphy 1990: 48). It is possible that remains of two individuals from the seventeenth or eighteenth century buried on a hillside near to Dunraven hill fort in Glamorgan may be the bodies of a suicides (Sell 1980; 2000). It has been suggested that a group of eighteenth- and nineteenth-century burials lying in the ruined nave of the Priory's church outside the official burial area on the former site of St Oswald's Priory in Gloucester may include suicides (Heighway and Bryant 1999: 100). It is possible that those carrying out the burials of people who had been excluded from the official cemetery chose a location that was close to the official burial ground, and which had had a religious significance in the past. Similar motivation may have lain behind the careful eighteenth-century supine west/east burial of a male in his forties, found in a disused oven in Bowthorpe, Norfolk, which had been built in the remains of an earlier church (Ayers 2001: 96). Another example is provided by the interment of the 15 year old male found with an eighteenth-century copper button on his chest during the excavation of Capel Teilo, Kidwelly (Jones n.d.). The chapel, which appears to have gone out of use during the eighteenth century, was not used for burial and the youth found under a layer of mortar to the east to the church buildings was probably a suicide or drowning victim. The burial of suicides in locations with ecclesiastical associations might relate to the development of a more compassionate attitude to suicide from the end of the seventeenth century, as described by MacDonald and Murphy (1990).

As the harshness of post-Reformation attitudes began to soften, many suicides were interred within churchyards, often on the north side of the church (Anderson 1987: 270; MacDonald and Murphy 1990: 48). The north side of the church was viewed as a less auspicious location for burial, and was generally underused until the nineteenth century pressures on graveyard space. This means that anomalous burials to the north may be more observable in rural locations where there were fewer interments. At Llanddewi Fach Church, Monmouthshire, for example, excavations on the north side of the church found only a nineteenth-century charnel pit and two isolated burials in the extreme north of the graveyard (*Archaeology in Wales* 1999:141). Excavations of eighteenth- and nineteenth-century burials on the north side of St Bartholomew's, Penn, found an adult female, aged between 30 and 40 who was interred with her head to the east, against usual burial practice. She was buried without a coffin, and the partial skeleton of a neonate was found in her pelvic region (Boyle 2002: 29). The contrasting orientation and the location of the burial to the north of the church raise the question of suicide, although the possible unbaptised state of the child may also have been a factor. Certainly, pregnancy outside of marriage provided a powerful reason for women to end their lives prematurely at this date (Malcolmson 1977). The social pressures on women to hide illegitimate babies are also seen in the register of St Bartholomew's which records the abandonment of a newborn baby at the church in 1750 (Boyle 2002: 35).

Central to the treatment of a suicide's corpse was their state of mind. Suicide was only seen as a felony if the individual was considered sane (MacDonald and Murphy 1990: 15). Furthermore attitudes towards suicide changed over time. Few deaths were ruled *felo de se* (self-murderers) prior to 1500 (Daniell 1998: 105). Instead many suicides were ruled to be accidental or the result of mental infirmity (Daniell 1998: 106). Religious, legal and governmental changes during the Tudor period led to a much stricter enforcement of the laws concerning suicide and the subsequent exclusion of their bodies from consecrated ground (MacDonald 1986: 57; MacDonald and Murphy 1990: 24). During the period following the Restoration a more sympathetic attitude emerged, and coroner's juries increasingly returning a verdict of *non compos mentis* in cases of suicide (MacDonald 1986: 58, 60). This allowed suicides to be interred within community burial grounds, albeit often on the unfavourable north side of the church (MacDonald and Murphy 1990: 213). As such, it seems likely that many later post-medieval suicides lie within churchyards and cemeteries indistinguishable from those who died of natural causes. Indeed, it was a combination of surviving coffin plates, osteological evidence and documentary sources that allowed the identification of two confirmed archaeological examples of suicides interred within recognised burial grounds. Both skeletons exhibited suspicious bullet wounds, one to the skull and the other through the mouth (Bowman *et al.* 1992: 92; Cox *et al.* 1990: 576), which were suggestive of suicide. This was confirmed by the identification of the individuals from coffin plates and location of additional evidence from documentary sources. Both individuals had committed suicide but been ruled *non compos mentis* by the coroner (Cox *et al.* 1990: 575; Bowman *et al.* 1992: 94) and both had been buried within a church. One individual was interred under the middle aisle of St Bride's Church London in 1821 and the other in the family vault at Christ Church Spitalfields, London in 1852 (Cox *et al.* 1990: 573; Bowman *et al.* 1992: 91).

The earlier of these two suicides is significant because it predates the Suicide Act of 1823 by two years. The Suicide Act prohibited the burials of suicides at crossroads with a stake through the heart and allowed their burial within churchyards, but only at night between nine and midnight (Anderson 1987: 270). The burial suggests that to some extent, this law only codified what was already happening. Indeed, by the early nineteenth century suicides were almost always determined to be *non compos mentis* and were interred in the usual burial grounds (MacDonald and Murphy 1990). However, the individual interred at St Bride's Church also demonstrates that before or after the Suicide Act, the wealthy were more able to circumvent traditional customs in order to bury a suicide according to regular procedures. There were exceptions to society's increasing leniency towards suicides. Verdicts of *felo de se* were still returned for those who killed themselves to escape punishment for crimes or were guilty of transgressions of acceptable behaviour (MacDonald 1986: 92–93; MacDonald and Murphy 1990: 136). Their corpses continued to be excluded from community burial grounds, and to be interred in the highway or at crossroads with a stake through them. It was as if having escaped the gallows, the state needed to control the condemned's interment (Gatrell 1994: 84). In 1812 following his suicide, the body of the murderer John Williams, still wearing a leg iron and surrounded by the bloody implements used in the murders, was drawn on a carriage past the homes of his victims and then deposited in a pit at a crossroads with a stake through his body (figure 5.8) (*The Times* 1st January 1812, p.4). Williams's body was

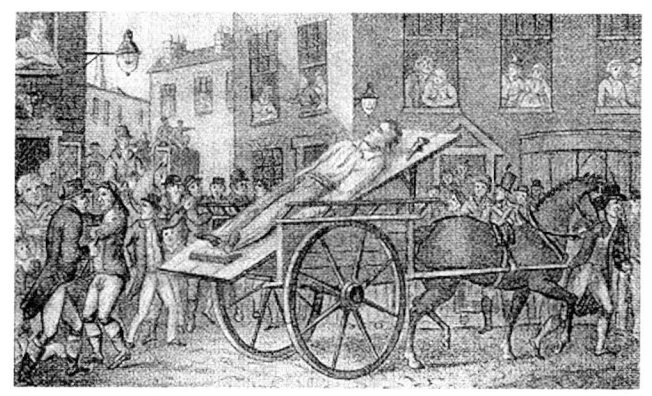

Figure 5.8 The body of murderer/suicide of John Williams being drawn though London's Streets prior to his burial at a crossroads. His body was buried, as was customary with suicides, with a stake through it at Cannon Street crossroads. Both crossroads burial and staking might originate as folk practices designed to prevent those who had died a 'bad death' from troubling the living. (Newgate Calendar)

accompanied by between 250 and 300 constables, many with drawn cutlasses and watched by the public, with the spectacle of a hanging being replaced by the display and desecration of the suicide's body. The passing of the Suicide Act in 1823 put an end to crossroad burials and staking of the bodies of suicides, instead requiring suicides to be interred in community churchyards and burial grounds (1823 4 Geo. 4 cap 52). However, the Suicide Act did not mean that suicides were treated the same as other interments, and it wasn't until the Interments (Felo de se) Act of 1882 that suicides could be buried outside the night time hours between nine and midnight (Anderson 1987: 275).

The excommunicated

Excommunication was the ecclesiastical court's ultimate punishment (Gittings 1984: 76). If rigorously enforced, excommunication led to an individual's exclusion from Christian society – a severe penalty given the importance of the church in late medieval and early modern society (Daniell 1997: 26). Excommunication was increasingly used in the aftermath of the Reformation, perhaps as a means of social control in turbulent times (Houlbrooke 1998: 335). During the early modern period, an individual could be excommunicated for a variety of offences, some serious, others trivial (Cressy 2000: 117). During 1635, parishioners at Walsall were excommunicated for laughing, talking or wearing hats in church, digging ditches on St Mark's Day and not attending services. In theory, those excommunicated were denied Christian burial and excluded from burial within the churchyard (Gittings 1984: 76). The *Hereford Journal* of 19th June 1783 records that a skeleton was discovered in 1783 in a paddock near Grantham, under a stone inscribed 'Here lies the body of Zacharias Laxton, deceased the 27th of August, 1667, being for his excommunication denied the usual place of burial' (Simpson and Roud 2000: 38). In other cases, the excommunicant was interred just outside the churchyard boundary. In 1619, Isabel Keames of Albrighton, Shropshire was buried in the hall orchard near to the church wall (Gittings 1984: 76). In some cases, the families of those denied churchyard burial may have sought burial locations that once had religious significance. Documentary sources mention the burial of excommunicants among the ruins of dissolved monastic houses (Hardy, Dodd and Keevill 2003: 519). Three burials from Eynsham Abbey in Oxfordshire were interred after the dissolution of the monastic house and probably constitute the graves of individuals excommunicated for Catholic recusancy. Not all excommunicants were denied churchyard burial. Some clergy allowed the burial of excommunicants on consecrated ground, provided it was at night, while some bishops would grant faculties allowing their interment within a churchyard, although this was often an expensive process (Gittings 1984: 77; Cressy 2000: 120). There is also evidence for the clandestine burial of excommunicants on consecrated ground. One of the more spectacular examples involved the burial of Mrs Horseman in the parish church at Horton in Oxfordshire in 1631 after the failure of an application for a faculty (Cressy 2000: 116, 121). The church's parish clerk arrived early one morning to find that during the night the doors had been unbarred, a grave dug and refilled in the chancel and a communion table placed on top.

The Unbaptised

In medieval society, baptism marked an individual's entry into Christian society and was considered necessary to remove the taint of original sin (Daniell 1998: 127; Coster 2000: 268). Those dying before baptism were condemned to eternal torment. By the later medieval period, this view was increasingly modified by consigning the unbaptised to Limbo rather than Hell. During the early modern period, the fate of the soul of the unbaptised remained a subject of debate (Fulke 1581: 44–52; Page 1637: 72), while the conventions governing the burial of the unbaptised are far from clear. An oath sworn by many seventeenth-century midwives required that those babies born stillborn were to be buried in "a secret place" (Gittings 1984: 83). Yet the burials of twenty-nine stillborn and unbaptised children; seven in the church, fourteen in the cellar under the church and eight in the churchyard, were recorded in the parish records of All Hallows, Honey Lane in London between 1600 and 1654 (Harding 1989: 122–3). The position of the Church itself was ambiguous; individual ministers were often left to decide whether to inter the unbaptised in consecrated ground (Cressy 1997: 114). The situation was further complicated by changes in theology in the aftermath of the Reformation resulting in the removal of Limbo, a territory in the late medieval Catholic Hell where unbaptised infants, and those non-Christians who had not been exposed to Christ's teachings for cultural or chronological reasons could pass their afterlives (Coster 2000: 270).

Every effort was made to ensure that the newborn was baptised to the extent of allowing lay baptism by midwives if the child was unlikely to survive long enough for a church baptism (Cressy 1997: 115). The sixteenth-century baptism register from St Michael le Belfry in York contains many references to baptism at home by the midwife (Berry and Schofield 1971: 462; n.21). This meant that the number of individuals dying unbaptised in the early modern period is likely to have been relatively small. For example, only five infants are recorded as dying unbaptised during an eleven year period at St Michael le Belfry (Berry and Schofield 1971: 462). As such, it is perhaps not surprising that there are few definite archaeological examples of infants interred away from consecrated ground. The graves of four infants were found at the Franciscan Priory of Lanercost in Cumberland (Whitworth 1998: 135). Three of the burials were cut through a layer of sandstone rubble, the result of the demolition or stripping after the dissolution of the priory. The size of the bones suggests the infants were either stillborn or newborn (Whitworth 1998: 136). These may have been the bodies of babies who were unbaptised and excluded from the consecrated ground, and were buried instead in a place which once had religious significance. That the burials were made with care is indicated by the associated evidence for individual interment within coffins. A small copper alloy pin, of a type commonly used to fasten shrouds and clothing after 1600 was also found (Whitworth 1998). Burial also continued at the Carmelite Friary in Aberdeen after the dissolution and destruction of the buildings and many of these later burials were children (Stone 1989: 42–43).

The fate of the souls of the unbaptised continued to be a subject of debate during the eighteenth and nineteenth centuries (Warden 1724; Verax 1748; *Hampshire Telegraph and Sussex Chronicle* August 4th 1849; *Birmingham Daily Post* May 8th 1873, p.8). It is difficult to determine to what extent the unbaptised were routinely excluded from normal burial grounds. There is certainly some evidence for their burial within churches and churchyards. A stillborn child was interred in the vault below Christ Church, Spitalfields in 1754 (Cox M. 1998: 118). The child, Master Chauvet, had no Christian name and may not have been baptised as there is no entry in the church's baptism register (Molleson and Cox 1993: 197; Cox M. 1998: 118). Elsewhere, a coffin at the Methodist burial ground at Carver Street in Sheffield contained the skeleton of female holding a neonate and there are six examples of infants buried with adults at St Martin's-in-the-Bull Ring, Birmingham (figure 5.9) (McIntyre and Willmott 2003: 26; Buteux and Cherrington 2006: 27). These burials may represent mothers and infants who died in childbirth, although the commonly reported practice of slipping the burial of an infant in with the next adult burial could also account for some of these double burials. In either

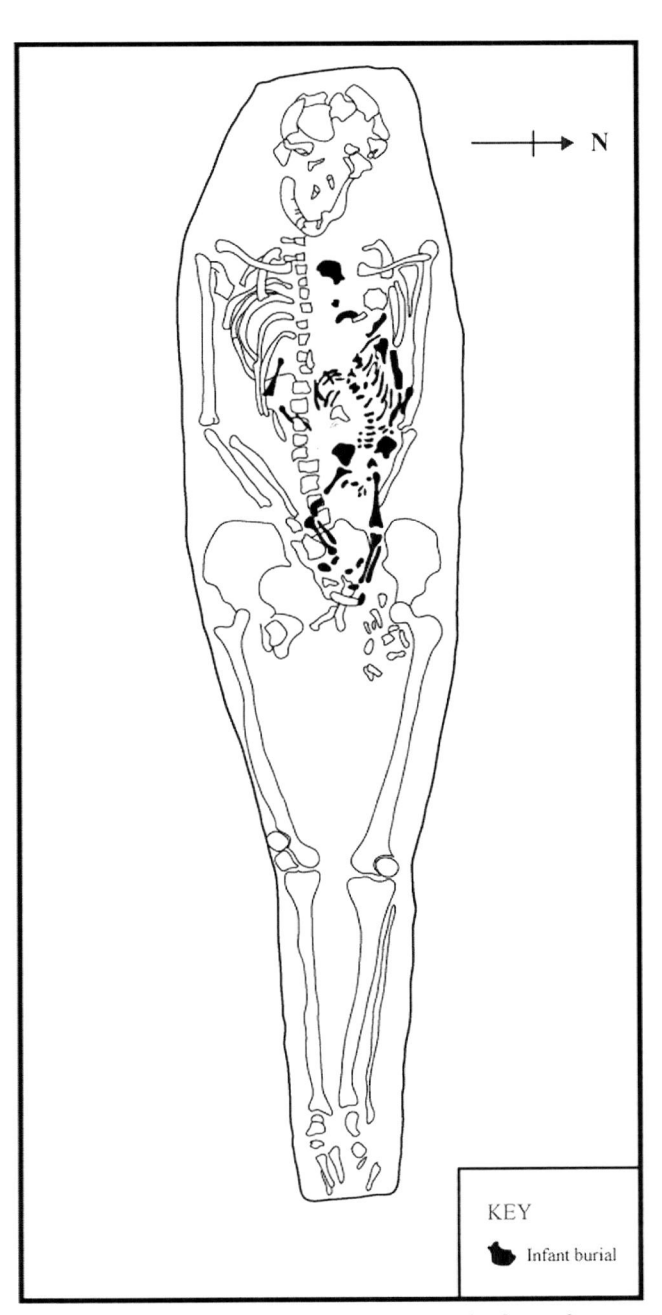

Figure 5.9 Burial of mother and neonate from the Carver Street Methodist Chapel, Sheffield (Debbie Miles-William adapted from McIntyre and Willmott 2003).

case it seems unlikely these infants would have survived long enough to be baptised, especially not if it required the attentions of a cleric. Thus it seems likely that, as in the early modern period, most of the unbaptised were interred within churchyards. There nevertheless appear to have been some exceptions: a group of eighteenth- and nineteenth-century burials lie within the ruined nave of St Oswald's Priory in Gloucester (Heighway and Bryant 1999: 100), outside the official area of the adjacent burial ground and the infants among this group may have been unbaptised. This is echoed at Jedburgh where the graveyard to the north of the abbey remained in use as the parish burial ground after the dissolution, while the area of the monastic cemetery appears to have been used to inter those excluded from the main graveyard (Lewis and Ewart 1995: 152). The isolated hillside grave of a two day old infant at Kiloran, Colonsay and Oransay, enclosed in a sub-rectangular wall may also represent an unbaptised child (Ponsford 2000: 326). Yet according to the inscription the child survived for two days after birth, sufficient time for baptism to have occurred and the unusual burial location may be the result of other factors. As in the early modern period, the attitudes of the local incumbent clergy would have been a key factor. One important difference compared with earlier periods was that the increasing numbers of non-conformist burial grounds as well as private and civic cemeteries were gradually eroding the Church of England's monopoly over burial location, offering those denied churchyard burial an acceptable alternative, at least in urban centres, and reducing the Anglican Church's ability to determine who was to be accorded a 'decent burial'. The advent of non-conformism had also created a new category of unbaptised individuals. Some dissenter groups such as the Baptists believed baptism should be delayed until a child had some understanding of the faith (Jupp 1997: 93). In areas lacking Baptist burial grounds if these children died before being baptised, they could be treated the same as unbaptised infants (Rugg 1998: 46; Stevens 2002: 332).

In contrast with mainland Britain, there has been a tradition of separate burial grounds for the unbaptised in Ireland, perhaps all of which had their origins in the post-medieval period (Finlay 2000: 408; Donnelly and Murphy 2008: 209). These burial grounds are known by a number of names – cillín, killen, callurgh and ceallúnach and often lie on marginal land or are associated with prehistoric monuments and abandoned ecclesiastical sites (figure 5.10) (Finlay 2000: 409). Sixty-one infant and two adult burials, dating to

Figure 5.10 Maamtrasna cillín, County Mayo. Both the commemorative cross and the fencing are recent introductions intended to demarcate the ground and provide a focus for remembrance. The elevated, rural location away from parish burial grounds is typical (Photograph courtesy of Ruthann O'Connor).

the nineteenth century, were recovered from a gravel bank near a series of enclosures and an early medieval burial ground at Johnstown in County Meath (Clarke 2002: 14–5), while a number of late cillín graves were found during the excavation of the early medieval settlement and cemetery at Reask in County Kerry (Fanning 1981: 74). Less common was the re-use of later secular buildings as at Castle Carra where fifteen infants and a child were buried within the remains of a tower house in County Antrim (Hurl and Murphy 1996). The use of former ecclesiastical sites, such as the abandoned church at Killalee in County Kerry, an early monastic enclosure at Caherlehillan, County Kerry and the monastic site at Inishcealtra, County Clare (de Paor 1972, 1973; Sheehan 1993, 1995, 1998, 2002; Dennehy and Lynch 2001: 22; Donnelly and Murphy 2008: 202), as cilliní may have provided a religious component to the burial of those excluded from consecrated ground (Finlay 2000: 411). At Kirk Field, Portmuck, County Antrim, human remains were found near a site reputed to be the location of a medieval abbey. Although the cemetery was primarily medieval in date, it seems to have continued in use as a burial ground for unbaptised infants and the poor well into the post-medieval period (Hurl 2001). There are some interesting parallels between this practice and the burial of infants and children among the ruins on monastic houses destroyed during the Reformation in mainland England and Scotland discussed above. In addition, there is a group of infants and children[8] buried within and around the ruins of an earlier church at Tintagel, Cornwall (figure 5.11) (Nowakowski and Thomas 1992: 27). This area of the churchyard at Tintagel had ceased to be used routinely for burial after the medieval period and perhaps was reserved for only certain types of burials such as the unbaptised who benefited from the sanctity of the earlier church. Some of the burials at Tintagel are accompanied by lumps of quartz, common in Irish cilliní, and the site would certainly be identified as a cillín had it been located across the Irish Sea. This raises interesting questions about how widespread cilliní and similar sites actually were, particularly in Scotland, the west of England and in Wales. The skeletons of three or more infants were found to the southeast corner of Capel Teilo in Kidwelly (Jones n.d.). The chapel, which was never routinely used for burial, went out of use during the

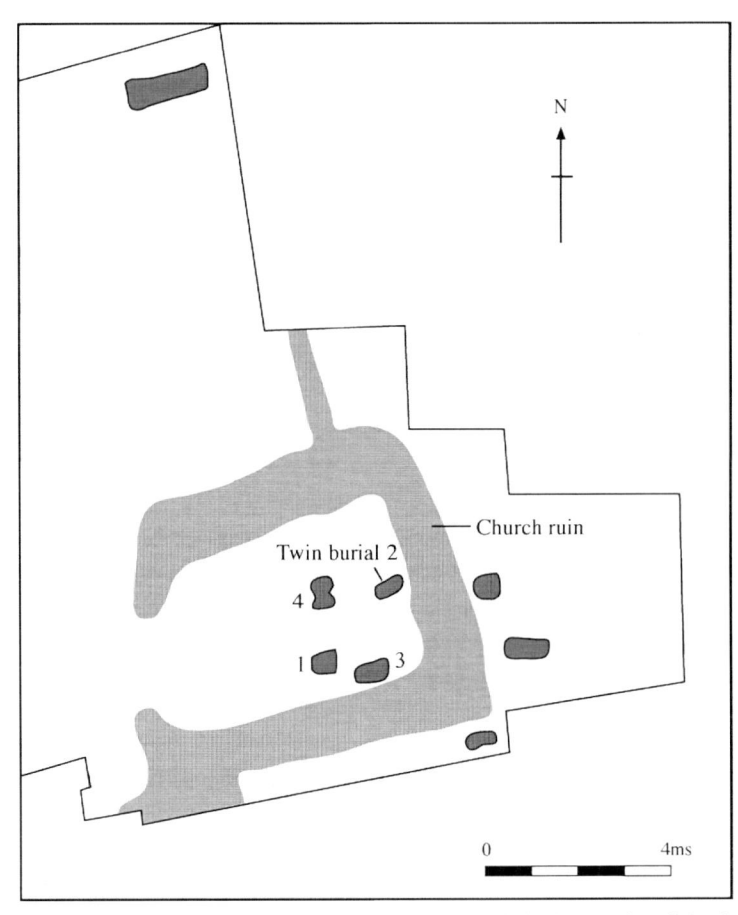

Figure 5.11 What appears to be a special cemetery for neonates and perhaps other liminal categories of the dead, at Tintagel in Cornwall. The tiny graves, dug in and around the ruins of the medieval church, are made as stone-lined cists or covered by two pieces of stone leaning against one another to make a 'tent'. Many features of these Tintagel burials including the ecclesiastical location, the preponderance of infant burials and the deposition of lumps of quartz with the burials, are associated with Irish cilliní (Plan drawn by Debbie Miles-Williams from Nowakowski and Thomas 1992).

eighteenth century and it is possible that these infants may have been unbaptised still-births or neonates. Recently McCabe has tentatively identified more than 20 sites in the west of Scotland as infant burial grounds in the Irish style (McCabe 2010). Returning to Ireland, a similar explanation may lie behind the cluster of infant burials found in the chancel of St Peter's Church in Waterford (Hurley and McCutcheon 1997: 221). The church itself went out of use during the early modern period, but burial continued on the site into the nineteenth century (Hurley and McCutcheon 1997: 190) and the infant burials probably belong to the period after the church went out of use (Hurley and McCutcheon 1997: 221). It is also worth noting that cillini were not the sole preserve of unbaptised infants. Adult burials were found during excavations at Killalee Church Killarney in County Kerry and Johnstown, County Meath, and we know from historical sources that these liminal burial grounds were used to inter others of marginal status such as suicides, strangers, criminals, excommunicates and the victims of famine or epidemic disease (Dennehy and Lynch 2001: 23; Clarke 2002: 15; Donnelly and Murphy 2008: 191). In addition, there are occasional examples of churchyards dedicated to women and children. Thirty-three burials of women and children were excavated within and around the ruined church of St Ronan's on Iona, thought to date to c.1600–1800 AD (O'Sullivan 1994: 333, 358). The church was probably in ruins by the 1640s and was definitely abandoned by 1795 (O'Sullivan 1994: 334). Documentary sources indicate the area was used as a women's cemetery during the post-medieval period until the mid to late eighteenth century, but this example of a single sex cemetery in lay use is exceptional.

Criminals

Despite their sins during life, prisoners were usually accorded a Christian burial during the early modern period (Gittings 1984: 67), including the majority of those executed for their transgressions. Often their bodies were given to family or friends for burial. When Richard Bigg died in prison in Evelchurch, Somerset, his body was taken back to his home in the parish of Wellow for burial. Alternatively, the bodies of prisoners would be interred in the churchyard nearest to the prison in which they died. Many of the unclaimed bodies of those dying in Newgate Prison were interred in London's New Churchyard during the early modern period (Harding 2002: 96). There are documented examples of cemeteries just for executed felons such as the new burial ground at Ringswell in Heavitree, Exeter consecrated in 1558 (Lepine and Orme 2003: 13), but such burial grounds seem to have been rare and the majority of prisoners were interred in parish churchyards.

Others, particularly murderers, were less fortunate and were simply interred in pits by the gallows (Bellamy 1979: 207). Sixty-four burials, tentatively dated to the sixteenth to eighteenth centuries were excavated from the partially infilled moat around Oxford Castle (Norton 2006: 12). While some bodies appear to have been interred with care, there are a number of prone[9] and multiple burials, including three individuals in a single grave. One adolescent male appears to have been interred with his legs bound up behind him (figure 5.12). The Castle served as the county gaol and the burials are almost certainly the unclaimed bodies of those individuals executed on the nearby gallows. Given their lack of regular alignment, the variation in their body positions and the apparent absence of coffins, it seems probable that these burials represent the careless disposal of unclaimed bodies on wasteland close to the gallows. The easy disposal of unwanted bodies of criminals may also explain early modern burials found at a number of other sites. A group of burials found on Hangman's Hill in Newton Longville in Buckingham are thought to be seventeenth-century criminals interred close to the gallows (Buckingham SMR record – 0188100000). The two mid-fourteenth- to seventeenth-century burials found during the excavation of Huntingdon castle mound are thought to be associated with the gallows known to have stood there during the post-medieval period (Vincent and Mays 2009: 1). Excavations in Eyre Square, Galway, in the vicinity of the site of the seventeenth-century town gallows, have uncovered the remains of at least five individuals. These include two carelessly interred north-south burials, the skull of a third individual and the partially excavated remains of a further two individuals (Lofqvist 2004; Quinn 2007: 58, 60–1). All were adults: three male and two individuals of indeterminate sex. Radiocarbon dates from two of the burials lay between 1650–1750 AD± 35 years (Quinn 2007: 121). The proximity of the burials to the seventeenth-century gallows suggest they may be criminals buried close to where they were executed (Lofqvist 2004: 29). However, it should be noted that remains of at least another 37 individuals have been encountered in other areas of the square, some with evidence for blunt force cranial trauma and with one instance of two individuals interred in a pit with opposing orientations (Quinn 2007: 43, 103, 107, 112). For much of the seventeenth century Eyre Square was an open area outside the city's main gate, and it is possible that the area may have been used to inter not only those dying on the gallows, but plague victims, fatalities of sieges during the Cromwellian and Williamite

Figure 5.12 Early modern burials from the filled-in moat of Oxford castle. Both of these burials are prone and neither was coffined. The angle of the arm of the burial on the left suggests that he was dumped rather than laid carefully in the grave. The burial on the right is that of a youth of about 15 years whose legs were drawn up – possibly bound – behind him. These are almost certainly the bodies of executed criminals (Photograph courtesy of Oxford Archaeology).

periods and, given the two infant burials recovered, the unbaptised (Quinn 2007: 14, 24, 90, 121). Six badly disturbed skeletons[10] were found on the south side of the castle mound at Norwich (Popescu 2009: 778). The bodies, all male, had been interred together arranged in three layers, each of two bodies placed side by side. Pins found in association with the bodies suggest they may have been interred in shrouds. The bodies, dated to the mid-seventeenth century, are thought to have been prisoners within the castle. Documentary evidence suggests that those executed at the castle were usually removed for burial (Popescu 2009: 900). Given these individuals were interred simultaneously; it is possible that they were victims of an epidemic within the gaol population (Popescu 2009:904). Alternatively the bodies may possibly be linked to riots during the Civil War that resulted in a number of individuals being executed within the castle (Popescu 2009: 900). Launceston Castle in Cornwall was also used as a prison and sixteen graves have been uncovered irregularly placed across the south-west bailey (Saunders 2006: 161). The burials are thought to date from the seventeenth and early eighteenth centuries and are probably individuals hanged within the bailey. Fourteen of the burials were male, one female and one of indeterminate sex (Mays and Keepax 2006: 431).

For those sentenced to death for witchcraft in England, death was usually by hanging and the disposal of the corpse in many ways comparable to other victims of the gallows (Gaskill 2005: 173). The bodies of witches were often buried in pits by the gallows, although they might be interred in prison burial grounds or in local churchyards on the north side (Gaskill 2005: 162). However unlike most other criminals, concerns about malevolent wandering spirits led in some instances to attempts to weigh down the body with stones, or to fix them to the ground with stakes. Occasionally the actions of the witch might be construed as treason for which the punishment for a woman was burning. The convicted witch Mary Lakeland was condemned to a traitor's death for the murder of her husband and burnt at the stake in 1645 at Ipswich (Gaskill 2005: 174–6). The situation in Scotland was slightly different: there, all those condemned to death for witchcraft were burnt at the stake.

During the early modern period, the one group of criminals specifically denied a Christian burial were those guilty of treason. The traditional punishment for treason was hanging, drawing and quartering for men. Women were burned because the exposure of the naked body necessary for partitioning the body was not considered acceptable for women (Gatrell 1994: 315–6). This particularly cruel and bloody punishment was designed to provide a grim reminder of the power of the state and the fate of those who betrayed the government. The body was often perceived as the source of criminal behaviour and vengeance was exacted by punishing the flesh (Porter 1991: 88). Unless the monarch granted an individual 'a nobleman's death' by beheading, traitors were initially hanged (Bellamy 1979: 202). In theory the individual should still be alive when removed from the gallows but this could depend on the attitudes of the government, sheriff and crowd (Bellamy 1979: 203). The body was then disembowelled and the heart removed, and the entrails burnt in a fire. During the medieval period treasonous thoughts were thought to have arisen in the body and these were purged by burning the entrails – a practice which persisted into the early modern period. The propaganda value of a traitor's execution did not end with their grisly death. Unlike the majority of the condemned, the interment of the bodies of most traitors occurred long after their death if it happened at all. The disembowelled body was cut into quarters and along with the head taken away to be parboiled and tarred (Owens 2005: 172). The remains were then displayed as a warning to others with parts of the body set on spikes throughout the city, often at gates or locations where the treason had occurred or gained support, as a warning to all (figure 5.13) (Bellamy 1979: 207–8; Richardson 1987: 34).[11] In 1606, eight members of the Gunpowder Plot conspiracy were hung drawn and quartered (Fraser 1996: 229–234), and parts of their bodies were exhibited in Westminster and London (Parliamentary archives 2009).

Heads and quarters often were mounted on city walls and gates. Eleven skulls, thirteen mandibles and eighteen neck vertebrae were found in a pit just outside the city walls in the Temple Bar area of Dublin (Simpson 1999: 3). Many of the bones exhibited wounds from sharp implements consistent with beheading. The heads were probably displayed on the city walls or at Dublin Castle prior to their disposal (Simpson 1999: 2). Similar origins have been suggested for the six post-medieval skulls found during the excavation of Galway's town walls (Walsh 2004: 22). The display of fragmented remains of executed traitors did not always occur. Those granted the privilege of being beheaded as opposed to hanged were usually placed in a coffin although the head might be retained for display (Bellamy 1979: 207). When Sir Thomas More was executed for treason in 1535, he was beheaded and his head was then mounted on a spike on London Bridge (Ackroyd 1998: 395). The rest of the corpse was interred in the church of St Peter ad Vincula within the Tower. At some point the head was recovered, encased in a lead box and eventually placed on his daughter Margaret Roper's coffin in the Roper Chantry in St Dunstan's Church, Canterbury (Tatton-Brown 1980: 238). The lead box containing the skull was later placed in a niche in the wall of the vault below the chantry (figure 5.14 shows a, perhaps rather fanciful, nineteenth-century depiction of the head) (Tatton-Brown 1980: 232). In contrast, when Oliver Plunkett, the archbishop of

Figure 5.13 A sixteenth-century image showing the display of severed heads above the gates of Dublin Castle (from Derricke 1581).

Figure 5.14 Thomas More's head. After More's execution and the brief public display of his head, it was taken by his daughter Margaret Roper and eventually deposited in a special niche in the Roper vault at St Dunstan's Church, Canterbury. This illustration is from the Gentleman's Magazine 7 (1837): 496.

Armagh, was executed for high treason at Tyburn in London in 1681, the body was hanged, drawn and quartered with the body parts being consigned to a fire (Kilfeather 2002: 230). The decapitated head, however, was rescued from the fire, which appears to have only caused limited damage to the rest of the body as the remains were examined by a surgeon after being burnt. The head and severed arms were kept for some time above ground in tin boxes while the rest of the body was buried, before all the remains were sent to Germany. The head was returned to Ireland during the eighteenth century and placed on display as a holy relic at St Peter's, Drogheda in 1921 (Kilfeather 2002: 229, 232) where it remains. The rest of the body was returned to Downside Abbey near Bath.

Even those posthumously convicted of treason could be denied a resting place in consecrated ground. When the monarchy was restored in 1660, Oliver Cromwell and the others involved in killing Charles I were convicted of high treason (Pearson and Morant 1935: 40). The body of Oliver Cromwell, who died in 1658, was exhumed, hanged and then decapitated (Pearson and Morant 1935: 43–44). His body was buried in a pit close to the gallows and his head mounted on the south-east end of Westminster Hall (Pearson and Morant 1935: 45–46).

Sentences of death by burning for women could be commuted to beheading (Bellamy 1979: 207). Traitors Anne Boleyn and Lady Jane Grey were sentenced to death by burning or beheading, and in both cases beheading was chosen. Burning was also the punishment for unrepentant heretics. This left little of the body for burial, yet these remains appear to have been collected, at least in some cases. When John Rogers was burnt in London some of the crowd collected his ashes and bones (Whitting 1998: 124), although whether this was for burial or retention as mementos is unclear.

From 1751, murderers were also denied Christian burial by the Act for the Better Preventing the Horrid Crime of Murder, better known as the Murder Act, which states that "in no case whatsoever the body of any murderer shall be suffered to be buried" unless first dissected (25 Geo. 2. CAP XXXVII: V). By the mid-eighteenth century, the death sentence was increasingly passed for relatively minor crimes so that it was felt an additional punishment was required to distinguish particularly serious crimes such as murder.

The practice of dissecting the corpses of murderers was already well established by 1751. An act of 1540 had granted the United Companies of Barbers and Surgeons the bodies of four executed criminals a year for dissection (Gittings 1984: 74; Richardson 1987: 32).[12] This number was increased by subsequent royal grants to ten (Gittings 1984: 74). At least some of these early victims of the surgeon's knife appear to have been subsequently buried in consecrated ground. Records from the Church of St Martin's Ludgate mention the burial of an anatomised corpse from the Royal College of Surgeons in 1615 (Gittings 1984: 75).

During the first half of the eighteenth century, anatomy became an increasingly essential element of medical training (Lineburgh 1988: 70). Moreover this training increasingly took the form of the students performing the dissection themselves often in a private anatomy school, rather than watching a public anatomisation. The increasing demand for corpses for dissection resulted in surgeons, anatomists and their agents not just taking the bodies to which they were entitled from the gallows, but attempting to claim those they had no right to, often with trouble or riots developing as family, friends and the crowd watching the execution tried to prevent them (Richardson 1987: 53; Lineburgh 1988: 79). Although the primary aim of the Murder Act was to augment the punishment for murder, the increased availability of corpses for dissections seems to have eased the conflicts seen around the gallows (Lineburgh 1988: 78).

What happened to the very fragmentary remains of those dissected after 1751 once the anatomists had finished is less clear, but it seems likely that few murderers sent for dissection would have received anything resembling a formal burial. Some of the remains would have been retained to form part of anatomical collections, which were used to illustrate normal anatomy and pathological conditions (Moore 2006: 119–20).[13] A collection of human remains, some exhibiting evidence for defleshing was found during excavations on the former site of the General Hospital in Nottingham (Chapman 1997: 37). A large proportion of the assemblage consisted of leg bones, particularly tibiae and femora (Chapman 1997: 38). Of the ten long bones present, three exhibited evidence for amputation, six showed significant pathological changes and one had been fitted with a hinge, suggesting it came from a skeleton used for anatomical teaching (Chapman 1997: 39, 44). It has been suggested that these bones were part of a teaching or reference collection, perhaps disposed of after the 1832 Anatomy Act made the retention of bodies as teaching skeletons illegal (Chapman 1997: 46). For those body parts not retained, it may simply have been a case of using the easiest means of disposal. A large quantity of mostly fragmentary human and animal remains was uncovered during renovation of 36 Craven Street in London (Hillson *et al.* 1998/9: 14–5). Many of the bones had been sawn up and others bore a variety of cut marks. Human skulls had been sectioned sagitally and transversely, with some exhibiting evidence for multiple trepanation cuts (Hillson *et al.* 1998/9: 16). Hillson *et al.* suggest that some of the cuts on human long bones may represent practice amputations. The assemblage also contained fragments of pottery, glassware and metal as well as traces of mercury. Mercury was often used as a marker in early anatomical preparations, as was the inorganic dye vermilion and the bright red dye was found outlining some dog vertebrae recovered from the site. The house was occupied by the anatomist William Hewson between 1772–4. He ran an anatomy school in Craven Street, although whether this was from number 36 is unknown. It seems likely that the remains, buried in the eighteenth-century back garden of the house in Craven Street, were either the product of Hewson's own research or perhaps from the anatomy school. Other anatomists used more elaborated means of disposal. The eighteenth-century anatomist John Hunter combined waste from the dissecting room of his private anatomy school with manure from his stables and used it as a fertiliser on his farm at Earl's Court (Moore 2006: 508), while an investigation into body snatching in Lambeth in 1795 heard that human flesh was being made into candles (Richardson 1987: 97). In some instances, human skin was used as book covers (figure 5.15).

Figure 5.15 Anthropodermic bibliopegy. This account of the trial and execution of the Jesuit Henry Garnet was bound in the subject's own skin (Photograph courtesy of Wilkinson's Auctioneers of Doncaster).

Dissection was not the only sentence available to a judge for the disposal of a murderer's corpse in the Murder Act. The body could also be 'gibbetted' or 'hung in chains' (Richardson 1987: 35; Gatrell 1994: 267). 'Hanging in chains' was a long-existing tradition and involved coating the body in tar and encasing it in an iron frame. This was then suspended from a gibbet in a prominent location, often close to the scene of the crime. In some rural areas, gibbets were placed in easily accessible, but marginal locations, such as moors, commons and beaches (Whyte 2003). The body of John Cliffen, was taken from his place of execution to Badley Moor where it was suspended from a scaffold lying on the parish boundary (Whyte 2003: 24). Pieces of the body would gradually fall to the ground below the gibbet as the corpse decayed. Disarticulated bone was found during the enlargement of the Royal Edward Dock at Avonmouth, Gloucestershire at the beginning of the twentieth century (Brett 1996: 118), which is likely to have come from the gibbet that stood nearby on Dunball Island. The gibbet denied the felon a grave and the iron cage had to be padlocked or riveted and the gibbet spiked with nails to prevent nocturnal raids by family or friends to retrieve the body (Richardson 1987: 36; Gatrell 1994: 87).

Executions had always been public spectacles but the eighteenth-century authorities became increasingly unhappy about the presence of the gallows crowd and their irreverence to the due process of law (Gatrell 1994: 59). In 1783 executions were moved from Tyburn to outside the debtor's door at Newgate Prison in London (Rumbelow 1982: 184). The change was instigated by the sheriffs because of the behaviour of the crowds. In 1802, a similar shift in location occurred in York when executions were moved from the Tyburn on Knavesmire to the female prison, which lay within the ruins of the medieval castle (York Archaeological Trust 1998: 6). The remains of five individuals, some with evidence of autopsy, interred within wooden coffins inside the castle are likely to be the unclaimed bodies of executed prisoners, probably dating from between 1802 and 1826. The eighteenth- or nineteenth-century burials found during the excavation of the Courthouse and Old Goal at Portlaoise are also probably those of executed prisoners (Keeley 1998: 14). The eighteenth century also saw a decline in convictions for treason, the number of traitors executed declining markedly after the Jacobite executions of the 1740s (Gatrell 1994: 298n). The ritualised mutilation of the body, long associated with a traitor's death also became increasingly rare, in part due to activities of penal reformers who increasingly sought to reform the mind rather than punish the body (Porter 1991: 92). The burning of women for treason was abolished by Parliament in 1790, and in 1814 Parliament decreed that traitors be beheaded after hanging. While the sentence of quartering remained on the statute books it was unlikely to be enacted (Gatrell 1994: 317, 320). Furthermore, in the age of reason scientific advances made it clear that death was the final punishment and the justification of further mutilation of the corpse became more problematic (Gatrell 1994: 16). The disposal of the traitor's corpse became something of a lottery, dependent on the nature of the treason and the status and connections of the victim. When Colonel Edward Despard was executed for treason in 1803, his corpse was interred in St Paul's Churchyard in London (Gatrell 1994: 88; Newgate Calendar 1926: 267). In contrast, despite the petitions to the king to allow their families to bury their bodies, the five Cato Street conspirators were interred in quicklime in unconsecrated ground inside Newgate prison in 1820 after being publicly hanged and then beheaded (Gatrell 1994: 302–308). The Cato Street conspirators are thought to have been the earliest burials in Birdcage Walk, a passage between the female wing and the outer wall which served as Newgate Prison's burial yard (Rumbelow 1982: 203). When the prison closed in 1902, the remains of ninety-two bodies were exhumed and reburied in the City of London cemetery (Rumbelow 1982: 209). Many of these burials are likely to have post-dated the Anatomy Act of 1832, which removed dissection as a punishment for murder.[14] The 1832 Act stipulated that the executed body of a murderer should either be to be placed on a gibbet or interred within the prison precinct where the individual had been detained (2 and 3 Will. 4 c.75). The latter was the fate of Allen Muir who was executed for murder on 4th of October 1843 and whose remains were recovered from beneath the floor of the passage leading from the courthouse to the prison courtyard at Perth (Addyman 2004: 92). The use of the gibbet was ended by the Capital Punishment Amendment Act of 1868, which also required those executed, regardless of crime, to be interred within the walls of the prison where they died, unless there was insufficient room (31 and 32 Vict. CAP XXIV).

Conclusion

Archaeological evidence from all chronological periods contains examples of atypical, deviant or strange burials (see for example Murphy 2008; Reynolds 2009). Yet in contrast to earlier periods, the wealth of surviving documentary sources in the post-medieval period provides an invaluable insight into social mores, while a combination of coffin plate and written evidence permits comparatively tight dating of many burials. This allows not only a greater understanding of the factors that may result in unusual burials but also helps us understand how these factors changed over time. This chapter grouped the causes of unusual burial into three broad categories: choice, circumstance and compulsion.

It is clear that the vast majority of the population of post-medieval Britain and Ireland were content to be interred according to contemporary norms. For those wishing a more individualistic interment, choice was constrained to some extent by available income and social and religious beliefs. Most of the individuals known to have chosen an atypical burial during the post-medieval period were reasonably wealthy and well educated. For those of lesser means, many of whom struggled to afford a basic funeral and interment, more individualistic burials were not an option. They were also not favoured among dissenting religious groups such as the Quakers. The degree of control exerted by the authorities, both ecclesiastical and secular, was also an important factor. The late seventeenth century saw an easing in the regulation and control of burial allowing a greater level of choice in the nature of interment (Gittings 2007: 325). The 1789 Act of Toleration gave further freedom of worship and burial to non-conformist communities while the College of Arms, a body which had strictly regulated aristocratic funerals, was abolished in the mid-seventeenth century (Gittings 2007: 324–5). The growing concern over potential health risks from inhumations in the early nineteenth century led to a raft of burial legislation in the middle part of that century which acted to tighten state control over burial and curtail individual choice. As such it is perhaps not surprising that many documented post-medieval examples of idiosyncratic burials date to the period between the Act of Toleration and the mid-nineteenth-century burial legislation (Gittings 2007: 323).

The frequency of unusual burials due to the circumstances of an individual's death followed two distinct patterns between 1600 and 1900. There was a constant small number of deaths due to accident, exposure or foul play. Many of these individuals would have been buried according contemporary custom in the usual burial grounds. However a small minority, due to the location of their deaths or the condition of their bodies, were interred close where they were found or left where they fell and not accorded the usual burial rites. The second pattern is more sporadic and is the result of natural and man-made catastrophes such as war, epidemics and famine. Examples affecting post-medieval Britain and Ireland include plague outbreaks of the sixteenth and seventeenth century, cholera epidemics of the nineteenth century, the Irish famine of the 1840s, and the English Civil War and Jacobite rebellions of the seventeenth and eighteenth centuries. In these situations, exceptionally high levels of mortality over a very short period of time overwhelmed existing burial resources resulting in a modification or abandonment of usual burial practices. In such cases, attempts were made to adhere to the conventions of a 'decent burial' for as long as possible, and it was only once the body count climbed that the usual funerary processes were gradually abandoned or adapted.

Unusual burial as a punitive measure declined during the period covered by this book. During the early modern period, those denied the usual burial rights of interment on consecrated ground due to ecclesiastical or secular transgressions included the unbaptised, excommunicants, suicides and some criminals. Differential treatment of these groups originated in the early medieval period, but the extent to which the exclusion was enforced varied between parishes and to some extent over time. Such was the importance of a normal burial that families of those excluded from the usual burial grounds would if necessary beg, bribe or even illicitly inter bodies of loved ones on consecrated ground to ensure that the appropriate rites were accorded an individual. As such, many individuals who might have been excluded from consecrated ground lie in parish churchyards. By the eighteenth and nineteenth centuries the diversification of burial locations in urban contexts meant that even if the local clergy excluded an individual from the parish churchyard other acceptable options were available. Moreover, nineteenth-century legislation such as the Suicide Act allowed, or in some cases compelled, interment within community burial grounds for those who would previously have been excluded. Growing secular regulation of burial during the nineteenth century saw concerns over potential health risks overriding the earlier ecclesiastical exclusion of certain groups. At a local level, the spread of garden cemeteries run by boards of governors resulted in the administration of burial sliding from ecclesiastical to secular control. By 1900, the only people routinely excluded from community burial grounds were criminals sent to the gallows. Their bodies had to be interred within prison walls, but at least they now had graves – something denied them by the 1751 Murder Act until 1832.

Notes

1 Prior to the Act of Toleration 1689 which allowed non-conformist groups to establish their own burial grounds, members of some dissenting communities interred their dead in gardens, orchards and fields (see chapter 4 for a more detailed discussion).

2   A second small cemetery of 26 individuals also thought to date from the seventeenth century has been excavated in Abingdon (Norton *et al.* 2005). The context for these burials is less clear but a Civil War date has been suggested.
3   See chapter 4.
4   See sections on the unbaptised, suicides and excommunicates later in this chapter for more details.
5   "Banker" may refer to a ship which worked the Newfoundland cod banks (Freeman 1985: 133).
6   The term suicide was not used until 1610 and did come into general use until the eighteenth century (MacDonald 1986: 53).
7   The office of the dead should not be used "for any that die unbaptised, or excommunicate, or have laid violent hands upon themselves" (Procter and Frere 1951: 636).
8   No bones survive but the size of the grave suggests the occupants were very young children or infants (Nowakowski and Thomas 1992: 28).
9   A high number of prone burials were found during excavations in the churchyard of St. Margaret in Combusto, which was used for both lay burial and for the burial of medieval Norwich's executed felons (Ayers 1990: 58) and in many late Saxon execution cemeteries (Reynolds 2009: 160–1).
10 A single bone from a juvenile was also recovered.
11 The remains of priests Lawrence Richardson and William Filby, along with that of Jesuit Thomas Cottam, were interred where they were executed due to concerns that the populace might object to seeing so many limbs set up over the London gates (*Lives of English Martyrs* – 1st series, ii 499).
12 Dissection and the treatment of the bodies of criminals is discussed in more detail in chapter 6.
13 See chapter 6 for a discussion of anatomical collections.
14 The Anatomy Act also required the remains of anyone dissected be given a Christian burial.

6 The medical body: the archaeological evidence for the use of the corpse in medical research and teaching

So far this book has considered aspects of the funerary process: how the corpse was dressed, the form and fittings of the grave and where the grave was located. A chapter on the medical use of the body might initially seem a little out of place. The subject is included both because much of the physical evidence for autopsy and dissection is found in burial contexts, and particularly because the corpse as a subject for medical enquiry challenged many of society's ideas about the acceptable treatment of the body and as such it provides a valuable insight into contemporary attitudes towards the dead and funerary practices. Dissection, while perhaps the best known method, was not the only way the dead were used to advance medical knowledge during the post-medieval period and this chapter examines the archaeological evidence for not only dissection, but also for autopsy, post-mortem surgery and the retention of body parts.

The study of normal and morbid anatomy in post-medieval Britain and Ireland

Perceptions about the functioning of the body changed in the seventeenth century when the medical writings of Hypocrites and Galen were challenged by new mechanical models of nature (Porter 2004: 50). This more functionalist approach envisioned the human body as a living machine (Porter 2004: 51). The new investigative climate favoured experimentation and observation over the teachings of ancient authorities (Pickstone 2000) and the internal working of the body became a subject for investigation (Warner 1995). The significance of this change in approach cannot be overemphasised. Throughout much of the medieval period in Britain and Ireland, the inner workings of the body were a subject of speculation and conjecture, but not experimentation. The body might be opened or dismembered to facilitate the burial of parts of the body in more than one location or as part of the embalming process (Gilchrist and Sloane 2005: 80; Litten 1991: 32–56),[1] but not as the subject of medical inquiry. This was not the situation elsewhere in Europe: scientific dissection was practiced in Italy from the late thirteenth century, and became increasingly commonplace during the fourteenth century; autopsies were also performed in late medieval Italy to determine cause of death (Park 1995: 114). Park has suggested that the common perception of death as a gradual process in Northern Europe, where the corpse was perceived as something from which the life gradually ebbed after death may have delayed the introduction of dissection in the British Isles (1995: 115).

It was only in the early modern period that the British medical fraternity accepted the potential value of opening the bodies of the dead (Park 1995: 131). Initially the focus was on normal anatomy, as the subject became part of the training of physicians and surgeons (Harley 1994a: 4). Anatomy classes took the form of lectures given while a corpse, fresh from the gallows, was dissected. The connection between dissection and judicial punishment was created in 1540, when Henry VIII granted the United Companies of Barbers and Surgeons the rights to four hanged felons for dissection (Gittings 1984: 74; Richardson 1987: 32). This number was then increased by subsequent royal grants to ten (Gittings 1984: 74). In addition, the College of Physicians was entitled to the bodies of up to four criminals a year for dissection in its charter of 1565 (Harley 1994a: 4). In early modernity the sense that the corpse retained some animation after death meant that the end of life did not necessarily mean the end of personhood. The ways in which the dead person continued to have relationships with the living are considered in Tarlow (2011) and in some ways the space left where Purgatory used to be was filled by the, strongly individuated, body itself. The dead body's personal identity was crucial in early modern judicial practices which sometimes extended the punishment of a deviant individual past the point of death, to be enacted on the corpse. For those guilty of certain crimes, death was just the beginning of their punishment as their bodies were drawn and quartered or hung in chains. Thus for the judiciary, dissection became one of an array of punitive measures at their disposal (Richardson 1987: 32). The link between judicial punishment and dissection was further reinforced by the 1751 Act for the Better Preventing the Horrid Crime of Murder, better known as the Murder Act (25 Geo. 2. C.37:5). By the mid-eighteenth century, the death sentence was increasingly passed for relatively minor crimes so that it was felt an additional punishment was required for murderers and this took the form of either dissection, with the body being delivered to surgeons for anatomisation, or being displayed in a gibbet. The act also specifically forbade the burial of anyone convicted of murder.

During the first half of the eighteenth century, anatomy became an increasingly important element of medical training (Linebaugh 1988: 70), and a good knowledge of anatomy was deemed to be essential for medical practitioners, especially surgeons. By the latter part of the eighteenth century, medical students were augmenting their standard training by taking courses in anatomy in privately-run anatomy schools and as fee-paying students attached to hospital physicians and surgeons (Gelfand 1985: 130; Lawrence 1995: 200). Anatomical training generally took the form of the student performing the dissection himself, rather than watching an anatomisation (Lawrence 1995: 199). The increasing demand for corpses for dissection resulted in surgeons, anatomists and their agents not just taking the bodies to which they were entitled from the gallows, but attempting to claim those they had no right to, often with trouble or riots developing as family, friends and the crowd watching the execution tried to prevent them (Richardson 1987: 53; Lineburgh 1988: 79). Although the primary aim of the Murder Act was to augment the punishment for murder, the increased availability of corpses for dissection seems to have eased the conflicts seen around the gallows (Lineburgh 1988: 78).

Yet while restoring relative peace at the gallows, the act failed to completely meet the anatomists' voracious need for fresh corpses. The 1828 Report of the Select Committee estimated that each student needed as least three corpses: two to learn anatomy and another for practicing surgical techniques (Report of Select Committee on Anatomy 1828: 4). In 1828, there were estimated to be approximately 800 medical students in London alone, of whom some 500 were thought to be involved in dissection. The number of students in the latter part of the eighteenth century was probably smaller but it is clear that there were insufficient numbers of hanged murderers to meet the requirements of the anatomists. Moreover, the private anatomy schools that provided much of anatomical training during this period were often not entitled to bodies from the gallows and had to look elsewhere for their raw materials (Richardson 1987: 40; Moore 2005: 77). A number of avenues were explored including purchasing the bodies of condemned not already destined for the dissecting room, stealing bodies from the gallows and bribing undertakers to remove bodies from coffins prior to interment (Moore 2006: 84). However, most bodies dissected in private anatomy schools were stolen from their graves by the so-called 'resurrectionists' (Richardson 1987: 54).

Outside medical circles, most of society was antagonistic to dissection. The activities of the resurrectionists and anatomists threatened the body's integrity and offended moral sensibilities by disrupting the usual conventions surrounding death and burial, while the dissection process had criminal connotations and provoked anxiety for complex reasons associated with self, privacy and personhood (Richardson 1989: 109; Rugg 1998: 48). Grave robbing violated the sanctity of the grave and was a matter of increasing concern as the body and its final resting place became more important as a focus for grief and mourning during the late eighteenth and nineteenth century (Jalland 1999a: 246; Tarlow 2000: 227). The history of use of the bodies of criminals for dissection had equated the process with judicial punishment in public perception (Richardson 1987: 32). As we have seen, the border between life and death in this period was not completely clear-cut, and a number of folk practices suggested that in certain contexts the corpse retained a degree of sentience for some time after death (Caciola 1996; Halliday 1997). Given the punitive associations of dissection, post-mortem anatomising of a body that retained its identity could be deeply distressing. Finally, there was the resurrection. The concept of bodily resurrection continued to influence ideas about death and the afterlife in the eighteenth and nineteenth century (Richardson 1987: 15, 76). If a body was fragmented, what would happen on the day of resurrection? Would the dissected be denied an afterlife? Although theologians stated unambiguously that a 'whole' corpse was not necessary for bodily resurrection to occur, popular anxieties remained. These concerns are comically reflected in a cartoon from 1782 of the day of judgement at William Hunter's Windmill Street anatomy school, depicting the newly risen dead looking for their missing body parts (figure 6.1).

The increasing levels of public disquiet about dissections and the activities of the anatomists combined with concerns over the largely unregulated anatomy schools led to the passing of the Act for Regulating Schools of Anatomy, better known as the Anatomy Act, in 1832 (2 and 3 Will. 4 c. 75). The act repealed the Murder Act of 1751, severing the connection between gallows and dissecting table and provided the medical profession with a far more plentiful supply of bodies: those of the very poor. The poor are not specifically mentioned in the Act, but it permits the "executor or other party having lawful

Figure 6.1 A cartoon from 1782 of the Day of Judgement at William Hunter's Windmill Street anatomy school, depicting the newly risen dead looking for their missing body parts (Photograph courtesy of the Wellcome Institute)

possession of the body of any deceased person…..to permit the body of such deceased person to undergo anatomical examination" (2 and 3 Will. 4 c.75). According to the act, "the party" could be the deceased's family, who in practice was unlikely to consent to a dissection. However the term also be applied to masters of workhouses and Poor Law guardians, those responsible for the unclaimed bodies of the poor (Richardson 1987: 206). The act had in effect removed the bodies of murderers from the dissecting room to replace them with the unclaimed corpses of the poor. This new supply of fresh corpses also removed the market for 'resurrected' bodies, ensuring those who could pay for burial could once more rest easy in their graves.

If dissection represented all that was abhorrent about the medical use of the dead, autopsies were a more respectable reason for carrying out a technically similar process (Crossland 2009a). The examined body of medico-legal autopsy incorporated two strands of mortuary tradition found throughout Europe and which allowed the exhumation and analysis of the body after death in circumstances where the cause of death was unclear. On the legal side, in England the dead body had been treated as evidence in coroners' inquests since the end of the twelfth century, although the practice predated the office of coroner (Hunnisett 1958). An indictment of homicide had to be made before the coroner with the body present (Hunnisett 1961:9), and although the bodies were not examined surgically, sometimes the coroner had to demand their exhumation in order to carry out his inquest (Hunnisett 1961:11). On the medical side, autopsy acted as a continuation of care for a patient after death (Harley 1994a: 27). Autopsy, like dissection, first appeared in Britain during the early modern period but had very different social connotations. Early autopsies were conducted to determine the cause of death of prominent individuals, particularly when there were suspicious circumstances. The post-mortem of Henry, Prince of Wales, in 1612 was conducted to eliminate the possibly of poisoning, as were those of James I and the Marquis of Hamilton (King and Meehan 1973; Harley 1994a: 7, 9). It was not until towards the end of the seventeenth century that the practice was drawn upon in homicide trials (Forbes 1985: 46–7; MacMahon 2006). Autopsies were less invasive and thus less destructive than dissections so potentially more acceptable. The scope of investigation was often limited to organs thought to be linked to the cause of death and examinations were usually confined to soft tissues (Harley 1994a: 5). The stripping and disarticulation of bones characteristic of dissection did not occur. Moreover, unlike dissections which were public affairs, autopsies took place in private homes or before an invited audience. During the eighteenth and nineteenth centuries, the autopsy of private patients was performed in increasing numbers as an extension of pre-mortem medical care, and usually by the same doctors (Harley 1994a: 10; Moore 2006: 231). The acceptance of autopsy by the elite, a marked contrast to the abhorrence with which dissection was regarded, can be attributed to several factors. The wealthy were used to the corpse being opened as part of the embalming process during the early modern period and this may have reduced the initial objections to autopsies (Martensen 1992: 523; Harley 1994a: 6).[2] In addition, in a period when curiosity and the acquisition of knowledge were increasingly valued, consenting to an autopsy was a mark of education. It could be understood both in terms of offering an explanation for the death of a loved one, and as having the potential to enhance medical understanding (Martensen 1992: 522). While autopsies were initially conducted to ascertain cause of death, it was not long before their potential value in the study of morbid anatomy was recognised (Martensen 1992: 519). Morbid anatomy, the study of the physical manifestations of disease, required corpses with a known clinical history (Harley 1994a: 3). Thus the bodies routinely used for dissection, which came from the gallows or the grave, were ill-suited for the study of disease, while the results of autopsies on private patients with known clinical histories were invaluable. As the potential value of autopsies was recognised they became more common and began to arouse more debate. By the early nineteenth century controversy arose in cases of undue enthusiasm by coroners, who were portrayed as pursuing knowledge for its own sake, rather than for the benefit of the family of the deceased (Burney 2000: 53–4). Post-mortems also started to be performed increasingly on a second group of individuals, patients in voluntary hospitals. These hospitals provided the only possible source of medical treatment for the poor in the eighteenth and nineteenth centuries (Fissell 1989: 36). Those who could afford it were treated at home. Hospital admission policies varied, but some required letters of admission and many barred individuals with certain conditions. For example Newcastle Infirmary excluded those suffering from measles, smallpox, consumption and infectious fevers (Start 2002: 114). Unless claimed by their families, the bodies of those who died in hospital were often subject to autopsy, dissection or post-mortem surgery prior to interment (Richardson 1987: 105–6; Moore 2005: 161).

The archaeological evidence for autopsy

The increased use of the body as an anatomical object, to enhance the understanding of normal and morbid pathology is evidenced by the archaeological record. Articulated skeletons with craniotomies and/or cuts to the bones of the thorax and spine have been found at a number of sites (see table 6.1). Of the thirty-one sites listed, twenty-four are churchyards or community burial grounds. The sample also includes two prison cemeteries and five hospital burial grounds. While the dividing line between dissection and autopsy can at times be blurred, the skeletal evidence for the medical investigation observed in the majority of the community churchyards and burial grounds in table 6.1 is more suggestive of autopsy as opposed to the higher levels of fragmentation associated with dissection. This is not unexpected. With the exception of St Benet Sherehog, most of churchyards and burial grounds in table 6.1 were in use during the eighteenth and nineteenth century, with the majority dating to between the late eighteenth and mid-nineteenth century. The Murder Act of 1751 was specifically designed to deny those sent to the anatomists for dissection a proper burial, while corpses acquired illegally from the resurrectionists, having been wrenched from their graves following one formal burial, were unlikely to be accorded a second. Thus between 1751 and the passing of the Anatomy Act in 1832 not only were subjects of dissection unlikely to be found in community churchyards or burial grounds, they were unlikely to be accorded formal burial at all. After 1832, the majority of bodies dissected were the unclaimed bodies of those dying in hospitals and workhouses and as such were usually interred in the burial grounds belonging to those institutions, although it should be noted that some workhouses and hospitals did use parish poor grounds (Welch 1994: 6; Morrison 1997: 99). When dealing with earlier material the situation is less clear cut and similar assumptions cannot be made as during the sixteenth and seventeenth centuries, some criminals subjected to the anatomist's knife are known to have been interred in churchyards, as discussed in chapter 5.

In contrast human remains from prison and hospital burial grounds do in some cases exhibit levels of fragmentation more indicative of dissection, although the evidence reveals how the lines between autopsy and dissection were not clearly drawn in practice (Crossland 2009a). The skulls of two individuals from the prison burial ground at Oxford Castle had been subjected to multiple craniotomies (Hacking 2006: 116–7) a level of medical intervention far in excess of what would be expected from an autopsy. These burials are thought to date between the sixteenth and eighteenth centuries (Norton 2006: 11–2) and thus may pre-date the Murder Act, which would explain the presence of dissected remains in a prison burial ground. The examples from York Prison are more ambiguous with the cut marks not differing markedly from those seen on bodies from churchyards or community burial grounds and may represent either autopsy or dissection (York Archaeological Trust 1998: 6). While the nature of the cut marks is suggestive of autopsy, the context appears to favour dissection. Moreover although high levels of skeletal fragmentation are associated with dissection, the only skeletal involvement required to remove and dissect all of the body's soft tissue is a craniotomy and the opening of the thoracic cavity. A similar challenge is presented by hospital burial grounds. The nature of the cut marks seen at Edinburgh Royal Infirmary and the Royal Naval Hospital at Greenwich are analogous to those seen in churchyards and probably represent autopsies although it is impossible to determine the extent of the fragmentation of the soft tissues. In contrast there is osteological evidence for greater division of the skeleton at the Newcastle Infirmary. While the cut marks seen in many articulated burials generally echo those found in skeletons from churchyards, there are some important differences (Boulter, Robertson and Start 1998: 138–9). Many of the skeletons have amputated limbs, including one individual having evidence of three separate operations, suggesting that some of the bodies were used to practice surgical techniques (Witkin 1997: 83). Another unusual finding was that a number of vertebrae were sawn transversely across (Boulter, Robertson and Start 1998: 138–9). The evidence seems to indicate that some individuals were simply subjected to an autopsy while others (such as the individual missing his entire lower body below the forth lumbar vertebrae) were subject to more invasive procedures (Nolan 1998: 49). The complete removal of the lower body was also observed in four individuals from the Royal London Hospital (Powers 2008: 47). One of these individuals also had multiple incisions made through the cranium.

Of the twenty-four churchyards and community burial grounds with autopsy evidence, eighteen were Anglican churchyards. Another, the Cross Bones burial ground, which was the parish poor ground, also lay under nominal Anglican control. The remaining sites included two Baptist burial grounds in London and Poole, a Methodist burial ground in Sheffield, a burial ground attached to a Catholic mission and the non-conformist City Bunhill burial ground. While this is a small sample, it does suggest autopsy was acceptable to some members of a number of different denominations. All bar one of the sites date to the eighteenth and nineteenth centuries. Increased evidence for autopsy might be expected in the eighteenth and nineteenth century as the procedure became more prevalent, and new approaches percolated through the medical fraternity. However, the general dearth of sixteenth- and seventeenth-century burial evidence may also account for the chronological distribution.[3] Eleven (45.8%) of the sites which yield post-mortem evidence are in London with another six located in large industrial towns, such as Birmingham. The remainder were found in market towns or rural locations. London was by a considerable margin the largest urban centre in Britain throughout the post-medieval period and approximately 12.5% of the sites in the gazetteer are in the metropolis including the majority of those with over one hundred excavated burials. As such, the high proportion of examples of autopsy from the city is not unexpected, particularly if the concentration of medical practitioners, anatomy schools and teaching hospitals in the metropolis is also considered. More interesting are the examples from the smaller towns of Poole, Barton-on-Humber and Bath, and the villages of Bathampton and Forest Hill, which illustrate that autopsy and medical enquiry were not the preserve exclusively of the urban medical practitioner and that by the nineteenth century, if not earlier, post-mortem examination had become part of the practice of the provincial doctor.

Those subjected to autopsy were most likely to originate from two distinct social groups. The first group were the poor and destitute from the voluntary hospitals. Once in hospital, the patients were placed under the authority of the medical staff and their families were not always in a position to resist demands for an autopsy (Richardson 1987: 47). The second group, at the other end of the scale, were members of the educated middle and upper classes. Those with means and education, particularly with a medical background, were likely to be able to afford private physicians and to subscribe to the developing scientific beliefs of the period, making them more likely to appreciate the value of autopsy. The presence of both groups can be detected to some extent in the archaeological record. Evidence for the post-mortem investigation of the bodies of patients has been encountered in a number of hospital burial grounds including Newcastle Infirmary, Edinburgh Royal Infirmary, the Royal London and the Royal Naval Hospital at Greenwich (figure 6.2). The co-operation of middle class families in post-mortem autopsy can be detected by examining the funerary context of those interred in churchyards and community burial grounds (table 6.2). While it was only possible to determine the funerary context of 31 autopsied individuals, the table demonstrates that several were interred in vaults, either below the church or within

6 The medical body: the archaeological evidence for the use of the corpse in medical research and teaching

Table 6.1. Archaeological examples of autopsy

Site	Date	Number autopsied/total number	% of skeletal assemblage	Nature of evidence	No of affected:[1] Males	Females	Sub-Adults	Reference
St Marylebone Church, London	18th–19th century	5/301	1.7	Craniotomies, cutmarks on ribs and sternum	2	0	3	Miles, Powers and Wroe-Brown 2008
Christ Church Spitalfields, London	1729–1867	7/968	0.72	Craniotomies, cutmarks on ribs and sternum, removal of spine	1?	1?	3	Molleson and Cox 1993
St Luke's Islington, London	18th–19th century	6/896	0.66	Craniotomy, sternotomy	5		1	Boyle 2005
Benet Sherehog Burial Ground	17th–19th century	1/212	0.47	Craniotomy			1	Miles and White 2008
St George Bloomsbury, London	1803–1856	4/111	3.6	Craniotomy, ribs and manubrium sawn through	4			Witkin and Boston 2006
Lower St Bride's Churchyard, London	Late 18th and 19th century	22/544	0.4	Craniotomies, cut ribs, cut clavicle	13[2]	5	1	http://www.museumoflondon.org.uk/English/Collections/OnlineResources/CHB/Database/Post-medieval+cemeteries/St+Brides+lower.htm
Cross Bones Burial Ground, London	Mainly 19th century	3/148	2.0	Craniotomy, cuts to neutral arches of vertebrae	1	1	1	Miles & Brickley 1999; http://www.museumoflondon.org.uk/English/Collections/OnlineResources/CHB/Database/Post-medieval+cemeteries/Cross+bones.htm
City Bunhill Burial Ground, Golden Lane, London	1833–1853	9/239	3.8	Craniotomy, cuts to mandible, manubrium, vertebrae, femur and ilium	2[3]	4	3	Connell and Miles 2010
Catholic Mission of St Mary & St Michael, London	1843–1854	7/747	0.93	Craniotomy	3	1	3	Miles and Powers 2006
Southwark Cathedral, London	18th century	1/24	4.1	Craniotomy		1		Dodwell 2001
Bow Baptist Church Burial Ground	1810–1837	1/348[4]	0.28	Craniotomy, cut ribs	1			Powers 2007
Castle Hill Chapel Cemetery, Northampton	Late 18th or early 19th	1/39	2.5	Craniotomy	1			Miller and Wilson 2005
Carver Street Methodist Chapel, Sheffield	1805–1855	4/136	2.9	Craniotomy				McIntyre and Wilmott 2003
St Martin's-in-the-Bull Ring, Birmingham	18th–19th century	7/505	1.4	Craniotomies	4	3		Brickley 2005
St Bartholomew's Church, Penn, Wolverhampton	18th–20th century	3/351	0.85	Craniotomies		1	2	Boyle 2002

The archaeological evidence for autopsy

Site	Date	Count	%	Evidence		Reference
Holy Trinity Church, Coventry	1776–c.1850	4/1706	0.23	Craniotomy		Soden 2000
West Butt Street Baptist Burial Ground, Poole	1735–1855	1/83[5]	1.2	Craniotomy	1	McKinley 2008
St Nicholas' Church, Bathampton, Somerset	19th century	1/6[6]	16.6	Craniotomy		Cox and Stock 1994
St Thomas a' Becket, Widcombe, Bath	16th century onwards	1/50	0.5	Craniotomy	1	Lewcun 1995
St Peter's Church, Barton-upon-Humber, Lincolnshire	Multi-period	1/651[7]	0.15	Craniotomy, removal of spine	1	Waldron 2007
St Nicholas' Church, Forest Hill, Oxfordshire	Probably 18th and 19th century	1/15	6.7	Craniotomy	1	Boston 2004
Churchyard of St John the Baptist, Cardiff	Early 19th century	2/32	6.25	Craniotomy	2	Tavener 1998b
Glasgow Cathedral	Post-medieval	3/79[8]		Craniotomy	2 unsexed adults	Driscoll 2002
St John the Baptist Church, Sligo	Late 18th to early 20th century	2/49	4.1	Craniotomy	2	Lynch 2002
Former female prison in York	Majority 1820–1826	1/5		Craniotomy, splayed ribs	1	Carrott et al. 1998
Oxford Castle	16th–18th century	2/64	3.1	Craniotomy	2	Hacking 2006
Newcastle Infirmary	1753–1845	7/440[9]	13.9	Craniotomy, post-mortem amputations, sawn vertebrae and ribs	5[10]	Boulter, Robertson and Start 1998
Royal London Hospital	1820–1854	62/170[11]		Craniotomy	38	
Royal Hospital Greenwich, London	1749–1857	4/107	3.7	Craniotomies	4[12]	Boston 2007
Edinburgh Royal Infirmary	1749–1803	2/6	33.3.	Craniotomies, cut marks on clavicles and manubrium	2	Henderson, Collard and Johnston 1996
Metropole Development, Clyde Street, Glasgow (hospital burial ground)	18th–19th century	1/2	50%	Craniotomy		Discovery and excavation in Scotland 2004: 68

1 Columns left blank if demographic information unavailable
2 Sex of three of the adults indeterminate
3 Sex of three of three individuals indeterminate
4 Preliminary findings
5 In situ remains only
6 Remains examined by osteologists
7 Only including skeletons in phases A and A/B
8 No of medieval and post medieval skeletons
9 Estimate based on evidence for craniotomies in 7 of the 56 articulated skeletons with crania. An additional 54 crania exhibiting evidence for autopsy/dissection were found among the disarticulated material
10 Numbers based on aritulated skeletons where sex could be estimated
11 Articulated burials examined osteologically. Preliminary data
12 97 of 105 adult skeletons from this site were male

6 The medical body: the archaeological evidence for the use of the corpse in medical research and teaching

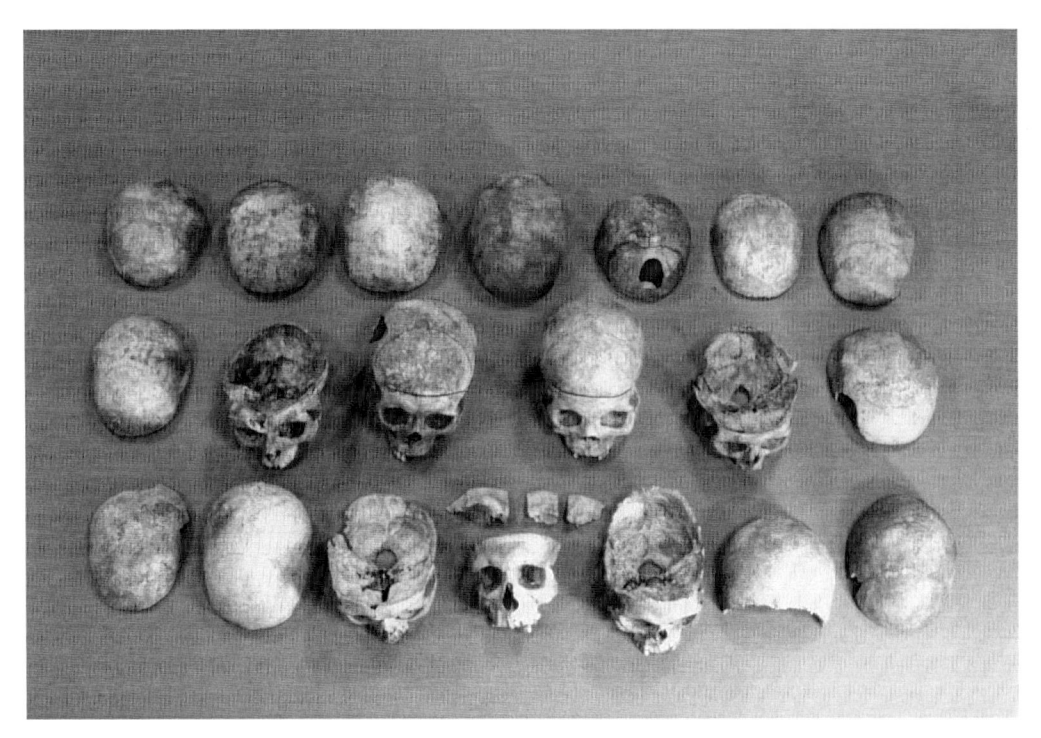

Figure 6.2 Some of the skulls recovered from the burial ground at the Newcastle Infirmary which had been subject to post-mortem investigation (Photograph courtesy of Andrew Chamberlain).

Table 6.2. Burial contexts of autopsied individuals from churchyards and community burial grounds

Site	Vault under church	Vault in churchyard	Stone/ brick-lined grave	Earth cut grave
Christ Church, Spitalfields, London	7			
St Luke's Islington	4[1]			
St George's Bloomsbury	4			
Catholic Mission of St Mary & St Michael, London				7[2]
St Martin's-in-the-Bull Ring, Birmingham		1[3]		
St Bartholomew's Penn, Wolverhampton		1		2
St Nicholas Bathampton			1	
St Thomas á Becket, Bath			1	
St Peter's, Barton-upon-Humber				1
St Nicholas', Forest Hill, Oxfordshire				1
West Butt Street Baptist Burial Ground, Poole				1[4]

1 It was only possible to determine the burial context of four of the autopsied individuals
2 All burials on site are from earth cut graves
3 It was only possible to determine the burial context of one of the autopsied individuals
4 All burials on site are from earth cut graves

the churchyard, and brick/stone-lined grave shafts. Burial in any of these contexts was rarely an inexpensive option and this suggests that these individuals came from relatively wealthy, and probably well-educated, families. Interestingly not all of those with autopsies came from wealthy contexts and there are also a number of individuals in earth-cut graves.[4] There are a number of factors which may account for this finding. While autopsy was initially confined to wealthy progressives, the procedure gradually became more widespread during the nineteenth century and the burial of autopsied bodies in earth-cut graves may provide an indication of the spread of the practice to other sectors of society. Alternatively, some of the individuals in earth-cut graves may have been hospital patients, subject to autopsy, and then interred either by their families or by the hospital authorities. Finally in some cases an individual's religious beliefs may have been a factor. Autopsied individuals in earth-cut graves were found in the Baptist burial ground in Poole and the burial ground associated with the Catholic Mission of St Mary and St Michael. All the burials from both of these sites were interred in earth-cut graves. It may be these individuals were relatively wealthy but a simple earth-cut grave among others of their own faith was more important than a more elaborate location elsewhere

Craniotomies (incisions that sectioned the skull) were the most common, and often only physical evidence for autopsy and account for most individuals in table 6.1. At the Royal London Hospital, craniotomies were present in 78% of the articulated skeletons with evidence for autopsy and whose skulls were present (Powers 2008: 47). There was marked variation in the location of the craniotomy cut within the sample. In some cases the horizontal cut is confined to the frontal parietal and occipital bones, while in other examples the cut is lower down the skull passing through the squamous part of the temporal bones. The top of the skull of a young adult male from the City Bunhill burial ground was removed by connecting a series of cuts (Connell and Miles 2010: 48). In some cases, the craniotomy was not just a horizontal section across the cranial vault. The skull of a young adult male from St Martin's-in-the-Bull Ring in Birmingham had a vertical cut in the coronal plane through the frontal bone with a second horizontal cut made through the occipital and parietal bones meeting the coronal cut (Brickley 2006: 147). Even more curious are the cut marks on another skull from the same site. Here a quasi roundel of bone has been cut from the frontal bone above the eyes while a second more conventional horizontal cut was then used to remove the skull cap. The considerable variation among the craniotomies can be attributed to a number of factors. In an era lacking a standardised medical education, much of the variation is likely to be a reflection of the differing practices and expertise of those performing the autopsy (Brickley 2006: 147; Miles, Powers and Wroe-Brown 2008: 147). In addition, the examples of craniotomies span a period of approximately a hundred years and some of the differences in technique may be a reflection of changes in methodology over time. In some instances, practical considerations could affect the location of the cranial cuts. The asymmetrical cuts on a male burial from the Royal London Hospital have been attributed to the subject's traumatic ankylosis (fusion) of the cervical vertebrae precluding the usual cuts being made (Powers 2008: 47).

Marks seen on the skull also illuminate other aspects of the autopsy. The skulls of individuals from Southwark Cathedral and Marylebone Church in London bore parallel cut marks on the side of the skull thought to be the result of a blade catching the skull while the scalp was being retracted prior to the removal of the skull cap (Dodwell 2001: 144; Miles, Powers and Wroe-Brown 2008: 147). Similar skinning marks were observed on a number of the autopsied skeletons from Lower St Bride's Churchyard in London (WORD database). The process of separating the skull cap from the rest of the cranium was not a simple matter of slicing through the bone and lifting off the top part. Chisels were often used to separate the cut part of the skull (Lee 1879: 26). The chipping present on the left side of the frontal bone of a skull from Marylebone Church marks the location of a series of leverage points used to remove the top of the skull (Miles, Powers and Wroe-Brown 2008: 147).

While craniotomies provide most of the evidence for autopsy in the dataset, there is some evidence for medical investigations on the post-cranial skeleton. This usually takes the form of cut marks on the ribs, sternum or clavicle such as the saw marks on the manubrium of an adult female from St Martin's-in-the-Bull Ring and on a young male interred at Marylebone Church in London (Brickley 2006: 146; Miles, Powers and Wroe-Brown 2008: 148). Cutting or bisecting the sternum was usually used to facilitate access to the thoracic cavity, allowing an examination of the heart and lungs. Another method of accessing the thoracic cavity was to cut the ribs as in the case of an adult male from Marylebone Church, who had diagonal cuts on the sternal ends of six right and five left ribs (Miles, Powers and Wroe-Brown 2008: 148). Cuts to the clavicles and sternal ends of the ribs to access the thoracic cavity were also observed on several individuals from Lower St Bride's Churchyard in London (WORD database). In a few cases the location of the cut marks may be indicative of a more limited examination of the thorax. One of the skeletons from Edinburgh Royal Infirmary had cut marks on the ends of the clavicles and manubrium (Henderson 1996: 937). There was no evidence for cut marks on the ribs and the position of the bones in the grave suggests that only the right clavicle had been displaced after death. It is possible that the ribs were cut through the costal cartilage (which connects the sternum and the ends of the ribs) to access the thorax and then restored to anatomical position prior to burial. Yet the location of the existing cut marks might be indicative of a post-mortem examination limited to the thyroid or aortic arch. A less common target for the anatomist's knife were the bones of the spine. Cut marks to the spine were found on individuals from Christ Church, Spitalfields and the Cross Bones burial ground, both in London (Molleson and Cox 1993: 87; Brickley and Miles 1999a: 45). The spine, ribs and sternum of an adult male at St Peter's Church at Barton-upon-Humber had been completely removed (Waldron 2007: 38). All the ribs of a male burial from St Bride's lower churchyard had severed ends where the thoracic part of the spine had been removed while the presence of cut fragments of the cervical vertebrae suggested that the upper spine had also been extracted (WORD database).

The skeletal evidence for post-mortem examination provides, at best, an incomplete picture of autopsy practices in the eighteenth and nineteenth century. It is possible to examine many of the internal structures of the body without having recourse to cutting bone. The skeleton does not shield the organs of the abdomen and their examination would leave no trace on skeletal remains. Furthermore, it is possible to access the thoracic cavity by cutting through the costal cartilage and dividing the sterno-clavicular joints, thus leaving no trace on the bones, as was recommended in late nineteenth-century post-mortem manuals (Lee 1879: 6; Harris 1887: 17–8). A male from Lower St Bride's Churchyard in London had cut marks on the ossified cartilage on one side of the manubrium but not on the other side where there was no ossification of the cartilage (WORD database). Not cutting the ribs had the added advantage of preventing the creation of sharp jagged edges, which could cut the hands and result in septic post-mortem wounds (Harris 1887: 18). Such an approach is suggested by the splayed position of the ribs of a nineteenth-century female skeleton from York Prison, which were left lying on top of her arms (Carrott *et al.* 1998: 4; York Archaeological Trust 1998: 14). There was no evidence for cut marks on her ribs or sternum suggesting the costal cartilage had been cut to open the thoracic cavity. This may account for the fact that craniotomies dominate the archaeological evidence for autopsy. Of the 62 skeletons exhibiting evidence of autopsy at the Royal London, 78% of the 50 with heads present had craniotomies, while only 23 (37%) of all the skeletons had cuts to the thoracic region (Powers 2008: 47). Moreover just because a craniotomy is the only visible evidence for autopsy on a skeleton it cannot be assumed that the thoracic cavity has not been opened. The situation is further complicated by the fact that poor skeletal preservation and methods of data collection may result in the under-recognition of autopsies in the archaeological record and bias the type of post-mortem modification observed. Bone preservation and the completeness of the skeleton have a significant effect on the quantity and quality of data recovered from a skeleton (Waldron 1987: 55). Thus, poor bone preservation or the survival of only part of the skeleton may obscure any evidence of autopsy. In addition structural differences in the bone can lead to differential preservation of different skeletal elements (Mays 1998: 23). The sternum and ribs, the site of any cut marks resulting from opening the thoracic cavity, tend to be under-represented in the archaeological record. This is due in part to the high proportion of less dense trabecular or spongy bone in these elements of the skeleton; even when they are present they may be highly fragmented. In contrast, the bones of the cranial vault are more robust. Hence evidence for the more extensive damage caused by a craniotomy might be observed on a poorly preserved skeleton while less overt cuts to the ribs and/or sternum could be obscured.

Detailed osteological analysis of all excavated post-medieval skeletal assemblages is not always feasible. Logistical considerations and limited resources may result in a sampling strategy being applied to maximise data recovered within the existing constraints, with detailed osteological analysis confined to only part of the excavated sample, and the remaining skeletons examined using low resolution methodologies. High resolution analysis at St Luke's Islington was confined to named individuals and those exhibiting unusual pathologies, surgical or dental interventions or exceptional levels of preservation (Boyle, Boston and Witkin 2005: 22). Low resolution analysis was used on the remaining skeletal material. In other cases, archaeological interventions are limited to a watching brief with osteological examination of the remains confined to observations made on site, as was the case at Ebenezer Chapel and Bond Street Congregational Chapel in Leicester (Jacklin 2006a: 1; Jacklin 2006b: 1). These variations in the nature of osteological analysis have the potential to affect not only the number of examples of autopsy observed but also the type of post-mortem intervention detected. A craniotomy, particularly if the skull is relatively well preserved, or a bisected sternum are more likely to be detected during limited osteological examinations than the more subtle cut marks on often fragmentary ribs.

Despite the limitations outlined above, it is still possible to draw a few tentative conclusions from the osteological evidence about the form of eighteenth- and nineteenth-century autopsies. As has already been discussed, the absence of cut-marks on the ribs and sternum cannot necessarily be treated as proof that the thoracic cavity has not been opened. Fortunately, the brain cannot be accessed without cutting the skull and, provided the skull is present and reasonably well preserved, the absence of craniotomy cuts can be taken as proof that the brain was not examined. Six individuals within the dataset, two from Spitalfields and the City Bunhill burial ground, and one each from the Cross Bones burial ground and Edinburgh Royal Infirmary burial ground have cut marks on the post-cranial skeleton but no evidence for craniotomies (Molleson and Cox 1993: 89; Henderson, Collard and Johnston 1996: 937; Brickley and Miles 1999a: 45; Connell and Miles 2010: 48). Morbid anatomy and forensic science were in their infancies during this period and there is little evidence for the standardisation of the form of the autopsy until the late nineteenth century. Descriptions in contemporary medical journals and newspapers suggest the brain, thoracic and abdominal cavities were the usual focus of post-mortem examinations (see for example *The Times* May 20th 1833; Johnson 1858: 493).

Yet, as demonstrated by the archaeological examples above, there was not necessarily a systematic examination of the body and an autopsy might not necessarily examine the brain, abdomen and thoracic cavity in all cases. Moreover, variations in the position of cut marks on the skull, ribs and sternum suggest the form that autopsies took was fluid rather fixed. In the absence of a standard methodology, a combination of clinical considerations and the need to respect the sensibilities of the families of wealthy subjects determined the location and extent of the post-mortem investigation. Designed to determine the cause of death, the post-mortem examination targeted the visible symptoms of disease. Thus while some post-mortems involved an examination of the brain and the organs of the thorax and abdomen, others confined investigation to those parts of the body thought to be diseased. Hence it seems probable that the lack of evidence for craniotomy on some autopsied individuals is because it was thought that an examination of the brain was unlikely to enhance the understanding of the cause of death. Symptoms prior to death may also account for some of the more atypical cut marks observed on the skeletons. Most of the post-cranial cut marks observed in the collected evidence are on the ribs or sternum and the majority are linked to opening the thoracic cavity, but occasionally they are found elsewhere such as on the spine as in individuals from the Cross Bones burial ground, City Bunhill burial ground and Christ Church Spitalfields, or on the lower leg as at Edinburgh Royal infirmary (Molleson and Cox 1993: 87; Henderson, Collard and Johnston 1996: 937; Brickley and Miles 1999a: 45; Connell and Miles 2010: 48). Two individuals from the City Bunhill burial ground had cut marks on the pelvis (Connell and Miles 2010: 48). Twenty-six (41.9%) of the autopsied individuals from the Royal London Hospital exhibited other cut marks outside those used to open the skull and thoracic cavity: locations included the pelvis, upper and lower limbs, and spine (Powers 2008: 47). In eleven of these cases, these less common post-mortem interventions formed the only evidence for autopsy. This suggests that in the absence of a standardised form, the nature of the post-mortem examination may have been determined in some instances by ante-mortem symptoms, particularly for those individuals interred within community burial grounds. The Royal London was a teaching hospital and while some of the more atypical cuts may be the result of clinical symptoms, it may be that some represent a more invasive investigation of the body than would have been conducted on private patients, or even the dissection of soft tissues. Symptoms may also explain some atypical craniotomy cuts, such as the roundel cut from the frontal bone of the skull of an individual from St Martin's-in-the-Bull Ring (Brickley 2006: 147).

The wishes of the relatives of deceased private patients could also determine the extent and location of any post-mortem investigation. Their permission was required prior to the performance of an autopsy, and not all were particularly happy at the thought of their loved one's body being cut open, even in the interest of science. Sometimes obtaining consent required a degree of compromise. When James Mason died in 1858 his father was reluctant to allow a post-mortem to be conducted (Chadwick 1858: 204). His consent was eventually obtained on the understanding that the autopsy be confined to only the abdominal cavity.

Demographic information was available for 141 (80.1%) of the individuals in table 6.1 and this is summarised in table 6.3. Among the 120 adults of known sex subjected to autopsy/dissection, 91 (75.8%) were males compared to only 29 (24.2%) females. The imbalance between the sexes appears to be present in all types of cemeteries, although the numbers from the prison sites are too small to allow any firm conclusions to be made. In addition, some of the imbalance between the sexes from the hospital sites can to be attributed to four male burials from the Royal Greenwich Hospital where 92.4% of the adult skeletons were male (Boston *et al.* 2008: 34). Although the numbers from the churchyards and community burial grounds are comparatively small, some tentative observations can be made. The evidence does suggest that sex may have influenced whether an individual was subject to autopsy. Females were either less likely

Table 6.3. Summary of demographic composition of examples of autopsy and dissection from different types of sites in table 6.1.

	Number of individuals				Number from all sites as % of all burials (n=141)
	Churchyards and community burial grounds	Hospital burial grounds	Prison burial grounds	All sites	
Adult males	42	47	2	91	64.5
Adult females	19	9	1	29	20.6
Children	20	1	-	21	14.9

to be subjected to the surgeon's knife after death than males, or the incisions were less aggressive and are less visible archaeologically. Many in the late eighteenth and nineteenth century found the dissection of a naked female body by male anatomists and students to be an intrusive violation of sexual privacy, almost a sexual assault (Rugg 1998: 48; *The Times* 9th December 1822), although there was a concomitant prurient interest in the post-mortem investigation of women's bodies as Michael Sappol has shown for North America (Sappol 2002). Thus while an autopsy was in theory a less invasive process, often performed by one of the doctors involved in treating the deceased during their final illness, it may have evoked the same concerns of sexual impropriety as dissection, resulting in unwillingness on the part of relatives to subject the bodies of female family members to an autopsy. Even less common was the surgical examination of the bodies of the young. Perhaps many of the causes of juvenile mortality were easily diagnosed or of less interest to physicians and thus the bodies of the young were less likely to be subject to medical investigations than those of adults. In some instances it appears that investigation of the cause of a child's death may have aided the parent's grieving process and potentially provided information to protect other siblings. The eighteenth-century anatomist, John Hunter, performed an autopsy on the ten-month son of a Mr Abbott, the fourth child his parents had lost suddenly at less than a year of age (Moore 2006: 235). The parents had sought out Hunter in an attempt to explain the loss of their children. Sadly, the autopsy provided no answers.

A variety of pathological lesions on some of the skeletons offer possible explanations for the post-mortem examinations (table 6.4). Tuberculosis was one of the great scourges of post-medieval Britain, causing significant mortality from the seventeenth century onwards and becoming the most common cause of death by the early nineteenth century (Roberts and Cox 2003: 338). Possible evidence of the disease is present in five of the individuals in table 6.4. Rib lesions, which may be indicative of tuberculosis, were found on the skeleton of George Walford at St Luke's Islington and on the remains of a young female from St Martin's-in-the-Bull Ring in Birmingham (Boyle *et al.* 2005: 252; Brickley and Buteux 2006: appendix 5). Interesting, the remains of George Walford had undergone both a craniotomy and a sternotomy, the latter presumably to allow an examination of the lungs. The calcified lung tissue found in an adult male and the infected elbow observed on an adolescent interred in the burial ground associated with Catholic Mission of St Mary and St Michael may also be the result of tuberculosis (Miles and Powers 2006: 31). A third individual from the mission burial ground had tuberculosis as well as another disease which became a significant problem during the post-medieval period: syphilis. Other conditions present in individuals subject to autopsy include rickets, healing rib fractures and facial cancer. The majority of the individuals subject to autopsy, however, exhibited no pathological changes to the skeleton and it is important to remember that not all diseases impact on the skeleton (Wood *et al.* 1992). Many diseases affect only the soft tissues while others,

Table 6.4. Individuals subject to autopsy exhibiting paleopathological lesions

Site	Biographical information	Pathological changes
St Marylebone Church London	5 year old child	Rickets
	4–5 year child	Infection from dental caries
	Young adult male	Rachitic changes and endocranial lesions
	Adolescent	Porotic hyperostosis and infection resulting from a dental abscess
St Luke's Islington, London	Thomas Tribe aged 53	Evidence for a facially disfiguring cancer
	George Walford aged 51	Active rib lesions – possibly tuberculosis
Catholic Mission of St Mary & St Michael, London	Adult female	Advanced syphilis and tuberculosis
	Adult male	Stellate lesion on left parietal and calcified lung tissue
	Adolescent	Evidence for infection around left elbow – possibly linked to tuberculosis
West Butt Street Baptist Burial Ground, Poole	5 year old child	Evidence for an extensive infection on left facial bones
St Martin's-in-the-Bull Ring	Young adult male	Healing rib fractures
	Adult female	Rib Lesions
	Young adult female	Sinisitis, cribra, periostitis
	Adult male	Healing rib fractures
	Young adult male	Small lytic lesion (?) on frontal

such as acute infections, kill so quickly that there is no time for any bony changes to occur (Roberts and Manchester 2005: 13). Furthermore some of the pathological conditions, which do result in changes to the skeleton, may not do so in all cases and the skeleton may only be affected in the later stages of the disease. The skeletal changes associated with syphilis only develop in the tertiary stage of the disease which occurs between two and ten years after infection (Ortner and Putscer 1985: 182), while the skeletal changes associated with tuberculosis only occur in 3–5% of infected individuals (Roberts and Manchester 2005: 188). Occasionally, when an individual can be identified from coffin plates it is sometimes possible to find documentary sources which explain the circumstances behind the post-mortem. George Warden, who was interred in his family's vault in the churchyard of St Martin's-in-the-Bull Ring in 1863, died from an overdose of the opium he had been taking to treat neuralgic pain while a student at Oxford according to his death certificate (Adams 2006: 199). The craniotomy cuts on his skull were the result of the two post-mortem examinations conducted on his remains by the Oxford coroner (Adams 2006: 199; Brickley 2006: 146).

The majority of individuals with craniotomies found in churchyards and burial grounds were interred with the skull caps removed during the post-mortem restored to anatomical position. By the late eighteenth century, the presentation of the corpse had become increasingly important[5] and this may explain the often fierce efforts that were made to conceal evidence of the post-mortem, thus making the body presentable for burial and avoiding further distress to the bereaved (Harris 1887: 77). In most cases the skull cap would have simply been repositioned and covered with the scalp to hold it in place. Oliver Cromwell was an early autopsy subject, as there were suspicions that his death in 1658 might be due to poisoning (Pearson and Morant 1935: 8). Needle holes found on his scalp indicate that it was sewn back in place to help secure the skull cap (Pearson and Morant 1935: 6, 7). While stitches were usually used to repair incisions in the scalp, fragments of hair and scalp fragments found adhering to a pin on the front of the skull of a young female interred in the late eighteenth century in Edinburgh Royal Infirmary's burial ground combined with the presence of copper alloy stains on skull may indicate that the skin was simply pinned rather than sewn back into place prior to burial (Henderson 1996: 937). While the scalp was usually sufficient to hold the skull cap in place, it does have a tendency to slip backwards creating a groove in the forehead and altering the features (Harris 1887: 77) and sometimes additional measures were required, as at St Peter's Church, Barton-upon-Humber in Lincolnshire where the two parts of a craniotomy were glued back together (Rodwell and Rodwell 1982: 306). The evidence of the methods used to secure the skull cap and repair the scalp would have been concealed by the hair or the funerary caps and bonnets of the period (Boyle, Boston and Witkin 2005: 251). Clothing may have been sufficient to obscure evidence of most abdominal and thoracic investigations once stitches had been used to close any incisions. A late nineteenth-century practical guide to post-mortems suggests cotton wool or linen be placed inside the body directly below the incisions in the chest and abdomen to prevent liquid leaking and staining the corpse's clothing (Harris 1887: 77–8). This packing could also be used to maintain a semblance of normal body shape masking the falling in of the sternum. Occasionally, the damage done to the body by the autopsy required the adoption of more extreme measures. An adult male interred at St Peter's church, Barton-upon-Humber had his spine, ribs and sternum removed as part of an autopsy and the vertebral column replaced with a piece of charred wood (figure 6.3) (Rodwell and Rodwell 1982: 306; Waldron 2007: 38). The body was then restored, using grass or moss to stuff the body cavities, to disguise the damage done by the post-mortem. The efforts made to hide the effects of the surgeon's knife are understandable when the consent of relatives was a necessary prerequisite for the majority of post-mortems. The return of an unsightly and obviously damaged corpse would do little to enhance the acceptability of the process.

There was no need to placate the sensibilities of relatives when interring the unclaimed bodies of hospital patients subject to autopsy and dissection. Yet even so there is evidence that some hospitals made at least some attempt to inter a presentable corpse. The skull cap of a young female from the Edinburgh Royal Infirmary discussed above had been returned to anatomical position following autopsy with the scalp used to hold the bone in place (Henderson, Collard and Johnston 1996: 937). Hospital regulations at Edinburgh required that bodies were sewn up and dressed on completion of an autopsy. While such regulations would have been primarily designed for those bodies being returned to their families after the autopsy, it is possible that the similar levels of care were extended to those interred by the hospital in their burial ground (Henderson, Collard and Johnston 1996: 939). Such regulations were not unique to Edinburgh. At St Bartholomew's in London a hospital beadle ensured that the body was sewn up and placed in a coffin after an autopsy (Lawrence 1996: 196). The hospitals of the eighteenth and nineteenth centuries were charitable institutions and charges of mutilation of the dead could stain their reputations

6 The medical body: the archaeological evidence for the use of the corpse in medical research and teaching

Figure 6.3 Skeleton 219, buried c. 1800 at St Mary's, Barton-upon-Humber. This individual has had his spine, ribs, pelvis and shoulders removed so that he was effectively "a skin bag" at the time of burial. His skull has been opened for the purposes of post-mortem inspection. However, those who buried him had gone to great lengths to restore his appearance for burial. In place of a spine a stake of wood had been inserted into the body cavity, which was probably then stuffed with some organic material, and his skull had been glued back together (Photograph courtesy of Warwick Rodwell).

and adversely affect their finances. At other institutions the evidence of care taken in reconstituting the body was more variable. At Newcastle Infirmary, some of those subjected to craniotomies were interred with the skull cap in approximate anatomical position (Nolan 1998: 46). Yet little attempt was made to mask the damage done by the surgeon's knife to other burials. One burial consisted of a prone torso with arms placed on top while the body of another interment had been sawn in half and the lower half below the fourth lumber vertebrae was missing (Nolan 1998: 46; Chamberlain 1999: 7). The latter was interred with a stone slab in the coffin to make up the weight of the lower body, perhaps to disguise the evidence of dissection and the absence of part of the body. Similar behaviour was observed at the Royal London Hospital where four individuals were interred without their lower bodies (Powers 2008: 47). One of these individuals was one of three bodies from the site interred without a skull, whose sawn cervical vertebrae indicated where their head had been removed. Variation in the treatment of those interred at Newcastle may be the result of a number of factors. The burial ground was in use for almost 100 years and it is possible that the regulations governing the burial of subjects of autopsy changed over this period. Perhaps there were differences in the requirements governing the interment of those subject to autopsy, as opposed to more invasive procedures. Alternatively there may have been practical considerations; while it could have been feasible to repair and conceal the results of an autopsy, such an undertaking is not always possible with more fragmented remains.

Less care appears to have been taken in the reconstruction of the remains of those interred in prison burial grounds. These actions undoubtedly reflect the legislation that denied murderers the right to burial between 1751 and 1832 as a means of extending punishment beyond death. The burials of two dissected felons from Oxford Castle, which probably predate the Murder Act, were interred with the fragmented remains of their skulls placed inside their chest cavities (Norton 2006: 12), while the splayed ribs of a late nineteenth-century female prisoner at York Prison suggest that little attempt had been made to repair the damage done when the chest was opened, although the skull cap had been replaced on top of the skull (Carrott et al. 1998: 4).

Archaeological evidence for dissection

In comparison with autopsies, there is less diagnostic evidence for dissection in the archaeological record. As discussed above, two of the burials from the sixteenth- to eighteenth-century prison cemetery at Oxford Castle were probably dissected. The skulls of these two individuals, both young adult males, had been subjected to multiple craniotomies and were then placed in their chest cavities prior to interment (figure 6.4) (Norton 2006: 12; Hacking 2006: 116–7). There is also a suggestion of dissection among some of the skeletal remains from the eighteenth- and nineteenth-century burial ground associated with the Newcastle Infirmary. The lower body of one individual was absent below the fourth lumber vertebrae, while the head and shoulders of another appears to have been retained for teaching purposes, possibly including dissection (Nolan 1998: 49). Other evidence for dissection has been found in dumps of medical waste (see table 6.5). Three of these sites can be linked to anatomical teaching establishments. An address in Craven Street, London, is known to have been home to the anatomist William Hewson between 1772 and 1774 (Hillson *et al.* 1999: 14). Hewson, a former pupil of John Hunter, ran an anatomy school in Craven Street and the assemblage containing skulls with sagittal and traverse craniotomies and long bones with practice amputations is probably linked to that establishment (Hillson *et al.* 1999: 14–5). The Old Ashmolean Museum in Oxford was the site of an anatomy school between 1683 and 1767 (Bennett, Johnston and Simcock 2000: 7, 23) and the collection of human and animal bones recovered from there is likely to be the result of clearing out that took place in 1781 (Bennett, Johnston and Simcock 2000: 27). The excavator suggested that the human bone, which included skulls with craniotomies and sawn bones, may have once formed part of a teaching collection on the growth and development of the skeleton (Bennett, Johnston and Simcock 2000: 51). The site at Surgeons' Square in Edinburgh lies to the north-east of Surgeons' Hall, and buildings to its west and east are known to have housed private anatomy schools (Henderson, Collard and Johnston 1996: 940). A small assemblage of bone, which includes a distal tibia

Figure 6.4 One of the burials from Oxford Castle moat. This individual, almost certainly an executed criminal, had been subject to post-mortem dissection and finally interred with the sawn-off part of his cranium in his chest cavity (Photograph courtesy of Oxford Archaeology).

6 The medical body: the archaeological evidence for the use of the corpse in medical research and teaching

Table 6.5. Non-funerary assemblages of human bone with evidence for medical intervention

Site	Date	Evidence for dissection	Evidence for retention for display	Evidence for post-mortem surgery	Animal bones present	Reference
Craven Street, London	1772–1777	Craniotomies, sawn bones	Evidence for preparation of samples including mercury	Trephination and amputation	Yes – including dogs, birds, fish and marine turtle	Hillson et al. 1999
Old Ashmolean Museum, Oxford	1683–1767	Craniotomies, sawn bones	Holes drilled through bones for suspension	No	Yes – including dog, racoon and manatee	Hull 2003
Surgeon's Square, Edinburgh	Mid 19th century	Sectioned bones	Possibly – collection included sectioned bones with pathological lesions	No	Yes – including brown bear and seal	Henderson, Collard and Johnston 1996
Nottingham General Hospital	Late 18th to early 19th century	No	Long bone fitted with iron hinge; bones with pathological lesions	No	No	Chapman 1997
Church Street, Romsey, Hampshire	Mid-19th century	Craniotomies, cut and saw marks on bones	No	No	No	Smith 1999
Royal London Hospital[1]	c.1820–1854	Craniotomies, sawn marks on ribs, vertebrae, clavicles, removal of head and lower body	Holes drilled through bones, wires and pins in bones, varnishing of bones, staining of bones, casts of blood vessels	Trephination	Yes – dog, rabbit, tortoise	Powers 2008

1 Assemblage from coffins and boxes containing dissected remains of more than one individual

and fibula sectioned coronally (along medial-lateral plane), is thought to be linked to one of these buildings (Henderson, Collard and Johnston 1996: 940). The fourth site, Church Street in Romsey, is a little more curious. The bones from this site, which include a sectioned femur and frontal bone as well as seven skeletal elements with fine superficial cuts, were found packed around a brick built-drain culvert (Smith 1999: 6–7). The house was occupied by a Dr. Beddome during the nineteenth century and it has been suggested that these bones may be the product of autopsies, although sectioning of long bones was not usually part of a post-mortem. Alternatively they may represent some type of private medical research. The lack of evidence for dissection in the archaeological record is perhaps not surprising as remains were often highly fragmented. An opponent of the 1832 Anatomy Act wrote that after dissection there was "little left but a series of disconnected bones denuded of flesh", and that three-quarters to two-thirds of the body had been wasted or consigned to troughs, pits and night carts (Roberts 1843: 9–10). The variety of methods used to dispose of the remains of dissected individuals has been considered in chapter 5.

Grave robbing can be dated back to the seventeenth century and bodies were being sold for profit by the early eighteenth century (Richardson 1987: 55). By the 1790s, one London gang were charging two guineas and a crown for adult bodies, and procuring children's bodies at six shillings for the first foot and then nine pence for every additional inch (Dopson 1949: 69). The fear of being untimely wrenched from the grave pervaded late eighteenth- and early nineteenth-century society. Whether the grave-robbers were really so prolific to warrant such widespread public panic is less clear. There is little direct evidence for their activities in the archaeological record. The lead coffin of Anna Barnard, who was interred in the Quaker Cemetery at Kingston-upon-Thames, had been ripped open at the head end and was empty except for a blonde hairpiece (Bashford and Sibun 2007: 111). The activities of the resurrectionists offer a likely explanation for the damage to the coffin and the absence of the body. The technique of breaking the coffin at the head end, and removing the body that way is described in a resurrectionist's memoir, discussed by Richardson (1987: 59). A further twenty-eight graves lacking any evidence for a body or a coffin were identified during excavations at the Quaker cemetery, their contents removed either by grave robbers or for interment elsewhere (Bashford and Sibun 2007: 114). Burial legislation of the 1850s resulted in the closure of many urban churchyards and burial grounds and there is some evidence for the exhumation of some bodies from these sites for interment elsewhere, often in garden cemeteries, as had been discussed in Chapter 4. An empty grave, which retained the impression of the coffin at the base of the cut, was also noted at the Baptist burial ground in Poole (McKinley 2008: 17). While it is possible that the occupant of this grave may have been removed by grave robbers, their activities tended to be primarily confined to cities with markets for fresh corpses such as London and Edinburgh. In some cases, the corpse never reached the grave and the rubble filling a coffin from the vault under Christ Church, Spitalfields may bear testament to the activities of a corrupt undertaker (Richardson 1987: 65; Molleson and Cox 1993: 205), who had sold the corpse to the anatomists prior to the funeral and used the rubble to disguise the absence of a body.

The paucity of archaeological evidence for the activities of the resurrection men is perhaps easily explained. The burgeoning urban populations of the industrial centres of eighteenth- and nineteenth-centuries overwhelmed existing graveyards and burial grounds, resulting in high levels of inter-cutting of burials.[6] In an era where it was not unknown for grave-diggers and sextons to use iron borers in an attempt to find room to inter another body (Chadwick 1843: 141; Mytum 1989: 291; Rugg 1998: 45) any empty graves resulting from the activities of the resurrectionists would be quickly obscured by later burials in many cemeteries, unless the individual was interred in a metal coffin. Anatomists would boast that no-one was beyond their reach and bodies are known to have been stolen to order (Richardson 1987: 63–64). In his evidence to the Select Committee in 1828 the surgeon Sir Astley Cooper said "there is no person, let his situation in life be what it may, whom, if I were disposed to dissect, I could not obtain" (Report of Select Committee on Anatomy 1828: 18). Yet much of the resurrectionist's trade involved targeting easy sources of bodies: primarily the graves of the poor (Richardson 1987: 61). In many inner city churchyards and burial grounds, the bodies of paupers and those of limited means were interred in mass graves and pits (Walker 1839: 139; Richardson 1989: 116; Brickley and Miles 1999a: 25).[7] These were graves initially dug to a great depth and left open while they gradually filled up over time. These open graves were popular targets for the resurrectionists and the flimsy wooden coffins of the poor offered little resistance, particularly when compared with the more robust triple-shelled coffins available to those with greater means (Richardson 1987: 60, 80). The absence of one or more bodies from these graves would not necessarily be noticeable in the archaeological record.

More visible archaeologically is the fear created by the activities of the resurrections as individuals sought to ensure their mortal remains did not end up on an anatomist's slab. This usually involved enhancing the protection provided to the body in the grave. For the wealthy, the use of brick-lined graves and private vaults, combined with triple-shelled coffins, all served to enhance security, but for some this was insufficient and additional measures were required (Richardson 1987: 80). While patents were filed for complex methods ensuring long-term occupancy of the grave, such as the Jarvis's Patent Coffin of 1810 (Litten 1991: 109–111), additional post-mortem security often took a simpler form of the addition of iron bars and straps to the coffin. At Christ Church Spitalfields, the outer wooden coffin of Mrs Mary Mason had three iron straps secured around it while the thin iron plate along the side of a coffin from St Oswald's Priory may represent the remains of an anti-resurrectionist device (Molleson and Cox 1993: 205; Heighway and Bryant 1999: 221). Interestingly, some of the most robust anti-ressurectionist defences were found on the coffin of the undertaker Mr. William Horne from Spitalfields. His triple-shelled coffin had two iron bars running the length of coffin supporting the lid of the wooden shell, the lead coffin had two iron bars nailed to the interior and the outer wooden coffin had two iron straps wrapped around it and secured with nails (Molleson and Cox 1993: 205). His profession would have made him more familiar with the activities of the resurrectionists than most. Indeed, some undertakers were known to accept bribes allowing the body to be stolen prior to interment (Richardson 1987: 65). Another method of ensuring the security of the grave was to use a mortsafe that could be placed above or around the coffin after burial and then removed once sufficient time had elapsed to allow putrefaction to set in thus rendering the body useless to the resurrectionists (figure 6.5) (Ritchie 1921). There were several types of mortsafes. The simplest consisted of a large grave-shaped stone, such as those found at Skene and Inverurie in Aberdeenshire, which were placed above the coffin (Ritchie 1921: 222). Others made from iron were more elaborate and could be placed around the coffin to prevent access. These consisted of iron cages which were inverted over the coffin containing the deceased, such as the examples unearthed in Oyne churchyard, Aberdeenshire in the 1910s or found at Auchlossan farm, Aberdeenshire (Ritchie 1921: 223–4).

Figure 6.5 Mortsafe from St Mary's, Holystone. This iron cage was designed to go deep into the grave around the newly buried coffin and thus to keep the burial safe from grave-robbers (Photograph courtesy of John Dalrymple).

Archaeological evidence for post-mortem surgery

While there is some evidence for the use of analgesics during the eighteenth century either in the form of small doses of opium administered prior to the operation or the use of tourniquets or clamps to apply pressure to deaden the nerves, most surgery was performed without anaesthesia until 1840s, often with the patient restrained (Porter 1996: 229; Witkin 1997: 20; Chamberlain 1999: 7). Under these circumstances surgery had to be quick and was not to be performed by the inexperienced, at least not on living patients (Porter 1996: 207). The dead however were another matter. Students were able to practice surgical techniques on a dead body without the complications of a moving patient or the prospect of an unfavourable outcome should they take too long. Any evidence for post-mortem surgery in the archaeological record is likely to be confined to those procedures which leave a trace on the skeleton which we can demonstrate occurred post-mortem and was not the product of surgery performed shortly before death. A number of the skulls found among the waste deposits associated with William Hewson's 1770s Craven Street anatomy school in London bore marks of specialised surgical instruments such as the trephine (Hillson *et al.* 1998/9: 16). The trephine was used to cut out circular discs of bone from the skull. The crania from Craven Street bear marks not only of completed holes but partially cut ones as well, with some skulls exhibiting multiple completed and uncompleted holes indicating their use for practicing surgery. A cranium from the Royal London had a trephine hole with ten clearly defined restarts (Powers 2008: 55). The cranium of an isolated skull found at Cotton Court, Hill Street in Belfast also exhibited marks from a trephine; in this case there were eleven separate cuts (figure 6.6). The skull is thought to have belonged to a medical student and was used to practice trepanation before being discarded in the back garden of the property (O Baoill, McQuaid and Buckley 2002: 7).

Six examples of post-mortem amputations were identified among the skeletal remains from the

Figure 6.6 The cranium of a skull found at Cotton Court, Hill Street in Belfast had eleven separate cuts made by a trephine. This was probably the product of a medical student practising trepanation on a dead body (Photograph courtesy of Laureen Buckley).

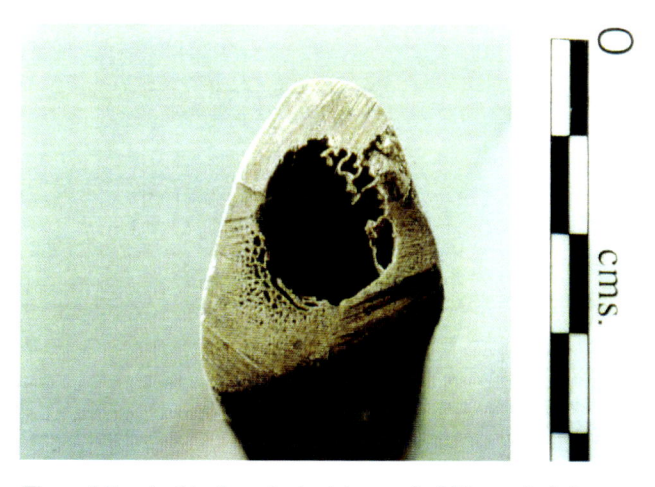

Figure 6.7 A tibia from the burial ground of Newcastle Infirmary had saw marks showing that the bone had been cut from 3 different directions. Such a process was far too slow and clumsy to have been used on a living patient and is therefore probably evidence of post-mortem surgery (Photograph courtesy of Annsofie Witkin)

Newcastle Infirmary's late eighteenth- and early nineteenth-century burial ground (Witkin 1997: 83, 87). On one bone, a tibia, the direction of sawing had changed several times, which indicates that the procedure would have been too slow to have been performed on a living patient with any chance of the individual surviving (figure 6.7) (Witkin 1997: 84; Chamberlain 1999: 7). The position of the cut on another bone, an ulna, was too high to have been performed ante-mortem, as there was no functional reason for retaining the elbow once the muscle insertions were removed (Witkin 1997: 88). Occasionally, the level of bone modification alone is suggestive of post-mortem surgery, such as in the case of the skeleton which has amputations to four bones; right humerus, right femur, right fibula and right tibia; representing three separate procedures (Boulter, Robertson and Start 1998: 138; Start 2002: 117; Witkin 1997: 89). It is unlikely that the leg was severed at both the thigh and calf for medical reasons. The same individual has also had a craniotomy, four cut ribs cut at the mid-shaft and the fifth thoracic vertebra had been transversely sectioned (Boulter, Robertson and Start 1998: 138). Cadavers were often in short supply and the use of a single body to practice multiple surgical techniques and for autopsy/dissection, as seen in this skeleton, was likely to have been common (Witkin 1997: 83). Indeed, similar evidence for multiple amputations was observed in a male burial from the Royal London whose tibiae, forearms and upper arms had been sawn through (Powers 2008: 47). The severed limbs had all been interred with the rest of the body.

The retention of body parts

The use of fresh cadavers in medical teaching and research was augmented by the use of preserved anatomical specimens. Anatomical collections contained both the mundane and exceptional, and were particularly useful in illustrating rare conditions and the complex, difficult-to-dissect parts of the body. A number of anatomical collections from the eighteenth and nineteenth century are still extant. The best known are those of John and William Hunter, which are housed in the Royal College of Surgeons in London and the Hunterian Museum in Glasgow respectively. In addition, skeletal material thought to have originated in anatomical collections has been excavated in Edinburgh, Nottingham, Oxford and London (see table 6.5).

The specimens in anatomical collections were usually a combination of skeletal samples and preserved soft tissue. The skeletal material consisted of single bones, some intact and others sectioned in different planes, and partial or complete skeletons, re-assembled using wires. Bones with copper stains from suspension wires and holes were found among the excavated material from the Old Ashmolean Museum, Oxford (Bennet, Johnston and Simcock 2000: 26; White 2003: 14–5). An ulna found among the disarticulated bone associated with Mercer's Hospital in Dublin had been perforated at the proximal end to allow the insertion of a copper hinge (Buckley and Hayden 2002: 170), and a right tibia found at Nottingham General Hospital had evidence for an iron hinge at the proximal end and a deeply incised slot on the distal end suggesting the bone was once part of anatomical teaching skeleton (Chapman 1997: 44). The hinge would have allowed flexion with the femur at the knee while the groove at the distal end would have housed a pivot for the foot (Chapman

1997: 45). Reference collections were also designed to illustrate morbid anatomy and many of the bones in the anatomical collection found at Nottingham exhibited pathological changes, such as rickets, osteomyelitis and septic arthritis (Chapman 1997: 39–43). High levels of pathological change were also observed among the bones from Surgeon's Square in Edinburgh including examples of Paget's disease, osteomyelitis and an ankylosed distal tibia and fibula that had been sectioned coronally to illustrate the ossified transverse and anterior tibiofibular ligaments (Henderson, Collard and Johnston 1996: 940).

Soft tissues could be preserved either by drying or preservation in alcohol (Knox 1836: 10, 13). Coloured solutions and mercury were often injected into specimens to highlight certain features, particularly the arterial, venous and lymphatic systems. The coloured solutions consisted of pigments combined with glue, varnish or wax to produce a substance that would solidify after injection, unlike mercury, which remained liquid after injection and could leach from the specimen (Knox 1836: 27–32). Specimens required regular care to prevent insect infestations or the evaporation of the liquids preserving wet samples (Knox 1836: 11, 16). Mercury in close proximity to some turtle bones and a dog vertebra outlined with the inorganic pigment vermilion were found during the excavations at Craven Street (Hillson *et al.* 1999: 16), suggesting that the preparation of specimens occurred on the premises. It has been proposed that some of the remains found during the excavation of the burial ground of the Royal London Hospital represented sporadic clear-outs of prepared specimens (Powers 2008: 56). Nine of the contexts with multiple remains contained evidence of prepared specimens (figure 6.8). Copper wires were found attached to an infant skull, a male pelvis, and a sacrum. Copper pins for articulating joints were found in a scapula and humerus from different contexts. Hands and feet articulated with wires and iron discs were also recovered. Five body portions had been stained bright red with the patination in some instances having a waxy appearance. A right parietal and tibia from one context exhibited evidence of varnishing (Powers 2008: 50, 56). In addition, some evidence for anatomical preparation and potential retention of entire

Figure 6.8 Grave at the Royal London Hospital containing a variety of human bones from several individuals which have been subject to cutting, either through surgery or in order to prepare anatomical specimens (Photograph courtesy of MOLA)

bodies was observed among the articulated burials from the Royal London Hospital. Wired specimens were observed in several contexts while an adult of indeterminate sex was accompanied in the grave by a number of irregular thin cylinders, up to c. 20mm in diameter, made from greyish clay or lime plaster (Powers 2008: 51, 56). It has been suggested that the latter may represent cast or calcified blood vessels (Powers 2008: 48, 51).

Animal bone was present in four of the assemblages in table 6.5. Approximately three-quarters of the animal bone recovered from the Old Ashmolean in Oxford was canine, from at least 24 individuals of a variety of breeds (Hamilton-Dyer 2003: 16–7). The dog bones had a bleached appearance and four had cut marks indicative of disarticulation or defleshing and two pelvic bones had been sawn in half. Animal bone was also recovered from Craven Street, the Royal London and Surgeon's Square. Exotic species were present at all four sites including racoon and manatee at Oxford (Hamilton-Dyer 2003: 17), seal and brown bear at Edinburgh (Henderson, Collard and Johnston 1996: 940), tortoise at the Royal London (Powers 2008: 51) and marine turtle at Craven Street, London (Hillson et al. 1999: 15). Animal bone was also recovered from fourteen of the contexts containing multiple disarticulated remains at the Royal London Hospital (Powers 2008: 51). These skeletons were often relatively complete and the wired vertebrae from a small mammal, possibly a rabbit were also recovered. The use of other species to better understand the structures and functions of human body has a long antiquity and appears in the writings of Aristotle and the Hippocratic school in the fourth century BC (Sandford, Lullerschmidt and Hutchinson 2002: 832). The concept was adopted by the British anatomists of the post-medieval period. "We can understand but little of our own structure unless we study that of other animals" wrote Alexander Munro, professor of medicine and anatomy at the University of Edinburgh in an essay on comparative anatomy published in 1744. The pioneering studies by William Harvey on the circulation of the blood and Thomas Willis on the anatomy of the brain in the seventeenth century drew heavily on animal experimentation (Harvey 1653; Willis 1681: 56). By the eighteenth century, the use of animals was an integral part of the work of anatomists such as John Hunter (Moore 2006: 23). The material from Craven Street has been linked to the anatomy school of one Hunter's students, William Hewson (Hillson et al. 1999: 16), whose work on blood used human and animal material and the publication of this work contains an appendix on the lymphatic systems of birds, fish and amphibians (Hewson 1772). Therefore, recovering animal bone from a dump of material from his anatomy school comes as no surprise, nor does the presence of animal bones at Oxford and Edinburgh. The use of animals for research had many advantages. They were easier to obtain than human remains and their exploitation had none of the moral complications or public relations problems associated with work on dead human bodies (Hull 2003: 23). Moreover, it was possible to perform experiments on living animals that were not legally or ethically acceptable on human subjects. New surgical procedures could be perfected on animals before they were used on patients (Moore 2006: 29), although it could be argued that the treatment some patients received in hospital constituted experimentation.

The origins of preserved human specimens in collections were the product of circumstance and changed over time. Early collections, such as the late seventeenth- and early eighteenth-century anatomy collection held in the anatomy school in the basement of the first Ashmolean, were likely to have derived largely from those executed at the gallows (Hull 2003: 21). The excavators note that the University at Oxford had legal access to the corpses of those executed at Oxford and Abingdon during the seventeenth and eighteenth centuries. The gallows would not have fulfilled all the school's requirements. Foetal bones were found during the excavation of material from Ashmolean's anatomy school (Bennett et al. 2000: 27; White 2003: 13) and it seems possible that the school sought to augment its teaching material by purchasing the remains of children and foetuses from parents or possibly ressurectionists (Hull 2003: 22).

The catalogues that describe in great detail the specimens in John Hunter's collection are usually silent as the origins of the human material (Clift 1825 and n.d.). It may simply be that this information was not deemed worth recording, yet for a small proportion of samples details of their origins are provided. One of the skeletons listed in a catalogue, compiled by William Clift after Hunter's collection had been moved to the Royal College of Surgeons after his death, was that of William Edward White who had been hanged for murder in 1773 (Clift 1800: 101). Among the pathological samples are specimens from patients Hunter treated either at St Georges Hospital or privately (Clift n.d: 18, 37, 49). In some cases the samples are the by-products of surgery such as parts of amputated limbs or excised tumours. Other specimens could only have been obtained after the death of the patient and while it seems unlikely that Hunter could have obtained parts of his deceased private patients without their consent, the situation pertaining to those he treated at St George's is less clear.

While the core of many private anatomical collections came from the dissecting room and the hospital, additional measures were often required to obtain

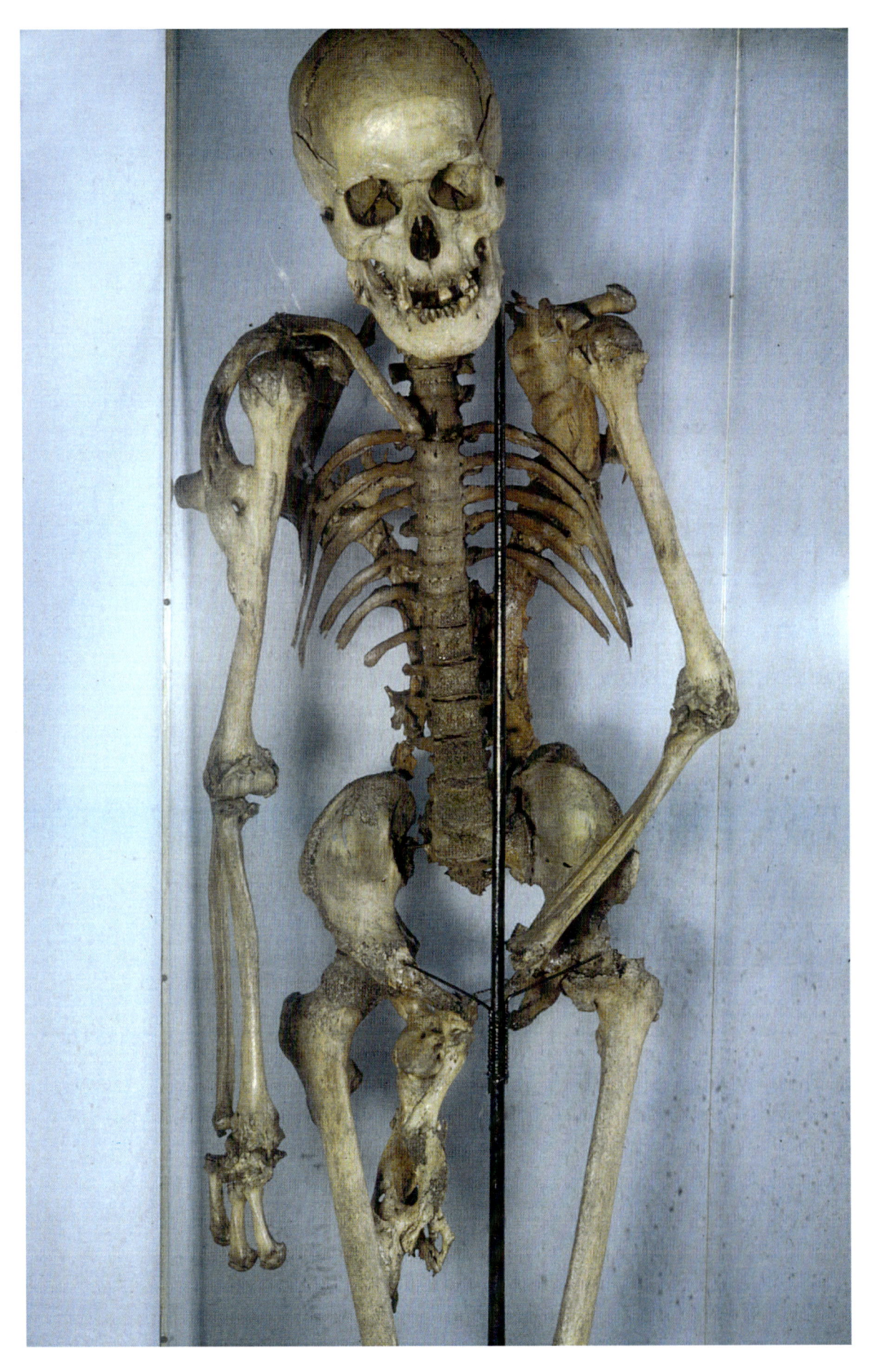

6 The medical body: the archaeological evidence for the use of the corpse in medical research and teaching

Figure 6.9 Skeleton of "Mr. Jeffs" purchased from another anatomist by John Hunter at auction in 1783 for 85 guineas. The skeleton exhibits bony growths resulting from the disease myositis ossificans (Photograph courtesy of the Hunterian Collection)

rare specimens. Resurrectionists would steal specific bodies to order for a price. The surgeon Astley Cooper's anatomical collection contained the ligatured aneurismal blood vessels of a patient he operated on some twenty years before his death. He had been notified of the individual's death by a local surgeon and commissioned two of his resurrectionists for seven guineas plus expenses to obtain the body (Richardson 1987: 64). Most private and institutional collections were enhanced by donations of rare and interesting specimens (Clift 1825; Cathcart 1893: v; Moore 2005: 468). Anatomical specimens could also be purchased at auctions, just like any other collectable. There were at least fourteen public auctions of anatomical preparations between 1746 and 1793, and probably many more private auctions. John Hunter's anatomical collection included a skeleton of "Mr. Jeffs"[8] purchased at auction in 1783 for 85 guineas (figure 6.9) (RCSHC/P 804). The skeleton exhibits bony growths resulting from the disease myositis ossificans and had previously been owned by another surgeon George Hawkins, whose death in 1783 led to the auction of his anatomical collection. Surviving auction catalogues not only provide evidence for the sale of whole or fragmented human remains, but give an indication of the size of some private collections. When the collection of "an eminent professor of anatomy" was auctioned in 1787, it consisted of 1328 lots including skeletal remains and preserved soft tissue, and was sold over 13 days (Anon 1787). Similarly the remains of Joshua Brookes's Museum were sold at auction over 23 days in 1830, with lots including wet and dry anatomical specimens, pathological samples, complete skeletons and disarticulated bone, which had been "allotted in small parcels, for the convenience of professional gentlemen, artists, sculptors, students etc" (Anon 1830).

Conclusion

The change in approach to medical teaching and research during the post-medieval period affected people's attitudes towards the corpse. In certain contexts the corpse had been transformed, either in its entirety or in pieces, into a source of knowledge. During the second half of the eighteenth century, the bodies of the dead became integral to the study of medicine as teaching aids in the study of anatomy and surgery and as the subject of research and experimentation. In some instances, bodies or body parts were retained in anatomical collections as reference materials. The importance of the dead to the medical profession also transformed the corpse into an object of exchange and commerce in the late eighteenth and early nineteenth century. The body became something to be bought, sold, exchanged and stolen. Whether illegal or legal, a fresh corpse could only be acquired at a cost. The resurrectionists stealing bodies needed to be paid. The bodies of criminals were free to those institutions legally entitled to them but money had to be given to the executioner and other officials to ensure the body was actually obtained and not lost to the gallows crowd. In addition, some criminals destined for the gallows but not the dissecting room would sell their bodies to pay for prison debts or funerary costs (Richardson 1987: 52). Commerce was not just confined to the initial acquisition of fresh corpses. Private anatomy schools would often sell dismembered body parts as a means to offset their running costs (Richardson 1987: 55) and many anatomical collections were augmented by specimens bought at auction. The clandestine trade in bodies came to an end with the passing of the Anatomy Act in 1832. The plentiful supply of the corpses of the poor meant there was no longer any need to pay the grave robbers or bribe officials to obtain a corpse from the gallows.

Notes

1. Also see discussion on embalming in chapter 2.
2. For a more detailed discussion of embalming see chapter 2.
3. See discussion of uneven chronological distribution of post-medieval burial evidence in chapter 1.
4. It is possible for a wealthy individual to have relatively basic funerary provision, it is less probable that a poor individual would have elaborate funerary provision.
5. See chapter 2.
6. See chapter 4.
7. See chapter 4.
8. The skeleton can still be seen in the Hunterian Museum at the Royal College of Surgeons in London.

7 Conclusions

The preceding chapters are a broad and general summary of the archaeological evidence, drawing out some of the major features of burial practices in the post-medieval period. Before moving on to the gazetteer, we will attempt to summarise some of the trends and themes that have emerged. Because of the way the information has been broken up for the purposes of the foregoing survey, this brief final evaluation will identify the particular times of greatest change, and look also at what remains largely unchanged through the period. Finally we will close with some reflections on how we would hope to see work in post-medieval burial archaeology progressing over the next few years, and an invitation to those involved in this area of study to help us to complete and update our gazetteer.

Trends and Themes

A number of general broad trends were operational over the whole of the post-medieval period. These include the gradual removal of death and burial from the control of the Church and into the hands of the State; a developing emphasis on the elaboration of the body and the memory of the deceased in mortuary and commemorative practices, as the Chantries Act removed the fate of any other person's soul from the control of the living; and an increase in the range of possibility and choice for the bereaved in their mortuary practices in terms of material culture and place of burial. In almost all the trends considered here, the rate of change was faster in cities than in the countryside, and faster in England than in other countries, perhaps because the rate and scale of urbanisation was greater in England than the other countries considered, and so much of our English data comes from cities, especially London.

It would not be correct to say that a religious understanding of the world was replaced over this period by a scientific one. Even in the nineteenth century there is little evidence of atheism or a totally secular outlook; and there is ample evidence of a developing empirical science from the sixteenth century onwards. However, it is certainly the case that regulation of the cultural and social process of death and disposal passed from the Church to the State, starting with the State's curtailment of the Church's ability to influence the fate of the soul through accepting endowments towards the repetition of masses and prayers. While the ceremonial aspects of burial remained in Church control, almost all the practicalities of disposal needed to comply with State regulation. Even such apparently private aspects of burial as the choice of textile in which to wrap the body were constrained by law under the various Burial in Woollen Acts, and by instituting a framework of inspections. Later the Law was to appropriate the corpse as a locus for the exercise of punishment. Meanwhile, attempts by the Church to demarcate acceptable religious and moral practice by excluding the bodies of suicides, the unbaptised, excommunicates, victims of drowning and others, were gradually eroded by law, in tune with a general change in public attitudes. In most archaeological periods archaeologists are probably justified in assuming that changing burial practices were the result of shifts in social and cultural relationships and beliefs. In contrast, during the post-medieval period much of the change we see was 'top-down', and accomplished by changes in legislation. Some of the acts with the greatest impact on burial practice are listed in Appendix 1.

The changes of the seventeenth century

Although the great dislocation between the medieval and the post-medieval period as it affected the relationship between the living and the dead took place when Purgatory disappeared from the thanatological landscape of most British Christians in the 1540s, it was not until the seventeenth century that the consequences of the religious Reformation became very clear in archaeologically-attested practices. A combination of factors is responsible for this. First, there is very little archaeological evidence for burial practices in the sixteenth century. Much of the evidence we do have for that period is atypical – burials of suspected recusants through the demolition layers of former monastic buildings for example. Secondly it is likely that in the politically and religiously unstable climate of the mid to late sixteenth century people were making conservative choices about burial ritual. However, the doctrinal changes of the Reformation affected directly and indirectly the relationship between the living and the dead which in turn had consequences for burial practices. A burial's proximity to the holiest places of the church – the high altar and the chancel – was no longer of spiritual significance and, for the first time, the churchyard began to be used for the display of prestigious memorials. In Scotland, where burial beneath the church floor was forbidden, in theory at least, new possibilities for high status memorials, such as burial aisles and mural tablets, came into use. Burial locations other than the parish churchyard became possibilities, at least in some areas, as dissenter and other unofficial burial places were established. Because the living were no longer empowered to have any effect on the fate of the soul, the focus of attention moved almost entirely onto the treatment of the body and the remembrance of the social and secular identity of the deceased.

Of all the changes in material practice that date to the post-medieval period, the near universal adoption of coffins is perhaps of the greatest significance. It indicates, among other things, a new sensitivity among the living to the treatment of the dead body. The living now had a degree of insulation from the physicality of burial and bodily decay. By the end of the seventeenth century, the body was most often encased in a coffin. This, in turn, enabled a new suite of material practices. Because the shroud no longer had the function of concealing and containing the body itself, a range of special grave clothes became more popular. These were designed to beautify the body, rather than to hide it, and include pinked, punched, frilled, gathered and embroidered ornamentation. The use of a wooden coffin also permitted the remains to be labelled, using tacks to form initials and dates, or by the application of engraved coffin plates which appear in increasing numbers from the seventeenth century. The exact purpose of a coffin plate is hard to explain, at least in practical terms, but their use is probably related to a developing identification of the modern self with a unique and individual body.

The Protestant Reformation of the sixteenth century constituted a radical break in religious history. However, it was not the only significant moment in a process of fragmentation of faith that continued up to the present. From a (relatively) unified Christian faith which was shared by nearly all the inhabitants of a parish, Britain and Ireland moved to a situation where adherence to Catholicism or Protestantism divided communities and then saw further fragmentation as the non-conformist Protestant denominations began to multiply. These breakdowns in religious affiliation had direct and far-reaching impact on burial practice. The dissenting Churches, especially Quakers, rejected conventional burial locations and orientations as superstitious, and therefore established their own burial grounds. These had the further advantage of freeing dissenters from dependence on the Established Church for permission to bury the dead as they wished.

Although this book has attempted to review only the below-ground archaeology of post-medieval death, it is worth noting that the seventeenth century saw the first of two significant rises in the number of commemorative monuments erected in Britain and Ireland. Most of them were inside ecclesiastical buildings, but the earliest surviving graveyard monuments in many parishes also belong to the seventeenth century. The second major increase in the number of memorial monuments took place in the late eighteenth and early nineteenth centuries, and comprised a rapid rise in the number of monuments erected outside in the churchyards. Where the seventeenth-century monuments were individually made and usually commemorated members of wealthy or titled families, the eighteenth- to nineteenth-century 'gravestone boom' was associated with the widespread availability of mass-produced and cheaply made stones which were erected in memory of those of more modest means.

Post-medieval commemoration served as a means of perpetuating a memory – an acceptably secular form of afterlife now that the soul of the deceased was generally out of bounds to the bereaved. A memorial monument also functioned to locate the body, something that was often important given the centrality of the corpse to rituals of disposal and memory.

The changes of the nineteenth century

The second key period of change is the first half of the nineteenth century. Social attitudes, new scientific understandings of disease and the body, and changing political and economic environments combined to produce a set of burial practices, many of which are broadly recognisable today. A knowledge of medicine that related disease to poor hygiene, together with the land pressures of urban development, growing acknowledgment of the rights of non-conformists and other factors detailed by Rugg (1998) informed policy decisions to close the overcrowded urban parish graveyards and replace them with new, spacious, suburban landscaped cemeteries.

It is also in the nineteenth century that, outside Ireland, the secular powers of the State finally eclipsed the Church in control over burial practice. The new, suburban cemeteries were one aspect of this. In them, members of the Established Church were treated no more favourably than adherents to any other denomination or faith. At the same time, social attitudes towards marginal or transgressive individuals like suicides and criminals also softened considerably, and they were no longer routinely excluded from normal burial. In the nineteenth century the practice of punishing the dead body by quartering, dissection or exposure finally came to an end. Perhaps it was not until then that rational, secular thought was sufficiently established to challenge these vengeful and gruesome punishments which were opposed by the educated on the grounds that they were brutalising, tasteless and logically absurd.

Cremation was eventually legalised in Britain in the nineteenth century, although it did not have a big impact on disposal practice among the majority of people until the twentieth century. The legalisation of cremation made little impact on the archaeological record, but is indicative of a change in attitudes towards the dead body and its decay, marking both a desire to avoid the process of decay altogether by accelerating it, and a decline in the influence of the Church. It is worth noting that Britain was unusual in the West in favouring cremations, by the middle of the twentieth century, over interment. In other European countries, including Ireland, the Catholic Church was more influential in discouraging or preventing cremation from being a significant option. Even after the practice had the official sanction of the Church in the 1960s it was unpopular, and cremation was not available in the Republic of Ireland until about 20 years ago. Even in mostly Protestant Northern Ireland, where it had been legal since 1948 (Northern Ireland having been excluded from the first cremation acts), it was not a popular choice (Mates 2005: 262–71). In England, disposal by cremation was encouraged because, among other reasons, it offered an efficient use of space on an overcrowded island.

The nineteenth century has been represented historically as a period when death, mourning and commemoration were subject to particularly extensive and ostentatious cultural elaboration (e.g. Curl 1993). Apart from the wealthy elite, such elaboration is not very evident in the below-ground archaeology, however. The integration of excavated archaeological burial sites with studies of standing commemorative monuments and other items of funerary culture, both durable and ephemeral, is urgently needed.

Some things never change

It is quite easy, as an archaeologist, to direct one's analysis and interpretation towards periods and places of change and variation in the past. Much more easily overlooked are the practices and features that remain essentially the same over time, or hardly vary across space. In fact there are many aspects of post-medieval burial practice which do not change over the whole period, and several that have continued for millennia or even since prehistoric times. The most enduring of these is probably a west-east orientation of the body, which has dominated interment from the beginning of churchyard burial until the rise of non-denominational cemeteries in the nineteenth to twentieth centuries. A preference for west-east orientation was adopted in early Christianity from prevailing pre-Christian practice. Only the need to use space as efficiently as possible in order to accommodate the highest number of bodies and thus to maximise income caused a change in practice over the last 150 years or so, and even now west-east burial is frequently the norm when space and circumstances permit. Only a small number of non-conformists, mainly Quakers, eschewed west-east burial for theological reasons.

Location of burial is another remarkably enduring tradition. Throughout the period considered in this volume – and for nearly 700 years before it – the majority of burials took place in parish churchyards. Although other kinds of burial ground were increasingly available, especially in urban areas, the parish churchyard continued to act as the main place of interment across most of Britain and Ireland, even in towns and even in the nineteenth century. The parish graveyard answered the needs of, and helped to produce, strong local and family bonds. Burial at the heart of the community, close to one's ancestors and kin and accessible to the bereaved, remained the 'gold standard'.

Washing and clothing the dead body was an essential part of the burial rite for all but the most hurried or dangerous of funerals. Again, this tradition is probably very deep in time but archaeological evidence is scanty for early periods. A simple, supine, extended burial, unaccompanied by any grave goods has been the most common form of burial in Britain and Ireland since the coming of Christianity. The post-medieval period did, however, see a change from interment in a shroud only to interment in a coffin for nearly everyone. In the middle ages, coffins were only standard in the funerals of those of wealth and high social status (and perhaps on some occasions as a means of enclosing the bodies of those who had died from certain infectious diseases). Ordinary people were wrapped in winding sheets that covered the body fully, including the face, before being laid in the grave.

In more general terms, however, burial remained one of the areas of practice in which the distinction between the wealthy elite and the rest of the people was observed and produced. In fact, as the religious interest in burial practice waned, its significance in the construction of social distinction might even have increased. In the absence of grave goods, the quality of the coffin was one indicator of wealth. Double or triple-shelled coffins lined with lead, expensive coffin fittings and beautiful funerary textiles, held in place and decorated with ornamental studs or 'coffin lace', were a demonstration of status as well as a response to concerns about grave robbers. Burial location could also indicate the status of the deceased or their families. Despite the official abandonment of Catholic doctrine in most of Britain, a grave beneath the floor of the church building continued to be considered more desirable than one in the churchyard. Even outside, a hierarchy of space from the favoured south and east sides to the undesirable north persisted, long after the point when such distinctions could have had any theological rationale. The grave itself was made differently according to the resources of those who bought and commissioned it. Wealthier families eschewed simple holes in the earth in favour of brick-lined shafts and vaults (which had the advantage of making subsequent interments in the same grave easier).

Geographically, normative burial practices were remarkable similar across all regions and countries. There are some variations in, for example, the wood from which coffins were made, and some local traditions in their shape too – such as the fishtail coffins known in the Birmingham area. But coffin furniture is more likely to reflect wealth than geography, especially in the nineteenth century when the manufacture and distribution of such artefacts occurred on an industrial scale. The relatively small number of fully published sites from Ireland makes it hard to draw firm conclusions, but the evidence currently available suggests that once again it is wealth and status rather than religion or nationality that is most likely to make a burial distinctive. The widespread use of unofficial cilliní burial grounds, however, is a practice strongly associated with Ireland, although in the course of compiling the material for this book we have identified a small number of sites outside Ireland which might belong to the same tradition – in Scotland and Cornwall principally.

What the future holds (we hope)

In writing this book, we have been aware of how new and how little developed is the archaeological study of post-medieval death and burial in Britain and Ireland, but also surprised at the number of sites which have been excavated. There have been a good number of excellent recent reports, and many units are making considerable efforts to publish their research in monograph form or as extensive journal articles. Others have made good use of the internet and have made some or all of their work accessible on their own websites or through the Archaeology Data Service. However, despite a flurry of good reports having reached publication in the last 5 years, it is still difficult to find enough data of the right quality and sufficiently standardised recording to undertake good comparative work on many aspects of mortuary archaeology. Many site reports remain unpublished and were not easily accessible: we were only able to find out about them through speculative visits and enquiries to active archaeological units. In part this is a consequence of dependence on developer funding and the costs of extensive post-excavation analyses (especially of human bone) outstripping the available budget. However, imaginative ways of getting at least an interim report into the public domain are much appreciated in such circumstances. It is still also the case that several publications say very little about burial practices. We were frustrated, for example, that were we unable to find out basic information like how many coffin plates were recovered, even from some of the major monograph publications. Published reports of multi-period sites, particularly those which were published more than 15 years ago, often pay little attention to post-medieval phases of use, reflecting a widespread lack of recognition of the value of studying post-medieval sites more generally. Among the 30–40 best reports there is a strong bias towards eighteenth- and nineteenth-century burial grounds, and towards cities, especially London.

Unlike archaeological reports of medieval and earlier cemeteries, where the human bone report can sometimes appear to be a flimsy afterthought to an archaeology of burial practices, the study of human bone often takes a leading role in post-medieval cemetery analysis and publication. Good bone reports are always to be applauded, but it is also important to consolidate our knowledge of the cultural mortuary practices which give the, often excellent, human bone analysis context and significance. This demands that the cultural history of death and disposal is given more than cursory consideration. It may be that in the case of burials from the last 500 years their cultural and historical context is considered to be already known, and similar to our own: a regular problem for post-medieval archaeology in all areas. Too frequently the bone report is entirely separate from the description of the archaeology. We have regularly been frustrated by the difficulty or impossibility of matching the individuals in the bone report with the burials mentioned in the text.

Post-medieval burial sites constitute a particular challenge to field archaeologists in Britain and Ireland. Few practitioners or academics have much training or

7 Conclusions

knowledge of this kind of site. Classic cemetery excavations tend to deal with far smaller numbers of inhumations – maybe only a few dozen – in which most grave cuts are well spaced and clearly separable. Many post-medieval cemeteries are quite different from this and present problems which demand a different approach to excavation and analysis from the full and detailed consideration customarily given each excavated medieval interment, for example. There may be thousands of burials. Moreover, they tend to be heavily disturbed and intercut, and burials are often placed on top of one another in a deep shaft containing ten or more individuals. Deposits are full of partial, disarticulated and redeposited remains. The basic task of attributing bones to individuals can be impossible under such circumstances, let alone making stratigraphic sense of the site, even under the best conditions. And post-medieval cemeteries are not usually excavated under the best conditions, but under great time pressure, severe budgetary constraints, and sometimes in forced collaboration with clearance companies, or in the face of hostility from funders, locals or even other archaeologists. Because of their size, decisions about sampling need to be taken; post-excavation analysis of human bone is expensive and therefore needs to be selective. Excavation is often only carried out on a tiny fraction of the whole site and is often rushed, or takes the form of very limited investigations and a watching brief. It is hard to secure adequate funding for excavating post-medieval sites when the general level of awareness and knowledge of their value is not high. There are few long-term, slow, research-led excavations of post-medieval cemeteries. They are usually only excavated in response to an immediate threat, so excavation with insufficient time and resources is the norm.

There are additional factors that constrain archaeological work on post medieval cemeteries. Ethical and political tensions that exist whenever we work on the bodies of the dead are often particularly sensitive when dealing with the recent dead, and there may be public resistance to excavation or to extensive study of the remains. In some cases, there may also be legitimate concerns about the health of excavators (Kneller 1998). Well-sealed lead-lined coffins containing surviving soft tissue are not normally opened, but are reburied instead. There is still some uncertainty about how long certain diseases might survive in such unusual conditions and the health risk of investigating bodies that might have died from smallpox, for example, normally outweighs the potential gains in our knowledge of burial practice. The modern attitude to the risks presented by the bodies of long-dead ancestors stand in contrast to those of the eighteenth century, where antiquarian investigations of the embalmed remains of the famous were frequent, and regularly included smelling, touching and even tasting the body liquor.

Given all these practical, logistical and technical difficulties, the excellent reports that have appeared recently are all the more admirable and welcome. In London particularly there are now several well-known and well-published sites, which starts to make it possible for archaeologists to compare a site with others. However, most reports are still very limited in their focus to the single site under study. When comparanda are mentioned, Spitalfields is still pre-eminent. Even 20 years after its original publication, the Spitalfields report is in many ways a model – it is thorough, analytical and intelligently integrates historical, archaeological and laboratory analysis. And yet it is in many ways an exceptional site. Because the project focused on the excavation of vaults beneath the church rather than the excavation of a churchyard, the population represented is atypically wealthy. It was also shaped by a large French Huguenot presence in the area. Perhaps there is no such thing as a typical post-medieval burial site, but it is hoped that in the future sites such as St Martin's-in-the-Bull Ring and the Kingston-upon-Thames Quaker cemetery – both excellent publications – will provide a wider range of sites for comparison.

For anyone planning the excavation and publication of a post-medieval burial site, here are our suggestions on some things it would be useful to see in the publication. There are also some recommendations for priorities in directing future research.

1. All publications of post-medieval cemeteries and burial grounds – and for that matter of burial grounds dating to any period – should contain an appendix listing, as far as possible, each burial – giving details such as age, sex, pathology and any other relevant aspects of skeletal analysis alongside features of the burial such as position, orientation, use of coffin, any associated finds or coffin furniture and so on. The identification number given to each burial should, as far as possible, be the same in plans and descriptions of the archaeology and in the osteoarchaeological report. This is a fundamental necessity if we are to be able to undertake large-scale analytical projects looking at more than a single site.

2. Many reports are good at including local historical details relevant to the site under examination, but wider understanding of the historical and archaeological context, including reference to comparable sites elsewhere and to regional, national and international social and economic history would make them more enjoyable to read and help to demonstrate the relevance of this field of study to an often sceptical public.

3. Although eighteenth- and nineteenth-century urban burial grounds are now reasonably well-known, we still have little information on early modern burial practice. Dating burials can be difficult or even impossible, especially in cases where interment has taken place in the same area for many centuries or even millennia, and there is little material culture and complex, disturbed stratigraphy. However, where possible, some attempt to phase and attribute a tentative date to burials would help us to fill this gap.

4. Excavation of post-medieval sites has been almost entirely reactive, in response to immediate threat, and the nature and level of archaeological investigation has often depended on the personal views of local decision-makers with regard to the archaeological value of such sites. A clearer research-driven agenda would identify the need to improve our knowledge of certain kinds of sites: early modern sites are not well known; rural sites and burial grounds in minor towns are under-represented. Sites outside London and the major cities need to be better known.

5. At present we know of no studies that have a sustained integration of above- and below-ground archaeology. While there are many good studies of memorial monuments, and increasing numbers of good excavation reports, the comparison of commemoration with actual practice is potentially a very fruitful and interesting area (Mytum's (forthcoming) preliminary attempts at such an analysis have yielded fascinating results suggesting, among other things, that commemorative monuments are much more susceptible to changes in fashion than the material culture of interment which is remarkably conservative).

6. We have attempted in this volume to include sites from around Britain and Ireland, but have not researched or tried to integrate sites from further afield, either in Europe or in North America or other English-speaking countries around the world. There is limitless scope for wider global perspectives.

7. We need more synthetic, interpretive, secondary work. This volume is intended to act as a guide to resources, but there is really a dearth of literature at the moment to which one might turn for an overview of post-medieval burial practice, or for an idea of what the archaeological data might mean. In their absence, the authors of site reports and the authors of this volume have turned either to another well-known site report, such as Spitalfields (Reeve and Adams 1993), or to works of social history (such as Gittings 1984 or Litten 1991), which are lively and informative books but do not foreground the material or spatial aspects of burial practice. There are no works of geographical comparison or synthesis at either the national or even the regional level by archaeologists.

This volume is an early attempt at a review of the data. The authors would welcome updates, corrections and revisions for possible future editions.

Appendix 1: Burial Legislation, c.1500–1902

Year	Citation	Title
1547	1 Edw. VI, c.14	An Acte wherby certaine Chauntries, Colleges, Free Chapells and the Possessions of the Same be given to the King's Majestie (Chantries Act)
1662	13 & 14 Cha. II c.4	An Act for the Uniformity of Publick Prayers; and Administration of the Sacraments, and other Rites and Ceremonies: And for Establishing the Form of Making Ordaining, and consecrating Bishops, Priests and Deacons of the Church of England
1666	18 & 19 Cha. II c.4	An Act for burying in woollen onely (Burial in Woollen Act)
1678	30 Cha. II c.3	An Act for burying in woollen
1680	32 Cha. II c.1	An additional Act for burying in woollen
1689	1 Wil & Mar. c.18	An Act for exempting their majesties Protestant Subjects, dissenting from the Church of England, from Penalties of certain Laws (Act of Toleration)
1751	25 Geo. II c.37	An Act for the better preventing the horrid Crime of Murder (Murder Act)
1808	48 Geo III c.75	An act providing suitable interment in church-yards or Parochial Burying Grounds in England, for such dead Human bodies as may be cast on Shore from the Sea, in cases of Wreck or otherwise (Burial of Drowned Persons Act)
1816	56 Geo III c.141	An Act for enabling Ecclesiastical corporate bodies, under certain circumstances, to alienate lands for enlarging cemeteries and churchyards (Burial Ground Act)
1823	4 Geo IV c.52	An Act to alter and amend the law relating to the interment of the remains of any person found Felo de se (Suicide Act)
1832	2 & 3 Gul. IV c.75	An Act for regulating Schools of Anatomy (Anatomy Act 1832)
1847	10 & 11 Vict c.65	An Act for consolidating in one Act certain provisions usually contained in Acts authorising the making of cemeteries (Cemetery Clauses Act 1847)
1850	13 & 14 Vict. c.52	An Act to make better provision for the interment of the Dead in or near the Metropolis (Burial Act 1850)
1852	15 & 16 Vict. c.85	An Act to amend the Laws concerning the burial of the dead in the metropolis (Burial Act 1852)
1853	16 & 17 Vict. c.134	An Act to amend the Laws concerning the Burial of the dead in England beyond the Limits of the Metropolis and to amend the Act concerning the Burial of the Dead in the Metropolis (Burial Act 1853)
1855	18 & 19 Vict. c.128	An Act further to amend the Laws concerning the Burial of the Dead in England (Burial Act 1855)
1855	18 & 19 Vict. c.68	An Act to amend the Laws concerning the Burial of the Dead in Scotland (Burial Act Scotland)
1856	19 & 20 Vict. c.98	An Act to amend the laws relating to the burial of the dead in Ireland (Burial Act Ireland)
1857	20 & 21 Vict. c.81	An Act to amend the Burial Act (Burial Act 1857)
1859	22 Vict. c.1	An Act more effectively to prevent the Danger to the Public Health from Places of Burial (Burial Act 1859)
1864	27 & 28 Vict. c.97	An Act to make further Provision for the Registration of Burials in England
1868	31 & 32 Vict. c.24	An Act to provide for the carrying out of Capital Punishment within Prisons (Capital Punishment Amendment Act)
1871	34 & 35 Vict. c.16	An Act to Amend the Act for Regulating Schools of Anatomy (Anatomy Act 1871)
1874	37 & 38 Vict. c.88	An Act to amend the Law relating to the Registration of Births and Deaths in England, and to consolidate the Law respecting the Registration of Births and Deaths at Sea
1875	38 & 39 Vict. c.55	An Act for consolidating and amending the Acts relating to Public Health in England (Public Health Act)
1880	43 & 44 Vict. c.41	An Act to amend the burial laws (Burial Laws Amendment Act)
1882	45 & 46 Vict. c.19	Interments (felo de se) Act

Appendix 1

Year	Citation	Title
1884	47 & 48 Vict. c.72	An Act for preventing the erection of Buildings on Disused Burial Grounds (Disused Burial Grounds Act)
1886	49 & 50 Vict. c.20	An Act to amend the Law in respect to the Discovery and Interment of Persons drowned
1886	49 Vict. c.21	An Act to amend the Burial grounds (Scotland) Act
1902	2 Edw. VII c.8	An Act for the regulation of the burning of human remains, and to enable burial authorities to establish crematoria (Cremation Act)

References

Ackroyd, P. 1998. *The Life of St. Thomas More*. London: Chatto and Windus.

Adams, J. 2006. The Parish, the Church, and the Churchyard. In Brickley, M. and Buteux, S. (eds) *St. Martin's Uncovered. Investigations in the Churchyard of St. Martin's-in-the-Bull Ring, Birmingham, 2001*. Oxford: Oxbow Books. pp. 6–23.

Adams, J., Buteux, S. and Cherrington, R. 2006. St. Martin's in Context: the Church and Funerals. In Brickley, M. and Buteux, S. (eds) *St. Martin's Uncovered. Investigations in the Churchyard of St. Martin's-in-the-Bullring, Birmingham, 2001*. Oxford: Oxbow Books. pp. 221–228.

Adams, J. and Colls, K. (eds) 2007. *'Out of Darkness, cometh Light'. Life and Death in nineteenth-century Wolverhampton; Excavation of the Overflow Burial Ground of St Peter's Collegiate Church, Wolverhampton 2001–2002*. British Archaeological Reports, (British Series) 442. Oxford: Archaeopress.

Addyman, T. 2000. The Tollbooth, Broad Street, Stirling. *Discovery and Excavation in Scotland* 1: 91–92.

Addyman, T., Connolly, D. and Macfadyen, K. 2002. Kilbarchan West Parish Church. *Discovery and Excavation in Scotland* 3: 98–99.

Allen, D. and Anderson, S. 1999. *Basing House, Hampshire: Excavations 1978–1991*. Hampshire Field Club Monograph 10. Hampshire: Hampshire Field Club and Archaeological Society.

Allen, T. 1990. Abingdon. *Current Archaeology* 121(1): 24–7.

Allen, T. 2006. *Abingdon Vineyard*. Unpublished manuscript held at Oxford Archaeology.

Anderson, O. 1987. *Suicide in Victorian and Edwardian England*. Oxford: Clarendon Press.

Anderson, S. 1996. *Human Skeleton Remains from the Castle Mound, Castle Mall, Norwich, excavated 1989–91 (68/69)*. English Heritage Laboratory Report.

Anderson, S. 1998. Pathology of some Seventeenth-century Prisoners from Norwich Goal. In Anderson, S. and Boyle, K. (eds) *Current and Recent Research in Osteoarchaeology. Proceedings of the Third Meeting of the Osteoarchaeological Group held in Leicester on 18th November 1995*. Oxford: Oxbow Books. pp. 39–41.

Anderson, S. and White, R. n.d. An Unknown Graveyard at Prestonpans. *East Lothian Life*. p. 23.

Anderson, T. 2002. A Nineteenth-century Post-mortem Specimen from Deal, Kent. *International Journal of Osteoarchaeology* 12: 216–219.

Anderson, T., O'Connor, S. and Ogden, A.R. 2004. An Early Eighteenth-century Denture from Rochester, Kent, England. *Antiquity* 78: 858–864.

Andrews, P. and Oakey, N. 1998. *Holy Trinity Church Centre, Coventry: Archaeological Excavation Assessment Report (43425b)*. Unpublished Wessex Archaeology Report.

Andrews, T. 1847. *A Cyclopedia of Domestic Medicine and Surgery; being an Alphabetical Account of the Various Diseases incident to the Human Frame; with Directions for their Treatment, and Performing the more Simple Operations of Surgery*. Glasgow: Blackie and Son.

Anon. 1641. *London's Lamentation; or, a Fit Admonishment for City and Countrey, wherein is described Certaine Causes of this Affliction and Visitation of the Plague*. London.

Anon. 1642. *True Newes out of Herefordshire. Being a Certaine and Exact Relation, of a Battle fought betweene the Lord Marqesse Hertford, the Lord Herbert and their Cavaliers, in number Six Thousand Men against the Earle of Stamford, his Forces in those Parts; being Trained Bands of that County, and Others Adjoying*. London: Fr. Wright.

Anon. 1644. *A Fuller Account of the Great Victory Obtained (through Gods providence) at Alsford, on Friday the 28th, of March, 1644. By parliamentary Forces, under the Command of Sir William Waller, Sir William Balfore, and Major General Browne, against the Forces Commanded by the Earl of Forth*. London: Laurance Blaiklock.

Anon. 1787. *A Descriptive Catalogue of a Very Extensive and Capital Collection of Anatomical Preparations, Original Casts of the Gravid Uterus Accurately Moulded from Nature, Coloured Anatomical Drawings, and Natural History: forming the Entire and Genuine Museum of an Eminent Professor of Anatomy, who has Declined Teaching. This collection has been the work of many years of extensive Practice and close application to this Study. which will be sold by auction by Mr. Hutchins, at his rooms, in King Street and Hart Street, Covent Garden, on Monday December the 10th, 1787, and the twelve following evenings (Sundays excepted), at Six o' clock. The while will be on view on Friday 7th and Saturday the 8th instant*. Copy held in Wellcome Library, London.

Anon. 1820. Correspondence. *Gentleman's Magazine* 90: 13–15.

Anon. 1830. *Museum Brookesium. A Descriptive and Historical Catalogue of the Remainder of the Anatomical and Zootomical Museum of Joshua Brookes Esq F.R.S., F.L.S., F.Z.S., and c. Comprising nearly Half of the Original Collection and Embracing an Almost Endless Assemblage of Every Species of Anatomical, Pathological, Obstetrical, and Zootomical Preparations, as well as Subjects in Natural History, of the Choicest and Rarest Species in Every Department: which will be sold by auction by Messers. Wheatley and Adlard at the theatre of Anatomy, Blenheim Street, Great Malborough Street, on Monday the 1st of March, 1830 and 22 following evenings (Saturdays and Sundays excepted) at half-past six o'clock precisely*. London: Richard Taylor.

Anon. 1844. *Proceedings of Society of Antiquaries of London* 1 (part 2): 47–48.

Anon. 1896. *Archaeologia Aeliana*: Or Miscellaneous Tracts Relating to Antiquity XVIII: 1–25.

Anon. 1926. *The Complete Newgate Calendar*. London: Navarre Society Ltd.

Anon. 2001. *Land off Sutton Road, Coxside, Plymouth, Devon. Archaeological Evaluation*. Unpublished Cotswold Archaeological Trust Report 01072.

Appleton-Fox, N. 1999. *Moreton Jeffries Church, Herefordshire: A Report on an Archaeological Evaluation*. Unpublished Marches Archaeology Report No. 90.

Arabaolaza, L., Ponce, P. and Boylston, A. 2007. Skeletal Analysis. In Adams, J. and Colls, K. (eds) *'Out of darkness, cometh light'. Life and Death in nineteenth-century Wolverhampton; Excavation of the Overflow Burial Ground of St Peter's Collegiate Church, Wolverhampton 2001–2002*. British Archaeological Reports (British Series) 442. Oxford: Archaeopress. pp. 39–70.

Ariès, P. 1962. *Centuries of Childhood*. London: Cape.

Ariès, P. 1974. *Western Attitudes toward Death from the Middle Ages to the Present*. London: Marion Boyars.

Ariès, P. 1981. *The Hour of our Death*. London: Penguin.

Arnold, C. 2006. *Necropolis. London and its Dead*. London: Pocket Books.

Aston, M. 1973. English Ruins and English History: The Dissolution and the Sense of the Past. *Journal of Warburg and Courtauld Institutes* 36: 231–255.

Aston, M. 2003. Public Worship and Iconoclasm. In Gaimster, D. and Gilchrist, R. (eds) *The Archaeology of Reformation 1480–1580*. Leeds: Maney Publishing. pp. 9–28.

Aston, M. and Bond, J. 1976. *The Landscape of Towns*. Archaeology in the Field Series. London: J.M. Dent.

Atkinson, J.A. and Photos-Jones, E. 1999. *Scottish Bloomeries Project: Interim Report*. Unpublished Glasgow University Archaeological Research Division Report.

Aubrey, J. 1881. *Remaines of Gentilisme and Judaisme*. London: Folklore Society.

Aveling, J.C.H. 1976. *The Handle and the Axe. The Catholic Recusants in England from Reformation to Emancipation*. London: Bland and Briggs.

Ayers, B. 1990. Norwich: ubi sepeliuntur suspensi... *Current Archaeology* 122: 56–59.

Ayers, B. 2001. Excavations at St. Michael's Church, Bowthorpe, 1984–5. In Beazley, O. and Ayers, B. (eds) *Two Medieval Churches in Norfolk*. East Anglia Archaeology Report 96. Dereham: Norfolk Museums and Archaeology Service. pp. 64–97.

Ayers, B. and Beazley, O. 2001. *Two Medieval Churches in Norfolk*. East Anglian Archaeological Report 96. Dereham: Norfolk Museums and Archaeology Service.

Baddeley, S. 1891. Salt Detested by Demons and Sorcerers. *Notes and Queries* 7 –XI (no. 266): 93.

Bagwell, T. and Tyers, I. 2001. *Dendrochronological Analysis of a Coffin Assemblage from Carver Street, Sheffield, South Yorkshire*. Unpublished Archaeological Research and Consultancy at the University of Sheffield Report.

Baillie, M. 1812. On the Embalming of Dead Bodies. *Transactions of a Society for the Improvement of Medical and Chirurgical Knowledge* 3: 7–23.

Barnet, M.C. 1972. The Cholera Epidemic in York. *Medical History* 16: 27–39.

Bashford, L. and Pollard, L. 1998. "In the burying place" – the Excavation of a Quaker Burial Ground. In Cox, M. (ed.) *Grave concerns. Death and Burial in England 1700–1850*. Council for British Archaeology Research Report 113. York: Council for British Archaeology. pp. 144–166.

Bashford, L. and Sibun, L. 2007. Excavations at the Quaker Burial Ground, Kingston-upon-Thames, London. *Post-medieval Archaeology* 41: 100–154.

Bateman, N. and Miles, A. 1999. St. Lawrence Jewry from the Eleventh to the Nineteenth Century. *Transactions of the London and Middlesex Archaeological Society* 50: 109–143.

Bayer, O.J. 1996. *Archaeological Excavation of Human Remains at Saunton Down End, Croyde Bay, Devon*. Unpublished Exeter Archaeology Report.

Beazley, O. 2001. Excavations in St Martin-at-Palace Church, 1987. In Beazley, O. and Ayers, B. (eds) *Two Medieval Churches in Norfolk*. East Anglian Archaeology Report 96. Dereham: Norfolk Museums and Archaeology Service. pp. 1–63.

Beckensall, S. 1998. A Watching Brief of British Telecom Trenches in the Market Place and Beaumont Street in 1990. In Cambridge, E. and Williams, A. (eds) Hexham Abbey. A Review of

References

Recent Work and its Implications. *Archaeologia Aeliana* (5th Series). 23: 60–63.

Beddoe, J. 1907. Report on two Skulls found at Great Depths at Bristol Dockgate and at Avonmouth Dock. *Proceedings of the Bristol Naturalists' Society* (4th Series.) 1: 61–65.

Bedwin, O. 1994/5. Hempstead, Church of St. Andrew, Essex. *Transactions of the Essex Society for Archaeology and History* 26: 226.

Belford, P. and Witkin, A. 2000. *Archaeological Recording and Osteological Analysis of Human Remains from the Site of the Graveyard of St. Paul's Church, Pinstone Street, Sheffield.* Unpublished Archaeological Research and Consultancy at the University of Sheffield Report.

Bell, C. 1799. *A System of Dissections Explaining the Anatomy of the Human Body, the Manner of Displaying the Parts and their Varieties in Disease. Volume the First Containing the Dissection of the Abdomen, Thorax, Pelvis, Thigh and Leg.* Edinburgh: Mundell and Son.

Bell, C. 1994. *St. Bartholomew's Church, Penn, West Midlands.* Unpublished Oxford Archaeological Unit Report.

Bellamy, J. 1979. *The Tudor Laws of Treason. An Introduction.* London: Routledge and Kegan Paul.

Bellamy, R.L. 1994. *The United Reform Chapel, Broad Street, Reading: a Recording Action During the Exhumation of Burials.* Unpublished Thames Valley Archaeological Services Report No 94/31. http://www.tvas.co.uk/Reports/pdf/URC94-31.pdf (accessed 30th March 2010).

Bendix, R. 1980. *Kings or People: Power and the Mandate to Rule.* Berkeley: University of California Press.

Bennett, H. 1975. A Murder Victim Discovered: Clothing and other Finds from an Early Eighteenth-century Grave on Arnish Moor, Lewis. *Proceedings of Society of Antiquaries of Scotland* 106: 172–183.

Bennett, J.A., Johnston, S.A. and Simcock, A.V. 2000. *Solomon's House in Oxford. New finds from the First Museum.* Oxford: Museum of the History of Science.

Bennett, P., Houliston, M. Ward, A. Excavations at St. George's Clocktower. http://www.hillside.co.uk/arch/clocktower/church.html (accessed 1st January 2010).

Berry, B.M. and Scofield, R.S. 1971. Age at Baptism in Pre-industrial England. *Population Studies* 25: 453–463.

Bevan, L. 2006. Jewellery and other Personal Items. In Brickley, M. and Buteux, S. (eds) *St. Martin's Uncovered. Investigations in the Churchyard of St. Martin's-in-the-Bull Ring, Birmingham, 2001.* Oxford: Oxbow Books. pp. 179–184.

Bevan, L. 2007. Small Finds. In Adams, J. and Colls, K. (eds) *"Out of Darkness, cometh Light". Life and Death in Nineteenth-century Wolverhampton.* British Archaeological Reports (British Series) 442. Oxford: Archaeopress. p. 35.

Biddle, M. 1972. Excavations at Winchester, 1970. Ninth Interim Report. *Antiquaries Journal* 52: 93–131.

Binford, L. 1971. Mortuary Practices: their Study and their Potential. *American Antiquity* 36(3:2): 6–29. Reprinted in Binford, L. 1972. *An Archaeological Perspective.* New York: Seminar Press.

Bishop, H. 1978. Excavations at the Church of Saints Peter and Paul, Healing. *Lincolnshire History and Archaeology* 13: 25–34.

Blackmore, W. 1775. Commentaries on the Laws of England. In Douglas, D. C. (ed.) *English Historical Documents.* Volume 10, 1714–1783. London: Eyre and Spottiswoode. pp. 89–93.

Blockley, K. 1996. Pershore Abbey. *Current Archaeology* 13: 216–221.

Blockley, K. 2000a. Pershore Abbey: Excavations in the Choir, Crossing and Transepts 1996. *Transactions of the Worcestershire Archaeology Society* 17: 1–52.

Blockley, K. 2000b. Pershore Abbey. *Church Archaeology* 4: 60–61.

Blockley, K., Sparks, M. and Tatton-Brown, T. 1997. *Canterbury Cathedral Nave. Archaeology, History and Architecture.* Archaeology of Canterbury. Volume 1. Canterbury: Published by the Dean and Chapter of Canterbury Cathedral and Canterbury Archaeological Trust.

Bloice, B. 1976. Excavation Round-up 1975. *London Archaeologist* 2(14): 370–372.

Bluer, D. 2002. *The Royal Foundation of St. Katherine, Butcher Row, Ratcliff, E14: An Archaeological Watching Brief Report.* Unpublished Museum of London Archaeological Service Report.

Bogan, P.P. 1999. The Ancient Catholic Cemetery of St. James in Winchester. In Winchester Catholic History Group (ed.) *St. Cross and the Cemetery of St. James, Winchester.* The Winchester Catholic History Group Publication No. 1. Winchester: Catholic History Group. pp. 16–84.

Bonner, D. 1994. *Archaeological Investigations at All Saints Church, Loughton, Milton Keynes.* Unpublished Buckinghamshire County Museum Archaeological Service Report.

Boore, E.J. 1985. Excavations at St Augustine the Less, Bristol, 1983–84. *Bristol and Avon Archaeology* 4: 21–33.

Boore, E.J. 1986. The Church of St. Augustine the Less, Bristol: an Interim Statement. *Transactions of the Bristol and Gloucestershire Archaeological Society* 104: 211–214.

Boore, E.J. 1989. Archaeology in Bristol, 1986–89. *Transactions of the Bristol and Gloucestershire Archaeological Society* 107: 246–248.

Boore, E.J. 1998. Burial Vaults and Coffin Furniture in the West Country. In Cox, M. (ed.) *Grave Concerns. Death and Burial in England 1700–1850*. Council for British Archaeology Research Report 113. York: Council for British Archaeology. pp. 67–84.

Boothroyd, N. 1998. *Watching Brief at St. Mary and All Saints' Church, Trentham, Staffordshire*. Unpublished Stoke on Trent City Museum Field Archaeology Unit Report.

Boston, C. and Boyle, A. n.d. *The Skeleton Assemblage from the Regal Cinema Site, Abingdon*. Oxford Archaeology unpublished document.

Boston, C. 2004. *St. Nicholas', Forest Hill, Oxfordshire: the Human Skeletal Assemblage*. Unpublished Oxford Archaeology Report.

Boston, C. 2005a. Appendix 10. Human Bone – Baptist Interments. In Brown, R. *Vancouver Centre and Clough Lane Car Park, King's Lynn Norfolk. Post-Excavation Assessment and Updated Project Design*. Unpublished Oxford Archaeology Report. pp. 121–159.

Boston, C. 2005b. *The Paddock, Royal Naval Hospital, Haslar, Gosport, Hants*. Unpublished Oxford Archaeology Report.

Boston, C. 2005c. Summary of Human Bone. In Norton, A., Laws, G. and Smith, A. *Abingdon West Central Redevelopment Area, Oxfordshire. Post-Excavation Assessment and Updated Project Design*. Unpublished Oxford Archaeology Report.

Boston, C. 2007. *The Royal Hospital Greeenwich London. Archaeological Excavation Report*. Unpublished Oxford Archaeology Report.

Boston, C. 2008. *Rycote Chapel. Coffins in the Crypt. Archaeological Watching Brief*. Unpublished Oxford Archaeology Report. http://ads.ahds.ac.uk/catalogue/library/greylit/details.cfm?id=4233 (accessed 13th February 2010).

Boston, C. 2009. Burial Practice and Material Culture. In Boston, C., Boyle, A. Gill, J. and Witkin, A. *"In the Vaults Beneath". Archaeological Recording at St. George's Church, Bloomsbury*. Oxford Archaeology Monograph no. 8. Oxford: Oxford Archaeological Unit. pp. 147–172.

Boston, C. and Boyle, A. 2005. Burial Practice and Material Culture. In Boyle, A., Boston, C. and Witkin, A. *The Archaeological Experience at St. Luke's Church, Old Street, Islington*. Unpublished Oxford Archaeology Report. pp. 82–101 http://lso.co.uk/downloadables/lumps/upload/277-12.pdf (accessed 10th January 2010).

Boston, C., Boyle, A., Gill, J. and Witkin, A. 2009. *"In the Vaults Beneath". Archaeological Recording at St. George's Church, Bloomsbury*. Oxford Archaeology Monograph no. 8. Oxford: Oxford Archaeological Unit.

Boston, C., Boyle, A. and Witkin, A. 2006. *"In the Vaults beneath" – Archaeological Recording at St. George's Church, Bloomsbury*. Unpublished Oxford Archaeology Report.

Boston, C., Witkin, A., Boyle, A. and Kitch, J. 2009. The Human Bone Assemblage. In Boston, C., Boyle, A., Gill, J. and Witkin, A. *"In the Vaults beneath". Archaeological Recording at St. George's Church, Bloomsbury*. Oxford Archaeology Monograph no. 8. Oxford: Oxford Archaeological Unit. pp. 103–138.

Boston, C., Witkin, A., Boyle, A. and Wilkinson, D.R.P. 2008. *'Safe moor'd in Greenwich Tier': A Study of the Skeletons of Royal Navy Sailors and Marines Excavated at the Royal Hospital Greenwich*. Oxford Archaeology Monograph 5. Oxford: Oxford Archaeological Unit.

Boucher, A. 2000. *The Chapter House Vestibule, Hereford Cathedral*. Unpublished Hereford Archaeological Services Interim Report, No. 461.

Boucher, A. and Crooks, K.H. 2001. *Chapter House Yard, Hereford: Archaeological Excavation and Survey*. Report no. 490. Unpublished Hereford Archaeological Services Report.

Boucher, A. and Hovered, T. 1997. *Cathedral Close, Hereford: Archaeological Investigations of voids at the east end of the Cathedral*. Hereford: Archaeological Investigations.

Boulter, S., Robertson, D.J. and Start, H. 1998. *The Newcastle Infirmary at the Forth, Newcastle upon Tyne. Volume II. The Osteology: People, Disease and Surgery*. Unpublished Archaeological Research and Consultancy at the University of Sheffield Report.

Bowler, D. 2002. Excavations and Watching Brief in Dunino Churchyard, Fife. *Tayside and Fife Archaeological Journal* 8: 125–137.

Bowler, D., Perry, D. and Middleton, M. 2000. Clearance and Survey at Edzell Old Church, Angus. *Tayside and Fife Archaeological Journal* 6: 136–153.

Bowman, J.E., MacLaughlin, S.M. and Scheuer, J.L. 1992. Burial of Early Nineteenth-century Suicide in the Crypt of St. Bride's Church, Fleet Street. *International Journal of Osteoarchaeology* 2: 91–94.

Bowsher, D. 1995. *Excavations at St. Paul's Churchyard, Site code CGD95*. Unpublished Museum of London Archaeological Service Report.

Bowsher, D., Holder, N. and Miles, A. 1997. *St. Paul's Churchyard, Covent Garden, WC2, City of Westminster. An Archaeological Investigation*. Unpublished Museum of London Archaeological Service Report.

Boyd, Z. 1629. *The Last Battell of the Soule in Death*. Edinburgh: Heires of Andro Hart.

Boyle, A. 1995. *A Catalogue of Coffin Fittings from St. Nicholas, Sevenoaks*. Unpublished Oxford Archaeology Report.

References

Boyle, A. 1998. High Wycombe, All Saints, Carrington Burial Vault. *Church Archaeology* 2: 60–61.

Boyle, A. 1999. A Grave Disturbance: Archaeological Perspectives on the Recently Dead. In Downes, J. and Pollard, T. (eds) *The Loved Body's Corruption*. Glasgow: Cruithne Press. pp. 187–199.

Boyle, A. 2002. *St. Batholomew's Church, Penn, Wolverhampton. Results of Investigations in the Churchyard*. Unpublished Oxford Archaeology Report.

Boyle, A. 2004. What Price Compromise? Archaeological Investigations at St. Bartholomew's Church, Penn, Wolverhampton. *Church Archaeology* 5/6: 69–79.

Boyle, A., Boston, C. and Witkin, A. 2005. *The Archaeological Experience at St. Luke's Church, Old Street, Islington*. Unpublished Oxford Archaeology Report. http://lso.co.uk/downloadables/lumps/upload/277-12.pdf (accessed 10th January 2010).

Boyle, A. and Hiller, J. 2004. Langley Marish, St. Mary. *Church Archaeology* 5/6: 117–118.

Boyle, A. and Keevill, G. 1998. "To the Praise of the Dead, and Anatomie": the Analysis of Post-medieval Burials at St. Nicholas, Sevenoaks, Kent. In Cox, M. (ed.) *Grave Concerns. Death and Burial in England 1700–1850*. Council for British Archaeology Research Report 113. York: Council for British Archaeology. pp. 85–99.

Boyle, A. and Witkin, A. 2004. *Devonport Buildings. King William Walk. Greenwich. London. Post-Excavation Assessment*. Unpublished Oxford Archaeology Report.

Brading, R., Lindsey, R., Higgins, P. and Whitehead, B. 1993. Bedhampton, St. Thomas' Church. In Hampshire County Council. *Archaeology in Hampshire*. Winchester: Hampshire County Council. pp. 56–57.

Bradley, A and Boyle, A. 2004. Moving the Dead of Islington. *The Archaeologist* 52: 16–17.

Brennand, M. 1999. *Report on an Archaeological Watching Brief at 27–28 Tombland, Norwich*. Unpublished Norfolk Archaeological Unit Report.

Brett, J. 1996. Archaeology and the Construction of the Royal Edward Dock, Avonmouth, 1902-8. *Archaeology of the Severn Estuary* 7: 115–120.

Brett, M. 2004. *Land to rear of Camden House, London Road, Stroud, Gloucestershire. Programme of Archaeological Recording*. Unpublished Cotswold Archaeology Report 04095.

Brickley, M. 2006. The People: Physical Anthropology. In Brickley, M. and Buteux, S. (eds) *St. Martin's Uncovered. Investigations in the Churchyard of St. Martin's-in-the-Bull Ring, Birmingham, 2001*. Oxford: Oxbow Books. pp. 90–151.

Brickley, M. and Buteux, S. 2006. *St. Martin's Uncovered. Investigations in the Churchyard of St. Martin's-in-the-Bull Ring, Birmingham, 2001*. Oxford: Oxbow Books.

Brickley, M. and Miles, A. 1999a. *The Cross Bones Burial Ground, Redcross Way Southwark London. Archaeological Excavations (1991–1998) for the London Underground Limited Jubilee Line Extension Project*. MoLAS Monograph 3. Lavenham: Museum of London Archaeological Services.

Brickley, M. and Miles, A. 1999b. The O'Meara Street Grouting Shaft Excavation. In Brickley, M. and Miles, A. (eds) *The Cross Bones Burial Ground, Redcross Way Southwark, London: Archaeological Excavations (1991–1998) for the London Underground Limited Jubilee Line Extension Project*. MoLAS Monograph 3. Lavenham: Museum of London Archaeological Services.

Briden, C. 1999. *Church of Saint Mary, Thirsk, North Yorkshire*. Report on a Watching Brief. Unpublished document.

Brittain, R.P. 1965. Cruentation in Legal Medicine and in Literature. *Medical History* 9(1): 82–88.

Brodie, A., Davies, J. and Croom, J. 1999. *The Hidden Architecture of English Prisons*. London.

Brooks, C. 1989. *Mortal Remains. The History and Present State of Victorian and Edwardian Cemeteries*. Exeter: Wheaton.

Brossler, A. 1999. High Wycombe, All Saints' Church. *Church Archaeology* 3: 50.

Brown, C. 1989. Urbanization and Living Conditions. In Pope, R. (ed.) *Atlas of British Social and Economic History*. London: Routledge. pp. 170–182.

Brown, J. 1981. The Search for Rank in Prehistoric Burials. In Chapman, R., Kinnes, I. and Randsborg, K. (eds) *The Archaeology of Death*. Cambridge: Cambridge University Press. pp. 25–37.

Brown, R. 2005. *Vancouver Centre and Clough Lane Car Park, King's Lynn, Norfolk*. Unpublished Oxford Archaeology Report.

Brown, T. 1966. The Triple Gateway. *Folklore* 77: 123–131.

Bruce, G. 2009. Fishergate, York: Mass Graves of the English Civil War? *Post-medieval Archaeology* 43: 353–355.

Brushfield, T.N. 1890. Strange Discovery in St. Mary-le-Port Church, Bristol, 1814. *Gloucestershire Notes and Queries* 4: 387–388.

Buchan, W. 1789. *Domestic Medicine or a Treatise on the Prevention and Care of Diseases by Regimen and Simple Medicines with an Appendix Containing a Dispensatory for the Use of Private Practiners*. London: W. Strahan.

Buckley, L. and Hayden, A. 2002. Excavations at St. Stephen's Leper Hospital, Dublin: a Summary

Account and an Analysis of Burials. In Duffy, S. (ed.) *Medieval Dublin III*. Dublin: Four Courts Press. pp. 151–194.

Buckley, L. and McConway, C. 2004. Wee Band of Brothers. *Archaeology Ireland* 18: 40.

Buckley, L. and Nellis, D. 2000. One Foot in the Grave. *Archaeology Ireland* 14(4): 5.

Burchill, R. 1994. *Archaeological Excavation of St. Thomas Burial Ground, St. Thomas Street, Bristol, Avon*. Unpublished Bristol and Region Archaeological Services Report BA/D132.

Burckhardt, J. 1878 [1937]. The Civilisation of the Renaissance in Italy (trans. S.G.C. Middlemore). London: Allen and Unwin.

Burke, P. 1997. Representations of the Self from Petrarch to Descartes. In Porter, R. (ed.) *Rewriting the Self: Histories from the Renaissance to the Present*. London: Routledge. pp. 17–28.

Burney, I. A. 2000. *Bodies of Evidence: Medicine and the Politics of the English Inquest, 1830–1929*. Baltimore: John Hopkins University Press.

Bury, S. 1984. *An Introduction to Rings*. London: Her Majesty's Stationery Office.

Buteux, S. and Cherrington, R. 2006. The Excavations. In Brickley, M. and Buteux, S. (eds) *St. Martin's Uncovered. Investigations in the Churchyard of St. Martin's-in-the-Bull Ring, Birmingham, 2001*. Oxford: Oxbow Books. pp. 24–89.

Buteux, S. 2003. *Beneath the Bull Ring: the Archaeology of Life and Death in Early Birmingham*. Studley: Brewin Books Ltd.

Buteux, V. 1996. *Archaeological Assessment of High Ercall, Shropshire*. CMHTS (Central Marches Historic Towns Survey). http://ads.ahds.ac.uk/catalogue/projArch/marches_eus_2005/downloads.cfm?CFID=3873547&CFtoken=32068166&ciunty=Shropshire&area=ercall (accessed 5th March 2010).

Butler, L.A.S. 1978. St. Martin's Church, Allerton Mauleverer. *Yorkshire Archaeological Journal* 50: 177–188.

Butler, L. and Morris, R. 1994. Derby Cathedral: The Cavendish Vault. *Derbyshire Archaeological Journal* 114: 14–28.

Bynum, C.W. 1995a. *The Resurrection of the Body in Western Christianity, 200–1336*. New York: Columbia University Press.

Bynum, C.W. 1995b. Why all the Fuss about the Body? A Medievalist's Perspective. *Critical Inquiry* 22(1): 1–33.

Bynum, C.W. 1998. Death and Resurrection in the Middle Ages: Some Modern Implications. *Proceedings of the American Philosophical Society* 142(4): 589–596.

Cachart, R. and Cox, A. 2001. Archaeological Excavations at the White Church, Comrie. *Tayside and Fife Archaeological Journal* 7: 118–128.

Caciola, N. 1996. Wraiths, Revenants and Ritual in Medieval Culture. *Past and Present* 152: 3–45.

Caldicott, D.K. 1989. *Hampshire Nunneries*. Bungay: Phillimore.

Caldwell, D.H. 1976. A Group of Post-medieval Burials at Haddington. *Transactions of East Lothian Antiquarian and Field Naturalists' Society* 15: 25–37.

Cale, K.L. 1999. *Archaeological Watching Brief, Saint Robert's Church, Pannal*. Unpublished Report.

Cale, K.L. 2000. *Archaeological Watching Brief, Saint Robert's Church, Pannal*. Unpublished Report.

Cameron, A. 2006. The Excavation. In *Excavation at Kirk of St. Nicholas*. Initial Report. http://www.aberdeencity.gov.uk/nmsruntime/saveasdialog.asp?lID=21646&sID=654 (accessed 4th April 2010).

Campbell, C. 1987. *The Romantic Ethic and the Spirit of Modern Consumerism*. Oxford: Blackwell.

Campbell, J. 1982. *The Anglo-Saxons*. London: Penguin Books.

Canterbury Archaeological Trust. 1998. *Archaeological Evaluation at River Parish Church, River, near Dover*. Unpublished Canterbury Archaeological Trust Report no. 1998/44.

Carlton, C. 1992. *Going to the Wars. The Experience of the British Civil Wars 1638–1651*. London: Routledge.

Carrott, J., Fryer, K., Hall, A., Hughes, P., Jaques, D., Johnstone, C. and Worthy, D. 1998. *Report on the Biological Remains from the Former Female Prison, York (Site code 1998.32)*. Reports from the Environment Archaeology Unit, York 98/21. http://www.york.ac.uk/inst/chumpal/EAU-reps/eau98-21.pdf (accessed 24th April 2010).

Cassell's Household Guide 1870. *Being a Complete Encyclopedia of Domestic and Social Economy and Forming a Guide to Every Department of Practical Life*. London: Cassell, Petter and Galpin. http://www.victorianlondon.org/cassells/cassells-35.htm#1 (accessed 10th April 2010).

Cathcart, C.W. 1893. *Descriptive Catalogue of Anatomical and Pathological Specimens in the Museum of the Royal College of Surgeons of Edinburgh*. Edinburgh: James Thin.

Centre for Archaeological Fieldwork 2002. *Investigations at St John's Church, County Antrim*. Unpublished Centre for Archaeological Fieldwork Report.

Chadwick, E. 1843. *Report on the Sanitary Condition of the Labouring Population of Great Britain. A supplementary Report on the Results of a Special Inquiry into the Practice of Interment in Towns*. London: W. Clowes and Sons. http://www.archive.org/stream/Reportonsanitary00chaduoft#page/n3/mode/2up (accessed 25th April 2010).

Chadwick, S.T. 1858. Case of Hepatic Abscess, Suddenly Fatal. *British Medical Journal* 1(63): 204–205.

References

Chamberlain, A. 1999. Teaching Surgery and Breaking the Law. *British Archaeology* 48: 6–7.

Chamberlain, A., McIntyre, L. and Pearson, N. 2008. *Mass Graves in a Medieval Cemetery: Skeletal Remains from the Barbican Site York*. Paper presented at British Association of Biological Anthropology and Osteoarchaeology Annual Conference, University of Oxford.

Chamberlain, A. and Sayer, D. 2001. *Forensic Anthropological Evaluation. Former Weslayan Methodist Chapel, New Street Barnsley*. Unpublished Archaeological Research and Consultancy at the University of Sheffield Report.

Channing, J. 1992. *Report on Archaeological monitoring and Excavations at Poolbeg Street, Dublin 2*. Unpublished John Channing Report.

Chapman, S. 1999. *An Archaeological Watching Brief during the Laying of Water and Electricity Services at St. Peter's Church, Belgrave, Leicester*. Unpublished University of Leicester Archaeological Services Report 99/15.

Chapman, S.J. 1997. The Finding of a Possible Reference Collection in the Grounds of a Victorian General Hospital, Nottingham, U.K. *Journal of Paleopathology* 9: 37–46.

Chave, S.P.W. 1969. Bones in Broadwick Street. *British Medical Journal* 1(5645): 710.

Cherry, J. 1972. Post-medieval Britain in 1971. *Post-medieval Archaeology* 6: 208–223.

Cherry, J. 1973. Post-medieval Britain in 1972. *Post-medieval Archaeology* 7: 100–117.

Cherry, J. 1974. Post-medieval Britain in 1973. *Post-medieval Archaeology* 8: 120–136.

Cherry, J. 1975. Post-medieval Britain in 1974. *Post-medieval Archaeology* 9: 240–260.

Cherry, J. 1976. Post-medieval Britain in 1975. *Post-medieval Archaeology* 10: 161–175.

Cherry, J. 1977. Post-medieval Britain in 1976. *Post-medieval Archaeology* 11: 87–100.

Cherry, J. 1978. Post-medieval Britain in 1977. *Post-medieval Archaeology* 12: 109–121.

Cherry, J. 1979. Post-medieval Britain in 1978. *Post-medieval Archaeology* 13: 273–284.

Cherry, J. 1980. Post-medieval Britain in 1979. *Post-medieval Archaeology* 14: 205–214.

Cherry, J. 1981. Post-medieval Britain in 1980. *Post-medieval Archaeology* 15: 225–232.

Cherry, J. 1982. Post-medieval Britain in 1981. *Post-medieval Archaeology* 16: 217–230.

Cherryson, A.K. 2007. Disturbing the Dead: Urbanisation, the Church and the Post-Burial Treatment of Human Remains in Early Medieval Wessex, c.600–1100AD. *Anglo-Saxon Studies in Archaeology and History* 14: 130–142.

Chisham, C. 2008. Coffin Wood Identification. In McKinley, J. *The Eighteenth-century Baptist Chapel and Burial Ground at West Butts Street, Poole*. Salisbury: Wessex Archaeology. pp. 47–49.

Ciaraldi, M. 2006. Plant Offerings. In Brickley, M. and Buteux, S. (eds) *St. Martin's Uncovered. Investigations in the Churchyard of St. Martin's-in-the-Bull Ring, Birmingham, 2001*. Oxford: Oxbow Books. pp. 184–186.

Clarke, A. 1994. *The Judge's Lodging: an Evaluation Report*. Unpublished York Archaeological Trust Report.

Clarke, L. 2002. An Early Medieval Enclosure and Burials, Johnstown, Co. Meath. *Archaeology Ireland* 16: 13–15.

Clay, P. 1981. The Small Finds – Non-structural. In Mellor, J.E. and Pearce, T. 1981. *The Austin Friars, Leicester*. Council for British Archaeology 35. Leamington: Council for British Archaeology/ Leicester County Council. pp. 130–145.

Clift, W. 1800. *Catalogue of the Museum. GB 0114 MS0007/1/1/1/4*. Held at the library of the Royal College of Surgeons.

Clift, W. 1825. *Additions to the Pathological Series in Spirit from 1800. Catalogue of the Papers of William Clift. GB 0114 MS0007/1/1/1/20*. Held at the Royal College of Surgeons.

Clift, W. n.d. *Hunterian Collection: A Catalogue of Morbid Preparations. Catalogue of the Papers of William Clift. GB 0114 MS0007/1/1/1/6*. Held at the Library of the Royal College of Surgeons.

Clough, S. 2007. *St. Ives and Hemingford Flood Alleviation Scheme, St. Ives, Cambridgeshire. Archaeological Investigation Report*. Unpublished Oxford Archaeology Report. http://theHumanjourney.net/pdf_store/hgrey/final_Report.pdf (accessed 8th February 2010).

Clyne, M. 2005. Archaeological Excavations at Holy Trinity Abbey, Lough Key, Co. Roscommon. *Proceedings of the Royal Irish Academy* 105C: 23–98.

Coates, G. and Litherland, S. 1996. *An Archaeological Salvage Recording and Watching Brief at the University of Wolverhampton, Wolverhampton, West Midlands*. BUFAC Project No. 417. Unpublished Birmingham University Field Archaeology Unit Report.

Cohen, N. 1995. The Birth of Church Archaeology in London. *London Archaeologist* 7: 315–320.

Cohen, N. 1999. *A Burying Ground for Protestant Dissenters 1783. Brentford Free Church, Boston Manor Road, Brentford, Middlesex TW8*. Unpublished MoLAS Report.

Colchester Archaeological Trust. 2000. *A Watching Brief at the Site of the former St. Paul's Church, Belle Vue Road, Colchester, Essex*. Unpublished Colchester Archaeological Report No. 137.

Coles, N.R. 1986. *Excavations on Flat Holm Island, South Glamorgan*. Unpublished Gwent-Glamorgan Archaeological Trust Report.

Coles, W. 1656. *The Art of Simpling*. London: Nath. Brook.

Colgrave, B. 1940. Anonymous Life of St. Cuthbert. In Colgrave, B. (ed.) *Two Lives of Saint Cuthbert*. Cambridge: Cambridge University Press. pp. 59–139.

Cooper, L. 1998. *An Archaeological Watching Brief and Archaeological Recording at Haymarket Towers, Leicester*. Unpublished University of Leicester Archaeological Services Report 98/146.

Connell, B. and Miles, A. 2010. *The City Bunhill Burial Ground, Golden Lane, London*. MOLA Archaeology Studies Series 21. London: Museum of London.

Coppack, G. 2000. *The White Monks. The Cistercians in Britain 1128–1540*. Stroud: Tempus.

Coster, Will. 2000. Tokens of Innocence: Infant Baptism, Death and Burial in Early Modern England. In Gordon, B. and Marshall, P. (eds) *The Place of the Dead: Death and Remembrance in Late Medieval and Early Modern Europe*. Cambridge: Cambridge University Press. pp. 266–287.

Cotswold Archaeological Trust. 2001. *Land off Sutton Road, Coxside, Plymouth, Devon*. Unpublished Cotswold Archaeological Trust Report 01072.

Courtney, P. and Courtney, Y. 1992. A Siege Examined: the Civil War Archaeology of Leicester. *Post-medieval Archaeology* 26: 47–90.

Coutts, C. and Parkhouse, J. 2000. *Leek Wootton, All Saints Church*. Unpublished Warwickshire Museum Field Services Report.

Cox, A. 1998. Grave Consequences: a Consideration of the Artefact Evidence from Four Post-medieval Graveyard Excavations. *Tayside and Fife Archaeological Journal* 4: 289–299.

Cox, M. 1996. *Life and Death in Spitalfields 1700 to 1850*. CBA Occasional Paper. York: Council of British Archaeology.

Cox, M. 1998. Eschatology, Burial Practice and Continuity: a Retrospection from Christ Church, Spitalfields. In Cox, M. (ed.) *Grave Concerns. Death and Burial in England 1700–1850*. Council for British Archaeology Research Report 113. York: Council for British Archaeology. pp. 112–125.

Cox, M., Molleson, T. and Waldron, T. 1990. Preconception and Perception: The lessons of a Nineteenth-century Suicide. *Journal of Archaeological Science* 17: 573–581.

Cox, M. and Stock, G. 1995. Nineteenth-century Bath-stone walled Graves at St. Nicholas's Church, Bathampton. *Proceedings of the Somerset Archaeology and Natural History Society* 138: 131–150.

Cowie, R., Bekvalac, J. and Kausmally, T. 2008. *Late Seventeenth- to Nineteenth-century Burial and Earlier Occupation at All Saints, Chelsea Old Church, Royal Borough of Kensington and Chelsea*. Museum of London Archaeology Service Archaeology Studies Series 18. London: Museum of London Archaeology Service.

Coyne, F. 2003. *Archaeological Excavations at Stradbally North, Castleconnell, Co. Limerick*. Unpublished Aegis Archaeology Report.

Coyne, F. and Lynch, L. 2003a. Stradbally North – Grave Concerns at Castleconnell. *Archaeology Ireland* 17: 14–16.

Coyne, F. and Lynch, L. 2003b. *A Post-medieval Burial Ground at Castle Connell, Co. Limerick*. Irish Post-medieval Archaeology Group Newsletter.

Cramp, R. 2005. *Wearmouth and Jarrow Monastic Sites*. London: English Heritage.

Crawley, P.E. *An Archaeological Watching Brief at St Michael's Church, Aylsham, 7402 AYL*. Unpublished Norfolk Archaeology Unit Report.

Cressy, D. 1989. *Bonfires and Bells: National Memory and the Protestant Calendar in Elizabethan and Stuart England*. London: Weidenfeld and Nicolson.

Cressy, D. 1997. *Birth, Marriage and Death: Ritual, Religion and the Life-cycle in Tudor and Stuart England*. Oxford: Oxford University Press.

Cressy, D. 2000. *Agnes Bowker's cat. Travesties and Transgressions in Tudor and Stuart England*. Oxford: Oxford University Press.

Crockett, A. 1994. *Holy Trinity Church, Cookham, Berkshire. Archaeological Watching Brief (Report No. W595)*. Unpublished Wessex Archaeology Report.

Croft, R.A. and Hollinrake, C. 1992. Frome Rook Lane Chapel. *Proceedings of the Somerset Archaeology and Natural History Society* 136: 180.

Crooke, H. 1631. *Microcosmographia: a Description of the Body of Man*. London: Thomas and Richard Cotes.

Crossland, Z. 2002. Violent Spaces: Conflict over the Reappearance of Argentina's Disappeared. In Schofield, J., Beck, C. and Johnson, W.G. (eds) *The Archaeology of 20th Century Conflict*. London: Routledge. pp. 115–131.

Crossland, Z. 2009a. Acts of Estrangement: the Making of Self and other through Exhumation. *Archaeological Dialogues* 16(1): 102–125.

Crossland, Z. 2009b. Of Clues and Signs: the Dead Body and its Evidential Traces. *American Anthropologist* 111(1): 69–80.

Crossland, Z. 2010. Materiality and Embodiment. In Hicks, D. and Beaudry, M. (eds) *The Oxford Handbook of Material Culture Studies* (Ms No. 19). Oxford: Oxford University Press. pp. 386–405.

Crothers, N. 1993. Further Excavations at Ballyrea Townland, Co Armagh. *Emania* 11: 49–54.

Crowfoot, E. 2001. Textiles. In Ayers, B. and Beazley, O. *Two Medieval Churches in Norfolk*. East Anglian

References

Archaeological Report 96. Archaeology and Environment Division, Norfolk. pp. 44–45.

Crowther, M.A. 1983. *The Workhouse System 1834–1929. The History of an English Institution.* London: Methuen.

Crouch, K.R. and Shanks, S.A. 1984. *Excavation in Staines 1975–76. The Friends' Burial Ground Site.* London and Middlesex Archaeological Society/Surrey Archaeological Society: Dorking.

Cullen, I. 1997. *Kilwinning Abbey (North Ayrshire), Report 454.* Unpublished Glasgow University Archaeological Research Division Report.

Cunliffe, B. and Garratt, B. 1994. *Excavations at Portchester Castle. Vol. V: Post-medieval 1609–1819.* London: Society of Antiquaries.

Curl, J.S. 1993. *A Celebration of Death: An Introduction to Some of the Buildings, Monuments and Settings of Funerary Architecture in the Western European tradition.* London: B.T. Batsford.

Dalglish, C. 2003. *Rural Society in the Age of Reason.* New York: Kluwer Academic/Plenum Press.

Daniell, C. 1997. *Death and Burial in Medieval England.* London: Routledge.

Daniels, R. 1986. The Excavation of the Church of the Franciscans, Hartlepool, Cleveland. *Archaeological Journal* 143: 260–304.

Dawkes, G. and Buckley, L. 2006. Bagnal's Castle, Newry: an Elizabethan Tower House and Cemetery. *Archaeology Ireland* 20: 31–33.

de Paor, L. 1972. *Inishcaltra (Holy Island).* www.excavations.ie 1972:0006.

de Paor, L. 1973. *Inishcaltra (Holy Island).* www.excavations.ie 1973:0006.

Deeves, S. 2001. *An Archaeological Watching Brief at 150–164 Goswell Road and 2–14 Seward Street, Islington, EC1.* Unpublished Pre-Construct Archaeology Report.

Deeves, S. 2002. *Assessment of an Archaeological Monitoring Exercise at 150–164 Goswell Road and 2–14 Seward Street, London, EC1.* Unpublished Pre-Construct Archaeology Report.

Defoe. D. 1722. *Journal of the Plague Year.* London: Bradbury and Evans.

Dekker, T. 1603. *The Wonderfull Yeare.* London: Thomas Creede.

Department for Transport Receiver of Wreck 2011. Wrecks Designated as Military Remains. http://www.dft.gov.uk/mca/mcga-environmental/mcga-dops_row_receiver_of_wreck/mcga-dops-row-protected-wrecks/mcga-dops-sar-row.htm (accessed 16th March 2011).

Dennehy, E.A. and Lynch, L.G. 2001. Unearthed Secrets: a Clandestine Burial-Ground. *Archaeology Ireland* 15: 20–23.

Diamond, A. S. 1955. The Cemetery of Resettlement. *Transactions of Jewish Historical Society of England* 19: 163–190.

Dillon, A. 2003. Praying by Number: The Confraternity of the Rosary and the English Catholic Community, c.1580–1700. *History* 88: 451–471.

Dinn, R. 1995. Death and Rebirth in Late Medieval Bury St. Edmunds. In Bassett, S. (ed.) *Death in Towns: Urban responses to the Dying and the Dead, 100–1600.* Leicester: Leicester University Press. pp. 151–169.

Divers, D. 1998. *An Archaeological Evaluation at Bermondsey Square, London. Borough of Southwark, SE1.* Unpublished Pre-Construct Archaeology Report.

Divers, D. 2001. *Assessment of an Archaeological Excavation at Southwark Cathedral. London Borough of Southwark SE1: Phases 1 and 2.* Unpublished Pre-Construct Archaeology Report.

Dobson, J. 1953. Some Eighteenth Century Experiments in Embalming. *Journal of the History of Medicine and Allied Sciences* 8: 431–441.

Dodwell, N. 2001. The Human Remains. In Divers, D. *Assessment of an Archaeological Excavation at Southwark Cathedral, London Borough of Southwark SE1: Phases 1 and 2.* Unpublished Pre-Construct Archaeology Ltd Report. pp. 141–145.

Donagan, B. 1998. The Casualties of War: Treatment of the Dead and Wounded in the English Civil War. In Gentles, I., Morrill, B. and Warden, B. (eds) *Soldiers, Writers and Statesmen of the English Revolution.* Cambridge: Cambridge University Press. pp. 114–132.

Donel, L. 1993. *Lincoln Castle Service Trenching. Archaeological Recording.* Report No. 59. Unpublished City of Lincoln Archaeological Unit Report.

Donnelly, J. and Murphy, E.M. 2008. The origins of cillíní in Ireland. In Murphy, E.M. (ed.) *Deviant Burial in the Archaeological Record.* Oxford: Oxbow Books. pp. 191–223.

Dopson, L. 1949. St. Thomas's Parish Vestry Records and a Body-snatching Incident. *British Medical Journal* 2: 69.

Doran, S. and Durstan, C. 2003. *Princes, Pastors and People: the Church and Religion in England 1500–1700.* London: Routledge.

Drage, C. 1989. Nottingham Castle. A Place full Royal. *Transactions of the Thoroton Society of Nottinghamshire* 93: 1–151.

Driscoll, S.T. 1994. Trial Excavations at Govan Old Parish Church. *Annual Report of the Society of Friends of Old Govan* 5: 2–14.

Driscoll, S.T. 2002. *Excavations at Glasgow Cathedral 1988–1997.* Society for Medieval Archaeology Monograph 18. Leeds: Society for Medieval Archaeology.

Driscoll, S.T. and Will, R.S. 1996. An Interim Report on the 1996 Excavations at Govan Old Parish

Church and Water Row. *Glasgow Archaeological Society Bulletin* 37: 4–7.

Driscoll, S.T. and Yeoman, P.A. 1997. *Excavations within Edinburgh Castle in 1988–91*. Society of Antiquaries of Scotland Monograph 12. Edinburgh: Sutton Publishing.

Drury, S. 1994. Funeral Plants and Flowers in England: Some Examples. *Folklore* 105: 101–103.

Duday, H. 2009. *The Archaeology of the Dead: Lectures in Archaeothanatology*. A.M. Cipriani and J. Pearce, transl. Oxford: Oxbow Books.

Duff, E.J. and Johnson, J.S. 1974. Some Social and Forensic Aspects of Exhumation and Reinterment of Industrial Revolution Remains. *British Medical Journal* 1974:1: 563–567.

Duffy, E. 1992. *The Stripping of the Altars: Traditional Religion in England, c. 1400–1580*. New Haven and London: Yale University Press.

Duffy, P. and Grant, N.M. 2006. *Galston Skeletal Analysis and Pottery Assessment Project 1753*. Unpublished Glasgow University Archaeological Research Division Report.

Duggan, D. 2003. Hale Church and St Paul's Church, Covent Garden. *Proceedings of the Hampshire Field Club and Archaeological Society* 58: 242–253.

Duncan, J.S. 1999. Excavations at Cladh na Sassunach. In Atkinson, J.A. and Photos-Jones, E. (eds) *Scottish Bloomeries Project: Interim Report*. Unpublished Glasgow University Archaeological Research Division Report. pp. 97–103.

Dyer, C. 1989. *Standards of Living in the Later Middle Ages: Social Change in England c. 1200–1520*. Cambridge: Cambridge University Press.

Dyer, C. 2002. *Making a Living in the Middle Ages: The People of Britain 850–1520*. New Haven: Yale University Press.

Dyer, C. 2003. The Archaeology of Medieval Small Towns. *Medieval Archaeology* 47: 85–114.

Dyson, L., Malt, R., and Wellman, T. 1987. *Excavations at Broad Street Station (LSS85), Part 3: The Cemetery*. Museum of London Archaeological Service Archive Report.

E.S. 1747. Of Burial Garlands. *Gentleman's Magazine* 17: 264–265.

Edmondson, G 1999. *Archaeological Observations and Recording at All Saints' Church, Ravensden, Bedfordshire*. Unpublished Bedfordshire County Archaeology Service Report.

Edwards, R.E. 1992. Trial Excavation and Salvage Recording at St. Oswald's Almshouses, Worcester. *Transactions of the Worcestershire Archaeological Society* 3 (Series 13): 181–191.

Egan, G. 1983. Post-medieval Britain in 1982. *Post-medieval Archaeology* 17: 185–204.

Egan, G. 1984. Post-medieval Britain in 1983. *Post-medieval Archaeology* 18: 307–326.

Egan, G. 1985. Post-medieval Britain in 1984. *Post-medieval Archaeology* 19: 159–192.

Egan, G. 1986. Post-medieval Britain in 1985. *Post-medieval Archaeology* 20: 333–360.

Egan, G. 1987. Post-medieval Britain in 1986. *Post-medieval Archaeology* 21: 267–294.

Egan, G. 1988. Post-medieval Britain in 1987. *Post-medieval Archaeology* 22: 189–232.

Egan, G. 1989. Post-medieval Britain and Ireland in 1988. *Post-medieval Archaeology* 23: 25–68.

Egan, G. 1990. Post-medieval Britain and Ireland in 1989. *Post-medieval Archaeology* 24: 159–212.

Egan, G. 2008a. Burial Finds. In Miles, M., White, W. and Tankard, D. (eds) *Burial at the Site of the Parish Church of St Benet Sherehog before and after the Great Fire: Excavations at 1 Poultry, City of London*. Museum of London Archaeology Service Monograph 39. Lavenham: Museum of London Archaeological Services. pp. 68–69.

Egan, G. 2008b. Burial Goods. In Miles, A., Powers, N. and Wroe-Brown, R. (eds) *St. Marylebone Church and Burial Ground in the 18th and 19th centuries. Excavations at St. Marylebone School, 1992 and 2004–6*. Museum of London Archaeology Service Monograph 46. London: Museum of London Archaeological Services. pp. 65–66.

Elliot, L. 2000. Swarkestone, St. James. *Church Archaeology* 4: 68–69.

Elliott, B. 1982. *Notes on the Rosary. England's First Non-denominational Cemetery*. Unpublished document held at Norfolk Historic Environmental Record.

Elliott, L. 1993a. *St. Nicholas' Church, Littleborough, Nottinghamshire: A Report on the Archaeological Recording, June 1993*. Unpublished Trent and Peak Archaeological Trust Report.

Elliott, L. 1993b. *St. Peter and St. Paul's Church, Bridge Street, Mansfield, Nottinghamshire. A Report on the Archaeological Recording, November-December 1993*. Unpublished Trent and Peak Archaeological Trust Report.

Elliott, L. 2000a. Archaeological Recording at St. Catherine's Church and the Willowby Burial Vault, Cossall, Nottinghamshire. *Transactions of the Thoroton Society of Nottinghamshire* 104: 83–97.

Elliott, L. 2000b. Cossall, St. Catherine. *Church Archaeology* 4: 73–74.

Ellis, H. 1853. Letters from a Subaltern Officer of the Earl of Essex's Army, Written in the Summer and Autumn of 1642; Detailing the Early Movements of that Portion of the Parliament Forces which was formed by the Volunteers of the Metropolis; and their Further Movements when Amalgamated with the Rest of the Earl of Essex's Troops. *Archaeologia* 35: 310–334.

Ellis, R. 1985. Excavations at 9 St Clare Street. *London Archaeologist* 5(05): 115–121.

References

Emery, P. 2006. End of the Line: St. Pancras Station. *British Archaeology* 88. http://www.britarch.ac.uk/ba/ba88/feat1.shtml (accessed 6th January 2010).

Ennis, T. 2000. *St. Mary and All Saints Church, Debden, Essex. Archaeological Monitoring and Excavation.* Unpublished Essex County Council Field Archaeology Unit Report.

Eogan, J. 2000. *Report on the Excavation of an Inhumation Cemetery at Mercer St, Dublin 2.* Unpublished Archaeological Development Services Ltd Report.

Essex County Council Field Archaeology Unit 2005. *United Reform Church/ Salvation Army Hall, Abbey Lane, Saffron Walden.* Unpublished Report.

Evans, D. 2004. *Land to rear of Camden House, London Road, Stroud, Gloucestershire. Programme of Archaeological Recording (Phase II).* Unpublished Cotswold Archaeology Report 04190.

Evans, D.T. 1999. The Former Female Prison: "Skeletons in the Cupboard". *Archaeology in York (Interim)* 23(1): 17–22.

Everson, P. and Stocker, D. 2003. The Archaeology of Vice-regality: Charles Brandon's Brief Rule in Lincolnshire. In Gaimster, D. and Gilchrist, R. (eds) *The Archaeology of the Reformation 1480–1580.* Leeds: Maney pp. 145–158.

Eyre-Morgan, G. 1995. *St. Winifred's Parish Church, Davenham, Cheshire. An Archaeological Survey of a Burial Vault and its Contents.* Unpublished University of Manchester Archaeological Unit Report.

Eyre-Morgan, G. 1997. The Investigation of a Burial Vault at St. Wilfred's Parish Church, Davenham, Cheshire. *Archaeology North-West* 2(6): 148–149.

Fanning, T. 1981. Excavation of an Early Christian Cemetery and Settlement at Reask, County Kerry. *Proceedings of the Royal Irish Academy C* 81: 67–172.

Farwell, D. 1988. *Archaeological Observations at Wimbourne Minster.* Unpublished Wessex Archaeology Report.

Fasham, P.J. and Keevill, G. 1995. *Brighton Hill South (Hatch Warren): an Iron Age Farmstead and Deserted Medieval Village in Hampshire.* Wessex Archaeology Report 7. Salisbury: Wessex Archaeology.

Ferguson, B. n.d. *Royal Mint Square, Cartwright Street, London E1. A Report on the Watching Brief.* Unpublished Museum of London Archaeological Services Report.

Ferris, I.M. 2002. Excavations at Greyfriars, Gloucester in 1967 and 1974–5. *Transactions of the Bristol and Gloucestershire Archaeological Society* 119: 95–146.

Fewer, T.G. 1998. An Apparent Funerary Anomaly from Seventeenth-century Waterford. *Journal of the Royal Society of Antiquaries of Ireland* 128: 17–25.

Fibiger, L. 2004. *Report on the Human Skeletal Remains, Carrickmines, Co. Dublin.* Unpublished Human Skeleton Report.

Filer, J. 1991a. Excavation Round-up 1990: part 1, City of London. *London Archaeologist* 6(10): 271–278.

Filer, J. 1991b. Excavation Round-up 1990: part 2, London Boroughs. *London Archaeologist* 6(11): 301.

Finch, E. 1999. *Archaeological Evaluations. St. Margaret's Church, Ipswich (IAS 7806).* Unpublished Suffolk County Council Archaeological Service Report.

Finch, J. 2003. A Reformation of Meaning: Commemoration and Remembering the Dead in the Parish Church, 1450–1640. In Gaimster, D. and Gilchrist, R. (eds) *The Archaeology of Reformation 1480–1580.* Leeds: Maney Publishing. pp. 437–449.

Finch, R.P. 1788. *A Sermon, preached at Christ Church, Middlesex, for the Benefit to the Humane Society on Sunday the 30th day of March at Parish Church with prefatory address and an Appendix containing some Select Accounts of Recovery in Various Cases of Suspended Animation.* London: John Nichols.

Finley, N. 2000. Outside of Life: Traditions of Infant Burial in Ireland from Cillín to Cist. *World Archaeology* 31: 407–422.

Fiorato, V., Boylston, A. and Knüsel. C. 2000. *Blood Red Roses. The Archaeology of a Mass Grave from the Battle of Towton AD 1461.* Oxford: Oxbow Books.

Fissell, M.E. 1989. The "Sick and Drooping Poor" in Eighteenth-century Bristol and its Region. *Journal of the Social History of Medicine* 2: 35–58.

Fitzpatrick, A.P. and Laidlaw, M. 2001. An Unusual Early Seventeenth-century Burial at the Roman Villa at Pinglestone Farm, Old Alresford. *Proceedings of the Hampshire Field Club and Archaeological Society* 56: 219–228.

Fletcher, M. 1994. *St. Bartholomew's Church, Westhoughton: Archaeological Evaluation Report.* Unpublished Greater Manchester Archaeological Contractors Report.

Foarde, G. 1995. *Naseby: the Decisive Campaign.* Whitstable: Prior.

Foarde, G. 2001. The Archaeology of Attack: Battles and Sieges of the English Civil War. In Freeman, P.M.W. and Pollard, A. (eds) *Fields of Conflict: Progress and Prospect in Battlefield Archaeology.* British Archaeology Report (International Series) 958. Oxford: Archaeopress. pp. 87–103.

Forbes, T. R. 1985 *Surgeons at the Bailey. English Forensic Medicine to 1878.* New Haven and London: Yale University Press.

Forsythe, W. 2007. On the Edge of Improvement: Rathlin Island and the Modern World. *International Journal of Historical Archaeology* 11(3): 221–240.

Foucault, M. 1977. *Discipline and punish: The Birth of the Prison.* New York: Pantheon Books.

Fowler, S. 2007. *Workhouse.* Kew: National Archives.

Fraser. A. 1996. *The Gunpowder Plot. Terror and Faith in 1605.* London: Arrow.

Fraser, D. 1976. Introduction. In D. Fraser (ed.) *The New Poor Law in the Nineteenth Century.* London: Macmillan. pp. 1–24.

Fraser, A.H. and Brown, M. 2008. Mud, Blood and Missing Men: Excavations at Serre, Somme, France. In Pollard, T. and Banks, T. (eds) *Scorched Earth: Studies in the Archaeology of Conflict.* Leiden: Koninklijke Brill. pp. 147–171.

Freeman, R. 1985. Post-medieval Burials near Dartmouth Castle. *Devon Archaeological Society* 43: 131–134.

Fritz, P.S. 1994–5. The Undertaking Trade in England: its Origins and Early Development, 1660–1830. *Eighteenth-Century Studies* 28: 241–253.

Fulke, W. 1581. *A Rejoinder to Bristows Replie in Defence of Allens Scroll of Articles and Booke of Purgatorie. Also the Cauils of Nicholas Sander D in Dintnitie about the Supper of our Lord and Apologie of the Church of England, Touching the Doctrine Thereof.* London: George Middleton.

Gaimster, D. and R. Gilchrist (eds) 2003. *The Archaeology of Reformation 1480–1580.* Leeds: Maney Publishing.

Gaimster, M. 2008. Post-medieval Fieldwork in Britain, Northern Ireland and the Channel Isles in 2007. *Post-medieval Archaeology* 42: 341–411.

Gale, R. 1986. *The Identification of Wood from Sites Excavated by the DUA.* AML Report 60/87.

Gale, R. 2006. Wooden Coffin Remains. In Brickley, M. and Buteux, S. (eds) *St. Martin's Uncovered. Investigations in the Churchyard of St. Martin's-in-the-Bull Ring, Birmingham, 2001.* Oxford: Oxbow Books. pp. 160–163.

Gaskill, M. 2005. *Witchfinders. A Seventeenth-century English Tragedy.* London: John Murray.

Gatrell, V.A.C. 1994. *The Hanging Tree: Execution and the English people 1770–1868.* Oxford: Oxford University Press.

Geary, P. 1994. Exchange and Interaction between the Living and the Dead in Early Medieval Society. In Geary, P. (ed.) *Living with the Dead in the Middle Ages.* London: Cornell University Press. pp. 77–92.

Gelfand, T. 1985. "Invite the Philosopher, as well as the Charitable": Hospital Teaching as Private Enterprise in Hunterian London. In Bynum, W.F. and Porter, R. (eds) *William Hunter and the Eighteenth-century Medical World.* Cambridge: Cambridge University Press. pp. 129–151.

Gent, T.H. 1998. *A Further Inhumation at Saunton Down End, Croyde Bay.* Unpublished Exeter Archaeology Report.

Gentles, T. 1996. Political Funerals during the English Revolution. In Porter, S. (ed.) *London and the Civil War.* London: Macmillan. pp. 205–224.

Germany, M. 1997. *St. Mary's Church Broomfield, Essex. Archaeological Watching Brief.* Unpublished Essex County Council Field Archaeology Group Report.

Germany, M. 1999. *St. Mary and All Saints Church, Debden Essex. Archaeological Evaluation.* Unpublished Essex County Council Field Archaeological Unit Report.

Gibson, D.J. 1994. *An Archaeological Site Evaluation at St. Andrew's Church, Impington, Cambridgeshire.* Unpublished Cambridge Archaeological Unit Report.

Gibson, M. 2008. *St. Mary the Virgin, Kirtlington. Archaeological Watching Brief Report.* Unpublished Oxford Archaeology Report.

Gifford and Partners. 1999. *St. Mary's Church, Southampton. Report of the Archaeological Evaluation.* Unpublished Gifford and Partners Report.

Gilchrist, R. 2003. "Dust to Dust": Revealing the Reformation Dead. In Gaimster, D. and Gilchrist, R. (eds) *The Archaeology of Reformation 1480–1580.* Leeds: Maney Publishing. pp. 399–414.

Gilchrist, R. 2008. Magic for the Dead? The Archaeology of Magic in Later Medieval Burials. *Medieval Archaeology* 52: 119–159.

Gilchrist, R. and Sloane, B. 2005. *Requiem: the Medieval Monastic Cemetery in Britain.* London: Museum of London Archaeology Service.

Gillian-Hurst, D. 1967. Post-medieval Britain in 1966. *Post-medieval Archaeology* 1: 107–121.

Gillian-Hurst, D. 1968. Post-medieval Britain in 1967. *Post-medieval Archaeology* 2: 175–194.

Gillian-Hurst, D. 1969. Post-medieval Britain in 1968. *Post-medieval Archaeology* 3: 193–212.

Gillian-Hurst, D. 1970. Post-medieval Britain in 1969. *Post-medieval Archaeology* 4: 174–188.

Gilmour, B.J.J. and Stocker, D.A. 1986. *St. Mark's Church and Cemetery.* The Archaeology of Lincoln, Volume XIII-1. London: Council for British Archaeology for the Trust for Lincolnshire Archaeology.

Girardon, S. and Heathcote, J. 1989. Excavation Round-up 1988: Part 2, London Boroughs. *London Archaeologist* 6(03): 72–80.

Gittings, C. 1984. *Death, Burial and the Individual in Early Modern England.* London: Routledge.

Gittings, C. 2007. Eccentric or Enlightened? Unusual Burial and Commemoration in England, 1689–1823. *Mortality* 12: 321–349.

Goldstein, L. 2004. Ancient Southwest Mortuary Practices: Perspectives from Outside the Southwest. In Mitchell, D., Brunson-Hadley, J.

and Lippert, D. *Ancient Burial Practices in the American Southwest: Archaeology, Physical Anthropology, and Native American Perspectives*. Albuquerque: University of New Mexico Press. pp. 249–255.

Goodall, H.G. 1970. A Seventeenth-century Vault in Blandford Parish. *Proceedings of the Dorset Natural History and Archaeology Society* 92: 153–155.

Graham, A.H. 1996. *St. Mary's Church, Whitelackington, Somerset. Archaeological records made during the Repair of the Southern Pew Platform*. Unpublished Report.

Grant, K. 2009. *An Enhanced Archaeological Watching Brief at St. John the Baptist Church, Southover High Street, Southover, Lewes, East Sussex*. Archaeology South-East Report 2009017. http://www.Archaeologyse.co.uk/ReportLibrary/2009/2009017-3587-Baptist-Church-Southover-Hight-Street.pdf (accessed 20th April 2011).

Graves, C.P. 1997. Social Space in the English Medieval Parish Church. In Bryant, C. and Jary, D. (eds) *Anthony Giddens: Critical Assessments*. Volume 4. London: Routledge. pp. 262–288.

Greatorex, P. 1993. Cathedral Close, Gloucester. *Transactions of the Bristol and Gloucestershire Archaeological Society* 111: 222.

Greenblatt, S. 1980. *Renaissance Self-fashioning, from More to Shakespeare*. Chicago: Chicago University Press.

Greenwood, P. and Maloney, C. 1993. Excavation Round-up 1992: part 1. *London Archaeologist* 7(2): 47–51.

Greenwood, P. and Maloney, C. 1994. London Fieldwork and Excavation Round-up 1993. *London Archaeologist* 7(8): 197–218.

Greenwood, P. and Thompson, A. 1992. Excavation Round-up 1991: Part 2, London Boroughs. *London Archaeologist* 6(15): 415–423.

Griffen, S. 2000. *Watching Brief at St. Oswald's Almhouses, Worcester*. Unpublished Worcestershire County Council Archaeological Services Report.

Groves, C. and Boswijk, G. 1998. *Tree-ring Analysis of Coffin Boards from the former Burial Ground of the Infirmary, Newcastle upon Tyne*. English Heritage Ancient Monuments Laboratory Report 15.

Guibert, P. 1639. *The Charitable Physitian with the Charitable Apothecary*. London: Thomas Harper.

Hacking, P. 2006. Human Bone. In Norton, A. (ed.) *Oxford Castle. Post-Excavation Analysis and Research Design*. Unpublished Oxford Archaeology Report. pp. 116–118.

Hadley, D. 2001. *Death in Medieval England*. Stroud: Tempus.

Haglund, W.D., Connor, M. and Scott, D.D. 2001. The Archaeology of Contemporary Mass Graves. *Historical Archaeology* 35: 57–69.

Haglund, W.D. 2002. Recent Mass Graves. In Haglund, W.D. and Sorg, M.H. (eds) *Advances in Forensic Taphonomy. Method, Theory and Archaeological Perspectives*. London: CRC Press. pp. 243–261.

Haigh, C. (ed.) 1987. *The English Reformation Revised*. Cambridge: Cambridge University Press.

Hair, N. 1995. *St. Thomas the Martyr Church, Upholland, Lancashire. Archaeological Evaluation* (LUAU PRN 1369). Unpublished Lancaster University Archaeological Unit.

Hall, D. 1989. Perth: the Excavations. In Stones, J.A. (ed) *Three Scottish Carmelite Friaries: Excavations at Aberdeen, Linlithgow and Perth 1980–1986*. Edinburgh: Edinburgh: Society of Antiquaries of Scotland. pp. 99–110 http://ads.ahds.ac.uk/catalogue/adsdata/PSAS_2002/pdf/Monogr_06/6_prelims.pdf?CFID=573996&CFTOKEN=39545028 (accessed 12th April 2010).

Hallam, T. 1999. *Archaeological Excavation of two Brick Burial Vaults at the Bull Hotel, Peterborough*. Unpublished Northamptonshire Archaeology Report.

Halliday, R. 1994. Wayside Graves and Crossroads Burials. *Norfolk Archaeology* 42(1): 80–83.

Halliday, R. 1997. Criminal Graves and Rural Crossroads. *British Archaeology* 25: 6.

Halliday, R. and Susser, B. 2002. The Ipswich Jewish community in the Eighteenth and Nineteenth Centuries. *Proceedings of the Suffolk Institute of Archaeology and History* 40: 151–163.

Hamilton-Dyer, S. 2003. Animal Bone. In Hull, G. The Excavation and Analysis of an Eighteenth-century Deposit of Anatomical Remains and Chemical Apparatus from the rear of the First Ashmolean Museum (now the Museum of the History of Science), Broad Street, Oxford. *Post-medieval Archaeology* 37: 1–28.

Hammond, S. and Ford, S. 2003. *Bonn Square Improvements, Oxford. An Archaeological Evaluation and Desk-based Assessment*. Unpublished Thames Valley Archaeological Services Report.

Hancox, E. 2006. Coffins and Coffin Furniture. In Brickley, M. and Buteux, S. (eds) *St. Martin's Uncovered. Investigations in the Churchyard of St. Martin's-in-the-Bull Ring, Birmingham, 2001*. Oxford: Oxbow Books. pp. 152–160.

Hannaford, H.R. 1995. *Archaeological Excavation of a Test Pit at Old Chad's Church, Shrewsbury*. Unpublished Shropshire County Council Archaeological Services Report.

Harding, C. 1987. Post-medieval Coffin Furniture. In Hurst, J.G. and Rahtz, P.A. *Wharram: A Study of Settlement in the Yorkshire Wolds, III: Wharram Percy: the Church of St. Martin*. Society of Medieval Archaeology Monograph 11. Leeds: Maney Publishing. pp. 150–153.

Harding, V. 1989. "And One More May be Laid There": the Location of Burials in Early Modern London. *The London Journal* 14: 112–129.

Harding, V. 1993. Burial of the Plague Dead in Early Modern London. In Champion, J.A.I. (ed.) *Epidemic Disease in London.* Centre for Metropolitan History Working Papers Series No. 1. London: Institute of Historical Research. pp. 53–64.

Harding, V. 1998. Burial on the Margin: Distance and Discrimination in Early Modern London. In Cox, M. (ed.) *Grave Concerns: Death and Burial in England 1700–1850.* Council for British Archaeology Research Report 113. York: Council for British Archaeology. pp. 54–64.

Harding, V. 2002. *The Dead and the Living in Paris and London, 1500–1670.* Cambridge: Cambridge University Press.

Hardy, A. 1999. *The Devonport Buildings, King William Walk, Greenwich. London Borough of Greenwich. Archaeological Watching Brief.* Unpublished Oxford Archaeology Report.

Hardy, A., Dodd, A. and Keevill, G.D. 2003. *Aelfric's Abbey. Excavations at Eynsham Abbey, Oxfordshire, 1989–92.* Thames Valley Landscapes Volume 16. Oxford: Oxford Archaeology.

Hare, J. 1993. Netley Abbey: Monastery, Mansion and Ruin. *Proceedings of the Hampshire Field Club and Archaeological Society* 49: 207–227.

Harley, D. 1994a. Political Post-mortems and Morbid Anatomy in Seventeenth-century England. *Social History of Medicine* 7: 1–28.

Harley, D. 1994b. Legal Medicine in Lancashire and Cheshire. In Clark, M. and Crawford, C. (eds) *Legal Medicine in History.* Cambridge: Cambridge University Press. pp. 45–63.

Harris, B., 2004. Public Health, Nutrition, and the Decline of Mortality: the McKeown Thesis Revisited. *Social History of Medicine* 17(3): 379–407.

Harris, T. 1887. *Post-mortem Handbook or How to Conduct Post-mortem Examinations for Clinical and for Medico-legal Purposes.* London: Smith, Elder and Co.

Hart, A. 2002a. Excavations in the Churchyard of St. Martin of Tours, Chelsfield. *Kent Archaeological Review* 149: 191–198.

Hart, A. 2002b. Trial Excavations in the Churchyard of St. Martin of Tours, Chelsfield. *Archives of the Orpington District Archaeological Society* 24: 21–31.

Harvey, W. 1653. *The Anatomical exercises of Dr. William Harvey professor of Physick, and Physician to the Kings Majesty, Concerning the Motion of the Heart and Blood.* London: Francis Leach.

Havis, R. 1995. St. Andrew's Church, Hatfield Peverel. *Essex Archaeology and History* 26: 277–279.

Hawes, W. 1780. *An Account of the Late Dr. Goldsmith's Illness, so far as Relates to the Exhibition of Dr. James' Powder. An Examination of the Rev. Mr. John Wesley's Primitive Physic: and an Address to the Public on Premature Death and Premature Interment.* London: W. Brown and H. Gardner.

Hay, D., Linebaugh, P., Rule J.G., Thompson, E.P. and Winslow, C. 1988. *Albion's Fatal Tree. Crime and Society in Eighteenth-century England.* London: Penguin Books.

Hayes, J.P., Williams, D.E. and Payne, P.R. 1983. Report of an Excavation in the Ground of St. Bartholomew's Chapel, Chatham. *Archaeologia Cantiana* 98: 177–189.

Heal, F. 2003. *Reformation in Britain and Ireland.* Oxford: Oxford University Press.

Heathcote, J. 1988. Excavation Round-up 1987 Part 1: City of London. *London Archaeologist* 5(14): 382–387.

Heawood, R. 2002. Excavations at Warrington Friary 2000. *Journal of the Chester Archaeological Society* 77: 131–185.

Heighway, C. 1999. *Church of St. Leonard, Upton St Leonards, Gloucester. Report of Archaeological Watching Brief.* Unpublished Past Historic (Unit) Report.

Heighway, C. and Bryant, R. 1999. *The Golden Minster. The Anglo-Saxon Minster and Later Medieval Priory of St. Oswald's at Gloucester.* Council for British Archaeology Research Report 117. York: Council for British Archaeology.

Heighway, C.M. and Litten, J.W.S. 1994. Investigations at St. Kenelm's Church, Sapperton. *Transactions of the Bristol and Gloucestershire Archaeological Society* 112: 111–126.

Henderson, D. 1996. The Skeletal Remains. In Henderson, D., Collard, M. and Johnston, D.A. 1996. Archaeological Evidence for Eighteenth-century Medical Practice in the Old Town of Edinburgh: Excavations at 13 Infirmary Street and Surgeons' Square. *Proceedings of the Society of Antiquaries of Scotland* 126: 936–938.

Henderson, D., Collard, M. and Johnston, D.A. 1996. Archaeological Evidence for Eighteenth-century Medical Practice in the Old Town of Edinburgh: Excavations at 13 Infirmary Street and Surgeons' Square. *Proceedings of the Society of Antiquaries of Scotland* 126: 929–941.

Henshall, A.S. and Maxwell, S. 1952. Clothing and Other Articles from a Late Seventeenth-century Grave on Gunnister, Shetland. *Proceedings of the Society of Antiquarians of Scotland* 86: 30–42.

Herbert, P. 1979. Excavations at Christchurch Greyfriars, 1976. *London Archaeologist* 3: 327–332.

Hewson, W. 1772. *Experimental Inquiry into the Properties of the Blood: with Remarks on Some of its Morbid Appearances: and an Appendix Relating to the Discovery of the Lymphatic System in Birds, Fish and the Animals called Amphibious.* London: T. Cadell.

References

Heys, F.G. 1958–60. Excavations at Castle Green. *Transactions of Woolhope Naturalists' Field Club* XXXVI: 343.

Hicks, M. 1990. *Redcross Way/ Union Street, Southwark: Archaeological Assessment.* Unpublished Oxford Archaeology Report.

Hiller, J. 1999a. *Church of St. Thomas of Canterbury, Elsfield, Oxon. Archaeological Field Evaluation Report.* Unpublished Oxford Archaeological Unit Report.

Hiller, J.R. 1999b. *Parish Church of St. Mary, Sulhamstead Abbots, West Berkshire. Archaeological Field Evaluation Report.* Unpublished Oxford Archaeological Unit Report.

Hillson, S., Waldron, T., Owen-Smith, B. and Martin, L. 1999. Benjamin Franklin, William Hewson and the Craven Street Bones. *Archaeology International* 2: 14–16.

Hoad, S. 1989. *Level III Archive Report on the Evaluation Project at Gowers Walk, E1.* Department of Greater London Archaeology (DGLA) Report.

Holder, N. and Jeffries, N. forthcoming. *Spitalfields: a History of the London Suburb from 1539 to the 1880s. Archaeological Excavations at Spitalfields Market, 1991–2007.* London: Museum of London Archaeology Monograph Series.

Holmes, B. 1896. *The London Burial Grounds.* London: T. Fisher Unwin.

Holmes, N. 1997. The Later Medieval and Post-medieval Coins. In Hill, P. (ed.) *Whithorn and St Ninian: the Excavation of a Monastic Town 1984–1991.* Stroud: Alan Sutton/Whithorn Trust. pp. 345–351.

Holmes, N.M. 1991. The Coins. In McCullagh, R. and McCormick, F. The Excavation of Post-medieval Burials from Braigh, Aignish, Lewis, 1989. *Post-medieval Archaeology* 25: 81–83.

Hood, J.S.R. 1980. Coffin Wood. In Shoesmith, R. Llangar. *Archaeologia Cambrensis* 129: 93–95.

Houlbrooke, R. 1989. Death, Church, and Family in England between the Late Fifteenth and the Early Eighteenth Centuries. In Houlbrooke, R. (ed.) *Death, Ritual, and Bereavement.* London: Routledge. pp. 25–42.

Houlbrooke, R. 1998. *Death, Religion and the Family in England, 1480–1750.* Oxford: Oxford University Press.

Howard, B. 1996. *Fareham Beach Burial.* Unpublished Report held at Hampshire SMR.

Howell, I. 2004. *St. George's Church, Hanworth.* Unpublished Museum of London Archaeological Services Report.

Hoyle, J. 1991a. *A Report on a Watching Brief at St. Edward's Church, Evenlode, June 1990.* Unpublished Gloucester County Council Archaeology Section Report.

Hoyle, J. 1991b. *Watching Brief at All Saints Church, Preston, Gloucestershire.* Unpublished Gloucestershire County Council Archaeology Section Report.

HRO 24M54/60, Alton Monthly Meeting Accounts: Account Book relating mainly to Building and Maintenance of Meeting House and Burial Ground, 1672–1810.

Hull, G. 2003. The Excavation and Analysis of an Eighteenth-century Deposit of Anatomical Remains and Chemical Apparatus from the rear of the First Ashmolean Museum (now the Museum of the History of Science), Broad Street, Oxford. *Post-medieval Archaeology* 37: 1–28.

Hume, L. 1994. *St. Mary's Church, Saltford: Site Specific Archaeological Evaluation in Advance of Proposed Development.* Unpublished Avon Archaeological Unit Report.

Hunnisett, R.F. 1958. The Origins of the Office of Coroner. *Transactions of the Royal Historical Society* (Fifth Series) 8: 85–104.

Hunter, J. 1972–4. The Church of St. Nicholas, Aberdeen. *Proceedings of the Society of Antiquaries of Scotland* 105: 236–247.

Hunter, W. 1776. *The Art of Embalming Dead Bodies, being the Substance of a Lecture Delivered by William Hunter M.D., January 13 1776.* Notes from Lecture held at Royal College of Surgeons, London.

Hunting, P. 1991. The New Churchyard. In Hunting, P. (ed.) *Broadgate and Liverpool Street Station.* London: Rosehaugh Stanhope Developments plc. pp. 31–37.

Hurl, D.P. 2001. Portmuck. www.excavations.ie. Site 2001:015.

Hurl, D.P. and Murphy, E.M. 1996. Life and Death in a County Antrim Tower House. *Archaeology Ireland* 10: 20–23.

Hurley, F.C. 2000. *Archaeological Monitoring at Western Road, Clonmel, Co. Tipperary.* Unpublished Report.

Hurley, M.F. and McCutcheon, S.W.J. 1997. St. Peter's Church and Graveyard. In Hurley, M.F. and Scully, O.M.D. (eds) *Late Viking and Medieval Waterford. Excavations 1986–1992.* Waterford: Waterford Corporation. pp. 190–227.

Hurley, M.F. and Sheehan, C.M. 1995. *Excavations at the Dominican Priory. St. Mary's of the Isle, Cork.* Cork: Cork Corporation.

Hurst, J.G. and Rahtz, P.A. 1987. *Wharram: A Study of Settlement in the Yorkshire Wolds, III: Wharram Percy: the Church of St. Martin.* Society of Medieval Archaeology Monograph 11. Leeds: Maney Publishing. pp. 150–153.

Hutchings, P. 1999. *St. Michael and All Angels Church, Wilmington, Dartford, Kent.* Unpublished Canterbury Archaeological Trust Report.

Ignatieff, M. 1978. *A Just Measure of Pain: the Penitentiary in the Industrial Revolution 1750–1850*. Columbia: Columbia University Press.

Iles, R. 1983. Avon Archaeology 1982. *Bristol and Avon Archaeology* 2: 52.

Irish Archaeological Consultancy Ltd n.d. *Stratigraphic Report on an Archaeological Excavation at 189–194 North King Street, Dublin 7*. Unpublished Irish Archaeological Consultancy Ltd Report.

Jacklin, H.A. 2006a. *Bond Street Congregational Chapel: The Human Remains and Burial Archaeology*. University of Leicester Archaeological Services Draft Report.

Jacklin, H.A. 2006b. *Ebenezer Chapel: The Human Remains and Burial Archaeology*. University of Leicester Archaeological Services Draft Report.

Jackson, R.G. and Stevens, D. 2002. *Archaeological Evaluation at Quakers Friars, Broadmead, Bristol*. Unpublished Bristol and Region Archaeological Services Report 926/2002.

Jackson, S. and Timmins, G. 1989. Demographic Changes 1701–1981. In Pope, R. (ed.) *Atlas of British Social and Economic History since c. 1700*. London: Routledge. pp. 134–148.

Jalland, P. 1999a. Victorian Death and its Decline 1850–1918. In Jupp, P. and Gittings, C. (eds) *Death in England. An Illustrated History*. Manchester: Manchester University Press. pp. 230–255.

Jalland, P. 1999b. *Death in the Victorian Family*. Oxford: Oxford University Press.

James, T. 1997. Excavations at Carmarthen Greyfriars, 1983–1990. *Medieval Archaeology* 41: 100–194.

Janaway, R. 1993. The Textiles. In Reeve, J. and Adams, M. 1993. (eds) *The Spitalfields Project. Volume 1 – the Archaeology. Across the Styx*. Council of British Archaeology Research Report 85. York: Council of British Archaeology. pp. 92–119.

Janaway, R. 1998. An Introductory Guide to Textiles from Eighteenth- and Nineteenth-century Burials. In Cox, M. (ed.) *Grave Concerns: Death and Burial in England 1700–1850*. Council for British Archaeology Research Report 113. York: Council for British Archaeology. pp. 17–32.

Jenner, M. 2005. Death, decomposition and dechristianisation? Public Health and Church Burial in Eighteenth-century England. *English Historical Review* 120: 615–632.

Johns, C. 1996. *St. Paternus Church, North Petherwin, Cornwall*. Unpublished Cornwall Archaeological Unit Report.

Johnson, H. 1858. Case of Suspected Poisoning by Lobelia inflate: with Appearances after Death. *British Medical Journal* 1(77): 493–495.

Johnson, M. 1996. *An Archaeology of Capitalism*. Oxford: Blackwell.

Jones, A.E. 1991. *St. Mary's Church, Ross: An Archaeological Evaluation. Report no. 173*. Unpublished Birmingham University Field Archaeology Unit Report.

Jones, C. 1999. *Archaeological Evaluation at the Church of St James the Great, Snitterfield, Warwickshire*. Warwickshire Museum Field Services Report.

Jones, G.R. n.d. *Excavations at Capel Teilo, Kidwelly, 1966–1969*. http://www.kidwellyHistory.co.uk/Articles/CapelTeilo/CapelTeilo.htm (accessed 24th July 2009).

Jones, N., Silvester, B. and Edwards, N. 2001. St. Cyngar's Church, Hope. *Archaeology in Wales* 41: 42–50.

Jones-Baker, D. 1977. *The Folklore of Hertfordshire*. Batsford: London.

Jupp, P.C. 1990. *From Dust to Ashes: The Replacement of Burial by Cremation in England 1840–1967*. London: The Congregational Memorial Hall Trust.

Jupp, P.C. 1997. Enon Chapel: No Way for the Dead. In Jupp, P.C. and Howarth, G. (eds) *The Changing Face of Death*. Basingstoke: Macmillan. pp. 90–104.

Jupp, P.C. 2006. *From Dust to Ashes: Cremation and the British way of Death*. Basingstoke: Palgrave Macmillan.

Katz, D.S. 1994. *The Jews in the History of England*. Oxford: Clarendon Press.

Keeley, V. 1998. *Final Report. Archaeological Investigation and Monitoring. Courthouse, Old Gaol/ Arts Centre, Portlaoise*. Unpublished Valerie Keeley Excavation Report.

Keen, L. and Hough, P. 1993. *Beeston Castle, Cheshire. A Report on the Excavation 1968–85*. London: English Heritage.

Kenworthy, J.B. 1980. *Excavations at Balmerino Abbey NE Fife*. Unpublished Report held by National Trust for Scotland.

Kilfeather, S. 2002. Oliver Plunkett's head. *Textual Practice* 16: 229–248.

King, H.A. 1993. *Clonmacnoise*. www.excavations.ie. Site 1993:186.

King, H.A. 1994. *Clonmacnoise*. www.excavations.ie. Site 1994:196.

King, H.A. 1995. *New Graveyard, Clonmacnoise*. www.excavations.ie. Site 1995:250.

King, L.S. and M. C. Meehan. 1973. A History of the Autopsy. A review. *American Journal of Pathology* 73: 514–545.

Kirk, L. 1998. The Excavation of a Quaker Burial Ground, 84 London Road, Kingston upon Thames. *London Archaeologist* 8(11): 298–303.

Kirk, L. and Start, H. 1999. Death at the Undertakers. In Downes, J. and Pollard, T. (eds) *The Loved Body's Corruption*. Glasgow: Cruithne Press. pp. 200–208.

References

Kjølbye-Biddle, B. 1992. Dispersal or Concentration: the Disposal of the Winchester Dead over 2000 years. In Bassett, S. (ed.) *Death in Towns*. Leicester: Leicester University Press. pp. 210–247.

Kneller, P. 1998. Health and Safety in Church and Funerary Archaeology. In Cox, M. (ed.) *Grave Concerns: Death and Burial in England 1700–1850*. Council for British Archaeology Research Report 113. York: Council for British Archaeology. pp. 181–189.

Knight, H. 2002. *Aspects of Medieval and Later Southwark. Archaeological Excavations (1991–8) for the London Underground Limited Jubilee Line Extension Project*. Museum of London Archaeological Service Monograph Series 13. London: Museum of London Archaeology Service.

Knox, F.J. 1836. *The Anatomist's Instructor and Museum Companion: being Practical Directions for the Formation and Subsequent Management of Anatomical Museums*. Edinburgh: Adam and Charles Black.

Krakowicz, R. and Rudge, A. 2004. *Masshouse Circus. Birmingham City Centre: Archaeological Recording 2002*. Unpublished Birmingham Archaeology Report 923.

Langstaff, G. 1842. *Catalogue of the Preparations illustrative of Normal, Abnormal and Morbid Structure, Human and Comparative, constituting the Anatomical Museum of George Langstaff*. London: John Churchill.

Lankstead, D. 2005. *The former Purimachas Factory Site, Waterloo Road, Bristol*. Unpublished Bristol and Region Archaeological Services Report.

Laqueur, T.W. 1983. Bodies, Death, and Pauper Funerals. *Representations* 1 (Winter 1983): 109–131.

Laqueur, T.W. 1989a. Bodies, Details and the Humanitarian Narrative. In Hunt, L. (ed.) *The New Cultural History*. Berkeley and Los Angeles: University of California Press. pp. 176–204.

Laqueur, T.W. 1989b. Crowds, Carnival and the State in English Executions, 1604–1868. In Stone, L., Beier, A.L., Cannadine, D. and Rosenheim, J.M. (eds) *The First Modern Society: Essays in English History in Honour of Lawrence Stone*. Cambridge: Cambridge University Press. pp. 205–355.

Laqueur, T. 1993. Cemeteries, Religion and the Culture of Capitalism. In Garnett, J. and Matthew, C. (eds) *Revival and Religion since 1700: Essays for John Walsh*. London and Rio Grande: Hambledon Press. pp. 183–200.

Lawrence, S.C. 1995. Anatomy and Address: Creating the Medical Gentlemen in Eighteenth-century London. In Nutton, V. and Porter, R. (eds) *The History of Medical Education in Britain*. Amsterdam: Rodopi. pp. 199–228.

Lawrence, S.C. 1996. *Charitable Knowledge: Hospital Pupils and Practitioners in Eighteenth-century London*. Cambridge: Cambridge University Press.

Le Goff, J. 1984. *The Birth of Purgatory*. London: Scolar Press.

Leach, P. and Sterenberg, J. 1992. *Holy Trinity Churchyard, Sutton Coalfield: An Archaeological Evaluation 1992*. Unpublished Birmingham University Field Archaeology Unit Report.

Leach, S. 1999. *Codford St. Peter, Wiltshire: Observations of Drainage Work Carried out at Codford St. Peter*. Unpublished AC Archaeology Report.

Leather, E.M. 1912. *The Folklore of Herefordshire*. Hereford: Jakeman and Cerver.

Lee, R.J. 1879. *Notes for Students. Pathological Anatomy. A Guide in the Post-mortem Room*. London: T. Richards.

Leech, R. 1981. *Early Industrial Housing: the Trinity area of Frome*. London: RCHME.

Lelong, O. 1999. Excavations at North Fasagh Settlement. In Atkinson, J.A. and Photos-Jones, E. (eds) *Scottish Bloomeries Project: Interim Report*. Unpublished Glasgow University Archaeological Research Division Report. pp. 81–97.

Lepine, D. and Orme, N. 2003. *Death and Memory in Medieval Exeter*. Exeter: Devon and Cornwall Records Society.

Lewcun, M. 1995. *Excavations at the Church of St. Thomas a' Becket, Widcombe, Bath*. Unpublished Bath Archaeological Trust Report.

Lewis, D. and Pikes, P.J. 2004. *The Tanyard and Quaker Burial Ground, Bromyard, Herefordshire: Archaeological Excavation and monitoring*. Unpublished Archenfield Archaeology Ltd Report. http://ads.ahds.ac.uk/catalogue/library/greylit/details.cfm?id=2714 (accessed 4th March 2010).

Lewis, J.H. and Ewart, G.J. 1995. *Jedburgh Abbey: The Archaeology and Architecture of a Border Abbey*. Society of Antiquaries of Scotland Monograph Series No. 10. Edinburgh: Society of Antiquaries of Scotland. http://ads.ahds.ac.uk/catalogue/library/psas/monograph10.cfm (accessed 23rd April 2010).

Lindley, P. 2007. *Tomb Destruction and Scholarship: Medieval Monuments in Early Modern England*. Donington: Shaun Tyas.

Lindsay, W.J. 1989. Linlithgow: The Excavations. In Stone, J.A. (ed.) *Three Scottish Carmelite Friaries. Excavations at Aberdeen, Linlithgow and Perth 1980–86*. Society of Antiquaries of Scotland Monograph Series No. 6. Edinburgh: Society of Antiquaries of Scotland. pp. 57–98 http://ads.ahds.ac.uk/catalogue/adsdata/PSAS_2002/pdf/Monogr_06/6_prelims.pdf?CFID=573996&CFTOKEN=39545028 (accessed 12th April 2010).

Linebaugh, P. 1988. The Tyburn Riot against the Surgeons. In Hay, D., Linebaugh, P., Rule, J.G., Thompson, E.P. and Winslow, C. (eds) *Albion's Fatal Tree: Crime and Society in Eighteenth-century England*. London: Penguin Books. pp. 65–117.

Linklater, A. 2004. St. Mary's Church, Chilham. Canterbury Archaeological Trust Annual Report 28 (2003–2004): 26–27.

Litten, J. 1991. *The English Way of Death. The Common Funeral since 1450*. London: Robert Hale.

Litten, J. 1997. The Funeral Trade in Hanoverian England 1714–1760. In Jupp, P.C. and Howarth, G. (eds) *The Changing Face of Death: Historical Accounts of Death and Disposal*. Basingstoke: Macmillan. pp. 48–61.

Litten, J.W.S., Dawson, D.P. and Boore, E.J. 1988. The Poulett Vault, Hinton St George. *Somerset Archaeology and Natural History* 132: 256–259.

Llewellyn, N. 1991. *The Art of Death: Visual Culture in the English Death Ritual c.1500–c.1800*. London: Reaktion Books.

Locock, M. 1993. *Excavations at Cwm Nash, Monknash, South Glamorgan*. Unpublished Gwent-Glamorgan Archaeological Trust Report 93/068.

Locock, M. 1994a. *Archaeological Excavation, Herbert Chapel, St. Mary's Priory Church, Abergavenny*. Unpublished Gwent-Glamorgan Archaeological Trust Report 94/060.

Locock, M. 1994b. *Archaeological Excavation, Herbert Chapel, St. Mary's Priory Church, Abervagenny, Gwent. A Report on Further Work*. Unpublished Gwent-Glamorgan Archaeological Trust Report 94/066.

Lofqvist, C. 2004. *Osteological Report on Human Skeletal Remains from Eyre Square, Galway City*. Unpublished Moore Archaeological and Environmental Services Ltd Report.

Lorimer, D.H. 1991. The Human Remains. In McCullagh, R. and McCormick, F. The Excavation of Post-medieval Burials from Braigh, Aignish, Lewis, 1989. *Post-medieval Archaeology* 25: 76–81.

Loudon, J.C. 1843. *On the Laying Out, Planting and Managing of Cemeteries and on the Improvement of Churchyards*. London: Longman, Brown, Green and Longmans.

Lucas, J. 1993a. *An Archaeological Evaluation in the Guildhall Graveyard, Leicester*. Unpublished Leicestershire Archaeological Unit Report.

Lucas, J. 1993b.The Guildhall Graveyard, St. Martins West, Leicester. *Transactions of Leicestershire Archaeological and Historical Society* 69: 126.

Lunn, P. 1991. Nutrition Immunity and Infection, In Schofield, R., Reher, D. and Bideau, A. (eds) *The Decline of Mortality in Europe*. Oxford: Oxford University Press. pp. 131–145.

Lynch, L. 2002a. Surgical Procedures in Nineteenth-century Sligo. *Paleopathology Association Irish Section News* 5: 5–7.

Lynch, L.G. 2002b.*Osteo-Archaeological Report on Human Skeletal Remains Excavated at Our Lady's Hospital, Manorhamilton, County Leitrim*. Unpublished AEGIS Archaeology Report.

Lyne, M. 1997. *Lewes Priory: Excavations by Richard Lewis 1969–82*. Lewes: Lewes Priory Trust.

McCabe, M. 2010. 'Through the Backdoor to Salvation: Infant Burial Grounds in the Early Modern Gaelhealtachd'. The 32nd Annual Conference of the Theoretical Archaeology Group. University of Bristol, Bristol, 17th–19th December 2010.

MacCulloch, D. 1991. The Myth of the English Reformation. *Journal of British Studies* 30: 1–19.

MacDonald, F. 1998. *Excavation of Human Remains at St. Peter's Church, Redcar*. Unpublished Tees Archaeology Report.

MacDonald, M. 1986. The Secularisation of Suicide in England 1660–1800. *Past and Present* 111: 50–100.

MacDonald, M. and Murphy, T.R. 1990. *Sleepless Souls: Suicide in Early Modern England*. Oxford: Clarendon Press.

MacFarlane, A. 1981. Death and the Demographic Transition: a Note on English Evidence on Death 1500–1700. In Humphreys, S. and King, H. (eds) *Mortality and Immortality: the Anthropology and Archaeology of Death*. London: Academic Press. pp. 249–259.

Mackie, D. 1994. *An Archaeological Evaluation at Castle Yard, Leicester*. Unpublished Leicestershire Archaeological Unit Report 94/27.

Mahoney, D. 2005. Appendix 9. Human Bone – Quaker Interments. In Brown, R. *Vancouver Centre and Clough Lane Car Park, King's Lynn Norfolk. Post-Excavation Assessment and Updated Project Design*. Unpublished Oxford Archaeology Report. pp. 76–120.

Malcolmson, R.W. 1977. Infanticide in the Eighteenth Century. In Cockburn, J.S. (ed.) *Crime in England 1550–1800*. London: Methuen and Co Ltd. pp. 187–209.

Maloney, C. 2000. London Fieldwork and Publication Round-up 1999. *London Archaeologist* 9(supp02): 35–63.

Maloney, C. 2001. Fieldwork Round-up 2000. *London Archaeologist* 9(supp03): 67–94.

Maloney, C. and Holroyd, I. 2002. London Fieldwork and Publication Round-up 2001. *London Archaeologist* 10(Supp01): 1–30.

Maloney, C. and Holroyd, I. 2003. London Fieldwork and Publication Round-up 2002. *London Archaeologist* 10(Supp02): 33–61.

References

Maloney, C. and Holroyd, I. 2005. London Fieldwork and Publication Round-up 2004. *London Archaeologist* 11(Supp01): 1–22.

Maloney, C. and Holroyd, I. 2006. Fieldwork Round-up 2005. *London Archaeologist* 11(Supp02): 22–53.

Manchester, K. 1983. Human Remains. In Mayes, P. and Butler, L. (eds) *Sandal Castle Excavations 1964–1973. A Detailed Archaeological Report.* Wakefield: Wakefield Historical Publication. pp. 337–339.

Mann, J. 1986. Small Finds. In Gilmour, B.J.J. and Stocker, D.A. (eds) *St. Mark's Church and Cemetery.* The Archaeology of Lincoln volume XIII-1. London: Trust for Lincolnshire Archaeology/Council for British Archaeology. pp. 41–42.

Mann, L.M. 1937. Notes on the Discovery of a Body in a Peat Moss at Cambusnethan. *Transactions of the Glasgow Archaeological Society* 9: 44–45.

Manning, A. 1998a. Carmarthen Greyfriars. *Church Archaeology* 2: 71.

Manning, A. 1998b. *Carmarthen Greyfriars, Carmarthen: The 1997 Rescue Excavations and Watching Brief on the Site of the choir and area north of the Friary.* Cambrian Archaeology Report. http://www.dyfedarchaeology.org.uk/Projects/CGF/1997Report.PDF (accessed 4th March 2010).

MAP Consultancy Ltd. 1996. *Norman Court, Grape Lane, York. Archaeological Watching Brief.* Unpublished MAP Consultancy Report.

MAP Archaeological Consultancy Limited. 1998. *All Saints Church, Pavement – York. Archaeological Excavations, phases I and II, Interim Report.* Unpublished MAP Archaeological Consultancy Ltd Report.

Marks, K. 2009/2010. The Archaeology of Anglo-Jewry in London, 1656–c.1850. *London Archaeologist* 12: 182–188.

Markus, T. 1993. *Buildings and Power: Freedom and Control in the Origin of Modern Building Types.* London: Routledge.

Marshall, P. 2002. *Beliefs and the Dead in Reformation England.* Oxford: Oxford University Press.

Martensen, R.L. 1992. "Habit of reason": Anatomy and Anglicanism in Restoration England. *Bulletin of the History of Medicine* 66: 511–535.

Martin, C. 2006. *A Glimpse of Heaven: Catholic Churches of England and Wales.* London: English Heritage.

Mary Henry Archaeological Services Ltd. 2000. *Pre-construction Testing, Western Road, Clonmel.* Unpublished Mary Henry Archaeological Services Ltd Report.

Mastin, J. 1818. *The History and Antiquities of Naseby in the County of Northampton.* London: J. Haddon.

Mates, L. 2005. Ireland. In Davies, D. and Mates, L. (eds) *Encyclopaedia of Cremation.* Farnham: Ashgate. pp. 262–271.

Mayes, P. and Butler, L. 1983. *Sandal Castle Excavations 1964–1973. A Detailed Archaeological Report.* Wakefield: Wakefield Historical Publication.

Maylan, C.N. 1993. Excavations at St. Mary's Priory, Usk. *Monmouthshire Antiquary* 9: 29–42.

Maynard, D. 1996. *Archaeological Excavation. Herbert Chapel, St. Mary's Priory Church, Abergavenny, Monmouthshire.* Unpublished Gwent-Glamorgan Archaeological Trust Report.

Mayo, C. 2002. *Assessment of Archaeological Excavation and Watching Brief at Southwark Cathedral, London Borough of Southwark SE1: Phase 3.* Unpublished Pre-Construct Archaeology Report.

Mays, S. 1998. *The Archaeology of Human Bones.* London: Routledge.

Mays, S, Harding, C. and Heighway, C. 2007. *Wharram. A Study of Settlement on the Yorkshire Wolds, XI: The Churchyard.* York University Archaeological Publications 13. York: York University.

Mays, S.A. and Keepax, C.A. 2006. Human Bones. In Saunders, A. (ed.) *Excavations at Launceston Castle, Cornwall.* Society for Medieval Archaeology Monograph 24. Leeds: Maney Publishing. pp. 431–445.

McCarthy, M. 2001. *Pre-Development Archaeological Testing at Shandon Court Hotel, Cork.* Unpublished Archaeological Services Unit, University College Cork Report.

McCullagh, R. and McCormick, F. 1991. The Excavation of Post-medieval Burials from Braigh, Aignish, Lewis, 1989. *Post-medieval Archaeology* 25: 73–88.

McIntyre, L. and Willmott, H. 2003. *Excavations at the Methodist Chapel Carver Street, Sheffield.* Unpublished Archaeological Research and Consultancy at the University of Sheffield. Project Report 507.

McKinley, J. 2008. *The 18th century Baptist Chapel and Burial Ground at West Butts Street, Poole.* Salisbury: Wessex Archaeology.

McKinley, J.I. and Manning, A. 2010. Late Medieval/Early Post-medieval Burial Remains from Boscombe Down Airfield, Amesbury. *Wiltshire Archaeology Magazine* 103: 320–323.

McMahon, V. 2006. Reading the Body: Dissection and the 'Murder' of Sarah Stout, Hertfordshire, 1699. *Social History of Medicine* 19(1): 19–35.

McNeill, P. 1883. *Tranent and its Surroundings.* Glasgow: John Menzies and Co.

McNichol, D., Clough, S. and Loe, L. 2007. *Hemingford Flood Alleviation Scheme, St. Ives, Cambridgeshire. Watching Brief and Excavation Report.* Unpublished Oxford Archaeology Report.

Melikian M. 2004a. *An Archaeological Watching Brief of the Exhumation of the Jesuit Cemetery at Whitelands College, Roehampton, London Borough of Wandsworth.* Unpublished AOC Report.

Melikian, M. 2004b. An Archaeological Watching Brief of the Exhumation of the Jesuit Cemetery at Manresa House, Roehampton. *London Archaeologist* 10(9): 230–233.

Mepham, L. and Avery, R. 2008. The Metalwork. In McKinley, J. *The Eighteenth-century Baptist Chapel and Burial Ground at West Butts Street, Poole*. Salisbury: Wessex Archaeology. pp. 37–47.

Mereweather, J. 1847. Account of the Opening of the Coffin of Joanna de Bohun in the Lady Chapel in Hereford Cathedral. *Archaeologia* 32: 60–63.

Merrifield, R. 1955. Witch Bottles and Magical Jugs. *Folklore* 66: 195–207.

Michell, D., Brunson-Hadley, J. and Lippert, D. 2001. *Ancient Burial Practices in the American Southwest: Archaeology, Physical Anthropology, and Native American Perspectives*. Albuquerque: University of New Mexico Press.

Miles, A. 1993. *Archaeological Investigations at St. James Garlickhythe Church (involving the North-east Burial Vault)*. Unpublished Museum of London Archaeological Services Report.

Miles, A. 1996. *St. Luke's Estate, Bath Street, London EC1. An Archaeological Watching Brief*. Unpublished Museum of London Archaeological Service Report.

Miles, A. 1997. *New Bunhill Fields Burial Ground, Gaskin Street, Islington Green, London N1, London Borough of Islington. An Archaeological Watching Brief*. Unpublished Museum of London Archaeological Service Report.

Miles, A. 1998. *The Burial Ground of St. John of Wapping Church, London, E1. London Borough of Tower Hamlets. An Archaeological Watching Brief*. Unpublished Museum of London Archaeological Services Report.

Miles, A. 2004. *St. Marylebone School, Marylebone High Street, Marylebone W1. An Archaeological Excavation*. Unpublished Museum of London Archaeological Service Report.

Miles, A. 2006. *The Crypt of St. Andrew, Holborn London EC4. An Archaeological Assessment and Updated Project Design*. London: Museum of London Archaeological Service Report.

Miles, A. and Powers, N. 2006. *Bishop Challoner Catholic Collegiate School, Lukin Street, London E1. Borough of Tower Hamlets. A Post-excavation Assessment and Updated Project Design*. Unpublished Museum of London Archaeological Service Report.

Miles, A. and Powers, N. 2007. *Bow Baptist Church Burial Ground, 2–25 Payne Road, London, E3. London Borough of Tower Hamlets*. Unpublished Museum of London Archaeological Services Report.

Miles, A., Powers, N. and Wroe-Brown, R. 2008. *St. Marylebone Church and Burial Ground: Excavations at St. Marylebone School, 1993 and 2004–6*. Museum of London Archaeological Service Monograph 46. London: Museum of London Archaeological Service.

Miles, A. and White, W. 2008. *Burial at the Site of the Parish Church of St. Benet Sherehog before and after the Great Fire*. Museum of London Archaeological Service Monograph 39. London: Museum of London Archaeological Service.

Miles, A.E.W. 1989. *An Early Christian Chapel and Burial Ground on the Isle of Ensay, Outer Hebrides, Scotland with a Study of the Skeletal Remains*. British Archaeological Report (British Series) 212. Oxford: Archaeopress.

Miller, P. 1993. *84, London Road, Kingston, Royal Borough of Kingston upon Thames. An Archaeological Evaluation*. Unpublished Museum of London Archaeological Services Report.

Miller, P. and Wilson, T. 2005. *Saxon, Medieval and Post-medieval Settlement at Sol Central, Marefare, Northampton: Archaeological Excavations 1998–2002*. Museum of London Archaeological Services Monograph 27. London: Museum of London Archaeological Services.

Miller, P. and Saxby, D. 2007. *The Augustinian Priory of St Mary Merton, Surrey: Excavations 1976–90*. Museum of London Archaeological Services Monograph 34. London: MoLAS.

Millett, M. 1983. Excavations at Cowdrey's Down Basingstoke Hampshire, 1978–81. *Archaeological Journal* 140: 151–279.

Milne, G. 1997. *St. Bride's Church London. Archaeological Research 1952–60 and 1992–5*. English Heritage Archaeological Report 11. London: English Heritage.

Mingay, G.E. 1994. *Land and Society in England, 1750–1980*. London: Longman.

Misson, H. 1719. *M. Misson's Memoirs and Observations in his Travels over England: with some Account of Scotland and Ireland. Dispos'd in Alphabetical Order*. London: D. Browne, A. Bell, J. Darby, A. Bettesworth, J. Pemberton et al.

Mitchell, S. and White, R. 2004. *Longdykes, Prestonpans, East Lothian*. Unpublished CFA Archaeology Report 944.

Moffett, C. and Hewlings, R. 2009. The anthropoid coffins at Farleigh Hungerford Castle, Somerset. *English Heritage Historical Review* 4: 55–71.

Moller, J. 2003. *Masonic Lodge, 12 Old Orchard Street, Bath. An Archaeological Watching Brief on the lowering of the floor level in the basement and other elements affected by the works*. Unpublished Bath Archaeological Trust Report.

Molleson, T. and Cox, M. 1993. *The Spitalfields Project. Volume 2. The Middling Sort, the Anthropology*. Council for British Archaeology Research Report 86. York: Council for British Archaeology.

Monaghan, J. 1997. *Roman Pottery from York (Archaeology of York 16/8)*. York: Council for British Archaeology.

References

Moore Group Archaeological and Environmental Services Ltd. 2001. *Archaeological Excavation at Our Lady's Hospital, Manorhamilton Co. Leitrim.* Unpublished Moore Archaeological and Environmental Services Ltd Report.

Moore Group Archaeological and Environmental Services Ltd. 2002. *Archaeological Excavation at Our Lady's Hospital, Manorhamilton Co. Leitrim.* Unpublished Preliminary Report. Moore Archaeological and Environmental Services Ltd Report.

Moore, D. 2003. *Report on Archaeological Excavation of Human Remains. Road Improvement works at Creagh Junction, Ballinasloe, Co. Galway.* Unpublished Moore Archaeological and Environmental Services Ltd Report.

Moore, D. and Rogers, T.V. 2002. *Archaeological Excavations at Our Lady's Hospital, Manorhamilton, County Leitrim.* Moore Group Unpublished Report.

Moore, R. 1998. *Church of St. Mary and St Nicholas, Spalding: Foundations for a New Vestry: Archaeological Watching Brief.* Unpublished Lindsey Archaeological Services Report.

Moore, W. 2006. *The Knife Man. Blood, Body Snatching and the Birth of Modern Surgery.* London: Bantam Press.

Moorhouse, S. 1971. Post-medieval Britain in 1970. *Post-medieval Archaeology* 5: 197–222.

Morgan, J. 1989. The Burial Question in Leeds in the Eighteenth and Nineteenth Centuries. In Houlbrooke, R. (ed.) *Death, Ritual and Bereavement.* London: Routledge. pp. 95–104.

Morris, R.J. 1976. *Cholera 1832: The Social Response to an Epidemic.* London: Croom Helm.

Morris, R. 1989. *Churches in the Landscape.* London: Phoenix.

Morrison, K. 1997. *The Workhouse: a Study of Poor-law Buildings in England.* Swindon: Royal Commission on the Historical Monuments of England.

Mossop, M. 2004. *St. Winnow Church, Lostwithiel, Cornwall.* Unpublished Cornwall Archaeological Unit Report.

Mottershead, G. 1999. *Bury Methodist Church, Union Street, Bury. Phase 2: Archaeological Evaluation and Phase 3: Exhumation.* Unpublished University of Manchester Archaeological Unit Report.

Mullet, M. 1991. *Sources for the History of English Non-Conformity 1660–1800.* London: British Records Association.

Mullet, M. 1996. *John Bunyan in Context.* Keele: Keele University Press.

Mumford, J. 2006. *9a Wood Street, Calne, Wiltshire.* Unpublished Archaeological Watching Brief Report.

Munro, A. 1744. *An Essay on Comparative Anatomy.* London: John Nourse.

Murphy, E.M. 2008. *Deviant Burial in the Archaeological Record.* Oxford: Oxbow Books.

Murphy, D. and Stirland, J. 2006. *Old Abbey Lane, Drogheda, Co. Louth.* Unpublished Archaeological Consultancy Services Report.

Murray, H. 1991. *The Garden of Death. The History of York Cemetery.* York: William Sessions.

Murray, A. 2000. *Suicide in the Middle Ages: the Curse on Self-murder (volume 2 of Suicide in the Middle Ages).* Oxford: Oxford University Press.

Murray, J.D. and Wills, O. 1997. *London Bridge Station Area 8, Station Approach, London SE1. Jubilee Line Extension Project, Contract 104. MoLAS Report.* Unpublished Museum of London Archaeological Services Report.

Mytum, H. 1988. A Newly Discovered Burial Vault in North Dalton Church, North Humberside. *Post-medieval Archaeology* 22: 183–187.

Mytum, H. 1989. Public Health and Private Sentiment: the Development of Cemetery Architecture and Funerary Monuments from the Eighteenth Century Onwards. *World Archaeology* 21: 283–297.

Mytum, H. 2007. Explaining Stylistic Change: a Comparison of Above- and Below-Ground Funerary Material Culture 1720–1870. Paper presented at Society for Historical Archaeology annual conference, Williamsburg, VA.

Napthan, M. 1994. *Evaluation to the Rear of Kingdom Hall, Leominster (Internal Report No. 264).* Unpublished Hereford and Worcester County Council, County Archaeological Service Report.

Newman, J. 1990. Ipswich, Francisan Way/Wolsey Street. *Proceedings of the Suffolk Institute of Archaeology and History* 37: 271–273.

Newman, P.R. and Roberts, P.R. 2003. *Marston Moor 1644. The Battle of the Five Armies.* Pickering: Blackthorn Press.

Newman, P.R. 1978. *Marston Moor 1644: the Sources and the Site.* Borthwick Papers 53. York: University of York, Borthwick Institute of Historical Research.

Nilsson Stutz, L. 2003. *Embodied Rituals and Ritualized Bodies: Tracing Ritual Practices in Late Mesolithic Burials.* Acta Archaeologica Lundensia, No 46, Stockholm: Almqvist and Wiksell.

Noel Hume, I. 1974. *All the Best Rubbish.* New York: Harper and Row.

Nolan, J. 1997. *The International Centre for Life: the Archaeology and History of the Newcastle Infirmary.* Unpublished Newcastle City Archaeology Unit Report.

Nolan, J. 1998. *The Newcastle Infirmary at the Forth, Newcastle upon Tyne. Volume 1. The Archaeology and History.* Unpublished Northern Counties Archaeological Services Report.

Norton, A. 2006. *Oxford Castle. Post-Excavation Analysis and Research Design.* Unpublished Oxford Archaeology Report.

Norton, A., Laws, G. and Smith, A. 2005. *Abingdon West Central Redevelopment Area, Oxfordshire. Post-excavation Assessment and Updated Project Design.* Unpublished Oxford Archaeology Report.

Nowakowski, J. and Thomas, C. 1990. *Excavations at Tintagel Parish Churchyard, Cornwall, Spring 1990.* Interim Report. Institute of Cornish Studies.

Nowakowski, J.A. and Thomas, C. 1992. *Grave News from Tintagel. An Account of a Second Season of Archaeological Excavation.* Truro: Cornwall County Council.

Ó Baoill, R., McQuaid, Y. and Buckley, L. 2002. Holier than Thou. Experimental Surgery in Olde Belfast. *Archaeology Ireland* 16: 7.

Ó Floinn, R. 1995. Recent Research into Irish Bog Bodies. In Turner, R.C. and Scaife, R.G. (eds) *Bog Bodies. New Discoveries and New Perspectives.* London: British Museum Press. pp. 137–145.

O'Byrne, E. 2003. The Walshes and the Massacre at Carrickmines. *Archaeology Ireland* 17: 8–11.

O'Shea, J. 1981. Social Configurations and the Archaeological Study of Mortuary Practices: a Case Study. In Chapman, R., Kinnes, I. and Randsborg, K. (eds) *The Archaeology of Death.* Cambridge: Cambridge University Press. pp. 39–52.

Oakey, N. 1999. *St. Peter's Church, Farmington, Gloucestershire. Archaeological Watching Brief.* Unpublished Cotswold Archaeological Trust Report.

Oakley, N. and Andrews, P. 1998. Coventry, Cathedral Priory Church of St. Mary. *Church Archaeology* 2: 61–63.

Ogden, A.R., Boylston, A. and Vaughan, T. 2005. Tallow Hill Cemetery, Worcester: The Importance of Detailed Study of Post-medieval Graveyards. In Zakrewski, S.R. and Clegg, M. (eds) *Proceedings of the Fifth Annual Conference of the British Association for Biological Anthropology and Osteoarchaeology.* British Archaeological Reports (International Series) 1383. Oxford Archaeopress. pp. 51–58.

Oman, C. 1974. *British Rings 800–1914.* London: B.T. Batsford Ltd.

O'Neil, R. 2006. *Assessment Report of Excavations at Sheffield Cathedral NW Car Park, Sheffield, South Yorkshire.* Unpublished Archaeological Research and Consultancy at the University of Sheffield Report.

Orr, S. 1921. Clothing found on a Skeleton at Quintfall Hill, Barrock Estate, near Wick. *Proceedings of the Society of Antiquaries of Scotland* 55: 213–221.

Ortner, D.J. and Putscher, W.G.J. 1985. *Identification of Pathological Conditions in Human Skeletal Remains.* Washington: Smithsonian Institute Press.

O'Sullivan, J. 1993. Archaeological Excavations at Cochpen Medieval Parish Church, Midlothian, 1993. *Proceedings of the Society of Antiquaries of Scotland* 125: 881–900.

O'Sullivan, J. 1994. Excavation of an Early Church and a Women's Cemetery at St. Ronan's Medieval Parish Church, Iona. *Proceedings of the Society of Antiquaries of Scotland* 124: 327–365.

O'Sullivan, J., Roberts, J. and Halliday, S. 2003. Archaeological Excavation of Medieval, Post-medieval and Modern Burials at Ennis Friary. *North Munster Antiquarian Journal* 43: 21–42.

Overton, M. 1996. *Agricultural Revolution in England: the Transformation of the Agrarian Economy 1500–1850.* Cambridge: Cambridge University Press.

Owens, M.E. 2005. *Stages of Dismemberment. The Fragmented Body in Late Medieval and Early Modern Drama.* Newark: University of Delaware Press.

Owen-Smith, B. and Martin, L. 1998/9. Benjamin Franklin, William Hewson and the Craven Street Bones. *Archaeology International* 2: 14–16.

Oxford Archaeological Unit 1992a. *Holy Trinity Church, Cookham, Berkshire: Archaeological Watching Brief.* Unpublished Oxford Archaeological Unit Report.

Oxford Archaeological Unit 1992b. *St. Mary's Church, Winkfield.* Unpublished Oxford Archaeological Unit Report.

Oxford Archaeological Unit 1992c. *St. Nicholas' Church, Newbury: Excavation of a Foundation for a Heating System.* Unpublished Oxford Archaeological Unit Report.

Oxford Archaeology 1992d. *St. Nicholas Church, Abingdon, Oxfordshire. Excavation 1992.* Unpublished Oxford Archaeological Unit Report.

Oxford Archaeological Unit 1993a. *Binfield Church, Berkshire: Archaeological Evaluation.* Unpublished Oxford Archaeological Unit Report.

Oxford Archaeological Services 1993b. *High Wycombe. All Saints Church.* Unpublished Oxford Archaeological Unit Report.

Oxford Archaeological Unit 1996. *St. Mary's Church, Beenham, Berkshire. Archaeological Watching Brief Report.* Unpublished Oxford Archaeological Unit Report.

Oxford Archaeological Unit 1999. *St. Mary's Church, Garsington, Oxfordshire: An Archaeological Watching Brief.* Unpublished Oxford Archaeological Unit Report.

Oxford Archaeology 2002. *St. Mary's Church, Langley Marish, Slough. Archaeological Excavation and Watching Brief.* Unpublished Oxford Archaeology Report.

References

Oxford Archaeology 2003. *St. Laurence Church, Appleton, Oxfordshire. Archaeological Watching Brief Report.* Unpublished Oxford Archaeology Report.

Oxford Archaeology 2008a. *All Saints Church, Laleham, Surrey. Archaeological Evaluation Report.* Unpublished Oxford Archaeology Report.

Oxford Archaeology 2008b. *St. Mary the Virgin Church, Long Crendon, Buckinghamshire. Archaeological Watching Brief.* Unpublished Oxford Archaeology Report.

Oxford Archaeology 2009. *St. Paul's Church, Hammersmith. Borough of Hammersmith and Fulham. Interim Archaeological Excavation Report Stage 1.* Unpublished Oxford Archaeology Report.

Page, N. 2001. Excavation in St. Peter's Church, Carmarthen, 2000. *Archaeology in Wales* 41: 51–61.

Page, N.A. 1994. *Archaeological Excavation, St. Mary's Church, Abergavenny.* Unpublished Gwent-Glamorgan Archaeological Trust Report 94/016.

Page, S. 1637. *The Broken Heart of David's Penance, Fully Exprest in Holy Meditations upon the 51 Psalm.* London: Nathanael Snape.

Palmer, M. and Neaverson, P. 1984. *Industry in the Landscape 1700–1900.* London: Routledge.

Parfitt, K. 1999. *Archaeological Observations at the East Barracks, Deal. 1999.* Unpublished Canterbury Archaeological Trust Report.

Parfitt, K. 2000. East Barracks, Deal. *Canterbury Archaeological Trust Annual Report* 24: 31–32.

Park, K. 1994. The Criminal and the Saintly Body: Autopsy and Dissection in Renaissance Italy. *Renaissance Quarterly* 47(1): 1–33.

Park, K. 1995. The Life of the Corpse: Division and Dissection in Late Medieval Europe. *Journal of the History of Medicine and Allied Sciences* 50: 111–132.

Parker Pearson, M. 1982. Mortuary Practices, Society and Ideology: an Ethnoarchaeological Study. In Hodder, I. (ed.) *Symbolic and Structural Archaeology.* Cambridge: Cambridge University Press. pp. 99–114.

Parliamentary Archives 2009. The Gunpowder Plot: Parliament and Treason 1605. http://www.gunpowderplot.parliament.uk/adults_plot_tte.htm (accessed 31st July 2009).

Parry, A. 1999. *Archaeological Evaluation of Land at Wilson Street, St. Paul's, Bristol.* Unpublished Bristol and Region Archaeological Services Report 673.

Patrick, C. 1999. *The Churchyard of St. Philip's Cathedral, Birmingham: An Archaeological Watching Brief.* Unpublished Birmingham University Field Unit Report 582.

Patrick, C. 2001. *The Churchyard of St. Philip's Cathedral, Birmingham. An Archaeological Watching Brief.* Unpublished Birmingham University Field Unit Report 701. http://ads.ahds.ac.uk/catalogue/adsdata/oasis_reports/birmingh2/ahds/dissemination/pdf/birmingh2-48957_1.pdf (accessed 12th February 2010).

Pearson, K. and Morant, G.M. 1935. *The Portraiture of Oliver Cromwell with Special Reference to the Wilkinson Head.* Cambridge: Cambridge University Press.

Phillips, M. 2000. *The Church of St. Mary the Virgin, Little Houghton, Northamptonshire: Archaeological Watching Brief.* Unpublished Bedford County Council Archaeology Service Report.

Phillpotts, C. 2003. The Houses of Henry VIII's Courtiers in London. In Gaimster, D. and Gilchrist, R. (eds) *The Archaeology of Reformation 1480–1580.* Leeds: Maney Publishing. pp. 299–309.

Pickstone, John V. 2000 *Ways of Knowing: a New History of Science, Technology and Medicine.* Manchester: Manchester University Press.

Pilkington, J. 2000. *Archaeological Watching Brief at former Moravian Chapel, Upper Maudlin Street, Bristol.* Unpublished Bristol and Region Archaeological Services Report 658/2000.

Pine, J. 2005. *Rotherwick Church, Rotherwick, Hook, Hampshire. An Archaeological Watching Brief.* Thames Valley Archaeological Services Ltd Report 05/102. http://www.tvas.co.uk/reports/pdf/RCR05-102wb.pdf (accessed 5th March 2010).

Plummer, A. and Scott, A. 1997. *The Church of St. Laurence Chorley, Lancashire: Archaeological Watching Brief.* Unpublished Lancashire University Archaeological Unit Report.

Plymouth and District Archaeological Society News. http://www.plymarchsoc.org.uk/pdas%20news%202.html (accessed 12th February 2010).

Pocock, M. 2006. *United Reform Church/Salvation Army Hall, Abbey Lane, Saffron Walden, Essex. Archaeological Monitoring and Recording of Grave Clearance.* http://ads.ahds.ac.uk/catalogue/library/greylit/details.cfm?id=1443 (accessed 13th April 2010).

Pollard, T. 1999. The Drowned and the Saved: Archaeological Perspectives on the Sea as Grave. In Downes, J. and Pollard, T. (eds) *The Loved Body's Corruption: Archaeological Contributions to the Study of Human Mortality.* Glasgow: Cruithne Press. pp. 30–51.

Pollard, T. and Ferguson, N. 2009. *Prestonpans Battlefield Archaeological Project* 12012. GUARD: Glasgow http://www.battleofprestonpans1745.org/heritagetrust/html/documents/Prestonpans PD_revised_.pdf (accessed 19th April 2011).

Ponsford, M. 1991. Post-medieval Britain and Ireland in 1990. *Post-medieval Archaeology* 25: 115–170.

Ponsford, M. 1992. Post-medieval Britain and Ireland in 1991. *Post-medieval Archaeology* 26: 95–156.

Ponsford, M. 1993. Post-medieval Britain and Ireland in 1992. *Post-medieval Archaeology* 27: 205–296.

Ponsford, M. 1994. Post-medieval Britain and Ireland in 1993. *Post-medieval Archaeology* 28: 119–184.

Ponsford, M. 2000. Post-medieval Britain and Ireland in 1998 and 1999. *Post-medieval Archaeology* 34: 207–391.

Ponsford, M. 2001. Post-medieval Britain and Ireland in 2000. *Post-medieval Archaeology* 35: 122–289.

Ponsford, M. 2002. Post-medieval Britain and Ireland in 2001. *Post-medieval Archaeology* 36: 173–288.

Ponsford, M. 2003. Post-medieval Britain and Ireland in 2002. *Post-medieval Archaeology* 37: 221–376.

Ponsford, M. 2004. Post-medieval Britain and Ireland in 2003. *Post-medieval Archaeology* 38: 229–401.

Ponsford, M. 2005. Post-medieval Fieldwork in Britain and Northern Ireland in 2004. *Post-medieval Archaeology* 39: 335–428.

Ponsford, M. 2006. Post-medieval Fieldwork in Britain and Northern Ireland in 2005. *Post-medieval Archaeology* 40: 316–410.

Ponsford, M. 2007. Post-medieval Fieldwork in Britain and Northern Ireland in 2006. *Post-medieval Archaeology* 41: 318–416.

Ponsford, M. and Jackson, R. 1995. Post-medieval Britain and Ireland in 1994. *Post-medieval Archaeology* 29: 113–194.

Ponsford, M. and Jackson, R. 1996. Post-medieval Britain and Ireland in 1995. *Post-medieval Archaeology* 30: 245–320.

Ponsford, M. and Jackson, R. 1997. Post-medieval Britain and Ireland in 1996. *Post-medieval Archaeology* 31: 257–332.

Ponsford, M. and Jackson, R. 1998. Post-medieval Britain and Ireland in 1997. *Post-medieval Archaeology* 32: 145–206.

Porter, E. 1969. *Cambridgeshire Customs and Folklore*. London: Routledge and Kegan Paul.

Porter, G. 1997. *Watching Brief at Paternoster Row, EC4, Site Code: PRN97*. Unpublished Museum of London Archaeological Service Report.

Porter, R. 1989. Death and the Doctors. In Houlbrooke, R. (ed.) *Death, Ritual and Bereavement*. London: Routledge. pp. 77–94.

Porter, R. 1991. Bodies of Thought: Thoughts about the Body in Eighteenth-century England. In Pittock, J.H. and Wear, A. (eds) *Interpretation and Cultural History*. Basingstoke: Macmillan. pp. 82–108.

Porter, R. 1996. Hospitals and Surgery. In Porter, R. (ed.) *The Cambridge Illustrated History of Medicine*. Cambridge: Cambridge University Press. pp. 202–245.

Porter, R. 1997. Introduction. In Porter, R. (ed.) *Rewriting the Self: Histories from the Renaissance to the Present*. London: Routledge. pp. 1–16.

Porter, R. 2004. *Flesh in the Age of Reason*. London: Penguin.

Porter, S. 1982. Death and Burial in a London Parish: St. Mary Woolnoth 1653–99. *London Journal* 8: 76–80.

Potts, R.U. 1920. St. Austin's Abbey, Canterbury: Abbot Roger II (1252–1272). *Archaeologia Cantiana* 34: 138–147.

Poulton, R. and Woods, H. 1984. *Excavations on the Site of the Dominican Friary at Guildford in 1974 and 1978*. Research Volume of the Surrey Archaeological Society No. 9. Guildford: Surrey Archaeological Society.

Power, C. 1997. Human Skeletal Remains – Emmet Street/Kickham Street (Clonmel Excavations-4). *Tipperary Historical Journal* 10: 112–123.

Powers, N. 2005. St Pancras Burial Ground, Camden. Museum of London Archaeological Service Annual Review. http://www.molas.org.uk/projects/annualreviews.asp?aryear=2004&category=12&section=1 (accessed 12th April 2010).

Powers, N. 2006. Archaeological Evidence for Dental Innovation: an Eighteenth-century Porcelain Dental Prosthesis Belonging to Archbishop Arthur Richard Dillon. *British Dental Journal* 201: 459–463.

Powers, N. 2007. The Human Bone. In Miles, A. and Powers, N. *Bow Baptist Church Burial Ground, 2–25 Payne Road, London, E3. London Borough of Tower Hamlets. A Post-Excavation Assessment and Updated Project Design*. Unpublished Museum of London Archaeological Service Report. pp. 16–26.

Powers, N. 2008. The Human Bone. In Vuolteenaho, J., Wood, L. and Powers, N. *Royal London Hospital, Whitechapel Road, London E1 1BB. The Post-excavation Assessment and Updated Project Design. Site code: RLP05*. Unpublished MOLA Report.

Powers, N. and Walker, D. 2004. *Selected Projects 2005. Human Osteology at St Marylebone, Westminter (MBH04)*. Museum of London Archaeological Service Annual Review 2005.

Priest, V. 1994. *Excavations of a Graveyard in Whatton, Nottinghamshire*. Unpublished Trent and Peak Archaeological Trust Report.

Procter, F. and Frere, W.H. 1951. *A New History of the Book of Common Prayer*. London: Macmillan and Co, Limited.

Prosser, L. and Hattersley, C. 2004. Milton, All Saints. *Church Archaeology* 5/6: 119.

Prynne, W. 1641. *Mount-Orgueil ... A Poem of The Soule's Complaint against the Body Hereto Annexed*. London: Michael Sparke Senior.

Pugin, A.W.N. 1844. *Glossary of Ecclesiastical Ornament and Costume*. London: Bernard Quaritch.

References

Quinn, B. 2007. *Report on the Results of Archaeological Monitoring for the Eyre Square Enhancement Scheme on Behalf of Galway City Council*. Unpublished Moore Group Unpublished Report.

Rahtz, P. 1970. Excavations on Glastonbury Tor, 1964–6. *Archaeological Journal* 127: 1–81.

Rahtz, P. and Watts, L. 2003. *Glastonbury: Myth and Archaeology*. Stroud: Tempus.

Rahtz, P. and Watts, L. n.d. *The Quaker Burial Ground at Helmsley: An Interim Report*. Unpublished Report held at the University of Bradford.

Rawnsley, S. and Reynolds, J. 1977. Undercliffe Cemetery, Bradford. *History Workshop Journal* 4: 215–221.

Razzel, P. and Spence, C. 2006. The Hazards of Wealth: Adult Mortality in Pre-twentieth-century England. *Social History of Medicine* 19: 381–405.

RCSHC/P 804 – Homo sapiens. http://surgicat.rcseng.ac.uk/(e2ahkg55ag1fxb45teaa4e55)/detail.aspx (accessed 13th November 2009).

Read, A. 1696. *Chirurgarum Comes: or the Whole Practice of Chirurgery. Began by the Learned Dr Read; Continued and Completed by a Member of the Royal College of Physicians in London. To which is Added by Way of an Appendix, two Treatise, one of Veneral Disease, the other Concerning Embalming*. London: Hugh Newman.

Redknap, M. 1985. Little Ilford, St Mary the Virgin 1984. *London Archaeologist* 5(02): 31–37.

Rees, A.R. and Strachan, R.J. 1998. Fowlis Wester Church. *Church Archaeology* 2: 68–69.

Rees, T. 2004. Excavation of a Post-medieval Chapel and Graveyard at Cille Bhrea, Lemlair, Highland. *Post-medieval Archaeology* 38: 181–209.

Reeve, J. and Adams, M. 1993. *The Spitalfields Project. Volume 1 – the Archaeology. Across the Styx*. Council of British Archaeology Research Report 85. York: Council of British Archaeology.

Report from the Select Committee on Anatomy. 1828. London: House of Commons, 22nd July 1828.

Reynolds, A. 2009. *Anglo-Saxon Deviant Burial Customs*. Oxford: Oxford University Press.

Richards, E. 1982. *A History of the Highland Clearances, Vol.1: Agrarian Transformation and the Evictions 1746–1886*. London: Croom Helm.

Richardson, B. 1982. Excavation Round-up 1981. *London Archaeologist* 4(06): 159–166.

Richardson, B. 1983. Excavation Round-up. *London Archaeologist* 4(10): 274–277.

Richardson, B. 1984. Excavation Round-up 1983. *London Archaeologist* 4(14): 384–391.

Richardson, B. 1986. Excavation Round-up. *London Archaeologist* 5(06): 157–164.

Richardson, R. 1988. *Death, Dissection and the Destitute*. London: Penguin.

Richardson, R. 1989. Why was Death so Big in Victorian Britain? In Houlbrooke, R. (ed.) *Death, Ritual and Bereavement*. London: Routledge. pp. 105–117.

Richmond, M. 1999. Archaeologia Victoriana: the Archaeology of the Victorian Funeral. In Downes, J. and Pollard, T. (eds) *The Loved Body's Corruption*. Glasgow: Cruithne Press. pp. 145–158.

Ritchie, J. 1921. Relics of the Body-snatchers: Supplementary Notes on Mortsafe Tackle, Mortsafes, Watch-houses, and Public Vaults, mostly in Aberdeenshire. *Proceedings of the Society of Antiquaries of Scotland* 55: 221–229.

Roberts, C. and Cox, M. 2003. *Health and Disease in Britain from Prehistory to the Present Day*. Stroud: Sutton Publishing.

Roberts, C. and Manchester, K. 2005. *The Archaeology of Disease*. Stroud: Sutton Publishing (3rd edition).

Roberts, E. 1989. The Lancashire Way of Death. In Houlbrooke R. (ed.) *Death, Ritual and Bereavement*. London: Routledge. pp. 188–207.

Roberts, I. 2002. *Pontefract Castle: Archaeological Excavations 1982–6*. Yorkshire Archaeology Monograph 8. Leeds: West Yorkshire Archaeological Service.

Roberts, J. 1994. *Nineteenth-century Burials at St. Mary's Churchyard, Buckden*. Unpublished Cambridgeshire County Council Archaeological Field Unit Report.

Roberts, W. 1843. *Mr. Warburton's Anatomy Bill, Thoughts on its Mischievous Tendency, with Suggestions for an Entirely New one founded upon an Available Anti-sceptic Process*. London: J. Olivier.

Robertshaw, A. and Kenyon, D. 2008. *Digging the Trenches: the Archaeology of the Western Front*. Barnsley: Pen and Sword Military.

Roche, J. 1989. *Archaeological Excavations at 95–105 Backchurch Lane. October 1988 – January 1989*. Unpublished Department of Greater London Archaeology Report.

Rodwell, W. 2007. Burial Archaeology. In Waldron, T. (ed.) *St. Peter's, Barton-upon-Humber, Lincolnshire. A Parish Church and its Community. Volume 2: The Human Remains*. Oxford: Oxbow Books. pp. 15–32.

Rodwell, W. and Rodwell, K. 1982. St. Peter's Church, Barton-upon-Humber: Excavation and Structural Study, 1978–81. *Antiquaries Journal* 62: 283–315.

Roffey, S. 2003. Deconstructing a Symbolic World: the Reformation and the English Medieval Parish Chantry. In Gaimster, D. and Gilchrist, R. (eds) *The Archaeology of Reformation 1480–1580*. Leeds: Maney Publishing. pp. 341–355.

Roffey, S. 2007. *The Medieval Chantry Chapel. An Archaeology*. Woodbridge: Boydell Press.

Rogers, P.W. 2006. Textiles. In Brickley, M. and Buteux, S. *St. Martin's Uncovered. Investigations in the*

Churchyard of St. Martin's-in-the-Bull Ring, Birmingham, 2001. Oxford: Oxbow Books. pp. 163–178.

Rogers, T., Fibiger, L., Lynch, L. and Moore, D. 2006. Two Glimpses of Nineteenth-century Institutional Burial Practice in Ireland: a Report on the Excavation of Burials from Manorhamilton Workhouse, County Leitrim and St Brigid's Hospital, Ballinasloe, County Galway. *Journal of Irish Archaeology* 15: 93–104.

Rowsome, P. 2000. *Heart of the City. Roman, Medieval and Modern London revealed by Archaeology at 1 Poultry*. London: English Heritage/Museum of London Archaeological Service.

Roy, M. and Toolis, R. 2005. *Parliament House. Phase 1C. Archaeological Evaluation. Data structure Report*. Unpublished AOC Report.

Roycroft, N. 2003. Industries and Uprisings at Carrickmacross. *Archaeology Ireland* 17: 5.

Ruby, J. 1995. *Secure the Shadow: Death and Photography in America*. Cambridge, Mass: MIT Press.

Rugg, J. 1997. The Origins and Progress of Cemetery Establishment in Britain. In Jupp, P.C. and Howarth, G. (eds) *The Changing Face of Death: Historical Accounts of Death and Disposal*. Basingstoke: Macmillan. pp. 105–119.

Rugg, J. 1998. A New Burial Form and its Meaning: Cemetery Establishment in the First Half of the Nineteenth Century. In Cox, M. (ed.) *Grave Concerns: Death and Burial in England 1700–1850*. Council for British Archaeology Research Report 113. York: Council for British Archaeology. pp. 44–53.

Rugg, J. 1999. From Reason to Regulation: 1760–1850. In Jupp, P.C. and Gittings, C. (eds) *Death in England: an Illustrated History*. Manchester: Manchester University Press. pp. 202–229.

Rumblelow, D. 1982. *The Triple Tree. Newgate, Tyburn and the Old Bailey*. London: Harrap.

Russell, B.E. 1998. *St. Margaret's Churchyard, Walmgate, York: Report of an Archaeological Evaluation*. York Archaeological Trust (1998 Field Report No. 28).

Ryder, P.F. 1993. *All Saints' Church, Lanchester: Archaeological Watching Brief*. Unpublished Report.

Ryder, P.F. 1998. Corbridge, St Andrew, The Winship Vault. *Church Archaeology* 2: 60.

Ryder, P.F. 2000. Houghton le Spring, St. Michael. *Church Archaeology* 4: 69.

Samuel, J. 2003. *The Infirmary Burial Ground, Johnny Ball Lane, Bristol*. Unpublished Bristol and Region Archaeological Services Report 1071/2003.

Sandford, G.M., Lullerschmidt, W.I. and Hutchinson, V.H. 2002. The Comparative Method Revisited. *Bioscience* 52: 830–836.

Sappol, M. 2002. *A Traffic of Dead Bodies: Anatomy and Embodied Social Identity in Nineteenth-Century America*. Princeton, N.J.: Princeton University Press.

Saunders, A. 2006. *Excavations at Launceston Castle, Cornwall*. Society for Medieval Archaeology Monograph 24. Leeds: Maney Publishing.

Saunders, N. 2007. *Killing Time: Archaeology and the First World War*. Stroud: Sutton Publishing.

Sawday, J. 1995. *The Body Emblazoned*. London: Routledge.

Saxby, D. 1998. *The Watch House, St. Mary Magdalen Churchyard, Bermondsey Square, London SE16*. Unpublished Museum of London Archaeological Service Report.

Sayer, D. and Symonds, J. 2004. Lost Congregations: the Crisis Facing Later Post-medieval Urban Burial Grounds. *Church Archaeology* 5/6: 55–61.

Scarisbrick, J.J. 1984. *The Reformation and the English People*. Oxford: Oxford University Press.

Schlee, D. 2009. *The Pembrokeshire Cemeteries Project Excavations at St. Brides Haven, Pembrokeshire*. Unpublished Dyfed Archaeological Trust Report. http://www.dyfedarchaeology.org.uk/projects/stbridescompletereport.pdf.

Schoenfeldt, M. 1999. *Bodies and Selves in Early Modern England*. Cambridge: Cambridge University Press.

Schofield, J. 1998. *Archaeology in the City of London, 1907–1991: A Guide to Records of Excavations by the Museum of London (Archaeological Gazetteer)*. London: Museum of London.

Schofield, J. with contributions by Brigham, T., Blackmore, L., Dyson T. and White, B. 1999. *The London Waterfront 1200–1750. An Archaeological Assessment of four Excavations in Thames Street, 1974–83 Part 1: the Potential of the Evidence* (Site codes: NFW74, SH74, SWA81, BIG82, archive Report). London: Museum of London.

Schofield, J. and Lea, R. 2005. *Holy Trinity Priory Aldgate, City of London. An Archaeological Reconstruction and History*. Museum of London Archaeological Service Monograph 24. London: Museum of London.

Scholz, S. 2000. *Body Narratives*. Basingstoke: Macmillan.

Scheuer, L. 2004. St. Brides Fleet Street: Studying the Skeletons of Known People. *Current Archaeology* 16: 437–444.

Schupbach, W. 1982. The Paradox of Rembrandt's 'Anatomy of Dr Tulp'. *Medical History, Supplement* 2.

Scott, I.R. 1996. *Romsey Abbey. Report on the Excavations 1973–1991*. Hampshire Field Club Monograph 8. Bodmin: Hampshire Field Club and Archaeological Society.

Seeman, E. 2010. Reassessing the "Sankofa Symbol" in New York's African Burial Ground. *The William and Mary Quarterly* 67(1): 101–122.

References

Sell, S.H. 1980. *The Discovery of a Human Burial at Trwyn-y-Witch, Dunraven, Southerndown.* Unpublished Gwent and Glamorgan Archaeological Trust Report.

Sell, S.H. 2000. *Glamorgan Coastal Hillforts: Erosion Monitoring and Assessment.* Unpublished Gwent and Glamorgan Archaeological Trust Report.

Sheehan, J. 1993. *Caherlehillan.* www.excavations.ie. Site 1993:118.

Sheehan, J. 1995. *Caherlehillan.* www.excavations.ie. Site 1995:133.

Sheehan, J. 1998. *Caherlehillan.* www.excavations.ie. Site 1998:268.

Sheehan, J. 2002. *Caherlehillan.* www.excavations.ie. Site 2002:0771.

Shelley, A. (ed.) 2004. *Excavations and Building Recording at Jarrold's Printing Works, Whitefriars, Norwich 2002–3. Assessment Report and Updated Project Design.* Unpublished Norfolk Archaeological Unit Report No. 908.

Shelley, A. and Forrest, K. 1996. *A Watching Brief at St. Saviour's Church, Norwich.* Unpublished Norfolk Archaeological Unit Report No. 191.

Shepherd Popescu, E. 2009. *Norwich Castle: Excavations and Historical Survey, 1987–98. Part II: c.1345 to Modern.* East Anglian Archaeology Report 132. Dereham: Norfolk Museums and Archaeology Service.

Sheppard, R. and Appleton, E. 1999. *Norbury Church. An Assessment of Drainage Problems and Related Excavations in the North Churchyard.* Unpublished Trent and Peak Archaeological Unit Report.

Sherlock, W. 1690. *A Practical Discourse concerning Death* (2nd ed). London: W. Rogers.

Shoesmith, R. 1980a. *Hereford City Excavations. Volume 1. Excavations at Castle Green.* Council for British Archaeology Research Report 36. London: Council for British Archaeology.

Shoesmith, R. 1980b. Llangar. *Archaeologia Cambrensis* 129: 64–132.

Shoesmith, R. and Hoverd, T. 1996. *Abbey Halls, Tewkesbury Abbey. Archaeological Recording and Historical Research.* Unpublished City of Hereford Archaeology Unit Report.

Sidebottom, P. 1995. *A Watching Brief at the Church of St John the Evangelist, Carlton in Lindrick, Nottinghamshire.* Unpublished Archaeological Research and Consultancy at the University of Sheffield Report.

Silveira, J. 1836. *An Account of the Catholic Burial Ground of St. James in the City of Winchester. Translation from Latin Manuscript held in Rome.* Hampshire Records Office document 37M48/46.

Sims, M. 2007. *Church of the Blessed Virgin Mary, Lillingstone Lovell, Buckinghamshire. Archaeological Watching Brief.* Unpublished Oxford Archaeology Report.

Sims, M. 2008. *New Boundary Wall, St. Mary's Church. Archaeological Watching Brief Report.* Unpublished Oxford Archaeology Report.

Sims, M. 2009. *St Laurence Church, South Hinksey, Oxford. Archaeological Watching Brief.* Unpublished Oxford Archaeology Report.

Simpson, L. 1999. *Emergency Excavation at No. 16, Eustace Street, Temple Bar, Dublin 2.* Unpublished Margaret Gowan and Co Ltd Report.

Simpson, J. and Roud, S. 2000. *A Dictionary of English Folklore.* Oxford: Oxford University Press.

Slater, D. 2002. *An Archaeological Watching Brief at St. Nicholas's Church, The Stowage, Deptford.* Unpublished Pre-construct Archaeology Report.

Smith, M.P. 1999. *Report on the Archaeological Watching Brief to the Rear of 2 Church Street, Romsey, Hampshire.* Unpublished Southampton City Council Archaeology Unit Report.

Smith, M.P. 2006. *Archaeological Watching Brief, Excavation and Building Recording at the Church of St. John the Baptist, Winchester, Hampshire.* Unpublished Southampton Archaeology Unit Report 741.

Snee, J. 1999. *Archaeological Watching Brief Report: St. James Church, Louth.* Unpublished Pre-Construct Archaeology (Lincoln) Report.

Snell, K. 1985. *Annals of the Labouring Poor.* Cambridge: Cambridge University Press.

Soden, I. 2000. *A Typical English Churchyard?* http://www.buildingconservation.com/articles/churchyard/churchyard.htm (accessed 18th November 2009).

Soden, I. 2003. The Conversion of Former Monastic Buildings to Secular use: the Case of Coventry. In D. Gaimster and R. Gilchrist (eds) *The Archaeology of Reformation 1480–1580.* Leeds: Maney Publishing. pp. 280–289.

Somerset SMR record 57136 – http://webapp1.somerset.gov.uk/her/details.asp?prn=57136 (accessed 15th July 2009).

Southern Archaeological Services Ltd. 1992. *Summary Report on the Evaluation at St. Thomas' Church, Bedhampton.* Unpublished Southern Archaeological Services Report.

Spencer-Wood, S.M. and Baugher, S. 2001. Introduction and Historical Context for the Archaeology of Institutions of Reform. Part I: Asylums. *International Journal of Historical Archaeology* 5(1): 3–17.

Spicer, A. 2000. "Defile not Christ's kirk with your Carrion": Burial and the Development of Burial Aisles in Post-Reformation Scotland. In Gordon, B. and Marshall, P. (eds) *Death and Remembrance in Late Medieval and Early Modern Europe.* Cambridge: Cambridge University Press. pp. 149–169.

Spicer, A. 2003. Iconoclasm and Adaptation: The Reformation of the Churches in Scotland and the Netherlands. In Gaimster, D. and Gilchrist, R. (eds) *The Archaeology of the Reformation 1480–1580.* Leeds: Maney Publishing. pp. 29–43.

Spurr, J. 1996. From Puritanism to Dissent, 1660–1700. In Durston, C. and Eales, J. (eds) *The Culture of English Puritanism 1560–1700.* Basingstoke: Macmillan. pp. 234–265.

Stafford, H. 1993. *Rook Lane Chapel, Frome.* Unpublished Somerset Buildings Preservation Trust Report.

Start, M. 2002. Morbid Osteology. In Arnott, R. (ed.) *The Archaeology of Medicine.* British Archaeological Report (International Series) 1046. Oxford: British Archaeological Reports. pp. 113–123.

Sterenberg, J. 1998. *St. Peter's Church, Barford, Warwickshire. An Archaeological Watching Brief 1998.* Unpublished Birmingham University Field Archaeology Unit Report.

Stevens, C. 2002. The Burial Question. *Welsh History Review* 21: 328–356.

Stevenson, B. 1995. The Social Integration of Post-Restoration Dissenters 1660–1725. In Spufford, M. (ed.) *The World of Rural Dissenters 1520–1725.* Cambridge: Cambridge University Press. pp. 360–387.

Stevenson, J. 1999. *An Archaeological Watching Brief at St. Nicholas Church, Shepperton.* Unpublished Surrey County Archaeological Unit Report.

Stirland, A.J. 2005. *The Men of the Mary Rose: Raising the Dead.* Stroud: Sutton Publishing.

Stock, G. 1998a. Quaker Burial: Doctrine and Practice. In Cox, M. (ed.) *Grave Concerns. Death and Burial in England 1700–1850.* Council for British Archaeology Research Report 113. York: Council for British Archaeology. pp. 129–142.

Stock, G. 1998b. The Eighteenth- and Early Nineteenth-century Quaker Burial Ground at Bathford, Bath, Northeast Somerset. In Cox, M. (ed.) *Grave Concerns. Death and Burial in England 1700–1850.* Council for British Archaeology Research Report 113. York: Council for British Archaeology. pp. 144–153.

Stone, J.A. 1989. Aberdeen: the Excavations. In Stone, J.A. (ed.) *Three Scottish Carmelite Friaries. Excavations at Aberdeen, Linlithgow and Perth 1980–86.* Society of Antiquaries of Scotland Monograph Series No. 6. Edinburgh: Society of Antiquaries of Scotland. pp. 35–52 http://ads.ahds.ac.uk/catalogue/adsdata/PSAS_2002/pdf/Monogr_06/6_prelims.pdf?CFID=573996&CFTOKEN=39545028 (accessed 12th April 2010).

Stone, L. 1977. *The Family, Sex and Marriage in England, 1500–1800.* London: Weidenfeld and Nicolson.

Stone, R. 1993. Old Bones: Excavations at Hereford Cathedral. *Rescue News* 59: 4.

Strachan, R.J. 1997. *Fowlis Wester Church, Perthshire and Kinross. Archaeological Excavations. Report No. 354.* Unpublished Centre for Field Archaeology Report.

Strange, J-M. 2005. *Death, Grief and Poverty in Britain, 1870–1914.* Cambridge: Cambridge University Press.

Susser, B. n.d. *An Account of the Old Jewish Cemetery on Plymouth Hoe.* Manuscript held in Parkes Collection at Southampton University (BZ 2301.G7S97).

Susser, B. 1993. *The Jews of South-West England.* Exeter: Exeter University Press.

Swedlund, A. 2009. *Shadows in the Valley: A Critical History of Illness, Death and Loss in New England, 1840–1916.* Boston: University of Massachusetts Press.

Swift, D. 2005. *Cable Trench between Finsbury Market and Devonshire Square, London, EC2 and EC3. An Archaeological Watching Brief Report.* Unpublished Museum of London Archaeological Service Report.

Sydes, B. 1984. *The Excavation of St. Wilfred's Church, Hickleton. An Interim Report.* Unpublished South Yorkshire County Council Archaeology Report.

Symonds, J. and Sayer, D. 2001. *Data Structure Report: Excavation of Skeletons from Sheffield Cathedral.* Unpublished Archaeological Research and Consultancy at the University of Sheffield Report.

Tait, C. 2002. *Death, Burial and Commemoration in Ireland, 1550–1650.* Basingstoke: Palgrave Macmillan.

Tarlow, S. 1992. Each Slow Dusk a Drawing-down of Blinds. *Archaeological Review from Cambridge* 11(1): 125–140.

Tarlow, S. 1995. What Dreams may Come: Metaphors of Death in Orkney. *Scottish Archaeological Review* 9/10: 110–114.

Tarlow, S. 1999a. *Bereavement and Commemoration: an Archaeology of Mortality.* Oxford: Blackwell.

Tarlow, S. 1999b. Wormie Clay and Blessed Sleep: Death and Disgust in Later Historical Britain. In Tarlow, S. and West, S. (eds) *The Familiar Past? Archaeologies of Later Historical Britain.* London: Routledge. pp. 183–198.

Tarlow, S. 2000. Landscapes of Memory: the Nineteenth-century Garden Cemetery. *European Journal of Archaeology* 3: 217–239.

Tarlow, S. 2002. The Aesthetic Corpse in Nineteenth-century Britain. In Hamilakis, Y., Pluciennik, M. and Tarlow, S. (eds) *Thinking through the Body. Archaeologies of Corporeality.* New York: Kluwer Academic/Plenum Publishers. pp. 85–97.

Tarlow, S. 2003. Reformation and Transformation: what happened to Catholic Things in a

Protestant World? In Gaimster, D. and Gilchrist, R. (eds) *The Archaeology of Reformation 1480–1580*. Leeds: Maney Publishing. pp. 108–121.

Tarlow, S. 2007. *The Archaeology of Improvement*. Cambridge: Cambridge University Press.

Tarlow, S. 2008. The Extraordinary Story of Oliver Cromwell's Head. In J. Robb and D. Bori (eds) *Past Bodies: Body-centred Research in Archaeology*. Oxford: Oxbow Books. pp. 69–78.

Tarlow, S. 2011. *Ritual, Belief and the Dead in Early Modern Britain and Ireland*. Cambridge: Cambridge University Press.

Tate, F. 1600. Of the Antiquity, Variety and Ceremonies of Funerals in England. Reprinted in Anon 1771. *A Collection of Curious Discourses written by Eminent Antiquarians upon Several Heads in our English Antiquities*. London: Ward J. Richardson. Volume I. pp. 215–221.

Tatton-Brown, T. 1980. The Roper Chantry in St. Dunstan's Church, Canterbury. *The Antiquaries Journal* 60: 227–246.

Tavener, N. 1998a. *Cardiff Centre for the Visual Arts, The Old Library, Trinity Street, Cardiff. Exhumation of Burials and Archaeological Excavation*. Unpublished Cambrian Archaeological Projects Report 36.

Tavener, N. 1998b. Exhumation of Burials and Excavations at the Old Free Library, Trinity Street, Cardiff. *Archaeology in Wales* 38: 74–78.

Taylor, A. and Preston, S. 2006. *St Michael's Church Parish Rooms, Church Lane, Warfield, Berkshire. An Archaeological Recording Action for The Warfield Churches*. Unpublished Thames Valley Archaeological Services Ltd. http://www.tvas.co.uk/reports/pdf/MCW03-60ex.pdf (accessed 30th March 2010).

Taylor, F. 1996. *Holy Trinity Church, Christchurch, Newport, Gwent*. Unpublished Monmouth Archaeological Society Report.

Terhune, A.M. and Terhune, A.B. 1980. *The Letters of Edward FitzGerald. Volume I 1830–1850*. Princeton: Princeton University Press.

Thomas, C. 1991. The Leather Shoes and Leggings. In Hodder, M.A. (ed.) Excavations at Sandwell Priory and Hall, 1982–88. *South Staffordshire Archaeological and Historical Society Transactions* 31: 102–111.

Thompson, N.P. and Ross, H. 1973. Excavations at the Saxon Church, Alton Barnes. *Wiltshire Archaeological Magazine* 68: 71–78.

Thompson, N.P. and Ross, H. 1998. *Former Female Prison, Castle Yard, York: Report of an Archaeological Evaluation (Field Report No.26)*. Unpublished York Archaeological Trust Report.

Thompson, A., Westman, A. and Dyson, T. (eds) 1998. *Archaeology in Greater London, 1965–1990: a Guide to Records of Excavations by the Museum of London*. London: Museum of London.

Thorn, J.C. 1981. The Burial of John Dygon, Abbot of St. Augustine's. In Detsicas, A. (ed.) *Collectanea Historica. Essays in Memory of Stuart Rigold*. Maidstone: Kent Archaeological Society. pp. 74–92.

Thorpe, C. 1998. *St. Miniver Parish Church: An Archaeological Watching Brief*. Unpublished Cornwall Archaeological Unit Report, Cornwall County Council.

Thorpe, C. 1999. *St. Andrew's Church, Stratton*. Unpublished Cornwall Archaeological Unit Report.

Thorpe, C. 2001a. *St. Felicitas Church, Phillack, Cornwall*. Unpublished Cornwall Archaeological Unit Report.

Thorpe, C. 2001b. *St. Mawgan in Pydar Church, Cornwall*. Unpublished Cornwall Archaeological Unit Report.

Thorpe, C. 2003. *Mullion Church, Cornwall*. Unpublished Cornwall Archaeological Unit Report.

Thorpe, R. 1991. *A Watching Brief at St. Paul's Church, Covent Garden, London*. Unpublished Central Archaeology Service Report.

Timbs, J. 1872. *Abbeys, Castles, and Ancient Halls of England and Wales: their Legendary Lore and Popular History*. London: Frederick Warne and Co.

Todd, M. (ed.) 1995. *Reformation to Revolution: Politics and Religion in Early Modern England*. London: Routledge.

Torrance, L.J. and Ford, S. 1992. *Church of St. James the Great, Ruscombe, Berkshire*. Report 91/15. Unpublished Thames Valley Archaeological Service Report.

Town, M. and Scurfield, C. 1999. *The Church of St. Lawrence*. Unpublished Lancaster University Archaeological Unit Report.

Tucker, S. 1996. *Area 3, Tower Street/ St. Thomas' Street (East Vent Shaft), Southwark SE1. Jubilee Line Extention Project, Contract 104. An Archaeological Excavation*. Unpublished MoLAS Report.

Turner, N. 1996. *St. Mary Magdalene Church, Hullavington, Wiltshire. Archaeological Watching Brief Report No. 96428*. Unpublished Cotswold Archaeological Trust Report.

Turner, R.C. 1995. Recent Research into British Bog Bodies. In Turner, R.C. and Scaife, R.G. *Bog Bodies. New Discoveries and New Perspectives*. London: British Museum Press. pp. 108–122.

Turner, T. 1997. *The Baptist Church, Coxwell Street, Cirencester, Gloucestershire: Archaeological Watching Brief*. Unpublished Cotswold Archaeological Trust Report 97843.

Tweddle, D., Moulden, J. and Logan, E. 1999. *Anglian York: a Survey of the Evidence (The Archaeology of York* 7:2) York: Council for British Archaeology.

Tyler, R. 2001. Archaeological Investigations during Refurbishments of St. Aldate's Church, Oxford. *Oxoniensia* 66: 369–409.

University of Manchester Archaeological Unit 1999. *Cathedral Yard, Manchester. An Archaeological Evaluation*. Unpublished University of Manchester Archaeological Unit Report.

University of Leicester Archaeological Services n.d. Vine Street, Leicester. http://www.le.ac.uk/ulas/projects/vine_st.html.

Verax. 1748. Observations on a Paragraph in Mr. White's second Defence of his Letters to a Dissenter. *Gentleman's Magazine* 18: 316.

Vincent, S. and Mays, S. 2009. *Huntingdon Castle Mound, Cambridgeshire. Osteological Analysis of the Huntingdon Castle Population*. Environmental Studies Report. English Heritage Archaeological Science Research Department Report Series no. 8.

Vuolteenaho, J., Wood, L. and Powers, N. 2008. *Royal London Hospital, Whitechapel Road, London E1 1BB. The Post-excavation Assessment and Updated Project Design. Site code: RLP05*. Unpublished MOLA Report.

W.H.B. 1918. Barnardiston Vaults in Kedington Church. *Proceedings of the Suffolk Institute of Archaeology and Natural History* 16: 44–48.

W.P. 1746. Letter. *Gentleman's Magazine* 16: 640.

Wakely, J. and Smith, A. 1998. A Possible Eighteenth- to Nineteenth-century Example of a Popliteal Aneurysm from Leicester. *International Journal of Osteoarchaeology* 8: 56–60.

Waldron, H. 1993. The Health of the Adults. In Molleson, T. and Cox, M. (ed.) *The Spitalfields Project. Volume 2: The Anthropology: the Middling Sort*. Council for British Archaeology Research Report 86 York: Council for British Archaeology. pp. 67–89.

Waldron, T. 1987. The Relative Survival of the Human Skeleton: Implications for Paleopathology. In Boddington, A., Garland, A.N. and Janaway, R.C. (eds) *Death, Decay and Reconstruction*. Manchester: Manchester University Press. pp. 55–64.

Waldron, T. 2007. *St. Peter's Barton-upon-Humber, Lincolnshire. A Parish Church and its Community*. Oxford: Oxbow Books.

Walker, G.A. 1839. *Gatherings from Graveyards; Particularly those of London with a Concise History of the Modes of Interment among Different Nations from the Earliest Periods and a Detail of Dangerous and Fatal Results produced by the Unwise and Revolting Custom of Inhuming the Dead in the Midst of the Living*. London: Longman and Company.

Walker, K.E. and Farwell, D.E. 2000. *Twyford Down, Hampshire. Archaeological Investigations on the M3 motorway from Bar End to Compton, 1990-1993*. Hampshire Field Club Monograph 9. Salisbury: Hampshire Field Club and Archaeological Society.

Walsh, G. 2004. Merchant's Road (E400/E915): Excavation. In Fitzpatrick, E., O'Brien, M. and Walsh, P. (eds) *Archaeological Investigations in Galway City. 1987–1998*. Bray: Wordwell. pp. 15–30.

Walsham, A. 2011. *The Reformation of the Landscape. Religion, Identity and Memory in Early Modern Britain and Ireland*. Oxford: Oxford University Press.

Walton Rogers, P. 2006. Textiles. In Brickley, M. and Buteux, S. (eds) *St. Martin's Uncovered. Investigations in the Churchyard of St. Martin's-in-the-Bull Ring, Birmingham, 2001*. Oxford: Oxbow Books. pp. 163–178.

Ward, A. and Anderson, T. 1990. Excavations at Rochester Cathedral. *Archaeologia Cantiana* 108: 91–151.

Ward, B. 1909. *The Dawn of the Catholic Revival in England*. Volume 1. London: Longmans, Green and Co.

Ward, S.W. 1997. *Chester Cathedral Excavations in 1996 and 1997*. Unpublished Chester City Council Report.

Ward. S.W. 1998. Archaeology in Chester Cathedral 1995–97. *Church Archaeology* 2: 39–44.

Ward, S.W. 2003. Dissolution or Reformation? A Case Study from Chester's Urban Landscape. Gaimster, D. and Gilchrist, R. (eds) *The Archaeology of Reformation 1480–1580*. Leeds: Maney Publishing. pp. 267–279.

Warden, J. 1724. *A Practical Essay on the Sacrament of Baptism*. Edinburgh: J. MacEuen.

Warner, John Harley 1995. The History of Science and the Sciences of Medicine. *Osiris* (2nd Series) 10: 164–193.

Watson, B. 1993. *109–153 Back Church Lane, London, E1. London Borough of Tower Hamlets. An Archaeological Evaluation*. London: Museum of London Archaeological Service (Unpublished Report).

Watt, T. 1991, *Cheap Print and Popular Piety, 1550–1640*. Cambridge: Cambridge University Press.

Watts, L. and Rahtz, P.A. 1985. *Mary-le-Port, Bristol, Excavations 1962–3*. Bristol: City of Bristol Museum and Art Gallery.

Watts, M.A. 1998. *Archaeological Recording During Drainage Works at St. Saviour's Church, Dartmouth (Report 99.25)*. Unpublished Exeter Archaeology Report.

Waughman, M. 1995. *The Carr House Sands Project Summary Report*. Unpublished Tees Archaeology Report.

References

Way, A. 1857. Notices of an Enamelled Chalice and of Other Ancient Reliques found on the Site of Rusper Priory. *Sussex Archaeological Collections* 9: 303–311.

Way, T. 1998. *Human Remains at St. Mary Magdalene Churchyard, Ickleton.* Unpublished Cambridgeshire County Council Archaeological Field Unit Report.

Webb, H. 2007. *St. Clement's Churchyard, The Plain, Oxford. Archaeological Watching Brief.* Unpublished Oxford Archaeology Report.

Webb, H. 2008. *Zion Baptist Chapel Calne Wiltshire. Archaeological Evaluation Report.* Unpublished Oxford Archaeology Report.

Webb, J.F. 1965a. *Eddius Stephanus: Life of Wilfred* In Farmer, D. H. (ed.) 1965. *The Age of Bede.* London: Penguin. pp. 105–184.

Webb, J.F. 1965b. (trans.) *Bede's Life of Cuthbert.* In Farmer, D. H. (ed.) 1965. *The Age of Bede.* London: Penguin. pp. 41–104.

Westman, A. 1992. Excavation Round-up 1991, Part 1: City of London. *London Archaeologist* 6(14): 388–392.

Weiss-Krejci, E. 2005. Excarnation, Evisceration and Exhumation in Medieval and Post-medieval Europe. In Rakita, G.F.M., Buikstra, J.E., Beck, L.A. and Williams, S.R. (eds) *Interacting with the Dead. Perspectives on Mortuary Archaeology for the New Millennium.* University Press of Florida: Gainesville. pp. 155–157.

Welch, K. 1994. *Eighteenth-century Burials at Old Addenbrooke's Hospital.* Cambridgeshire County Council Archaeological Field Unit Report.

Wenham, P. 1970. *The Siege of York 1644.* York: Sessions Book Trust.

Whitaker, D.K. 1993. Oral Health. In Molleson, T. and Cox, M. (eds) *The Spitalfields Project. Volume 2. The Middling Sort, the Anthropology.* Council for British Archaeology Research Report 86. York: Council for British Archaeology. pp. 49–66.

White Marshall, J. and Walsh, C. 1994. Illaunloughan: Life and Death on a Small Early Monastic Site. *Archaeology Ireland* 8(4): 24–28.

White Marshall, J. and Walsh, C. 2005. *Illaunloughan Island: An Early Medieval Monastery in County Kerry* Dublin: Wordwell Books.

White, B. 2003. Human Bone. In Hull, G. The Excavation and Analysis of an Eighteenth-century Deposit of Anatomical Remains and Chemical Apparatus from the rear of the First Ashmolean Museum (now the Museum of the History of Science), Broad Street, Oxford. *Post-medieval Archaeology* 37: 1–28.

White, R. 2004. *St. Mary's Star of the Sea, Leith (area A), Archaeological Evaluation and Excavation.* Unpublished CFA Archaeology Report 931.

White, S. 2002. A Burial ahead of its Time? The Crookden Burial Case and the Sanctioning of Cremation in England and Wales. *Mortality* 7(2): 171–190.

White, W. 1978. Changing Burial Practice in Late Medieval England. *The Ricardian* 4 (63): 23–30.

White, W. 1986. *The Human Skeletal Remains from the Broadgate Site LSS85 – some Interim comments. Archive Report.* Unpublished Museum of London Archaeological Service Report.

White, W. 1987. *The Human Skeletal Remains from the Broadgate Site (HUM 01/87). Archive Report.* Unpublished Museum of London Archaeological Service Report.

Whitting, R. 1998. *Local Responses to the English Reformation.* Basingstoke: Macmillan.

Whitworth, A.M. 1998. Lanercost Priory Excavations in 1994. *Transactions of Cumberland and Westmorland Antiquarian and Archaeological Society* 98: 133–143.

Whyte, N. 2003. The Deviant Dead in the Norfolk Landscape. *Landscapes* 4: 24–39.

Wichbold, D. and Brown, D.L. 1993. St. Peter's Church, Ipsley, Redditch, Hereford and Worcester. *West Midlands Archaeology* 8: 36.

Wiggins, M. 1995. *St. Martin's Church Hall, High Street, Ruislip. An Archaeological Watching Brief.* Unpublished Museum of London Archaeological Service Report.

Wildman, J. 1998. *An Archaeological Investigation of the Site of a New Vestry at St. Mary's Church, Church Street, West Chiltington, West Sussex.* Unpublished Southern Archaeology Ltd Report.

Wilkinson, D. and McWhirr, A. 1998. *Cirencester Anglo-Saxon Church and Medieval Abbey.* Unpublished Cirencester Archaeological Trust Ltd Report.

Williams, B. (ed) 2000. Review of Archaeology 1999–2000. *Bristol and Avon Archaeology* 17: 139–151.

Williams, D.N. 1998. *St. Mary's Priory Church, Abergavenny, Monmouthshire: An Archaeological Evaluation.* Unpublished Archaeological Investigations Ltd Report 343.

Willis, J. 2003. Archaeological Review. *Transactions of the Bristol and Gloucestershire Society* 121: 267–289.

Willis, T. 1681. *Dr. Willis's Practice of Physick being all the Medical Works of that Renowned and Famous Physician .. done into English by S.P. Esq.* London : T. Dring, C. Harper, J. Leigh.

Willmott, H. 2008. Glass. In Miles, A. and White, W. (eds) *Burial at the Site of the Parish Church of St. Benet Sherehog before and after the Great Fire.* Museum of London Archaeological Service Monograph 39. London: Museum of London Archaeology Service. p.68.

Witkin, A. 1997. *The Cutting Edge. Aspects of Amputation in the Late Eighteenth and Nineteenth Century.* MSc Dissertation University of Sheffield and Bradford.

Witkin, A. and Boston, C. 2006. The Human Remains. In Boston, C., Boyle, A. and Witkin, A. *"In the Vaults Beneath" – Archaeological Recording at St. George's Church, Bloomsbury.* Unpublished Oxford Archaeology Report. pp. 44–99.

Wood J.W., Milner G.R., Harpending H.C. and Weiss K.M. 1992. The Osteological Paradox: Problems of Inferring Prehistoric Health from Skeletal Samples. *Current Anthropology* 33(4): 343–370.

Woolgar, A. 1994. *O'Meara Street, Southwark SE1. London Borough of Southwark. Jubilee Line Extension Project, contract 103, Southwark Station and Running Tunnels: Grout Shaft Extension. Updated Project Design/Assessment Report.* Unpublished Museum of London Archaeological Service Report.

WORD database – http://www.museumoflondon.org.uk/download/chb/PMSBL/PMSBL_path.lst (accessed 26th July 2009).

Wragg, K. 1993. *Sincil Bank, West (Watermains Relay, Archaeological Recording).* Unpublished City of Lincoln Archaeological Unit Report no. 88.

Wroe-Brown, R. 2001. *St. Paul's Cathedral Choir Practice Facilities, London EC4.* Unpublished Museum of London Archaeological Service Report.

York Archaeological Trust. 1998. *Former Female Prison, Castle Yard, York. Report on an Archaeological Evaluation.* Unpublished York Archaeological Trust Report 26.

York Archaeological Trust - York Archive Gazetteer. http://www.iadb.co.uk/gaz/help.php.

Youngs, S.M., Gaimster, D.R.M. and Barry, T. 1988. Medieval Britain and Ireland in 1987. *Medieval Archaeology* 32: 225–314.

Post-medieval burial gazetteer

The following gazetteer includes the main sites at which post-medieval burials have been archaeologically excavated. All accounts of articulated or partly articulated human remains from the post-medieval period are noted, where known, as are all records of coffins and vaults. Disarticulated human bone is included when it has been shown to come from a discrete feature of context such as a charnel pit. For reasons of space, human remains that have not been assigned a date or date range are not included. Disarticulated bone when it is not in a clear context is also omitted. Memorials and above-ground records of cemeteries are not included, except when associated with an excavated burial. Published references to effigy monuments, death masks, graveyards and grave markers, mausoleums and other iconography of death are discussed where relevant in the main text but are not normally noted in the gazetteer.

Sites are organised alphabetically by country, then by (old) county and by site name. All sites are organised by historic counties. London and Dublin are listed separately. Each entry gives the name of the site (as published), the type of site, the approximate date, the number of bodies excavated and the date of excavation, followed by a very brief summary text and references. Full references are included in the 'References' section.

Abbreviations
ADS: Archaeology Data Service   BIAB: British and Irish Archaeological Bibliography

Notes
The York Archive Gazetteer is a computerised database of sites investigated by the York Archaeological Trust, accessible online via the Archaeological Data Service website. Discovery and Excavation in Scotland is also accessible through the ADS.

England

Bedfordshire

All Saints Church, Ravensden

Grid Reference	TL 0700 5400
Cemetery type	Churchyard
Date of cemetery	Post-medieval
Number of bodies excavated	24
Date of excavation	1999

The disturbed remains of 24 burials were noted in the area of the vestry extension in 1999 by Bedfordshire County Archaeology Service.

References
BIAB 2001 supp; Edmondson 1999; ADS

St. Mary's Church, Bedford

Grid Reference	TL 05 49
Cemetery type	Churchyard
Date of cemetery	Brick vault c.1772; post-medieval bone
Number of bodies excavated	1 + disarticulate
Date of excavation	1990

Four test pits excavated within the churchyard revealed human bone. Also, a trench across sacristy revealed a brick vault with a lead-lined coffin of a child, probably Edmund Greene (d.c.1772).

References
BIAB 1990; ADS

Berkshire

Binfield Church, Binfield

Grid Reference	SU 8433 7217
Cemetery type	Churchyard
Date of cemetery	19th century
Number of bodies excavated	3
Date of excavation	1993

A brick vault containing three early nineteenth-century coffined burials, with lead inner shells and partially preserved exterior wooden shells, was recorded.

References
BIAB Supp 1994:448–9; Oxford Archaeology Unit 1993a; ADS

Church of St. James the Great, Rushcombe

Grid Reference	SU 798 762
Cemetery type	Churchyard
Date of cemetery	Post-medieval
Number of bodies excavated	13+
Date of excavation	1992

Articulated inhumations, disarticulated human bone and 13 lead coffins were recorded below the chancel floor.

References
BIAB supp 3/1992:337; Torrance and Ford 1992

Holy Trinity Church, Cookham

Grid Reference	SU 8970 8550
Cemetery type	Churchyard
Date of cemetery	18th–19th century
Number of bodies excavated	At least 3
Date of excavation	1992–1994

In 1992, post-medieval burials were recorded pre-dating a vault containing a coffin and loose bones. In 1993, a post-medieval inhumation was observed during restoration work on the chancel. In 1994, two eighteenth- to nineteenth-century burials were located.

References
ADS; Oxford Archaeology Unit 1992a; Crockett 1994; BIAB 1998:1994

Parish Church of St. Mary, Sulhamstead Abbots

Grid Reference	SU 6450 6792
Cemetery type	Churchyard
Date of cemetery	Post-medieval?
Number of bodies excavated	5
Date of excavation	1999

Five graves, probably post-medieval in date, were uncovered during an evaluation excavation in 1999. Articulated human remains found in two of them.

References
BIAB 10.1/1999:481; Hiller 1999b

St. Mary the Virgin Church, Reading

Grid Reference	SU 714 733
Cemetery type	Churchyard
Date of cemetery	Post-medieval
Number of bodies excavated	At least 1
Date of excavation	1992

Human remains, including an articulated skeleton, were recorded and reburied during a watching brief. A number of late eighteenth- and early nineteenth-century gravestones were also recorded.

References
Ponsford and Jackson 1996:245

St. Mary's Church, Beenham

Grid Reference	SU 5910 6850
Cemetery type	Churchyard
Date of cemetery	18th–19th century
Number of bodies excavated	Not specified
Date of excavation	1996

Burial vaults of eighteenth- and nineteenth-century date revealed during replacement of wooden floor of the nave and aisles of church.

References
BIAB 1996:445; Oxford Archaeology Unit 1996; ADS

St. Mary's Church, Chieveley

Grid Reference	SU 48 73
Cemetery type	Churchyard
Date of cemetery	Post-medieval
Number of bodies excavated	1
Date of excavation	1997

Post-medieval burial vault and the lower half of a child's skeleton were observed in a watching brief during the construction of French drains.

References
ADS

St. Mary's Church, Langley Marish, Slough

Grid Reference	TQ 00450 79550
Cemetery type	Churchyard
Date of cemetery	Late 18th–19th century
Number of bodies excavated	At least 7
Date of excavation	1992, 2000

In 1992, human bone was observed in trenches during a watching brief. Two brick vaulted tombs were noted within the church. Excavations in 2000 opened two early nineteenth-century vaults, each containing a single interment; one in a wooden coffin and the other in triple-shelled coffin. Two infant burials, members of the Macintosh family, were recovered from beneath a grave slab. A number of earth cut graves were also revealed, most if not all thought to date to the later eighteenth and early part of nineteenth century.

References
ADS; Oxford Archaeology 2002

St. Mary's Church, Winkfield

Grid Reference	SU 9044 7242
Cemetery type	Churchyard
Date of cemetery	19th century
Number of bodies excavated	1
Date of excavation	1992

Single nineteenth-century burial was observed in a construction trench during the excavation of foundations for an extension to the church.

References
BIAB Supp 3/1992; Oxford Archaeological Unit 1992b; ADS

St. Michael's Church Parish Rooms, Warfield

Grid Reference	SU 8800 7217
Cemetery type	Churchyard
Date of cemetery	19th–early 20th century
Number of bodies excavated	Unspecified
Date of excavation	2004

Several burials of nineteenth- and early twentieth-century date in wooden and wood/lead coffins were recorded in two brick vaults during an archaeological evaluation.

References
Ponsford 2004:242; Taylor and Preston 2006

St. Nicholas' Church, Newbury

Grid Reference	SU 4706 6710
Cemetery type	Churchyard
Date of cemetery	Post-medieval
Number of bodies excavated	3 tombs and numerous burials
Date of excavation	1992

Three tombs and numerous burials identified.

References
BIAB; Oxford Archaeology Unit 1992c

The United Reform Chapel, Broad Street, Reading

Grid Reference	SU 7140 7342
Cemetery type	Non-conformist burial ground
Date of cemetery	Late 18th–19th century
Number of bodies excavated	148
Date of excavation	1994

Forty-seven vaulted brick-lined burial shafts, some containing coffin supports, and three earth cut graves were located in the general area of the vestry, the schoolroom, and behind the chapel. The burials and vault lay in an area known as the 'burial ground' in the early nineteenth century. A total of 148 individuals were recorded during exhumation for reburial and the vaults were also examined and recorded. Bodies were oriented with heads to west or south, following the axis of the shaft within which they were deposited. A variety of lead and wood coffins were recorded. The lead coffins showed no decoration. Examples were found of coffins with textile covering and iron or brass stud decoration. One shaft contained fragments of leather with iron stud decoration attached. Details of coffin furniture and manufacture were recorded where possible. Most coffin plates were lead, with some iron and brass plates also noted. One individual was buried with two hair combs. A finger ring of twisted gold wire was also recovered.

References
BIAB; Ponsford and Jackson 1996:245; Bellamy 1994

Buckinghamshire

All Saints Church, High Wycombe

Grid Reference	SU 865 935
Cemetery type	Churchyard
Date of cemetery	19th century
Number of bodies excavated	3 burials vaults – 7 coffins
Date of excavation	1993, 1997

The Carrington vault was initially examined during the relaying of the church floor in 1993. Four years later the vault and its contents were fully recorded. The brick vault contained shelves that formed 15 coffin niches. The vault contained seven coffins; five were of triple-shelled construction with velvet outer coverings and brass or tin fittings. The remaining two coffins had lead shells, one with an inner wooden shell. The latter may have originally possessed an outer lead shell but the other was covered with ornate lettering suggesting there was no other outer covering. The most elaborate coffin was that of Robert 1st Baron Carrington, which had a funerary coronet on the lid. The body inside one of the coffins had been covered in a layer of white powder, thought to be quicklime.

References
BIAB supp 4/1993:456; Ponsford 2000:224; Oxford Archaeological Unit 1993b; Boyle 1998; Brossler 1999

All Saints Church, Loughton

Grid Reference	SP 8375 3788
Cemetery type	Churchyard
Date of cemetery	Post-medieval
Number of bodies excavated	124 inhumations at least 14 of which were Victorian
Date of excavation	1994

Medieval and post-medieval human remains were removed during work on the north side of the graveyard of All Saints Church. The top of a large vault was also uncovered during the excavations. 124 inhumations were exposed, many inter-cutting, and not in close alignment with each other, although all were oriented with heads generally to the west. Three burials were found with associated copper alloy shroud pins, and 43 were found with associated small iron coffin nails, many still adhering to fragments of wood.

Fourteen burials could be dated to the Victorian period by the associated coffin furniture, which included handles, brass plates and decorative metal strips. One individual was found within a fairly intact coffin, made of oak, with decorative brass plates, handles and large bolts attached. A large depositum plate was fixed to the lid. The inscription was illegible, but traces of red paint were noted. A late seventeenth- or eighteenth-century 'steeple-bottle' containing several copper pins was found between the left humerus and upper chest of an young adult (burial 106). The bottle was sealed with the remnants of a cork pierced by a number of pins. The liquid found in the bottle was thought to be human urine on the basis of similar finds known from elsewhere. The bottle is thought to be a late seventeenth- or eighteenth-century witch bottle.

References
BIAB supp 5/1994:479; Bonner 1994

Langley Marish, St. Mary

Grid Reference	TQ 00 79
Cemetery type	Churchyard
Date of cemetery	Predominantly late 18th–19th century
Number of bodies excavated	Unknown
Date of excavation	1992, 2001

Large quantities of human bone were observed during a watching brief in 1992. In 2001, excavations to the north side of St. Mary's Church, prior to construction of an outbuilding, uncovered a number of predominately eighteenth- and nineteenth-century burials and three brick vaults. The burials were interred in wooden coffins, although one lead coffin was recovered from one of the brick-built vaults. Some of later wooden coffins were more elaborate being adorned with coffin fittings.

References
Boyle and Hiller 2004; ADS

St Mary the Virgin Church, Long Crendon

Grid Reference	SP 697 090
Cemetery type	Churchyard
Date of cemetery	Post-medieval
Number of bodies excavated	At least 2 post-medieval
Date of excavation	2007

Fifteen inhumations were uncovered during a watching brief. Coffin fittings dating from the eighteenth- to nineteenth-century were found with two of the burials. Seven post-medieval copper-alloy buttons were found with one of the burials.

References
Oxford Archaeology 2008b

St Peter and St Paul's Church, Olney

Grid Reference	SP 88 50
Cemetery type	Churchyard
Date of cemetery	Post-medieval
Number of bodies excavated	1
Date of excavation	1995

Post-medieval human remains and grave were uncovered.

References
ADS

Cambridgeshire

All Saint's Church, Kirtling

Grid Reference	TL 6870 5760
Cemetery type	Churchyard
Date of cemetery	17th century

Number of bodies excavated	3
Date of excavation	1997?

A sixteenth-century burial vault belonging to the North family was surveyed. The entrance lay below a chest tomb for Edward, 1st Baron North (1496–1564) in sixteenth-century North Chapel. The vault was constructed in brick and enlarged in the seventeenth century and again in the nineteenth century when another chamber was excavated at the south end of the late seventeenth-century vault. Five interments were observed within the original sixteenth-century vault. All were within lead shells and two had outer wooden cases. They include the double shell coffin of Charles 5th Baron North and Lord Grey of Rolleston (d. 1690) and two triple shell coffins of the twentieth century. The other two lead shells were originally encased within fabric-covered outer cases and were provisionally associated with late seventeenth century North family members commemorated on ledgers in the chancel. The surviving seventeenth-century coffin furniture included a pierced iron grip-plate with lobed terminals with a rectangular ball-shaped iron grip. Three of the interments in the north half of the vaults were laid on brick plinths. A small charnel deposit was also recorded.

The more recent North family interments at the south end of the seventeenth-century vault overlay white marble ledgers commemorating Maria North (d. 1841) and John Crichton Stuart, Marquis of Bute (d. 1848) in adjacent brick graves or a brick vault constructed below their ledgers. Further brick graves or vaults within the North Chapel and Chancel are suggested by the presence of ledgers and mural monuments.

References
Ponsford and Jackson 1998:145

All Saints' Church, Milton

Grid Reference	TL 480 629
Cemetery type	Churchyard
Date of cemetery	18th–19th century
Number of bodies excavated	6
Date of excavation	2000–1

A late eighteenth-century vault was temporally opened during a watching brief at All Saints' Church. The lime washed vault, which was slightly flooded, contained six lead lined coffins with decayed upholstery studs, fabric covers and name plates.

References
Prosser and Hattersley 2004

Bull Hotel, Peterborough

Grid Reference	TL 1920 9890
Cemetery type	Non-conformist burial ground
Date of cemetery	18th–19th century
Number of bodies excavated	1
Date of excavation	1999

Burial vaults from an eighteenth-nineteenth-century chapel or meeting house were recorded. Single skeleton was excavated.

References
BIAB supp. 1999 10.2/1999:750; Hallam 1999; ADS

Hemingford Grey

Grid Reference	TL 29645 71228
Cemetery type	Quaker burial ground
Date of cemetery	1680s–1720s
Number of bodies excavated	16
Date of excavation	2006

Sixteen complete or partial skeletons were excavated from a small Quaker cemetery in the village of Hemingford Grey. The cemetery is thought to date from the 1680s to the 1720s. The burials were in coffins with coffin fittings and decorations in the form of metal plates and upholstery pins. The coffins were largely decayed, but fragments of wood survived. The large quantities of shroud pins suggest bodies were shrouded in more tailored shifts that had been pinned in place. Two copper alloy aglets were recovered from graves.

References
McNichol, Clough and Loe 2007

Huntingdon Castle Mound

Grid Reference	TM 39695 80356
Cemetery type	Execution victims
Date of cemetery	15th–17th century
Number of bodies excavated	At least 2
Date of excavation	1967

Fifty-five skeletons were uncovered during excavations of Huntingdon Castle Mound. The majority date to the late Saxon period but two have been radiocarbon dated to between the mid-fifteenth and seventeenth centuries. These burials may be associated with the gallows that are known to have stood in this area during the post-medieval period.

References
Vincent and Mays 2009

Old Addenbrooke's Hospital, Cambridge

Grid Reference	TL 4510 5787
Cemetery type	Hospital cemetery
Date of cemetery	1772–1778
Number of bodies excavated	5
Date of excavation	1994

Five disturbed individual burials were recorded during the monitoring of service trenches. All were buried within coffins. All the burials were supine, extended and oriented with their heads to the west. Two were found with copper alloy pins, probably from shrouds. The location of the burials outside a churchyard and the evidence of physiological stress on some bones suggest that the graves were those of poor patients from the hospital. It seems probable that the burials therefore date to between 1772 and 1778 when the poor who had no subscriber willing to pay for their burial were interred in the hospital grounds. A piece of land, already consecrated, at the rear of the hospital was set aside for these burials. Human remains were previously uncovered in the same location in 1895.

References
Welsh 1994

St. Andrew's Church, Impington

Grid Reference	TL 4480 6320
Cemetery type	Churchyard
Date of cemetery	19th century
Number of bodies excavated	10
Date of excavation	1994

Ten incomplete nineteenth-century skeletons were noted.

References
BIAB supp 5/1994; Gibson 1994

St. Mary Magdalene Church, Ickleton

Grid Reference	TL 4900 4400
Cemetery type	Churchyard

Date of cemetery	Post-medieval?
Number of bodies excavated	4
Date of excavation	1998

Disarticulated human bone was recorded along with four extended supine inhumations (left in situ). All were oriented west-east with their heads to west. Juvenile and infant bones made up a large proportion of the recovered material, possibly due to the shallow depth of the area excavated.

References
Way 1998

St. Mary's Churchyard, Bucken

Grid Reference	TL 1920 6765
Cemetery type	Churchyard
Date of cemetery	Late 19th century
Number of bodies excavated	6 grave cuts, 3 partially excavated.
Date of excavation	1994

An archaeological evaluation occurred in the churchyard to the west of St. Mary's Buckden. Six grave cuts were identified. Three were partially excavated and found to contain coffin fittings dating to the late nineteenth century.

References
Roberts 1994

Cheshire

Beeston Castle, Cheshire

Grid Reference	SJ 538 592
Cemetery type	War burials
Date of cemetery	1645
Number of bodies excavated	3
Date of excavation	1968–73

Three burials were excavated lying alongside the curtain wall on north side of the inner ward of the castle. All burials were young males and are thought to have been Royalist casualties of the siege of the castle during the Civil War.

References
Keen and Hough 1993

Chester Cathedral

Grid Reference	SJ 406 664
Cemetery type	Churchyard
Date of cemetery	Early post-medieval
Number of bodies excavated	Unspecified
Date of excavation	1998

Brick-built burial vaults were found under the aisle containing relatively elaborate burials. Numerous single burials also found under the nave. The majority exhibited no evidence for the use of coffins suggesting simple shroud burials. The burials are thought to be of late medieval to early post-medieval date.

References
Ward 1997; Ward 1998

St. Wilfred's Church, Davenham

Grid Reference	SJ 66 71
Cemetery type	Churchyard
Date of cemetery	Post-medieval
Number of bodies excavated	Unspecified
Date of excavation	1995

A post-medieval burial vault and coffin were recorded.

References
ADS; Eyre-Morgan 1995; Eyre-Morgan 1997

Warrington Friary

Grid Reference	SJ6063 8797
Cemetery type	Churchyard
Date of cemetery	c.1292–1800
Number of bodies excavated	Unknown
Date of excavation	2000

The site of the Augustinian friary was excavated in 2000. Friary was probably dissolved in 1539 and sold in 1540. The friary church passed to the rector of Warrington and appears to have been used for worship until 1640s. The church was destroyed after sustaining damage during the Civil War, with the area becoming a burial ground.

References
Heawood 2002

Cornwall

Launceston Castle

Grid Reference	SX 330 846
Cemetery type	Prison cemetery
Date of cemetery	Uncertain
Number of bodies excavated	16
Date of excavation	1961–1983

Sixteen randomly orientated graves were found scattered across the south-west bailey of the castle. The burials are thought to be linked to the gaol and are presumably felons that had been hanged in the bailey. One burial has injuries suggestive of hanging. The burials are thought to date to the first half of the eighteenth century although some may date to the late seventeenth century. Hanging ceased at the castle in 1821, the gaol being abandoned in 1840. Any burials are likely to pre-date the gaol's closure and possibly the end of hanging at the castle. A number of graves contained iron nails and fragments of wood indicative of the use of coffins. Buttons and other dress fittings were found with a number of the interments suggesting clothed interment. A strike-a-light was found with one of the burials.

References
Saunders 2006

Mullion Church

Grid Reference	SW 6790 1920
Cemetery type	Churchyard
Date of cemetery	17th–18th century
Number of bodies excavated	5
Date of excavation	2003

Five graves were recorded during drainage work around the church. All burials were in coffins. One adult burial in a wooden coffin with 16 nails was radiocarbon dated to c. AD 1666–1756. One grave contained the remains of an adult male and a juvenile. Another burial was stratigraphically dated to the late eighteenth or early nineteenth century. There was no evidence for coffin fittings

References
Thorpe 2003

St. Andrew's Church, Stratton

Grid Reference	SS 2315 0648
Cemetery type	Churchyard
Date of cemetery	Post-medieval

Number of bodies excavated	3
Date of excavation	1999

The graves of William Toms (d.1861) and that of his wife Elizabeth (d.1854) were recorded. The inside of the brick-lined burial vault containing the coffin of Elizabeth Toms had been whitewashed and then decorated with black painted lines. A third undated burial with no evidence of a coffin was recorded

References
Thorpe 1999

St. Felicitas Church, Phillack

Grid Reference	SW 5653 3842
Cemetery type	Churchyard
Date of cemetery	Post-medieval
Number of bodies excavated	Unknown
Date of excavation	2001

Two graves and a charnel pit were observed in the course of a watching brief during the construction on the south side of the church. Wood stains suggest that both burials were in wooden coffins, with nails recovered from one of the burials. An early post-medieval date is suggested for the burials due to their presence of coffins.

References
Thorpe 2001a

St. Mawgan in Pydar Church

Grid Reference	SW 8722 6596
Cemetery type	Churchyard
Date of cemetery	15th–17th century
Number of bodies excavated	20
Date of excavation	2001

Seventeen graves containing a minimum of twenty individuals, buried in at least three family plots, were recorded during the extension of the church. A fifteenth- to seventeenth-century date has been suggested for the burials as they lack the long cists of the tenth to fourteenth century and the elaborate coffin fittings of eighteenth and nineteenth centuries.

References
Thorpe 2001b

St. Miniver Parish Church

Grid Reference	SW 9646 7707
Cemetery type	Churchyard
Date of cemetery	Post-medieval
Number of bodies excavated	1
Date of excavation	1997

Graves marked with memorial slabs dating to eighteenth and nineteenth centuries were recorded. A coffin was observed within one of the vaults. The coffin appears to be of oak with an interior lined with fabric. There is a silver tinned breastplate, with a black painted inscription. Corroded iron coffin fittings were present.

References
BIAB supp. 8/1997:582; Thorpe 1998

St. Paternus Church, North Petherwin

Grid Reference	SX 2818 8962
Cemetery type	Churchyard
Date of cemetery	1810–1855
Number of bodies excavated	Unknown
Date of excavation	1996

Four burials were recorded during a watching brief to upgrade utilities at the church. Two brick-lined graves with slate lids were identified in another trench. No coffins or burial furniture were identified.

References
Johns 1996

St. Winnow Church, Lostwithiel

Grid Reference	SX 11530 56970
Cemetery type	Churchyard
Date of cemetery	Post-medieval
Number of bodies excavated	1
Date of excavation	2004

Articulated human bone and coffin nails from a single burial recorded during a watching brief. The remains are likely to be of eighteenth- or nineteenth-century date and were preserved in situ.

References
Mossop 2004

Tintagel Churchyard

Grid Reference	SX 05 88
Cemetery type	Churchyard
Date of cemetery	Post-medieval
Number of bodies excavated	8
Date of excavation	1990–1992

Eight post-medieval graves of children were recorded in Tintagel Parish Churchyard. Graves were constructed by digging a small grave pit into the compacted rubble demolition layers and building a tent or cist-like structure into the grave pit.

References
Nowakowski and Thomas 1990; Nowakowski and Thomas 1992

Cumberland

Church of St. Lawrence, Morland

Grid Reference	NY 5980 2255
Cemetery type	Churchyard
Date of cemetery	Post-medieval
Number of bodies excavated	1?
Date of excavation	1999

At least one post-medieval burial was recorded during an archaeological evaluation prior to a proposed development.

References
Town and Scurfield 1999

Lanercost Priory, Brampton, Cumberland

Grid Reference	NY 55 63
Cemetery type	Post-dissolution
Date of cemetery	Post-medieval
Number of bodies excavated	4
Date of excavation	1994

Four infant burials and two associated and unexcavated grave cuts, also probably of infants, were found near the exterior wall on the north-east side of Lanercost Priory (to the north of the Lady Chapel). Nails and a small copper alloy pin were found in association with the burials. The size of the bones of the infants suggested that they were either still born or neonates. The lack of any records or grave-markers and their burial outside the recognised churchyard suggest that they may have been unbaptised. Although the priory went out of use as a religious house after the Dissolution, the burials appear to post-date this. They cut through an area of compact sandstone fragments that may have been associated with the demolition and stripping of the Priory after its dissolution.

References
Whitworth 1998

Derbyshire

Church of St. Mary and St. Barlok, Norbury

Grid Reference	SK 1250 4240
Cemetery type	Churchyard
Date of cemetery	19th century?
Number of bodies excavated	12
Date of excavation	1999

Twelve burials, probably nineteenth century, were recorded. There is a suggestion that the area was not used for burials until eighteenth century.

References
Sheppard and Appleton 1999

Derby Cathedral: The Cavendish Vault

Grid Reference	SK 351 365
Cemetery type	Churchyard
Date of cemetery	1607–1848
Number of bodies excavated	46
Date of excavation	1977

The contents of the Cavendish family vault, which lies below the south aisle of Derby Cathedral, were recorded in 1977. The vault contained 44 seventeenth- to nineteenth-century coffins, placed in stone-built tiers of shelving, and two burial drums. The majority of coffins had an outer wooden shell, often with cloth covers surviving and coffin fittings, with a inner lead shell. The coffin of an individual that died in Rome had a glass inspection panel used to identify the body. Two burial drums are thought to contain the entrails of corpses which had been embalmed.

References
Butler and Morris 1994

St James Church, Swarkestone

Grid Reference	SK 372 286
Cemetery type	Churchyard
Date of cemetery	19th century
Number of bodies excavated	1
Date of excavation	Unknown

An isolated nineteenth-century burial was discovered to the east of the chapel during a watching brief.

References
Elliot 2000

St. Mary's Church, Scopton

Grid Reference	SK 1927 3020
Cemetery type	Churchyard
Date of cemetery	18th–19th century
Number of bodies excavated	5
Date of excavation	2004

Five articulated burials were uncovered with associated coffin fittings indicating an eighteenth- to nineteenth-century date. Disarticulated remains were also recorded.

References
O'Neill pers. comm.

Devon

Athenaeum burial ground, Plymouth

Grid Reference	SX470560
Cemetery type	Hospital cemetery?
Date of cemetery	18th–early 19th century
Number of bodies excavated	20
Date of excavation	2007

Twenty skeletons thought to be more than 300 years old were uncovered in Plymouth. Two skeletons had leg amputation – one healed and the other occurring peri-mortem. The site is thought to be a burial site associated with the naval hospital.

References
Plymouth District Archaeological Society News

Exeter Cathedral

Grid Reference	SX 921 926
Cemetery type	Churchyard
Date of cemetery	Post-medieval
Number of bodies excavated	Unknown
Date of excavation	1970s

Post-medieval burials uncovered during excavations in the Cathedral Close

References
ADS

Near One Gun Point and Dartmouth Castle, Dartmouth

Grid Reference	SX 88 50
Cemetery type	Stranger burials
Date of cemetery	Post-medieval
Number of bodies excavated	8
Date of excavation	1985

Eight post medieval burials were excavated near One Gun Point, outside of any recognised churchyard and nearby Dartmouth Castle. Several burials have been found in the area previously. The individuals were in separate grave cuts, some inter-cutting. Seven of the burials seem to have been buried in wooden coffins, indicated by the presence of nails. Two of the burials were in very tightly fitting rectangular or trapezoidal coffins. Three of the individuals were oriented approximately north-east to south-west with heads to the south. The other five were buried approximately east-west, with their heads to the south-east. Burials thought to post-date 1600 due to the presence of clay pipes in the fill and the fragment of pine attached to one of the coffin nails. The churchyard of St Petrox Church, 200m away, was enclosed in 1600 and the modern boundaries are thought to parallel those of the early modern period, indicating that these burials were deliberately placed outside the churchyard. It has been suggested that the site was used to bury foreigners who died on ships coming into port. The lack of a mass grave suggests that they are not shipwreck victims, but the placement and orientation is consistent with other graves of apparent foreigners at ports or near the sea.

References
Freeman 1985

Saunton Down End, Croyde Bay

Grid Reference	SS 4335 3873
Cemetery type	Drowning victims
Date of cemetery	16th century
Number of bodies excavated	Unknown
Date of excavation	1903, 1996–8

In 1998, a sixteenth-century inhumation was found near to the location of burials found in 1906 and 1996. It has been suggested that the remains were of a mariner who had drowned at sea and was buried near the beach. Other inhumations were found eroding out of the cliff-face in 1996 formed a group and were thought to be contemporaneous shipwreck victims.

References
Bayer 1996; BIAB supp. 9/1998:565; BIAB supp. 7/1996:477; Gent 1998

St. Saviour's Church, Dartmouth, Devon

Grid Reference	SX 87 51
Cemetery type	Churchyard
Date of cemetery	17th–early 18th century
Number of bodies excavated	1 and disarticulated bone
Date of excavation	1998

Excavations in the churchyard uncovered a single inhumation and disarticulated remains, thought to be post-medieval in date, outside the modern churchyard.

References
ADS; Watts 1998

Sutton Harbour, Sutton Road, Plymouth

Grid Reference	SX 4860 5420
Cemetery type	Prison cemetery
Date of cemetery	18th century
Number of bodies excavated	19
Date of excavation	2001

A shallow mass grave, thought to date to eighteenth century and containing 19 individuals, was found set back from the harbour waterfront. Fourteen individuals survived mostly intact. The bodies were interred 'head to toe' and within coffins. The skeletons were mostly male and the aged between 17 and 25, with one juvenile and two older individuals also recorded. Evidence of rickets and possible club foot was noted. The site was formerly the location of a prison and the burials are thought to be eighteenth-century prisoners, possibly French.

References
Ponsford 2003:234–5; Anon 2001

Dorset

Baptist Burial Ground, Wear Butts, Poole

Grid Reference	SZ 00930 90760
Cemetery type	Baptist burial ground
Date of cemetery	1735–1855
Number of bodies excavated	83
Date of excavation	2002

Excavations in 2001 on the site of a former Baptist burial ground uncovered the in situ remains of 83 individual in 81 graves. The graves were orientated approximately southeast to northwest with the majority interred in coffins. The coffins were of yew and elm and were adorned with locally made coffin furniture. Most of the bodies appear to been dressed in shrouds often pinned together. A five year-old child had been subject to an autopsy. One grave was empty with only an impression of the coffin remaining in its base. The burial ground was in use between 1735 and 1855 and served two Baptist communities in Poole.

References
Ponsford 2002:187; McKinley 2008

Blandford Parish Church,

Grid Reference	ST 8855 0631
Cemetery type	Churchyard
Date of cemetery	Mid–late 17th century
Number of bodies excavated	7
Date of excavation	1970

Mid-seventeenth-century coffins and coffin plates were recorded in a vault built out from the east side of Blandford Parish Church. Five large lead coffins and one small baby's coffin were noted, as well as a partially disintegrated wooden coffin. The latter contained the body of a young girl and many bay and rosemary twigs and leaves.

References
Goodall 1970

Minster Churchyard, Wimbourne Minster

Grid Reference	SU 1000 4010
Cemetery type	Churchyard
Date of cemetery	Post-medieval
Number of bodies excavated	Unknown
Date of excavation	1988

A post-medieval vault and human remains observed during a watching brief in churchyard during a paving/drainage scheme.

References
ADS; Farwell 1988

Durham

All Saints' Church, Lanchester

Grid Reference	NZ 17 46
Cemetery type	Churchyard
Date of cemetery	19th century
Number of bodies excavated	Unknown
Date of excavation	1992

Nineteenth-century burials were recovered from the graveyard during a watching brief prior to construction of a new visitor centre

References
ADS; BIAB supp. 3/1992:370; Ryder 1993

St. Michael's Church, Houghton le Spring

Grid Reference	NZ 34 49
Cemetery type	Churchyard
Date of cemetery	18th–19th century
Number of bodies excavated	Unknown
Date of excavation	1999

Eighteenth and nineteenth-century vaults observed during building works in 1999.

References
Ryder 2000

The Carr House Sands Project, Hartlepool

Grid Reference	NZ 52 31
Cemetery type	Isolated burial
Date of cemetery	Post-medieval
Number of bodies excavated	1
Date of excavation	1995

A single inhumation was found by contractors working on the new sea defences between Hartlepool and Seaton Carew. The adult male had been buried in sand dunes, which were later covered by a sea wall and promenade constructed in c.1900. The individual had pipe facets on his teeth and was accompanied with a fragment of clay pipe, suggesting a post-medieval date.

References
ADS; Waughman 1995

Essex

Bannister's Green

Grid Reference	TL 69 20
Cemetery type	Quaker burial ground
Date of cemetery	Late 17th–early 18th century
Number of bodies excavated	9
Date of excavation	1947

Nine coffined burials were uncovered during excavation of a mound, thought to have been the site of a windmill. Little wood survived, but coffin handles were found with some inhumations. The mound is known as Quaker's mound and it is thought that the burials are late seventeenth- and early eighteenth-century Quakers.

References
Essex SMR record 1256

Church of All Saints, Hutton

Grid Reference	TQ 631 950
Cemetery type	Churchyard
Date of cemetery	1779
Number of bodies excavated	1
Date of excavation	1991

Excavations for a drain uncovered a vault in the south-west corner of the church. The vault contained only one coffin, presumed to be that of Thomas Hills, the name on grave marker who died in 1779.

References
Essex SMR record 5353

Church of St. Andrew, Hempstead, Uttlesford

Grid Reference	TL 63 37
Cemetery type	Churchyard
Date of cemetery	17th century or earlier
Number of bodies excavated	2
Date of excavation	1994

Excavations below the brick floor of the Harvey vault found a small pit, containing the remains of two adults. These burials, probably formerly in the churchyard, had most likely been moved as a result of construction of the Harvey vault. The Harvey vault contains a number of coffins including some seventeenth-century lead coffins with modelled faces.

References
BIAB supp. 5:550–1; Bedwin 1994/5; ADS

Holy Trinity Church, Rayleigh

Grid Reference	TL 8080 9090
Cemetery type	Churchyard
Date of cemetery	Mid-18th century onwards
Number of bodies excavated	Over 100
Date of excavation	1994

Over 100 graves were revealed during a watching brief in advance of building works. Forty of these had been identified by grave markers prior to excavation. Grave types encountered included earth cut, brick-lined and corbelled. The cemetery appears to date from the twelfth century, but only burials from the mid-eighteenth century onwards could be dated and identified.

References
BIABsupp. 5/1994:546

Little Easton

Grid Reference	TL 6045 2350
Cemetery type	Churchyard
Date of cemetery	17th century
Number of bodies excavated	1
Date of excavation	Unknown

A coffin dating to the 1660s was recorded in the east chamber of the Maynard vault, with appliquéd coats of arms. The vault also contained a small brick bin for charnel.

References
Litten 1991: 95–6

St. Andrew's Church, Hatfield Peverel

Grid Reference	TL 788 117
Cemetery type	Churchyard
Date of cemetery	18th century
Number of bodies excavated	25
Date of excavation	1989

Twenty-five coffins, the earliest dating to 1778, were noted from within a vault on the south side of the church. The majority were single break coffins of wood inside outer lead shells. Some of the later coffins had outer wooden shells. One lead coffin dated 1799 contained a child's remains. One black coffin had ornate brass fittings. Some names plates were present for the Wright and Firman families.

References
Havis 1995

Saint Mary's Cathedral, Chelmsford

Grid Reference	TL 7082 0694
Cemetery type	Churchyard
Date of cemetery	Post-medieval
Number of bodies excavated	13
Date of excavation	1995

Three test pits were excavated in the cathedral grounds and another at the junction of the chapter house and north transept. Articulated skeletons were excavated and reburied.

References
BIAB supp 6/1995:209

St Mary and All Saints Church, Debden

Grid Reference	TL 5513 3322
Cemetery type	Churchyard
Date of cemetery	Post-medieval
Number of bodies excavated	8
Date of excavation	1999

The positions of approximately 33 graves were recorded during excavations to the north and east of the existing vestry. At least thirteen were part excavated including that of an infant or small child. Three graves contained coffin nails, one of which also produced a coffin handle, a coffin plate and decayed wood. Decayed wood was also found in a second grave. The shape of some graves suggests that coffin use was not universal.

References
BIAB supp. 10.2/1999:713; Germany 1999; Ennis 2000

St. Margaret's Churchyard, Chelmsford

Grid Reference	TQ 73 95

Cemetery type	Churchyard
Date of cemetery	Post-medieval
Number of bodies excavated	Unknown
Date of excavation	1982

Post-medieval human remains were noted.

References
ADS

St. Mary the Virgin, Ramsden Crays

Grid Reference	TQ 70800 93350
Cemetery type	Churchyard
Date of cemetery	17th century and later
Number of bodies excavated	Unknown
Date of excavation	2002?

Inhumations were noted during archaeological monitoring of drainage trenches. A seventeenth century or later date has been suggested for the remains.

References
Ponsford 2003:237

St. Mary's Church, Broomfield

Grid Reference	TL 7050 1050
Cemetery type	Churchyard
Date of cemetery	19th–early 20th century
Number of bodies excavated	6+
Date of excavation	1996

Two brick vaults and six inhumations from early nineteenth to early twentieth century were recorded, as well as some shallower nineteenth-century grave cuts.

References
BIAB supp. 7/1996:502; Germany 1997

St. Mary's Church, Great Bentley

Grid Reference	TM 10 20
Cemetery type	Churchyard
Date of cemetery	18th–19th century
Number of bodies excavated	Unknown
Date of excavation	1987

A watching brief prior to construction to the south of the church revealed an eighteenth- or nineteenth-century brick-lined vault and additional burials of a similar period.

References
Essex SMR record 7261

St. Mary's Church, Maldon

Grid Reference	TL 80 00
Cemetery type	Churchyard
Date of cemetery	Post-medieval
Number of bodies excavated	2
Date of excavation	1989

A test pit was dug to the south side of the church prior to construction of a new church hall. Two intact burials, dating to eighteenth and nineteenth century, with the remains of coffins, coffin fittings and coffin studs were uncovered. Charnel was found below and above the burials.

References
ADS

St. Michael, Manningtree

Grid Reference	TM 107 318
Cemetery type	Unknown
Date of cemetery	Early 17th century
Number of bodies excavated	Unknown
Date of excavation	1974

Early seventeenth-century foundations were noted together with associated graves.

References
Cherry 1975:240

St. Paul's Church, Belle Vue Road, Colchester

Grid Reference	TL991260
Cemetery type	Churchyard
Date of cemetery	1869–1900
Number of bodies excavated	4
Date of excavation	2001

Four burials, including a child, were excavated during a watching brief at St. Paul's Church. The graves were unmarked and thought to be burials of the residents of the nearby Essex Hall asylum. Two burials appeared to have been in coffins.

References
Colchester Archaeological Trust 2000

United Reform Church/ Salvation Army Hall, Abbey Kane, Saffron Waldon

Grid Reference	TL 536 383
Cemetery type	Non-conformist burial ground
Date of cemetery	1694–1870
Number of bodies excavated	117+
Date of excavation	2005

Archaeological monitoring on development in the the area of the United Reform Church graveyard identified 117 grave cuts aligned east-west. A third of the graves contained structures, either brick-lined, chambered or vaulted. The vaults had half-brick width ledges for wooden structures or bath stone slabs to support the coffin. Two lead coffins were found in the vaults. The remaining 70% of graves were earth-filled features containing a varying number of interments. Coffin fittings and nails accompanied the inhumations. Grave goods were confined to buttons and a bone comb.

References
Field Archaeology Unit, Essex County Council 2005; Pocock 2006

Gloucestershire

All Saints Church, Preston, Gloucestershire

Grid Reference	SP 044 009
Cemetery type	Churchyard
Date of cemetery	Post-medieval
Number of bodies excavated	Unknown
Date of excavation	1991

Post-medieval human remains were noted during a watching brief.

References
ADS; Hoyle 1991b

Baptist Burial Ground, Redcross Street

Grid Reference	ST 59563 73191
Cemetery type	Baptist burial ground
Date of cemetery	Late 17th century – cleared 1926
Number of bodies excavated	Unknown

Post-medieval burial gazetteer

Date of excavation   1982

The Baptist Burial Ground was founded in the late seventeenth century and cleared in 1926, with the remains re-interred in Greenbank cemetery. However, a watching brief in 1982 recorded burials across much of the site, particularly along its eastern end.

References
Iles 1983

Bristol Royal Infirmary Burial Ground

Grid Reference	ST 58656 73336
Cemetery type	Hospital cemetery
Date of cemetery	1757–1857
Number of bodies excavated	c.1000
Date of excavation	2002

More than 1000 bodies dating to the late eighteenth and early nineteenth century were removed from the Royal Infirmary Burial Ground. Some skeletal material was sent to Bristol University for analysis. The bodies were not buried in coffins. This, together with their burial in the infirmary ground, suggests that those buried here were probably all paupers.

References
Samuel 2003; Willis 2003

Camden House, Stroud

Grid Reference	SO85300492
Cemetery type	Baptist burial ground
Date of cemetery	19th–early 20th century
Number of bodies excavated	26
Date of excavation	2004

Excavations on the site of the former Baptist burial ground, which was in use between 1844 and 1914, located 26 full or partial grave cuts. The size and shape of the grave cuts were recorded, but the inhumations were not excavated. There was some variation in the size and shape of the grave cuts due to multiple burials within single plots.

References
Evans 2004; Brett 2004

Church of St. Leonard, Upton St. Leonards, Gloucester

Grid Reference	SO 8620 1500
Cemetery type	Churchyard
Date of cemetery	Late 18th–early 19th century
Number of bodies excavated	5
Date of excavation	1999

Five burials, dating to the late eighteenth-early nineteenth century, two with deposition plates, and one with coffin handles, were recorded.

References
BIAB supp. 10.2/1999:1029–30; Heighway 1999

Gloucester Cathedral

Grid Reference	SO 831 188
Cemetery type	Churchyard
Date of cemetery	17th century?
Number of bodies excavated	12
Date of excavation	1992

Twelve inhumations of probable seventeenth-century date recorded.

References
BIAB supp. 3/1992:396; Greatorex 1993

Greyfriars, Gloucester

Grid Reference	SO 8314 1836
Cemetery type	Unknown
Date of cemetery	Post-medieval
Number of bodies excavated	Unknown
Date of excavation	1967, 1974–5

Human remains noted

References
Ferris 2002

Mary-le-Port Church, Bristol

Grid Reference	ST 58990 73024
Cemetery type	Churchyard
Date of cemetery	17th–19th century
Number of bodies excavated	Unknown
Date of excavation	1814, 1962–3

Post medieval burials were cleared by workmen with limited recording. Eighteenth- and nineteenth-century brick family burial vaults, coffins and coffin furniture were noted. A seventeenth-century burial was exhumed in the nineteenth century.

References
Watts and Rahtz 1985; Brushfield 1890

Moravian burial ground, Bristol

Grid Reference	ST 58717 73420
Cemetery type	Non-conformist burial ground
Date of cemetery	Post-medieval
Number of bodies excavated	Unknown
Date of excavation	1993, 1999

The Moravian chapel was cleared in 1973 but found to have many burials still remaining during development work in 1993. Several family vaults and brick graves containing burials were recorded, together with some of the coffin furniture.

References
Pilkington 2000; Williams 2000

Royal Edward Docks, Avonmouth

Grid Reference	ST 50904 78518
Cemetery type	Gibbet
Date of cemetery	Post-medieval
Number of bodies excavated	unknown
Date of excavation	1902–1908

Human remains were recovered from below the low tide mark during the construction of Royal Edward Docks. The remains were thought to be associated with a gibbet that was located on Dunball Island into the nineteenth century.

References
Beddoe 1907; Brett 1997

Southgate Gallery, Southgate Street, Gloucester

Grid Reference	SO 82 18
Cemetery type	Unknown
Date of cemetery	Medieval and later
Number of bodies excavated	100
Date of excavation	

One hundred burials were recovered from cemeteries associated with Medieval church of St. Owen and later nonconformist chapels and Royal Infirmary.

References
BIAB supp. 2/1990–1:143–4

St Margaret's Chapel, London Road, Gloucester

Grid Reference	SO 8415 1890
Cemetery type	War burials
Date of cemetery	Post-medieval
Number of bodies excavated	2
Date of excavation	1990

Medieval burials were found to the south of St Margaret's Chapel and to the west of St Margaret's Almshouses. Also found were two burials, possibly in the same grave cut, on a northwest-southeast alignment. It has been suggested that they may be Civil War casualties.

References
Ponsford 1991:130

St. Augustine the Less, Bristol

Grid Reference	ST 5849 7272
Cemetery type	Churchyard
Date of cemetery	Late 17th–early 19th century
Number of bodies excavated	Unknown
Date of excavation	1988

Excavation occurred at the site of a previously demolished church and churchyard. From the late seventeenth century to the early nineteenth century almost the entire under-floor area was in use for burial vaults and brick-lined graves of which 93 had been recorded by 1983. A high density of burials was found beneath the nineteenth-century vestry. Several inhumations in the north and south aisles were cut by brick-lined graves and vaults. Graves below the early eighteenth-century aisle extension had been removed before rebuilding. Five nineteenth-century lead coffined burials were uncovered and were re-interred elsewhere. Four triple coffin burials were also recorded beneath the heating ducts installed in the nineteenth century. Much coffin furniture was recovered, including coffin plates, escutcheons, decorated grips and grip-plates and upholstery pins.

References
Egan 1984:307–8; Egan 1985:159; Egan 1989:25–7; Boore 1985, 1986 & 1998

St. Edward's Church, Evenlode

Grid Reference	SP 2206 2907
Cemetery type	Churchyard
Date of cemetery	Post-medieval
Number of bodies excavated	Unknown
Date of excavation	1990

Grave cuts and post-medieval coffin were noted.

References
BIAB supp. 2/1990–1:140; Hoyle 1991a

St. John the Baptist, Cirencester

Grid Reference	SP 0233 0210
Cemetery type	Churchyard
Date of cemetery	18th–19th century
Number of bodies excavated	4 + 24
Date of excavation	2000–3

In 2000, trenches to the north and east of the lady chapel uncovered medieval and post-medieval burials. Further work in 2002–3 located 8 graves. The burials were recorded and left in situ. Four are probably late medieval and four of eighteenth- to nineteenth-century date. Excavations between 1964–6 of the site of Cirencester Abbey uncovered 24 skeletons. The burials were thought to be part of the churchyard of St. John's and to be post-medieval in date.

References
Ponsford 2004:258; ADS; Wilkinson and McWhirr 1998

St. Kenelm's Church, Sapperton, near Stroud

Grid Reference	SO 947 034
Cemetery type	Churchyard
Date of cemetery	Post-medieval
Number of bodies excavated	Unknown
Date of excavation	Unknown

Single case coffins found in Atkyns vault, Sapperton.

References
Heighway and Litten 1994

St. Mary's Church, Bitton

Grid Reference	ST 6820 6933
Cemetery type	Churchyard
Date of cemetery	Late 18th–early 19th century
Number of bodies excavated	6 and charnel
Date of excavation	1988

Six articulated adult coffined burials and charnel were recorded in the late eighteenth-century rectangular-plan barrel vault belonging to the Creswicke family. An extended burial with head to the west and traces of wooden coffin was located near the entrance against the north wall. A lead coffin, with lid decorated with a diaper pattern lay to the south of the entrance. Four more lead coffins were found in the southern half of vault, also with heads to the west. These four lead coffins were originally triple-shell with inner wooded shell and outer wooden case covered with velvet, probably red, attached by upholstery pins. Coffin grips dating to the eighteenth and early nineteenth centuries were also recorded, usually with winged cherub heads and made of brass or iron with copper alloy decoration. Four depositum-plates made of brass or copper alloy recorded details of individual Creswicke family members from 1799 to 1834. In the south-east corner was a pile of carefully arranged disarticulated human bone. This contained long bones and six skulls, all from adult individuals. It has been suggested that these were the earliest burials, probably interred in single shell coffins, and moved to make space for later burials. A single burial near the entrance to the vault may have been a family servant.

References
Egan 1989:25–6; Boore 1989; Boore 1998

St. Oswald's Priory, Gloucester

Grid Reference	SO 8300 1898
Cemetery type	Churchyard
Date of cemetery	Few post-Reformation, rest 18th- and 19th-century
Number of bodies excavated	124
Date of excavation	1970s

The priory was dissolved in 1537 and the north aisle of the priory church was converted into small parish church. The site was excavated in the 1970s. Ten burials dating to c.1540–1650 were excavated from in front of the sixteenth- to seventeenth-century altar. Only three of these burials were in coffins, all rectangular in shape, and none of these had fittings. A further 114 eighteenth- and nineteenth-century burials were also recovered. Half of these burials had coffins. The majority of coffins were wooden, either rectangular or single-break, with only one triple shelled coffin recovered from the site. A number of eighteenth- and nineteenth-century coffin fittings were also recovered. Three brick-lined graves were present, two rectangular and one shouldered brick grave, as well as earth cut graves. One coffin had a very thin iron plate, possibly the remains of an iron shell used in the nineteenth century as an anti-resurrectionist safeguard.

References
Heighway and Bryant 1999

St. Peter's Church, Farmington

Grid Reference	SP 1365 1528
Cemetery type	Churchyard
Date of cemetery	1778
Number of bodies excavated	1
Date of excavation	1999

A disturbed, stone lined grave was found to the south of the chancel containing the remains of the triple shell coffin of Charles Miller (d. 1778). Fragments of a decorated stone chest tomb were found in the backfill of the grave.

References
BIAB supp. 10.2/1999:1021–2; Oakey 1999

St. Thomas' Church burial ground, Bristol

Grid Reference	ST 59106 72788
Cemetery type	Churchyard
Date of cemetery	Medieval onwards
Number of bodies excavated	Unknown
Date of excavation	1994

Archaeological evaluation in churchyard noted quantities of disarticulated bones. Part of a brick burial shaft and a burial vault were exposed. The vault contained a lead coffin.

References
Burchill 1994

Tewkesbury Abbey (Abbey Halls)

Grid Reference	SO 8910 3240
Cemetery type	Churchyard
Date of cemetery	19th century
Number of bodies excavated	1
Date of excavation	1996

Human bones were found in the basement of early nineteenth-century National School, probably a child burial. These appear to have been disturbed during the construction of the school. To rear of the school lay the Russell Almshouses, founded in the late seventeenth century and replaced 1831–2.

References
BIAB supp. 7/1996:522; Shoesmith and Hoverd 1996

The Baptist Church, Coxwell Street, Cirencester

Grid Reference	SP 0216 0214
Cemetery type	Baptist burial ground
Date of cemetery	18th–19th century
Number of bodies excavated	3
Date of excavation	1997

Three graves containing burials dated by coffin fittings to eighteenth to nineteenth century. One grave was a brick lined vault containing two burials originally separated by coffin supports.

References
BIAB supp. 8:627; Turner 1997

The Society of Friends' Burial Ground, Quaker's Friars (Priors' burial ground), Bristol

Grid Reference	ST 59302 73315
Cemetery type	Quaker burial ground
Date of cemetery	1669 onwards
Number of bodies excavated	Unknown
Date of excavation	2002, 2006

Archaeological investigations on the south and east of the burial ground recorded in situ post-medieval inhumations.

References
Jackson and Stevens 2002; Ponsford 2003:230–1

The Tabernacle, Penn Street, Bristol

Grid Reference	ST 59390 73355
Cemetery type	Non-conformist burial ground
Date of cemetery	18th–19th century
Number of bodies excavated	Unknown
Date of excavation	2006

The Tabernacle Chapel was built in 1753 for a Methodist society. The crypt contains a number of brick vaults. The chapel later became a Congregation chapel. The building was demolished in 1958. The crypt was excavated in 2006 by Cotswold Archaeology with human remains and coffins being recovered from the brick vaults within the crypt.

References
http://www.cotswoldarch.org.uk

Waterloo Road, Old Market, Bristol

Grid Reference	ST 60040 73260
Cemetery type	Non-conformist burial ground
Date of cemetery	18th–19th century
Number of bodies excavated	Unknown
Date of excavation	2005

Several infant burials were noted in the area of an eighteenth-century burial ground. Most, if not all, were in coffins. One infant burial had a complete cup found alongside its skull. No human remains were removed.

References
Lankstead 2005

Wilson Street, St. Paul's, Bristol

Grid Reference	ST 5959 7370
Cemetery type	Private burial ground
Date of cemetery	19th century
Number of bodies excavated	Unknown
Date of excavation	1999

Excavations occurred on the site of a nineteenth-century infant burial ground. North and east limits of the cemetery are bounded by a cobbled alley and garden boundary wall.

References
ADS; Parry 1999; Ponsford 2000:222

Hampshire

2, Church Street, Romsey

Grid Reference	SU 3525 2145
Cemetery type	Medical waste
Date of cemetery	19th century
Number of bodies excavated	Minimum of 2
Date of excavation	1999

Human remains were found packed around an early twentieth-century drain. The disarticulated remains exhibited evidence for deliberate post-mortem modification – either as the result of autopsy or dissection. Bones are linked to occupation of house by Dr. Beddome in mid-nineteenth century.

References
BIAB supp. 10.2/1999:865; Smith 1999

Church of St. John the Baptist, Winchester

Grid Reference	SU 48702 29452
Cemetery type	Churchyard
Date of cemetery	1747–1855
Number of bodies excavated	10
Date of excavation	2006

Excavations in the churchyard of St. John the Baptist in 2006 uncovered the remains of ten individuals: three adults and seven children. The individuals had been interred in coffins. Coffin furniture recovered from the graves included grip plates, coffin plates and nails. Upholstery nails and studs used to decorate coffins were also recovered. The coffins appear to have been made entirely of wood.

References
Smith 2006

Colewort Barracks, Portsmouth

Grid Reference	SZ 6335 9975
Cemetery type	Plague victims
Date of cemetery	Early–mid 17th century
Number of bodies excavated	Unknown
Date of excavation	1984

Excavations of the power station coal yard adjacent to St. George's Road, Portsmouth identified the remains of Colewort barracks and a number of burials. The chapel of St Mary was known to be situated in the area along with a burial ground known as Colewort Garden, which was in use until 1817. However, the burials are not thought to have been part of this burial ground but associated with the plague outbreak

References
ADS; Egan 1985:162

Cowdrey's Down, Basingstoke

Grid Reference	SU 656 533
Cemetery type	War burials
Date of cemetery	Possible Civil War burials
Number of bodies excavated	2
Date of excavation	1979

Two burials were uncovered in 1979. One was a mature male and the other of uncertain age and sex. There was little dating evidence apart from hobnails found in one of the graves and a sherd of late sixteenth- to seventeenth-century pottery. A post-medieval date for the burials was tentatively suggested.

References
Cherry 1979:273; Cherry 1980:205; Millett 1983

Land opposite Pinglestone Farm, Old Alresford

Grid Reference	SU 5820 3340
Cemetery type	Isolated burial
Date of cemetery	Early 17th century
Number of bodies excavated	1
Date of excavation	1997

Early seventeenth-century burial of a 30–40 year-old man lying supine in a shallow grave, with the head to the west, was found around 1km away from Old Alresford, and outside consecrated ground. Eight English silver coins, a copper alloy ring and an iron sewing ring were found in a group below the pelvis, possibly held in a purse or other container at the time of deposition. Two copper alloy lace tags or lace ends were found on the body. Staining indicated that they were originally next to the waist. They were probably originally attached to a doublet. A coin was also found in the throat region, and hand bones were also found by the skull suggesting that animals had disturbed the grave.

References
BIAB supp. 8/1997:707; Fitzpatrick and Laidlaw 2001

Lower Canal Walk, Southampton

Grid Reference	SU 4214 1110
Cemetery type	Isolated burial
Date of cemetery	Post-medieval
Number of bodies excavated	Unknown
Date of excavation	1957

An isolated skeleton, thought to be of post-medieval date, found on the site of a former bicycle warehouse

References
ADS

Porchester Castle

Grid Reference	SU 625 029
Cemetery type	Prison cemetery
Date of cemetery	Mid-18th century
Number of bodies excavated	5
Date of excavation	1971–2

Two grave pits were discovered; both had been partly destroyed by later rubbish pits. One pit contained the remains of three skeletons and the arm of a fourth. One of the skeletons was interred with a rosary. The second pit contained a single skeleton. The burials are thought to be associated with use of the castle to hold prisoners during the 7 years war in the eighteenth century.

References
Cherry 1971:197; Cherry 1973:100; Cunliffe and Garratt 1994

Rotherwick Church, Rotherwick, Hook

Grid Reference	SU 7120 5625
Cemetery type	Churchyard
Date of cemetery	Post-medieval
Number of bodies excavated	11
Date of excavation	2005

Eleven post-medieval graves, including partially preserved wooden coffins with brass fittings were observed. Some headstones were also recorded and an eighteenth- to nineteenth-century brick vault noted.

References
Pine 2005

Royal Naval Hospital, Haslar

Grid Reference	SZ 6150 9849
Cemetery type	Hospital cemetery
Date of cemetery	1753–1859
Number of bodies excavated	19
Date of excavation	2005

Nineteen burials from cemetery of Royal Naval Hospital at Haslar were recorded during an archaeological evaluation. The burials were male or of undetermined sex with some individuals being interred in coffins. Burials were very simple with no evidence for coffin fittings or other forms of adornment. One grave contained three individuals one above the other.

References
Boston 2005b

Solent Breezes, Fareham

Grid Reference	SU 49 04
Cemetery type	Isolated burial
Date of cemetery	18th-19th century
Number of bodies excavated	1
Date of excavation	1996

The shallow grave of a young female was found on a beach near Fareham lying between the low and high water marks. The remains are estimated to be between one and two hundred years old.

References
Howard 1996

St. James' Church, Bramley

Grid Reference	SU 6542 5899
Cemetery type	Churchyard
Date of cemetery	Post-medieval
Number of bodies excavated	22
Date of excavation	1993

Remains of twenty-two individuals, thought to be of post-medieval date, were recovered and reburied prior to the construction of a new church hall.

References
BIAB supp. 4:587

St. John's Church, French Street, Southampton

Grid Reference	SU 41 11
Cemetery type	Churchyard
Date of cemetery	Post-medieval
Number of bodies excavated	Unknown
Date of excavation	2000–1

Post-medieval cemetery and vault

References
ADS

St. Mary's Church, Hale

Grid Reference	SU 1784 1865
Cemetery type	Churchyard
Date of cemetery	Late 18th–mid-19th century
Number of bodies excavated	12
Date of excavation	2001

The brick burial vault of May family was recorded. It was built in 1792 within the existing transept, and closed in 1856. It contained twelve family members and one governess. The burials were left in place and the vault construction, coffins and coffin furniture recorded. At the west end, coffins were supported by an unusual pre-constructed iron framework made to fit the vault.

References
Ponsford 2002:216

St. Mary's Church, Overton

Grid Reference	SU 5148 4998
Cemetery type	Churchyard
Date of cemetery	Late 18th–early 20th century
Number of bodies excavated	92
Date of excavation	1994, 1998

A watching brief in 1994 to the north of the church led to the recovery of human remains dating to the late eighteenth and nineteenth century. There may have been earlier material present that was not so well preserved. In 1998, graves and brick vaults were noted during a watching brief to the north side of the church. The burials dated from 1790 to the 1880, with one twentieth-century grave. Nineteenth-century coffin furniture was recovered, mostly fragments of thin tin plating. The earliest datable burial was from 1843. Burial on the north side of the church began after 1790 after the burial of the Rev. Thomas. Subsequently prominent local families also buried in this area. This part of the churchyard therefore seems to have come into use at a later date than other parts.

References
Ponsford and Jackson 1995:115; Ponsford 2000:283; BIAB supp. 9:630

St. Mary's Church, Southampton

Grid Reference	SU 4262 1166
Cemetery type	Churchyard
Date of cemetery	Post-medieval
Number of bodies excavated	1+
Date of excavation	1999

Excavation revealed an articulated skeleton. A tomb containing disarticulated bone was also noted. Two deep grave cuts, which cut through earlier fills were also excavated and recorded.

References
BIAB 10.1/1999:469; Gifford and Partners 1999

St. Peter's Church, Soberton

Grid Reference	SU 6095 1680
Cemetery type	Churchyard
Date of cemetery	19th century or later
Number of bodies excavated	Unknown
Date of excavation	2003?

Archaeological evaluation prior to development to the north of the church uncovered nineteenth-century burials.

References
Ponsford 2004:290–1

St. Thomas' Church, Bedhampton, Havant

Grid Reference	SU 7025 0641
Cemetery type	Churchyard
Date of cemetery	Post-medieval
Number of bodies excavated	Unknown
Date of excavation	1992

A post-medieval feature was located in churchyard to north-east of church, containing the articulated and disarticulated remains of several individuals

References
BIAB supp 3/1992:194; Southern Archaeological Services Ltd 1992; Brading et al. 1993

Winchester Cathedral, Cathedral Green, Winchester

Grid Reference	SU 483 293
Cemetery type	Churchyard
Date of cemetery	Post-medieval
Number of bodies excavated	Unknown
Date of excavation	1970

Excavations on the site of the Wessex Hotel in 1961 and the eastern part of the Cathedral Green uncovered post-medieval burials and indicated the eastwards spread of the cathedral burial ground into those areas.

References
Moorhouse 1971:197; Biddle 1972; Kjolbye-Biddle 1992

Herefordshire

Civil War Mass Grave, Gasworks Lane, Ledbury

Grid Reference	SO 7040 3715
Cemetery type	War burials
Date of cemetery	17th century
Number of bodies excavated	Unknown
Date of excavation	19th century

A mass grave from the Civil War was uncovered during the building of the Hereford and Gloucester canal.

References
SMR record

Hereford Cathedral, Chapter House Yard

Grid Reference	SO 50 39
Cemetery type	Churchyard
Date of cemetery	Post-medieval
Number of bodies excavated	Unknown
Date of excavation	1999–2000

A number of interventions in the vicinity of the Cathedral have encountered burials, some dating to the post-medieval period, including a brick lined grave and lead lined coffin noted during test pitting and radar survey in 1993.

References
Stone 1993; Boucher and Hovered 1997; Boucher 2000; ADS; Boucher and Crooks 2001; BIAB supp. 8/1997:334

Kingdom Hall (former), South Street, Leominster

Grid Reference	SO 4962 5883
Cemetery type	Quaker burial ground
Date of cemetery	1660–1904
Number of bodies excavated	40
Date of excavation	1994

Part of the burial ground associated with the meeting house of the Society of Friends was found to the east of the meeting house. It was in use from 1660 to c.1904 and was densely packed with graves aligned west-east. Evidence of 40 burials was recovered and all were left in situ. Much disarticulated bone was also present. The probable town ditch was also obscured by and cut by many graves.

References
BIAB supp. 5/1994:297–8; Napthan 1994; Ponsford and Jackson 1995:115; ADS; SMR record

Post-medieval churchyard, St. Mary's, Ross-on-Wye

Grid Reference	SO 5979 2405
Cemetery type	Churchyard
Date of cemetery	Post-medieval
Number of bodies excavated	Unknown
Date of excavation	1991

Evaluation trenches in the churchyard revealed post-medieval inhumations.

References
Jones 1991; ADS; SMR record

St. Guthlac's in Hereford Castle, Castle Green

Grid Reference	SO 5124 3956
Cemetery type	Churchyard
Date of cemetery	18th century
Number of bodies excavated	Unknown
Date of excavation	1960

Limited excavations in 1960 uncovered an early cemetery and some eighteenth-century burials.

References
Heys 1958–60; Shoesmith 1980a

St. Peter's Church, Ipsley, Redditch

Grid Reference	SP 06 66
Cemetery type	Churchyard
Date of cemetery	19th–20th century
Number of bodies excavated	Unknown
Date of excavation	1993

Some nineteenth- to early twentieth-century inhumations were removed and reburied during a watching brief.

References
BIAB supp. 4/1993:625; Wichbold and Brown 1993

The Church, Moreton Jefferies

Grid Reference	SO 60 48
Cemetery type	Churchyard
Date of cemetery	Post-medieval
Number of bodies excavated	Unknown
Date of excavation	1999

Crypt containing post-medieval coffins

References
ADS; Appleton-Fox 1999

Hertfordshire

Tilehouse Street Baptist Churchyard, Hitchin

Grid Reference	TL 1811 2895
Cemetery type	Churchyard
Date of cemetery	17th century onwards
Number of bodies excavated	Unknown
Date of excavation	1978

Grave memorials were surveyed in 1978 and graves dating to between 1702 and 1939 were recorded during 1979. The original chapel existed between 1692 and 1843 when it was replaced by a larger church in a different part of the churchyard. Majority of burials were interred before 1850. Several types of burials were recorded. These included simple wood coffins in unmarked earth graves and a large number of burials, often in elaborate wood and lead coffins, in well-made brick family vaults. About 150 memorial stones were recorded, of which c.85 were in situ. Many graves had no marker.

References
Cherry 1980:205–6

Kent

Bell Vault, Milton Church, Thanington Without

Grid Reference	TR 12043 55693
Cemetery type	Churchyard
Date of cemetery	1820s–1850s
Number of bodies excavated	Unknown
Date of excavation	Unknown

Three of the coffins within the Bell vault dated to 1827, 1836 and 1855 provide a good illustration of changes in coffin styles during the nineteenth century.

References
Litten 1991

Canterbury Cathedral

Grid Reference	TR 15 57
Cemetery type	Churchyard
Date of cemetery	16th–18th century
Number of bodies excavated	6
Date of excavation	1993

During excavations in the nave of the cathedral, six in situ burials were uncovered dating to the sixteenth to eighteenth centuries. Three were in lead coffins that narrowed towards the foot. None of the coffins were opened. Three in situ burials with evidence for wooden coffins were also observed including one burial surrounded by clench nails.

References
Blockley, Sparks and Tatton-Brown 1997

Culpepper vault, Hollingbourne

Grid Reference	TQ 842 551
Cemetery type	Churchyard
Date of cemetery	17th century
Number of bodies excavated	Unknown
Date of excavation	Unknown

The Culpepper vault in Hollingbourne Church contains a number of seventeenth-century lead coffins without outer wooden cases. The coffins were decorated with incised or appliqué inscriptions and decorative lead work.

References
Litten 1991

East Barracks, Deal

Grid Reference	TR 3760 5190
Cemetery type	Hospital cemetery
Date of cemetery	1795–c.1860
Number of bodies excavated	16
Date of excavation	1999

Human remains were recovered from the area of the former Royal Naval Hospital (1795–c.1860). The graves of four children and five adults (three male and two unsexed) were located within the known burial ground of the hospital. One of the adult male skeletons showed evidence of cranial surgery suggestive of autopsy. The top of the cranium had been removed and was not found with the body. This burial dates to between 1812 and the 1860s. Nineteen grave markers (some still legible) are still standing in the burial ground. A further seven burials (two juvenile and five adults) were found behind the hospital to the north, lying outside the limits of the later burial ground. These are likely to have been associated with the earlier Naval Hospital, prior to the purchase of the hospital by the Admiralty. It is suggested that patients were mostly British servicemen and some Russian prisoners of war.

References
ADS; BIAB supp. 10.2/1999:883; Parfitt 1999; Parfitt 2000; Anderson 2002

River Parish Church, River, near Dover

Grid Reference	TR 2905 4346
Cemetery type	Churchyard
Date of cemetery	17th century onwards
Number of bodies excavated	Unknown
Date of excavation	1998

Several burials and grave shafts were noted, dating to seventeenth century and later.

References
BIAB supp. 9/1998:350; Canterbury Archaeological Trust 1998

Rochester Cathedral

Grid Reference	TQ 743 685
Cemetery type	Churchyard
Date of cemetery	Post-medieval
Number of bodies excavated	63
Date of excavation	1990

Excavations in the former lay cemetery of Rochester Cathedral revealed 63 burials of which 35 are thought to be of post-medieval date. Two skeletons lay on layers of bitumen from the bases of their coffins. Coffin fittings were observed with some of the burials. The remains of an infant were found lying on the knee of an adult skeleton.

References
Ward and Anderson 1990; Ponsford 1991:115

St. George's Clocktower

Grid Reference	TR 15 57
Cemetery type	Churchyard
Date of cemetery	Post-medieval
Number of bodies excavated	Unknown
Date of excavation	1991

Excavations prior to a retail development revealed a large number of post-medieval burials associated with St. George's Church.

References
Bennett, Houliston and Ward n.d.

St. Mary's Church, Chilham

Grid Reference	TR 0688 5365
Cemetery type	Churchyard
Date of cemetery	16th–early 17th century
Number of bodies excavated	1
Date of excavation	2002

Graves and human remains were exposed. One was dated through associated pottery to the sixteenth or early seventeenth century.

References
Linklater 2004

St. Michael and All Angels Church, Wilmington, Dartford

Grid Reference	TQ 5381 7348
Cemetery type	Churchyard
Date of cemetery	Post-medieval
Number of bodies excavated	Unknown
Date of excavation	1999

Construction of a new church building revealed post-medieval burials.

References
BIAB supp. 10.2/1999; Hutchings 1999

St. Nicholas, Sevenoaks Church

Grid Reference	TQ 5312 5431
Cemetery type	Churchyard

Date of cemetery	1550–1875
Number of bodies excavated	256
Date of excavation	1993

Excavation of the interior of St. Nicholas' Church, Sevenoaks revealed 256 burials dating from 1550 to 1875. Eighteenth- and nineteenth-century human remains were removed by a commercial clearance company. Low resolution recording took place during this process. As at Spitalfields, the sequence of coffins within vaults was often reversed. Two pairs of dentures were recovered from the lead coffin of Maria West buried in 1785. They included real teeth as well as teeth made from porcelain. A number of wooden coffins dating to the eighteenth and nineteenth centuries contained flower petals, located both above and below the human remains. Floral wreaths were also noted, as were bunches of lavender and rosemary in the coffin of Peter Nouaille, a Huguenot who died 1845 aged 79. The body of nighteenth-century silk weaver was buried in a darned hooded cotton nightshirt. A facecloth and knitted nightcap were also recorded.

References
Boyle 1995; Boyle and Keevill 1998

The Roper Chantry, St. Dunstan's Church, Canterbury

Grid Reference	TR 1424 5831
Cemetery type	Churchyard
Date of cemetery	Early 18th-century burials
Number of bodies excavated	5 and a head
Date of excavation	1978

The main burial vault of the Roper family in their Chantry Chapel was opened and recorded in 1978. The vault contained five lead coffins and a number of lead coffin plates dating to the first half of the eighteenth century. Iron handles were attached to one lead coffin, while a hole in another coffin allowed the corpse wrapped in a shroud to be observed. It is possible that at least one of the coffins may have had an outer wooden shell. The coffins were laid on a floor of unmortared bricks embedded in sand. A small brick lined cist of charnel pit was cut into the floor at the south end of the vault. The pit had been covered by a wooden lid. The wood does not survive but the corroded remains of two iron rings used to raise the lid survive in situ. The pit contained the disarticulated remains of at least eight skeletons, possibly the remains of earlier occupants of the vault relocated to make space for later interments. A lead box containing the fragmentary remains of a human skull was found in a niche in the north wall behind an iron grate. Head thought to be that of Sir Thomas More as his daughter married into the Roper family and the head is reputed to have been placed on her coffin in the vault.

References
Tatton-Brown 1980

Lancashire

Bury Central Methodist Church, Union Street, Bury, Greater Manchester

Grid Reference	SD 8060 1070
Cemetery type	Churchyard
Date of cemetery	Post-medieval
Number of bodies excavated	Unknown
Date of excavation	1999

In situ human remains were revealed for later exhumation.

References
BIAB 10.1/1999:405; Mottershead 1999

Cathedral Yard, Manchester

Grid Reference	SJ 8387 9871
Cemetery type	Churchyard
Date of cemetery	Post-medieval
Number of bodies excavated	Unknown
Date of excavation	1999

Inhumations were recovered from along the length of Cathedral Yard.

References
BIAB 10.1/1999:406; University of Manchester Archaeological Unit 1999

Church of St. Laurence, Chorley

Grid Reference	SD 5830 1170
Cemetery type	Churchyard
Date of cemetery	19th century
Number of bodies excavated	Unknown
Date of excavation	1997

A two-chambered brick vault contained nineteenth-century burials, some in lead coffins, and a large amount of disarticulated human bone. Most of the human remains were disturbed, but two undisturbed graves were also recorded.

References
ADS; BIAB supp. 8/1997:766–7; Plummer and Scott 1997

St. Anne's Parish Church, Copp, Great Eccleston

Grid Reference	SD 4211 3946
Cemetery type	Churchyard
Date of cemetery	19th century
Number of bodies excavated	4
Date of excavation	2002?

Unmarked nineteenth-century graves were located. Four were recorded.

References
Ponsford 2003:283

St. Bartholomew's Church, Westhoughton, Greater Manchester

Grid Reference	SD 5620 0600
Cemetery type	Churchyard
Date of cemetery	18th–19th century
Number of bodies excavated	Unknown
Date of excavation	1994

An evaluation in advance of demolition and rebuilding led to the identification of three phases of burial activity. Phase 1 dated to the period of the 1731 chapel that previously existed on the site and its associated graves. Phase 2 encompassed a line of burial vaults probably dating from c1825 rebuilding. Phase 3 dated to the 1870 church which stood on the site at the time of the archaeological recording.

References
BIAB supp. 5/1994:284; Fletcher 1994

St. Thomas the Martyr Church, Up Holland

Grid Reference	SD 5240 0510
Cemetery type	Churchyard
Date of cemetery	Possibly 18th century
Number of bodies excavated	2
Date of excavation	1995

Two poorly preserved burials, probably eighteenth century or earlier were identified. Pottery of medieval and later date and clay pipe fragments were also retrieved.

Leicestershire

Church of St. Mary and St. Hardulph, Breedon on the Hill

Grid Reference	SK 405 233
Cemetery type	Churchyard
Date of cemetery	Post-medieval
Number of bodies excavated	c.70
Date of excavation	1987

Excavations to the south and the east of church located 70 post-medieval burials.

References
Youngs, Gaimster and Barry 1988: 260

Church of St. Mary the Virgin, Ashby Road, Coleorton

Grid Reference	SK 404 175
Cemetery type	Churchyard
Date of cemetery	Post-medieval
Number of bodies excavated	Unknown
Date of excavation	1997

Post-medieval human remains were found at intervals within service trench.

References
ADS

East Bond Street Congregational Chapel

Grid Reference	SK 5855 0474
Cemetery type	Non-conformist burial ground
Date of cemetery	1824–1890
Number of bodies excavated	101
Date of excavation	2006

More than 100 nineteenth-century burials were uncovered during excavations at the Bond Street Congregational Chapel. The burials were interred in coffins, many with coffin fittings and coffin plates in earth graves and brick-lined grave shafts. Organic preservation was good with survival of wood from coffins and fabric covered coffins. One coffin contained wood shavings and fabric, possibly acting as a pillow. The inside of a number of brick-lined graves were painted in a variety of colours.

References
Jacklin 2006a

Ebenezer Chapel

Grid Reference	SK 5844 0472
Cemetery type	Non-conformist burial ground
Date of cemetery	1802–late 19th century
Number of bodies excavated	75
Date of excavation	2006

Seventy-five nineteenth-century burials were uncovered during excavations at Ebenezer Chapel. The burials were interred in wooden coffins either in earth graves or in brick-lined graves. Many of the coffins were accompanied with coffin fittings and coffin plates. Shroud pins and buttons were recovered from many graves. One burial had pennies covering both eyes.

References
Jacklin 2006b

Haymarket Towers, Leicester

Grid Reference	SK 58 04
Cemetery type	Non-conformist burial ground
Date of cemetery	19th century
Number of bodies excavated	4
Date of excavation	1996–7

Five graves containing four skeletons were uncovered during an watching brief and archaeological recording at Haymarket Towers. The burials are remnants of the graveyard of the Congregation Chapel. Two of the individuals lay in a brick built grave vault and there was an infant burial in a wooden coffin.

References
Cooper 1998

Leicester Castle

Grid Reference	SK 582 041
Cemetery type	Churchyard/Plague burials
Date of cemetery	17th century?
Number of bodies excavated	Unknown
Date of excavation	1951

Excavations in 1951 on Castle View revealed human inhumation burials cut into the castle ditch fills without coffins or grave goods and laid in rows with their feet to the east. Documentary references suggest these may be plague burials. Excavations in the castle yard in 1994 uncovered four burials and a quantity of disarticulated bone. Human remains are thought to have once been part of the medieval to post-medieval cemetery of St. Mary de Castro.

References
Mackie 1994

St. Peter's Church, Belgrave, Leicester

Grid Reference	SK 5929 0716
Cemetery type	Churchyard
Date of cemetery	Post-medieval
Number of bodies excavated	Unknown
Date of excavation	1999?

Articulated and disarticulated human remains noted.

References
BIAB supp. 10.2/1999:629; Chapman 1999

The Guildhall, Leicester

Grid Reference	SK 5845 0444
Cemetery type	Churchyard
Date of cemetery	1760–1849
Number of bodies excavated	Unknown
Date of excavation	1993–5

Eighteenth and nineteenth-century burials from the Western Burial ground, formerly part of the graveyard of St. Martin's Cathedral, were uncovered. Some burial were accompanied by coffin name plates. Most bone recovered was disarticulated, and thought to represent a minimum number of 125 individuals. The position of two lead coffins was also noted.

References
BIAB supp. 4/1993:317; Lucas 1993a; Lucas 1993b; Wakely and Smith 1998

Vine Street Baptist Chapel

Grid Reference	SK 5835 0490
Cemetery type	Baptist burial ground
Date of cemetery	19th century

References
ADS; BIAB supp. 6/1995:297–8; Hair 1995

Number of bodies excavated	Unknown
Date of excavation	2006

Ten burials, and an infant in a casket, were excavated. All were orientated north-south and in coffins with fittings. Most burials were to the north of the chapel.

References
University of Leicester Archaeological Services n.d.

Lincolnshire

64 Steep Hill, Lincoln

Grid Reference	SK 97 71
Cemetery type	Unknown
Date of cemetery	Post-medieval
Number of bodies excavated	Unknown
Date of excavation	1978

Human remains observed during re-flooring are thought to be part of a post-medieval cemetery.

References
ADS

Church of St. Mary and St. Nicholas, Spalding

Grid Reference	TF 2503 2242
Cemetery type	Churchyard
Date of cemetery	Medieval–Post-medieval
Number of bodies excavated	35
Date of excavation	1998

Excavations revealed thirty-five closely packed and inter-cutting medieval and post-medieval burials.

References
BIAB supp. 9/1998:750; Moore 1998

Lincoln Castle Service Trenching, Lincoln

Grid Reference	SK 9747 7187
Cemetery type	Unknown
Date of cemetery	Post-medieval
Number of bodies excavated	Unknown
Date of excavation	1993

Burials from debtor's graveyard, along with features associated with the former prison were noted in the service trench.

References
BIAB supp. 4/1993:675; Donel 1993

Sincil Bank West/ Pennell Street, Lincoln

Grid Reference	SK 97 70
Cemetery type	Unknown
Date of cemetery	Post-medieval
Number of bodies excavated	Unknown
Date of excavation	1992–3

Post-medieval human remains noted

References
ADS; Wragg 1993

St. James' Church, Louth, East Lindsey

Grid Reference	TF 3265 8737
Cemetery type	Churchyard
Date of cemetery	Post-medieval
Number of bodies excavated	23
Date of excavation	1999?

Twenty-three burials and a large amount of disarticulated human bone was revealed and later reburied

References
BIAB supp. 10.2/1999:643; Snee 1999

St. Mark's Church and Cemetery, Lincoln

Grid Reference	SK 97377081
Cemetery type	Churchyard
Date of cemetery	Mid-16th century–c.1871
Number of bodies excavated	187
Date of excavation	1976–7

The site of medieval parish church of St. Mark's was excavated. The church lies south of Lincoln's walled centre in the suburb of Wigford. One hundred and eighty-seven post-medieval burials were excavated. Fourteen were dated to the sixteenth and seventeenth centuries. These included two burials in an unmortared cist and a single burial in the south porch floor. Another burial within the church was associated with traces of a wooden coffin. One of the burials outside the church was accompanied by traces of a wooden coffin and brass coffin studs.

Sixty-four burials were dated to c.1720–1786. Although some of the buried were in wooden coffins, the majority of these burials lack any evidence for a coffin. A large brick vault with three lead coffins lay in the south-east corner of the chancel. Another vault containing four lead coffins lay on the south side of the north-east chapel.

One hundred and two burials were dated to c.1786–1871. A number of these burials contained evidence for wooden coffins, often accompanied by iron handles and other coffin fittings. Five brick-lined graves lay to the south of the church, one of which contained two burials, the upper being supported by a course of stone slabs. Another two burials were contained in the remains of what had been a multiple vault. Seven burials were dated to the period 1871–2; three had wooden coffins.

References
Gilmour and Stocker 1986

St. Peter and St. Paul's Church, Healing

Grid Reference	TA 21 10
Cemetery type	Churchyard
Date of cemetery	18th–19th century
Number of bodies excavated	Unknown
Date of excavation	1975

Human remains were excavated at the church of Saints Peter and Paul. A bone pit was found next to the south exterior wall. Another small pit had been dug into a bank of redeposited natural material. Coffin plates from the eighteenth to nineteenth centuries were recorded. They were made of tin or silvered tin. Silvered iron coffin handles decorated with two cherubs were also recorded

References
Bishop 1978

St. Peter's Church, Barton-upon-Humber

Grid Reference	TA 0347 2194
Cemetery type	Churchyard
Date of cemetery	Post-medieval
Number of bodies excavated	Unknown
Date of excavation	1978–81

Several hundred post medieval burials were excavated from graves and vaults within the nave and aisles of St Peter's and from outside the church, south of the tower. Although the graves produced few coffin plates or grips, a number of nineteenth-century burials were found with grave goods including coins and a fob watch. Two bodies were found wearing leather trusses, and two were buried with porcelain vessels. Evidence for autopsy was found in one burial. The spinal column and ribcage had been completely removed. A charred wooden stake had been placed in the body to replace the spine. The top of the skull had been removed and then subsequently glued back in place.

References
Rodwell and Rodwell 1982; Waldron 2007

London

1 Watling Street, City of London

Grid Reference	TQ 3226 8108
Cemetery type	Churchyard
Date of cemetery	17th century
Number of bodies excavated	Unknown
Date of excavation	1954

Excavations by Guildhall Museum in 1954 revealed the burial ground associated with the Church of St. John the Evangelist. Seventeenth-century coffins and inhumations were recorded, as were charnel pits.

References
SMR record

1, Poultry (site of St. Benet Sherehog), City of London

Grid Reference	TQ 3258 8110
Cemetery type	Churchyard
Date of cemetery	c.1666–19th century
Number of bodies excavated	212
Date of excavation	1994

Over 200 burials post-dating the Great Fire were excavated from the site of St Benet Sherehog, a medieval church destroyed in the fire. While the church was not rebuilt, its burial ground continued in use as an additional place of burial for the parishes of St Benet's and St Stephen Walbrook until the mid-19th century. All burials were within wooden coffins, many with metal fittings and some with name plates. The family vault of Michael Davison Esq. (d. 1676), which contained two lead coffins and three wooden coffins, and the monument to Mayor John Maurois (d. 1673) were also recorded. Evidence for autopsy was present

References
Ponsford and Jackson 1995:115; BIAB supp. 5/1994:567; Rowsome 2000; Miles and White 2008

179–181 Whitechapel Road E1

Grid Reference	SU 7025 0641
Cemetery type	Workhouse
Date of cemetery	18th–19th century
Number of bodies excavated	60
Date of excavation	2006/7

Sixty burials thought to be associated with the Whitechapel workhouse were excavated.

References
Greater London Archaeology Advisory Service Annual Review 2007 http://www.english-heritage.org.uk/content/imported-docs/f-j/glaas-2007tagged.pdf

21–29 Mansell Street, E1, City of London

Grid Reference	TQ 33810 81190
Cemetery type	Non-conformist burial ground
Date of cemetery	18th century
Number of bodies excavated	100
Date of excavation	1982

One hundred burials were found on the north side of a wall, which presumably bounded the eighteenth-century non-conformist burial ground that is historically documented in the area. Most remains were found stacked in wooden coffins (up to nine deep), organised in close rows. Ages have been estimated for 74 individuals, of which 57 were adults, seven children, and ten infants.

References
Egan 1983:191

252b Gray's Inn Road, Camden

Grid Reference	TQ 3076 8237
Cemetery type	Churchyard
Date of cemetery	1754–1853
Number of bodies excavated	Unknown
Date of excavation	1993

A watching brief was conducted in the area of the detached burial ground of St Andrew's Holborn, which was in use during the period 1754–1853. The burial ground had already been partially cleared, probably between 1871 and 1896, but the deepest burials had been left in situ. Coffins were noted and left undisturbed and a brick burial vault of the late eighteenth to early nineteenth-centuries, together with undisturbed contents, was also noted. Disarticulated bone from the graveyard soil was collected for reburial. Some gravestones were also recorded.

References
Ponsford 1994:120; BIAB supp. 4/1993:549

31–32 Ely Place, Camden

Grid Reference	TQ 3146 8164
Cemetery type	Prison cemetery
Date of cemetery	Post-medieval, possibly civil war
Number of bodies excavated	Unknown
Date of excavation	1990/1?

Excavations revealed a number of skeletons including two possibly dating to Civil War period when the site was used as a prison and hospital.

References
ADS; Ponsford 1991:130–1

36–44 Gower's Walk

Grid Reference	TQ 3417 8116
Cemetery type	Non-conformist burial ground
Date of cemetery	Post-medieval
Number of bodies excavated	Unknown
Date of excavation	2005

MoLAS excavated two areas in Gower's Walk. The second area revealed a section of a dissenter's burial ground with a test pit revealing an in situ west-east burial in a wooden coffin.

References
Hoad 1989

37–39 Artillery Lane

Grid Reference	TQ 335 817
Cemetery type	Epidemic disease
Date of cemetery	17th century or earlier
Number of bodies excavated	Unknown
Date of excavation	1976

Remains of a plague pit exposed and recorded during building works.

References
Cherry 1977:91

43–51 St. Mary Axe, City of London

Grid Reference	TQ 3327 8132
Cemetery type	Churchyard
Date of cemetery	Medieval/post-medieval
Number of bodies excavated	9 + disarticulate
Date of excavation	1950–1

Building work in 1950–1 uncovered a pit containing 150 skeletons. A nineteenth-century clay pipe was found at the bottom of the pit suggesting that the bones were found and reinterred in 1860 when an office building was constructed on the churchyard of St. Mary Axe. Excavation in 1989–90 by MoLAS revealed nine burials and rediscovered the charnel pit seen in 1950–1.

References
SMR record

61, Queen Street/Upper Thames Street (site of St. Martin Vintry Church) EC4, City of London

Grid Reference	TQ 32452 80843
Cemetery type	Churchyard
Date of cemetery	17th century
Number of bodies excavated	1
Date of excavation	1956–7

1956–7 excavations found a complete London delftware plate, c.1680, inverted over abdomen of male skeleton in a coffin.

References
Noel Hume 1974; Cohen 1995

75–82 Farringdon Street (St Bride's Lower Churchyard) EC4

Grid Reference	TQ 3158 8132
Cemetery type	Churchyard
Date of cemetery	1770–1849
Number of bodies excavated	606
Date of excavation	1991–2

606 burials dating from between 1770 and 1849 were recovered from a burial ground founded in 1610. Most were buried in elm coffins stacked up to eight deep, in nine intercutting north-south rows across site. A brick burial vault at the west end of the site contained 47 coffined burials and 75 individuals pushed to far end of vault to create more space. Twenty-two individuals exhibiting evidence of autopsy were found, all eighteenth to early nineteenth century in date.

References
http://www.museumoflondon.org.uk/English/Collections/Online Resources/CHB/Database/Post-medieval+cemeteries/St+Brides +lower.htm; Ponsford 1993:229; Greenwood and Maloney 1993: 48

9, St. Clare Street, EC3, City of London

Grid Reference	TQ 3372 8106
Cemetery type	Churchyard
Date of cemetery	Post-medieval
Number of bodies excavated	Unknown
Date of excavation	1983

Post-medieval burials found cutting medieval deposits.

References
Thompson, Westman and Dyson 1998:248; Richardson 1984:390–1; Ellis 1985:115–21

95–105 Back Church Lane, E1/109–153 Backchurch Lane, E1

Grid Reference	TQ 3421 8124
Cemetery type	Private burial ground
Date of cemetery	c.1776–1854–6
Number of bodies excavated	Unknown
Date of excavation	1988, 1993

Excavations were conducted on the site of a private burial ground established in the late eighteenth century and closed in 1855–57. Burials were found in stacks of four to seven coffins deep. Some of the coffins contained sawdust or animal hair/straw pillows

References
Girardon and Heathcote1989: 79; Roche 1989; Watson 1993; Thompson, Westman and Dyson 1998:238;

All Hallows by the Tower Churchyard, Bywater Street

Grid Reference	TQ 3337 8068
Cemetery type	Churchyard
Date of cemetery	19th century
Number of bodies excavated	Unknown
Date of excavation	1996

A nineteenth-century brick vault was noted in 1996, along with disturbed human remains and other graveyard deposits. Excavations in 1999 recovered inhumations, coffins and coffin furniture. Three examples of post-mortem or autopsy were encountered. The upper part of the skulls had been sawn and removed, but there was no evidence on the ribs or sternum.

References
ADS; Ponsford and Jackson 1997:257; Maloney 2000:35–63

All Saints Parish Church, Church Street, West Ham, Newham

Grid Reference	TQ 3728 7748
Cemetery type	Churchyard
Date of cemetery	Late 18th–19th century
Number of bodies excavated	Unknown
Date of excavation	1984, 2001

Archaeological recording of brick burials vaults and burials was undertaken.

References
Egan 1985:161; Ponsford 2002:204; Maloney 2001:84

Anderson's Yard, Islington

Grid Reference	TQ 3175 8370
Cemetery type	Private burial ground
Date of cemetery	1788–1853
Number of bodies excavated	Unknown
Date of excavation	1993

The site includes the probable remains of 'Jones Burial Ground' a private profit-making cemetery founded in 1788 by the minister of the nearby chapel on Gaskin Street. When the ground was closed in 1853, a number of bodies were exhumed for reburial elsewhere. Empty grave cuts were located, cut into the original ground surface. Also in situ wooden coffins were found in the deeper waterlogged parts of the site, with disarticulated human remains and coffin fragments above this.

References
Ponsford 1994:121

Artillery Ground, Spitalfields Market

Grid Reference	TQ 334 819
Cemetery type	Isolated burial
Date of cemetery	1640–1650s?
Number of bodies excavated	2
Date of excavation	1991–2007

Two adult males were found in north-south orientated graves placed between the star fort and the boundary wall of the artillery ground. The burials appear to post-date the star fort and these individuals are thought to have been members of one of groups using the artillery ground, killed in either a military accident or during the failed Presbyterian and City backed counter revolution against Parliament in 1647.

References
Holder and Jeffries forthcoming

Billingsgate Lorry Park, Lower Thames Street, City of London

Grid Reference	TQ 3300 8065
Cemetery type	Churchyard
Date of cemetery	15th–17th century
Number of bodies excavated	50+
Date of excavation	1982

Excavations in area of the former church of St Botolph (church destroyed in the Great Fire) recorded some high-status burials beneath the floor, some dating to the mid fifteenth to seventeenth century. These produced evidence of shrouds and coffins (sometimes decorated with copper studs), and iron coffin furniture. Coffin nails on one coffin were arranged into the date 1665. A number of burials found in voids indicative of coffins.

References
Egan 1983:185; Richardson 1983:274

Bishop Challenor's School, Commercial Road, Tower Hamlets

Grid Reference	TQ 3535 8115
Cemetery type	Catholic burial ground
Date of cemetery	1843–1854
Number of bodies excavated	742
Date of excavation	2004/5

Excavation of the former burial ground on the south side of the Roman Catholic Church of St Mary's and St Michael's which was in use for eleven years during the nineteenth century. Seven hundred and forty two burials in wooden coffins were excavated. They had been placed in deep graves, stacked upon one another (adults at the bottom children and infants on the top), but with no inter-cutting of the graves and the excavator suggests that this indicates a well planned and laid out cemetery. Dates from the coffin plates suggest that each day represents a single day's burials. There was also very little disarticulated human bone in the graveyard soil. The skeletal remains were well preserved, including a large number of infants in the uppermost layers of burials. Approximately one-quarter of burials contained legible coffin plates. Some grave goods, including crucifixes, have been noted, together with fragments of clothing. Evidence of autopsies was also recorded.

References
Powers 2005; Miles and Powers 2006

Bow Baptist Church Burial Ground, Payne Road, Tower Hamlets

Grid Reference	TQ 37698 83071
Cemetery type	Non-conformist burial ground
Date of cemetery	1810–1837
Number of bodies excavated	348
Date of excavation	2005–2006

Three hundred and forty eight burials from the Bow Baptist Church Burial Ground were uncovered during excavations at Payne Road in 2006. All burials were orientated west to east, with the majority interred in wooden coffins although seven lead coffins were recovered: two from the general burial ground and five from one of the two brick lined vaults. The presence of buttons and other types of clothing fasteners indicate that a few individuals had been interred in clothes. Tortoiseshell combs were found in two graves and coins had been placed on the body of a few burials. One example of autopsy was recorded.

References
Miles and Powers 2007

Brentford Free Church, Boston Manor Road, Brentford, Hounslow, Greater London

Grid Reference	TQ 1770 7765
Cemetery type	Non-conformist burial ground
Date of cemetery	1782–1856
Number of bodies excavated	23
Date of excavation	1999

The commercial clearance of the churchyard and recording of eight brick burial vaults was undertaken in 1999. Twenty-three coffins were recorded ranging in date from the late eighteenth to mid nineteenth century. Twelve coffins had legible plates. Some of the vaults had been cleared in the late nineteenth century and mid-twentieth century.

References
Cohen 1999; Ponsford 2000:249; BIAB supp 10.2/1999:791

Burial ground of St. John of Wapping Church

Grid Reference	TQ 34650 80125
Cemetery type	Churchyard
Date of cemetery	Post-medieval
Number of bodies excavated	c.430
Date of excavation	1997–8

The church began as a chapel of ease, becoming a parish church in 1694. It was built on swampy land and became unusable by the mid-eighteenth century although the site continued in use as the main parish burial ground until 1854. The commercial clearance of the burial ground of St Johns was monitored. Around 430 burials were exhumed, of which 126 had legible coffin plates. A communal burial vault in the northeast corner of the site contained forty-one separate coffins. Ten family burial vaults were also located along the south boundary wall containing forty-four coffins. A re-interment pit was noted in the centre of the southern part of the site, which contained the disarticulated remains of over 1,700 individuals. Disarticulated bone representing approximately 100 individuals was also found in a construction trench around the apse of the church. Dating evidence suggests most of the excavated burials are from mid-18th to mid-19th century.

References
Ponsford and Jackson 1998:145–6; Miles 1998

Campbell's Tomb, St. Margaret's Church, Barking and Dagenham

Grid Reference	TQ 44084 83905
Cemetery type	Churchyard
Date of cemetery	Post-medieval
Number of bodies excavated	Unknown
Date of excavation	1985

A brick vault, built in 1645, was found during excavations at the eastern end of of St. Margaret's Parish church. Eight coffins were removed and examined along with a quantity of disarticulated bone.

References
ADS; Richardson 1986:157

Chelsea Old Church (St. Luke's), 2–4 Old Church Street, Kensington and Chelsea

Grid Reference	TQ 2708 7765
Cemetery type	Churchyard
Date of cemetery	Late 17th–mid 19th century?
Number of bodies excavated	288
Date of excavation	1999, 2000

Archaeological excavations were undertaken in the post-medieval cemetery and burial vault in the churchyard of Chelsea Old Church. A total of 290 skeletons were recovered dating from the end of the seventeenth century to the mid nineteenth century, including two foetuses. Two brick burial vaults and two brick built tombs were present in the churchyard. Many of the graves contained several stacked burials. Most of the coffins were of wood, surviving only as dark brown organic deposits. Nine lead coffins were also recovered. Coffin plates and other coffin fittings accompanied many of the burials. Nineteen individuals could be identified, at least in part, from coffin plates, including two members of the Hand family. A further seven were identified from other sources. Fragments of textiles were recovered from several burials. Other associated finds include coins, pins and fastenings from clothing.

References
ADS; Ponsford 2001:148; Ponsford 2002:201; Maloncy and Holroyd 2002:17–8; Cowie et al. 2008

Christ Church Burial Ground, Newgate Street, City of London

Grid Reference	TQ 3194 8137
Cemetery type	Churchyard
Date of cemetery	18th–19th century
Number of bodies excavated	12
Date of excavation	1998/9?

After the Reformation the conventual church of the Christchurch Greyfriars was used as a parish church and was then rebuilt by Wren in 1704. Excavations in south aisle of the church in 1976 uncovered nine damaged lead coffins. Six had inscriptions dating from 1770 to 1803. In addition three burials in wooden coffins were also identified, possibly also of post-medieval date.

References
Herbert 1979; Ponsford 2000:239; Richardson 1982:161; Filer 1991a:273

Christ Church, Spitalfields

Grid Reference	TQ 3377 8178
Cemetery type	Churchyard
Date of cemetery	1729–1867
Number of bodies excavated	1000+
Date of excavation	1984, 2003

In 1984, the first major church crypt excavation project exhumed 983 individuals, all of whom had been placed in the vault between 1729 and 1867. Of these almost half were identified from accompanying coffin plates. The vast majority of coffins were the single break type, with single, double and triple shelled examples recovered. Coffins were of wood or wood and lead with one iron example. Large quantities of coffin fittings of lead, iron and brass accompanied the burials. Other coffin types included one trapezoid coffin and three rectangular examples. Most of the coffins were covered in fabric although a few had been painted or limewashed. Textile preservation was good allowing the recovery of shrouds, funerary clothing, pillows and mattresses. Although grave goods were uncommon, jewellery, coins and a small wooden barrel were found within the coffins. In 2003, a further 78 burials were exhumed from three small crypts at the east end of the Church, 23 in lead coffins with 22 individuals identified from coffin plates. Some infant bones were also found within the vault.

References
Cox, Molleson and Waldron 1990; Molleson and Cox 1993; Reeve and Adams 1993; Cox 1996, 1998; Ponsford 2004:280

City Bunhill Burial Ground, Golden Lane/Whitecross Street.

Grid Reference	TQ 32390 82040
Cemetery type	Non-conformist burial ground
Date of cemetery	Post-medieval
Number of bodies excavated	248
Date of excavation	2006

A total of 248 burials were recorded during the excavation of part of the burial ground, which was founded in the seventeenth century. All burials were aligned west to east, and had been interred in wooden coffins. No intercutting of burials was observed. Information was obtained on 20 burials from accompanying coffin plates.

References
www.molas.org.uk

College Hill, EC4

Grid Reference	TQ 3250 8087
Cemetery type	Churchyard
Date of cemetery	18th–19th century?
Number of bodies excavated	24
Date of excavation	1949

Excavations in 1949 revealed 24 burials, thought to be eighteenth-nineteenth century on the south-east area of the church. Human bones and coffins were recorded.

References
Greater London SMR

Craven Street

Grid Reference	TQ 302 804
Cemetery type	Medical waste
Date of cemetery	1772–4
Number of bodies excavated	Disarticulated
Date of excavation	1998

Fragmentary bones were uncovered by builders digging foundations during the renovation of Benjamin Franklin's home on Craven Street in 1997. The bones represented the remains of at least four adults and six children, with a number of bones bearing saw and drill marks. The remains are thought to be linked to William Hewson, who lived at Craven Street from 1772 to 1774. Hewson, a student of William Hunter, started his own anatomy school in Craven Street in 1772 after arguing with Hunter. Further excavation in the basement in 1998 revealed more human and animal bones. Remains recovered included human bones with a variety of cut marks and the bones of dogs, turtles, birds and fish. The remains appear to have been deposited in a carefully constructed burial pit. Human skulls had been sectioned on the sagittal and transverse planes. A number exhibited multiple trephination cuts, possibly representing practising of surgical techniques. Some of the cuts observed on long bones may also represent practice amputations.

References
Hillson *et al.* 1999

Cross Bones burial ground (St Saviour's Burial Ground), Redcross Way, and Union Street

Grid Reference	TQ 32450 80050
Cemetery type	Churchyard
Date of cemetery	16th century onwards.
Number of bodies excavated	147
Date of excavation	1990

In 1993, St Saviour's Burial Ground (1665–1853) was excavated in advance of the Jubilee line extension. Parish burials of paupers were made at this site in the nineteenth century and documents record that 18% of burials came from the parish workhouse. One hundred and sixty individuals were exhumed, with a high proportion of infants. Most of the remains probably dated from the late nineteenth century. All were found in coffins of variable quality. The majority were made of 'deal' (pine, spruce or larch soft woods). Only 23% showed evidence of decoration such as studs or fittings. Three individuals (one adult and two children) were found with associated clothing, the adult in boots and trousers and the children in coarsely woven shrouds, one with woollen booties. Two skeletons showed evidence of autopsy.

References
Brickley and Miles 1999a

Davenant Centre, E1

Grid Reference	TQ 3440 8180
Cemetery type	Epidemic disease
Date of cemetery	17th–18th century
Number of bodies excavated	Unknown
Date of excavation	1977

The observation of contractors' trenches revealed burials associated with a known burial ground of seventeenth to nineteenth century. In 1832, a cholera pit was dug on land adjoining the cemetery for 196 victims of the disease.

References
ADS

Feeney Neil Sarcophagi, Guildhall, City of London

Grid Reference	TQ 32 81
Cemetery type	Unknown
Date of cemetery	Post-medieval
Number of bodies excavated	2
Date of excavation	2004

Two sarcophagi have been recorded from a crypt, the Feeney Neil room, at the Guildhall.

References
www.molas.org.uk

Great St. Helen's Church, Bishopgate

Grid Reference	TQ 3320 8128
Cemetery type	Churchyard
Date of cemetery	Post-medieval
Number of bodies excavated	Unknown
Date of excavation	1993

One inhumation was uncovered in a trench against the west wall of the church. This burial was cut by a large charnel pit of later date.

References
Ponsford 1994:120

Jesuit Cemetery, Manresa House, Whitelands College, Roehampton

Grid Reference	TQ 22191 73612
Cemetery type	Catholic burial ground
Date of cemetery	1867–1962
Number of bodies excavated	28 pre-1901
Date of excavation	2004

The Jesuit cemetery at Manresa House was in use from 1867 to 1962. One hundred and eight male individuals (73 ordained priests, including a bishop and an archbishop, 26 brothers and 4 priests in training) were exhumed for reburial. They were buried up to four deep, in rows oriented east to west, each grave plot capped with a headstone lying flat above it. Although all burials were aligned east-west, 80% were buried with their heads to the west and 18% with heads to the east. All were supine with arms at sides or crossed over the torso. Many were buried in vestments. 32% were buried with a rosary or crucifix, which were found around the neck, in the hands, or placed on the torso. All except two coffins were wooden. Three were of double shell construction and one substantial oak coffin was also noted. Two lead coffins were present. One, that of Archbishop Goodier, had an outer wooden shell that was left intact. The other lead coffin was of triple shell construction. Most coffins were lined with tar and packed with sawdust or newspaper. One contained a limestone packing and one had traces of horse hair. Grips and grip plates and breast plates were noted. The last were found with 47% of burials and were usually cruciform, rectangular or shield shaped, and made of lead, iron or copper alloy. A number of coffins had crucifixes at the head end.

References
Melikian 2004a; Melikian 2004b

Mary Ann Buildings, Lewisham

Grid Reference	TQ 375 776
Cemetery type	Churchyard
Date of cemetery	Post-medieval
Number of bodies excavated	2
Date of excavation	1993

Two skeletons were found during recording work at Mary Ann Buildings. Burials are probably associated with a nearby church cemetery.

References
Greenwood and Maloney 1994: 209

Mitre Street (29–31 and 32–34), City Of London

Grid Reference	TQ 3343 8116
Cemetery type	Churchyard
Date of cemetery	Post-medieval
Number of bodies excavated	Unknown
Date of excavation	1986

Burials in lead and wood coffins were observed during work in the graveyard of St. Katharine Cree Church in 1986. In 1990, excavations uncovered 59 burials.

References
Egan 1987:268

Monument Street/17 Fish Street, City of London

Grid Reference	TQ 32 80
Cemetery type	Churchyard
Date of cemetery	Post-medieval
Number of bodies excavated	26
Date of excavation	1987?

Twenty-six burials from St. Michael's Crooked Lane were uncovered. The remains were re-interred on site.

References
Heathcote 1988:386

New Bunhill Fields Burial Ground, Gaskin Street, Islington Green, Islington

Grid Reference	TQ 31727 83734
Cemetery type	Non-conformist burial ground
Date of cemetery	Late 18th–1853
Number of bodies excavated	c.14,300
Date of excavation	1996, 2004

The commercial clearance of 14,300 burials from the unconsecrated non-conformist New Bunhill Fields Burial ground, opened in late eighteenth century, was archaeologically monitored. One thousand, four hundred and sixty eight nineteenth-century coffin plates were collected from the burial ground, providing a useful comparison with contemporaneous coffin furniture recorded from intramural burials, as at Spitalfields. In 2004, two burial vaults recorded. One contained four lead coffins of the Maitland family, dating from 1775 to 1785. The second vault contained wooden coffins.

References
Ponsford and Jackson 1997:275; BIAB supp 8/1997:660–1; Miles 1997; Maloney and Holroyd 2005:11

New Churchyard

Grid Reference	TQ 33100 81700
Cemetery type	Municipal cemetery
Date of cemetery	1569–1720
Number of bodies excavated	400+
Date of excavation	1985–6

Over 400 post-medieval burials were excavated from the former New Churchyard, which was in use between 1569 and 1720. It has been suggested that some bodies may be from the nearby Bethlem Hospital. A large number of infant burials were noted in the first season of excavations. There were few primary burials cut into the imported soil brought in when the burial ground was created, and these were usually without coffins. These were cut by pit interments containing between four and sixteen individuals, which may be linked to an outbreak of the plague. Most of the subsequent burials were within coffins, some with decorative studding. All of the burials were orientated east to west. Twenty-six coffins were decorated and twenty-four had iron breastplates. Two brick-built vaults were recorded, the larger of which contained six lead outer coffins that contained highly decorated inner wooden shells. Lead breastplates on exterior coffins were dated to between 1686 and 1714.

In 2004 disarticulated human bone from at least 20 individuals and two articulated skeletons were found at the western end of Liverpool Street. These were probably from the 'New Cemetery', or 'Bethlem Church Ground', associated with the Priory and Hospital of Saint Mary Bethlehem formerly found near Liverpool Street

References
White 1986; Dyson, Malt and Wellman 1987; White 1987; Hunting 1991; Swift 2005

O'Meara Street (no. 49), Southwark

Grid Reference	TQ 3239 8027
Cemetery type	Quaker burial ground
Date of cemetery	1666–1860
Number of bodies excavated	11 and disarticulate
Date of excavation	1994

A small scale excavation noted a burial pit containing the disturbed remains of a minimum of nine individuals, variably oriented. The bodies appear to have been buried at least three deep, and were probably paupers. In addition, a pit and two more graves containing human remains and coffin fittings were also uncovered. These remains appear to be associated with a former Quaker burial ground, in use by 1666 and cleared in 1860 when a contemporary account noted that nearly a thousand skeletons and nineteen lead coffins were removed. The wooden coffins had disintegrated, leaving only fragments of wood. Traces of deal coffin bases were recovered, but the oak and elm sides and coffin tops had decayed. Few handles were recovered. Some of the lead coffins were opened, including that of Elizabeth Crosby (d. 1765) which had an intact inner wooden shell. The body was in an ornamented shroud and had been wrapped in a linen winding sheet and packed around with wool. The feet were left bare. Another body was found buried with a tortoiseshell comb, and the area around the head had been packed with feathers.

References
BIAB supp. 5/1994:589–90; Brickley and Miles 1999b; Woodger 1994

Pasternoster Row, City of London

Grid Reference	TQ 3212 8102
Cemetery type	Churchyard
Date of cemetery	Post-medieval
Number of bodies excavated	Unknown
Date of excavation	1999?

Post-medieval burials, from north-east corner of medieval churchyard of St. Paul's were excavated and re-interred.

References
Ponsford 2000:239

Paternoster Row, City of London, EC4

Grid Reference	TQ 3212 8102
Cemetery type	Churchyard
Date of cemetery	Post-medieval
Number of bodies excavated	4
Date of excavation	1997–8

Four burials were observed during a watching brief in a British Telecom inspection manhole. The burials were orientated west-east and there were associated coffin nails.

References
Porter G 1997

Public Conveniences, St Paul's Churchyard

Grid Reference	TQ 3031 8084
Cemetery type	Unknown
Date of cemetery	1630s–1853
Number of bodies excavated	8
Date of excavation	1995

Seven graves containing eight bodies were excavated in St. Paul's Churchyard. All burials were in wooden coffins, some of which were decorated with iron studs. One had a very decayed breastplate and two had coffin handles. Two of the graves contained multiple stacks of burials. Two bodies had been removed prior to the construction of public conveniences in 1888. A square brick structure is thought to be the remains of a box tomb.

References
Bowsher 1995

Quaker Burial Ground, 84, London Road, Kingston upon Thames

Grid Reference	TQ 1865 6930
Cemetery type	Quaker burial ground
Date of cemetery	1664–1814
Number of bodies excavated	390
Date of excavation	1993, 1996

In 1993, trial trenching located twenty-six graves from a burial ground of the Religious Society of Friends (Quakers) in use between 1664 and 1814. A further 364 graves were excavated from the burial ground in 1996 in advance of development. While the density of burials varied, there was much inter-cutting of graves, and variation in orientation. Only 10% were oriented west to east in the usual Christian manner. A mid-eighteenth-century brick burial vault belonging to the Barnard family was found in the middle of the site containing a total of sixteen lead coffins. The majority of skeletons were supine with arms at sides, indicating that the limbs had been tied, although there was some variation in the position of bodies. Some shroud pins were found associated with skulls. Elements of burial clothing were preserved in three coffins. These included the remains of leather caps found with two skeletons, leather ties in the sternum area of another skeleton and cuff links with another. The lead coffins also contained traces of winding sheets and occasional imprints of mattress pillows and coffin linings. One skeleton was found with four walnuts buried with it, of which three were in situ: one placed in the mouth and two others between the knees and feet. The wooden coffins showed some variation from plain rectangular boxes to others with decorative elements, including elaborate grips and escutcheons and cloth covering and upholstery studs. Wooden coffins were also found with viewing windows. There were some double graves where bodies were buried together, and one grave contained the remains of two partially burnt individuals.

References
Bashford and Pollard 1998; Kirk 1998; Bashford and Sibun 2007

Royal Mint Square, (former Aldgate burial ground), E1

Grid Reference	TQ 34000 80730
Cemetery type	Churchyard
Date of cemetery	1615–late 18th century
Number of bodies excavated	210
Date of excavation	2005

In 2005, a number of burials associated with the parish church of St Botolph in Aldgate High Street were excavated. The burial ground was consecrated in 1615 and by the late eighteenth century was derelict. Two hundred and thirty eight burials were recorded, of which 28 were left in situ. The majority were interred in wooden coffins, some with traces of name plates, two of which were partially legible. The graves usually contained between two and five individual burials stacked one above the other. Evidence was found for the disturbance of graves during the period of the burial ground's use, and the consequent deposition of disarticulated bone into charnel pits.

References
Bloice 1976:372; Thompson, Westman and Dyson 1998:247; Ferguson n.d.

Southwark Cathedral

Grid Reference	TQ 3270 8033
Cemetery type	Churchyard
Date of cemetery	Post-medieval
Number of bodies excavated	57
Date of excavation	2000–1

Excavations uncovered 57 burials in the cathedral's south churchyard. Evidence for the use of wooden and lead coffins was present and there was one iron coffin. A number of burials were accompanied with coffin fittings. One individual exhibited evidence of autopsy.

References
Mayo 2002

Southwark Cathedral, Montague Close

Grid Reference	TQ 3270 8037
Cemetery type	Unknown
Date of cemetery	18th century
Number of bodies excavated	24
Date of excavation	1999?

Part of an eighteenth-century cemetery was found during the excavation of the extension to Montague Chamber's light-well. Twenty-four burials were recovered. The majority came from three adjacent multiple graves. The top of the skull of one of the burials had been removed as part of an autopsy.

References
Divers 2001; Mayo 2002

St. Andrew's Church, Holborn Viaduct, City of London

Grid Reference	TQ 3147 8152
Cemetery type	Churchyard
Date of cemetery	1691–1852
Number of bodies excavated	1794
Date of excavation	2001

1,055 lead coffins and 739 wooden coffins dating to between 1691 and 1853 were recorded during the clearance of a church crypt. Some lead coffins were inscribed with personal details, directly into the lead. 995 coffins had partially legible nameplates, mostly of lead although some brass plates were also recorded. The occasional iron plate was preserved well enough to be legible.

References
Ponsford 2002:193; Ponsford 2003:242; Maloney and Holroyd 2003 supp. 2:38; Miles 2006

St. Bartholomew's Hospital, 150–64 Goswell Road/2–14 Seward Street, Islington

Grid Reference	TQ 6295 8245
Cemetery type	Hospital cemetery
Date of cemetery	Late 18th–early 19th century
Number of bodies excavated	550
Date of excavation	2001

Work on the site of the late eighteenth- to early nineteenth-century burial ground associated with St. Bartholomew's Hospital revealed 550 densely packed burials. Initial rows of coffins were placed on brick markers or spacers. Large burial pits in south-west corner contained 100 burials. The excavators suggest that these were pauper burials from the hospital. Some showed evidence of medical research. Charnel areas were also noted.

References
Deeves 2001; Ponsford 2002:200

St. Botolph, Aldgate, City of London

Grid Reference	TQ 3358 8120
Cemetery type	Churchyard
Date of cemetery	Post-medieval
Number of bodies excavated	Unknown
Date of excavation	1990

Excavations in the crypt of the church noted many post-medieval burials. A head found at the Holy Trinity, Minorites (said to belong to Henry, Duke of Suffolk, executed 1554) was moved to St. Botolph in 1899 and is thought to have been interred within the church after the Second World War.

References
Ponsford 1991:116

St. Bride's, Fleet Street

Grid Reference	TQ 3155 8114
Cemetery type	Churchyard
Date of cemetery	Analysed remains from 1740–1852.
Number of bodies excavated	At least 227 post-medieval
Date of excavation	1952–3

St. Bride's church was destroyed during the Blitz and excavations were conducted in 1952–3 prior to rebuilding. Approximately 5000 burials were recovered from within the church and its vaults. Remains of 227 individuals from coffins with plates giving biographical information were retained. Dates of death of these individuals ranged between 1740 and 1852.

References
Bowman, Maclaughlin and Bowman 1992; BIAB supp 4/1993:553; Milne 1997; Scheuer 2004

St. Ethelburga the Virgin, Bishopsgate, City of London

Grid Reference	TQ 3318 8136
Cemetery type	Churchyard
Date of cemetery	18th–19th century
Number of bodies excavated	2
Date of excavation	2001?

Archaeological recording occurred during clearance following terrorist activity in 1993. Two stacked lead coffins were noted in south aisle, the upper one had a coffin plate dating to 1838. Both coffins were left in place.

References
Ponsford 2002:191–2

St. George the Martyr

Grid Reference	TQ 32481 79785
Cemetery type	Churchyard
Date of cemetery	Mid-18th–early 19th century
Number of bodies excavated	Unknown
Date of excavation	2004/5

Lead and wooden coffins sealed below a layer of charnel backfill below the floor of the nave and crypt were recorded. The coffin plates dated from the mid-eighteenth to early nineteenth century. The coffins appear to have been displaced from their original location, probably during late-nineteenth-century refurbishment. The burial ground of St George's had been converted into a public park in 1887. In 2004, two backfilled brick structures, possibly vaults were recorded as well as re-deposited eighteenth- and nineteenth-century gravestones.

References
www.molas.org.uk

St. George's Bloomsbury, Camden

Grid Reference	TQ 3025 8150
Cemetery type	Churchyard
Date of cemetery	1800–1856
Number of bodies excavated	781
Date of excavation	2003

Archaeological recording was undertaken during the clearance of the crypt below St. George's Church in 2003. Details of 781 coffins, all triple shelled, were recorded and osteological analysis of 111 skeletons was undertaken. There were some surviving textiles and several burials had been interred wearing bridges and dentures. The coffin of a young girl was found to contain two death masks and a plaster effigy of a right hand while another burial contained a snuff box.

References
Boston, Boyle and Witkin 2006; Boston et al. 2009

St. George's Church, Hanworth

Grid Reference	TQ 11252 71883
Cemetery type	Churchyard
Date of cemetery	Post-medieval
Number of bodies excavated	6
Date of excavation	2004

Six inhumations were found to the north of the church in an area approximately 5m x 5m. Some evidence for burial within coffins was found. All individuals were buried at a relatively shallow depth, and, where orientation could be discerned, were aligned with their heads to the east. The excavators suggest that this was a pauper plot. Four brick burial vaults were also recorded.

References
Howell 2004; Maloney and Holroyd 2005:10

St. James Garlickhythe Church, Garlick Hill, EC4

Grid Reference	TQ 3238 8085
Cemetery type	Churchyard
Date of cemetery	18th–19th century
Number of bodies excavated	5
Date of excavation	1992

A burial vault in the north-east of the church was recorded, as were five lead coffins found within it. Four of the coffins were arranged in two stacks. The position of the fifth was unclear as it was much distorted possibly due to having exploded. A seventeenth-century desiccated corpse, known as 'Jimmy Garlick,' was recovered from this church and put on display in the nineteenth century.

References
BIAB supp. 3/1992:408; Westman 1992:391; Greenwood and Maloney 1993:49; Ponsford 1993:206; Miles 1993

St. James, Bowling Green Lane, Islington

Grid Reference	TQ 31 82
Cemetery type	Churchyard
Date of cemetery	c.1660–1853
Number of bodies excavated	700
Date of excavation	2007–8?

The site of the cemetery of St. James, Bowling Green Lane, Islington, which was associated with St. James Clerkenwell, was cleared prior to development. Seven hundred burials were archaeologically excavated while the rest of the site was cleared by an exhumation contractor.

References
www.aocarchaeology.com

St. Lawrence Jewry Burial Vaults, Guildhall Yard, Guildhall Bollards, City of London

Grid Reference	TQ 32476 81329
Cemetery type	Churchyard
Date of cemetery	1819–1845
Number of bodies excavated	61
Date of excavation	1998

A sealed burial vault at the east end of St Lawrence Church was emptied of 61 lead-lined coffins dating from the early to mid-nineteenth century. The individuals buried there were drawn from the middle classes, many working in occupations associated with drapery, the main trade of the local area. The coffins were recorded, but not opened. The age at death was recorded for 59 individuals – the two with no recorded age at death were infants, who had probably died at birth or soon afterwards.

References
Bateman and Miles 1999; Ponsford 2000:237

St. Luke's Estate, Bath Street, London

Grid Reference	TQ 32581 82562
Cemetery type	Poor burial ground
Date of cemetery	17th–19th century
Number of bodies excavated	1+ disarticulated
Date of excavation	1996

A watching brief in a known seventeenth- to nineteenth-century burial ground identified a charnel pit and neonate burial.

References
BIAB supp. 7/1996:539; Miles 1996

St. Luke's Islington

Grid Reference	TQ 32320 82424
Cemetery type	Churchyard
Date of cemetery	18th–19th century
Number of bodies excavated	1053
Date of excavation	2000

1,053 burials of eighteenth- to nineteenth-century date were excavated from the crypt and churchyard of St Luke's. Seven hundred and twelve coffins, made of lead, wood, zinc and iron, were recorded and reburied. Textiles including coffin linings and mattresses were recovered. A flower arrangement was noted lying on top of a young woman's coffin (died 1830). The taxonomy of coffin furniture developed at Spitalfields has been expanded based on this site and St George's Bloomsbury. Evidence of post mortem autopsy was found in four cases.

References
Bradley and Boyle 2004; Boyle, Boston and Witkin 2005

St. Martin of Tours, Chelsfield, Bromley

Grid Reference	TQ 547 164
Cemetery type	Churchyard
Date of cemetery	c.1600
Number of bodies excavated	1
Date of excavation	2001

A single articulated and uncoffined burial dating to c.1600 was recorded.

References
Hart 2002a, 2002b

St. Martin's Church, High Street, Ruislip

Grid Reference	TQ 0916 8756
Cemetery type	Churchyard
Date of cemetery	18th–19th century
Number of bodies excavated	16
Date of excavation	1995

Sixteen burials in substantial wood coffins were uncovered during excavations prior to the extension of the church hall. A metal plaque from one of the coffins suggests a eighteenth- or nineteenth-century date for the burials.

References
Wiggins 1995; Ponsford and Jackson 1996:266

St. Mary Aldermanbury Church, Aldermanbury, EC2, City of London

Grid Reference	TQ 32412 81443
Cemetery type	Churchyard
Date of cemetery	19th century
Number of bodies excavated	Unknown
Date of excavation	1968

Nineteenth-century coffin plates were recorded from vaults within the church, including the Hogg family vault. A burial pit was noted under the nave containing human remains and a charnel house at south-east corner of church.

References
ADS

St. Mary Magdalen Churchyard, The Watch House, Bermondsey Square

Grid Reference	TQ 32481 79785
Cemetery type	Churchyard
Date of cemetery	Mid-late 18th century–early 19th century
Number of bodies excavated	15
Date of excavation	1998

Fifteen complete and partial skeletons of mid-late eighteenth- to early nineteenth-century date were recovered from the churchyard of St Mary Magdalen. The graves had been cut in three parallel rows aligned west-east, and individuals were buried up to 5 deep within a single plot. Decayed remains of handles, nails and studs indicated that each had been buried within a wooden coffin.

References
Saxby 1998; Divers 1998

St. Mary the Virgin, Manor Road, Bexley

Grid Reference	TQ 49 73
Cemetery type	Churchyard

Date of cemetery	Post-medieval
Number of bodies excavated	Unknown
Date of excavation	1999

Post-medieval vault and human remains were noted.

References
Maloney 2000

St. Marylebone Church, Marylebone High Street, Marylebone, Westminster

Grid Reference	TQ 2830 8197
Cemetery type	Churchyard
Date of cemetery	18th–19th century
Number of bodies excavated	c.350
Date of excavation	1992, 2004–6

A series of archaeological interventions between 1992 and 2005 resulted in the recording of over 300 burials from the graveyard and church of St. Marylebone. Three brick burial vaults containing 23 burials (21 in lead coffins and two in wooden coffins) were identified within the excavation area. One hundred and seven named individuals were at least partially identified from coffin plates. A total of 57 lead coffins were recorded during all excavations. The remaining burials were interred in wooden coffins, often represented by dark organic stains. Coins were found over the eyes of a three year-old. Shroud pins were found in several burials while others contained buttons, suggestive of clothed burial. Three individuals were found wearing dental prostheses and five individuals exhibited evidence of autopsy.

References
Miles, Powers and Wroe-Brown 2008

St. Mary's Church, Church Road, SW13

Grid Reference	TQ 220 765
Cemetery type	Churchyard
Date of cemetery	Post-medieval
Number of bodies excavated	Unknown
Date of excavation	1987–1983

Post-medieval burials were noted.

References
Thompson, Westman and Dyson 1998:171

St. Mary's Church, Ealing

Grid Reference	SU 3669 1246
Cemetery type	Churchyard
Date of cemetery	Post-medieval
Number of bodies excavated	Unknown
Date of excavation	1994

Single brick-lined graves or vaults were recorded in the central nave, aisle and elsewhere. Two large vaults were recorded, one on the north side of the nave in front of the chancel arch, and the other to the east of the chancel arch on the north side of the chancel. The contents (particularly skeletal material) were poorly preserved, although there was some preservation of cloth and wood and botanical remains. Previously concealed seventeenth- to nineteenth-century ledger slabs were also recorded.

References
Ponsford and Jackson 1995:113–4

St. Mary's Church, Little Ilford, Newham

Grid Reference	TQ 4290 8526
Cemetery type	Churchyard
Date of cemetery	17th–18th century
Number of bodies excavated	Unknown
Date of excavation	1984

Seventeenth to eighteenth-century burials in the chancel and nave, and the Lethieullier family vault, were recorded. The remains of Charles Lethieullier (d. 1759) were examined. The inner lead shell was full of liquid similar to honey. A viscera chest was opened and the well-preserved heart and soft organs found sitting on bran inside. Waxed paper was used between the top of the sides of the coffin and the lid in order to reduce odours.

References
Egan 1985:161; Redknap 1985:31–7; Litten 1991

St. Mary's Road, Ealing, Greater London

Grid Reference	TQ 1770 7975
Cemetery type	Churchyard
Date of cemetery	18th–19th century
Number of bodies excavated	Unknown
Date of excavation	2002?

The brick vault associated with the Georgian church was recorded. Three lead coffins were recorded and left in situ.

References
Ponsford 2003:244; Maloney and Holroyd 2003:40

St. Nicholas, Deptford

Grid Reference	TQ 3740 7775
Cemetery type	Churchyard
Date of cemetery	Post-medieval
Number of bodies excavated	1
Date of excavation	2002

Disarticulated bone and a human burial were observed during a watching brief.

References
Slater 2002; Maloney and Holroyd 2003:48

St. Olave's Cemetery

Grid Reference	TQ 3281 8027
Cemetery type	Non-conformist burial ground?
Date of cemetery	Post-medieval
Number of bodies excavated	21
Date of excavation	1995

In 1995, part of a post-medieval cemetery was noted. A total of 21 burials excavated, including three coffins stacked on top of each other in a single grave. Burials may be part of a cemetery on land leased by St. Olave's Church and called the Flemish Churchyard on a nineteenth-century plan

References
Murray and Willis 1997; Knight 2002

St. Pancras Burial Ground, Camden

Grid Reference	TQ 29 81
Cemetery type	Churchyard
Date of cemetery	1793–1854
Number of bodies excavated	Unknown
Date of excavation	2004

The excavation of the extension of St Pancras burial ground (used between 1793 and 1854) recorded burials of all social classes, including nobility and workhouse inhabitants. Evidence of autopsies and probable anatomical dissections of both human and animal bone was also noted. 82% of the dated burials were interred between 1793 and 1812. Arthur Richard Dillon (1721–1806), Archbishop of Narbonne and Primate of Languedoc was buried wearing porcelain dentures and other individuals were found with dental fillings of gold and another grey metal.

References
Powers 2005, 2006; Maloney and Holroyd 2003:35–6

St. Paul's Cathedral Crypt

Grid Reference	TQ 3207 8112
Cemetery type	Churchyard
Date of cemetery	Post-medieval
Number of bodies excavated	4
Date of excavation	200–1

Excavations in the south transept of St. Paul's Cathedral revealed four burials in two grave cuts. One held the coffins of Dorathy Spencer (d.1687) and an unknown child. The other the stacked coffins of Lawrence Spencer (Clerk of Works during the construction of the Cathedral – d.1719–20) and his son, also called Lawrence (d.1719–20). All were interred in wooden coffins. The earlier coffins of Dorathy and the infant were decorated with decorative iron plates, while the later coffins of father and son had copper alloy studs.

References
Ponsford 2001:142; Maloney 2001:72; Wroe-Brown 2001

St. Paul's Church, Covent Garden, Westminster

Grid Reference	TQ 3031 8084
Cemetery type	Churchyard
Date of cemetery	18th–19th century
Number of bodies excavated	7 graves
Date of excavation	1991, 1995

A crypt and remains of six to twelve individuals were located during a watching brief in 1991. Further archaeological investigation of the site in 1995 uncovered another seven graves containing eight burials. All were in wooden coffins, dating from the eighteenth to mid-nineteenth century. Some were decorated with iron studs; one with decayed breast plates and two with handles. One grave contained stacked burials up to five deep.

References
Thorpe 1991; BIAB supp 8/1997:651; Ponsford and Jackson 1996:246; Bowsher, Holder and Miles 1997; Duggan 2003

St. Paul's Church, Hammersmith

Grid Reference	TQ 2327 7846
Cemetery type	Churchyard
Date of cemetery	1828–1853
Number of bodies excavated	80 burials
Date of excavation	2009

Eighty post-medieval burials were uncovered during excavations in the western churchyard of St. Pauls's Church. The land forming this part of the churchyard was acquired in 1828 with most burial ceasing in 1853. Where shape could be determined, all coffins were single-break. The majority of coffin fittings were of iron. Twenty-six of the thirty-one graves contained multiple interments, with a maximum of five coffins observed. Small shell buttons were found in the pelvic are of several male interments. A large horn or tortoiseshell comb was found by the head of one of the female burials. Four craniotomies were observed.

References
Oxford Archaeology 2009

St. Paul's Graveyard, Deptford High Street, Lewisham

Grid Reference	TQ 3728 7748
Cemetery type	Churchyard
Date of cemetery	19th century
Number of bodies excavated	20
Date of excavation	2000

A brick barrel vaulted tomb on the north side of church was recorded as were brick lined graves either side of the south entrance into the crypt. Twenty burials in wooden coffins with nineteenth-century grips were excavated from a shaft excavated for a soakaway on the south side of the church.

References
Ponsford 2001:150

St. Peter Cornhill, City of London

Grid Reference	TQ 3302 8111
Cemetery type	Churchyard
Date of cemetery	Post-medieval
Number of bodies excavated	Unknown
Date of excavation	1990

Post-medieval brick burial vaults, memorial stones, lead coffins, coffin fragments and disarticulated human remains were found during excavations. An empty burial vault cleared in the nineteenth century, probably before 1889 refurbishment, was also recorded.

References
ADS; Filer 1991a:277; Ponsford 1991:119

St. Sepulchre North Churchyard, Snow Hill Court, Newgate Street, City of London

Grid Reference	TQ 3178 8148
Cemetery type	Churchyard
Date of cemetery	Post-medieval
Number of bodies excavated	Unknown
Date of excavation	2001

Post-medieval burials were recorded in three trial excavations

References
Ponsford 2002:195

St. Thomas' Hospital

Grid Reference	TQ 3286–7 8014–8
Cemetery type	Hospital cemetery
Date of cemetery	17th century
Number of bodies excavated	239
Date of excavation	1991

Excavations in 1991 uncovered a burial ground of the early seventeenth century containing the remains of 227 individuals. The burials had been interred in at least 16 intercutting pits. The bodies appear to have been interred in shrouds and are thought to be part of St. Thomas Hospital cemetery. Excavations as part of the extension to the Jubilee line identified more burials probably associated with the hospital's seventeenth-century burial ground. In area 3, the remains of twelve burials were recovered from two grave pits. There was no evidence for coffins. In area 4 one post-medieval skeleton was recorded.

References
Greenwodd and Thompson 1992:420; Tucker 1996; Knight 2002

The Chapel Undercroft, Lincoln's Inn, Camden

Grid Reference	TQ 3103 8143
Cemetery type	Unknown
Date of cemetery	Late 18th–early 19th century

Number of bodies excavated	1
Date of excavation	1991

Some disturbance to vault burials was noted. Adult inhumation below the ledger slab of Polydore Plumtree (d. 1777) was recorded and reburied. A slab was found within another grave shaft, warning grave diggers that they were near the top of the coffin of Peter Holford (d. 1804). This was also recorded and reburied.

References
Ponsford 1992:96

The Royal Foundation of St. Katherine, Butcher Row, Ratcliff

Grid Reference	TQ 36000 81000
Cemetery type	Churchyard
Date of cemetery	19th century
Number of bodies excavated	2
Date of excavation	2002

Nineteenth-century burials were removed by a non-archaeological contractor. An elaborate burial vault, containing two lead coffins with coffin fittings, was archaeologically recorded.

References
Bluer 2002; Maloney and Holroyd 2003

The Royal Hospital Greenwich

Grid Reference	TQ 3830 7785
Cemetery type	Hospital cemetery
Date of cemetery	1747–1856
Number of bodies excavated	107
Date of excavation	1999

A series of excavations were conducted between 1999 and 2001 at Devonport Buildings. The site encompassed an area used as a burial ground by the Royal Hospital Greenwich between 1749–1856 to inter retired members of the Royal Navy. A total of 107 skeletons were recovered from 55 graves. The majority were older males, but a small number of women and adolescents were also present. Evidence for wooden coffins, in the form of nails and coffin fittings, and shrouds were recovered from many graves. Several individuals exhibited evidence of autopsy.

References
Boston et al. 2008

The Royal London Hospital, Whitechapel Road, E1

Grid Reference	TQ 34743 81695
Cemetery type	Hospital cemetery
Date of cemetery	1820–1854
Number of bodies excavated	265
Date of excavation	2005

Archaeological investigations took place at the Royal London prior to redevelopment. Excavation of area A of the site uncovered 265 "burials". 177 of these were articulated inhumations, 66 of whom exhibited evidence for autopsy. The remaining 89 "burials" consisted of coffin-loads of disarticulated remains. In the western end of the cemetery the graves were shallow and the coffins poorly preserved. In the east side of the cemetery the grave cuts were deeper and containing stacked coffins, usually five or more deep. A group of burials in the south-east corner appear to consist of several rows of stacked up coffins up to four or five high. The stacked burials appear to have been laid on the contemporary ground surface and covered with a layer of rubble. Factors behind the mass burial are unclear but they may relate to epidemic disease or the need to dispose of old anatomical specimens. This burial ground, which was established to the east of the extended east wing of the hospital, lies outside any of the burial grounds shown on plans and maps of the hospital. The cemetery appears to have been established to dispose of the remains of those subjected to post-mortem procedures in the adjacent medical school.

Excavation of a second area (B) to the west of area A uncovered several rows of burials. A total of 28 grave cuts were found to contain between two and six individuals along with disarticulated dissected human and animal bone. Lack of documentary sources makes dating the burials problematic but the available evidence suggests the area was used for burial by the hospital between c. 1820 and 1854. The burials from area B probably date to c.1830–1854 which is when this area lay within the hospital burial ground.

References
Vuolteenaho, Wood and Powers 2008

Therese House, 29–30 Glasshouse Yard EC1

Grid Reference	TQ 32040 82050
Cemetery type	Non-conformist burial ground
Date of cemetery	Post-medieval
Number of bodies excavated	7
Date of excavation	2005, 2006

Seven post-medieval burials were located within test pits. The individuals were aligned north to south and were buried in wooden coffins. The excavator suggests that these were probably associated with a non-conformist chapel known from eighteenth-century maps of the area. Another, possibly earlier, burial aligned east to west was recorded, as well as the edge of a large post-medieval rubbish pit. Further excavation in 2006, revealed additional north-south burials.

References
Maloney and Holroyd 2006

Norfolk

27–8 Tombland, Norwich

Grid Reference	TG 2336 0878
Cemetery type	Churchyard
Date of cemetery	Post-medieval
Number of bodies excavated	1
Date of excavation	1999

A single male inhumation was uncovered, probably from the cemetery of the now demolished Church of St. Cuthbert.

References
BIAB supp. 10.2/1999:743; Brennand 1999

Castle Mound, Castle Mall, Norwich

Grid Reference	TG 23 08
Cemetery type	Prison cemetery
Date of cemetery	17th century
Number of bodies excavated	7
Date of excavation	1989–91

The remains of seven seventeenth-century burials were found during excavations at Norwich Castle. All six adults were male. The bodies appear to have been interred together, packed two abreast in three layers. The burials were aligned roughly east-west, three has their heads to the east and three to the west. All of the burials were supine. Shroud pins were found with two of the burials and fragments of a leather belt were found adhering to the foot of one of the skeletons. The burials are thought to have been prisoners at the castle but the burials may be linked to executions following riots during the civil war.

References
Anderson 1996; Anderson 1998; Shepherd Popescu 2009

General Baptist Chapel, Priory Yard, Norwich

Grid Reference	TG 235 098
Cemetery type	Baptist burial ground
Date of cemetery	1726–1856
Number of bodies excavated	63
Date of excavation	2002

Sixty-three burials were recovered during excavations of the burial ground of General Baptists at Priory Yard. The excavated area was part of extension to the burial ground, which was in use between 1726 and 1854. Most burials were in coffins in earth-cut graves with one brick-built vault containing coffins. Although coffin plates were found with many burials, the only legible coffin plates were found on the coffins from the brick-built vault. The burial of an adolescent of c.17–18 was found with a teacup placed over the left-side of the chest, roughly in area of the heart.

References
Shelley 2004

Old Hunstanton Churchyard

Grid Reference	TF 6893 4201
Cemetery type	Unknown
Date of cemetery	Post-medieval
Number of bodies excavated	Unknown
Date of excavation	Unknown

Skeletal remains from Old Hunstanton Churchyard were recorded.

References
ADS

St Martin-at-Palace, Norwich

Grid Reference	TG 2347 0911
Cemetery type	Churchyard
Date of cemetery	Medieval–post-medieval
Number of bodies excavated	47
Date of excavation	1987–8

The remains of 47 burials of medieval and post medieval date were recorded, of which 27 were articulated burials in the nave and tower of the church. Further graves were found in the nave, the south aisle and the chancel. Most burials were orientated with their heads to the west, except for three of the five recorded infant burials, which were buried with the head to the east. The majority of the burials were found with their hands by the sides. One adult was found with its left arm bent and cradling a neonate. A large number of graves produced evidence of coffins and three lead coffins were also recorded. The majority of coffins were made of elm, though ash and oak were recorded. Coffin grips and fittings were of iron, some with non metallic plating. The burial shafts were painted white interior, while vaults were not painted. Only four breast plates were recorded from coffins. Coffin studs were usually arranged in linear or trefoil designs, as well as dot in circle or floral motifs. One fragment was found with a possible letter and full stop in small studs. Evidence for woollen coffin coverings, dyed blue and purple, was found on the back of several grip plates and beneath the decorative copper alloy studs. Some evidence was also found for linings. Nineteen copper alloy pins of different sizes and style of manufacture were found. Nine came from coffins, one of which was attached to human hair. Pins from an elm and an oak coffin were associated with un-dyed silk ribbons. The specialist report on the textiles suggests that all were used to attach funeral caps and dated to the late eighteenth to early nineteenth centuries. A similar bow of blue silk ribbon was noted on the head of another individual. An iron hook was found in a coffin, and was probably used to hold clothing in place. Evidence was also found of a possible shroud and of machine knitted cotton fabric possibly supplied by relatives rather than the undertakers. Fragments of fine gilded sheet, two lace tags and a Victoria penny from 1900 were also recovered.

References
Ayers and Beazley 2001

St. Giles-on-the-Hill, Norwich

Grid Reference	TG 2256 0860
Cemetery type	Unknown
Date of cemetery	18th–19th century
Number of bodies excavated	3
Date of excavation	2004

An eighteenth- or nineteenth-century vault containing three coffins, two adults and one child, was recorded as part of a watching brief.

References
Excavations and Surveys in Norfolk in 2004 (available online)

St. Mary's Church, Thrigby

Grid Reference	TG 1605 1239
Cemetery type	Churchyard
Date of cemetery	1779–1808
Number of bodies excavated	5
Date of excavation	2003?

A brick burial vault containing five lead coffins dating between 1779 and 1808 was recorded. Each contained the body of an elderly woman. One coffin had an "ornate cover of wood and leather". On top of these were two infant coffins. Another female skeleton found in a corner of the vault packed between a coffin and the wall and had been excarnated. It was suggested that the skeleton was left after its wooden coffin had decayed completely, before the final lead coffin had been inserted.

References
Ponsford 2004:307

St Michael's Church, Aylsham

Grid Reference	TG 1773 0910
Cemetery type	Churchyard
Date of cemetery	18th century
Number of bodies excavated	1
Date of excavation	2004

Three post-medieval brick crypts were identified during a watching brief. One earth cut grave thought to be of post-medieval date was also identified.

References
Crawley 2005

St. Michael's Church, Bowthorpe, Norwich

Grid Reference	TG 1924 2701
Cemetery type	Isolated burial
Date of cemetery	18th century
Number of bodies excavated	1
Date of excavation	2004

Excavations in St Michael's Church, west of the medieval core of

Norwich, located a post-medieval inhumation in an oven or corn-dryer. The tower of the church had been used as a chimney for the oven in the eighteenth century before its destruction before 1790. The body of a man in his 40s lay with the head to the west in the oven in a supine extended position. The head lay on the floor of the oven with the rest of the body extending into the stoke hold. Bricks had been removed to enable body to lay flat. The report suggests that the tower was destroyed deliberately, perhaps soon after the inhumation was placed there.

References
Ayers and Beazley 2001

St. Peter's Southgate Church, Argyle Street, Norwich

Grid Reference	TG 2377 0775
Cemetery type	Churchyard
Date of cemetery	19th century
Number of bodies excavated	Unknown
Date of excavation	1997

Nineteenth-century post-medieval graves were noted during a watching brief.

References
Ponsford and Jackson 1998:146

St. Saviour's Church, Norwich

Grid Reference	TG 2366 0807
Cemetery type	Churchyard
Date of cemetery	Post-medieval
Number of bodies excavated	Unknown
Date of excavation	1996

Several brick vaults were recorded below the altar area of the church, one of which included four lead coffins of the Beevor family. Individual vaults were also observed beneath the vestry.

References
BIAB supp. 7/1996:674; Shelley and Forrest 1996

Vancouver Centre, King's Lynn (Baptist cemetery)

Grid Reference	TF 61871 20003
Cemetery type	Baptist burial ground
Date of cemetery	c.1773–1841
Number of bodies excavated	18
Date of excavation	2002–3

A small Baptist cemetery was excavated prior to the construction of a car park in King's Lynn. Eighteen burials were excavated with the majority interred within single shell wooden coffins, although there was a triple shell coffin with a middle layer of iron. One of the coffins lay on two transverse wooden slats.

References
Brown 2005; Boston 2005a

Vancouver Centre, King's Lynn (Quaker cemetery)

Grid Reference	TF 61871 20003
Cemetery type	Quaker burial ground
Date of cemetery	1780–1835
Number of bodies excavated	34
Date of excavation	2002–3

A small Quaker cemetery was excavated prior to the construction of a car park in King's Lynn. Thirty-four bodies were recovered, some from earth cut graves and others from brick lined graves. The coffins were mainly wood with simple fittings, although there was one zinc coffin.

References
Brown 2005

Northamptonshire

Castle Hill Chapel Cemetery, Northampton

Grid Reference	SP 7508 6047
Cemetery type	Non-conformist burial ground
Date of cemetery	Late 18th–early 19th century
Number of bodies excavated	39, only 12 lifted
Date of excavation	1988–1992

Thirty-nine burials thought to have been part of the Castle Hill Chapel cemetery were uncovered during a watching brief. All burials were west-east, except a juvenile interred north-south. Evidence for coffins was found with six burials, in the form of coffin nails or coffin fittings. Shroud pins were found with six burials. One skeleton exhibited evidence for autopsy in the form of a craniotomy.

References
Miller and Wilson 2005

College Street Chapel, Northampton

Grid Reference	SP 75 60
Cemetery type	Unknown
Date of cemetery	Post-medieval
Number of bodies excavated	Unknown
Date of excavation	1985–6

Post-medieval human remains noted.

References
ADS

St. Mary the Virgin, Church of Little Houghton

Grid Reference	SP 80 59
Cemetery type	Churchyard
Date of cemetery	Post-medieval
Number of bodies excavated	Unknown
Date of excavation	1999

In situ burials and disarticulated bones were noted during a watching brief. The remains of a brick lined vault or grave were noted.

References
ADS; BIAB supp.10.2/1999:678; Phillips 2000

St. Peter's Churchyard, Oundle

Grid Reference	TL 042 882
Cemetery type	Churchyard
Date of cemetery	Post-medieval
Number of bodies excavated	Unknown
Date of excavation	1988

A brick-lined vault containing a single burial and wooden coffin fragments was recorded. One piece had the letter 'W' picked out in brass studs.

References
Egan 1989:27–8

Northumberland

Jarrow

Grid Reference	NZ 33 65
Cemetery type	Churchyard
Date of cemetery	Post-medieval

Number of bodies excavated	119
Date of excavation	1960s

119 post-medieval burials were uncovered during excavations at Jarrow and form part of the churchyard associated with St. Paul's. The largest group of burials were 78 infant burials lying just to the north of the chancel. These individuals may have been interred within a relatively short period of time and perhaps are related to cholera epidemics of the nineteenth century.

References
Cramp 2005

Market Place and Beaumont Street, Hexham

Grid Reference	NY 93 64
Cemetery type	Churchyard
Date of cemetery	Post-medieval
Number of bodies excavated	16
Date of excavation	1990

Part of the conventual cemetery was excavated producing the skeletal remains of 16 individuals. Those in the examined section were in layers without coffins or shrouds. A group of disarticulated bones was found just below the road and pavement surfaces.

References
Beckensall 1998

St. Andrew, The Winship Vault, Corbridge

Grid Reference	NY 988 644
Cemetery type	Churchyard
Date of cemetery	19th century
Number of bodies excavated	2
Date of excavation	1997

Two coffins were observed during a watching brief carried out during repairs of a brick vault thought to date to the eighteenth century. The two coffins in the vault are thought to date to the early nineteenth century.

References
Ryder 1998

The Infirmary, The Forth International Centre for Life, Newcastle upon Tyne

Grid Reference	NZ 4243 5636
Cemetery type	Hospital cemetery
Date of cemetery	1753–1845
Number of bodies excavated	210
Date of excavation	1996–7

Two hundred and ten in situ burials were excavated from the burial ground associated with Newcastle Infirmary (in use between 1753 and 1845). The remains of a minimum of 407 further individuals were recovered from charnel deposits. These seem to date from a partial clearance of the cemetery in 1852 after which the infirmary buildings were extended. Of the in situ burials, c. 62 were in coffins. Sixteen of these coffins, all of the flat-lidded single break type, were well preserved. No personal details were recorded on the coffins. Timbers from 19 coffins were analysed and found to be predominantly of softwood boards of one of three different conifers. Two of the analysed boards were beech. There was extensive evidence for surgery and both post-mortem autopsy and anatomist activity, including c. 200 amputated limbs and 60 craniotomies. The majority of human remains showing evidence of post-mortem dissection were found in the earlier parts of the cemetery, indicating that this activity predated the Anatomy Act of 1832.

References
Ponsford and Jackson 1997:283; Nolan 1997 & 1998; Boulter, Robertson and Start 1998; Groves and Boswijk 1998; Chamberlain 1999; Start 2002

Nottinghamshire

28, Church Street, Whatton

Grid Reference	SK 74 39
Cemetery type	Churchyard
Date of cemetery	15th–18th century
Number of bodies excavated	20
Date of excavation	1993?

The burials of a minimum of 20 individuals were recorded to the east of the current churchyard boundary. They were later in date than deposits incorporating fourteenth- to fifteenth-century pottery but earlier than enclosure (1790), so a fifteenth- to eighteenth-century date was suggested for the burials.

References
ADS; BIAB supp. 3/1992:565; Priest 1994

Church of St. Helens, Burton Joyce

Grid Reference	SK 6478 4380
Cemetery type	Churchyard
Date of cemetery	Post-medieval
Number of bodies excavated	1
Date of excavation	1996

One inhumation was noted during excavations within the nave aisles.

References
ADS

Church of St. John the Evangelist, Carlton-in-Lindrick

Grid Reference	SK 589 839
Cemetery type	Churchyard
Date of cemetery	Post-medieval
Number of bodies excavated	2
Date of excavation	1995

Two articulated burials in two grave cuts were uncovered. Disarticulated remains were also recorded with associated coffin fittings indicating a post-medieval date for the burials.

References
Sidebottom 1995

Church of the Holy Rood, Edwalton

Grid Reference	SK 5900 3500
Cemetery type	Churchyard
Date of cemetery	Post-medieval
Number of bodies excavated	Unknown
Date of excavation	1996

Numerous inhumation burials identified and handed over for reburial.

References
ADS

Church of the Holy Trinity, Lambley, Gedling

Grid Reference	SK 63 45
Cemetery type	Churchyard
Date of cemetery	Post-medieval
Number of bodies excavated	1

Date of excavation 1998

Post-medieval grave and human remains were noted.

References
ADS

Church Walk/Church Street, Newark

Grid Reference	SK 7990 5392
Cemetery type	Unknown
Date of cemetery	Post-medieval
Number of bodies excavated	3
Date of excavation	1995/6?

Remains of three skeletons were located and removed.

References
ADS; BIAB supp 7/1996:714

Nottingham Castle

Grid Reference	SK 56 39
Cemetery type	War burials
Date of cemetery	Post-medieval
Number of bodies excavated	1
Date of excavation	

Single inhumation of young male found in area of Castle Green. It has been suggested that the inhumation may have been a Civil War fatality

References
Drage 1989

Nottingham General Hospital

Grid Reference	SK 568 397
Cemetery type	Medical waste
Date of cemetery	Late 18th–early 19th century
Number of bodies excavated	Min. 5
Date of excavation	1994

Excavations in the grounds of the former General Hospital found the disarticulated skeletal remains, mostly long bones, from a minimum of five individuals. Of the ten long bones, six showed evidence of gross pathology and three showed evidence of amputation. A tibia had been fitted with a hinge consistent with its use as part of an articulated skeleton used in teaching anatomy. Chapman suggests that the bones were originally part of a teaching or reference collection from the hospital. They might have been disposed of subsequent to the 1832 Anatomy Act

References
Chapman 1997

St. Nicholas' Church, Littleborough

Grid Reference	SK 8240 8260
Cemetery type	Churchyard
Date of cemetery	16th–19th century
Number of bodies excavated	Unknown
Date of excavation	1998

Burials were revealed inside St Nicholas Church, when drainage pipes were being laid along the south and east walls of the chancel. There was no evidence of burials prior to 1539, and the absence of grave markers suggested that they had been interred before the 1830s. To the north of the church the drainage pipe extended outside into the graveyard, which was found to have been artificially raised in this area. Only one burial was found from this trench.

References
Elliott 1993a

St. Peter and St. Paul's Church, Bridge Street, Mansfield

Grid Reference	SK 5400 6100
Cemetery type	Churchyard
Date of cemetery	Post-medieval
Number of bodies excavated	Unknown
Date of excavation	1993

Movement of gravestones noted, probably as a result of boundary changes. Two brick vaults sealed with stone slabs were also observed. One contained a lead coffin.

References
BIAB supp. 4/1993:740; Elliott 1993b

Willoughby Vault, St. Catherine's Church, Cossall

Grid Reference	SK 4836 4227
Cemetery type	Churchyard
Date of cemetery	17th–18th century
Number of bodies excavated	12
Date of excavation	1999

Fifteen earth-cut graves, four of which contained visible human skeletal material (including two infant burials) were found beneath the floor of the chancel, nave and aisles. The graves were probably from the churchyard and predate the construction of this part of the church in 1842. The infant burials probably post-date the Reformation as they cut the foundation of the chapel altar in the east end of the south aisle. Four copper alloy pins found with one of the infants, three by the head and one over the ribs, indicating a probable shroud or winding sheet. A possible coffin nail was also found at the foot of the grave. The other infant burial produced similar finds, including a copper alloy pin, a small iron nail and three encrusted pieces of iron which the excavator interprets as possible bracket coffin fittings. The Willoughby vault contained eight visible coffins dating from the seventeenth century and later, five of lead and three of stone, and charnel, including seven skulls as well as pelvic and long bones.

References
Elliott 2000a; Elliott 2000b

Oxfordshire

102, Bayswater Road, Oxford

Grid Reference	SP 58880 08025
Cemetery type	Unknown
Date of cemetery	Post-medieval
Number of bodies excavated	Unknown
Date of excavation	1994

Post-medieval human remains were noted.

References
ADS

Abingdon Vineyard, Lay Cemetery, Abingdon

Grid Reference	SU 4985 9725
Cemetery type	Unknown
Date of cemetery	c.1645–1661
Number of bodies excavated	285
Date of excavation	1988–1993

Excavations in the Vineyard, Abingdon in the area of the former Abbey revealed a civil war cemetery northwest of the convent ditch, which ran across the site and formed the western boundary of the medieval lay cemetery. Nearly 300 regularly and closely spaced burials were excavated from an estimated 500. There was no evidence of inter-cutting of graves. The vast majority of graves were orientated north to south. All age groups were represented, as were both sexes. Most burials were associated with coffin nails or shroud pins, or both in a few cases. An ornamental coffin plate dating to between 1650 and 1675 was recovered from one grave. A silver penny of Charles I was found associated with one burial, and another was found with two Scottish silver shillings of James VI or Charles I. There were some multiple burials. In particular nine male individuals, one of whom was found with a musket ball between the ribs, were buried in a single grave. Allen suggests that this grave corresponds to the documented burial of nine prisoners from the town gaol in the Burial Register for 1644–5.

References
Allen 1990; Allen 2006

Bonn Square, Oxford

Grid Reference	SP 5118 0615
Cemetery type	Churchyard
Date of cemetery	Post-medieval
Number of bodies excavated	Unknown
Date of excavation	1874

Post medieval charnel pit, inhumation, tomb and other human remains were noted in the former graveyard of St Peter-le-Bailey, located on Bonn Square in 1874. Refurbishment of the square in 2008 revealed disarticulated bone and burial vaults.

References
http://www.thehumanjourney.com; ADS; Hammond and Ford 2003; Ponsford 2004:308

Church of St. Thomas of Canterbury, Elsfield

Grid Reference	SP 5407 0998
Cemetery type	Churchyard
Date of cemetery	Post-medieval
Number of bodies excavated	2
Date of excavation	1999

Two articulated skeletons were revealed, but not fully excavated. One grave had coffin handles suggestive of an early to mid-nineteenth century date.

References
BIAB 10.1/1999:459; Hiller 1999a

Eynsham Abbey

Grid Reference	SP 4325 0925
Cemetery type	Isolated burial
Date of cemetery	Late 16th–mid-17th century
Number of bodies excavated	3
Date of excavation	1989–92

Three burials (one male and two female) were found cut into the demolition debris layer at the west end of the refectory. The presence of nails suggests these individuals were interred in wooden coffins.

References
Hardy, Dodd and Keevill 2003

Freelands House, Oxford, Oxfordshire

Grid Reference	SP 5262 0449
Cemetery type	Isolated burial
Date of cemetery	Post-medieval
Number of bodies excavated	1
Date of excavation	1922

A skeleton in a pit-like grave was found to the west of Freelands House in 1922. The skull was fractured and the burial may have been linked to the civil war.

References
ADS

Museum of the History of Science (Old Ashmolean Museum)

Grid Reference	SP 5149 0645
Cemetery type	Medical waste
Date of cemetery	1683–1781
Number of bodies excavated	Minimum of 18
Date of excavation	1999

The Old Ashmolean Museum was the location of the University's Anatomy school until 1781. Human and animal skeletal remains, together with chemical apparatus, clay tobacco pipes, glass, and other refuse, were found during refurbishment of the Museum. It has been suggested that these materials were deposited when the basement was converted into a chemical laboratory in 1781. The human bones exhibited evidence for dissection and display such as holes drilled in some bones, attached wires and copper staining.

References
Bennett *et al.* 2000; Hull 2003

Oxford Castle/Oxford Prison

Grid Reference	SP 5098 0613
Cemetery type	Prison cemetery
Date of cemetery	16th–18th century
Number of bodies excavated	64
Date of excavation	1999–2002

Fifty-nine burials were recovered from the ditch between the motte and bailey of Oxford Castle. The bodies are thought to date from the sixteenth to eighteenth centuries and are likely to be prisoners who were executed at the prison or died while there. A number of burials exhibit unusual features, including prone burials and multiple burials. Evidence for dissection was present.

References
Norton 2006

Rycote Chapel, Thame

Grid Reference	SP 667 046
Cemetery type	Private Chapel
Date of cemetery	1649–1889
Number of bodies excavated	24
Date of excavation	2004

In 2004, the 24 coffins in the crypt below Rycote Chapel, a private chapel at Rycote Park near Thame in Oxfordshire, were recorded. The coffins represented six generations of the Bertie family. The earliest identified burial, in the only anthropoid coffin, dated to 1649. The remaining burials were in triple-shelled single break coffins with the last interment dating to 1884.

References
Boston 2008

St. Aldate's Church, Oxford

Grid Reference	SP 51350 06000
Cemetery type	Churchyard
Date of cemetery	18th–19th century
Number of bodies excavated	c.50
Date of excavation	1999

Approximately 50 grave structures dating to the eighteenth and nineteenth centuries were uncovered, including earth cut graves and brick lined shaft graves in an area previously part of the churchyard. There was some preservation of wooden coffins. One of the intramural shaft graves (dating to the mid nineteenth century) used stone slabs to separate the coffins rather than iron bars. A large stone built charnel pit was also noted in the centre of the chancel. Stone memorial slabs were also recorded. A two year-old child was found with a musket ball in the cranial cavity.

References
Tyler 2001

St Clement's churchyard, The Plain, Oxford

Grid Reference	SP 523 059
Cemetery type	Churchyard
Date of cemetery	18th–19th century
Number of bodies excavated	16
Date of excavation	2007

Sixteen west-east aligned earth-cut graves and a brick lined burial shaft were uncovered during a watching brief on the former site of the St Clements Churchyard. Burial is thought to have ceased on the site in 1828. Coffin fittings accompanying the burials suggest an eighteenth- to nineteenth-century date for the burials.

References
Webb 2007

St. Laurence Church, Appleton

Grid Reference	SP 445 015
Cemetery type	Churchyard
Date of cemetery	Mid-18th–early 19th century
Number of bodies excavated	30
Date of excavation	2002–3?

Excavations prior to the extension and refurbishing of church uncovered a total of 30 burials. Twenty-six of these were in earth cut graves of unknown date. A total of 10 brick-lined barrel vaulted graves were identified during the excavations. A number were empty or were not excavated. A total of four burials were observed within the brick-lined graves. One was in a triple shelled coffin, another lay in the remains of wooden coffins. Coffin fittings associated with the burials in the vaults suggest a mid eighteenth- to mid nineteenth-century date for the burials

References
Oxford Archaeology 2003

St. Laurence Church, South Hinksey

Grid Reference	SP 5096 0398
Cemetery type	Churchyard
Date of cemetery	18th–19th century
Number of bodies excavated	3
Date of excavation	2009

Three post-medieval graves were revealed during a watching brief prior to construction work. Coffins fittings found with two of the burials dated to the eighteenth or nineteenth century

References
Sims 2009

St. Mary's Church, Banbury

Grid Reference	SP 454 405
Cemetery type	Churchyard
Date of cemetery	Post-medieval
Number of bodies excavated	2
Date of excavation	2008

A watching brief prior to the renovation of a boundary wall revealed a brick lined grave containing two burials, possibly of seventeenth-century date

References
Sims 2008

St. Mary's Church, Garsington

Grid Reference	SP 58 02
Cemetery type	Churchyard
Date of cemetery	Post-medieval
Number of bodies excavated	1
Date of excavation	1994

Excavation of soakaway trenches revealed some disarticulated bone and partially exposed an in situ Victorian burial. A watching brief in 1997 located an undated burial vault.

References
ADS; Oxford Archaeological Unit 1999

St Mary the Virgin Church, Kirtlington

Grid Reference	NGR SP 500 196
Cemetery type	Churchyard
Date of cemetery	Post-medieval
Number of bodies excavated	37
Date of excavation	2007

Thirty-seven burials were excavated from the north and west of the churchyard during an archaeological watching brief. One was in a coffin with fittings indicative of a post-medieval date. Fittings from another two coffins were uncovered, which dated to the eighteenth to nineteenth century.

References
Gibson 2008

St. Nicholas' Church, Abingdon

Grid Reference	SU 4983 9708
Cemetery type	Churchyard
Date of cemetery	Post-medieval
Number of bodies excavated	c.7
Date of excavation	1993

Excavations in the cemetery of St Nicholas, (in use until 1881) revealed a minimum of seven post-medieval/Victorian graves, three of which were brick-lined, in the eastern half of a trench placed on the north of the church. The skeletal remains were left in situ.

References
Oxford Archaeology 1992; Ponsford 1994:122

St. Nicholas' Church, Chadlington

Grid Reference	SP 332 211
Cemetery type	Churchyard
Date of cemetery	Post-medieval
Number of bodies excavated	1
Date of excavation	2007

A watching brief revealed a probably post-medieval burial and a brick lined grave. The brick lined grave was not opened but the remains of a burial were observed within.

References
Webb 2008

St. Nicholas' Church, Forest Hill, Oxfordshire

Grid Reference	SP 58 07
Cemetery type	Churchyard

Date of cemetery	Post-medieval, possibly Georgian or Victorian
Number of bodies excavated	15
Date of excavation	Unknown

Fifteen graves, including two brick lined shaft graves, were excavated. The burials were all west-east, with coffin fittings suggesting a post-medieval, probably Georgian or Victorian, date for the burials. One individual has undergone a postmortem. All bar one burial were in wooden coffins, the majority of which had coffin fittings. One burial was in a triple-shelled coffin.

References
Boston 2004

St. Nicholas Church, Rotherfield Greys

Grid Reference	SU 7263 8231
Cemetery type	Churchyard
Date of cemetery	18th–19th century
Number of bodies excavated	Unknown
Date of excavation	2003

Burials and coffin fittings and furniture of eighteenth- and nineteenth-century date were recorded in churchyard.

References
Ponsford 2004:308

The Regal Cinema Site, Abingdon

Grid Reference	SU 4962 9702
Cemetery type	War burials
Date of cemetery	17th century
Number of bodies excavated	26
Date of excavation	1995, 2002

Excavations revealed a post-medieval cemetery of 18 individuals in 1995. The skeletons were assessed in situ. During a second phase of excavation in 2002, these skeletons were re-exposed and re-excavated. Another eight skeletons were discovered during this phase of excavation. Residual pottery and the nature of the burial practices, in unadorned wooden coffins, suggest an early post-medieval date for the burials, probably seventeenth century. While most burials were single inhumations, four graves contained multiple burials of two or three individuals.

References
Boston 2005c; Norton, Laws and Smith 2005; Boston and Boyle n.d.

Shropshire

Broseley Pipeworks

Grid Reference	SJ 6720 0230
Cemetery type	Quaker burial ground
Date of cemetery	Post-medieval
Number of bodies excavated	Unknown
Date of excavation	1990s

Burials associated with the Society of Friends Burial Ground were noted.

References
BIAB supp. 8/1997:889

High Ercall, Ercall Magna

Grid Reference	SJ 594 173
Cemetery type	Isolated burial
Date of cemetery	Post Civil War, pre 18th–19th century
Number of bodies excavated	1
Date of excavation	1977

In 1977 a skeleton was found cut into a ditch around a manor house dating from the Civil War. The remains are thought to be pre-eighteenth/nineteenth century. The articulated remains of a horse, possibly a burial, were found in the same area in 1991.

References
ADS; Buteux 1996

Old St Chad's Church, Shrewsbury

Grid Reference	SJ 492 123
Cemetery type	Churchyard
Date of cemetery	Late Saxon–Post-medieval
Number of bodies excavated	Unknown
Date of excavation	1889–90

Crypt with late Saxon to post-medieval burials was recorded.

References
ADS; Hannaford 1995

St. Andrew's, Ashford Bowdler

Grid Reference	SO 519 706
Cemetery type	Churchyard
Date of cemetery	19th century?
Number of bodies excavated	3
Date of excavation	2003?

Three skeletons and associated finds probably nineteenth century in date were recorded.

References
Ponsford 2004:310

The Railway Station, Shrewsbury

Grid Reference	SJ 494 129
Cemetery type	Isolated burial
Date of cemetery	16th century?
Number of bodies excavated	1
Date of excavation	1902–3

The station yard was excavated in 1902–03 revealing the partial skeleton of young man associated with lime traces. This has been interpreted as an illicit burial. Other things found included bronze 'bodkin', an Elizabethan silver coin and a knife blade.

References
ADS

Wenlock Priory, Much Wenlock

Grid Reference	SJ 625 001
Cemetery type	Churchyard
Date of cemetery	16th century
Number of bodies excavated	1
Date of excavation	1982

A sixteenth-century coffin burial of a priest was found on the south side of the chapel. This included a brown-glazed ceramic vessel of the type usually identified as a salt. It has been suggested that this was used instead of the metal mortuary chalice usually found in graves of priests.

References
Egan 1983:185

Somerset

Fore Street, Wellington

Grid Reference	ST 1379 2046
Cemetery type	Non-conformist burial ground
Date of cemetery	1680–mid-19th century
Number of bodies excavated	c.100
Date of excavation	2002

Around 100 individuals (male, female and juvenile) were found in a pit in the centre of Wellington, in the area of a non-conformist burial ground in use from 1680 to the mid-nineteenth century.

References
www.thisisthewestcountry.co.uk

Glastonbury Tor

Grid Reference	ST 515 386
Cemetery type	Isolated burial
Date of cemetery	1741
Number of bodies excavated	1
Date of excavation	1964–6

A post-medieval burial was found at the east end of Glastonbury Tor. The individual had been buried in a coffin and the remains are thought to be those of John Rawls, whose burial on the Tor in 1741 was recorded in the burial register of St. John's Church, Glastonbury.

References
Rahtz 1971; Rahtz and Watts 2003

Hinton St. George

Grid Reference	ST 4183 1270
Cemetery type	Private chapel
Date of cemetery	16th–19th century
Number of bodies excavated	41
Date of excavation	1981, 1987

An assessment of the Poulett Vault, which lies below the family chapel, recorded 39 coffins. The vault was built in the sixteenth century and then extended in the nineteenth century. The extension of the vault contained seventeenth- to nineteenth-century triple shelled coffins. The older part of the vault contained at least 22 poorly stacked coffins, including one, possibly two, anthropomorphic lead shells.

References
Egan 1988:189–91; Litten, Dawson and Boore 1988

Masonic Hall, 12 Old Orchard Street, Bath

Grid Reference	ST 752 646
Cemetery type	Catholic burial ground
Date of cemetery	1808–1850's
Number of bodies excavated	Unknown
Date of excavation	2003

Originally the building was a theatre, then converted to Catholic Chapel in 1808, remaining in use until the 1850s when it became the Masonic Hall. The basement contained eleven ashlar-lined tombs, each with up to three lead coffins inside. One lead coffin was found outside the tombs.

References
Moller 2003; Ponsford 2004:241

Quaker Burial Ground at Bathford

Grid Reference	ST 7851 6710
Cemetery type	Quaker burial ground
Date of cemetery	1734–1845
Number of bodies excavated	Unknown
Date of excavation	1993

Human remains were recorded during their removal for exhumation elsewhere. The burial ground was founded in 1734 and was in use until 1845. The majority of burials were earth cut graves, oriented north-south with the head to the south. A number of walled graves and lead coffins were also noted, within which bodies were buried with their heads to the north. The walled graves were made of Bath stone ashlar and there was some variation in their construction. Of the ten lead coffins, eight were buried in walled graves. The lead coffins had no external decoration. Traces of elm coffins were also noted. A variety of eighteenth-century grips and grip-plates recovered, made of iron or tin, one dating to around 1775. There were some similarities to coffin furniture known from London. Eight coffin name plates were also noted; the majority were shield shaped, but two were rectangular. There was some evidence of textile coverings for the coffins and some fragments of textile linings were also noted. Some traces of clothing were noted, including woven textile, felt and flock. One skeleton in a lead coffin was found with the remains of a cloth over the face.

References
Stock 1998b

Rook Lane Chapel, Frome

Grid Reference	ST 7753 4787
Cemetery type	Non-conformist burial ground
Date of cemetery	End of 17th–early 19th century
Number of bodies excavated	Unknown
Date of excavation	1992–3

Several brick-lined shaft graves of the eighteenth century or early nineteenth century were recorded during rescue excavations and the restoration of the Nonconformist Chapel.

References
Ponsford 1993:207; Stafford 1993; Croft and Hollinrake 1992

St. Mary Magdalene Church, Taunton

Grid Reference	ST 2288 2463
Cemetery type	Churchyard
Date of cemetery	Post-medieval
Number of bodies excavated	Unknown
Date of excavation	1992

Excavations on the north-east side of the church revealed disturbed human bone and thirteen burials (one of which was within a vault). Brickwork from the vault suggested an eighteenth- to nineteenth-century date. The remaining twelve burials could not be directly dated. All were aligned east to west. Associated unstratified coffin fittings of eighteenth- to nineteenth-century date suggested that they are of this date or earlier.

References
Ponsford 1993:207; ADS

St. Mary's Church, Saltford

Grid Reference	ST 6855 6750
Cemetery type	Churchyard
Date of cemetery	1792–20th century
Number of bodies excavated	5
Date of excavation	1994

Six trenches revealed earth cut and stone capped burials of the nineteenth and twentieth centuries. A brick arched burial vault containing at least five individuals was also recorded. These burials dated to between 1792 and 1824. An area of eighteenth- and nineteenth-century infant burials was also noted.

References
BIAB supp. 5/1994:158; Hume 1994

St. Mary's Church, Wedmore

Grid Reference	ST 4347 4793
Cemetery type	Churchyard
Date of cemetery	Post-medieval
Number of bodies excavated	6
Date of excavation	1992

Excavation on the north-east side of church revealed disturbed bone and six burials. One burial was within a vault with associated monument above it to James Hardwick (d. 5 Nov 1836).

References
Ponsford 1993:208; ADS

St. Mary's Church, Whitelackington

Grid Reference	ST 3796 1526
Cemetery type	Churchyard
Date of cemetery	Post-medieval
Number of bodies excavated	Unknown
Date of excavation	1989

In 1989 a small excavation revealed the disarticulated remains of eight individuals, disturbed by four later burials in wooden coffins. The latter were left undisturbed. Associated post-medieval artefacts, including coffin handles and fittings, were noted. In 1996, graves were recorded during construction work in the south aisle. Some had been inserted beneath the floors between the box pews.

References
BIAB supp. 7/1996:744; Graham 1996

St. Nicholas's Church, Bathampton

Grid Reference	ST 7770 6660
Cemetery type	Churchyard
Date of cemetery	19th century
Number of bodies excavated	Unknown
Date of excavation	1992–3

Building works to the north-east of the church disturbed twenty walled graves made of Bath stone ashlar blocks, as well as 26 interstitial earth graves mostly of nineteenth century date. All individuals appeared to be of high social and economic status. Coffins, made of elm, were preserved as were coffin fittings and furnishings including textiles, which were recorded where possible. Coffin plates were of a variety of shapes and these showed no correlation with either gender or status. Several individuals were wrapped in winding sheets and one male adult had his jaw tied closed. The faces of most individuals were covered with sheets. The remains of David Dallas (d. 1829 aged 28) were buried in a militaristic suit of felt-like fabric with shoulder pads and trousers with plain metal buttons down sides. Another skeleton (Mary Hume d. 1843 aged 75) was found with two narrow hallmarked gold rings on one finger of her left hand, and a set of sprung dentures. These had gold springs and a combination of natural 'Waterloo' and ceramic teeth. One individual (Lt. Gen. Sir Thomas Dallas GCB, d. 1839 aged 81) showed evidence of cranial autopsy.

References
BIAB supp. 4/1993:241; Cox and Stock 1995

St. Peter's, Exton

Grid Reference	SS 926 337
Cemetery type	Churchyard
Date of cemetery	1608
Number of bodies excavated	1
Date of excavation	1984

During a church recording, a single break gable lidded elm coffin, with its outer surface covered in pitched cambric or linen with black headed upholstery nails, was discovered

References
Litten 1991

St. Thomas a Becket Church, Widcombe, Bath

Grid Reference	ST 760 639
Cemetery type	Churchyard
Date of cemetery	16th century onwards
Number of bodies excavated	50
Date of excavation	1995

Fifty in situ inhumations, dating from the sixteenth century onwards were recorded. Forty were adult, three children and seven infants. The majority of coffin furniture came from the upper layer of burials. One lead coffin was recorded in the open cemetery, as well as traces of wooden coffins with grips and name plates. Two walled graves of Bath-stone ashlar, dating to 1833 and 1836 were surveyed. The first contained only one studded wooden coffin of a 16 year-old woman with a square copper alloy name plate. The second walled grave was of similar construction and was built for the Hedger family of Widcombe. It was placed over an earlier earth burial with a flat memorial stone to Matilda Maria Hedger died aged around 10 years in 1825. There was also a metal name plate in the shape of a shield on the coffin. Her skull showed evidence of post-mortem cranial autopsy. A one month-old male baby was added six months later, without an additional inscription. The walled grave was erected in 1833 to receive remains of Francis Hedger aged 52 in 1833. He was wrapped in a plain shroud and buried in a triple shell coffin with a copper alloy shield-shaped name plate. The coffin rested on iron bars, as did a similar coffin for his wife, Sarah, deposited 1843. She also had a copper alloy name shield. Sarah was wrapped in a carefully arranged shroud with ribbing over the chest and her head was on a pillow of similar fabric.

References
Lewcun 1995; Ponsford and Jackson 1996:245

Staffordshire

Church of St. Michael the Archangel, Rushall, Walsall

Grid Reference	SP 0249 9990
Cemetery type	Churchyard
Date of cemetery	17th–19th century
Number of bodies excavated	79
Date of excavation	2003?

Seventy-nine burials were recorded, of which 37 were in situ, mostly of nineteenth-century date, but some dating back to the seventeenth century.

References
Ponsford 2004:318

Lichfield Cathedral, Lichfield

Grid Reference	SK 117 097
Cemetery type	Churchyard
Date of cemetery	Post-medieval
Number of bodies excavated	Unknown
Date of excavation	1992 and 1994

A survey of tombs within the cathedral identified a small number of burials dating to the sixteenth to eighteenth centuries. Only three brick-built vaults containing lead-lined coffins were located. The stone-built tomb of Bishop John Hackett (d. 1671) was partially exposed, and the now-unmarked burial in a lead-lined coffin of Bishop Richard Smallbroke (d. 1794) was also located. Other graves contained plain timber coffins with iron fittings. In five cases, all dating to the early eighteenth century, initials and dates of the deceased were formed by hammering brass tacks into the lid. In two coffins the corpse was laid on a bed of lime-plaster and in another it was on a bed of coal dust.

References
Ponsford and Jackson 1995:116

Mayfield

Grid Reference	SK 1585 4523
Cemetery type	War burials
Date of cemetery	Post-medieval
Number of bodies excavated	Unknown
Date of excavation	Unknown

Human remains, possibly from a seventeenth-century battle cemetery were noted.

References
ADS

St. Bartholomew's Church, Penn, Wolverhampton

Grid Reference	SO 8945 9529
Cemetery type	Churchyard
Date of cemetery	Late 18th–20th century
Number of bodies excavated	372
Date of excavation	1999

In 1994, excavations revealed the graves and articulated remains of more than twenty individuals dating to the nineteenth century, as well as several of an earlier date. Brick burial vaults, probably also nineteenth century, were noted. In 1999, 372 burials from the rural churchyard of eighteenth- to nineteenth-century date were recorded and moved. The majority were buried in shrouds in earth cut graves or within wooden coffins. Triple shell lead and wooden coffins were encountered, often in brick-shaft graves or extra-mural brick vaults. Some coffins showed traces of outer fabric covers. A wide variety of coffin fittings were found, some of which were similar to examples known from Christ Church Spitalfields, and others were unique to the site. Most appear to have been made in Birmingham. Three skeletons showed evidence of cranial post-mortem surgery. The remains of wreaths were found on the coffins of several burials including a woman who died aged 33 in 1806 and a 63 year-old woman who died in 1897.

References
Bell 1994; Boyle 2002; Boyle 2004

St. Mary and All Saints' Church, Trentham

Grid Reference	SJ 8654 4091
Cemetery type	Churchyard
Date of cemetery	Mid-16th–late 18th century
Number of bodies excavated	5
Date of excavation	1998

Five burials noted dating from between mid-16th century to late 18th century were uncovered.

References
ADS; Boothroyd 1998; BIAB supp. 9/1998:845

University of Wolverhampton, Wolverhampton

Grid Reference	SO 9150 9890
Cemetery type	Churchyard
Date of cemetery	19th century
Number of bodies excavated	4
Date of excavation	1996

Four disturbed burials were uncovered within a brick-lined vault in the north-east corner of a nineteenth-century overspill graveyard for St. Peter's Church.

References
BIAB supp. 7/1996:789; Coates and Litherland 1996

Suffolk

Barnardiston Vaults, Kedington Church

Grid Reference	TL 705 4705
Cemetery type	Churchyard
Date of cemetery	16th century onwards.
Number of bodies excavated	46
Date of excavation	1915

Coffins dating to between the sixteenth to nineteenth centuries were recorded in the vault with the majority of datable remains being seventeenth century and later. The north vault held nine well preserved lead coffins enclosed in shells of wood. The oldest dated to 1700, 1704 and 1728. The eastern vault held eight lead coffins which had previously been enclosed in outer wooden shells. The south and south-eastern vault held 37 coffins, most dilapidated with no visible inscriptions. Most of the outer shells were of oak. Some anthropomorphic lead coffins were observed. These included three infant coffins, two of which were dated to 1671.

References
W.H.B. 1918:44–8

Francisan Way/Wolsey Street, Ipswich

Grid Reference	TM 16 44
Cemetery type	Post-dissolution
Date of cemetery	Early post-medieval
Number of bodies excavated	56
Date of excavation	1990

Fifty-six human burials may indicate the post-dissolution reuse of the friary as a hospital. No evidence for coffins. It has been suggested that the site may have used to bury paupers or plague victims. One skeleton was found with manacles on wrists.

References
BIAB supp. 2/1990:257–8; Newman 1990

St. Margaret's Church, Ipswich

Grid Reference	TM 1660 4485
Cemetery type	Churchyard
Date of cemetery	Post-medieval
Number of bodies excavated	Unknown
Date of excavation	1999

Skeletons and coffin fittings were recorded.

References
BIAB 10.1/1999:337; Finch 1999

Surrey

All Saints Church, Laleham

Grid Reference	TQ 035 715
Cemetery type	Churchyard
Date of cemetery	Post-medieval
Number of bodies excavated	5
Date of excavation	2008

Five burials were excavated during an archaeological evaluation. The accompanying coffin fittings indicate a post-medieval date. Medieval burials were also uncovered.

References
Oxford Archaeology 2008

Friends' Burial Ground, High Street, Staines

Grid Reference	TQ 035 715
Cemetery type	Quaker burial ground
Date of cemetery	1849–1944
Number of bodies excavated	78
Date of excavation	1975–6

Seventy-eight graves dating from 1849 to 1944, many containing multiple interments, were uncovered at Jordan's Quaker Burial Ground, Buckinghamshire. Of these, 34 graves were excavated. 31 were brick lined and contained up to four individual burials, stacked on top of each other and separated by stone flagstones. Wood and lead coffins were recovered with a variety of brass coffin furniture. Some shallow earth-cut graves were also noted, located between the vaults. The axis of the burials was north to south with the head to the south where it could be discerned.

References
Crouch and Shanks 1984

St. Nicholas Church, Shepperton

Grid Reference	TQ 0770 6661
Cemetery type	Churchyard
Date of cemetery	Post-medieval
Number of bodies excavated	7
Date of excavation	1999

Brick tombs, disarticulated and articulated human burials were uncovered, including seven complete burials aligned east to west.

References
BIAB supp. 10.2/1999:944–5; Stevenson 1999

Sussex

De la Warr vault, Withyham

Grid Reference	TQ 4939 3556
Cemetery type	Churchyard
Date of cemetery	16th–17th century
Number of bodies excavated	3
Date of excavation	Unknown

A vault containing an early example of a gable-lidded single break coffin, containing the remains of Lady Margaret Howard (d. 1591), was recorded. Also present were two anthropomorphic coffins containing infants dating to 1615 and 1618.

References
Litten 1991

St. John the Baptist Church, Southover High Street, Southover, Lewes

Grid Reference	TQ 412096
Cemetery type	Churchyard
Date of cemetery	18th Century
Number of bodies excavated	Unknown
Date of excavation	2009

An archaeological assessment prior to the construction of a new chapter house uncovered eighteenth-century graves.

References
Grant 2009

St. Mary's Church, Church Street, West Chiltington

Grid Reference	TQ 0901 1833
Cemetery type	Churchyard
Date of cemetery	Late 19th century.
Number of bodies excavated	Unknown
Date of excavation	1998

Burials from the last quarter of the nineteenth century, overlying earlier burials were recorded, as well as many other burials.

References
BIAB supp. 9/1998:905; Wildman 1998

Warwickshire

28 High Street, Alcester

Grid Reference	SP 0900 5734
Cemetery type	Quaker burial ground
Date of cemetery	1677–1835
Number of bodies excavated	6–12
Date of excavation	2003?

Six to twelve burials were located, probably from the former Quaker Meeting House graveyard which was in use between 1677 and 1835.

References
Ponsford 2004:319

All Saints Church, Leek Wootton

Grid Reference	SP 2885 6875
Cemetery type	Churchyard
Date of cemetery	Post-medieval
Number of bodies excavated	3
Date of excavation	2000

Two eighteenth-century gravestones were recovered inside church. These belonged to the Mallory family and had been laid over a brick built vault containing three lead coffins. One of these still showed traces of the outer wood coffin with double copper alloy studded decoration and a fabric cover.

References
BIAB supp. 10.2/1999:1132; Coutts and Parkhouse 2000

Church of St. James the Great, Snitterfield

Grid Reference	SP 2187 6008
Cemetery type	Churchyard
Date of cemetery	Late 19th century
Number of bodies excavated	Unknown
Date of excavation	1999

Late nineteenth-century inhumations were recorded.

References
BIAB supp 10.1/1999:590–1; Jones 1999

Church of St. Mary and St. Bartholomew, Hampton in Arden, Solihull

Grid Reference	SP 2030 8075
Cemetery type	Churchyard
Date of cemetery	18th–20th century
Number of bodies excavated	Unknown
Date of excavation	2002

Eighteenth- to twentieth-century burials recorded, removed and reburied within the churchyard. Some burials also recorded from church interior on north side of chancel, but few datable.

References
Ponsford 2003:298

Holy Trinity Church, Coventry

Grid Reference	SP 3350 7910
Cemetery type	Churchyard
Date of cemetery	1776–1850s
Number of bodies excavated	1706
Date of excavation	1997

A total of 1706 burials and associated coffins and coffin fittings were recorded and recovered during excavations on the site of Coventry cathedral, which had been reconsecrated in 1776 as an overspill churchyard for the adjacent Holy Trinity Church. Some of the coffins had floral wreaths still lying on top. Four individuals exhibited evidence of autopsy. The contorted position of the arms of one of the burials have led to suggestions that this individual may have been interred alive, but comatose.

References
BIAB supp. 8/1997:504; Andrews and Oakey 1998; Oakley and Andrews 1998; Soden 2000

Holy Trinity Churchyard, Sutton Coldfield

Grid Reference	SP 1219 9628
Cemetery type	Churchyard
Date of cemetery	Mid-18th century–1880s
Number of bodies excavated	At least 30
Date of excavation	1992

Post-medieval burials were recorded, including information on their age and state of preservation in the original churchyard and its 1832 extension. Coffin fittings and coffin nails were associated with many of the burials. The burials have been dated to between mid-eighteenth century to 1880s.

References
BIAB supp 3/1992:309; Leach and Sterenberg 1992

Park Street Burial Ground

Grid Reference	SP 0737 8709
Cemetery type	Churchyard
Date of cemetery	1810–1873
Number of bodies excavated	11
Date of excavation	2002

Excavations at the Park Street burial ground, a detached burial ground of St. Martin's-in-the-Bullring, uncovered the remains of eleven individuals with associated coffin fittings and nails.

References
Krakowicz and Rudge 2004

St Martin's Church, Bull Ring, Birmingham

Grid Reference	SP 07 86
Cemetery type	Churchyard
Date of cemetery	Majority from late 18th–mid-19th
Number of bodies excavated	857
Date of excavation	1974, 2001

In 2001, a total of 857 burials, mainly from the late eighteenth century and the first half of the nineteenth century were excavated on the north side of the church. The earliest dated burial was from the 1720s in an earth cut grave with copper alloy lettering remaining from where it had been attached to the coffin lid. Burial more or less ended in 1863 when the first public cemetery in Birmingham opened. Bodies were interred with the head to the west, and supine, usually in a wooden coffin with metal fittings. Charnel pits were also noted.

Seven hundred and forty nine of the burials were in inter-cutting earth graves, sometimes with two or more interments stacked above each other. One double burial was found with two adults, tightly shrouded, lying side by side with arms crossed over their chests. Coffins in the earth cut graves appear to have been of single wooden case 'single break' construction with iron grips, where these could be distinguished. In 27 cases the wood could be identified: it was mostly elm, with oak and pine used occasionally. Twenty-three brick lined graves were recorded, scattered among the earth cut graves and covered with a barrel vault or with flat slabs. Of the burials in brick-lined graves, one individual in a 'fish-tail' coffin was found with a tortoiseshell hair slide. Another grave containing an adult, a juvenile and an infant, contained a complete necklace consisting of pink glass beads with a copper alloy pendant inlaid with a cut glass rose attached. Eleven brick vaults were excavated, also of late eighteenth and nineteenth century in date. One male individual was found wearing the gold mourning ring of Mr Thomas Martin, died 1808, and a gold wedding ring was found with an 81 year-old woman, who was also buried with her dentures. A hair pin, hair combs and grips were also found.

In terms of textiles, wool coffin linings, funerary garments trimmed with silk and satin, silk hair ribbons, covered buttons and a face cloth were noted, as well as shroud pins and hooks. One male individual was buried in a pair of unfashionable, heavily darned and multicoloured socks. The remains of wreaths survived in four vaults. These were mainly composed of the tough leaves and twiggy elements of evergreen trees or shrubs. Box, juniper and privet were noted, with box the most prevalent. A number of single case and double case wooden coffins were found in brick lined graves and vaults. Only half of the coffins from the vaults were of triple shell lead lined construction. As with the earth cut graves, elm was the most common wood, with oak appearing occasionally. Grips were mostly of copper alloy, and grip plates were of copper alloy, iron, lead or tin/nickel. Eight coffins from the vaults showed evidence of textile covers, and linings and shroud fragments were found from vaults and earth cut graves. Evidence was found for post mortem cranial surgery.

References
ADS; Buteux 2003; Brickley and Buteux 2006

St. Peter's Church, Barford

Grid Reference	SP 2730 6090
Cemetery type	Churchyard
Date of cemetery	18th–19th century
Number of bodies excavated	Unknown
Date of excavation	1998

Two grave markers and associated remains recorded. One green sandstone headstone was associated with a coffin. The headstone dated the interment to 1775. The other marker was a red sandstone vault lid with no associated remains identified. Numerous burials, some of eighteenth- and nineteenth-century date, were noted.

References
BIAB supp. 9/1998:882; Sterenberg 1998

St. Phillip's Cathedral Churchyard, Birmingham

Grid Reference	SP 0710 8710
Cemetery type	Churchyard
Date of cemetery	Early 18th century–mid-19th century
Number of bodies excavated	At least 30
Date of excavation	1999

Brick burial vaults and the remains of 22 individuals were recorded in the churchyard. The burial vault of Baldwin Family, which contained four fish-tailed lead coffins and one individual interred in a wooden coffin, and Harrison family, which contained eight burials, were recorded. Many of the burials in the vaults were in fish-tailed coffins.

References
ADS; BIAB supp. 10.2/1999:1079; Patrick 1999 and 2001

Tysoe, Stratford on Avon

Grid Reference	SP 3523 4586
Cemetery type	War burials
Date of cemetery	Possibly 17th century
Number of bodies excavated	1
Date of excavation	Late 19th century

Skeleton found in the nineteenth century with point of sword sticking into the breast bone, thought to date to the seventeenth century and linked to the Battle of Edgehill.

References
ADS

Wiltshire

9a Wood Street, Calne

Grid Reference	ST 997 712
Cemetery type	Quaker burial ground
Date of cemetery	1696–mid 19th century
Number of bodies excavated	2
Date of excavation	2006

Two skeletons were uncovered during a watching brief on the site of a Quaker cemetery in use between the late seventeenth and mid nineteenth century. A coffin handle removed from one of the graves was dated to the late eighteenth or early nineteenth century.

References
Mumford 2006

Boscombe Down Airfield, Amesbury

Grid Reference	SU 176 393
Cemetery type	Isolated burial
Date of cemetery	15th–17th century
Number of bodies excavated	1
Date of excavation	2009

A watching brief undertaken prior to construction work uncovered the shallow burial of a young adult male. There was no evidence for a coffin and the burial appeared to have been orientated north-south.

References
McKinley and Manning 2010

Lydiard Tregoze

Grid Reference	SU 1040 8475
Cemetery type	Churchyard
Date of cemetery	Mid 17th century
Number of bodies excavated	1
Date of excavation	Unknown

The western St. John vault contained a lead coffin of mid-seventeenth-century date with grip plates and handles

References
Litten 1991

St. Mary Magdalene Church, Hullavington

Grid Reference	ST 8940 8205
Cemetery type	Churchyard
Date of cemetery	19th century
Number of bodies excavated	10
Date of excavation	1995–6

Disturbed and disarticulated human bone was recorded as well as ten unmarked burials. Coffin fittings associated with three of the burials suggest a nineteenth-century date.

References
BIAB supp. 7/1996:816; Turner 1996

St. Peter's Church, Codford

Grid Reference	ST 966 399
Cemetery type	Churchyard
Date of cemetery	Late 18th–19th century
Number of bodies excavated	Unknown
Date of excavation	1999

The rapid recording of late eighteenth-century and nineteenth-century brick vaults on south side of church was undertaken.

References
ADS; Leach 1999

The Saxon Church, Alton Barnes

Grid Reference	SU 109 621
Cemetery type	Churchyard
Date of cemetery	18th century
Number of bodies excavated	1
Date of excavation	1971–2

A late eighteenth-century child's wooden coffin decorated with brass studs was recorded. Traces of heart shaped iron coffin handles and tin or tin alloy grip plate impressed with cherub design were noted.

References
Thompson and Ross 1973

Wilton

Grid Reference	SU 0990 3109
Cemetery type	Unknown
Date of cemetery	Post-medieval
Number of bodies excavated	Unknown
Date of excavation	1961

Burials were found with seventeenth-century pottery in 1961.

References
ADS

Zion Baptist Chapel, Calne

Grid Reference	SU 009717
Cemetery type	Baptist burial ground
Date of cemetery	19th century
Number of bodies excavated	10
Date of excavation	2008

An archaeological evaluation on the site of the burial ground belonging to the Zion Baptist Chapel uncovered six earth cut graves, two brick lined grave shafts and two stone lined grave shafts. Not all features were fully excavated but coffins were observed in two of the earth-cut graves and the brick- and stone-lined grave shafts. One of the coffins appears to be of wood and zinc construction.

References
Webb 2008

Worcestershire

Baptist Church, Bewley

Grid Reference	SO 787 752
Cemetery type	Baptist burial ground
Date of cemetery	Post-medieval
Number of bodies excavated	Unknown
Date of excavation	1992

Coffined interments were recovered from within the crypt of the eighteenth-century church/chapel.

References
BIAB supp. 3/1992:475; Ponsford 1993:206

Civic Square, Oldbury

Grid Reference	SO 9898 8956
Cemetery type	Unknown
Date of cemetery	1529–1855
Number of bodies excavated	20
Date of excavation	2003

Twenty partial and complete burials within coffins were noted in a service trench, but not excavated. Coffins were mostly of simple plank construction. No coffin plates or other furniture was observed. One brick-lined grave and a brick crypt were also identified. More graves were found to the south. Documentary evidence dates the use of the graveyard to between 1529 and 1855.

References
Ponsford 2004:309–10

Pershore Abbey, Pershore

Grid Reference	SO 947 457
Cemetery type	Churchyard
Date of cemetery	Late 17th–early 19th century
Number of bodies excavated	Unknown
Date of excavation	1996–7

Burials dating from the late seventeenth to early nineteenth century were recorded from brick-lined barrel roofed burial vaults, located in the south transept, the crossing, the central aisle of the choir and in front of the entrance to the Lady Chapel. The roofs of six vaults were removed and produced evidence of coffins. All datable coffins were nineteenth century and the latest recorded coffin dated to 1854. The coffins were either wooden or of triple shell construction. Some had cloth coverings. Coffin fittings, including brass studs, name plates, decorative coffin plates and grips, were recovered. Two of the interior lead shells were decorated with rectangular patches of white paint. Two vaults contained a large amount of disarticulated bone, mostly long bones and skulls, which had probably been inserted when the church was restored in the 1860s.

References
Blockley 1996; Blockley 2000a; Blockley 2000b

St. Oswald's Almshouses, Worcester

Grid Reference	SO 8481 5565
Cemetery type	Unknown
Date of cemetery	18th–19th century
Number of bodies excavated	Unknown
Date of excavation	1998, 1999

Vaults containing articulated human remains dating to the eighteenth and nineteenth centuries were recorded. Coffin furniture was also retrieved. Documents record an almshouse and chapel associated with the graveyard in the late eighteenth to late nineteenth centuries.

References
BIAB supp. 10.2/1999:1144; Edwards 1992; Griffin 2000

Tallow Hill, Worcester

Grid Reference	SO 856 550
Cemetery type	Garden cemetery?
Date of cemetery	1823–1895
Number of bodies excavated	9
Date of excavation	2002

Part of Tallow Hill cemetery in Worcester was excavated in 2002. The cemetery was established by an Act of Parliament in 1792 to cope with increasing population of Worcester. It is an inner city cemetery in an industrial part of the city. The remains of nine individuals were recovered, one from a deep grave, two children from a brick-lined vault and six adults from a second brick-lined vault. All burials were in wooden coffins. One individual had perimortem cuts to the manubrium and underside of medial clavicle – thought to be the result of the undertaker cutting through the pectoral girdle to wedge body into coffin.

References
Ogden, Boylston and Vaughan 2005

Yorkshire

All Saints' Church, Pavement, York

Grid Reference	SE 6014 5171
Cemetery type	Churchyard
Date of cemetery	17th–19th century
Number of bodies excavated	17
Date of excavation	1995

Seventeen post-medieval burials dating from the seventeenth to nineteenth century were excavated from within and around All Saints' Church, with associated evidence for coffins and coffin fittings. One female skull was still wearing a funerary bonnet.

References
MAP Archaeological Consultancy Ltd 1998

Carver Street Methodist Chapel, Sheffield

Grid Reference	SK 3525 8725
Cemetery type	Non-conformist burial ground
Date of cemetery	1805–1855
Number of bodies excavated	101
Date of excavation	1999

Carver Street Methodist Chapel was the major non-conformist burial ground for Sheffield from 1806 to 1855. Excavation of the burial ground on the southwest corner of the chapel revealed the remains of 101 articulated human skeletons, as well as the disarticulated remains of up to 30 other individuals. A total of 47 grave cuts were identified, containing from one to eight individuals, all oriented with heads to the west. Bodies were buried within wooden coffins, usually made of oak with baseboards of Scots pine. Coffin fragments of elm were also identified. Coffin fittings were recorded, as well as traces of textiles, buttons and clay pipes. Four copper coins were found at the head of one skeleton. Small coffins for infant burials were noted, as well as one case where an adult female had been buried with a neonate resting on her chest. Five skulls showed evidence of craniotomy.

References
McIntyre and Willmott 2003; Bagwell and Tyers 2001

Clementhorpe, York

Grid Reference	SE 603 501
Cemetery type	Epidemic disease
Date of cemetery	16th–17th century
Number of bodies excavated	Unknown
Date of excavation	1996

Individual burials and one group burial were found on the site of the nunnery of St Clement. It was suggested that these inhumations relate to the use of the site for plague lodges from the mid-sixteenth century until the early seventeenth century

References
Cherry 1977:93

Former Female Prison, Castle Yard, York

Grid Reference	SE 6057 5147
Cemetery type	Prison cemetery
Date of cemetery	Majority 1802–1826
Number of bodies excavated	Unknown
Date of excavation	1998

Late eighteenth or early nineteenth-century burials were found overlaying earlier material, including burials dating to the ninth to eleventh centuries. They were located in the area of York Castle associated with a women's prison, county gaol and assize courts during the eighteenth and nineteenth centuries. The female prison is known to have been in use from the early 1780s until 1900 when it became a military prison. From 1802 public executions by hanging took place near the prison at the 'New Drop' between the assize courts and the bailey wall. Between 1868 and 1896 executions took place at the north end of the female prison, within the prison walls. Of five graves noted, four were cut in a line running east-west. All individuals had been buried in coffins (indicated by staining and the presence of coffin wood and nails) and were supine with their heads to the west. A female skeleton was found with a number of bone buttons in the abdominal area. Two individuals showed possible evidence of post mortem surgery. Skeleton 9056 (possibly a man, older than 25 years) had no sternum and the ribs appeared to have been pulled apart prior to burial, although no cut marks were noted on the bone. Bone and copper alloy buttons were also found in the abdominal area. Another skeleton, probably of a young woman around 25 years old, had the top of the cranium removed. The chest cavity had also been opened and the ribs had been left lying on top of the arms. The remains are suggested to be those of executed criminals, probably dating to between 1802 and 1826,

References
Thompson and Ross 1998; BIAB supp. 9/1998:395–6; Evans 1999

Friends Burial Ground, Bishopshill, York

Grid Reference	SE 6016 5138
Cemetery type	Quaker burial ground
Date of cemetery	Post-medieval
Number of bodies excavated	Unknown
Date of excavation	1973

Post-medieval inhumations were excavated, along with earlier material.

References
Monaghan 1997: 829, 908, 1125–6, 1128–9, 1147; Tweddle, Moulden and Logan 1999

Helmsley Quaker Burial Ground

Grid Reference	SE 614 837
Cemetery type	Quaker burial ground
Date of cemetery	Post-medieval
Number of bodies excavated	10
Date of excavation	1996

Ten graves, all aligned approximately west-east, were excavated. Seven contained human remains. Shroud pins were recovered from three graves. All burials were in wooden coffins with coffin fittings.

References
Rahtz and Watts n.d.

The Judge's Lodging, York

Grid Reference	SE 6012 5201
Cemetery type	Unknown
Date of cemetery	Post-medieval
Number of bodies excavated	9
Date of excavation	1994

Excavations revealed a minimum of nine burials, all oriented east-west, cut through older layers containing disarticulated human bone. Associated coffin nails and wood stains indicated the presence of coffins.

References
BIAB supp. 5/1994:368; Clarke 1994

Norfolk Street Upper Chapel (Unitarian), Sheffield

Grid Reference	SK 3541 8725
Cemetery type	Non-conformist burial ground
Date of cemetery	1723–1854
Number of bodies excavated	4+
Date of excavation	2006

The remains of four articulated skeletons were recovered from within the precincts of the Upper Chapel (Unitarian). The Chapel was built in 1700. Burials are recorded between 1723 and 1854.

References
O'Neill pers comm.

Norman Court, Grape Lane, York

Grid Reference	SE 6031 5202
Cemetery type	Non-conformist burial ground
Date of cemetery	Post-medieval
Number of bodies excavated	1
Date of excavation	1996

A burial associated with the Grape Lane Chapel, possibly remains of William Wren, the chapel preacher was uncovered.

References
BIAB supp 7/1996:697; MAP Consultancy Ltd 1996

North Dalton Church

Grid Reference	SE 9345 522
Cemetery type	Churchyard
Date of cemetery	18th century
Number of bodies excavated	3
Date of excavation	1980s

An eighteenth-century vault containing three coffins, all oriented east-west, was recorded. The first coffin that appears to have been placed in the vault had collapsed and was only partially visible. A double row of bronze pins could be observed. The second coffin had also partially collapsed. Its lid was edged with a double band of alternating brass pins, and its sides were decorated with a single line of bronze pins. In the centre of the lid was an inscription within a shield, made out in pins dated to 1748. Traces of inner lining were visible. The third (and probably more recent) coffin was smaller with no brass pins, although it had a corroded lid design. Each section of the coffin had been covered separately with fabric before being put together, and there were also traces of an inner fabric lining. The interior had also been coated in pitch. Woody vegetation could be seen inside the second coffin, close to the head

References
Mytum 1988

Pinstone Street, Peace Gardens, Sheffield

Grid Reference	SK 3540 8710
Cemetery type	Churchyard
Date of cemetery	1743–1860s
Number of bodies excavated	13
Date of excavation	1997–8

Thirteen articulated skeletons and the remains of a minimum of three disarticulated individuals were noted in the burial ground of the former St Paul's Church, which was in use from 1743 to the 1860s. There was evidence of 'stacking' of multiple burials. Coffins had been packed with sawdust and wood shavings. Inscribed tin coffin plates were also recorded.

References
Belford and Witkin 2000

Pontefract Castle, Wakefield

Grid Reference	SE 460 223
Cemetery type	War burials
Date of cemetery	17th century
Number of bodies excavated	3
Date of excavation	1982

Three graves, and three possible grave cuts, containing skeletons of probable Civil War victims were found in the Elizabethan Chapel. In contrast to other deposits associated with the chapel, these had been left relatively undisturbed.

References
Egan 1983:187; Roberts 2002

Rose and Crown, Lawrence Street, York

Grid Reference	SE 6116 5140
Cemetery type	War burials
Date of cemetery	Post-medieval, possibly Civil War
Number of bodies excavated	1
Date of excavation	1977

A post-medieval inhumation, possibly Civil War victim of siege of Walmgate Bar, was uncovered.

References
York Archaeological Trust – York Archive Gazetteer

Sandal Castle

Grid Reference	SE 433 418
Cemetery type	War burials
Date of cemetery	1645
Number of bodies excavated	9
Date of excavation	1964–1973

Nine skeletons were buried in bailey of Sandal Castle. All burials were male and exhibited evidence of perimortem trauma and weapons injuries. The burials are thought to be Royalist casualties from siege of 1645.

References
Mayes and Butler 1983

Sheffield Cathedral, Sheffield

Grid Reference	SK 3540 8750
Cemetery type	Churchyard
Date of cemetery	Late 18th–mid-19th century
Number of bodies excavated	140+
Date of excavation	1994, 2000, 2004/5

In 1994 excavations in front (south) of the Cathedral revealed grave cuts and articulated human remains and inscribed grave slabs. The area was known to have been used for burial until the late nineteenth century. An area from where burials were thought to have been removed was also evaluated, indicating that this was the case, except for some articulated remains which had been left on the western and eastern margins of the area. Further excavations in 2000 in the north-west car park revealed a minimum of eleven post-medieval burials in five graves. Additional excavations in 2004/2005 revealed a further 80 graves containing 140 articulated skeletons probably dating from the late eighteenth to mid nineteenth century. There was evidence of 'stacking' of multiple burials. Shroud pins and coffin fittings (grip handles, nails and studs), including a few inscribed tin plates, were recovered. Three individuals had coins placed over their eyes. A single bracelet of glass beads, three earrings and several clay wig curlers were also present. Disarticulated remains of a minimum of 440 individuals were recovered mostly around the buttresses of the Chapel of the Holy Spirit, where they were probably reburied during construction of the Chapel in the 1930s and 1940s.

References
Symonds and Sayer 2001; O'Neill 2006

St Crux, The Shambles, York

Grid Reference	SE 6050 5182
Cemetery type	Churchyard
Date of cemetery	Post-medieval
Number of bodies excavated	Unknown
Date of excavation	1976, 1989

Excavations in 1976 revealed the remains of a number of human skeletons presumed to be from the former St Crux churchyard. In 1989, more articulated human remains thought to belong to the same burial ground were recorded.

References
York Archaeological Trust – York Archive Gazetteer

St. Helen's Square, York

Grid Reference	SE 6017 5196
Cemetery type	Churchyard
Date of cemetery	Late 17th–early 18th century
Number of bodies excavated	12
Date of excavation	1984, 1988–9

Excavations occurred ahead of construction in St Helen's

churchyard, which was closed in 1730 after which the site was levelled. Twelve individuals, mostly adults were identified buried in shrouds near the boundary wall of the graveyard. Six more articulated skeletons were then found closer to the church. Of these, three were children. Most of these were buried in wooden coffins. All seem to date to the late seventeenth century.

References
Egan 1990:160

St. Lawrence Church Hall, Lawrence Street, York

Grid Reference	SE 6122 5132
Cemetery type	Churchyard
Date of cemetery	Post-medieval
Number of bodies excavated	Unknown
Date of excavation	1989

Post-medieval human remains were excavated

References
ADS

St. Margaret's Churchyard, Walmgate, York

Grid Reference	SE 6090 5153
Cemetery type	Churchyard
Date of cemetery	18th–19th century
Number of bodies excavated	18
Date of excavation	1998

Seven trenches were opened, some of which provided evidence for around eighteen post-medieval burials, most with evidence for coffins.

References
BIAB supp. 9/1998:395; Russell 1998

St. Martin's Church, Allerton

Grid Reference	SE 41 57
Cemetery type	Churchyard
Date of cemetery	Unknown
Number of bodies excavated	2
Date of excavation	1970s

A vault was encountered during excavations within the chancel. Most of the burials had been removed in 1862. Two nineteenth-century adult wooden coffins, possibly with inner lead shells remained and these were removed for burial elsewhere.

References
Butler 1978

St. Peter's Church, Redcar

Grid Reference	NZ 6000 2400
Cemetery type	Churchyard
Date of cemetery	Post-medieval
Number of bodies excavated	1
Date of excavation	1997

A juvenile skeleton was excavated and re-interred

References
BIAB supp 8/1997:228; MacDonald 1998

St. Robert's Church, Pannal

Grid Reference	SE 3040 5160
Cemetery type	Churchyard
Date of cemetery	Post-medieval
Number of bodies excavated	Unknown
Date of excavation	1999

Inhumations and funerary structures were recovered from waterlogged contexts. Human remains were poorly preserved and crushed.

References
BIAB supp 10.2/1999:1171–2; Cale 1999; Cale 2000

St. Sampson's Church, Church Street, York

Grid Reference	SE 6040 5190
Cemetery type	Churchyard
Date of cemetery	Post-medieval
Number of bodies excavated	Unknown
Date of excavation	1979, 1981

In 1979, three human burials were observed in a contractor's trench within the churchyard to the west of St Sampson's Church. In 1981, a number of Victorian graves were excavated and the human remains removed.

References
York Archaeological Trust – York Archive Gazetteer

St. Wilfred's Church, Hickleton

Grid Reference	SE 484 053
Cemetery type	Churchyard
Date of cemetery	18th–19th century
Number of bodies excavated	13
Date of excavation	1983

Thirteen post-medieval skeletons were recovered during excavations in 1983.

References
Sydes 1984

Wesleyan Methodist Chapel, Barnsley

Grid Reference	SE 437 405
Cemetery type	Non-conformist burial ground
Date of cemetery	1804–1874
Number of bodies excavated	At least 3
Date of excavation	2001

The remains of at least three individuals discovered during renovation work on a nightclub. Pottery associated with burials suggests a nineteenth-century date for the inhumations. They are thought to be associated with the former New Street Methodist Chapel. The location of the remains is indicative of burial within the walls of the original chapel.

References
Chamberlain and Sayer 2001; Sayer and Symonds 2004

Wharram Percy Church, Wharram Percy

Grid Reference	SE 858 641
Cemetery type	Churchyard
Date of cemetery	18th-19th century
Number of bodies excavated	64+
Date of excavation	1962–74

Over 64 post-medieval burials were recovered during excavations at Wharram Percy. Those with coffin fittings dated to the mid-eighteenth to mid-nineteenth centuries. A number of coffins were covered with woollen fabrics, with colours including dark blue and dark red. The wood used for coffins included pine and oak – in some cases in the same coffin.

References
Harding 1987; Hurst and Rahtz 1987; Mays et al. 2007

Ireland

Antrim

Bushfoot Strand, Portballintrae

Grid Reference	J 414 875
Cemetery type	Isolated burial
Date of cemetery	Late 17th–18th century
Number of bodies excavated	1
Date of excavation	1999?

A coffin burial was found in the sand dunes outside Portballintrae. The burial was oriented east-northeast to west-southwest with some wood and iron nails in situ. The upper part of the male skeleton was no longer present. Radiocarbon analysis dated it to the late seventeenth to eighteenth century.

References
Ponsford 2000:312

Castle Carra, Cushendun

Grid Reference	D2497346
Cemetery type	Cillín
Date of cemetery	Post-medieval
Number of bodies excavated	16
Date of excavation	1996?

The burials of fifteen infants and a child were found within Castle Carra, a tower house. The site is thought to have served as a cillín.

References
Hurl and Murphy 1996

Cotton Court, Hill Street/Waring Street, Belfast

Grid Reference	J 34 74
Cemetery type	Medical waste
Date of cemetery	Late 18th–early 19th century
Number of bodies excavated	1
Date of excavation	2002

An isolated skull found during excavations at Cotton Court. Skull has eleven trephination holes cut with a trepine. Skull was thought to have been used to practise surgery and then dumped in the back garden.

References
O'Baoill, McQuaid and Buckley 2002

Kirk Field, Portmuck

Grid Reference	D 4603 0222
Cemetery type	Cillín
Date of cemetery	Post-medieval
Number of bodies excavated	65
Date of excavation	2001

Poorly preserved human remains were found during landscaping of a stream bank. They were located in an area called Kirk Field in Portmuck, near the reputed site of a medieval abbey. The cemetery contained primarily medieval cist burials, although interment continued into the post-medieval period. At this date the top of the bank slope seems to have been used as a cillín for unbaptised children and the poor, as it contained mostly simple shallow child burials. A total of 65 burials were recovered along with a large amount of disarticulated bone.

References
www.excavations.ie Site 2001:15

Lancasterian Street, Carrickfergus

Grid Reference	J 414 875
Cemetery type	Unknown
Date of cemetery	Post-medieval
Number of bodies excavated	1
Date of excavation	1995

A fragment of skull was found in the sixteenth-century defensive ditch, together with pottery, leather, tiles, cloth, and iron blades.

References
Ponsford and Jackson 1995:251

St. John's Church, Ballyharry

Grid Reference	J4636 9798
Cemetery type	Churchyard
Date of cemetery	18th–19th century
Number of bodies excavated	2
Date of excavation	2002?

Human remains were discovered beneath the aisle of the late sixteenth / early seventeen-century church of St John's, which was probably a Church of Ireland foundation. The remains of two wooden coffins were recorded. The upper body was oriented with the head to east. The lower coffined burial had the head oriented to the west. Decorative copper alloy studs were noted on the coffins. Five skulls were also found: three at the west end and two at the east end of the grave cut. Disarticulated bone and coffin furniture was also recovered. Although the burials could date to the seventeenth century, the coffin style suggests a date no earlier than the eighteenth century. They appear to have been deposited before restoration of the church in the 1820s.

References
Centre for Archaeological Fieldwork 2002; Ponsford 2003:306

Armagh

Navan Fort Environs, Ballyrea

Grid Reference	H 845 449
Cemetery type	Isolated burial
Date of cemetery	1478–1651
Number of bodies excavated	1
Date of excavation	1992

Excavation of primarily medieval contexts on the site of the visitor's centre near Navan Fort revealed the extended supine burial of a child, of around ten years of age. No evidence for a coffin or grave goods were present. The body was oriented approximately west-east, with the skull facing to the north, and both arms flexed. The right hand would have rested on the upper chest and the left hand by the left shoulder. Radiocarbon dating gave a date of 1478 – 1651 AD.

References
Ponsford 1993:274; Crothers 1993

Cavan

Clough, Oughter Castle

Grid Reference	H 357 078
Cemetery type	War burials
Date of cemetery	Post-medieval
Number of bodies excavated	2
Date of excavation	1987

Excavations occurred at the thirteenth- to seventeenth-century castle. Two burials in shallow graves were found to the south-east of the castle, possibly linked to the Cromwellian siege of 1653.

Clare

Ennis Friary, Ennis

Grid Reference	R 333 780
Cemetery type	Friary
Date of cemetery	Mid-to-late 17th century–1890s
Number of bodies excavated	c.56
Date of excavation	1997

Excavations occurred in the east range and cloister of Ennis Friary in an area used as a cemetery from the mid to late seventeenth century until the 1890s. Some 90 unmarked graves were revealed. The graves were usually shallow and closely packed. There was some evidence of burial in shrouds.

References
Ponsford and Jackson 1998:146; O'Sullivan, Roberts and Halliday 2003

Cork

Dominican Priory, St. Mary's of the Isle, Cork

Grid Reference	W671715
Cemetery type	Churchyard
Date of cemetery	16th century
Number of bodies excavated	53
Date of excavation	1993

Excavations at the site of the Dominican Priory uncovered a large number of burials. Fifty-three of these burials were dated to the early to mid-sixteenth century and were interred in the cloister ambulatories. One grave contained wood staining indicative of the presence of coffins. No nails were recovered. Another burial dated to the late fourteenth to sixteenth century contained a rosary of 42 bone beads, which appears to have been placed in the hands of the deceased.

References
Hurley and Sheenan 1995

St. Anne's Graveyard, Shandon

Grid Reference	W 6731 7239
Cemetery type	Churchyard
Date of cemetery	Post-medieval
Number of bodies excavated	Unknown
Date of excavation	2001

Excavation was carried out prior to building works in the parish of Shandon outside the walled medieval city of Cork. An 1869 map showed St Anne's Graveyard in the area of proposed development. There was evidence of nineteenth-century disturbance to the cemetery. Buried grave markers, disarticulated bone and several articulated human skeletons were found, oriented with the head to the west. These were recorded and left in situ. One skeleton was found with a wooden and cord set of rosary beads wrapped around the distal end of the radius. A piece of the shroud had survived around the rosary beads. Fragments of metal were found on the upper vertebrae of the same individual. The excavator noted that these could derive from a coffin breastplate or possibly be part of the shroud. Wooden coffin fragments and metal handles and nails were also found around and overlying the skeleton. There was no evidence of a grave cut.

References
McCarthy 2001

St. Nicholas's Church, Cove Street, Cork

Grid Reference	W 6736 7140
Cemetery type	Churchyard
Date of cemetery	Post-medieval
Number of bodies excavated	Unknown
Date of excavation	2002

Inhumations were uncovered during excavations prior to the conversion of St. Nicholas's Church into offices. The burials, which were thought to be associated with the eighteenth-century church or its earlier medieval incarnation, were left in situ.

References
www.excavation.ie Site 2002:0275

Down

Bagenal's Castle, Newry

Grid Reference	J08732615
Cemetery type	Post-dissolution
Date of cemetery	1550–1650
Number of bodies excavated	33
Date of excavation	2006?

Nicholas Bagenal was granted the Cistercian abbey at Newry in the 1540s and built a tower-house, possibly incorporating the Abbot's residence. A cemetery of 33 individuals, men, women and infants has been excavated to the north of the tower-house with the burials dug through the foundations of the monastic buildings. The burials have been dated to between 1550 and 1650 and are thought to have been retainers of the Bagenal family. Trauma from sharp implements, probably swords was found on the skulls of three of the individuals.

References
Dawkes and Buckley 2006

Dublin

141–143 James Street, Dublin

Grid Reference	31408 188878
Cemetery type	Unknown
Date of cemetery	Post-medieval
Number of bodies excavated	6
Date of excavation	1999

Evidence of a burial ground located in an area where there had previously been a post-medieval industrial complex. Five extended inhumations were recovered within a squarish grave cut c. 2m x 2m in size in the south-east of the site. These were all young male adults between 17 and 30 years old. Subsequent work located an isolated burial of an adult female in the north-west part of the site. Disarticulated human bone representing at least four individuals, including a young child was found in dumped deposits across the site. Properties were constructed on the site in the eighteenth century.

References
www.excavations.ie Site 1999:211

16 Eustace Street, Dublin

Grid Reference	O 156 341
Cemetery type	Executed criminals
Date of cemetery	Post-1600
Number of bodies excavated	Unknown
Date of excavation	1997

A collection of eleven skulls, thirteen mandibles and eighteen vertebrae were found in a pit in an area lying outside the city

References
Egan 1988:194–5

walls. The bone lay within reclamation layers which have been dated to the 1600s onwards. Many of the bones exhibited evidence of trauma in the form of slash and chop wounds and are though to belong to royal enemies decapitated in the mid to late seventeenth century. No remains of the post-cranial skeletons were found other than the neck vertebrae. The excavator suggests that the heads were displayed on the city walls.

References
Ponsford and Jackson 1998:167; Simpson 1999

189–194 King Street North/ Green Street, Dublin

Grid Reference	31513 23465
Cemetery type	Churchyard/Cillín
Date of cemetery	18th–20th century
Number of bodies excavated	c.487
Date of excavation	1997, 1998, 1999–2000

In 1998, excavations occurred on the site of a detached burial ground associated with church of St. Michan during the mid-eighteenth century. The area may have been used informally for burials of the poor prior to this. Burial is thought to have come to an end in 1787 if not earlier. A layer of rubble was revealed containing disarticulated skeletal material overlying 18 fully articulated and extended human skeletons. Adult male, adult female and infant burials were noted. All graves were oriented east-west except for two infant burials, which were oriented approximately north-south and were found just inside the site at the Green Street side. Further excavations between 1999 and 2000 recovered c. 469 articulated human skeletons along with disarticulated human remains of at least 134 individuals. Many burials had associated with evidence for coffin use and shroud pins. There was evidence for multiple burials in single graves over a short period of time. Nine infant burials cut through the rubble layer sealing the site point to the later use of the disused cemetery as a cillín.

References
Irish Archaeological Consultancy Ltd n.d.; Buckley and Nellis 2000:5

39 Francis Street, Dublin

Grid Reference	O 148 337
Cemetery type	Isolated burial
Date of cemetery	Post-medieval
Number of bodies excavated	1
Date of excavation	1994

A partial isolated burial was identified in the vicinity of the medieval Franciscan Friary. This was found in the base of cultivated soil containing seventeenth- and eighteenth-century pottery.

References
www.excavations.ie Site 1994.68

Carrickmines Castle

Grid Reference	32185 22404
Cemetery type	War burials
Date of cemetery	17th century
Number of bodies excavated	17
Date of excavation	2001

Two mass graves containing a total of fifteen individuals, with a single inhumation lying between the graves and another prone burial lay to the north-east, were uncovered during excavations at Carrickmines Castle. The mass graves contained bodies of women and children, while the isolated prone burial was male. The skeletons of seven individuals exhibit peri-mortem trauma and a musket ball was found in one of the mass burials. Burials thought to be victims of the massacre that followed the end of the siege in 1642.

References
Fibiger 2004

Davis Place (off French Street), Dublin

Grid Reference	315008 233704
Cemetery type	Churchyard
Date of cemetery	17th century
Number of bodies excavated	4
Date of excavation	2001

Excavations revealed coffin fittings and nails, shroud-pins, seventeenth-century pottery, clay pipe fragments and two pieces of glazed floor tile. The layer containing this material was cut by burials. Six juveniles, one adolescent, four young adults and four middle adults were recovered. The adults included five males and two females. Copper-alloy shroud-pins, a possible lace tag and a belt-buckle were found in association with the burials. Three sequentially organised grave orientations were identified, the earliest of which (Phase I) was represented by the graves of two individuals oriented north–south, followed by ten individuals oriented south-west/north-east (Phase II) and finally four with an east–west orientation (Phase III). The latest burials may be associated with the churches of St Nicholas of Myra. The burials of Phases I and II, were mainly coffin burials, and it is suggested that they date from no later than the seventeenth century and may have been aligned on an element of the medieval friary of St Francis, or on posited later structure which pre-dated the later church.

References
www.excavations.ie Site 1999:196 and 2001:257

Dublin Institute of Technology, Aungier Street/Peter Row

Grid Reference	O 153 334
Cemetery type	Churchyard
Date of cemetery	1711–1840
Number of bodies excavated	At least 2
Date of excavation	2001

Articulated and disarticulated human bone and a human skull were found in the area of a known Huguenot cemetery, attached to the chapel of St Peter built around 1711. Two skeletons oriented east-west and within grave-cuts were recorded. Eighteenth-century pottery sherds were found within the grave cuts. The chapel of St Peter was demolished in 1840, when the human remains were moved to Mount Jerome cemetery. The area excavated had been separated from the original cemetery by a change in the southern boundary in the late nineteenth century and was thus missed when the cemetery was cleared.

References
www.excavations.ie Site 2001:363

John Dillon Street, Dublin

Grid Reference	O142338
Cemetery type	Churchyard
Date of cemetery	17th century–early 19th century
Number of bodies excavated	13
Date of excavation	2001

Thirteen burials associated with parish church of St. Nicholas of Myra were uncovered during a rescue excavation. The burials are thought to date to between the seventeenth century and the building of the present church early in the nineteenth century

References
www.excavations.ie Site 2001:388

Lower Stephen Street, Dublin

Grid Reference	O 157 338
Cemetery type	Medical waste?
Date of cemetery	13th–17th century
Number of bodies excavated	26
Date of excavation	1991

Excavations in the area of St. Stephen's leper hospital in Dublin uncovered burials dating from the medieval to post-medieval period. The leper hospital was suppressed in 1542 although it continued to function until 1604 and the graveyard appears to have continued in use until the eighteenth century. Eight burials, four adults and four infants, were dated to the seventeenth century. Decayed wood and corroded coffin nails were associated with five of the burials, while copper-alloy shroud pins were found with four of the burials. A further four in situ burials have been dated to the eighteenth to nineteenth century. The graveyard became the site of the Mercer Hospital from 1734 and the College of Dublin Society of Surgeons from 1796 and an ulna, perforated at the proximal end to allow the insertion of a hinge, has been linked to teaching at the College during the nineteenth or twentieth century.

References
Eogan 2000; Buckley and Hayden 2002

Poolbeg Street, Dublin

Grid Reference	O 162 343
Cemetery type	Non-conformist burial ground
Date of cemetery	1752–c.1850
Number of bodies excavated	7
Date of excavation	1992

Seven burials in coffins thought to be associated with an eighteenth-century Lutheran church were excavated on the south side of Poolbeg Street.

References
Channing 1992

St. Luke's Church, The Coombe, Dublin

Grid Reference	31495 23340
Cemetery type	Churchyard
Date of cemetery	Post-medieval
Number of bodies excavated	Unknown
Date of excavation	2001

St Luke's was built between 1713 and 1716, supposedly for a Huguenot congregation, although there is no evidence for this in the parish registers. Excavations took place in advance of construction, at either end of the north side of the church with a third trench against the eastern precinct wall. This last contained an infant burial. Although few human remains were found, other excavations in the very north of the churchyard resulted in the removal of 168 burials and large quantities of disarticulated human remains.

References
www.excavations.ie Sites 2001:372 and 2001:373

Trinity College Library Extension, Dublin

Grid Reference	O168339
Cemetery type	Medical waste
Date of cemetery	Post-medieval
Number of bodies excavated	250+
Date of excavation	1999

Assessment of the area of extension to the Berkeley Library revealed a pit containing a large amount of animal (including camel) and human bone. The human bones showed evidence of dissection, with lateral and longitudinal cut or saw marks found on femurs and skulls, which were the most common human skeletal elements in the pit. More human bone was found piled within shallow trenches against the base of two eighteenth-century boundary walls. These remains were most often clustered in groups of two or three individuals, both adults and children. Two additional pits were found also containing human bone, although at a lower density. One was located against one of the boundary walls at its western end and the other was found against the east face of the second wall. The two walls enclosed an area called the 'Physick Garden'. The excavators estimate that more than 250 individuals were represented in total from these contexts. Associated finds are dated to the eighteenth and nineteenth centuries and included pottery, glass, copper wiring and a small metal canula probably used in dissection. The foundations of a possible detached extension were also uncovered (possibly a bath house) to the Anatomy House, known to have been located in the area until 1820, when it was demolished.

References
www.excavations.ie Site 1999:231

Wolfe Tone Park, Dublin

Grid Reference	31545 23445
Cemetery type	Churchyard
Date of cemetery	1709–1886
Number of bodies excavated	Unknown
Date of excavation	1999–2001

Wolfe Tone Park was originally a graveyard for St Mary's Church, which was built between 1697 and 1702. The earliest interments probably date from 1709. In 1886 the graveyard was redesigned as a garden/park, and many of the grave-slabs now line its enclosing walls. In 2001 excavations exposed articulated in situ burials but these were left undisturbed. Disarticulated human bone was recovered from topsoil and deeper deposits, along with clay pipe fragments, glass, coffin nails and ceramic bottle stoppers. Large amounts of human bone were recovered from the context beneath the topsoil, mostly in the south-eastern corner of the site. The large amount of re-deposited skeletal material may be related to the construction of a pond and flowerbeds as part of the conversion of the graveyard into a park. There was evidence that an attempt had been made to bury several skulls together in a shallow pit.

References
www.excavations.ie Site 1999:238 and 2001:387

Galway

Eyre Square, Galway City

Grid Reference	1302 2251
Cemetery type	Executed criminals
Date of cemetery	17th century
Number of bodies excavated	3
Date of excavation	2003

Two male burials orientated north to south and the skull of a third individual were found during excavations in Eyre Square in Galway City. The skeletons were found close to the site of the city gallows and it has been suggested that these individuals, who have tentatively been dated to the seventeenth century, were executed criminals.

Subsequent excavations at Eyre Square have uncovered the articulate and disarticulate remains of at least another 42 individuals. Among the articulated burials were two adults interred in the same pit in opposing orientations. A further two burials were found in the vicinity of the gallows, radiocarbon dated to c.1650–1730. While most of the remains found around the square were from adults at least two infant burials were also found. Evidence for blunt force cranial trauma was observed on a number of individuals (not those associated with the gallows). It is possible that Eyre Square was used to inter those dying on the gallows as well as the unbaptised and fatalities of the numerous sieges experienced by Galway in the late seventeenth and early eighteenth centuries.

References
Quinn 2007

Merchant's Road, Galway

Grid Reference	M 300 254
Cemetery type	Executed criminals
Date of cemetery	17th–19th century
Number of bodies excavated	5 skulls
Date of excavation	1987

Excavation in area of old city wall revealed a bastion and a part of an outer revetment wall, probably dating to the 1640s when the city defences were strengthened. Six isolated skulls found in rubble layer are associated with an eighteenth-century wall.

References
Egan 1988:195; Walsh 2004

St. Brigid's Hospital, Ballinsloe

Grid Reference	18660 23090
Cemetery type	Hospital cemetery
Date of cemetery	Mid–late 19th century
Number of bodies excavated	12
Date of excavation	2002

Twenty-six graves thought to date to the mid- to late-nineteenth century were identified on grounds of St. Brigid's Hospital. Twelve of the burials in unadorned spruce coffins were excavated and they are thought to be inmates of Connaught Asylum.

References
Moore 2003; Rogers et al. 2006

Kerry

Illaunloughan

Grid Reference	V 362 733
Cemetery type	Cillin
Date of cemetery	Post-medieval
Number of bodies excavated	Unknown
Date of excavation	1995?

Infant burials dating from the cillin phase were discovered overlying drystone huts

References
White Marshall and Walsh 1994; White Marshall and Walsh 2005

Killalee Church, Killarney

Grid Reference	9347 9274
Cemetery type	Cillin
Date of cemetery	Post-medieval
Number of bodies excavated	4
Date of excavation	2000

Excavations on the site of an abandoned medieval church revealed 23 graves that formed part of a cillin. Four graves were fully excavated and the remains of two infants and two adults were recovered. Coins accompanying one of the burials dated to 1737 and 1738. Shroud pins and textiles were recovered from two of the burials.

References
Dennehy and Lynch 2001

Reask

Grid Reference	365043
Cemetery type	Cillin
Date of cemetery	Post-medieval?
Number of bodies excavated	Unknown
Date of excavation	1972–5

A number of burials associated with the later use of the site of an early medieval settlement and burial ground as a children's cemetery were excavated.

References
Fanning 1981

St. Bredan's Cathedral, Ardfert

Grid Reference	Q 786 214
Cemetery type	Churchyard
Date of cemetery	Post-medieval
Number of bodies excavated	Unknown
Date of excavation	1989, 1990, 1991, 1992, 1995

The site of the cathedral, which was burnt and abandoned in the sixteenth century, has been used for burial up to the present and was subjected to a series of excavations in the 1980s and 1990s. In 1989, a dense concentration of post-medieval burials were encountered inside the north and west doorways of the cathedral. In 1991, seventeenth- and eighteenth-century human remains (dated by shroud pins) were excavated from the interior of the cathedral. Two seventeenth-century Cork City of Refuge tokens were found on the left and right shoulders of one skeleton. In 1992, the lack of later (eighteenth and nineteenth century) burials was noted on the north side of the graveyard, although many infant graves were found by the north wall dating from the medieval period onwards.

References
www.excavations.ie Sites 1989:051, 1991:062 and 1992:098

Kildare

Convent of Mercy, Sallins Road, Naas

Grid Reference	N28902212
Cemetery type	Churchyard
Date of cemetery	18th–19th century, probably pre-1839
Number of bodies excavated	42
Date of excavation	2005

Forty burials were recovered during excavations in the grounds of the Convent of Mercy in Naas. The burials are thought to date to the eighteenth and nineteenth centuries, predating the foundation of the convent in 1839 and possibly associated with the Catholic Church of St Mary and St David. Fragments of coffin wood and in some cases metal coffin fittings found with a number of burials suggest nearly all of the burials were in coffins.

References
www.excavations.ie Site 2005:772

Graney East, Castledermot

Grid Reference	281742 183906
Cemetery type	Unknown
Date of cemetery	Medieval–early modern
Number of bodies excavated	Unknown
Date of excavation	1999, 2000

In 1999 archaeological monitoring of a quarry site at Graney East, c.4km south-west of Castledermot, revealed an extended inhumation of a young adult female. The skeleton was oriented with the head to the west. No grave cut could be determined. Medieval and post-medieval pottery was found associated with the skeleton. The remains of a nunnery founded around 1200 and in existence until its suppression in 1539 were known to be located in the western part of the field under study. In 2000 an additional adult female skeleton was found during monitoring of top-soil stripping. This could not be excavated in situ, but appeared to have been lying in an extended position within a grave-cut oriented east-north-east to west-south-west. An additional group of articulated human remains were found lying in a natural sand-filled depression within gravels. The burial ground appears to have extended over 11.8m north–south x 9.6m, and burials were at least 0.4m below the existing surface. Burials were mostly orientated west-east, although some had been disturbed by later burials.

References
www.excavations.ie Sites 1999:383, 2000:484 and 2001:643

Kill, Monasterevin

Grid Reference	26455 20939
Cemetery type	Cillín
Date of cemetery	Post-medieval?
Number of bodies excavated	At least 1
Date of excavation	2002

Investigations on the site of a children's burial ground uncovered the remains of an infant.

References
www.excavations.ie Site 2002:0958

Leitrim

Manorhamilton Workhouse

Grid Reference	18925 33939
Cemetery type	Workhouse cemetery
Date of cemetery	Mid – late 19th century
Number of bodies excavated	73
Date of excavation	2001–2002

Seventy-three burials were excavated from the cemetery of Manorhamilton Workhouse Cemetery. The individuals were interred in plain wooden coffins with no decoration or fittings. Fabric found within the coffins is thought to be shrouding material. Three individuals were interred with rosaries and three coffins contained organic matter thought to be straw. The burials are thought to date to the mid- to late nineteenth century.

References
Moore Group Archaeological and Environmental Services 2001; Lynch 2002b; Moore and Rogers 2002; Rogers *et al*. 2006

Laois

Old Gaol And Courthouse, Church Street, Portlaoise

Grid Reference	S 470 984/2470 1984
Cemetery type	Prison cemetery
Date of cemetery	18th-19th century
Number of bodies excavated	8
Date of excavation	1996, 1998

In 1996 two human skeletons were found in the courtyard of a late eighteenth-century gaol that was in use until 1830 and adjoined the courthouse. The skeletons were male and aged 23–25 and 25–30. One had been disturbed and was incomplete. Traces of a coffin were found associated with one of the skeletons. This appears to have been slightly too small for the body. Both skeletons were oriented north-south, with their heads to the south. Part of a third skeleton was noted but not excavated. In 1998, six skeletons were found during monitoring of foundation trenches. All were supine, and orientated approximately north-south, and all except one had their heads to the south. Two skeletons were complete but the others had been disturbed and truncated in some cases. One burial found with a copper pin, with a fragment of preserved fragment of cloth, at the neck, thought to be remnants of a shroud. Nails indicated the presence of coffins and their position led the excavator to suggest that they were built of several pieces of wood tacked onto a frame. One coffin had a thin iron band running down the centre of the lid. While this may have been used to hold the coffin together, observation of an impressed flower motif and swirls on the iron band suggests that it was also decorative. The apparently careful construction of the coffin contrasts with the way in which the bodies were apparently squashed into coffins that were too small, and the lack of the usual east-west orientation suggesting that the metal band may have been reused. The burials are thought to be associated with the gaol which was built in 1789 and date to the late eighteenth or nighteenth centuries.

References
www.excavations.ie sites 1996:224 and 1998:370; Keeley 1998

Limerick

Sheares Street, Kilmallock

Grid Reference	R 6061 2781
Cemetery type	Isolated burial
Date of cemetery	Unknown
Number of bodies excavated	1
Date of excavation	2000

An adult human skeleton was found in a shallow grave cut into a field ditch just to the west of Sheares Street in the medieval walled town of Kilmallock. The town appears to have extended into this area sometime in the sixteenth century.

References
www.excavations.ie Site 2000:587

Stradbally North, Castleconnell

Grid Reference	R 661 624
Cemetery type	Unknown
Date of cemetery	15th–17th century
Number of bodies excavated	13
Date of excavation	2003

Thirteen burials from ten graves were uncovered during excavations at Castleconnell. Artefacts from one of the graves suggest a seventeenth-century date, although individuals may have been interred at this site over a long period of time. There was no evidence for the use of coffins, but the arrangement of some of the bodies suggests some were shrouded. The graves were very narrow and the bodies appeared to have been interred rapidly. The remains of a belt were found with one burial.

References
Coyne and Lynch 2003a and b; Coyne 2003;

Louth

5 Seatown, Dundalk

Grid Reference	J 051 075
Cemetery type	Churchyard
Date of cemetery	Medieval–modern
Number of bodies excavated	Unknown
Date of excavation	1991

Human bone was found during the renovation of outbuildings to the rear of No. 5, Seatown, Dundalk. The human remains probably came from the graveyard associated with the Priory and Hospital of St Leonard, founded in the late twelfth century. After the dissolution the church remained in use until the nineteenth century. The last known burial in the graveyard dated to 1876. The excavated graves were carefully ordered in rows, all orientated consistently and with no apparent inter-cutting. Both adult and juvenile remains were recovered. The possible remains of a coffin were found associated with one of the burials.

References
Ponsford 1992:100

Church Lane, Carlingford

Grid Reference	J18991141
Cemetery type	War burials
Date of cemetery	17th century
Number of bodies excavated	4
Date of excavation	2003

Four burials, three in a single grave, were found during excavations in Church Lane. All burials exhibited peri-mortem trauma and are thought to date to the seventeenth century.

References
Buckley and McConway 2004

Holy Trinity Church, Carlingford

Grid Reference	J 189 120
Cemetery type	Churchyard
Date of cemetery	Medieval–post-medieval
Number of bodies excavated	22
Date of excavation	1992, 1999

In 1991 building works exposed 20 extended and inter-cutting inhumations in shallow graves beneath the floor boards of Holy Trinity Church. All were oriented with heads to the west and were deposited in visible grave cuts with no evidence of coffins or clothing. In some cases individuals had been reburied in later graves. Some of this disturbance may date to nineteenth-century renovations. The disarticulated remains of at least 32 individuals were also identified. Of the 20 in situ inhumations, ten were males, six were females and four were juveniles. Of the rest, at least 15 were male, nine were female and four were juveniles. Two bones were dated by C14. One dates to AD 1517–1666 (calibrated), and the other to AD 1442–1650.

In 1999 two extended inhumations, both oriented east-west, and one cutting the other, were located in the churchyard during building works. The individuals were buried in shallow graves, with no visible marker present. Nails provided evidence that they were originally buried in coffins. A bone pin/handle was found in the machined-off topsoil less than a metre away from the later of the two burials. Both burials were cut by drains dating to the nineteenth century and the late nineteenth/early twentieth century. These burials are similar to, and may be contemporaneous with, those excavated in 1992.

References
www.excavations.ie Sites 1992:133 and 1999:554

Old Abbey Lane, Drogheda

Grid Reference	30857 27521
Cemetery type	Post-dissolution
Date of cemetery	17th century
Number of bodies excavated	8
Date of excavation	2006

The Abbey of St. Mary D'Urso in Drogheda was dissolved in 1540 and its lands and building leased. It is unclear whether the associated hospital continued in use. The hospital and its buildings passed to ownership of Corporation in 1555–6 and although little is known of the site's use under the Corporation, the buildings appear to have fallen into decay. Excavation prior to demolition of derelict properties on the site uncovered eight burials cut through seventeenth-century reclamation layers. A sixteenth- to seventeenth-century St. Patrick's halfpenny was found below one of the burials.

References
Murphy and Stirland 2006

Townparks, Dundalk

Grid Reference	30435 30742
Cemetery type	Cillin
Date of cemetery	Post-medieval
Number of bodies excavated	3
Date of excavation	2000

Test-trenching carried out along the proposed storm-water pipelines in Dundalk revealed human remains at the north end of Laurels Road. The disarticulated remains of a minimum of three infants, were found in a garden soil of the seventeenth to eighteenth centuries. The area is known locally as a former burial ground for unbaptised children.

References
www.excavations.ie Site 2000:0680

Meath

Johnstown

Grid Reference	27600 24000
Cemetery type	Cillin
Date of cemetery	19th century
Number of bodies excavated	63
Date of excavation	2002

The remains of 61 infants and two adults were excavated from the site of cillin within an early medieval enclosure close to an early medieval cemetery. The burials are thought to be 100–200 years old.

References
Clarke 2002

Monaghan

Cloughvalley Upper

Grid Reference	284278 305094
Cemetery type	Other
Date of cemetery	18th–19th century
Number of bodies excavated	16
Date of excavation	2003

Archaeological excavations prior to road construction uncovered a small burial ground of fourteen graves containing fourteen articulated burials and the disarticulated remains of a further three individuals. Most of the remains were adult, although the remains of two children were recovered. The burials were supine and all interred with their heads to the west. All the burials appeared to have been wrapped in shrouds, with a fragment of textile recovered from one of the burials. Partial stone linings were found in many of the graves. An iron object, possibly a knife, was found in one of the graves and two small metal pins were recovered from another. It is thought to be a small family burial ground of the eighteenth to early nineteenth centuries, although it may represent a famine cemetery.

References
www.excavations.ie Site 2003:1485

Lisanisk Ringfort

Grid Reference	285030 303700
Cemetery type	Isolated burial
Date of cemetery	17th century
Number of bodies excavated	1
Date of excavation	2003

A burial was found in the outer ring of the ringfort. It is thought to date to the seventeenth century and may possibly be a murder victim or be linked to the rising of 1641–7.

References
Roycroft 2003; www.nra.ie/Archaeology/ArchaeologyRoad Schemes

Offaly (Kings)

Clonmacnoise

Grid Reference	N 011 308
Cemetery type	Post-dissolution
Date of cemetery	Post-medieval
Number of bodies excavated	2
Date of excavation	1993

After removal of three stone crosses into the Visitors' Centre on the site of the monastery of Clonmacnoise, the site of the crosses were examined. Two post-medieval burials were found beneath the base of the north cross (a millstone). The north cross had been situated at the east end of a rectangular structure, believed to be the burial place of the Malone family. It was suggested that the cross was moved to its present position after 1738 after the burials had been placed there. "Modern" burials were also uncovered during limited excavations associated with the south and west cross.

References
Ponsford 1994:123; www.excavations.ie Sites 1993:186, 1994:196 and 1995:250

Roscommon

Holy Trinity Abbey, Lough Key

Grid Reference	18335 30446
Cemetery type	Post-dissolution
Date of cemetery	Early modern
Number of bodies excavated	6
Date of excavation	1991–2

At least six burials were found cut through the clay floor of the chancel after the site was abandoned by monks in c.1606–7. Two of the burials were in coffins. The total number of burials dating to the post-dissolution period cannot be determined due to the difficulties in distinguishing them from late medieval burials

References
Clyne 2005

Sligo

8–9 Lower Abbey Road, Sligo

Grid Reference	G 695 359
Cemetery type	Isolated burial
Date of cemetery	17th century
Number of bodies excavated	3
Date of excavation	1998

Three poorly preserved human burials were found overlying an infilled medieval lime kiln in an area next to Sligo Dominican Priory. Associated pottery suggested a seventeenth century date. The burials do not seem to derive from a formal burial ground.

References
www.excavations.ie Site 1998:580

St. John the Baptist, Sligo

Grid Reference	G6836
Cemetery type	Churchyard
Date of cemetery	Late 18th–early 20th century
Number of bodies excavated	49
Date of excavation	2001

Excavations in the cemetery attached to St. John the Baptist Church in Sligo in 2001 uncovered 49 inhumations, dating from the late eighteenth to early twentieth century. Craniotomies were observed in two individuals.

References
Lynch 2002a

Tipperary

Cormac's Chapel, Cashel

Grid Reference	S 075 410
Cemetery type	Churchyard
Date of cemetery	Post-medieval burials within chapel
Number of bodies excavated	11
Date of excavation	1992–3

In 1993 the area between Cormac's Chapel and the cathedral chancel was excavated, as well as the north tower, chancel and approximately half of the nave of the chapel. Much of the interior of the chapel had been disturbed by seventeenth- and eighteenth-century burials.

References
wwe.excavations.ie Site 1993:203

"Rose Ville", Western Road, Clonmel

Grid Reference	22026 12237
Cemetery type	Hospital cemetery
Date of cemetery	1841–1870
Number of bodies excavated	12
Date of excavation	2000

Twelve articulated skeletons were revealed during excavations in the area of a known burial-ground. There was no evidence of grave-cuts or coffins. A large amount of disarticulated bone was also recovered. Documentary sources indicate that victims of infectious diseases at the nearby Fever Hospital were interred in this area during the nineteenth century. Contemporary maps suggest that the burial ground, which was in use between 1841 and the 1870s, was probably created during the famine, in response to the increased rates of disease, infection and mortality.

References
Mary Henry Archaeological Services Ltd 2000; Hurley 2000; www.excavations.ie Site 2000:933

Emmet Street/ Kickham Street, Clonmel

Grid Reference	S203225
Cemetery type	Unknown
Date of cemetery	Post-medieval
Number of bodies excavated	Unknown
Date of excavation	1997

Human skeletal remains were uncovered.

References
Power 1997

Parnell Street, Clonmel

Grid Reference	S 206 243
Cemetery type	Unknown
Date of cemetery	17th century
Number of bodies excavated	23
Date of excavation	1994

Excavations identified of part of a previously unrecorded burial ground thought to be 250–300 years old. Twenty-three male skeletons were recovered, aged between thirteen and mid-40s, buried in unmarked shallow pits. The burials were aligned east-west with the head to the west in most cases and most of the burial pits contained two or more individuals. Pistol balls were found lodged in the thoraxes of two individuals. The jaws of several individuals showed evidence of pipe smoking. Three spherical buttons found with one of the burials are suggestive of a mid seventeenth-century date.

References
Ponsford 1994:141

Tyrone

Cookstown

Grid Reference	H 804 768
Cemetery type	Other
Date of cemetery	Post-medieval
Number of bodies excavated	Unknown
Date of excavation	1982

Burials had disturbed earlier deposits.

References
Egan 1983:186

Waterford

St. Peter's Church, Waterford City

Grid Reference	S6011
Cemetery type	Churchyard
Date of cemetery	12th–19th century
Number of bodies excavated	2000
Date of excavation	1986, 1988, 1990

Two thousand human skeletons dating from the twelfth to nineteenth centuries were recorded and 285 (primarily medieval in date) underwent laboratory analysis. All burials were oriented west-east, except for one early to mid seventeenth-century burial, which was aligned north-south. Fewer suggests that this grave could be explained in terms of a different religious identity.

References
Hurley and McCutcheon 1997; Fewer 1998

Westmeath

Friars Mill Road, Mullingar

Grid Reference	243850 253189
Cemetery type	Epidemic disease
Date of cemetery	19th century
Number of bodies excavated	4
Date of excavation	1999

Archaeological excavation prior to a development at Friars Mill Road, Mullingar, revealed a single extended inhumation of a young adult male in a shallow grave oriented north-south and containing eighteenth and nineteenth-century pottery sherds. The graveyard boundaries shown on the 1854 town map indicate that this area was previously associated with the local church. Later excavations further south in the grounds of the Manse house found three more inhumations in shallow graves, some covered in lime and associated with nineteenth-century pottery. A coffin handle was recovered from the fill of the third burial. It was suggested that these burials may date to a mid-nineteenth-century cholera epidemic.

References
www.excavations.ie site 1999:870 and 871

Scotland

Aberdeenshire

Aberdeen Blackfriars

Grid Reference	NJ 938 064
Cemetery type	Post-dissolution
Date of cemetery	Late 14th–17th century
Number of bodies excavated	122
Date of excavation	1980–1

One hundred and twenty-two intercutting burials were uncovered during excavations at Aberdeen Blackfriars. Radiocarbon dates suggest a late fourteenth- to seventeenth-century date for the burials, although it is unclear how long burial persisted on the site after the Reformation. It has been suggested that the post-reformation burials may be victims of famine, plague or those with family links to the Friary who continued to use the site after the Reformation.

References
Stone 1989

East Kirk of St. Nicholas, Aberdeen

Grid Reference	NJ 941 062
Cemetery type	Churchyard
Date of cemetery	Post-medieval
Number of bodies excavated	Unknown
Date of excavation	2005–6

Excavation within the East Kirk revealed well-preserved burials, together with coffins, iron fittings, hair and textiles, all in a good state of preservation. An area on the south side of the choir appears to have been used for the burial of young children including neonates. Some nails were found in the soil associated with these burials, but there was little evidence for coffins, although they were used for older children buried at the Kirk. An older adult male was found buried within a wooden coffin. A baby, probably shrouded within a coffin had subsequently been buried near the feet of the burial with its head to the NW. One coffin was found with four copper coins placed on its lid dating to the seventeenth century, while a coin from 1590s was found with another burial. Evidence for the presence of a floral arrangement was found in one coffin. A small number of brooches were found in situ including a heart-shaped brooch, and beads of bone, glass, ceramic and jet were recovered. Several pairs of glasses were also excavated. Copper alloy pins were also found associated with the burials.

References
Hunter 1972–4; Ponsford 2007:390; Cameron 2008

York Place, Aberdeen

Grid Reference	NJ 954 061
Cemetery type	Isolated burial
Date of cemetery	17th century
Number of bodies excavated	Unknown
Date of excavation	1987

Disarticulated human bone was found in a beach-sand deposit in an area traditionally understood to be where plague victims were buried. The excavators suggest that these remains date to the 1647 plague, as a contemporary source mentions burial in the sands. The bones were probably disturbed in 1891 when the sewers were laid.

References
Egan 1988:214

Angus

Bishop's Close and Church Lane, Brechin

Grid Reference	NO 601 598
Cemetery type	Churchyard
Date of cemetery	Post-medieval
Number of bodies excavated	Unknown
Date of excavation	1995

Several inhumations were cut by a sewage pipe in Church Lane. They are probably from the church graveyard, which previously extended beyond the present day boundaries.

References
Ponsford and Jackson 1996:247

The Town House, High Street, Montrose

Grid Reference	NO 7144 5778
Cemetery type	Churchyard
Date of cemetery	19th century
Number of bodies excavated	Unknown
Date of excavation	1999?

An 1819 vault contained two table tombs, two horizontal gravestones and four commemorative plaques, all older than the vault. Excavation indicated that the table tombs were in situ, but the horizontal slabs had been moved. Three unidentified graves were also noted, two of which predated the table tombs.

References
Ponsford 2000:325

Argyllshire

Duart Point, Mull

Grid Reference	NM 748 355
Cemetery type	Drowning victims
Date of cemetery	17th century
Number of bodies excavated	Unknown
Date of excavation	1992, 2003

In 1992 a small shipwreck, probably of mid 17th century date, was located close to the shore. Human remains have been noted on board the wreck, together with finds that suggest the presence of high status individuals on the ship. The ship might be HMS Swan, lost in 1653.

References
Ponsford 1993:223

Kiloran, Colonsay

Grid Reference	NR 9813 9728
Cemetery type	Isolated burial
Date of cemetery	Post-medieval
Number of bodies excavated	1
Date of excavation	1999–2000?

A grave with an inscription to a newborn child who survived only two days, was found on hillside, enclosed by a sub-rectangular mortared wall.

References
Ponsford 2000:326

Lismore Parish Church

Grid Reference	NM 860 435
Cemetery type	Churchyard
Date of cemetery	Post-medieval
Number of bodies excavated	1
Date of excavation	1994

Single adult inhumation, probably late in date was found in the churchyard to the north of the parish church. This inhumation was possibly disturbed or re-interred. Two small pits containing charcoal were found in the same trench.

References
Ponsford and Jackson 1995:118

St. Ronan's Medieval Parish Church, Iona

Grid Reference	NM 284 241
Cemetery type	Churchyard
Date of cemetery	Post-medieval
Number of bodies excavated	29
Date of excavation	1993?

Bones from twenty adult skeletons, plus four juveniles and five infants, were excavated and analysed from the post-medieval women's cemetery at St Ronan's Parish Church. The church was to remain in use, particularly for burial until the mid-seventeenth century, but with few organised services. The majority of the human remains were excavated from within the church where there was a clear preference for burial at the east end, close to the altar. All burials were supine, with heads to the west and usually with arms folded across the pelvis. Some nails were found within the fill of graves suggesting that coffins were used, and in one case fragments of coffin wood were also identified. Three bronze pins and three carved and polished bone pins were also found, although only one came from a clearly defined grave cut. These may have been used to fix shrouds. Small white quartz pebbles were found within the fill of some graves. The use of St Ronan's as a women's cemetery may have some time depth, perhaps dating back to the medieval period, although this could not be verified as the older human remains were poorly preserved.

References
O'Sullivan 1994

Ayrshire

Hogg Hall, Galston Parish Church

Grid Reference	NS 5000 3669
Cemetery type	Churchyard
Date of cemetery	18th–19th century
Number of bodies excavated	25
Date of excavation	2003, 2004

In 2003, disarticulated human bone and two intact graves were encountered during excavations. One grave contained fragments of skull from an articulated skeleton, with a shroud pin and three coffin nails. In 2004, 23 fairly undisturbed articulated burials were located within the burial ground. Most burials were associated with shroud pins. Fragments of wooden coffins and coffin nails were also noted. The artefacts suggested an eighteenth- to nineteenth-century date. Disarticulated remains of at least 72 individuals were also recovered.

References
Discoveries and Excavations in Scotland N.S. 2003:53; Discoveries and Excavations in Scotland N.S. 2004:51; Ponsford 2004:349; Duffy and Grant 2006

Kilwinning Abbey

Grid Reference	NS 303 432
Cemetery type	Churchyard
Date of cemetery	Post-medieval
Number of bodies excavated	Unknown
Date of excavation	1996?

The upper part of a single skeleton with was observed during a watching brief. Corroded iron from the chest area may be the remains of a coffin plate.

References
ADS; Cullen 1997

Caithness

Quintfall Hill, Barrock Estate, near Wick

Grid Reference	ND35 town
Cemetery type	Isolated burial
Date of cemetery	Late 17th–early 18th century
Number of bodies excavated	1
Date of excavation	1920

The skeleton of a man dressed in a patched and mended suit of clothing was found buried in peat at Barrock near Wick. The body was prone, with the arms straight along sides. He was wearing a suit and wrapped in plaid or blanket. A cap and shoes were found above the knees. No mention of a grave cut was made in the published report. There was evidence of a blow to the skull suggesting that the individual met a violent death. In the pocket of suit was a leather purse with 19 bawbees or Scots sixpenny pieces All dated to the reign of Charles II except one of William and Mary, indicating a date of 1694 or later.

References
Orr 1921

East Lothian

Longdykes, Prestonpans, near Edinburgh

Grid Reference	NT 395 745
Cemetery type	Churchyard
Date of cemetery	Late medieval–post-medieval
Number of bodies excavated	8
Date of excavation	Unknown

Five articulated skeletons and the disarticulated remains of a further three individuals were recovered during excavations within the churchyard of St. Andrew's Church at Prestonpans. Radiocarbon dating of three of the burials suggests the cemetery was in use between the fourteenth and seventeenth centuries.

References
Mitchell and White 2004; Anderson and White n.d.

St. Andrew's Old Church and Kirkyard, Anchor Green, Kirkness

Grid Reference	NT 5540 8556
Cemetery type	Churchyard
Date of cemetery	12th–17th century
Number of bodies excavated	30–40
Date of excavation	1999–2005

Excavations in the churchyard of St Andrews Old Church recovered between 30 and 40 inhumations dating to between the twelfth and seventeenth century, with most probably dating to the end of this period. St Andrews Old Church was a pre-Reformation church, of which only the porch still stood at the time of the excavations, the rest of the church having collapsed into the sea due to coastal erosion in the 1660s. Although there is some evidence for the continuing use of the churchyard after this date, it seems largely to have been abandoned after the collapse of the church. The site had been excavated in the 1950s and in the recent excavations a charnel pit was noted containing approximately 30 inhumations, probably reburied from the earlier excavations. Pre-Reformation burials associated with shroud pins were found at a significantly deeper level than the later coffined burials, which also produced evidence of shroud pins. The human skeletal remains were well preserved and coffin traces were also evident, including iron nails and corner braces.

References
Ponsford 2001:199

St. Mary's Parish Church, Haddington

Grid Reference	NT 518 673
Cemetery type	Churchyard
Date of cemetery	Late 17th–early 19th century
Number of bodies excavated	17
Date of excavation	1974

At least 17 coffins from the seventeenth to late nineteenth centuries were recorded along with associated fittings. The lead coffin of the Duke of Lauderdale (d. 1682) was opened. Inside was an inner wooden coffin containing the remains of an embalmed and shrouded body, resting on sawdust. The interior of the inner coffin was sealed with a probable mixture of lanolin and gum ammoniacal. Apart from a black silk ribbon holding back the hair at the back of the skull, the body appeared to be wearing no clothes other than the shroud. It was wrapped in layers of coarse linen impregnated with lanolin, and the whole tied up with linen tapes. An associated lead box contained a red earthenware canopic jar of globular form. Other coffins, including one of a child, were covered in velvet and divided into panels marked by brass studs.

References
Cherry 1975:240; Caldwell 1976

Fife

Balmerino Abbey, Fife

Grid Reference	NO 358 246
Cemetery type	Post-dissolution
Date of cemetery	16th–early 17th century
Number of bodies excavated	9
Date of excavation	1980

Excavations outside the west door of the Cistercian Abbey uncovered evidence for reconstruction after the English attack in 1547. Nine inter-cutting burials were cut through the reconstruction evidence. These belonged to an early post-Reformation cemetery, sealed by building debris from the mid-seventeenth century

References
Kenworthy 1980; Cherry 1981:225–6

Christ's Kirk on the Green, Leslie, Kirkcaldy

Grid Reference	NO 255 020
Cemetery type	Churchyard
Date of cemetery	17th–19th century
Number of bodies excavated	At least 45
Date of excavation	1993

Excavations around the Kirk, built in 1820 on the site of an earlier structure, revealed tightly spaced burials, which were recorded and removed. Initial excavations revealed the remains of at least 4 complete burials along with disarticulated bone. Associated shroud pins suggest a seventeenth- or eighteenth-century date for the burials. These were left in situ. In 1993–4, forty-one complete and partial burials within the interior of the church were recorded and removed. Nineteen were simple shroud burials and 22 were coffin burials. Artefacts recovered included an incomplete copper alloy button of a type introduced in the early nineteenth century, and an eighteenth-century cufflink from a shroud burial. Groups of pins were found in several graves. Their positions indicated that they were used to secure simple textile shrouds, pinned at waist and shoulder. A smaller quantity of pins was found with later coffined burials. A small clump of sheep's wool was found beneath one of the coffin burials, probably thrown into the grave before deposition of the coffin.

References
Cox 1998

Dunino Churchyard

Grid Reference	NO 541 109
Cemetery type	Churchyard
Date of cemetery	17th–early 20th century
Number of bodies excavated	At least 2
Date of excavation	1997

Excavation during building works revealed re-deposited human bone and two infant burials probably of nineteenth- or early twentieth-century date which were left in situ.

References
Cox 1998; Bowler 2002

St. Andrew's Public Library, St. Andrews

Grid Reference	NO 5089 1667
Cemetery type	Churchyard
Date of cemetery	1410–1600
Number of bodies excavated	70
Date of excavation	2003

Seventy articulated skeletons and quantities of disarticulated human bone were uncovered in graveyard of parish church of the Holy Trinity. The graveyard is known to have been used from AD1410–1600.

References
Ponsford 2004:464

Inverness-shire

Isle of Ensay

Grid Reference	NF 975 869
Cemetery type	Churchyard
Date of cemetery	c.1500–late 19th century
Number of bodies excavated	416
Date of excavation	1960s-1990s

Over 400 post-medieval burials were recovered from a wind eroded burial ground close to the north-west shore of the isle of Ensay in the Outer Hebrides. The burials date from c.1500 to the late nineteenth century, with the later burials encased in wooden coffins. The earliest burials lack any evidence for the use of coffins. Coffin use increased in mainland Scotland in the seventeenth century, but appears to have been later on this largely treeless island. Three neonate burials were found above the sand-buried wall of the burial ground.

References
Miles 1989

Lanarkshire

Cambusnethan

Grid Reference	NS 8143 5467
Cemetery type	Isolated burial
Date of cemetery	c.1680–90
Number of bodies excavated	1
Date of excavation	1932

A post-medieval bog body was found in Cambusnethan. The body was laid in a shallow grave with pieces of wood placed above it, perhaps originally used to transport the body to burial location. Surviving clothing included a jacket, cap, shoes and stockings. A cut in area of cap corresponding to the back of the head suggest this individual may have been murdered and illicitly disposed of.

References
Mann 1937

Glasgow Cathedral, City of Glasgow

Grid Reference	NS 605 655
Cemetery type	Churchyard
Date of cemetery	Post-medieval
Number of bodies excavated	82+
Date of excavation	1992–1997

A total of 77 burials were excavated in the autumn and winter of 1992–3. In the Lower Church the majority appeared to be early nineteenth century in date. Those in the nave dated from before the twelfth century to the nineteenth century. Coffin fittings were also recovered as was a large amount of disarticulated bone. Excavations continued in later 1993, in the north-west corner of the Session Room in Glasgow Cathedral, effectively extending the trench previously excavated in 1992/93. Five burials were found, of which four were excavated. These seemed to date to the early nineteenth century, and to be contemporaneous with previously recovered inhumations from the same general area. In 1996/7 human remains were found outside eighteenth-century boundary wall. The cemetery may have been more extensive previously or they may have come from a peripheral or unconsecrated burial ground.

References
Ponsford and Jackson 1995:118; Driscoll 2002

Govan Old Parish Church and Water Row, Govan

Grid Reference	NS 5534 6590
Cemetery type	Churchyard
Date of cemetery	19th century
Number of bodies excavated	At least 8
Date of excavation	1994, 1996

In 1994 excavations in the churchyard found four graves of which one was definitely post-medieval in date and the others were probably medieval. One trench located close to the south-east corner of the church, revealed three modern burials, one of which was an infant, but with no associated artefacts to give a more precise dating estimate. A trench was placed next to the north boundary of the churchyard, within a Victorian burial layer. Good evidence for nineteenth-century burial furnishings was recovered. One of the trenches was later re-opened and extended to reveal a number of eighteenth- and nineteenth-century graves, of which two were fully excavated. Portions of seven burials were examined and coffin fittings were noted. One burial contained two individuals, possibly mother and child.

References
Driscoll 1994; Driscoll and Will 1996; Ponsford and Jackson 1995:118–9; Ponsford and Jackson 1997:289–91

Metropole Development, Clyde Street, Glasgow

Grid Reference	NS 591 647
Cemetery type	Hospital cemetery
Date of cemetery	Post-1773
Number of bodies excavated	2
Date of excavation	2004

A test pit placed close to the heart of the medieval burgh of Glasgow produced the skeletal remains of two individuals, including skull fragments. These were found in the area of the town's hospital and burial ground, which was in use from 1773. One of the skulls showed evidence of having been opened after death. The excavators suggest that this was often done to the insane after death.

References
Discovery and Excavation in Scotland New Series 2004:68

Midlothian

13, Infirmary Street, Edinburgh

Grid Reference	NT 2608 7343
Cemetery type	Hospital cemetery
Date of cemetery	17th–18th century
Number of bodies excavated	6
Date of excavation	1992–3

A number of human burials were discovered during building works at the former church of Lady Hay of Yester (in existence from 1647 to 1803). Six near-complete supine extended inhumations with their heads to the west were recovered, along with disarticulated human bone. The human remains provided good evidence for post-mortem surgery and tooth removal. The Royal Infirmary is known to have used the graveyard as a burial ground for the unclaimed dead from 1749 to the beginning of the nineteenth century. The top of the cranium of one skeleton had been sawn off and replaced before burial, and there was evidence that the skin and hair covering it had also been replaced. Some of the disarticulated bone also exhibited evidence of surgery.

References
Ponsford 1994:123; Henderson, Collard and Johnstone 1996

20 Calton Road, Edinburgh

Grid Reference	NT 264 739
Cemetery type	Churchyard
Date of cemetery	1688–1775
Number of bodies excavated	1
Date of excavation	1997?

A single inhumation of a young adult female buried in a coffin was uncovered. The area was probably used as a graveyard around Canongate Kirk, c. 1688–1775.

References
Ponsford 2001:203–4

Almond Valley Pipeline, Newbattle Abbey

Grid Reference	NT 3310 6587– 3373 6666
Cemetery type	Churchyard
Date of cemetery	Medieval–post-medieval
Number of bodies excavated	125
Date of excavation	2001?

One hundred and twenty-five inhumations were removed from the medieval and post-medieval cemetery associated with Newbattle Abbey. Nine stone-capped graves probably of relatively late date were noted to the west of the abbey

References
Ponsford 2002:268

Cockpen Medieval Parish Church

Grid Reference	NT 3267 6333
Cemetery type	Churchyard
Date of cemetery	Medieval– post-medieval
Number of bodies excavated	Unknown
Date of excavation	1993

Archaeological work carried out during conservation uncovered burials of medieval and post-medieval date.

References
O'Sullivan 1995

Greyfriars Tollbooth and Highland Kirk, Cramond, City Of Edinburgh

Grid Reference	NT 2557 7337
Cemetery type	Churchyard
Date of cemetery	Post-medieval
Number of bodies excavated	29
Date of excavation	2003

Disturbed human skeletal remains and articulated skeletons were recorded in graves cut into the subsoil within the churchyard of Greyfriars Tollbooth and Highland Kirk. Twenty discrete groups of bone were located from a minimum number of 29 individuals. Coffin handles, nails and wood fragments were also recovered.

References
Discovery and Excavation in Scotland New Series 2003:70; Ponsford 2004:359

Parliament House, Edinburgh

Grid Reference	NT 2571 7353
Cemetery type	Churchyard
Date of cemetery	Late 15th century–c.1566
Number of bodies excavated	96
Date of excavation	2004

Ninety-six inhumations, arranged in rows and oriented west-east were recovered from the probable southward extension of St Giles' Church. This was extended from the later fifteenth century and was out of use by 1566. A group of six skeletons may have been interred in a mass grave; one of the bodies was lying prone with arms spread eagled, suggesting the body had been dumped.

References
Discovery and Excavation in Scotland New Series 2003; Roy and Toolis 2005

St. Mary's Star of the Sea, Constitution Street, Edinburgh

Grid Reference	NT 271 762
Cemetery type	War burials
Date of cemetery	c.1500–1631
Number of bodies excavated	5
Date of excavation	2004

Four north-south burials were found on a site of domestic habitation not far from Constitution Street in Leith. There was no evidence for the use of coffins and it has been suggested that these burials on unconsecrated ground may be soldiers killed during one of the sieges in Leith. The burials lie only some 100m from Commercial Street where the defensive line is thought to have run.

References
Discovery and Excavation in Scotland New Series 2004:57; White 2004

Surgeon's Square, Edinburgh

Grid Reference	NT 2623 7352
Cemetery type	Medical waste
Date of cemetery	18th–19th century
Number of bodies excavated	Unknown
Date of excavation	1996

A small assemblage of human and animal bone was excavated from accumulated deposits in Surgeons' Square, to the north-east of the former Surgeons' Hall. The faunal remains included brown bear and seal. A minimum of five individuals were represented by the human bone, including a child of 6–8 years old. 37% of the human bone showed evidence of dissection, including sectioned bones. Also an iron or steel pin had been inserted into the side of a tubercular lumbar vertebra. There were high levels of severe pathological lesions. This, taken together with the unusual faunal assemblage, suggests that the bones were used as part of teaching collections at one of the private surgery and anatomy schools that were found on the Square during the eighteenth and early nineteenth centuries.

References
Henderson, Collard and Johnstone 1996

The Coal Yard, Edinburgh Castle

Grid Reference	NT 2511 7349
Cemetery type	War burials
Date of cemetery	1689
Number of bodies excavated	15 +2
Date of excavation	1988–91

Fifteen burials were uncovered in a small cemetery by the fortifications at the entrance to Edinburgh Castle. All individuals were male with the majority being young adults. All were interred in coffins without coffin fittings in shallow graves. There was no evidence for clothing but small wire pins were found with several of the burials suggesting the use of shrouds. Two burials found during excavations in Princes Street Gardens during the 1960s are thought to have been part of the same cemetery. Two of the graves were cut into a demolition layer which contained a coin dating to c.1686. The cemetery is though to date to the 1689 siege of the castle by supporters of William and Mary when food and water were in short supply and epidemics were reported.

References
Driscoll and Yeoman 1997

Moray

High Street, Elgin, Moray

Grid Reference	NJ 213 627
Cemetery type	Churchyard
Date of cemetery	Post-medieval
Number of bodies excavated	23
Date of excavation	1995

Work to the east and west of St Giles' Church uncovered 23 skeletons and disarticulated bones.

References
Ponsford and Jackson 1996:247

Orkney Isles

Newark, Sanday

Grid Reference	HY 5747 0413
Cemetery type	Churchyard
Date of cemetery	Post-medieval
Number of bodies excavated	8
Date of excavation	2000

Eight burials exposed in the sea bank were excavated and removed. Three further burials were noted. The majority were aligned northwest to southeast and appear to have been interred in shrouds given the lack evidence for coffins. A single grave was constructed with stone sides and cover, though only the head end was visible in section. One of the burials was prone.

References
Ponsford 2001:244

Perthshire

Blackfriars, Perth

Grid Reference	NO 119 233
Cemetery type	Post-dissolution
Date of cemetery	Post-medieval
Number of bodies excavated	15
Date of excavation	1982

A prone skeleton was found lying north-south across a ditch, dating to the period of the Reformation and thought either to be a fresh burial exhumed during the demolition of the Friary or an illicitly dumped murder victim. Another fourteen graves were found cut into the demolition rubble. Five graves contained articulated skeletons with the others either empty or containing disarticulated bone. Two of the skeletons lay in coffins. It's not clear why these burials are here, although it has been suggested that they may form part of a plague cemetery or part of a later burial ground.

References
Hall 1989

Fowlis Wester Church

Grid Reference	NN 928 241

Cemetery type	Churchyard
Date of cemetery	17th century onwards
Number of bodies excavated	5
Date of excavation	1997

Five skeletons were excavated prior to the underpinning of the eastern gable wall of Fowlis Wester Church. All burials are thought to post-date the refurbishment of the church in 1641. One skeleton had coins dating to 1642–1650 over its eye-sockets.

References
Strachan 1995; Rees and Strachan 1998

Greyfriars Burial Ground, Perth

Grid Reference	NO 120 232
Cemetery type	Churchyard
Date of cemetery	Post-medieval
Number of bodies excavated	Unknown
Date of excavation	1997, 2001?

Test-pits were placed against the east wall of Greyfriars burial ground. The burials were recorded in situ.

References
Ponsford and Jackson 1998:147; Ponsford 2001:247

Kinnoull Parish Church, Perth

Grid Reference	NO 123 233
Cemetery type	Churchyard
Date of cemetery	Post-medieval
Number of bodies excavated	50+
Date of excavation	1995

Excavations at Kinnoull parish church in the southwest corner of the graveyard revealed the remains of more than 50 burials, most within coffins. One of the later coffins contained fragments of coarse woollen lining or covering as well as compressed wood shavings or straw covered with tar-like substance. Small pieces of twine or rope found with another graveyard burial, probably belonging to the internal furnishings of the coffin. Copper alloy, glass and mother of pearl buttons were found in association with several burials. Four small copper alloy eyelets were found with a child burial, lying in a line in the chest area. A cord to fasten the burial garment would have passed through these. A fragmentary safety pin was also noted with one of later burials. Several pins and pin fragments were also found, some closely associated with coffined burials. A half penny of Queen Victoria (1837–1860) was found on the chest of a child burial. An oyster shell with a single roughly square perforation through the thicker end was also found in the grave cut of one of the deepest burials.

References
Cox 1998

Perth Prison, Perth

Grid Reference	NO 117 222
Cemetery type	War burials
Date of cemetery	Post-medieval
Number of bodies excavated	Unknown
Date of excavation	1999

Human remains were found on the north side of Perth Prison, at the southern edge of the road between the perimeter wall and a nineteenth-century building known as the Old Laundry, when new sewer pipe was being laid. Further human and coffin remains were recovered and thought to be of French prisoners of war who had died while being held at the depot during the Napoleonic Wars. The human remains were examined forensically and later returned to the prison and reburied adjacent to where they were found.

References
Ponsford 2001:248

White Kirk, Dunira Street, Comrie

Grid Reference	NN 7728 2194
Cemetery type	Churchyard
Date of cemetery	17th century–1805
Number of bodies excavated	Unknown
Date of excavation	1999

Excavations occurred on the site of the former White Church, built in 1805 to replace an earlier church. Disarticulated human remains were recovered from the pre-White Church deposits. Four complete articulated burials including coffin fittings and furnishings were recorded as well as grave cuts containing the remains of coffined burials. All were oriented approximately west-east in rows running north-south and predate 1805. The coffins were of flat-lidded, single break construction, made of pine planks with oval iron grips, some of which were bound with a narrow textile bandage. Iron loops, used to lower the coffin into the grave, were also recorded. Wood shavings were found inside one coffin. The imprint of a finely woven textile was noted on the exterior surface of some coffin brackets. The excavators suggest that a mort cloth covered the coffin and decayed in situ. Two of the complete burials contained a coin placed below the body. A total of ten coins were found in graveyard soil in close association with the coffined burials. Where the date was visible, they were minted between 1639 and 1697. Other artefacts included a pale blue glass bead, a small copper alloy brooch or earring decorated with a vine motif and a copper alloy lace tag. These are interpreted as coming from personal garments rather than from specialist grave clothing. A large number of copper alloy pins were also recovered.

References
Ponsford 2001:245–6; Cachart and Cox 2001

Renfrewshire

Kilbarchan Old West Parish Church, Kilbarchan

Grid Reference	NS 401 632
Cemetery type	Churchyard
Date of cemetery	Late 18th–early 19th century
Number of bodies excavated	64
Date of excavation	2002

Sixty-four burials were excavated with the majority lying in wooden coffins. The upper burials tended to have good skeletal preservation, while the lower burials, from more waterlogged deposits had preserved coffin traces but little bone. One individual had been buried with a gold ring. Some of the burials from poorer simple coffins had evidence of notches in their teeth consistent with weaving activity; weavers are known to have lived and worked locally. Ceramics found in the grave fills suggested a date of late eighteenth to early nineteenth century.

References
Ponsford 2003:358–9

Neilston Parish Church, Neilston

Grid Reference	NS 4801 5736
Cemetery type	Churchyard
Date of cemetery	18th–19th century
Number of bodies excavated	27
Date of excavation	2003

Disarticulated human bone was found above articulated skeletons inside the church. Finds included a seventeenth-century coin as well as earlier artefacts. In the graveyard 27 articulated skeletons were found, of which four were removed, and the others recorded in situ. An eighteenth- to nineteenth-century date was suggested by the associated lead lined coffins, coffin handles, and shroud pins.

References
Discovery and Excavation in Scotland New Series 2003:67; Discovery and Excavation in Scotland New Series 2004:51; Ponsford 2004:355

Ross and Cromarty

Arnish Moor, Lewis

Grid Reference	NB 386 305
Cemetery type	Isolated burial
Date of cemetery	18th century
Number of bodies excavated	1
Date of excavation	1964

The clothed body of a possible murder victim was found about two feet below the surface of a peat bank on Arnish Moor, south of Stornoway, near the junction of the Grimshader road with the Stornoway-Harris road. The body was a young man, around 20–25 years old, and was laid on his back, with his head to the north-west. Although the skeletal preservation was poor, the peat had preserved some dark hair and nails as well as woollen clothing and other artefacts. The individual was wearing a thigh length jacket over a knee-length shirt and undershirt. A knitted bonnet was found on the head. Cloth stockings were wrapped over the feet with rags, and were gathered below the knee with strips of cloth. All the clothing was much patched and mended. There was no trace of shoes or breeches. The clothing suggests an early eighteenth-century date for the burial. A small striped woollen bag was also found. This contained a wooden comb made of birch, a small block of oak, a horn spoon repaired with rivets, two sharpened quills, probably pens, and three clews of wood. Three lengths of wood were also found. No coins were found with the body. There was evidence of a skull injury, probably the result of a blow with an object with "a defined striking surface" – consistent with an attack from the rear and appears to be the cause of death.

References
Bennett 1975

Braigh (Broad Bay), Aignish, Lewis

Grid Reference	NB 4801 3220
Cemetery type	Drowning victims
Date of cemetery	Post-medieval
Number of bodies excavated	11
Date of excavation	1989

Eleven individuals buried in two groups, were found during excavations in sand dunes at Braigh, Aignish. The bodies were orientated north-south and most appeared to have been male in their late teens or early twenties. There was an older individual and one juvenile and one possible female. One individual was buried with a purse of coins and an iron whittle tang knife. The associated coins provide a suggested date of around 1700. Two lead objects were also recovered. Their orientation combined with burial outside consecrated ground, and foreign coins suggest that they were shipwreck victims, and were not local to the area.

References
McCallagh, Roderick and McCormick 1991

Cille Bhrea, Lemlair

Grid Reference	NH 57 62
Cemetery type	Churchyard
Date of cemetery	16th–19th century
Number of bodies excavated	50
Date of excavation	1998

Coastal erosion at the east end of Cille Bhrea chapel and graveyard led to the exposure of human bone. Subsequent excavations recorded 50 graves which were eroding into the Cromarty Firth. Coffin fittings dated some of the graves to the sixteenth to eighteenth century. Seven radiometric dates confirmed burials as belonging to the seventeenth to nineteenth centuries.

References
Rees 2004

Cladh na Sasunnach, Fasagh, Gairloch

Grid Reference	NH 0070 6595
Cemetery type	Other
Date of cemetery	Post-medieval
Number of bodies excavated	Unknown
Date of excavation	1997

The excavations were conducted of a cemetery located 620m to the north-west of an early seventeenth-century ironworks at Fasagh, located next to Lochan Cladh na Sasunnach. Twenty-three graves were identified, marked by angular boulder cairns. One grave was excavated and produced a small piece of waterlogged wood, probably from a coffin, and iron nails. There seem to be few similarities between these nails and those produced at the iron works although the connection between the cemetery and ironworks is unclear.

References
Ponsford and Jackson 1998:200; Atkinson and Photos-Jones 1999

Fisherman's Mission, North Beach Street, Stornaway, Lewis

Grid Reference	NB 422 327
Cemetery type	Churchyard
Date of cemetery	Post-medieval
Number of bodies excavated	Unknown
Date of excavation	2000?

The disturbed remains of several individuals as well as clay pipe fragments and iron nail with wood traces were found on the site of the former church and graveyard of St. Lennan.

References
Ponsford 2001:272–3

Point Street, Stornaway, Lewis

Grid Reference	NB 4219 3278
Cemetery type	Churchyard
Date of cemetery	Post-medieval
Number of bodies excavated	Unknown
Date of excavation	2000?

Human remains were noted during a watching brief, probably from graveyard associated with the early seventeenth-century church of St. Lennan.

References
Ponsford 2001:273

Roxburghshire

Jedburgh Abbey, Roxburgh

Grid Reference	NT 650 204
Cemetery type	Churchyard/post-dissolution use
Date of cemetery	18th–19th century

Number of bodies excavated   Unknown
Date of excavation   1990

A trench excavated in the presbytery revealed several burials, including a burial in a lead coffin encased in timber planks. Traces of textile and thin copper beaten into shell-like patterns were attached to the exterior of the coffin. The human remains were well preserved and articulated with some hair still attached to the skull. There was no lid to the coffin. The burial was probably of the late eighteenth or nineteenth century. More graves were noted to the east but were not excavated. A second cluster of post-medieval burials was found to the north-east of the chapter house. These burials were all in simple pits with no evidence for coffins, shrouds or burial goods. The graveyard to the north of the church was used as the parish churchyard after the dissolution. Excavations suggest that the monastic cemetery continued in use although the lack of organisation of the burials suggests that the area may have been used to inter those excluded from the main churchyard.

References
Ponsford 1991:118–9; Lewis and Ewart 1995

Shetland Isles

Gunnister

Grid Reference	HU 328 732
Cemetery type	Isolated burial
Date of cemetery	Late 17th century
Number of bodies excavated	1
Date of excavation	1951

Skeletal remains and well-preserved clothing and artefacts were found in a shallow grave in a peat bog in an isolated part of the moor near Gunnister, Shetland. A fully clothed male individual had been laid supine with the head towards the east-southeast. The body was buried only 30 inches deep, although the peat was up to 4 ft deep. The well preserved woollen clothing included a long coat with short wide legged breeches, a shirt and outer jacket, which was somewhat ragged in appearance, and a leather belt with a brass buckle. Long, knitted socks and knitted gloves were also found. He also wore a knitted cap and had another inside his clothing (possibly in an internal pocket) wrapped around a horn spoon. Inside the breeches on the left side were a small horn with a plug of spruce, and a knitted purse which held a folded silk ribbon and three late seventeenth-century coins. These were of low value, two Dutch and one Swedish, dating to 1690, 1681 and 1683 respectively. A stick made of birch lay across the legs. At the feet were a small wooden tub made of Scots pine, two lengths of woollen cord, an ash knife handle and two pierced and curved tablets of wood, one of oak, one of Scots pine. It has been suggested that the remains were those of a traveller who had died on the moor in adverse weather conditions, probably during winter, and was buried where he fell when found later in the year.

References
Henshall and Maxwell 1952

Stirlingshire

Stirling Castle

Grid Reference	NS 790 940
Cemetery type	Churchyard
Date of cemetery	Post-medieval
Number of bodies excavated	10
Date of excavation	1997

Ten inhumations (nine adults and one child) and a charnel pit were found in association with the chapel. The dating of the burials is unclear and some are likely to be linked to the pre-1530s structure, but at least one burial was associated with post-1530s chapel.

References
Ponsford and Jackson 1998:152–3; Ponsford 2000:369

The Toll Booth, Stirling

Grid Reference	NS 793 936
Cemetery type	Prison cemetery
Date of cemetery	19th century
Number of bodies excavated	At least 1
Date of excavation	1999

Historical records note that executed prisoners were buried within the confines of the Tollbooth. Disturbed human remains were discovered during a watching brief. Later work recovered the poorly preserved remains of a tall elderly man in a pine coffin, located beneath the original pend below the county house that led from the jail wynd into the prison courtyard. A turned bone trouser button and a pair of well-preserved boots were associated with the inhumation. The coffin was orientated north-south, on the same orientation as the pend. Historical documents and newspaper articles suggest that the remains were of Allan Mair, the last person hanged at Stirling, who was executed in 1843 for the murder of his wife.

References
Ponsford 2001:264; Discovery and Excavation in Scotland New Series 1999/2000

Sutherland

Cladh ne-h-aiteg, Kinlochbervie

Grid Reference	NC 202 585
Cemetery type	Isolated burial
Date of cemetery	Post-medieval
Number of bodies excavated	At least 5
Date of excavation	2003

Disturbed human remains were noted eroding out of the dunes. The disarticulated remains of at least five individuals were subsequently recovered and analysed.

References
Discovery and Excavation in Scotland New Series 2003:86

West Lothian

Linlithgow Blackfriars

Grid Reference	NT 300 676
Cemetery type	Post-dissolution
Date of cemetery	Late 15th–early 17th century
Number of bodies excavated	6
Date of excavation	1983–4

A group of five graves were uncovered in claustral area of the friary, thought to date between the late fifteenth and early seventeenth century. A sixth grave, the supine east-west burial of a child between four and eight years, was found to the west of the church and is thought to post-date the friary.

References
Lindsay 1989

Wales

Caernarvonshire

St. Catherine's Church, Criccieth

Grid Reference	SH 5006 3832
Cemetery type	Churchyard
Date of cemetery	19th century–20th century
Number of bodies excavated	Unknown
Date of excavation	1993

Building works on north side of the north aisle led to graveyard recording and excavation. Burials dating to the nineteenth and twentieth century were exhumed alongside the north wall of the north aisle. The majority of the graves were lined with brick walling. No finds predating the nineteenth century were found.

References
Archaeology in Wales 1993:85; Ponsford 1994:124

Carmarthenshire

Capel Teilo, Kidwelly

Grid Reference	SN 4356 0740
Cemetery type	Isolated burial
Date of cemetery	18th century?
Number of bodies excavated	At least 1
Date of excavation	1966–9

Excavations of a disused chapel uncovered the burial of a fifteen year-old male to the east of the Chapel. The burial had an eighteenth-century copper button on its chest and may represent the interment of a suicide or drowning victim. In addition, the superficial burials of at least three infants were encountered to the south-east of the chapel.

References
Jones n.d.

Carmarthen Greyfriars

Grid Reference	SN 4150 1980
Cemetery type	Post-dissolution
Date of cemetery	Post-dissolution?
Number of bodies excavated	51
Date of excavation	1997

Around 51 post-medieval burials were recorded during excavation in advance of redevelopment. They came from an extension to a smaller medieval graveyard, located on its east and south sides, providing evidence that the cemetery continued after the Dissolution.

References
James 1997; Ponsford and Jackson 1998:148; Manning 1998a; Manning 1998b

St. Nicholas' Church, Trelech

Grid Reference	SO 499 054
Cemetery type	Churchyard
Date of cemetery	18th–19th century
Number of bodies excavated	Unknown
Date of excavation	1995

Excavation to the north-west of the church tower, near the boundary of graveyard found 15 poorly preserved inhumations with grave markers. The most complete graves within the trench were of children. One adult inhumation was found in a coffin within a brick vault with traces of foliage carved on the collapsed lip of the coffin. One burial had disturbed previous interments and the backfill of the grave contained at least three individuals. Textiles and coffin fittings were recovered. Later excavations in a room to the north of the tower revealed three in situ burials and a large amount of disarticulated human bone.

References
Archaeology in Wales 1995:74–5; Ponsford and Jackson 1996:248; Ponsford and Jackson 1997:260

St. Peter's Church, Carmarthen

Grid Reference	SN 4152 2022
Cemetery type	Churchyard
Date of cemetery	18th–19th century
Number of bodies excavated	Unknown
Date of excavation	2000

Eighteenth- and nineteenth-century vaults containing coffins and covered with ledger stones were recorded in St. Peter's Churchyard. Escutcheons appear to have been removed from the lids of some coffins. A decorated and inscribed breast plate was also noted in one vault. A late seventeenth-century shaft grave contained a lead box with the head of St. Richard Steele (d.1729) inside. His body had been disturbed in 1876 and put on display before the head was re-buried. Box leaves were recovered from one burial.

References
Page 2001

Denbighshire

St. Michael's Church, Abergele

Grid Reference	SH 945 776
Cemetery type	Churchyard
Date of cemetery	Post-medieval
Number of bodies excavated	6
Date of excavation	2005/6

Six post-medieval burials were encountered during small-scale excavations at St. Michael's Church in Abergele. Post-medieval coins and pewter buttons recovered may have been associated with disturbed burials.

References
http://www.cpat.org.uk/projects/longer/abergele/abergele/abergele.htm

Flintshire

St. Cyngar's Church, Hope

Grid Reference	SJ 30965 58388
Cemetery type	Churchyard
Date of cemetery	18th century
Number of bodies excavated	2
Date of excavation	1997

Preliminary clearance in 1997 revealed a lead coffin beneath the floor, its lid embossed with the initial WH, a date of 1746 and a skull and crossed bones. This was left in situ. Later recording revealed a wooden coffin overlain by grey-brown loam with re-deposited mortar. This contained a Charles II coin and a George III halfpenny dated 1769.

References
Jones, Silvester and Edwards 2001

Glamorgan

Cardiff Free Library, Trinity Street, Cardiff

Grid Reference	ST 1831 7635

Cemetery type	Churchyard
Date of cemetery	Early 19th century
Number of bodies excavated	32
Date of excavation	1997

Work to the north of the Old Library (built 1882) led to excavation in the southern part of the former churchyard of St. John the Baptist. This part of the churchyard appears to have been in use for a short time in the early nineteenth century when it was created as an extension of the existing churchyard. Thirty-two individuals were excavated for reburial. All graves and vaults were orientated approximately east-west. Nine graves contained single individuals, another six contained multiple interments. Two vaults were recorded. One large brick vault in the south-west corner of the area under excavation contained six individuals; another near the library contained a single individual. Pottery and coffin furniture suggested a mid-nineteenth century date for the graves. The burials were in coffins with one individual in a tin or metal plate coffin. Possibly evidence for autopsy was found on two skulls.

References
Tavener 1998a and 1998b

Cwmnash, Monknash

Grid Reference	SS 905 701
Cemetery type	Post-dissolution
Date of cemetery	16th–17th century
Number of bodies excavated	3
Date of excavation	1993

Three burials, orientated east-west, were exposed eroding out of a cliff at the outflow of the Blaen-y-cwm valley, west of Monknash Grange. Three mostly intact individuals were retrieved, although the fill contained disarticulated remains from a further 11 individuals, all male and most 17–30 in age, although two may have been over 40. In one grave, a disturbed skull had been reburied with other bones at the foot of the grave, marked by a stone. Radiocarbon analysis dates the burials to the early post-medieval period. The inhumations probably derived from a cemetery used before St Mary Monknash was given burial rights in 1607. A holy well is nearby, and there is also evidence for a small circular chapel.

References
Ponsford 1994:126; Archaeology in Wales 1993:86; Locock 1993

Dunraven

Grid Reference	SS 8867 7279
Cemetery type	Isolated burial
Date of cemetery	Post-medieval
Number of bodies excavated	2
Date of excavation	1980

Two burials found on an eroding slope on Trwyn y Witch near the Dunraven Hillfort. Radiocarbon dating suggests a post-medieval date.

References
Sell 1980 and 2000

Flat Holm Island

Grid Reference	ST 218 648
Cemetery type	Drowning victims
Date of cemetery	Mid-18th–mid-19th century
Number of bodies excavated	3
Date of excavation	1986

Skeletal remains were exposed by tidal erosion of the cliff at Flat Holm Island in the Bristol Channel. Three male skeletons were found interred together in a pit also containing nineteenth-century rubbish. The pit underlay a boundary wall known to exist by 1885. Datable finds around burials suggest a mid-eighteenth- to mid-nineteenth-century date for the burials. The human remains included an oriental and a Caucasian whose left leg had been amputated after death. It appears the individuals were in an advanced state of decay when interred. It has been suggested that the three individuals had drowned at sea. It is known that ships were wrecked with some frequency in this area in the early nineteenth century.

References
Archaeology in Wales 1986:62; Coles 1986; Egan 1987:280

Merionenthshire

Llangar Church

Grid Reference	SO 064 425
Cemetery type	Churchyard
Date of cemetery	Post-medieval
Number of bodies excavated	52
Date of excavation	1974

Fifty-two articulated skeletons were found during excavations in advance of conservation works. Coffined intramural burials were also recorded. Fragments of a silver pin were found near the head of one individual. One male burial was found with traces of box and viola near his head and stomach respectively. A cluster of eight infant burials was found just east of the centre of the church. A coffined burial of 1687 was decorated with copper studs and covered in bark. A similar infant coffin of 1688 was also recorded.

References
Shoesmith 1980b

Pennal Churchyard, Meirionnydd

Grid Reference	SH 699 003
Cemetery type	Churchyard
Date of cemetery	19th century
Number of bodies excavated	174
Date of excavation	1991

Machine excavation within the churchyard revealed post-medieval burials. Little human bone remained with only fragmentary coffin furniture. Of 174 burials, only 17 were intact. These were nineteenth-century interments (one within a lead coffin) within brick or stone vaults on bases made from thin rectangular slabs of slate laid parallel. Brass and iron coffin furniture was identified, including handles, mounts, and fragments of thin escutcheons.

References
Archaeology in Wales 1993:86–87; Ponsford 1994: 125

Monmouthshire

Holy Trinity Church, Christchurch, Newport

Grid Reference	ST 894 346
Cemetery type	Churchyard
Date of cemetery	19th century
Number of bodies excavated	Unknown
Date of excavation	1996?

A brick vault was noted, which contained a burial dated 1861.

References
Ponsford and Jackson 1997:260; Taylor 1996

Llanddewi Fach Church,

Grid Reference	SO 3319 0558
Cemetery type	Churchyard

Date of cemetery	Post-medieval
Number of bodies excavated	2
Date of excavation	1999

A shallow charnel pit containing disarticulated human bone was found to the north of the church (possibly associated with nineteenth-century alterations within the church). Two burials were also found at the extreme north end of the churchyard, but no other burials were observed in the area.

References
Archaeology in Wales 1999:141; Ponsford 2000:382

St. Mary's Church, Undy

Grid Reference	ST 440 868
Cemetery type	Churchyard
Date of cemetery	Post-medieval
Number of bodies excavated	2
Date of excavation	1996?

Large amount of disarticulated bone and two post-medieval burials were uncovered in a soakaway dug off the north-east corner of the church.

References
Ponsford and Jackson 1997:260

St. Mary's Priory, Abergavenny

Grid Reference	SO 3010 1413
Cemetery type	Churchyard
Date of cemetery	17th–19th century
Number of bodies excavated	Unknown
Date of excavation	1994, 1996, 1999?, 2000

A number of archaeological interventions in the 1990s and 2000 have uncovered post-medieval brick burial vaults and burials, with coffins and coffin furniture.

References
Locock 1994a and b; Maylan 1993; Page 1994; Ponsford and Jackson 1995:120; 1997:259–60; Maynard 1996; Williams 1998; Archaeology in Wales 1999:139–40 and 2000:140; Ponsford 2001:279–80

St. Tudor's Church, Mynydd Islwyn, Caerphilly

Grid Reference	ST 1932 9392
Cemetery type	Churchyard
Date of cemetery	Post-medieval
Number of bodies excavated	Unknown
Date of excavation	2000, 2002

Two parallel extended post-medieval skeletons and disarticulated remains were found during excavations at St. Tudor's Church.

References
Archaeology in Wales 2000:136; Archaeology in Wales 2002:136

Pembrokeshire

St. Bride's Haven, Pembrokeshire

Grid Reference	SM 8021 1094
Cemetery type	Churchyard
Date of cemetery	Post-medieval
Number of bodies excavated	1
Date of excavation	2009

Stone lined cists had been noted eroding out of the Old Red sandstone cliffs to the north of St. Bride's parish church. Small-scale excavations were undertaken in 2009 to determine the extent and nature of the archaeological remains to determine the best way to manage the site. The cist cemetery lies c.50m to the north of the churchyard associated with St. Bride's Church and has traditionally been associated with a medieval chapelry. Excavations revealed portions of five burials. Four of the burials contained evidence for stone cists while the fifth contained no evidence for a cist. Radiocarbon analysis of one of the cist burials gave an early medieval date, but the burial from the earth cut grave gave an early modern date. It is possible that the churchyard was in constant use from the early medieval period to the early modern period. Alternatively the post-medieval burial was denied interment in St. Bride's Churchyard and was therefore buried in this early cemetery.

References
Schlee 2009

St. Ismael's Church, Camrose

Grid Reference	SM 9271 2006
Cemetery type	Churchyard
Date of cemetery	18th–early 19th century
Number of bodies excavated	8–9
Date of excavation	2000/1?

Natural clay subsoil was cut by seven or eight burials of eighteenth- to early nineteenth-century date, aligned on the churchyard path. Another burial was found opposite the church tower, cut from a higher level and probably of later nineteenth-century date. None of the burials were associated with above ground markers.

References
Ponsford 2002:284–5; Archaeology in Wales 2001:165

Index

Page numbers in italics should indicate references in the site gazetteer; those in bold refer to figures.

A

Aberdeen Blackfriar's *253*
Aberdeen Cathedral 82
Abingdon Abbey 82
Abingdon Vineyard, Oxfordshire 23, **109**, *231*
Abingdon West 24
Act for Burying in Woollen Only 24, 26, 44, 156
Act for Regulating Schools of Anatomy 134
Act for the Uniformity of Public Prayers 89
Act of Toleration 81, 103, 131
Act of Uniformity 37
affidavit for burial in woollen clothing 24, **25**
Aldgate Burial Ground, Royal Mint Square *222*
All Hallows by the Tower Churchyard, Bywater Street *217*
All Hallows, Honey Lane, London 122
All Saints Church, High Wycombe *198*
All Saints Church, Hutton *204*
All Saints Church, Kirtling, Cambridgeshire 66, *198*
All Saints Church, Laleham *238*
All Saints Church, Lanchester *203*
All Saints Church, Leek Wootton *238*
All Saints Church, Loughton, Buckinghamshire 76, *198*
All Saints Church, Milton *199*
All Saints Church, Pavement, York 28, *241*
All Saints Church, Preston, Gloucestershire *205*
All Saints Church, Ravensden *196*
All Saints Parish Church, Church Street, West Ham, Newham *217*
Almond Valley Pipeline, Newbattle Abbey *257*
Alton, Hampshire 90
Amersham, Buckinghamshire 90
amputation
  healed *202*
  peri-mortem *202*
  post-mortem 137, 150, 151, *220*, *230*, *263*
anatomical teaching establishments 147–150
Anatomy Act 1832 17, 98, 129, 130, 136, 149, 155, *230*, *231*
Anderson's Yard, Islington *217*
animals, use of in anatomical training 153, *220*, *225*, *248*
anthropologie du terrain 26
Apes, Henry (burial, suicide) 119
Archaeological Data Service 159, 196
Ariès, Philippe 13
Aristotle and the Hippocratic school 153
Arnish Moor, Lewis 117, *260*
Artillery Ground, Spitalfields Market *218*
Ashton-under-Lyme, Lancashire 41

Athenaeum burial ground, Plymouth *202*
Aubrey, John 73
Auchlossan farm, Aberdeenshire 150
Augustinian Friary, Hull 57, 78
Augustinian Priory of Lanercost, Cumberland 85
Austin Friars, Leicester 24
autopsy 39, 130, 133, 137, 143, 145, 146, 149, *209*, *216*, *217*, *218*, *220*, *222*, *224*, *225*, *227*, *229*, *230*, *234*, *236*, *239*, *263*
  conducted to detect poisoning 135, 145
  imbalance between sexes present in 143
Averie, William (ledger stone of) 49, 69
Aylesbury, battle of 107

B

Backchurch Lane Burial Ground, London 94
Bagenal, Nicholas 84, *246*
Bagenal's Castle, County Down 84, 108, *246*
Baillie, Matthew 42
Baldwin family vault, St Phillips Cathedral, Birmingham *240*
Ballinasloe and District Lunatic Asylum, County Galway 54, 71
Ballingall, Colonel David James (body of) 102
Ballingall, Dorcas 102
Balmerino Abbey, Fife *256*
Bannister's Green, Essex *204*
Baptist Burial Ground, Redcross Street *205*
Baptist Burial Ground, West Butts, Poole 56, 60, 66, 72, 73, 91, 93, 140, *203*
Baptist Church, Bewley *241*
Baptist Church, Coxwell Street, Cirencester *208*
Barbican, York 111
Barbour, George 82
Barling's Abbey 81
Barnard, Ramsden (coffin of) 79
Barnardiston vault in Keddington Church, Suffolk 48, *237*
Basil Brown, Mrs. 100
Basing House, North Hampshire 109
Baskerville, John (interment of) 105
Beaufort, Thomas, Duke of Exeter (embalming of) 39
Bede-roll 9
Beeston Castle, Cheshire 109, *200*
beheading as punishment 127, 128, 130
Bell Vault, Milton Church, Thanington Without *211*
Beswick, Hannah (body of) 41
Bethlehem Hospital, London 87, 88, *221*
bier-right (*see* cruentation)

265

Bigg, Richard (body of) 125
Bilingsgate Lorry Park, Lower Thames Street, City of London *218*
Binfield Church, Binfield 196
Bird, Pastor John 91
Bishop Challenor's School, Commercial Road, Tower Hamlets *218*
Bishop's Close and Church Lane, Brechin *254*
Black Death (*see also* disease, epidemic and pit, plague) 14, 46
black, coffins painted 69, *204*
Blackfriar's, Perth *258*
Blandford Parish Church 58, 78, *203*
body
   and mind, Cartesian distinction between 12
   as a scientifically anatomised material object 13
   as machine 133
   changing disciplinary practices around 16
   in relation to the self 12
   in relation to the soul 10, 12, 22
body, dead
   agency of 18
   as central to the grieving process 47, 60, 102
   attributed sentience of 20
   female (negative valuation of) 13
   lack of theological grounds for disposal of 10
   of marginalised classes and individuals 19
   retention of a personal and social identity of 11, 33
Bolton Priory, West Yorkshire 82
Bonn Square, Oxford *232*
Book of Common Prayer 89, 119
Boscombe Down Airfield, Amesbury *240*
Bow Baptist Church, London 72, *218*
Bowthorpe, Norfolk 119
Boyce, William (undertaker) 50
Boyd, Zacharie 10
Braigh, Aignish, Isle of Lewis 73, 115, **116**, 117, *260*
Braying Hertfordshire 39
Brechin Cathedral 82
Brentford Free Church, Boston Manor Road, Brentford, Hounslow, Greater London *218*
Bristol Royal Infirmary Burial Ground *206*
Bromyard, Herefordshire 91
Brook, Sarah (body of) 26
Broseley Pipeworks *234*
Browett, Ann Maria (interment of) 33, 34
Bull Hotel, Peterborough *199*
Bumpstead, Alice (bequest of) 24
Bunyan, John (burial of) 89
Burrowes, Silvester (burial of) 89
Burckhardt, Jakob 12
burial
   as a Christian act of mercy 71
   as determined by manner of death 21
   at crossroads 119
   atypical 2, 105
   civil war *200, 207, 211, 231, 232, 243*
   clandestine 121
   denial of, to those convicted of murder 128
   east–west orientated 72, *202, 205, 220, 227, 242, 243, 247, 250, 251, 261, 263*
   horse *234*
   in effigy 40
   in quicklime 112, *198*
   legal strictures surrounding 20
   north–south orientated 72, 107, 117, 119, 125, *215, 218, 227, 229, 238, 240, 247, 250, 253, 258–261*
   of criminals 125, 130, 131, *199, 242, 248, 249*
   of drowning victims 73, 113,115, **116**, 117, 120, *203, 262*
   of epidemic disease victims (*see also* pit, plague and disease, epidemic) 17, 24, **25**, 113, 88, 125
   of foreigners 115, *202, 260*
   of murder victims 73, 117, *252, 256, 258*
   of suicides 10, 88, 89, 115, 117 121, 125, 131, 156, 158, *262*
   of suspected witches 10, 126
   of the unbaptised 85, 117, 121, 126, 131, *201, 249*
   of those executed for treason 112, 126, 127, 130
   pauper's 71, 88, 94, *206, 223, 237*
   premature (fear of) 39, 112, *239*
   priest's *234*
   Royalist *200*
   secular control of 87
   state regulation of 44
   transition in control of 156
   west–east orientated 22, 72, 73, 172, *211, 216, 224, 229, 233, 234, 242, 245, 250, 253, 258*
   with objects of personal significance 28
   without appropriate rites 108
burial grounds
   Anglican control over 19
   Baptist 31, 50, 56, 60, 66, 72, 73, 90, 137, 140, *203*
   conversion to public spaces 100
   Jewish 88–89
   Methodist 73, 122, 137
   non-conformist 9, 89
   non-parochial 86, **87**, 88, 94
   privately owned 94, 99
   Quaker 10, 23, 28, 32, 34, 42, 45, 49, 50, 59, 60, 63, 66, 69, 72, 74, 90, 112, *203, 211, 221, 234, 238, 240*
   use after closure of church or monastery 11, 82–83, 93, 122, *253, 261, 262*
burial plots, re-use of 16
Burial Laws Amendment Act of 1880 103
Burial of the Dead in the Metropolis Act 1852 99, 101
burning (as punishment for criminal offences) 126–128, 130
burning at the stake 43
Burrowes, Silvester (burial of) 89
Bury Central Methodist Church, Union Street, Bury, Greater Manchester *213*
Bushfoot Strand, Portballintree *245*
Butler, Martha (coffin of) 56
Bynum, Caroline 12

C

Calvinist Methodist Chapel, Islington 90
Cambusnethan *256*
Camden House, Stroud *206*

Campbell's Tomb, St Margaret's Church, Barking and Dagenham *219*
cancer, facial 144
Canongate Kirk, 20 Calton Road, Edinburgh *257*
Canterbury Cathedral 47, *212*
Capel Teilo, Kidwelly 119, 124, *261*
Capital Punishment Amendment Act 1868 130
Cardiff Free Library, Trinity Street, Cardiff *262*
Carlingford, County Louth 107
Carmarthen Greyfriars 83, *261*
Carmelite Friary, Aberdeen 82, 85, 122
Carmelite Friary, Perth 82, 117, 119
Carnwath Chapel, Lanarkshire 85
Carrickmacross, County Monaghan 117
Carrickmines Castle, County Dublin 107, *247*
Carrington vault, All Saints Church, High Wycombe 53, 78, 112, *198*
Carrington, Elizabeth (possible cholera death) 112
Carrington, Robert (coffin of) 78, *198*
Carver Street Methodist Chapel, Sheffield 56, 57, 73, 91, 122, *241*
Cassell's Household Guide 33, 41, 42, 57
Castle Carra, Cushenden, County Antrim 124, *245*
Castle Hill Chapel Cemetery, Northampton *229*
Castle Mound, Castle Mall, Norwich *227*
Cathedral Yard, Manchester *213*
Catholic Relief Acts, 1778 96
Cato Street plot 112, 130
Cavendish vault at Derby Cathedral, Derbyshire 40, 41, 47, 108, *202*
Cavendish, Colonel Charles 40, 108
Cavendish, Elizabeth (coffin of) 41
Cavendish, Henry 40
Cavendish, Mary 40
cemeteries as a place for the improvement of the living 102
Cemeteries Clauses Act 99
Cemetery, 102 Bayswater Road, Oxford *231*
Cemetery, 141–143 James Street, Dublin *246*
Cemetery, 64 Steep Hill, Lincoln *215*
Chantries Act 46, 85, 156
Charles I 39
charnel deposit *199, 204, 205, 207, 213, 217, 220, 223, 224, 230–233, 239, 255*
charnel house 93
Chelsea Old Church, 2–4 Church Street, London 28, 50, 53, 56, 93, *219*
Cheriton, Hampshire, battle of 108
Chesney, Everilda (interment with husband's uniform) 28
Chester Castle *200*
cholera 15, 99, 111, 112, 113, 131, *230, 253*
Christ Church Burial Ground, Newgate Street, City of London *219*
Christ Church Spitalfields 23, 26, 27, 28, 30–34, 36, 38, 39, 41, 49, 50, 51, 53, 54, 56, 57, 61, 69, 70, 72, 77, 101, 120, 122, 141, 142, 143, 150, 160, *219*
Christ's Kirk on the Green, Leslie, Kirkcaldy 77, *256*
Church Lane, Carlingford *251*
Church of Lady Hay of Yester, 13 Infirmary Street, Edinburgh *257*

Church of the Holy Rood, Edwalton *230*
Church of the Holy Trinity, Lambley, Gedling *230*
Church Walk/Church Street, Newark *231*
Churchyard, 28 Church Street, Whatton, Nottinghamshire *230*
Churchyard, 9 St Clare Street, EC3, City of London *217*
churchyards, overcrowding of 16, 91
Cille Bhrea, Lemlair 56, *260*
cillín 76, 117, **123**, 124, 159, *245, 247, 249, 250, 251*
Cisterian Abbey of Newry, County Down 84
City Bunhill Burial Ground, London 32, 79, 141, 142, 143, *219*
City of London Cemetery 99, 130
Civil War Mass Grave, Gasworks Lane, Ledbury *210*
Civil War 14, 24, 38, 40, 107, 108, 109, 111, 126, 131, *200, 216, 228, 231, 234*
Cladh na Sasunnach, Fasagh, Gairloch *260*
Clarendon Code 89
Clementhorpe, York *242*
Cliffen, John (body of, post-execution) 130
Clift, William (skeleton of) 153
Clogh Oughter Castle, County Cavan 109
Clonmacnoise, County Offaly 83, *252*
Clough, Oughter Castle *245*
Cloughvalley Upper, Monaghan *251*
Cockpen Medieval Parish Church, Midlothian *257*
coffin accoutrements
  escutcheon 67, 70, *207, 222, 262, 263*
  furniture 160, *199, 206, 207, 209, 210, 218, 245, 262, 263, 264*
  grip-plate, coffin 66, **68**, 69, 70, 72, 79, *199, 207, 215, 220, 239, 240*
  handle 66, **68**, 70, *204, 215, 222, 224, 226, 228, 232, 236, 240, 243, 253, 257, 260, 263*
  lace 69, 159
  lining 34, *224, 243*
  mattress 34, *219*
  mort cloth 66, 69, *198, 199, 202, 207, 219, 228, 235–239, 243, 244, 255, 259, 261*
  nails 57, 59, 69, *198, 201, 202, 204, 218, 221, 229, 231, 232, 239, 242, 248, 255*
  pillows 34, *217, 219*
  pin or nail, upholstery 60, *199, 207, 209, 222, 236*
  plate **58**, 60, 61, **63**, **65**, 66, **68**, 69, 70, 72, 97, 120, 145, *198, 199, 204, 206, 207, 209, 213, 214, 218, 219, 223, 226, 228, 232, 241, 243, 255*
  sheet 28, 34, *228, 236*
  studs 59, 60, 69, *209, 215, 218, 224, 226, 228, 229, 238, 243, 245, 255, 263*
coffin decoration
  as medium for social display 50
  as status indicator 45, 57
  lid motifs **68**, 70
coffin fittings as conditioned by profession 71–72
coffin forms
  post-medieval **48**
  standardisation of 80
coffin maker 23, 50
coffin nails piercing the body 57
coffin use, increase over time in 44

coffin types
   'adult pauper' 54, 69, 70
   anthropoid 39, 47, **48**, 49, 51, *204, 235, 237*
   fishtailed 48, **49**, 72, 159, *239, 240*
   gable-lidded 49, *236, 238*
   glass-windowed 41, **42**, *202*
   lead 27, 33, 39, 41, 45, 47, **48**, 49, 51, 53, 54, 56, 58, 59, 61, 78, 82, 108, 112, 149, *196, 198, 203–205, 207, 208, 211–216, 218–223, 225–229, 231, 235–238, 240, 255, 261–263*
   single-break 48, 49, 50, 80, *204, 219, 226, 230, 232, 238, 239*
   triple-shelled 27, 50, 51, 60, 70, 78, 159, *199, 207, 208, 219, 220, 229, 232–237, 239*
coffin, near-universal adoption of 157
coffin, parish, 45–**47**
coffin, wood types used in the construction of 54–57
coin placed in the mouth of a corpse 73
coins, placed over eyes of a corpse 31, *214, 225, 243*
Colewort Barracks, Portsmouth *209*
collections, anatomical 151–152, *227*
College Hill, EC4, London *219*
College of Arms 49, 50, 131
College of Physicians 133
College Street Chapel, Northampton *229*
commemorative practices 11–13, 19, 30, 36, 77, 102, 156–158
   and bereavement 19
   archaeological study of 1
   monuments 20, 100, 157, 161
   mourning rings 35, 36
   Orcadian 13
   the church as a focus of 103
Convent of Mercy, Salins Road, Naas *249*
Cookstown, Tyrone *253*
Cooper, Sir Astley (surgeon) 149, 155
Cork City of Refuge tokens 73, *249*
Cormac's Chapel, Cashel *252*
coronet, funerary 78
corpse
   association of dental prostheses with 32, 33, *213, 223, 225, 226, 236, 239*
   beautiful 14, 30, 44
   coiffure of 32, *243*
   display or presentation of 22, 34, 44
   dressing of 19, 22, 24, 158
   keeping vigil over 38
   restoration of after autopsy or dissection 145, **146**
   sleeping 33, 34, 43
corpse-washing 22, 43, 158
   antiquity of tradition 22, 44
   of St Cuthbert 22
Cotton Court, Hill Street/Waring Street, Belfast *245*
counter-Reformation, Catholic 11
Court of Augmentations 81
Cowdrey's Down, Basingstoke *209*
craniotomy 137, **140**, 141–143, 145, 147, 151, *212, 216, 226, 229, 230, 237, 239, 242, 257*
craniotomy, as part of embalming 42
Craven Street, London (anatomy school) *219*

Cremation Act 1902
cremation 42, 158
cremation, ban on 43
Cremationist movement 43
crematorium, Milan 43
crematorium, Woking 43
Creswicke vault, St Mary's Church, Bitton, South Gloucestershire 112, *207*
Cromwell, Oliver 39, 40, 88, 128, 145
Crosby, Elizabeth (coffin of) *221*
Cross Bones cemetery, London 26, 30, 54, 56, 70, 97, 137, 141, 142, 143, *220*
Croyde Bay, Devon 115, 117
cruentation 11
Culloden, battle of 106
Culpepper vault, Hollingbourne Church *212*
Cutler, Sir Jarvis 109

D

da Vinci, Leonardo 12
Dallas, David (burial of) 28, *236*
Dallas, Lt. Gen. Sir Thomas (burial of) *236*
Daubney, Margareta (coffin of) 57
Davenant Centre, E1, London *220*
Davidson family vault, St Benet Sherehog 50, *216*
Davidson, Judith (coffin of) 59
Davis Place (off French Street) Dublin *247*
De La Warr vault, Withyham, Sussex 70, *238*
de Lacy family (Earls of Lincoln) 81
death
   archaeology of 19
   as a departure from systemic equilibrium 17
   as process 11
   complexity of beliefs regarding 18
   early modern perception of 26
death and sleep, analogy between 26, 44, 79
death anniversaries (month's mind, year's mind) 9
death masks, interment with 77, *223*
death ritual, resistance to change in 20
Despard, Colonel Edward (interment post-execution) 130
deviant burial (*see* burial, atypical)
Dillon, Archbishop Arthur Richard 33, *225*
Directory for the Publique Worship of God, 1644 89
disease, epidemic 15, 21, 45, 87–89, 93, **111**–113, 115, 125, 126, 131, *209, 214, 227, 253, 254, 258*
dissection, anatomical
   as necessary training for medical practitioners 134
   bodies stolen to order for 149, 155
   contribution to embalming 41
   evidence for 133, *225, 232*
   hostility toward 18
   in contrast to autopsy 136
   lack of archaeological evidence for 149
   link with judicial punishment 133, 158
   medical waste resulting from 6, 7, 147, *208, 209, 219, 223, 231, 232, 245, 248, 258*
   sexual impropriety of 144
   use of murderers' corpses in 112, 128
   use of paupers' bodies in 17, 134–135
   use of quicklime to prevent 112

Dissenters 9, 10, 20, 89–91, 94, 97, 98, 102–105, 123, 131, 157
Dissenter's burial ground, 36–44 Gower's Walk *216*
Dissolution 81–83, 85, 86, *201, 202, 262*
Dominican Priory (post-medieval isolated burial) 8–9 Lower Abbey Road, Sligo *252*
Dominican Priory, St Mary's of the Isle, Cork *246*
Dowager Duchess of Atholl 33
Downside Abbey, Bath 128
Drowned Persons Act 117
Duart Point, Mull 113, *254*
Dublin Institute of Technology, Aungier Street/Peter Row *247*
Duday, Henri 26
Duffy, Eamonn 12
Duke of Lauderdale 25, 40, 51, 59, *255*
Dunfermline Abbey 82
Dunino Churchyard *256*
Dunraven, Glamorgan 119, *263*
Dunster, Abbot John (grave of) 58
Dyer, Christopher 15
Dygon, Abbot John (grave of) 24, 58

E
East Barracks, Deal *212*
East Bond Street Congregational chapel, Leicester 34, 142, *214*
East Kirk, St Nicholas's Church, Aberdeen 73, *253*
Ebenezer Chapel, Leicester 31, 142, *214*
Edgehill, battle of *240*
Edinburgh Castle 111
Edinburgh Royal Infirmary 71, 137, 141–143, 145
Edward I 88, 128
Edward VI 11
Edwards, David 53
Edzell Old Church, Angus 85
Elizabeth I 11, 81
Ely Place, Camden, London 108
embalming 39, 40, 133, 136
embalming, decline in 41
Emmet Street/Kickham Street, Clonmel *253*
Enlightenment 26
Ennis Friary, Ennis *246*
Enon Baptist Chapel, London 54, 94, 96
Evelyn Street cemetery 102
evergreens as symbols of the immortality of the soul 78
excommunicates, interment of 83, 86, 121, 125, 131
Executed criminal burial ground, 16 Eustace Street, Dublin *246*
executions, public 16
Exeter Cathedral *202*
Eynsham Abbey, Oxfordshire 83, 121, *232*
Eyre Square, Galway City *248*
Eyre Square, Galway 125

F
fabric, covering coffin with (*see* mort cloth)
factory production, rise of 15
faculty for the removal of remains 102
famine 113, 115, 125, 131, *253*

feast, mourner's 71
Feeney Neil Sarcophagi, Guildhall, City of London *220*
felo de se 119, 120
Felsted, Essex 90
Fisherman's Mission, North Beach Street, Stornoway, Lewis *260*
Fitzalan Chapel at Arundel 86
Flat Holm Island, Bristol Channel 115, 117, *263*
floral wreaths, use of in funerary practice 79, *213, 239*
Foljambe family monument in Chesterfield, Derbyshire 23
Fore Street, Wellington *235*
Former Female Prison, Castle Yard, York *242*
Fowlis Wester Church, Perthshire 31, *258*
fractures, rib 144
Franciscan Friary (post-medieval isolated burial) 39 Francis Street, Dublin *247*
Franciscan Friary of Creevelea, County Leitrim 84
Franciscan Priory of Lanercost, Cumberland 122
Franciscan Way/Wolsey Street, Ipswitch *237*
Franklin, Benjamin (house of) *220*
Freelands House, Oxford *232*
Friar's Mill Road, Mullingar *253*
Friends Burial Ground, Bishopshill, York *242*
Friends Burial Ground, High Street, Staines *238*
funeral
    as reflective of political sympathies 20
    as social investment 19

G
Gainsborough, battle of 108
garlands, use of in funerary practice 78
Gathering from Graveyards 98, 99
General Baptist Chapel, Priory Yard, Norwich 77, *228*
General Board of Health 99
General Hospital, Nottingham 129
gibbet, use of 11, 21, 130, 134, *206*
Glasgow Cathedral, City of Glasgow 36, 47, 56, 85, 108, 112, *256*
Glastonbury Tor 105, *235*
Gloucester Cathedral *206*
Gloucester, Humphrey Duke of 39
Gorefields Nunnery, Buckinghamshire 73
Govan Old Parish Church and Water Row, Govan *257*
Gowland, John (bodies of his family) 102
Graney East, Castledermot *250*
grave goods and clothing 73–78
    aglets *199, 228, 247, 259*
    amulets 76
    bells 77
    buttons 30, *198, 200, 205, 214, 218, 242, 253, 256, 259, 262*
    ceramics 77, *208, 217, 228, 234, 244, 247, 252, 263*
    chin strap 25
    coins 73, 77, 111, 115–118, *209, 216, 218, 219, 225, 234, 242, 243, 249, 254, 258–262*
        earth blessed by a priest 86
    comb, hair 31, *198, 205, 239*
    comb, tortoiseshell 31, 32, *218, 221, 226*
    eyelets *259*
    feathers *221*

grave goods and clothing *(cont'd)*
  finger rings 34, 36, *198*
  funeral cap or bonnet **28**, 32, *228*
  jar, canopic 40, *255*
  manacles *237*
  pin, hair 32, *228*, *239*
  pipe, clay *202*, *204*, *217*, *242*, *248*, *260*
  rosary 113, *209*, *220*, *246*, *250*
  sheep's wool, interment with 77, *256*
  shroud pin 23, **24**, 122, 126, *198*, *199*, *201*, *214*, *222*, *227*, *229*, *242*, *243*, *247*, *248*, *249*, *255*, *256*, *258*, *260*
  shroud 22, **23**, **27**, 30, 43, 80, *200*, *203*, *218*, *219*, *227*, *236*, *237*, *246*, *252*
  teeth, "Waterloo" 33, *236*
  walnuts, interment accompanied by 76, *222*
  white quartz 76, *254*
  winding sheet 46, 158, *221*, *222*, *231*, *236*
  witch-bottle **76**, *198*
grave robbing 81, 82, 98, 134, 149, 155, 159
grave, brick lined 27, 31, 53, 54, **60**, 61, 149, *198*, *201*, *204*, *205*, *207*, *208*, *211*, *214*, *215*, *225*, *229*, *233*, *235*, *237*, *239*, *241*
grave, earth-cut 33, 53, 54, 61, 69, 79, 137, *228*, *231*, *233*, *238*
grave, mass 107, **111**, 112, *211*, *258*
Graveyard of St Katherine Cree *221*
Great Fire of London 45, 93, *216*, *218*
Great St Helen's Church, Bishopsgate *220*
Greene, Edmund (coffin of) *196*
Greenhead Moss, Lanarkshire 117
Greyfriar's Burial Ground, Perth *259*
Greyfriar's Tollbooth and Highland Kirk, Cramond, City of Edinburgh *257*
Greyfriars, Gloucester *206*
Greyfriars, Hartlepool 58
grief, separation 13, 44
Guildford Friary 57, 82
Gunnister, Shetland Islands 73, 117, *261*
Gunpowder Plot 127

H

Hackett, Bishop John (tomb of) *237*
Haddenham, Cambridgeshire 90
Haigh, Christopher 12
Haines family vault 100
Haines, Campbell Lloyd (coffin of) 100
Haines, Eliza (coffin of) 34, 100
Hand, Richard Gideon (grave of) 28
hanging in chains (*see also* gibbet) 129
hanging, death by 121, 126, 130, *200*, *261*
hanging, signs of on a corpse *200*
Hangman's Hill, Newton Longville, Buckingham 125
Hanham, Major (cremation of) 43
Hardwick, James (burial monument of) *236*
Harrison family vault, St Phillips Cathedral, Birmingham *240*
Harrison, Catherine (shroud of) 26
Harrison, Hannah (coffin of) 79
Harvey family vault, Church of St Andrew, Hempstead, Uttlesford *204*

Harvey, William (anatomist) 153
Hathersage, Derbyshire (Catholic interments at) 86
Hawes, William 23
Haymarket Towers, Leicester *214*
Heaven 8, 18
Hedger family vault, St Thomas a Becket Church, Widcombe, Bath *236*
Hell 8, 121, 122
Helmsley Quaker Burial Ground *242*
Hemingford Grey, Cambridgeshire 24, 46, 66, 72, 90, *199*
Henry Crookenden (exhumation and cremation of) 43
Henry V 39
Henry VIII 8, 11, 37, 39, 81, 86, 133
Henry, Prince of Wales 135
Hereford Cathedral 24, 57, *211*
Hewson, William (anatomist) 129, 147, 150, 153, *220*
High Ercall, Ercall Magna *234*
High Street, Elgin, Moray *258*
Highgate, London 98
Hills, Thomas (coffin of) *204*
Hinton St George, Somerset *235*
HMS Swan *254*
Hogg family vault, St Mary Aldermanbury Church *224*
Hogg Hall, Galston Parish Church, Ayrshire *255*
Holford, Peter (coffin of) *227*
Holy Trinity Abbey, Lough Hey, Roscommon 82
Holy Trinity Abbey, Lough Key *252*
Holy Trinity Church, Carlingford *251*
Holy Trinity Church, Christchurch, Newport *263*
Holy Trinity Church, Cookham 197
Holy Trinity Church, Coventry 39, 79, 94, *239*
Holy Trinity Church, Rayleigh *204*
Holy Trinity Church, Sutton Coldfield *239*
holy water, use of in funerary practice 77
Horne, William (burial of) 150
hospitals
  as charitable institutions 145
  fever 113, *252*
  leper *247*
House of Dr Beddome, 2 Church Street, Romsey *208*
Howard, Lady Elizabeth (coffin of) 49
Howard, Lady Margaret (coffin of) *238*
Huguenot 27, 79, 160, *213*, *247*
Hume, Colonel John (interment of) 31
Hume, Mary (burial of) 33, 36, *236*
humours, bodily 17
Hunter, John (anatomist) 129, 144, 147, 153
Hunter, William (anatomist) 41, 134, *220*
Hunterian Museum, Glasgow 151
Huntingdon Castle 125, *199*

I

identity, Catholic 19
Illaunloughan *249*
immigration into cities 15
Improvement 16
influenza 87
Inishcealtra, County Clare 76
Interments (Felo de se) Act of 1882 121
Isle of Ensay *256*

J

Jacobite uprising 107, 130
James I 135
Jarrow, Northumberland *229–230*
Jarvis Patent Coffin 1810 150
Jedburgh Abbey, Roxburgh *260*
Jenkins, William (coffin of) 71
Jesuit Cemetery, Manresa House, Whitelands College, London 37, 97, *220*
jewellery, as heirloom 36
John Dillon Street, Dublin *247*
Johnstown, County Meath 124, 125, *251*
Jones Burial Ground 94, *217*
Joshua Brookes's Museum 155

K

Keames, Isabel (burial of) 121
Kensal Green, London 98
Kilbarchan Old West Parish Church 79, *259*
Kill, Monasterevin *250*
Killalee Church, Killarney, County Kerry 125, *249*
Kiloran, Colonsay and Oransay 123, *254*
Kilwinning Abbey, Ayrshire *255*
Kingdom Hall (former), South Street, Leominster *211*
Kinnoull Parish Church, Perth *259*
Kirk Field, Portmuck *245*
Kirkstall Abbey 73

L

lace tags (*see* aglets under grave goods)
Laines, Thomas (funeral of) 71
Lakeland, Mary (burning at the stake) 126
Lancasterian Street, Carrickfergus *245*
Lanercost Priory, Brampton, Cumberland *201*
Langley Marish, St Mary *198*
Laqueur, Thomas 16
Latimer, Sarah (body of) 26
Launceston Castle, Cornwall 76, 126, *200*
Leicester Castle *214*
Lethieullier, Charles (coffin of) 40
Lewes Priory 81–82
Lewis, Mary Lucy 34
Lewis, Thomas 99
Lichfield Cathedral, Lichfield *236*
Limbo 121, 122
Lincoln Castle Service Trenching *215*
Lindsay family 85
Linlithgow Friary, West Lothian 82
Lisanisk Ringfort *252*
Lismore Parish Church *254*
Little Easton, Essex *204*
Little Ilford, Newham, London 69
Llanddewi Fach Church, Monmouthshire 120, *263*
Llangar Church, Merionethshire 56, 59, 66, 78, *263*
London Poor Union 71
Longdykes, Prestonpans, near Edinburgh *255*
Lower Canal Walk, Southampton *209*
Lower Stephen Street, Dublin *248*
Ludovic Stuart, Duke of Richmond and Lennox 39
Lumbye, Richard (excommunicated papist) 86
Lydiard Tregoze, Wiltshire *240*

M

Mackenzie, General Sir Alexander (shroud of) 26
Maitland family vault, New Bunhill Fields, London *221*
Manorhamilton workhouse, County Leitrim 37, 50, 54, 71, *250*
Manse House, Mullingar, County Tyrone 112
manufacture, shift in markets for 15
Market Place and Beaumont Street, Hexham *230*
Marranos 88
Marston Moor, battle of 106, 107, 108
Martin, Thomas (mourning ring of) *239*
Martyn, Dr William (interment of) 105
Marvell, Andrew 10
Mary Ann Buildings, Lewisham *220*
Mary I 11
Mary Rose 37, 113
Mary-le-Port Church, Bristol *206*
Mason, James (autopsy of) 143
Mason, Mary (coffin of) 150
Masonic Hall, 12 Old Orchard Street, Bath *235*
  use as a Catholic Chapel 96
Maurois, John (monument to) *216*
May family vault, St Mary's Church, Hale *210*
Mayfield, Staffordshire *237*
Maynard family vault, Little Easton *204*
Mayo, Bishop (interment of) 24
measles 136
medical dressing, retention of in burial 30
medical knowledge, gendered 17
Melrose Abbey 82
memento mori 78
Mercer's Hospital, Dublin 151, *248*
Merchant's Road, Galway *249*
mercury 41, 129, 152
Methodism 91
Metropole Development, Clyde Street, Glasgow *257*
Metropolitan Interments Act 1850 99, 101
midwives, baptism by 122
Miller, Charles (coffin of) *208*
Minister Churchyard, Wimbourne Minster *203*
Misson de Valbourg, Henri 38, 39
Mitre Street (29–31 and 32–34) City of London *221*
Monument Street/17 Fish Street, City of London *221*
Moravian Burial Ground, Bristol *206*
More, Sir Thomas (head of) 127, *213*
Morris, Catherine (shroud of) 26
mortality
  among the poor 15
  child and infant 14
  urban 15
mortsafe **150**
Mullion Church *200*
Munro, Alexander (anatomist) 153
Murder Act 128, 130, 131, 134, 136, 137, 145

N

Naseby, battle of 106–108
Navan Fort Environs, Ballyrea *245*

Neath Abbey 82
Neilston Parish Church *259*
Netley Abbey 81
New Bunhill Fields Burial Ground, London 26, 27, 61, 88, 89, 94, 99, 101, *221*
New Churchyard, London 24, 45, 49, 87, 88, 89, 113, 125, *221*
Newark, Sanday *258*
Newarke, Leicester 107
Newcastle Royal Infirmary 54, 56, 57, 71, 136, 146, 147, 151
Newgate Prison 125, 130
non compos mentis 120
Non-conformist burial ground, 21–29 Mansell Street, City of London *216*
Norfolk Street Upper Chapel (Unitarian), Sheffield *242*
Norman Court, Grape Lane, York *242*
North Dalton Church 50, *243*
North family vault, All Saints Church, Kirtling *199*
North Fasagh, Loch Maree 96
Nottingham Castle *231*
Nottingham General Hospital 151, *231*
Nouaille, Peter (coffin of) 79, *213*

O

Old Abbey Lane (Abbey of St Mary d'Urso), Drogheda, County Louth 73, *251*
Old Addenbrooke's Hospital, Cambridge 71, 96, *199*
Old Alresford, Hampshire 73, 118
Old Ashmolean Museum, Oxford 147, 151, 153, *232*
Old Gaol and Courthouse, Church Street, Portlaoise 57, 130, *250*
Old Hunstanton Churchyard *228*
Old St Chad's Church, Shrewsbury *234*
O'Meara Street (no. 49), London 32, 91, 101, *221*
One Gun, Dartmouth, Devon 115, *202*
opium, administration of prior to surgery 150
Oxford Castle/Oxford Prison 125, 146, 147, *232*
Oyne churchyard, Aberdeenshire 150

P

Parish Church of St Mary, Sulhamstead Abbots 197
Park Street Burial Ground *239*
Park, Katherine 11
Parliament House, Edinburgh *257*
Parnell Street, Clonmel *253*
Paternoster Row, City of London *221*
Pennal Churchyard, Meirionnydd *263*
Pershore Abbey, Pershore 70, *241*
Perth Prison 109, *259*
Phelps, William (coffin of) 61
Phillips, Jane Emily (funeral wreaths of) 79
Pinglestone Farm, Old Alresford (land opposite) *209*
Pinstone Street, Peace Gardens, Sheffield *243*
pipe facets present on teeth *204, 253*
pit, plague 107, **114**, *217, 220, 221, 237*
plague lodge *242*
Plague pit, 37–39 Artillery Lane, London *217*
plague victims, bans within churches 112
plague, nonspecific (*see* disease, epidemic)

plantation of criminals in American colonies 17
plants used in funerary practice
    bay laurel 78–79, *203*
    box 78–79, *239, 262, 263*
    hyssop 78
    juniper 79, *239*
    lavender 79, *213*
    oak 78
    privet *239*
    rosemary 78–79, *203, 213*
    yew 79
Plumtree, Polydore (ledger slab of) *227*
Plunkett, Archbishop Oliver (execution of) 128
Point Street, Stornoway, Lewis *260*
pollution, urban
    as deleterious to moral well-being 99
    effluvias 16
    miasmas 16, 43, 54
Pontefract Castle, Yorkshire 109, *243*
Poolbeg Street, Dublin *248*
Poor Law 135
Portballintree, County Antrim 115
Portchester Castle 36, 108, *209*
post-medieval sites, perceived lack of value of 159–161
postmortem (*see* autopsy)
post-mortem punishment 43, 157
post-Reformation 72, 82, 120
Poulett vault in Hinton St George, Somerset 48, *235*
poverty, scriptural valourisation of 9
Pratt, Honoretta (corpse of) 112
prayers
    denial of their potency on behalf of the deceased 19, 46, 85
    for the soul of the deceased 8
pre-Reformation 86, *255*
Presbyterian Church of Regent Square, London 94
Prestonpans, battle of 106
Price, Jesu Grist (cremation of) 43
Priory and Hospital of St Leonard, 5 Seatown, Dundalk *251*
Prison cemetery, 31–32 Ely Place, Camden *216*
prisoners of war 108, 109, *202, 212, 259*
Private Burial Ground 95–105 Back Church Lane, E1/109–153 Backchurch Lane, E1 *217*
Protection of Military Remains Act 113
Public Conveniences, St Paul's Churchyard *222*
Public Health Act of 1948 99
public health, concern for 98
Purgatory 8–9, 10
Purgatory, abolition or rejection of 38, 46 60, 85, 103, 133, 156
Puritans 9

Q

Quaker Burial Ground, Bathford, Somerset 72, 94, *235*
Quaker Burial Ground, Kingston-upon-Thames 28, 34, 38, 42, 46, 49, 59, 60, 66, 69, 72, 74, 90, 91, 93, 112, 160
Quaker cemetery, 9a Wood Street, Calne, Wiltshire 91, *240*

Quaker Meeting House Graveyard, 28 High Street, Alcester *238*
Quaker rejection of burial on consecrated ground 85, 90, 91, 105
quartz, use of in a funerary context 76, 77
Quintfall Hill, Barrock Estate, nearWick *255*
Quintfall Hill, Wick, Caithness 73, 76, 117

R
Rawls, John (burial of) 105, **106**, *235*
Reask, County Kerry 76, 124, *249*
recusant, Catholic 83, 86, 121
reference skeleton, anatomical **154**, 155
Reformation 1, 2, 8, 9, 11, 12, 19, 23, 37, 38, 45, 46, 71, 81–83, 85, 87, 103, 105, 121, 156, 157
Renaissance 12
Restoration 120
resurrectionists (*see* grave robbing)
rickets 144, *203*
Rievaulx Abbey, Yorkshire 117
ring, mourning 35, **36**
ring, wedding 35
Ringwood, Hampshire 100
River Parish Church, River, near Dover *212*
Rochester Cathedral *212*
Rogers, John (burning of) 128
Romantic movement 13
Romsey, Hampshire 82
Rook Lane Chapel, Frome *235*
Roper Chantry, St Dunstan's Church, Canterbury 127, *213*
Roper family 85
Roper, Margaret (coffin of) 127
rosary 36–38
Rosary, Norwich 97
Rose and Crown, Lawrence Street, York *243*
Rose Ville, Western Road, Clonmel *253*
Rosewell, Thomas (burial of) 89
Rotherwick Church, Rotherwick, Hook *209*
Royal College of Surgeons 128, 151
Royal Edward Dock, Avonmouth, Gloucestershire 130, *206*
Royal George 115
Royal Hospital Greenwich 143, *227*
Royal Injunction of 1538 37
Royal London Hospital 113, 137, 141–143, 146, 150–153, *227*
Royal Naval Hospital, Haslar, Greenwich 137, *209*
Royal Oak 113
Rusholme Road cemetery 102
Russell, William (undertaker) 50
Rycote Chapel, Thame *232*

S
Sale, Bridget (coffin of) 53
salt, use of in funerary practice 77–78
Sandal Castle, Yorkshire 109, *243*
'sanofka' symbol 59
Sappol, Michael 144
Saunton Down End, Croyde Bay *202*
Scapa Flow, Orkney 113

school, anatomy 98
scientific curiosities, embalmed individuals displayed as 42
security, post-mortem 149–150, *208*
self
  emotional 14
  gendered 13
  individualistic and autonomous 13
  knowledge 18
self-fashioning 12, 13
Sheares Street, Kilmallock *250*
Sheffield Cathedral 36, *243*
Sheldon, John (surgeon) 41
Shrawley, Reginald (interment of) 23
Shrewsbury, Elizabeth, Countess of (coffin of) 47
shroud, linen 24–26
shroud, woollen 24, 44
Sincil Bank West/Pennell Street, Lincoln *215*
Smallbroke, Bishop Richard (coffin of) *237*
smallpox 136, 160
smallpox, vaccination against 18
Society of Friends 90, 94
soft tissue, preservation of 152
Solent Breezes, Fareham *210*
Solent Waters 113
Southgate Gallery, Southgate Street, Gloucester *206*
Southwark Cathedral, Montague Close, London 141, *222*
Spa Fields Clerkenwell, London 94
Spencer, Dorothy (coffin of) 66, 69, *226*
Spencer, Lawrence (coffin of) 69, *226*
St Aldgate's Church, Oxford *232*
St Andrew, the Winship Vault, Corbridge *230*
St Andrew's Church, Ashford Bowdler *234*
St Andrew's Church, Hatfield Peverel *204*
St Andrew's, Hempstead, Uttlesford *204*
St Andrew's Church, Impington *199*
St Andrew's Church, Stratton *200*
St Andrew's Old Church and Kirkyard, Anchor Green, Kirkness *255*
St Andrew's Public Library, St Andrews *256*
St Andrew's Holborn, 252b Gray's Inn Road, Camden, London 33, 48, 97, *216*, *222*
St Anne's Graveyard, Shandon *246*
St Anne's Parish Church, Copp, Great Eccleston *213*
St Anne's, Middlesex 112
St Ann's, Shandon, County Cork 37
St Augustine the Less, Bristol *207*
St Augustine's Abbey, Canterbury, Kent 24, 58
St Barnabas's Church, West Kensington, London 28
St Bartholomew's Church, Penn 79, 120, *237*
St Bartholomew's Church, Westhoughton, Greater Manchester *213*
St Bartholomew's Hospital, Islington, London 145, *223*
St Benet Sherehog, 1 Poultry, London 45, 57, 59, 78, 136, *216*
St Botolph's Church, Aldgate, London *218*, *223*
St Brendan's Cathedral, Ardfert, County Kerry 73, *249*
St Bride's Church, Fleet Street, London 120, 141, 142, *217*, *223*
St Bride's Churchyard, 75–82 Farringdon Street, EC4, London *217*

Index

St Bride's Haven, Pembrokeshire *264*
St Brigid's Hospital, Balinsloe *249*
St Catherine's Church, Cricceth *262*
St Clement's Churchyard, The Plain, Oxford *233*
St Crux, The Shambles, York *243*
St Cuthbert (coffin of) 57
St Cuthbert's Church, 27–8 Tombland, Norwich *227*
St Cyngar's Church, Hope, Flintshire 53, *262*
St Edward's Church, Evenlode *207*
St Ethelburga the Virgin, Bishopsgate, City of London *223*
St Felicitas Church, Phillack *201*
St George the Martyr, London *223*
St George's Bloomsbury, Camden, London 26, 33, 34, 51, 53, 54, 61, 63, 66, 69, 70, 77, 101, 102, 112, *223*
St George's Chapel, Windsor 40
St George's Church, Hanworth *223*
St George's Clocktower *212*
St George's Hospital, London 153
St Giles-on-the-Hill, Norwich *228*
St Guthlac's, Hereford Castle, Castle Green *211*
St Helen's Church, Abingdon 108
St Helen's Church, Burton Joyce *230*
St Helen's Square, York *243*
St Ismael's Church, Camrose *264*
St James cemetery, Liverpool 102
St James Church, Swarkestone *202*
St James Garlickhythe Church, Garlick Hill, EC4 *223*
St James, Bowling Green Lane, Islington *224*
St James the Great Church, Rushcombe 196
St James the Great Church, Snitterfield *238*
St James's Church, Bramley *210*
St James's Church, Louth, East Lindsay *215*
St John Canterbury, hospital of 23
St John of Wapping Church, London 50, *218*
St John the Baptist Church, Southover High Street, Southover, Lewes *238*
St John the Baptist Church, Winchester *209*
St John the Baptist, Cirencester *207*
St John the Baptist, Sligo *252*
St John the Evangelist Church, Carlton-in-Lindrick *230*
St John the Evangelist Church, 1 Watling Street, London *216*
St John's Church, Ballyharry *245*
St John's Church, French Street, Southampton *210*
St Kenelm's Church, Sapperton, near Stroud *207*
St Laurence Church, Appleton *233*
St Laurence Church, Chorley *213*
St Laurence Church, South Hinksey *233*
St Lawrence Church Hall, Lawrence Street, York *244*
St Lawrence Church, Morland *201*
St Lawrence Jewry Burial Vaults, Guildhall Yard, Guildhall Bollards, City of London *224*
St Leonard's Church, Upton St Leonard's, Gloucester *206*
St Luke's Church, Islington 28, 34, 36, 41, 53, 69, 70, 79, 142, 144, *224*
St Luke's Church, The Coombe, Dublin *248*
St Luke's Estate, Bath Street, London *224*
St Margaret's Chapel, London Road, Gloucester *207*
St Margaret's Church, Ipswitch *237*
St Margaret's Church, Westminster 93
St Margaret's Churchyard, Chelmsford *204*
St Margaret's Churchyard, Walmgate, York *244*
St Mark's Church and Cemetery, Lincoln 28, 30, *215*
St Martin of Tours, Chelsfield, Bromley *224*
St Martin-at-Palace, Norwich 69, *228*
St Martin's Church, Allerton *244*
St Martin's Church, Birmingham 94
St Martin's Church, High Street, Ruislip *224*
St Martin's Church, Ludgate, London 128
St Martin's Church, Wharram Percy 56, 69, *244*
St Martin's Vintry Church, 61 Queen Street/Upper Thames Street, EC4, London 77, *217*
St Martin's-in-the-Bull Ring, Birmingham 26, 31, 34, 36, 49, 51, 53, 54, 60, 61, 63, 69–71, 93, 100, 122, 141, 143–145, 160, *239*
St Mary Aldermanbury Church, Aldermanbury, EC2, City of London *224*
St Mary and All Saints Church, Debden *204*
St Mary and St Barlok Church, Norbury *202*
St Mary and St Bartholomew Church, Hampton in Arden, Solihull *239*
St Mary and St Hardulph Church, Breedon on the Hill *214*
St Mary and St Michael, London (Catholic mission) 28, 30, 32, 36, 97, 140, 144
St Mary and St Nicholas Church, Spalding *215*
St Mary Axe, 43–51, City of London *217*
St Mary Colechurch 49
St Mary Magdalene Church, Hullavington *240*
St Mary Magdalene Church, Ickleton *199*
St Mary Magdalene Church, Taunton *235*
St Mary Magdalene Churchyard, The Watch House, Bermondsey Square 97, *224*
St Mary Monknash, Cwm Nash, Monknash, Glamorgan 82, *263*
St Mary Sandwell, Staffordshire 24
St Mary Spital, London 87
St Mary the Virgin Church, Ashby Road, Coleorton *214*
St Mary the Virgin Church, Kirtlington *233*
St Mary the Virgin Church, Long Crendon *198*
St Mary the Virgin Church, Ramsden Crays *205*
St Mary the Virgin Church, Reading 197
St Mary the Virgin, Church of Little Houghton *229*
St Mary the Virgin, Manor Road, Bexley *224*
St Mary Woolnoth 38
St Mary's, Ross-on-Wye *211*
St Marylebone, London 30, 31, 53, 77, 93, 97, 100, 141, *225*
St Mary's Cathedral and Benedictine Priory 81
St Mary's Cathedral, Chelmsford *204*
St Mary's Church, Banbury *233*
St Mary's Church, Bedford 196
St Mary's Church, Beenham 197
St Mary's Church, Bitton *207*
St Mary's Church, Broomfield *205*
St Mary's Church, Bucken *200*
St Mary's Church, Chieveley 197
St Mary's Church, Chilham *212*
St Mary's Church, Church Road, SW13 *225*
St Mary's Church, Church Street, West Chiltington *238*

St Mary's Church, Ealing 225
St Mary's Church, Garsington 233
St Mary's Church, Great Bentley 205
St Mary's Church, Haddington, East Lothian 40, 85, 255
St Mary's Church, Hale 210
St Mary's Church, Langley Marish, Slough 197
St Mary's Church, Little Ilford 40, 225
St Mary's Church, Maldon 205
St Mary's Church, Overton 210
St Mary's Church, Salford 235
St Mary's Church, Scopton 202
St Mary's Church, Southampton 210
St Mary's Church, Thrigby 228
St Mary's Church, Undy 264
St Mary's Church, Warwick 93
St Mary's Church, Wedmore 236
St Mary's Church, Whitelackton 236
St Mary's Church, Winkfield 197
St Mary's Priory, Abergavenny 264
St Mary's Road, Ealing, Greater London 225
St Mary's Star of the Sea, Constitution Street, Edinburgh 258
St Mawgan in Pydar Church 201
St Michael and All Angels Church, Wilmington, Dartford 212
St Michael le Belfry, York 122
St Michael the Archangel Church, Rushall, Walsall 236
St Michael, Manningtree 205
St Michael's Church Parish Rooms, Warfield 197
St Michael's Church, Abergele 262
St Michael's Church, Aylsham 228
St Michael's Church, Bowthorpe, Norwich 228
St Michael's Church, Houghton le Spring 203
St Michan Church, 189–194 King Street North/Green Street, Dublin 247
St Miniver Parish Church 201
St Nicholas's Church, Forest Hill, Oxfordshire 30, 66
St Nicholas, Sevenoaks, Kent 27, 33, 34, 79, 212
St Nicholas, Deptford 225
St Nicholas's Church, Abingdon 233
St Nicholas's Church, Bathampton, Somerset 26, 27, 28, 31, 32, 34, 36, 236
St Nicholas's Church, Chadlington 233
St Nicholas's Church, Cove Street, Cork 246
St Nicholas's Church, Forest Hill, Oxfordshire 233
St Nicholas's Church, Littleborough 231
St Nicholas's Church, Newbury 197
St Nicholas's Church, Rotherfield Greys 234
St Nicholas's Church, Shepperton 238
St Nicholas's Church, Trelech 262
St Olave's Cemetery 225
St Oswald's Almshouses, Worcester 241
St Oswald's Priory, Gloucester 45, 47, 66, 82, 119, 123, 150, 207
St Pancras Burial Ground, Camden 225
St Pancras Old Church, London 33, 79
St Paternus Church, North Petherwin 201
St Paul's Cathedral 66, 69, 226
St Paul's Church, Belle Vue Road, Colchester 205
St Paul's Church, Covent Garden, Westminster 226

St Paul's Church, Hammersmith, London 32, 226
St Paul's Church, Sheffield 34, 93
St Paul's Graveyard, Deptford High Street, Lewisham 226
St Peter and St Paul's Church, Bridge Street, Mansfield 231
St Peter and St Paul's Church, Olney 198
St Peter Cornhill, City of London 226
St Peter-le-Bailey, Oxford 232
St Peter-le-Poore, London 53
St Peter's and St Paul's Church, Healing 215
St Peter's Church, Barford 239
St Peter's Church, Barton-upon-Humber, Lincolnshire 30, 31, 35, 36, 77, 141, 145, 215
St Peter's Church, Belgrave 214
St Peter's Church, Carmarthen 79, 262
St Peter's Church, Codford 240
St Peter's Church, Farmington 208
St Peter's Church, Ipsley, Redditch 211
St Peter's Church, Redcar 244
St Peter's Church, Soberton 210
St Peter's Church, Waterford City 253
St Peter's Churchyard, Oundle 229
St Peter's Southgate Church, Argyle Street, Norwch 229
St Peter's, Drogheda 128
St Peter's, Exton, Somerset 49, 68, 236
St Peter's, Waterford 36, 125
St Peter's, Wolverhampton 36, 41, 77, 79, 94
St Petrox Church, Dartmouth 117, 202
St Phillip's Cathedral, Birmingham 26, 31, 49, 53, 73, 79, 240
St Robert's Church, Pannal 244
St Ronan's Church, Iona 76, 125, 254
St Sampson's Church, Church Street, York 244
St Saviour's Church, Dartmouth, Devon 203
St Saviour's Church, Norwich 229
St Sepulchre North Churchyard, Snow Hill Court, Newgate Street, London 226
St Stephen Walbrook 94
St Thomas a Becket Church, Widcombe, Bath 236
St Thomas of Canterbury Church, Elsfield 232
St Thomas the Martyr Church, Up Holland 213
St Thomas's Church Burial Ground, Bristol 208
St Thomas's Church, Bedhampton, Havant 210
St Thomas's Hospital 226
St Tudor's Church, Mynydd Islwyn, Caerphilly 264
St Wilfred's Church, Davenham 200
St Wilfred's Church, Hickleton 244
St Winnow Church, Lostwithiel 201
Steele, Sir Richard (head of) 262
Stirling Castle 261
Stradbally North, Castleconnell, County Limerick 24, 250
Stringfield, Anna (interment of) 77
Sturminster Newton, Dorset 43
Suicide Act of 1823 120, 121, 131
Surgeon's Square, Edinburgh 147, 152, 153, 258
surgery, post-mortem 151, 242
Sutton Harbour, Sutton Road, Plymouth 203
Swallow, Margaret (wedding ring of) 34
Swedlund, Alan 19
syphilis 144, 145

Index

T

Tallow Hill, Worcester *241*
Tate, Francis 23, 38
Taunton, Somerset 107
Temple Bar, Dublin 127
Test Acts 9
Tewkesbury Abbey *208*
The Carr House Sands Project, Hartlepool *203*
The Chapel Undercroft, Lincoln's Inn, Camden *226*
The Church, Morton Jeffries *211*
The Coal Yard, Edinburgh Castle *258*
The Guildhall, Leicester *214*
The Infirmary, The Forth International Centre for Life, Newcastle upon Tyne *230*
The Judge's Lodging, York *242*
The Lancet (medical journal) 99
The Railway Station, Shrewsbury *234*
The Regal Cinema Site, Abingdon *234*
The Royal Foundation of St Katherine, Butcher Row, Ratcliff *227*
The Saxon Church, Alton Barnes *240*
The Society of Friends' Burial Ground, Bristol *208*
The Tabernacle Penn Street, Bristol *208*
The Toll Booth, Stirling *261*
The Town House, High Street, Montrose *254*
The United Reform Chapel, Broad Street, Reading 197
Therese House, 29–30 Glasshouse Yard EC1 *227*
Thomas Drummond, Reverend 97
Tilehouse Street Baptist Churchyard, Hitchin *211*
Tintagel, Cornwall 76, 124, *201*
tobacco, use by coffin-bearers 39, 53
Toms, Elizabeth (grave of) *201*
Toms, William (grave of) *201*
tourniquets or clamps, use of prior to surgery 150
Townparks, Dundalk *251*
Towton, battle of 106
trauma, peri-mortem *243*, *247*
trephine 150, *245*
trephine, cuts made by **151**, *220*, *245*
Trinity College Library Extension, Dublin *248*
tuberculosis 144, 145, *258*
Tunbridge Wells 40
Tychbourne, Nicholas (recusant denied interment) 83
typhus 15, 87, 99, 113
Tysoe, Stratford on Avon *240*

U

Undercliffe Cemetery, Bradford 99
undertaking
　duties 23
　rise of profession 20
United Company of Barbers and Surgeons 128, 133
United Reform Church/Salvation Army Hall, Abbey Kane, Saffron Waldon *205*
University of Wolverhampton *237*

V

Van Butchell, Maria (body of) 41
Vancouver Centre (Baptist Cemetery at King's Lynn) *229*
Vancouver Centre (Quaker Cemetery at King's Lynn) 31, 34, 50, 63, 72, 73, *229*
Victoria, Queen 22, 81
Vine Street Baptist Chapel *214*

W

wakes 38, 39, 43
Walden, George (interment of) 145
Walford, George (skeleton of) 144
Walker, Dr George 98
Wall, Matthew (revival of) 39
Walmgate Bar, siege of *243*
Warden, Joseph (coffin of) 71
Warden, Mary Elizabeth (burial of) 79
Warrington Friary, Cheshire 83, *200*
water as a barrier to undead 119
Waterloo Road, Old Market, Bristol *208*
Wenlock Priory, Much Wenlock *234*
Wesleyan Methodist Chapel, Barnsley *244*
West Hill Cemetery, Winchester 98
West, Maria (coffin of) 33
Westmorland, Countess of (relocation of the tomb of) 82
White Kirk, Comrie, Pershire 69, 73, *259*
White, Charles (surgeon) 41
Whitechapel Church, London 98, 112
Whitechapel workhouse, 179–181 Whitechapel Road, E1 *216*
Whitefriars, Doncaster 82
Whitehall Conference of 1655 88
Wick, J.H. (undertaker) 71
Wilkinson Head, the 40
Williams, John (post-mortem display of) 120, **121**
Willis, Thomas (anatomist) 153
Willoughby vault in St Catherine's Church, Cossall, Nottinghamshire 50, 86, *231*
Willoughby, George (coffin of) 86
Wilson Street, St Paul's, Bristol *208*
Wilton, Wiltshire *240*
Winchester Cathedral, Cathedral Green, Winchester *210*
Winchester prison 83
witchcraft 12, 76, 126
Wolfe Tone Park, Dublin *248*
Woodchurch, Kent 115
Woolman, John (interment of) 89
workhouses 16, 17, 35, 37, 50, 54, 57, 70, 71, 96, 113, 135, 136
Wren, William (possible burial of) *242*

Y

York Archive Gazetteer 196
York Cemetery 97, 98, 113
York Place, Aberdeen 113, *254*
York Prison 137, 146

Z

Zion Baptist Church, Calne, Wiltshire *241*

Leicester Archaeology Monographs

This series was established in 1993 to publish work related to the research interests and activities of the School of Archaeology & Ancient History, including the work of the University of Leicester Archaeological Service (ULAS). The most recently published titles are listed below and can be ordered through bookshops, or direct at http://shop.le.ac.uk/

More information can be found at: http://www2.le.ac.uk/departments/archaeology/research/monographs

Hoards, Hounds and Helmets: A conquest-period ritual site at Hallaton, Leicestershire. (2012)
By Vicki Score *et al.* (ISBN 978-0-9560179-6-3)

Bronze Age Ceremonial Enclosures and Cremation Cemetery at Eye Kettleby, Leicestershire. (2011)
By Neil Finn (ISBN 978-0-9560179-5-6)

Two Iron Age 'Aggregated' Settlements in the Environs of Leicester. Excavations at Beaumont Leys and Humberstone. (2011)
By John Thomas (ISBN 978-0-9560179-4-9)

Debating Urbanism: Within and Beyond the Walls A.D 300–700. (2010)
Edited by Denis Sami and Gavin Speed (ISBN 978-0-9560179-2-5)

The Hemington Bridges: The excavation of three medieval bridges at Hemington Quarry, near Castle Donington, Leicestershire. (2009)
By Susan Ripper and Lynden P. Cooper (ISBN 978 0-9560179-1-8)

From Captivity to Freedom: Themes in Ancient and Modern Slavery. (2008)
Edited by Constantina Katsari and Enrico Del Lago (ISBN 978 0-9560179-0-1)

Monument, Memory and Myth, Use and re-use of three Bronze Age barrows at Cossington, Leicestershire. (2008)
By John Thomas (ISBN 978-0-9538914-8-1)

The Archaeology of the East Midlands. An Archaeological Resource Assessment and Research Agenda. (2006)
Edited by Nicholas J. Cooper (ISBN 978-0-9538914-7-4)

Coins, cult and cultural identity: Augustan coins, hot springs and the early Roman baths at Bourbonne-les-Bains. (2005)
By Eberhard Sauer (ISBN 0-9538914-4-5)

Ethnography and Archaeology in Upland Mediterranean Spain. Manolo's world: Peopling the recent past in the Serra de L'Altmirant. (2004)
By Neil Christie, Paul Beavitt, Josep A. Gisbert Santonja, Joan Seguí and Maria Victoria Gil Senís
(ISBN 0-9538914-6-1)

Re-Searching the Iron Age. (2003)
Edited by Jodie Humphrey (ISBN 0-9538914-5-3)

The Prehistory of the East Midlands Claylands. (2002)
By Patrick Clay (ISBN 0-9538914-2-9)

For further information (including trade purchases), please contact:

Leicester Archaeology Monographs c/o School of Archaeology & Ancient History,
University of Leicester, University Road, Leicester LE1 7RH, UK

Tel: +44 (0)116 252 2611; Fax: +44 (0)116 252 5005; Web: arch-anchist@le.ac.uk